Complete ♓

Pisces 2023

Monthly astrological forecasts for 2023

TATIANA BORSCH

Translated from Russian by Sonja Swenson
Translation copyright © Coinflow Limited, Cyprus
AstraArt Books is an imprint of Coinflow limited, Cyprus
Published by Coinflow Limited, Cyprus
For queries please contact: tatianaborsch@yahoo.com

ISBN978-9925-609-09-3 (paperback)
ISBN 978-9925-609-10-9 (ebook)

Contents

2023 –The Great Transition Continues

In previous forecasts, I have described the unique transition period in which the world finds itself.

I will summarize for those who have not read my predictions for 2020, 2021, and 2022.

We have entered a period of changes, and the world has come to a fateful point, where everything that seemed constant and unshakable no longer is. If that is the case, then what awaits us?

From an astrological perspective, 2020, 2021, and 2022 are extensions of one long period, and cannot be divided. This is a time of major changes in every nation, home, and individual.

There is no comparison for this period in modern history. In fact, humanity has not lived through a period quite like this for a very long time.

The astrological explanation for this is that we are living through a grandiose shift in eras. The Age of Pisces, which lasted for 2,160 years, is transitioning into the Age of Aquarius.

2023 fits naturally into this complex sequence. This is an important and critical watershed.

During the first half of 2023, we see a natural continuation of a very complicated period that began in 2022. The confrontation between East and West will continue in Ukraine, as will rivalry between the United States and China, along with financial and economic crises that have beset the entire world.

As of June 2022, when this forecast is being written, I can predict that in the fall of 2022, that is in October and November, the conflict between Russia and the West in Ukraine will reach a new level. Russia's advancements will force the West, including the United States, to take on a more active role in the face of the invasion in Ukraine, as the entire world risks being dragged into a new war.

The stars predict that the war in Ukraine may come to an end in January-February 2023. Ukraine will be divided into two zones of influence, with much of its territory falling under Russia's shadow. Volodymyr Zelenskyy will lose his grip on power and may flee the country, and Ukrainian leadership will be replaced. Peace initiatives that might otherwise be capable of changing this tragic situation will constantly be thwarted. In January 2023, aggressive Mars will no longer be in retrograde, and by February, there will be a light at the end of the tunnel. Initially, it will be just a flicker, but it is certainly better than nothing.

Gradually, the countries involved in this conflict will come to realize that they need to hold constructive negotiations in order to meet all of society's healthy demands and trends. These talks will not be swift, and they will probably only bear fruit in the second half of 2023.

Overall, despite Ukraine's valiant efforts both militarily and politically, along with support from the West, Russia will prevail, militarily, geopolitically, and ideologically.

This will seriously alter the geopolitical landscape on the global stage. In time, Asia and Russia will dominate the world's economy. The events of this year are just one more step in the transition as global influence shifts eastward. Tensions between the United States and Asian countries will only heat up.

In late 2022 and early 2023, many countries' economies will descend into chaos, and a general financial crisis will drag down banks, companies, and the entire planet's population.

In many Western countries, antiwar sentiment will be palpable, and there may be demonstrations, protests, and other expressions of dissatisfaction with governments.

In Russia, the fall of 2022 and first half of 2023 will see widespread changes in the structures of power. Western sanctions will lead to serious economic losses, forcing Russia to find a way to survive in the face of Western and American economic aggression.

The worst economic crisis will take place in the United States. The fall of 2022 and during the first half of 2023 may be the worst period it has faced in recent memory. There may be serious confrontations between political parties, which might throw American society as a whole off balance. During the fall of 2022 and first half of 2023, President Biden will experience serious difficulties. The stars predict he will face worsening health, along with serious destabilization of the entire American financial system. (A president's horoscope is responsible for much of what will happen to his or her country). During the same period, Bident's great foe, former President Trump, is expected to become much more active and powerful.

European countries will not be spared, either. In France, opposition to President Macron's policies will grow and Macron will lose some of his influence.

In Germany, Chancellor Olaf Scholz will become more aggressive during the fall. Despite his outward calm, he may turn out to be an active supporter of Western support for Ukraine. This will lead to a backlash in German society, and by May 2023, Scholz will be in a much weaker position than he is today.

From November 2022 to May 2023, the United Kingdom may see changes in leadership. This will be a period full of obstacles, including serious financial difficulties, demonstrations by those who disagree with the political power structure, and a trend of separatism in the various regions. In June-July, things will calm down significantly, and the British financial and political system will manage to recover.

The second half of May will also be a time of challenges. Jupiter will square Pluto during this time, with support from aggressive Mars. We can expect cataclysms and changes in many countries' governments here. Serious acts of terrorism cannot be ruled out, either.

During the second half of 2023, Jupiter will transition from the bellicose sign of Aries into the more peaceful sign of Taurus, and its favorable aspect with Saturn in June gives reason to hope that things are likely to improve.

That process will not be overnight, however. We see evidence of that in Uranus, which will be in the sign of Taurus, at the same degrees as during the period of World War II. Taurus symbolizes life and all its peaceful manifestations, while Uranus is the symbol of renewal through destruction. That portends a break with old structures, which may unleash war, death, and political and economic clashes.

All of these painful processes will eventually lead to the birth of a new, modern world, but that will not be completed until after 2025.

Looking at the future, I predict that in late 2022, and early 2023, economic, political, and social, as well as personal crises will reach a peak. Remember, we are blessed to live in an era of great change, and historical events certainly do leave their mark on our personal lives.

I also predict that during the second half of 2023, we will reach the halfway point on this long and winding road, and this may be the most complicated part of that trajectory. After this point, people will begin looking for a way to resolve the world's most pressing problems, and the light at the end of the tunnel may start to glimmer a bit brighter. Of course, this is inevitable, but step by step, people will start to tackle the many challenges we face. This is a gradual, sometimes painful process. But there is hope that Fate will have less unpleasant surprises in store for us and life will start running a bit more smoothly. It will never go back to exactly the way it was, but as this period draws to a close, we will see that in one way or another, all of these changes are for the best.

Money

We may face a global banking system crisis, which is likely to happen in November-December 2022. I believe it would be wiser to hold your money in something tangible, like real estate, land, or gold, than in the banking system or simply on paper. Purchasing power may experience a serious decline.

Health

Health-wise, anyone with thyroid problems or cardiovascular disease or any illnesses involving the blood vessels of the brain should be particularly cautious. We see this as Uranus transits into Taurus.

Pluto is still in Capricorn, which exacerbates musculoskeletal and bone disorders. Teeth are also in Pluto's crosshairs, so it is best to treat them quickly!

Cancer cases may rise, so do not hesitate to visit the doctor quickly, as cancer is only treatable in the early stages.

In 2023, Saturn is transiting into Pisces – this may lead to problems for those with various types of diabetes or problems involving the legs.

During the spring and fall of 2023, more outbreaks of unknown diseases and viruses are possible.

Nature

In 2023, various natural anomalies that the world has been struggling with may continue. Jupiter in Aries might cause fires, which will be a destabilizing factor during the winter and spring of 2023.

However, in early May, when Jupiter transitions into Taurus, we can expect to see significant improvements in agriculture. Harvests will be more abundant, which, in many countries, will mean a way out of the food crisis. Many countries will also be able to invest more in agriculture production and processing, which will only revive small towns and villages.

Fashion

Jupiter will be in Aries during the first half of 2023, and this promises all shades of red, which will be on models everywhere during this period. Many people will instinctively be drawn to red, as Aries's energy simply hangs in the air. Military-inspired dress may also be on the runways.

During the second half of 2023, Jupiter will transition into Taurus, which is primarily green in color. This is a great color, as it symbolizes growth and rebirth. Taurus's second color is pink, which symbolizes romanticism, softness, love for sensual pleasures and enjoyment. The fashion world may respond in kind with light, floaty fabrics and perhaps a new focus on femininity.

Have a wonderful year! Don't be afraid of crises, as they bring with them new opportunities!

Always,

Tatiana Borsch

2023 Overview for Pisces

A new cycle that you began in 2022 is continuing in your favor. Saturn is moving into your sign, which will mean discipline and responsibility. Be ready for setbacks as part of this harsh test.

Work. During the first half of 2023, you will be busy with work, new goals, and new ideas. You may be seeing your current long-term projects continue with success, whether you are a business owner or manager. The most optimistic months for you here are March, April, and May.

You may see pleasant changes, and for employees that may include a new job or a significant promotion where you are now, with a corresponding pay raise.

The most difficult period in the first half of 2023 will be January. During this time, you may still be grappling with thorny issues that appeared in the fall or winter of 2022, and that might include disagreements with a business partner, or difficulties related to real estate. However, by March, most of this will be resolved.

In May, Jupiter will change position and open new horizons. You will step up your communication with colleagues from other cities or abroad, and you might renew old ties or perhaps meet new colleagues.

Business owners and managers will be thinking about opening their business in another city or abroad, and you may find yourself frequently on the road or even moving.

Employees can count on working in another city or abroad, or perhaps frequent business travel.

However, there is always a fly in the ointment. Here, that will be some opposition that will arise during the fall of 2023. In October and November, many Pisceans will have to deal with audits and inspections, or possibly legal difficulties. Your partnership with colleagues from other cities or abroad will give you pause, as well. There may be issues involving business partners, or perhaps your work will clash with the laws of another country or even claims from leadership. However, any troubles that crop up during this period will be favorably resolved by the second half of December.

Money. 2023 is a great time for your bank account. You will have regular income and significantly more of it, too. Many Pisceans will reach the next level, and that should last for a long time. Your expenses will likely be related to major purchases, perhaps related to work, or alternatively, your personal life.

Love and family. Your romantic life is stable. If in 2022, you met someone important, now, your relationship may be on the upswing. If you do not have a partner yet, there is hope of meeting someone, and you can count on this relationship in the spring or summer of 2023. In many cases, that might happen on a business trip or among people who have come from afar.

If you are planning a move to another city or abroad, you can be sure to see that happen from May to September. The fall will probably not be particularly favorable for this, as you will be putting out all kinds of fires. That includes logistics, laws in other countries, and difficulties involving someone in your circle.

From October to November, you might face problems involving relatives. That may be a quarrel with a close relative, or perhaps a difficult situation has beset someone you love. You will only resolve this just before the holidays.

Health. In 2023, you will be changing the way you think about your body. Severe Saturn, which has long been in your sign, will force you to leave behind bad habits, take care of yourself, and do what you can to lead a healthy lifestyle.

January

New York Time			London Time		
Calendar Day	Lunar Day	Lunar Day Start Time	Calendar Day	Lunar Day	Lunar Day Start Time
01/01/2023	11	12:58 PM	01/01/2023	10	12:31 PM
02/01/2023	12	1:32 PM	02/01/2023	11	12:56 PM
03/01/2023	13	2:10 PM	03/01/2023	12	1:27 PM
04/01/2023	14	2:53 PM	04/01/2023	13	2:05 PM
05/01/2023	15	3:42 PM	05/01/2023	14	2:51 PM
06/01/2023	16	4:36 PM	06/01/2023	15	3:45 PM
07/01/2023	17	5:32 PM	07/01/2023	16	4:45 PM
08/01/2023	18	6:31 PM	08/01/2023	17	5:50 PM
09/01/2023	19	7:30 PM	09/01/2023	18	6:56 PM
10/01/2023	20	8:29 PM	10/01/2023	19	8:04 PM
11/01/2023	21	9:28 PM	11/01/2023	20	9:11 PM
12/01/2023	22	10:28 PM	12/01/2023	21	10:19 PM
13/01/2023	23	11:29 PM	13/01/2023	22	11:28 PM
15/01/2023	24	12:32 AM	15/01/2023	23	12:40 AM
16/01/2023	25	1:38 AM	16/01/2023	24	1:54 AM
17/01/2023	26	2:47 AM	17/01/2023	25	3:11 AM
18/01/2023	27	3:56 AM	18/01/2023	26	4:28 AM
19/01/2023	28	5:05 AM	19/01/2023	27	5:42 AM
20/01/2023	29	6:08 AM	20/01/2023	28	6:46 AM
21/01/2023	30	7:02 AM	21/01/2023	29	7:38 AM
21/01/2023	1	3:55 PM	21/01/2023	1	8:55 PM
22/01/2023	2	7:49 AM	22/01/2023	2	8:17 AM
23/01/2023	3	8:28 AM	23/01/2023	3	8:48 AM
24/01/2023	4	9:01 AM	24/01/2023	4	9:13 AM
25/01/2023	5	9:32 AM	25/01/2023	5	9:34 AM
26/01/2023	6	10:01 AM	26/01/2023	6	9:54 AM
27/01/2023	7	10:30 AM	27/01/2023	7	10:14 AM
28/01/2023	8	11:00 AM	28/01/2023	8	10:35 AM
29/01/2023	9	11:33 AM	29/01/2023	9	11:00 AM
30/01/2023	10	12:10 PM	30/01/2023	10	11:29 AM
31/01/2023	11	12:52 PM	31/01/2023	11	12:04 PM

You can find the description of each lunar day in the chapter "A Guide to The Moon Cycle and Lunar Days"

You are right in the middle of everything this January – friends, loved ones, a multitude of family obligations – when it rains, it pours! But you can handle it all with aplomb!

Work. Generally speaking, you are on a positive streak. Entrepreneurs and managers will be making new plans related to expanding their business and new financial opportunities. For now, things might just be in the planning stage, but in the very near future, you will make them come to life.

In some cases, your business expansion may be related to acquiring new production facilities or moving to a new office. Most likely, these bothersome tasks began in the fall or winter of last year and are finally coming to a close.

Your social circle may be expanding, too. In the first half of the month, you will see old friends, and closer to the end of the month, expect to make some new ones.

Remember that the last 10 days of the month is the best time for anything work-related, and the first 20 days are better for assessing your position and getting together with old friends and like-minded people. You might take a trip or be in contact with a colleague from afar.

Money. Your finances are not looking their best in January. You have a lot of expenses, and right now, they may be more than you earn. However, things will improve significantly later on, perhaps even by February.

Additionally, you can count on support from loved ones, your better half, or your parents.

Love and family. You will have some fateful events in your personal life this month. Many families will be busy with improving their home, repairs, or even building a new house. Most likely, these are tasks you began last year, and they are coming to a close.

You might be pouring most of your financial and organizational resources into a loved one.

During the first 10 days of January, many Pisces will find the time to take a trip. This will be a chance to relax from both work and household responsibilities.

Health. In January, you are feeling energetic and have no reason to fear falling ill.

February

New York Time			London Time		
Calendar Day	Lunar Day	Lunar Day Start Time	Calendar Day	Lunar Day	Lunar Day Start Time
01/02/2023	12	1:38 PM	01/02/2023	12	12:48 PM
02/02/2023	13	2:30 PM	02/02/2023	13	1:39 PM
03/02/2023	14	3:26 PM	03/02/2023	14	2:37 PM
04/02/2023	15	4:24 PM	04/02/2023	15	3:41 PM
05/02/2023	16	5:23 PM	05/02/2023	16	4:47 PM
06/02/2023	17	6:22 PM	06/02/2023	17	5:54 PM
07/02/2023	18	7:22 PM	07/02/2023	18	7:02 PM
08/02/2023	19	8:22 PM	08/02/2023	19	8:10 PM
09/02/2023	20	9:22 PM	09/02/2023	20	9:19 PM
10/02/2023	21	10:24 PM	10/02/2023	21	10:28 PM
11/02/2023	22	11:27 PM	11/02/2023	22	11:40 PM
13/02/2023	23	12:33 AM	13/02/2023	23	12:54 AM
14/02/2023	24	1:40 AM	14/02/2023	24	2:09 AM
15/02/2023	25	2:46 AM	15/02/2023	25	3:22 AM
16/02/2023	26	3:50 AM	16/02/2023	26	4:28 AM
17/02/2023	27	4:47 AM	17/02/2023	27	5:24 AM
18/02/2023	28	5:36 AM	18/02/2023	28	6:09 AM
19/02/2023	29	6:19 AM	19/02/2023	29	6:44 AM
20/02/2023	1	2:09 AM	20/02/2023	1	7:09 AM
20/02/2023	2	6:55 AM	20/02/2023	2	7:11 AM
21/02/2023	3	7:28 AM	21/02/2023	3	7:35 AM
22/02/2023	4	7:58 AM	22/02/2023	4	7:56 AM
23/02/2023	5	8:28 AM	23/02/2023	5	8:16 AM
24/02/2023	6	8:59 AM	24/02/2023	6	8:38 AM
25/02/2023	7	9:32 AM	25/02/2023	7	9:02 AM
26/02/2023	8	10:08 AM	26/02/2023	8	9:30 AM
27/02/2023	9	10:49 AM	27/02/2023	9	10:03 AM
28/02/2023	10	11:34 AM	28/02/2023	10	10:44 AM

You can find the description of each lunar day in the chapter "A Guide to The Moon Cycle and Lunar Days"

You are about to begin a calm, romantic, and even sensual month. Indulge in relaxation, good friends, and anything else your sensitive soul desires.

Work. If you want to busy yourself with work this month, or simply can't get away from it, you will be able to calmly deal whatever comes your way.

Managers and business owners should keep in mind that during the first 10 days of February, they may face various problems with partners from other cities or abroad, or see old legal issues suddenly rear their heads once again. These inconveniences will not have any significant consequences, but they will remind you of some problems in your recent past.

The last 20 days of the month, things are looking up. You will be busiest and most successful from February 20 to 28. You may expect new job offers or invitations to conduct new business.

Money. February is kind to your finances. You will have regular income, and significantly more of it during the last 10 days of the month. During this time, Jupiter and Venus, the most favorable planets in the sky, will be in the financial sector of your sky, which means that you may see a windfall. Buy a lottery ticket, go to the races, or otherwise test the capricious financial Fortune!

Love and family. February is a positive time for your personal life. Couples, whether married or not, may be focused on their future home, and though some roadblocks are likely during the first 10 days of the month, they will not cast a shadow over the atmosphere of the entire month.

Your relationship with relatives will improve significantly this month, and you are likely to be the one leading the charge. If you recently had a sudden argument or a relationship has cooled, you will be able to fix things.

Any trips planned for February will be very successful. Overall, February will be harmonious and calm, allowing you to smooth over all of the ups and downs of a very difficult 2022.

Health. You are feeling a little less energetic this month, and that will be especially noticeable during the Full Moon on February 4-5. Elderly people and those who are weakened are advised to take it easy and take care of themselves during this time. Those who are young and healthy should keep in mind that our bodies are especially vulnerable during the last month right before our birthdays.

This is the time to be kind to yourself, break any bad habits, visit a cosmetologist, massage therapist, and, if you can, visit a health resort or spa.

March

New York Time			London Time		
Calendar Day	Lunar Day	Lunar Day Start Time	Calendar Day	Lunar Day	Lunar Day Start Time
01/03/2023	11	12:24 PM	01/03/2023	11	11:33 AM
02/03/2023	12	1:19 PM	02/03/2023	12	12:29 PM
03/03/2023	13	2:16 PM	03/03/2023	13	1:31 PM
04/03/2023	14	3:15 PM	04/03/2023	14	2:36 PM
05/03/2023	15	4:15 PM	05/03/2023	15	3:44 PM
06/03/2023	16	5:14 PM	06/03/2023	16	4:52 PM
07/03/2023	17	6:15 PM	07/03/2023	17	6:00 PM
08/03/2023	18	7:15 PM	08/03/2023	18	7:09 PM
09/03/2023	19	8:17 PM	09/03/2023	19	8:19 PM
10/03/2023	20	9:20 PM	10/03/2023	20	9:31 PM
11/03/2023	21	10:25 PM	11/03/2023	21	10:44 PM
13/03/2023	22	12:31 AM	12/03/2023	22	11:58 PM
14/03/2023	23	1:37 AM	14/03/2023	23	1:11 AM
15/03/2023	24	2:40 AM	15/03/2023	24	2:18 AM
16/03/2023	25	3:37 AM	16/03/2023	25	3:16 AM
17/03/2023	26	4:28 AM	17/03/2023	26	4:03 AM
18/03/2023	27	5:12 AM	18/03/2023	27	4:41 AM
19/03/2023	28	5:50 AM	19/03/2023	28	5:10 AM
20/03/2023	29	6:23 AM	20/03/2023	29	5:35 AM
21/03/2023	30	6:54 AM	21/03/2023	30	5:57 AM
21/03/2023	1	1:26 PM	21/03/2023	1	5:26 PM
22/03/2023	2	7:24 AM	22/03/2023	2	6:17 AM
23/03/2023	3	7:55 AM	23/03/2023	3	6:38 AM
24/03/2023	4	8:27 AM	24/03/2023	4	7:01 AM
25/03/2023	5	9:03 AM	25/03/2023	5	7:28 AM
26/03/2023	6	9:43 AM	26/03/2023	6	9:00 AM
27/03/2023	7	10:27 AM	27/03/2023	7	9:38 AM
28/03/2023	8	11:16 AM	28/03/2023	8	10:25 AM
29/03/2023	9	12:10 PM	29/03/2023	9	11:19 AM
30/03/2023	10	1:07 PM	30/03/2023	10	12:19 PM
31/03/2023	11	2:05 PM	31/03/2023	11	1:24 PM

You can find the description of each lunar day in the chapter "A Guide to The Moon Cycle and Lunar Days"

Your greatest skill is the ability to juggle several tasks at the same time. This month will be your chance to show off that ingenuity, and Fortune is sure to appreciate it.

Work. Workplace events this month promise to serve you well. This is a great time for launching new projects and profiting from those you already started.

Employees can count on a promotion and salary raise, or perhaps additional responsibilities. In any case, the stars predict this will be extremely favorable to you.

The best time for anything work-related is the first or last 10 days of the month. During the second 10 days, you might run into some misunderstandings, which likely stem from issues from the past.

You are likely to experience disagreements with partners from other cities or abroad, or possibly problems involving land or real estate. In any case, there will not be any serious consequences, and things will quickly fall into place.

Money. Your finances are stable, with a strong upward trend. You might even say that money grows on trees for you this spring, as you enjoy various material benefits and other things of monetary value.

Expect the greatest sums of money on March 2, 4, 5, 13, 15, 22, 23, and 31.

Love and family. You will be so focused on work this month, that you may not have much time left over for your personal life. Even so, there are no problems on the horizon here, and everything will go as planned.

Spouses who get along might be working on home improvements, and you can expect some minor spats during the second 10 days of the month.

Couples who are divorcing or splitting up may run into past problems resurfacing. This time, things will be settled peacefully, likely because the worst is already behind you. Any loose ends will be dealt with calmly, without arguments, demands, or insults.

Health. This month, you are feeling energetic enough and have no reason to fear falling ill.

April

New York Time			London Time		
Calendar Day	Lunar Day	Lunar Day Start Time	Calendar Day	Lunar Day	Lunar Day Start Time
01/04/2023	12	3:04 PM	01/04/2023	12	2:30 PM
02/04/2023	13	4:04 PM	02/04/2023	13	3:38 PM
03/04/2023	14	5:04 PM	03/04/2023	14	4:46 PM
04/04/2023	15	6:05 PM	04/04/2023	15	5:56 PM
05/04/2023	16	7:07 PM	05/04/2023	16	7:06 PM
06/04/2023	17	8:11 PM	06/04/2023	17	8:18 PM
07/04/2023	18	9:16 PM	07/04/2023	18	9:32 PM
08/04/2023	19	10:23 PM	08/04/2023	19	10:47 PM
09/04/2023	20	11:30 PM	10/04/2023	20	12:02 AM
11/04/2023	21	12:34 AM	11/04/2023	21	1:11 AM
12/04/2023	22	1:33 AM	12/04/2023	22	2:12 AM
13/04/2023	23	2:25 AM	13/04/2023	23	3:02 AM
14/04/2023	24	3:10 AM	14/04/2023	24	3:41 AM
15/04/2023	25	3:48 AM	15/04/2023	25	4:12 AM
16/04/2023	26	4:22 AM	16/04/2023	26	4:38 AM
17/04/2023	27	4:53 AM	17/04/2023	27	5:00 AM
18/04/2023	28	5:22 AM	18/04/2023	28	5:20 AM
19/04/2023	29	5:52 AM	19/04/2023	29	5:40 AM
20/04/2023	1	12:15 AM	20/04/2023	1	5:15 AM
20/04/2023	2	6:23 AM	20/04/2023	2	6:02 AM
21/04/2023	3	6:57 AM	21/04/2023	3	6:27 AM
22/04/2023	4	7:35 AM	22/04/2023	4	6:56 AM
23/04/2023	5	8:18 AM	23/04/2023	5	7:32 AM
24/04/2023	6	9:06 AM	24/04/2023	6	8:15 AM
25/04/2023	7	9:59 AM	25/04/2023	7	9:07 AM
26/04/2023	8	10:55 AM	26/04/2023	8	10:06 AM
27/04/2023	9	11:53 AM	27/04/2023	9	11:09 AM
28/04/2023	10	12:52 PM	28/04/2023	10	12:15 PM
29/04/2023	11	1:52 PM	29/04/2023	11	1:23 PM
30/04/2023	12	2:51 PM	30/04/2023	12	2:30 PM

You can find the description of each lunar day in the chapter "A Guide to The Moon Cycle and Lunar Days"

This month, you will be able to tackle any task with inspiration and ingenuity. That gives you a chance to succeed in anything, whether political or personal. You have a lot to do, but anything worth doing is difficult!

Work. In April, issues that were a thorn in your side before are now favorably resolved. That may involve old legal troubles that kept you up at night for some time. Alternatively, you are smoothing over a tough relationship with colleagues in other cities or abroad. You will not avoid every argument, but close to the end of the month, your partners who live faraway will reach a compromise. You will give it everything you've got, and your efforts will pay off.

You might take a successful trip or plan one.

For anything work-related, the second half of April is ideal. Here, you will see positive changes in areas that have posed a challenge in the past, and you will see that nothing is insurmountable.

Money. Financially, April is looking very promising for you. You will have regular income, and significantly more of it. You might even say that this is the first glimmer of the success that awaits in the very near future. Expect the largest sums on April 1, 2, 10-12, 19, 20, 28, and 29.

Love and family. In your personal life, things are going great. Your relationship with relatives has seen some challenges, but you are now close to a resolution. You might be the one to take the first step, and your family member is sure to respond in kind.

Single people might have a fateful meeting while traveling or among people from somewhere faraway. You might both be on the road when this happens! If you recently me someone and began a romance, now is the time to think about how to strengthen your relationship. You might have serious talks while on a trip, and this is especially likely during the last 10 days of April or in May.

Health. Jupiter and Neptune are both in y our sign, which means a powerful burst of energy, and it's up to you how you decide to use it. In any case, you have no reason to fear falling ill.

May

New York Time			London Time		
Calendar Day	Lunar Day	Lunar Day Start Time	Calendar Day	Lunar Day	Lunar Day Start Time
01/05/2023	13	3:52 PM	01/05/2023	13	3:39 PM
02/05/2023	14	4:53 PM	02/05/2023	14	4:48 PM
03/05/2023	15	5:56 PM	03/05/2023	15	6:00 PM
04/05/2023	16	7:02 PM	04/05/2023	16	7:14 PM
05/05/2023	17	8:09 PM	05/05/2023	17	8:30 PM
06/05/2023	18	9:18 PM	06/05/2023	18	9:47 PM
07/05/2023	19	10:25 PM	07/05/2023	19	11:00 PM
08/05/2023	20	11:27 PM	09/05/2023	20	12:06 AM
10/05/2023	21	12:22 AM	10/05/2023	21	1:01 AM
11/05/2023	22	1:10 AM	11/05/2023	22	1:43 AM
12/05/2023	23	1:50 AM	12/05/2023	23	2:16 AM
13/05/2023	24	2:24 AM	13/05/2023	24	2:43 AM
14/05/2023	25	2:55 AM	14/05/2023	25	3:05 AM
15/05/2023	26	3:24 AM	15/05/2023	26	3:25 AM
16/05/2023	27	3:53 AM	16/05/2023	27	3:45 AM
17/05/2023	28	4:23 AM	17/05/2023	28	4:05 AM
18/05/2023	29	4:55 AM	18/05/2023	29	4:28 AM
19/05/2023	30	5:31 AM	19/05/2023	30	4:55 AM
19/05/2023	1	11:55 AM	19/05/2023	1	4:55 PM
20/05/2023	2	6:11 AM	20/05/2023	2	5:27 AM
21/05/2023	3	6:57 AM	21/05/2023	3	6:08 AM
22/05/2023	4	7:48 AM	22/05/2023	4	6:56 AM
23/05/2023	5	8:44 AM	23/05/2023	5	7:53 AM
24/05/2023	6	9:42 AM	24/05/2023	6	8:55 AM
25/05/2023	7	10:41 AM	25/05/2023	7	10:01 AM
26/05/2023	8	11:40 AM	26/05/2023	8	11:07 AM
27/05/2023	9	12:39 PM	27/05/2023	9	12:14 PM
28/05/2023	10	1:38 PM	28/05/2023	10	1:22 PM
29/05/2023	11	2:38 PM	29/05/2023	11	2:30 PM
30/05/2023	12	3:39 PM	30/05/2023	12	3:40 PM
31/05/2023	13	4:43 PM	31/05/2023	13	4:52 PM

You can find the description of each lunar day in the chapter "A Guide to The Moon Cycle and Lunar Days"

In May, you might think about making some serious changes in your life. Only you can decide what they will look like, but the stars advise that change is imminent.

Work. In May, your professional activities will take your attention somewhere far away, perhaps abroad. That may involve picking up old partnerships, or possibly a move or opening business in another city or abroad.

Negotiations on this topic may drag on all month long, but the most positive aspects will shine through during the last 10 days of May. During the first 20 days, you can expect setbacks at work, whether due to red tape or difficult colleagues in other cities or abroad. By the last 10 days of May, however, things will settle down and you will find the right path.

Any travel planned for May is sure to turn out successfully, especially if you have been to the same destination before. The same goes for old partners you may begin corresponding with once again.

Money. Financially, May is looking great. You will have a regular income, and this will continue into the future. Expect the largest sums to come in on May 7, 8, 15-17, 25, and 26.

Love and family. Your personal life looks agitated and turbulent.

Some Pisceans will make plans related to a move, and that may be to another city, abroad, or possible simply a new home. For now, you are in the planning stage, but during the year, these plans are sure to come to life.

Many Pisceans might take a trip to a place you have been before for a spring break.

Your relationship with relatives is much more active than before. You might take a trip together or see your family members living in another city or abroad.

Health. This month, your spirit might turn out to be much stronger than your body. Take care of yourself! Saturn is firmly and permanently ensconced in your sign and is telling you the same.

This advice is particularly important for those who are elderly or weakened.

June

New York Time			London Time		
Calendar Day	Lunar Day	Lunar Day Start Time	Calendar Day	Lunar Day	Lunar Day Start Time
01/06/2023	14	5:50 PM	01/06/2023	14	6:07 PM
02/06/2023	15	6:59 PM	02/06/2023	15	7:24 PM
03/06/2023	16	8:08 PM	03/06/2023	16	8:41 PM
04/06/2023	17	9:14 PM	04/06/2023	17	9:52 PM
05/06/2023	18	10:14 PM	05/06/2023	18	10:53 PM
06/06/2023	19	11:06 PM	06/06/2023	19	11:41 PM
07/06/2023	20	11:50 PM	08/06/2023	20	12:19 AM
09/06/2023	21	12:27 AM	09/06/2023	21	12:48 AM
10/06/2023	22	12:59 AM	10/06/2023	22	1:11 AM
11/06/2023	23	1:29 AM	11/06/2023	23	1:32 AM
12/06/2023	24	1:57 AM	12/06/2023	24	1:52 AM
13/06/2023	25	2:26 AM	13/06/2023	25	2:11 AM
14/06/2023	26	2:56 AM	14/06/2023	26	2:33 AM
15/06/2023	27	3:30 AM	15/06/2023	27	2:57 AM
16/06/2023	28	4:08 AM	16/06/2023	28	3:27 AM
17/06/2023	29	4:51 AM	17/06/2023	29	4:04 AM
18/06/2023	1	12:39 AM	18/06/2023	30	4:49 AM
18/06/2023	2	5:40 AM	18/06/2023	1	5:39 AM
19/06/2023	3	6:34 AM	19/06/2023	2	5:42 AM
20/06/2023	4	7:31 AM	20/06/2023	3	6:43 AM
21/06/2023	5	8:30 AM	21/06/2023	4	7:47 AM
22/06/2023	6	9:29 AM	22/06/2023	5	8:54 AM
23/06/2023	7	10:28 AM	23/06/2023	6	10:01 AM
24/06/2023	8	11:27 AM	24/06/2023	7	11:07 AM
25/06/2023	9	12:25 PM	25/06/2023	8	12:14 PM
26/06/2023	10	1:25 PM	26/06/2023	9	1:22 PM
27/06/2023	11	2:27 PM	27/06/2023	10	2:32 PM
28/06/2023	12	3:31 PM	28/06/2023	11	3:44 PM
29/06/2023	13	4:37 PM	29/06/2023	12	4:59 PM
30/06/2023	14	5:46 PM	30/06/2023	13	6:15 PM

You can find the description of each lunar day in the chapter "A Guide to The Moon Cycle and Lunar Days"

Jupiter's movements always bring change, and June is no different. Something that seemed like science fiction is quickly becoming reality.

Work. Once again, most Pisceans are developing their relationship with colleagues in other cities or abroad, this month. You might be renewing old ties, holding negotiations with past partners, or even go on a trip. June 10-19 is the best time for this.

Additionally, business owners and managers at every level may face difficulties involving colleagues. It seems that someone who is supposed to help you will instead throw a wrench in your plans.

Employees are advised to be careful with colleagues and avoid any intrigue on your team. Stay neutral – it is better, this way. You may also have to make a tough decision if you work with colleagues from faraway.

Money. Your finances are stable in June. You will have your regular income and expenses are low. For now, things are looking good.

Love and family. Your personal life is no less important than work, this month. Many Pisceans will be taking care of major issues involving your home. You may be getting a summer home ready, or perhaps looking for real estate faraway. You are noticeably spending much more time with relatives, and you may see family members living in other cities or abroad.

Near the end of the month, you will spend a lot of time with your children. You will be happily reunited, whether you have been separated by time or distance.

Health. This month, you are energetic enough and have no reason to fear falling ill. However, all month long, especially after June 20, you are advised to be careful when traveling and driving.

July

New York Time			London Time		
Calendar Day	Lunar Day	Lunar Day Start Time	Calendar Day	Lunar Day	Lunar Day Start Time
01/07/2023	15	6:54 PM	01/07/2023	14	7:30 PM
02/07/2023	16	7:58 PM	02/07/2023	15	8:37 PM
03/07/2023	17	8:55 PM	03/07/2023	16	9:33 PM
04/07/2023	18	9:44 PM	04/07/2023	17	10:16 PM
05/07/2023	19	10:25 PM	05/07/2023	18	10:49 PM
06/07/2023	20	11:00 PM	06/07/2023	19	11:15 PM
07/07/2023	21	11:31 PM	07/07/2023	20	11:38 PM
09/07/2023	22	12:01 AM	08/07/2023	21	11:58 PM
10/07/2023	23	12:29 AM	10/07/2023	22	12:18 AM
11/07/2023	24	12:59 AM	11/07/2023	23	12:39 AM
12/07/2023	25	1:32 AM	12/07/2023	24	1:02 AM
13/07/2023	26	2:08 AM	13/07/2023	25	1:30 AM
14/07/2023	27	2:49 AM	14/07/2023	26	2:04 AM
15/07/2023	28	3:36 AM	15/07/2023	27	2:46 AM
16/07/2023	29	4:28 AM	16/07/2023	28	3:36 AM
17/07/2023	30	5:24 AM	17/07/2023	29	4:34 AM
17/07/2023	1	2:33 PM	17/07/2023	1	7:33 PM
18/07/2023	2	6:22 AM	18/07/2023	2	5:37 AM
19/07/2023	3	7:21 AM	19/07/2023	3	6:43 AM
20/07/2023	4	8:20 AM	20/07/2023	4	7:50 AM
21/07/2023	5	9:19 AM	21/07/2023	5	8:56 AM
22/07/2023	6	10:17 AM	22/07/2023	6	10:03 AM
23/07/2023	7	11:15 AM	23/07/2023	7	11:09 AM
24/07/2023	8	12:15 PM	24/07/2023	8	12:17 PM
25/07/2023	9	1:16 PM	25/07/2023	9	1:27 PM
26/07/2023	10	2:20 PM	26/07/2023	10	2:39 PM
27/07/2023	11	3:26 PM	27/07/2023	11	3:53 PM
28/07/2023	12	4:33 PM	28/07/2023	12	5:07 PM
29/07/2023	13	5:39 PM	29/07/2023	13	6:16 PM
30/07/2023	14	6:39 PM	30/07/2023	14	7:17 PM
31/07/2023	15	7:32 PM	31/07/2023	15	8:07 PM

You can find the description of each lunar day in the chapter "A Guide to The Moon Cycle and Lunar Days"

In July, you seem to be receiving favorable attention from all ends. Wherever you are – on a beach on the Indian Ocean or just in nature near home, it is impossible to not take notice of you!

Work. During the first 20 days of July, you would do best to focus on relaxing rather than stress at work. The exception to this is people working in creative professions – actors, artists, musicians, and anyone who works with words. If that is you, expect a successful tour, recognition, and a handsome financial reward.

If various circumstances have forced you to spend your summer days at work, the stars recommend renewing old ties, and making new connections, as well. You might find yourself talking to old colleagues from other cities or abroad or even going on a trip.

Things will not run so smoothly after July 20. Expect unexpected and unpleasant surprises. Your relationship with some partners will grow much more difficult, and you may see claims against one another and open conflict.

You can expect your relationship with a colleague from faraway to worsen during the last 10 days of July, as well. You may have to reconsider some matters at work and things might drag out, or perhaps some colleagues will suddenly change the rules of the game.

During the last 10 days of July, managers should keep a close eye on their subordinates and avoid taking their word for things. Trust, but verify, in order to avoid mistakes or misunderstandings.

Employees should also be careful during this period and avoid placing too much trust in their colleagues. Stay out of any gossip on your team.

Money. July might be an inconsistent time for your finances. You have a lot of expenses, and most of the time, they are related to your personal life, romance, or your family.

Love and family. The stars predict that during the first 20 days of July, you would do well to relax and spend time with your loved ones. You might take a trip, which will turn out well. Take a few days to visit the beach, or simply take time off of work in order to restore your body and soul.

You might renew ties with old friends or former lovers, or expect to make new friends, as well, who may turn out to be useful at work.

Parents will manage to spend time with their children, while couples will dote on each other. During the last 10 days of July, however, clouds will begin to gather on your hitherto sunny horizon. Those whose relationships were already rocky are the ones most likely to suffer. Built-up resentment will boil over and possibly take a turn for something more serious. Your partner may become aggressive, or start being unpleasant and offensive. Keep your emotions in check and remember that poor peace is better than a good war.

Health. Overall, you are healthy, attractive, and dynamic. With that, you have no reason to fear falling ill.

August

New York Time			London Time		
Calendar Day	Lunar Day	Lunar Day Start Time	Calendar Day	Lunar Day	Lunar Day Start Time
01/08/2023	16	8:17 PM	01/08/2023	16	8:45 PM
02/08/2023	17	8:56 PM	02/08/2023	17	9:15 PM
03/08/2023	18	9:30 PM	03/08/2023	18	9:40 PM
04/08/2023	19	10:01 PM	04/08/2023	19	10:02 PM
05/08/2023	20	10:31 PM	05/08/2023	20	10:22 PM
06/08/2023	21	11:01 PM	06/08/2023	21	10:44 PM
07/08/2023	22	11:33 PM	07/08/2023	22	11:07 PM
09/08/2023	23	12:09 AM	08/08/2023	23	11:33 PM
10/08/2023	24	12:49 AM	10/08/2023	24	12:05 AM
11/08/2023	25	1:34 AM	11/08/2023	25	12:44 AM
12/08/2023	26	2:24 AM	12/08/2023	26	1:32 AM
13/08/2023	27	3:18 AM	13/08/2023	27	2:27 AM
14/08/2023	28	4:16 AM	14/08/2023	28	3:29 AM
15/08/2023	29	5:14 AM	15/08/2023	29	4:34 AM
16/08/2023	1	5:38 AM	16/08/2023	30	5:41 AM
16/08/2023	2	6:13 AM	16/08/2023	1	10:38 AM
17/08/2023	3	7:12 AM	17/08/2023	2	6:47 AM
18/08/2023	4	8:10 AM	18/08/2023	3	7:54 AM
19/08/2023	5	9:09 AM	19/08/2023	4	9:00 AM
20/08/2023	6	10:08 AM	20/08/2023	5	10:07 AM
21/08/2023	7	11:08 AM	21/08/2023	6	11:16 AM
22/08/2023	8	12:10 PM	22/08/2023	7	12:25 PM
23/08/2023	9	1:13 PM	23/08/2023	8	1:37 PM
24/08/2023	10	2:18 PM	24/08/2023	9	2:49 PM
25/08/2023	11	3:22 PM	25/08/2023	10	3:59 PM
26/08/2023	12	4:23 PM	26/08/2023	11	5:02 PM
27/08/2023	13	5:18 PM	27/08/2023	12	5:56 PM
28/08/2023	14	6:06 PM	28/08/2023	13	6:38 PM
29/08/2023	15	6:48 PM	29/08/2023	14	7:12 PM
30/08/2023	16	7:24 PM	30/08/2023	15	7:39 PM
31/08/2023	17	7:57 PM	31/08/2023	16	8:03 PM

You can find the description of each lunar day in the chapter "A Guide to The Moon Cycle and Lunar Days"

This month, you might find yourself in a sticky situation – it will be impossible to move forward, but you certainly don't want to stay where you are. Don't make any sudden moves and stay right where you are.

Work. Your main problem during this wonderful summer month will be a shaky relationship with colleagues in other cities or abroad. Many managers, business owners, and anyone whose job involves travel, business trips, or even those just hoping to open their business in another city or abroad can expect much of the same. All month long, you will have to grapple with delicate work-related matters, no matter how many times you come back to the same issues.

You may face conflict with certain partners, and this time, it is worth being patient and flexible.

In all difficult situations, you can count on help from old friends or people who are highly placed in society. They will act as intermediaries, allies, and even your assistants. This is especially relevant when it comes to legal issues.

Employees may face gossip and various types of disagreements on their team. If this describes you, try to stay above the fray and avoid any intrigue.

All Pisces, regardless of their career path, should be especially careful when checking any information that comes their way, be conscientious with documents, and never rush things. That is the only way to see yourself through this month.

Money. Despite the hurdles at work, you will not face any money issues in August. Things are predictable and reasonable in this area of your life, and whatever you put in you will get back.

Love and family. If you are more focused on your personal life, here you will not be spared, either.

Those who have moved somewhere faraway may face obstacles including the laws of foreign countries and various domestic concerns.

If you are part of a turbulent couple, your relationship is still far from ideal, and it is likely that you are the culprit for the lion's share of this situation. Either harshness or excessive restraint- the qualities that your harsh Uncle Saturn gave you- may lead to alienation or outright conflict.

Your relationship with relatives looks complicated, but that is only temporary, especially if you don't sweat the small stuff and treat those around you with respect.

Health. In August, you are feeling rather tired, so it is worth letting your body take a break and perhaps visiting a spa. If you are unable to do that, try to spend more time in nature, which you are sure to find time to do in August.

September

New York Time			London Time		
Calendar Day	Lunar Day	Lunar Day Start Time	Calendar Day	Lunar Day	Lunar Day Start Time
01/09/2023	18	8:28 PM	01/09/2023	17	8:24 PM
02/09/2023	19	8:59 PM	02/09/2023	18	8:46 PM
03/09/2023	20	9:32 PM	03/09/2023	19	9:09 PM
04/09/2023	21	10:07 PM	04/09/2023	20	9:34 PM
05/09/2023	22	10:46 PM	05/09/2023	21	10:05 PM
06/09/2023	23	11:30 PM	06/09/2023	22	10:43 PM
08/09/2023	24	12:19 AM	07/09/2023	23	11:28 PM
09/09/2023	25	1:13 AM	09/09/2023	24	12:21 AM
10/09/2023	26	2:09 AM	10/09/2023	25	1:21 AM
11/09/2023	27	3:08 AM	11/09/2023	26	2:25 AM
12/09/2023	28	4:07 AM	12/09/2023	27	3:31 AM
13/09/2023	29	5:05 AM	13/09/2023	28	4:38 AM
14/09/2023	30	6:04 AM	14/09/2023	29	5:45 AM
14/09/2023	1	9:40 PM	15/09/2023	1	2:40 AM
15/09/2023	2	7:03 AM	15/09/2023	2	6:52 AM
16/09/2023	3	8:02 AM	16/09/2023	3	7:59 AM
17/09/2023	4	9:02 AM	17/09/2023	4	9:07 AM
18/09/2023	5	10:03 AM	18/09/2023	5	10:16 AM
19/09/2023	6	11:06 AM	19/09/2023	6	11:27 AM
20/09/2023	7	12:10 PM	20/09/2023	7	12:39 PM
21/09/2023	8	1:13 PM	21/09/2023	8	1:48 PM
22/09/2023	9	2:13 PM	22/09/2023	9	2:52 PM
23/09/2023	10	3:09 PM	23/09/2023	10	3:48 PM
24/09/2023	11	3:58 PM	24/09/2023	11	4:33 PM
25/09/2023	12	4:41 PM	25/09/2023	12	5:09 PM
26/09/2023	13	5:18 PM	26/09/2023	13	5:38 PM
27/09/2023	14	5:52 PM	27/09/2023	14	6:03 PM
28/09/2023	15	6:24 PM	28/09/2023	15	6:25 PM
29/09/2023	16	6:55 PM	29/09/2023	16	6:46 PM
30/09/2023	17	7:27 PM	30/09/2023	17	7:08 PM

You can find the description of each lunar day in the chapter "A Guide to The Moon Cycle and Lunar Days"

September will open your world a bit wider than you are used to. Try to appreciate the perspective of your opponents, partners, or simply people you frequently interact with. If you do, solving many of your problems will become much easier and faster.

Work. Your relationship with business partners will be the most important theme for you this month. Business owners and managers at every level will face the difficult task of smoothing over ties with colleagues in other cities or abroad and reining in an opponent who has proven him or herself to be a loose cannon. Try to be flexible and diplomatic, even patient. These qualities will get you through the first two weeks of September, which will be the most difficult period this month.

You may also experience misunderstandings with your subordinates, who might not be shouldering their responsibilities, for various reasons. In some cases, this may boil down to outright sabotage, and it is worth keeping this in mind if you are a business owner or manager.

Employees can expect competition and ill will on the part of their team this month. Do your job in good faith and avoid any gossip.

If you are planning any business travel, be attentive with any documents and don't skip over the details. That is very pertinent during the first half of September, when Mercury, the planet that rules connections, contacts, and any travel, will be in retrograde.

Money. Financially, you can count on September to be neutral. You will not see any major windfalls, but you will also not incur any losses. To summarize, it is what it is.

Love and family. It is hard to rewrite the rules of your relationship when you are right in the thick of it. So avoid that, especially if you feel like you do not have the upper hand right now. If you do not appreciate how your partner is conducting him or herself, it is worth waiting it out.

Those who are moving somewhere faraway or simply to a new

home might be working with their partner to solve problems, and, fortunately, with each new day there are less problems to solve. Your relationship with relatives is also improving, and the stars give much of the credit for this to your spouse or partner.

If you plan to travel in September, select a place you have been before. That goes for the entire month, but especially during the first two weeks.

Health. In September, you are feeling rather sluggish, so don't overdo it, and try to strike a balance between work and play.

October

New York Time				London Time		
Calendar Day	Lunar Day	Lunar Day Start Time		Calendar Day	Lunar Day	Lunar Day Start Time
01/10/2023	18	8:02 PM		01/10/2023	18	7:33 PM
02/10/2023	19	8:40 PM		02/10/2023	19	8:02 PM
03/10/2023	20	9:23 PM		03/10/2023	20	8:38 PM
04/10/2023	21	10:11 PM		04/10/2023	21	9:21 PM
05/10/2023	22	11:04 PM		05/10/2023	22	10:12 PM
07/10/2023	23	12:01 AM		06/10/2023	23	11:11 PM
08/10/2023	24	12:59 AM		08/10/2023	24	12:14 AM
09/10/2023	25	1:58 AM		09/10/2023	25	1:20 AM
10/10/2023	26	2:57 AM		10/10/2023	26	2:27 AM
11/10/2023	27	3:56 AM		11/10/2023	27	3:34 AM
12/10/2023	28	4:54 AM		12/10/2023	28	4:40 AM
13/10/2023	29	5:54 AM		13/10/2023	29	5:48 AM
14/10/2023	30	6:54 AM		14/10/2023	30	6:56 AM
14/10/2023	1	1:55 PM		14/10/2023	1	6:55 PM
15/10/2023	2	7:55 AM		15/10/2023	2	8:06 AM
16/10/2023	3	8:59 AM		16/10/2023	3	9:17 AM
17/10/2023	4	10:03 AM		17/10/2023	4	10:29 AM
18/10/2023	5	11:07 AM		18/10/2023	5	11:40 AM
19/10/2023	6	12:08 PM		19/10/2023	6	12:46 PM
20/10/2023	7	1:05 PM		20/10/2023	7	1:44 PM
21/10/2023	8	1:55 PM		21/10/2023	8	2:32 PM
22/10/2023	9	2:38 PM		22/10/2023	9	3:09 PM
23/10/2023	10	3:16 PM		23/10/2023	10	3:40 PM
24/10/2023	11	3:50 PM		24/10/2023	11	4:05 PM
25/10/2023	12	4:21 PM		25/10/2023	12	4:27 PM
26/10/2023	13	4:51 PM		26/10/2023	13	4:48 PM
27/10/2023	14	5:22 PM		27/10/2023	14	5:09 PM
28/10/2023	15	5:55 PM		28/10/2023	15	5:32 PM
29/10/2023	16	6:32 PM		29/10/2023	16	4:59 PM
30/10/2023	17	7:13 PM		30/10/2023	17	5:31 PM
31/10/2023	18	8:00 PM		31/10/2023	18	6:11 PM

You can find the description of each lunar day in the chapter "A Guide to The Moon Cycle and Lunar Days"

In October, you will have to strike a healthy balance between your desires and reality. Sometimes, the spirit is willing, but the flesh is weak.

Work. October is not a particularly successful month for you at work. Most likely, things are not as exciting as you would like.

The main task for any business owners or managers might be strengthening your relationship with colleagues from other cities or abroad. If you are thinking about doing business somewhere faraway from home, you will need to get a handle on who you will have to work with.

During the first 20 days of October, your relationship is progressing fairly well. You might be meeting, holding negotiations, or traveling to see colleagues from faraway. There may be some disagreements over financial issues. You may need to recognize that not all of your expectations will come true, and your expenses may be higher than you initially intended.

After October 20, you will be dealing with a different type of problem. One way or another, it will involve colleagues from somewhere faraway. You may see disagreements among the people who you need to work with, or possibly involving the laws of other countries, which you will need to overcome. There is hope that by December, this will be resolved.

Money. October is contradictory for your finances. You have a lot of expenses, and your income is low, and you can expect to spend the most during the first half of the month. There is hope that during the difficult days, a loved one or old friend will lend a hand.

Love and family. You are seeing a lot of ups and downs in your personal life. Those who are moving somewhere faraway will still be dealing with various tasks related to that difficult endeavor.

Couples may argue, and you will be the culprit. Lately, you have been rigid and unbending, and that may cause major problems in your relationships. Your partner seems a lot more flexible and diplomatic than you, and the stars confirm that he or she will have a lot to deal with. Keep that in mind and watch yourself.

Your relationship with relatives will be stable, constructive, and important until October 20. A family member may be useful in helping you solve a lot of problems. After that date, however, family members will bicker, and this time, you will end up acting as the referee capable of bringing your loved ones together again.

Health. In October, you are feeling sluggish, so take care of yourself. Be careful when driving and traveling, as the last 10 days of October will be the most difficult period for this.

November

New York Time				London Time		
Calendar Day	Lunar Day	Lunar Day Start Time		Calendar Day	Lunar Day	Lunar Day Start Time
01/11/2023	19	8:52 PM		01/11/2023	19	7:00 PM
02/11/2023	20	9:49 PM		02/11/2023	20	7:57 PM
03/11/2023	21	10:47 PM		03/11/2023	21	9:00 PM
04/11/2023	22	11:47 PM		04/11/2023	22	10:06 PM
05/11/2023	23	11:46 PM		05/11/2023	23	11:13 PM
07/11/2023	24	12:45 AM		07/11/2023	24	12:20 AM
08/11/2023	25	1:43 AM		08/11/2023	25	1:26 AM
09/11/2023	26	2:42 AM		09/11/2023	26	2:33 AM
10/11/2023	27	3:42 AM		10/11/2023	27	3:41 AM
11/11/2023	28	4:43 AM		11/11/2023	28	4:50 AM
12/11/2023	29	5:46 AM		12/11/2023	29	6:02 AM
13/11/2023	1	4:27 AM		13/11/2023	30	7:15 AM
13/11/2023	2	6:51 AM		13/11/2023	1	9:27 AM
14/11/2023	3	7:57 AM		14/11/2023	2	8:28 AM
15/11/2023	4	9:01 AM		15/11/2023	3	9:38 AM
16/11/2023	5	10:00 AM		16/11/2023	4	10:40 AM
17/11/2023	6	10:53 AM		17/11/2023	5	11:31 AM
18/11/2023	7	11:39 AM		18/11/2023	6	12:12 PM
19/11/2023	8	12:18 PM		19/11/2023	7	12:44 PM
20/11/2023	9	12:52 PM		20/11/2023	8	1:10 PM
21/11/2023	10	1:23 PM		21/11/2023	9	1:32 PM
22/11/2023	11	1:52 PM		22/11/2023	10	1:52 PM
23/11/2023	12	2:22 PM		23/11/2023	11	2:12 PM
24/11/2023	13	2:53 PM		24/11/2023	12	2:34 PM
25/11/2023	14	3:27 PM		25/11/2023	13	2:58 PM
26/11/2023	15	4:05 PM		26/11/2023	14	3:27 PM
27/11/2023	16	4:49 PM		27/11/2023	15	4:03 PM
28/11/2023	17	5:39 PM		28/11/2023	16	4:48 PM
29/11/2023	18	6:35 PM		29/11/2023	17	5:42 PM
30/11/2023	19	7:33 PM		30/11/2023	18	6:43 PM

You can find the description of each lunar day in the chapter "A Guide to The Moon Cycle and Lunar Days"

Multitasking is your forte, and here, you are able to show that ability off to those around you. The obstacle course continues!

Work. In November, you are hardly ever seen at home. Travel, meetings, and negotiations are your backdrop all month.

Your links to colleagues in other cities and abroad are the most important issue in your professional life right now, but in mid-November, you might experience some hiccups here. Your colleagues might act in poor faith, and your efforts alone will make it possible to restore balance to this relationship. Friends and like-minded people will have your back, so your foes will eventually have to give in.

Employees should be careful during the last 10 days of the month. During this time, there is a high likelihood of disagreements with managers, who may grow excessively demanding, among other things. It is also likely that you have a hand in some of this, yourself. Seek out any weak links in your work and do what you can to fix them while you can.

Money. Your finances are stable, but that's all. You will not see any surprises, whether pleasant or not.

Love and family. November is a relatively peaceful time in your personal life. Couples might go on a trip together, but the stars do urge you to avoid doing that between November 10 and 20, when aggressive Mars will be in conflict with unpredictable Uranus, which means there is a likelihood of incidents on the road.

During the same period, you might see conflicts among your close relatives. This situation is nothing new to you, and its roots began in the recent past.

Those who are moving to another city or abroad will face a variety of difficulties, so consider other options and take any necessary measures. You're only as strong as your weakest link during this difficult time!

Health. You are active, energetic, and the picture of health this month. The stars urge you to be careful when traveling and driving. From November 10 to 20, there is a very high chance of road accidents.

If you are elderly or weakened, take any preventive measures you can when it comes to chronic illnesses, in order to avoid any serious complications.

The most difficult period is the New Moon, from November 12 to 14.

December

New York Time			London Time		
Calendar Day	Lunar Day	Lunar Day Start Time	Calendar Day	Lunar Day	Lunar Day Start Time
01/12/2023	20	8:33 PM	01/12/2023	19	7:49 PM
02/12/2023	21	9:34 PM	02/12/2023	20	8:57 PM
03/12/2023	22	10:33 PM	03/12/2023	21	10:04 PM
04/12/2023	23	11:31 PM	04/12/2023	22	11:11 PM
06/12/2023	24	12:29 AM	06/12/2023	23	12:17 AM
07/12/2023	25	1:28 AM	07/12/2023	24	1:24 AM
08/12/2023	26	2:28 AM	08/12/2023	25	2:32 AM
09/12/2023	27	3:30 AM	09/12/2023	26	3:42 AM
10/12/2023	28	4:34 AM	10/12/2023	27	4:54 AM
11/12/2023	29	5:40 AM	11/12/2023	28	6:08 AM
12/12/2023	30	6:46 AM	12/12/2023	29	7:21 AM
12/12/2023	1	6:32 PM	12/12/2023	1	11:32 PM
13/12/2023	2	7:49 AM	13/12/2023	2	8:28 AM
14/12/2023	3	8:46 AM	14/12/2023	3	9:25 AM
15/12/2023	4	9:36 AM	15/12/2023	4	10:11 AM
16/12/2023	5	10:18 AM	16/12/2023	5	10:47 AM
17/12/2023	6	10:55 AM	17/12/2023	6	11:15 AM
18/12/2023	7	11:27 AM	18/12/2023	7	11:38 AM
19/12/2023	8	11:56 AM	19/12/2023	8	11:59 AM
20/12/2023	9	12:25 PM	20/12/2023	9	12:19 PM
21/12/2023	10	12:55 PM	21/12/2023	10	12:39 PM
22/12/2023	11	1:27 PM	22/12/2023	11	1:02 PM
23/12/2023	12	2:02 PM	23/12/2023	12	1:28 PM
24/12/2023	13	2:43 PM	24/12/2023	13	2:00 PM
25/12/2023	14	3:30 PM	25/12/2023	14	2:41 PM
26/12/2023	15	4:23 PM	26/12/2023	15	3:30 PM
27/12/2023	16	5:20 PM	27/12/2023	16	4:28 PM
28/12/2023	17	6:20 PM	28/12/2023	17	5:33 PM
29/12/2023	18	7:21 PM	29/12/2023	18	6:40 PM
30/12/2023	19	8:21 PM	30/12/2023	19	7:48 PM
31/12/2023	20	9:20 PM	31/12/2023	20	8:56 PM

You can find the description of each lunar day in the chapter "A Guide to The Moon Cycle and Lunar Days"

Your decisive attitude toward work is paying off – you have accomplished a lot and are celebrating the holidays with the satisfaction of a job well done. You took the bull by the horns!

Work. You have a lot of work this month, and you are able to handle most of it with flying colors.

Your relationship with colleagues from other cities or abroad will be smooth and predictable. You may get some help here from old friends or someone highly placed in society. Thanks to your shared success, you are able to handle it all with aplomb and be very productive.

Your relationship with management or representatives from official bodies may also take some work this month. The former mostly concerns employees, while the latter will impact business owners. Here, you will see some clouds gather, but be flexible and diplomatic, and you will be able to shelter yourself from the storm.

Overall, however, you will make progress and cover a lot of ground.

The stars recommend being more attentive with your contacts and documents during the second half of the month. From December 12 to January 3, Mercury, the planet responsible for connections and contacts will be in retrograde, which means you may see some quarreling with like-minded people. There is no hostility, but you may find yourself coming back to the same issues over and over again.

Money. Your finances are looking good in December, and you will have regular income, which will increase significantly. Your expenses are low and mostly pleasant in nature.

Love and family. Your personal life may be looking uncertain. In some cases, you are pouring all of your efforts into work, and in others, after a difficult autumn, there is neither peace nor war in your relationships.

Pisces moving somewhere faraway might successfully overcome various problems, which will fade a bit more with each passing day.

Your relationship with relatives will also soften. Your problems will be surmountable, and you will tie up loose ends either this month or a little later on.

Travel is likely in December, and it is a good idea to prepare carefully, if that is going to take place during the second half of the month. It is also best to select a place you have been to several times in the past.

Health. In December, you are healthy, energetic, and ready to move mountains. You may not have to, though – the mountains may simply move to make way for you.

Pisces Description

Sign. Feminine, water, mutable.

Ruler. Neptune, Pluto.

Exaltation. Venus.

Positive traits. Highly imaginative, kind, adaptable, tranquil, peaceful, receptive, impressive, modest, compassionate, caring, delicate, gentle, idealistic, religious, deep.

Negative traits. Passive, shy, fanatical, impractical, fantastical, slovenly, volatile, unreliable, self-indulgent, overly sensual, malleable, submissive, dependent, moody, lazy, apathetic.

Weaknesses in the body. Legs – ankles, toe joints, toes. Tendons and ligaments. Digestive, lymphatic, and endocrine systems, heart and circulatory system.

Metal. Platinum and tin.

Minerals. For a talisman – amethyst and chrysolite. Opal, jasper, and coral are compatible.

Numbers. 3, 11, 19.

Day. Thursday.

Color. Purple and indigo.

Pisces energy

Pisces is influenced by the energies of both Neptune and Jupiter. In ancient cultures, Neptune was revered as the ruler of the seas. He represents the primal ocean and chaos where all opportunities lie, but nothing ever comes to life on its own. Neptune is the highest faith, psychic phenomena, hypersensitivity, deep and intuitive understanding of things and capacity for unearthly love. All of these traits are inherent to Pisces, and generous Jupiter bestows them with confidence in their own importance, a happy life, and great vitality.

Astrological portrait of Pisces

Pisces closes the Zodiac. This sign is a mirror of all the others, with a focus on their strengths and weaknesses. Pisces is a self-redeemer who is able to purify others by taking on the negativity. That is Pisces's greatest mission. Empathy, compassion, and the ability to reflect the qualities of any other sign with detachment are her main traits. "I feel, therefore I am" is Pisces's motto. However, in their negative manifestations, Pisces are ambivalent, unreliable, and prone to betrayal at any time. They make big promises and hardly ever follow through. They seek their own benefits and are very dishonest. Pisces always reflect their environment, which will determine their behavior. They are easily influenced by others, though this is usually unconscious. Without even realizing it, they take on the feelings and thoughts of whomever they are talking to. They can get carried away and simply go with the flow like water, not trying to change their own destiny. Pisces lack willpower and the ability to stand on their own two feet or have the inner core they need to resist the influence of others. Pisces is symbolized by two fish swimming in opposite directions. One fish is living, while the other is depicted as dead. This is Pisces – the living fish is in harmony with God and one with the cosmos. The dead Pisces is illusions, speculation of one's own weakness, opportunism, and chaos. At their worst, Pisces are capable of showing the vile human traits, only to be tormented by remorse afterward.

Pisces is a wise sign, with an understanding of others' suffering. They are capable of sacrificing themselves to help others. They are humane, merciful, and optimistic. But they are also overly sensitive and feel others' pain as their own. Pisces make good psychologists, and they are drawn to that which is hidden. They like to wrap their lives in mystery and express themselves symbolically. They tend to fantasize a lot. Others may not always understand Pisces, which causes her to suffer. She hates arguments and scandal but would rather tolerate evil and injustice than actually fight them. She has a good sense of humor, is friendly, humble, and calm. This draws many people in and opens doors. Pisces wants financial well-being but is rarely able to gain it on her own. As Pisces ages, she is eventually able to achieve peace and prosperity.

Pisces's great task is to carry divine love into the world, have compassion for her neighbors, and help them in their spiritual development. Nearly all Pisces are creative – many are musicians, artists, writers, performers, psychologist, or mystics.

How to recognize Pisces by appearances

Pisces is a sign that is constantly changing. Their appearance is a reflection of their inner state. Pisces tend to have large, deep, and alluring eyes, with an inward or wandering gaze that makes them look mysterious and almost absent. Pisces hardly ever look others in the eye. Their eyelids often appear red and irritated. Their skin is soft, pale, and almost transparent. Their hair is thin rather than thick, and their hands are small and soft, even in men. Pisces tend to gain weight, but they keep an eye on their figure.

Charting Pisces's Fate

Pisces's life path is often difficult and full of ups and downs. If she is not guided by someone else's strong hand, she may not achieve success. Pisces needs something or someone to stimulate and inspire her, especially among men. Female Pisces are often strong-minded, strong-willed individuals who forge their own path in life and are very successful in all of their endeavors.

A Guide to The Moon Cycle and Lunar Days

Since Ancient times, people have noticed that the moon has a strong influence on nature. Our Earth and everything living on it is a single living being, which is why the phases of the moon have such an effect on our health and mental state, and therefore, our lives. Remember Shakespeare and his description of Othello's jealousy in his famous tragedy:

"It is the very error of the moon, She comes more nearer Earth than she was wont And makes men mad."

If our inner rhythm is in harmony with that of the cosmos, we are able to achieve much more. People were aware of this a thousand years ago. The lunar calendar is ancient. We can find it among the ancient Sumerians (4000-3000 BC), the inhabitants of Mesopotamia, Native Americans, Hindus, and ancient Slavs. There is evidence that the Siberian Yakuts had a lunar calendar, as did the Malaysians.

Primitive tribes saw the moon as a source of fertility. Long before Christianity, the waxing moon was seen as favorable for planting new crops and starting a new business, for success and making money, while the waning moon was a sign that business would end.

What are the phases of the moon?

Phase 1 – new moon

- 2 – waxing crescent moon
- 3 – first quarter moon
- 4 – waxing gibbous moon
- 5 – full moon
- 6 – waning gibbous moon
- 7 – third quarter moon
- 8 – waning crescent moon

To simplify things, we can divide the month into two phases:
Waxing crescent moon - before the full moon
Waning crescent moon - after the full moon

New Moon

We cannot see the new moon, as it is hidden. People might complain about feeling weak, mental imbalance, and fatigue. During this time, we want to avoid taking on too much or overdoing things. Generally, people are not very responsive and react poorly to requests, which is why it is best to look out for yourself, while not keeping your plate too full.

The new moon is a bad time for advertising – it will go unnoticed. It is not worth preparing any presentations, parties, or loud gatherings. People are feeling constrained, not very social, and sluggish.

This is also a less than ideal time for surgery, as your recovery will be slow, and the likelihood of medical error is high.

It is also difficult to get an accurate diagnosis during the new moon – diseases might seem to be hidden, and doctors might not see the real underlying cause of what ails you.

The new moon is also a bad time for dates, and sexual encounters may be dissatisfying and leave you feeling disappointed. Ancient astrologers did not advise planning a wedding night during the new moon.

Waxing Crescent Moon

It is easy to identify a waxing crescent moon. If you draw an imaginary line between the two "horns", you should see the letter P. The waxing moon is then divided into one and two quarters.

During the first quarter moon, we need to focus on planning – setting goals and thinking of how we will set about achieving them. However, it is still a good idea to hold back a bit and not overdo things. Energy levels are still low, though they are growing along with the moon. It is still a good idea to avoid any medical procedures during this time.

The second quarter is a time for bold, decisive action. Things will come easy, and there is a greater chance of a lucky break. This is a good time for weddings, especially if the moon will be in Libra, Cancer, or Taurus. Nevertheless, it is a good idea to put off any advertising activities and public speaking until closer to the full moon, if you can.

Full Moon

During the full moon, the Earth is located between the sun and the moon. During this time, the moon is round and fully illuminated. This takes place during days 14-16 of the lunar cycle.

During the full moon, many people feel more vigorous than usual. They are emotional, sociable, and actively seeking more contact, so this may be a good time for any celebrations.

However, be careful not to drink too much – you can relax to the point that you lose control, and the consequences of that can be very unpleasant. If you are able to stick to moderation, there is no better time for a party!

The full moon is also the best time for advertising, as not only will your campaign be widely seen, people will be apt to remember it.

The full moon is also a favorable time for dates, and during this time, people are at their most open, romantic, and willing to tell each other something important that might take their relationship to the next level of trust and understanding.

Moreover, during the full moon, people feel a surge of energy, which may lead to hyperactivity, restlessness, and insomnia.

It will be harder to keep your emotions in check. You might face conflicts with friends, disasters, and accidents. During the full moon, any surgeries are **not a good idea**, as the risk of complications and bleeding is on the rise. Plastic surgery is also a bad idea, as swelling and bruises might be much worse than in another lunar phase. At the same time, the full moon is a good time to get an accurate diagnosis.

During this time, try to limit your calories and liquid intake (especially if you deal with bloating and excess weight), as your body is absorbing both calories and liquids faster during the full moon, and it can be very difficult to get rid of the weight later on.

Waning Crescent Moon

The full moon is over, and a new phase is beginning – the waning moon. This is a quieter time, when all of the jobs you started earlier are being partly or entirely completed (it all depends on the speed and scale).

Surgery will turn out much better if it is performed during the waning moon. Your recovery will be faster, and the likelihood of complications is much lower. If you have any plans to lose weight, the waning moon is the best time to do that. This is also a good time for quitting bad habits, such as smoking or cursing.

The waning moon can also be divided into the third and fourth quarters.

Third quarter - this is a favorable period, and you are able to resolve a lot of problems without conflict. People are calming down and ready to listen and take in information, while still being active. However, this is not the best time to begin any major projects, especially if you are unsure if you will be able to complete them by the start of the new lunar month.

The third quarter is a good time to get married, especially if the moon is in Cancer, Taurus, or Libra.

Fourth quarter – This is the most passive period of the lunar cycle. You are not as strong as usual. Your energy is lagging. You will be tired until reaching a new beginning. The best thing you can do as the lunar cycle comes to an end is to get things in order, and avoid anything that might get in your way at work or in personal relationships. Examine your successes and failures.

Now, let's discuss the lunar days in greater detail. For centuries, people around the world have described the influence of lunar days, and modern astrologers only add to this work, as they compare old texts to modern life.

The 1ˢᵗ lunar day

The first lunar day is extremely important for the rest of the lunar month. This is a much-needed day to carefully plan your activities and lay the groundwork for the rest of the lunar month. Remember that the first lunar day is not a good day for major activities, but rather for sitting down and planning things.

Avoid conflicts on this day, unless you want them to overshadow the rest of the month. Try to see the positive side of things and imagine that the lunar month will bring you good things both at work and in love. The more vividly you can imagine this, the sooner your desires will come to fruition. Perhaps it would be a good idea to jot down plans that will bring you closer to achieving your dreams. This is the best time for both manifesting and making wishes!

This is also a favorable day when it comes to seeking a new job or starting an academic program.

It is fine to go out on a date on the first lunar day, but limit any sexual contact, as your energy levels are low, and you are likely to end up disappointed.

Getting married on the first lunar day is not recommended.

Avoid getting a haircut – there are many indications that cutting your hair on the first lunar day will have a negative effect on your health and life expectancy.

Under no circumstances should you undergo any major cosmetic procedures, including plastic surgery. Energy levels are low, your skin is dull and almost stagnant. The results will not live up to your expectations, and in the worst-case scenario, you will end up looking worse than before. It is common for cosmetic procedures performed on this day to be disappointing or even useless. Even the best surgeons are less capable.

Your good dreams on the first lunar day foretell happiness and joy. Bad ones usually do not come true.

The 2nd lunar day

This is considered a lucky day, and is symbolized by a cornucopia. It is not an exaggeration to say that the second lunar day is a favorable time for both work and love. It is a time for action, and a great period to work on yourself, look for a new job, start something new, or complete any financial transaction, whether a sale or purchase. This is also a great time for creative and scientific insights, and a good time for any meeting – whether political or romantic.

Any romantic dates or sexual encounters during the second lunar day are unlikely to disappoint. This is also a good day for weddings or taking a trip with someone special.

During the second lunar day, the moon is beginning its waxing phase, which is a good time for anything you might to do nourish and restore your skin. This is a great time for any cosmetic procedures aimed at preservation, though it is best to put off any plastic surgery until the waning moon. If that is not possible, then the second lunar day is acceptable, if not ideal, and you will not run into any complications.

Folklore tells us that this is not a good day for a haircut, as that may lead to arguments with a loved one.

This is the best time for exercise – your body is in good shape, and you are able to handle new exercise regimens. If the moon happens to be in Scorpio, though, be careful.

This is a good day for anything positive, but avoid any conflicts, discussions about the status of your relationship, or litigation.

Dreams of the second lunar day are usually not prophetic.

The 3rd lunar day

On this day, we are usually able to make out a thin sliver of the lunar crescent. It is a longstanding tradition to show money during the new month – it is believed that as the moon grows, so will your savings.

However, astrological systems around the world consider this an unlucky, unfavorable day. It is not a good idea to travel, begin any new business, or give into your bad mood.

You might run into many a lot of problems at work on this day, which will cause you a lot of anxiety. However, it is a good day to take a step back and identify and set about fixing any flaws and shortcomings. Remember that everything tends to look worse on this day than it actually is.

It is not the time to ask management for anything – you are likely to walk away disappointed, and end up unfairly reprimanded rather than receiving a promotion or raise. Instead, focus on areas of work that need to be smoothed over or studied further. It will be clear what problems you are facing, and you will easily be able to find a remedy.

Do not rush to criticize your loved ones – things may not be as they appear. "Measure twice and cut once" is your motto on this day.

This is not a good day to get married, as the couple is likely to have a turbulent, short-lived marriage.

You can schedule a cosmetic procedure for this day, but only if it is relatively minor. Plastic surgery should wait.

Do exercises as usual, without overdoing it or adding any new routines.

Dreams on this day do not mean anything.

The 4th lunar day

These are relatively neutral days, in that they are unlikely to bring anything bad, but they also will not bring you any windfalls. The fourth lunar day is symbolized by a tree of paradise, the tree of knowledge, and the choice between good and evil. Things ultimately depend on us and our final decisions.

This is a great day for anything money-related – signing contracts, agreements, or even taking on credit. There also a lot of contradictions on this day – on one hand, we are likely to receive money, which is a good thing, but on the other, we will have to give some of it away, which is never particularly fun or pleasant. There is good reason to consider all of your opportunities and possibilities before acting.

It is not a good day to get married, as the wedding will not be as fun as you had hoped. However, the fourth lunar day is, in fact, a good day for sex and conceiving a healthy child.

Be careful on this day if you happen to engage in any physical exercise, as it is not a good idea to overeat or abuse alcohol. Take care of yourself. Any illnesses which began on this day may be extremely dangerous, if they are not dealt with immediately.

Cosmetic procedures are not contraindicated, as long as they are to preserve your appearance. Plastic surgery can be performed if you truly feel it is necessary.

However, avoid getting a haircut, as it is unlikely to grow back healthily, and will become brittle and dull. However, if the moon is in Leo, you can disregard this advice.

Dreams may turn out to be real.

The 5th lunar day

Traditionally, the fifth lunar day is one of the worst of the lunar month. It is symbolized by a unicorn. Unicorns need to be tamed, but only a virgin is capable of doing so. Many people will feel drained on this day, or frustrated with themselves, those around them, and life in general.

Try to avoid arguments- any conflicts are likely to drag out for a long time, and then you may be overcome with guilt. This advice is relevant for both work and love.

exual encounters may be pleasant, but this is not a good day to plan a wedding, as it is likely to lead to a marriage full of unpleasant incidents.

Do not start any new businesses, or ask those around you for favors- you may be misunderstood and rejected.

It is fine to engage in physical exercise, but if you overdo it on this day, you may injure yourself.

Your energy levels are low. Cosmetic procedures may not be effective, and avoid any plastic surgeries.

It is good if you dream something connected with the road, trips or with movement in general. A bad dream might be a sign of a health problem which should be addressed.

The 6th lunar day

The symbol of the sixth lunar day is a cloud and a crane. This is a philosophical combination that suggests that it is not worth rushing things on these days. This is a very positive, lucky day for both work and love. Creative work will be especially successful, as will any attempts at opening a new business in your field.

The sixth lunar day is a good time for resolving any financial matters. There is one limitation, however – do not give anyone a loan, as they may not pay it back. But you can certainly sponsor and support those who are more vulnerable than you.

This day is a good time to go on a trip, whether close to home or far away.

This is also a good day for dates, weddings, and marriage proposals. Remember that energy is more romantic than sexual, so it is better to give the gift of roses and a bottle of champagne than hot, passionate sex.

It is a good idea to get some exercise, but do not overdo things, though you will probably not want to, either.

Cosmetic procedures will be successful, and you can even have plastic surgery performed, so long as the moon is not in Scorpio.

It is still a good idea to avoid getting your hair cut, as you might "cut off" something good in addition to your hair.

It is better to not discuss dreams as they are usually true. Your dreams of this day can remind you of something that needs to be completed as soon as possible.

The 7ᵗʰ lunar day

This is also a favorable lunar day, and it is symbolized by a fighting cock, which is an Avestan deity. Avoid any aggression on this day, and instead work on yourself, spend time at home or in nature. Avoid discussing the status of your relationship with anyone, arguing, or wishing bad things on anyone. Everything will come back to haunt you, remember, silence is golden.

Business negotiations and contracts will be successful. You can find support, sponsors, and people ready to help you in both words and deeds.

Lighten up with your colleagues and subordinates. Pay attention not only to their shortcomings, but also to their skills. This is a good day for reconciliation and creating both political and romantic unions.

The seventh lunar day is good for traveling, no matter how near or far from home.

It is also a favorable time for love and marriage.

Exercise moderately, and any plastic surgeries will go very smoothly, as long as the moon is not in Scorpio.

Dreams of this day may become a reality.

The 8ᵗʰ lunar day

The symbol for this day is a Phoenix, which symbolizes eternal rebirth and renewal, because this day is a great time for changes in all areas of your life. Your energy is likely to be high, and you want to do something new and unusual. This is a good time to look for a new job or begin studying something. Any out-of-the-box thinking is welcome, along with shaking things up a bit in order to improve your life.

However, avoid any financial transactions, as you may incur losses.

Avoid aggression. You can share your opinion by presenting well-founded arguments and facts, instead.

The phoenix rises from the ashes, so this is a good time to be careful with electrical appliances and fire in general. The risk of housefires is high.

Avoid any major financial transactions on the eighth day, as you may end up facing a series of complications. You can pay people their salaries, as this is unlikely to be a large sum.

This is a good day for weddings, but only if you and your future spouse are restless, creative souls and hope to achieve personal development through your marriage.

Any cosmetic procedures and plastic surgeries will go well today, as they are related to rebirth and renewal. Surgeons may find that they are true artists on this day!

You can try to change your hairstyle and get a fashionable haircut on this day.

You can trust your dreams seen on this day.

The 9th lunar day

The ninth lunar day is not particularly auspicious, and is even referred to as "Satan's" day. You may be overcome with doubt, suspicions, even depression and conflicts.

Your self-esteem will suffer, so don't overdo things physically, and avoid overeating or abusing alcohol.

This is a negative day for any business deals, travel, or financial transactions.

This is a particularly bad day for any events, so keep your head down at work and avoid any new initiatives.

It is better to avoid getting married on "Satan's" day, as the marriage will not last very long. Avoid sex, as well, but you can take care of your partner, listen them, and support them however they need.

Any cosmetic procedures will not have a lasting effect, and avoid any plastic surgery. A haircut will not turn out as you hoped.

Dreams of this day are usually prophetic.

The 10th lunar day

This is one of the luckiest days of the lunar month. It is symbolized by a spring, mushroom, or phallus. This is a time for starting a new business, learning new things, and creating.

The 10th lunar day is particularly lucky for business. Networking and financial transactions will be a success and bring hope. This is an ideal time for changing jobs, shifting your business tactics, and other renewals.

This is a perfect time for people in creative fields and those working in science, who may come up with incredible ideas that will bring many successful returns.

This is a very successful day for building a family and proposing marriage. This is a good time for celebrations and communication, so plan parties, meet with friends, and plan a romantic date.

One of the symbols for this day is a phallus, so sexual encounters are likely to be particularly satisfying.

The 10th lunar day is the best time to begin repairs, buying furniture, and items for home improvement.

You can exercise vigorously, and cosmetic procedures and plastic surgery will be very effective.

Dreams of this day will not come true.

The 11th lunar day

This is one of the best lunar days, and seen as the pinnacle of the lunar cycle. People are likely to be energetic, enthusiastic, and ready to move forward toward their goals.

The 11th lunar day is very successful for any financial transactions or business deals and meetings.

You might actively make yourself known, approach management to discuss a promotion, or look for a new job. This is an auspicious time for advertising campaigns, performances, and holding meetings.

Any trips planned will be a great success, whether near or far from home.

Romantic relationships are improving, sex is harmonious, and very desired.

Weddings held on this day will be fun, and the marriage will be a source of joy and happiness.

Exercise is a great idea, and you might even beat your own personal record.

This is an ideal time for any cosmetic procedures, but any more serious plastic surgeries might lead to a lot of bruising and swelling.

A haircut will turn out as you had hoped, and you can experiment a bit with your appearance.

You can ignore dreams of this day – usually they do not mean anything.

The 12th lunar day

This day is symbolized by the Grail and a heart. As we move closer to the full moon, our emotions are at their most open. During this time, if you ask someone for something, your request will be heeded. This is a day of faith, goodness, and divine revelations.

For business and financial transactions, this is not the most promising day. However, if you help others on this day, your good deeds are sure to come back to you.

This is a day for reconciliation, so do not try to explain your relationships, as no one is at fault, and it is better to focus on yourself, anyway.

Avoid weddings and sex on this day, but if you want to do what your partner asks, there is no better time.

Many may feel less than confident and cheerful during this day, so take it easy when working out. Avoid overeating, stay hydrated, and avoid alcohol.

The 12th lunar day is not the best for getting married or having sex, but the stars would welcome affection and a kind word.

Avoid getting a haircut, or any plastic surgeries. This is a neutral day for minor cosmetic procedures.

Nearly all dreams will come true.

The 13th lunar day

This day is symbolized by Samsara, the wheel of fate, which is very erratic and capable of moving in any direction. This is why the 13th lunar day is full of contradictions. In Indian traditions, this day is compared to a snake eating its own tail. This is a day for paying off old debts and returning to unfinished business.

Avoid beginning any new business on this day. It is preferable to finish old tasks and proofread your work. Information you receive on this day may not be reliable and must be verified.

It is worth resolving financial problems very carefully, and avoid arguments and conflict.

Do not change jobs on this day or go to a new place for the first time. Do not sit at home alone, though, go see old friends, parents, or older family members.

Minor cosmetic procedures are welcome on this day, but avoid any plastic surgery, as you may experience major swelling and bruising. Avoid any haircuts, too.

As a rule, all dreams will come true.

The 14th lunar day

It's a full moon! The 14th lunar day is one of the happiest, and it is symbolized by the trumpet. Pay attention – you may run into new, much-needed information. Networking will be successful, and you can confidently sign agreements, meet with people, and attend fun gatherings or other leisure activities. This is one of the best days for advertising, performances, and concerts, and those working in creative professions should keep this in mind, as should those who work in politics. Do not sit in place on this day – you need to get out and see others, make new connections, and try to be visible.

This is one of the best days for communication with and making requests from management, as your initiatives will be noticed and welcome. You might talk about a promotion, raise, or something similarly related to professional growth.

Couples will see their relationship is moving along well on this day, and it is also a good day for getting married.

Any sex on this day will be vigorous and memorable for a long time. The full moon is the best time for conceiving a child.

Any cosmetic procedures will be effective, but avoid any major changes to your appearance, as there is a high likelihood of bleeding and bruising. A haircut will turn out well.

Your dreams of this day will be more or less doubtful.

The 15th lunar day

It's a full moon! This day is symbolized by a serpent of fire. This is the energy peak of the entire lunar cycle, and a lot will depend on where you are focusing your energy.

You might face a lot of temptations on this day, for example, you might tell someone else's secret or your own to others, and come to regret it for a long time. The stars suggest exercising restraint in both your words and actions, as the 15th day of the lunar cycle is a day of deception and weaknesses.

This is a very active time, and many people might take unnecessary risks. This is not the best day for signing any agreements or contracts. For any performances, concerts, or advertising, however, this is one of the best days of the month.

You can get married on the 15th day, but only if you know each other well and have carefully considered your partnership, without any hasty decisions. This is also a favorable day for a second marriage.

Your romantic relationship is looking wonderful – you are on cloud 9, writing poetry, and deeply convinced of how right your partner is for you – and they feel the same way. It is important that this does not suddenly lead to an abrupt disappointment.

Avoid getting any haircuts on the 15th day of the month, as you may end up with a headache.

Conservative cosmetic procedures and creams will be very effective, but avoid any injections or plastic surgery today. Bleeding, swelling, and bruising are all but guaranteed.

Dreams on the 15th day nearly always come true.

The 16th lunar day

This day is symbolized by a dove. The full moon is over, and the moon is now in its waning phase. Usually, after the turbulent days of the full moon, people feel a bit under the weather. They are not cheerful, and want to avoid excess worry and give themselves a chance to breathe.

Don't ignore your body's wishes, take it easy with physical activities, and take some time for yourself. You might spend time in nature, in the forest, or at a country home.

The 16th day of the lunar month is a time for moderation in all areas – your behavior, eating, and even in your clothes. If you overate during the full moon period, now is the time to diet a bit or at least avoid fatty foods and meat.

This is not a promising day for resolving any financial matters. Keep your documents in order and get ready for any future meetings, instead. If you help a loved one, your good deed will come back 100 times over.

Avoid getting married today, as well as sex.

Cosmetic procedures are likely to be a success, especially if they are related to cleansing your skin, but it is best to avoid any plastic surgery or injections. Your body is not ready to accept them. A haircut will turn out as you hoped.

Any dreams are likely to come true, but that also depends on a correct interpretation.

The 17th lunar day

This day is represented by a vine and bell. It is a happy day and both successful and fun-filled. It is also a good time for negotiations, concluding small business deals, shaking up staffing, and creativity. However, you should keep in mind that the 17th day is only favorable for minor business, and you should avoid starting any major events.

Avoid any major financial transactions on this day. Do not give anyone money as a loan or borrow anything yourself, either.

Any travel, whether for business or pleasure, is likely to be a success.

The 17th day is a great time to get married, and an ideal day for dates. Any sexual encounters will bring you happiness and joy.

Avoid getting your hair cut on this day, but cosmetic procedures and plastic surgery will be a success. Women will look better than usual.

Your dreams are likely to come true in three days.

The 18th lunar day

This day is represented by a mirror. It is a difficult, and generally unpromising day, too. Just as the mirror reflects our imperfections back to us, we need to remember that moderation and modesty are key.

The 18th day is not a favorable time for any business meetings or financial transactions. You can, however work on jobs you already began. It is, however, a positive day for those who work in research or the creative fields.

Your motto of the day is to keep a cool head when it comes to your opportunities and the opportunities of those around you. This is relevant for both work and romantic relationships. It is not a good time to criticize others – any conflicts or arguments may lead to lasting consequences, which you do not need.

Avoid getting married on this day, as well as sexual encounters, which are likely to be disappointing. It is a good time to take a trip together, which will only be good for your relationship.

Avoid getting your hair cut, though this is a relatively neutral day for a haircut, which might turn out well, and though it will not exceed your expectations, it will also not leave you upset. Avoid any plastic surgeries.

Dreams on this day will come true.

The 19th lunar day

This is a very difficult day and it is represented by a spider. The energy is complicated, if not outright dangerous. Don't panic or get depressed, though – this is a test of your strength, and if you are able to hold onto all you have achieved. This is relevant for both work and love. On the 19th day, you should avoid taking any trips.

The energy of the 19th lunar day is very unfavorable for beginning any major projects, and business in general. Work on what you started earlier, get your affairs in order, think over your ideas and emotions, and check to make sure that everything you have done hitherto is living up to your expectations. Do not carry out any financial transactions or take out any loans – do not loan anyone else money, either. Do not ask your managers for anything as they are unlikely to listen to what you have to say, and make judgments instead.

This is a day when you might face outright deception, so do not take any risks and ignore rumors. Do not work on anything related to real estate or legal matters.

This is a very hard time for people with an unbalanced psyche, as they may experience sudden exacerbations or even suicidal ideations.

This is a very unlucky day to get married. Sexual encounters might be disappointing and significantly worsen your relationship.

Avoid any haircuts or cosmetic procedures or surgeries.

Your dreams of this day will come true.

The 20th lunar day

This is also a difficult day, though less so than the 19th. It is represented by an eagle. This is a good time to work on your own development and spiritual growth, by speaking to a psychologist or astrologer.

Avoid pride, anger, arrogance, and envy.

The 20th lunar day is a good time for people who are active and decisive. They will be able to easily overcome any obstacles, flying over them just like an eagle. If you have to overcome your own fears, you will be able to do so – don't limit yourself, and you will see that there is nothing to be afraid of. It is a good day for any financial transactions, signing contracts, and reaching agreements, as well as networking.

The 20th lunar day is a favorable time for those who work in the creative fields, as they will be able to dream up the idea that will open up a whole host of new possibilities. Avoid conflicts – they may ruin your relationship with a lot of people, and it will not be easy to come back from that.

This is a lucky day for getting married, but only if you have been with your partner for several years, now. Sexual encounters will not be particularly joyful, but they also will not cause you any problems.

Avoid getting your hair cut, but you can certainly get it styled. The 20th lunar day is a good day for those who are looking to lose weight. You will be able to do so quickly, and it will be easy for you to follow a diet.

Cosmetic procedures will be a success, as will any plastic surgeries.

Pay attention to dreams of this day as they are likely to come true.

The 21st lunar day

This is one of the most successful days of the lunar month, and it is symbolized by a herd of horses – imagine energy, strength, speed, and bravery. Everything you think up will happen quickly, and you will be able to easily overcome obstacles. A mare is not only brave but also an honest animal, so you will only experience this luck if you remember that honesty is always the best policy.

This is also a favorable day for business. Reaching new agreements and signing contracts, or dealing with foreign partners – it is all likely to be a success. Any financial issues will be resolved successfully.

Those in the creative world will be able to show off their talent and be recognized for their work. Anyone involved in the performing arts can expect success, luck, and recognition. A galloping herd of horses moves quickly, so you might transition to a new job, move to a new apartment, or go on a business trip or travel with your better half.

The 21st lunar day is one of the best to get married or have a sexual encounter.

This is a great time for athletes, hunters, and anyone who likes adventurous activities.

But for criminals and thieves, this is not a lucky or happy day – they will quickly be brought to justice.

Any haircuts or cosmetic procedures are likely to be a huge success and bring both beauty and happiness. You will recover quickly after any surgeries, perhaps without any swelling or bruising at all.

Dreams tend to not be reliable.

The 22nd lunar day

This day will be strange and contradictory. It is symbolized by the elephant Ganesha. According to Indian mythology, Ganesha is the patron saint of hidden knowledge. so this is a favorable day for anyone who is trying to learn more about the world and ready to find the truth, though this is often seen as a hopeless endeavor. This is a day for philosophers and wisemen and women. However, it is an inauspicious day for business, and unlikely to lead to resolving financial issues, signing contracts, agreements, or beginning new projects. You can expect trouble at work.

For creative people, and new employees, this is a successful day.

This is a good day for apologies and reconciliation.

Avoid getting married, though you can feel free to engage in sexual encounters.

For haircuts and cosmetic procedures, this is a fantastic day. Surgeries will also turn out, as long as the moon is not in Scorpio.

Dreams will come true.

The 23rd lunar day

This is a challenging day represented by a crocodile, which is a very aggressive animal. This is a day of strong energy, but it is also adventurous and tough. Your main task is to focus your energy in the right direction. There may be accidents, arguments, conflicts, fights, and violence, which is why it is important to strive for balance and calm.

Keep a close eye on your surroundings – there may be traitors or people who do not wish you well, so be careful.

However, this is still a favorable day for business – many problems will be resolved successfully. You are able to sign contracts and receive credit successfully, as long as you remain active and decisive in what you do.

This is not a day for changing jobs or working on real estate transactions or legal proceedings. This is not a favorable day for traveling, no matter how near or far you plan on going.

This is not a promising day to get married – things may end in conflict, if not an all-out brawl.

Sexual relations are not off the table, as long as the couple trusts one another.

Haircuts or cosmetic procedures will not turn out as you had hoped, so avoid them.

Dreams during this lunar day usually mean something opposite of what awaits you, so you can disregard them.

The 24th lunar day

This is a neutral, calm day that is symbolized by a bear. It is favorable for forgiveness and reconciliation.

This is also a good day for learning new things, reading, self-development, and taking time to relax in nature.

This is a great day for any type of financial activity, conferences, academic meetings, and faraway travel.

The 24th lunar day is a good time for love and getting married, as any marriage will be strong and lasting.

Cosmetic procedures and plastic surgery will be a success, and you can expect a speedy recovery.

Avoid getting a haircut on this day, however, as your hair will likely thin and grow back slowly.

Dreams of this lunar day are usually connected with your personal life.

The 25th lunar day

This is still another quiet day, symbolized by a turtle.

Just like a turtle, this is not a day to rush, and it is best to sit down and take stock of your life. This is a good time for resolving any personal problems, as the moon's energy makes it possible for you to calm down and find the right path.

This is also not a bad day for business. It is believed that any business you begin on this day is sure to be a success. This is especially the case for trade and any monetary activities.

The 25th lunar day is not a good day to get married, especially if the couple is very young.

This is a neutral day for sexual encounters, as the moon is waning, energy is low, so the decision is yours.

Avoid any cosmetic procedures, except those for cleansing your skin. This is not a favorable day for haircuts or plastic surgery – unless the moon is in Libra or Leo.

You can have a prophetic dream on this day.

The 26th lunar day

The 26th lunar day is full of contradictions and complicated. It is represented by a toad.

It is not time to start or take on something new, as nothing good will come of it. Avoid any major purchases, as you will later come to see that your money was wasted. The best thing you can do on this day is stay at home and watch a good movie or read a good book.

Avoid traveling on this day, as it may not turn out well.

The 26th lunar day is a negative day for any business negotiations and starting new businesses. Do not complete any business deals or financial transactions. Your colleagues may be arguing, and your managers may be dissatisfied. But if you have decided to leave your job, there is no better time to do so.

This is not a good day to get married, as both partners' expectations may fall flat, and they will soon be disappointed.

The waning moon carries a negative charge, so avoid any haircuts and surgeries, though you can get cosmetic procedures if they are relatively minor.

Your dreams will come true.

The 27th lunar day

The 27th lunar day is one of the best days of the month, and it is represented by a ship. You can boldly start any new business, which is sure to be promising. This is a great day for students, teachers, and learning new things. Any information that comes to you on this day may be extremely valuable and useful to you.

The 27th day is good for communication and travel, whether near or far from home, and no matter whether it is for work or pleasure.

This is also a good day for any professional activities or financial transactions. If there are people around you who need help, you must support them, as your good deeds will come back 100-fold.

Romantic dates will go well, though any weddings should be quiet and subdued. This is a particularly good day for older couples or second marriages.

The waning moon means that hair will grow back very slowly, but in general, you can expect a haircut to turn out well. This is a great day for plastic surgery or cosmetic procedures, as the results will be pleasing, and you will have a speedy recovery, without any bruising or swelling, most of the time.

However, beware if the moon is in Scorpio on this day – that is not a good omen for any plastic surgery.

Do not pay any attention to dreams on this day.

The 28th lunar day

This is another favorable day in the waning moon cycle, and it is represented by a lotus. This is a day of wisdom and spiritual awakening. If possible, spend part of the day in nature. It is important to take stock of the last month and decide what you need to do during its two remaining days.

This is a good time for any career development, changing jobs, conducting business, decision-making, and signing agreements, as well as going on a trip. You might conclude any business deal, hold negotiations, work with money and securities.

This is also a good day for any repairs or improvements around your home or apartment.

Anyweddingstodayshouldbesubduedandmodest,andrestrictedtofamily members only. A loud, raucous wedding might not turn out very well.

Your hair will grow slowly, but any haircuts will turn out very elegant and stylish. Cosmetic procedures and surgeries are not contraindicated. You will recover quickly with little bruising and swelling.

Do not take any dreams too seriously.

The 29th lunar day

This is one of the most difficult days of the lunar month, and it is considered a Satanic day, unlucky for everyone and everything. It is symbolized by an octopus.

This is a dark day, and many will feel melancholy, depression, and a desire to simply be left alone. This is a day full of conflict and injuries, so be careful everywhere and with everyone. If you can, avoid any travel, and be particularly careful when handling any sharp objects. Do not engage in any business negotiations, sign any contracts, or take part in any networking.

Astrologers believe that anything you start on this day will completely fall apart. For once and for all, get rid of things that are impeding you from living your life. This is a good time to avoid people who you do find unpleasant.

This is also a time for fasting and limitations for everyone. Do not hold any celebrations, weddings, or have sexual relations – these events may not turn out as you hoped, and instead bring you nothing but suffering and strife.

Avoid getting a haircut, as well, as it will not make you look more beautiful and your hair will come back lifeless and dull. Cosmetic procedures can go ahead, but avoid any surgeries.

Dreams are likely to be true.

The 30th lunar day

There is not always a 30th lunar day, as some lunar months have only 29 days. This day is represented by a swan. The 30th lunar day is usually very short, and sometimes, it lasts less than an hour. This is a time for forgiveness and calm.

You might take stock of the last month, while also avoiding anything you do not need around you. Pay back loans, make donations, reconcile with those who recently offended you, and stop speaking to people who cause you suffering.

This is a good time for tying up loose ends, and many astrologers believe that it is also a good day to start new business.

However, avoid celebrations or weddings on this day. Spouses will either not live long, or they will quickly grow apart.

Do not get a haircut on this day, though cosmetic procedures are possible, as long as you avoid any surgeries.

Dreams promise happiness and should come true.

A Guide to Zodiac Compatibility

Often, when we meet a person, we get a feeling that they are good and we take an instant liking to them. Another person, however, gives us immediate feelings of distrust, fear and hostility. Is there an astrological reason why people say that 'the first impression is the most accurate'? How can we detect those who will bring us nothing but trouble and unhappiness?

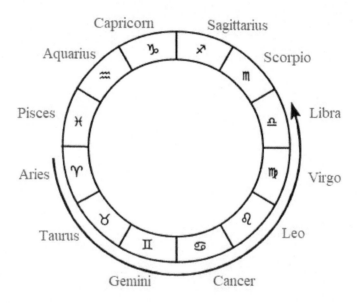

Without going too deeply into astrological subtleties unfamiliar to some readers, it is possible to determine the traits according to which friendship, love or business relationships will develop.

Let's begin with problematic relationships - our most difficult are with our **8ᵗʰ sign**. For example, for Aries the 8ᵗʰ sign is Scorpio, for Taurus it is Sagittarius and so on. Finding your 8th sign is easy; assume your own sign to be first (see above Figure) and then move eight signs counter clockwise around the Zodiac circle. This is also how the other signs (fourth, ninth and so on) that we mention are to be found.

Ancient astrologers variously referred to the 8th sign as the symbol of death, of destruction, of fated love or unfathomable attraction. In astrological terms, this pair is called 'master and slave' or 'boa constrictor and rabbit', with the role of 'master' or 'boa constrictor' being played by our 8th sign.

This relationship is especially difficult for politicians and business people.

We can take the example of a recent political confrontation in the USA. Hilary Clinton is a Scorpio while Donald Trump is a Gemini - her 8th sign. Even though many were certain that Clinton would be elected President, she lost.

To take another example, Hitler was a Taurus and his opponents – Stalin and Churchill - were both of his 8th sign, Sagittarius. The result of their confrontation is well known. Interestingly, the Russian Marshals who dealt crushing military blows to Hitler and so helped end the Third Reich - Konstantin Rokossovsky and Georgy Zhukov - were also Sagittarian, Hitler's 8th sign.

In another historical illustration, Lenin was also a Taurus. Stalin was of Lenin's 8th sign and was ultimately responsible for the downfall and possibly death of his one-time comrade-in-arms.

Business ties with those of our 8th sign are hazardous as they ultimately lead to stress and loss; both financial and moral. So, do not tangle with your 8th sign and never fight with it - your chances of winning are remote!

Such relationships are very interesting in terms of love and romance, however. We are magnetically attracted to our 8th sign and even though it may be very intense physically, it is very difficult for family life;

'Feeling bad when together, feeling worse when apart'.

As an example, let us take the famous lovers - George Sand who was Cancer and Alfred de Musset who was Sagittarius. Cancer is the 8th sign for Sagittarius, and the story of their crazy two-year love affair was the subject of much attention throughout France. Critics and writers were divided into 'Mussulist' and 'Sandist' camps; they debated fiercely about who was to blame for the sad ending to their love story - him or her. It's hard to imagine the energy needed to captivate the public for so long, but that energy was destructive for the couple. Passion raged in their hearts, but neither of them was able to comprehend their situation.

Georges Sand wrote to Musset, "*I don't love you anymore, and I will always adore you. I don't want you anymore, and I can't do without you. It seems that nothing but a heavenly lightning strike can heal me by destroying me. Good-bye! Stay or go, but don't say that I am not suffering. This is the only thing that can make me suffer even more, my love, my life, my blood! Go away, but kill me, leaving.*" Musset replied only in brief, but its power surpassed Sand's tirade, "*When you embraced me, I felt something that is still bothering me, making it impossible for me to approach another woman.*" These two people loved each other passionately and for two years lived together in a powder keg of passion, hatred and treachery.

When someone enters into a romantic liaison with their 8th sign, there will be no peace; indeed, these relationships are very attractive to those who enjoy the edgy, the borderline and, in the Dostoevsky style, the melodramatic. The first to lose interest in the relationship is, as a rule, the 8th sign.

If, by turn of fate, our child is born under our 8th sign, they will be very different from us and, in some ways, not live up to our expectations. It may be best to let them choose their own path.

In business and political relationships, the combination with our **12th sign** is also a complicated one.

We can take two political examples. Angela Merkel is a Cancer while Donald Trump is a Gemini - her 12th sign. This is why their relations are strained and complicated and we can even perhaps assume that the American president will achieve his political goals at her expense. Boris Yeltsin (Aquarius) was the 12th sign to Mikhail Gorbachev (Pisces) and it was Yeltsin who managed to dethrone the champion of Perestroika.

Even ancient astrologers noticed that our relationships with our 12th signs can never develop evenly; it is one of the most curious and problematic combinations. They are our hidden enemies and they seem to be digging a hole for us; they ingratiate themselves with us, discover our innermost secrets. As a result, we become bewildered and make mistakes when we deal with them. Among the Roman emperors murdered by members of their entourage, there was an interesting pattern - all the murderers were the 12th sign of the murdered.

We can also see this pernicious effect in Russian history: the German princess Alexandra (Gemini) married the last Russian Tsar Nicholas II (Taurus) - he was her 12th sign and brought her a tragic death. The wicked genius Grigory Rasputin (Cancer) made friends with Tsarina Alexandra, who was his 12th sign, and was murdered as a result of their odd friendship. The weakness of Nicholas II was exposed, and his authority reduced after the death of the economic and social reformer Pyotr Stolypin, who was his 12th sign. Thus, we see a chain of people whose downfall was brought about by their 12th sign.

So, it makes sense to be cautious of your 12th sign, especially if you have business ties. Usually, these people know much more about us than we want them to and they will often reveal our secrets for personal gain if it suits them. However, the outset of these relationships is, as a rule, quite normal - sometimes the two people will be friends, but sooner or later one will betray the other one or divulge a secret; inadvertently or not.

In terms of romantic relationships, our 12th sign is gentle, they take care of us and are tender towards us. They know our weaknesses well but accept them with understanding. It is they who guide us, although sometimes almost imperceptibly. Sexual attraction is usually strong.

For example, Meghan Markle is a Leo, the 12th sign for Prince Harry, who is a Virgo. Despite Queen Elizabeth II being lukewarm about the match, Harry's love was so strong that they did marry.

If a child is our 12th sign, it later becomes clear that they know all our secrets, even those that they are not supposed to know. It is very difficult to control them as they do everything in their own way.

Relations with our **7th sign** are also interesting. They are like our opposite; they have something to learn from us while we, in turn, have something to learn from them. This combination, in business and personal relationships, can be very positive and stimulating provided that both partners are quite intelligent and have high moral standards but if not, constant misunderstandings and challenges follow. Marriage or co-operation with the 7th sign can only exist as the union of two fully-fledged individuals and in this case love, significant business achievements and social success are possible.

However, the combination can be not only interesting, but also quite complicated.

An example is Angelina Jolie, a Gemini, and Brad Pitt, a Sagittarius. This is a typical bond with a 7th sign - it's lively and interesting, but rather stressful. Although such a couple may quarrel and even part from time to time, never do they lose interest in each other.

This may be why this combination is more stable in middle-age when there is an understanding of the true nature of marriage and partnership. In global, political terms, this suggests a state of eternal tension - a cold war - for example between Yeltsin (Aquarius) and Bill Clinton (Leo).

Relations with our **9th sign** are very good; they are our teacher and advisor - one who reveals things we are unaware of and our relationships with them very often involve travel or re-location. The combination can lead to spiritual growth and can be beneficial in terms of business.

Although, for example, Trump and Putin are political opponents, they can come to an understanding and even feel a certain sympathy for each other because Putin is a Libra while Trump is a Gemini, his 9th sign.

This union is also quite harmonious for conjugal and romantic relationships.

We treat our **3rd sign** somewhat condescendingly. They are like our younger siblings; we teach them and expect them to listen attentively. Our younger brothers and sisters are more often than not born under this sign. In terms of personal and sexual relationships, the union is not very inspiring and can end quickly, although this is not always the case. In terms of business, it is fairly average as it often connects partners from different cities or countries.

We treat our **5th sign** as a child and we must take care of them accordingly. The combination is not very good for business, however, since our 5th sign triumphs over us in terms of connections and finances, and thereby gives us very little in return save for love or sympathy. However, they are very good for family and romantic relationships, especially if the 5th sign is female. If a child is born as a 5th sign to their parents, their relationship will be a mutually smooth, loving and understanding one that lasts a lifetime.

Our **10th sign** is a born leader. Depending on the spiritual level of those involved, both pleasant and tense relations are possible; the relationship is often mutually beneficial in the good times but mutually disruptive in the bad times. In family relations, our 10th sign always tries to lead and will do so according to their intelligence and upbringing.

Our **4th sign** protects our home and can act as a sponsor to strengthen our financial or moral positions. Their advice should be heeded in all cases as it can be very effective, albeit very unobtrusive. If a woman takes this role, the relationship can be long and romantic, since all the spouse's wishes are usually met one way or another. Sometimes, such couples achieve great social success; for instance, Hilary Clinton, a Scorpio is the 4th sign to Bill Clinton, a Leo. On the other hand, if the husband is the 4th sign for his wife, he tends to be henpecked. There is often a strong sexual attraction. Our 4th sign can improve our living conditions and care for us in a parental way. If a child is our 4th sign, they are close to us and support us affectionately.

Relations with our **11th sign** are often either friendly or patronizing; we treat them reverently, while they treat us with friendly condescension. Sometimes, these relationships develop in an 'older brother' or 'high-ranking friend' sense; indeed, older brothers and sisters are often our 11th sign. In terms of personal and sexual relationships, our 11th sign is always inclined to enslave us. This tendency is most clearly manifested in such alliances as Capricorn and Pisces or Leo and Libra. A child who is the 11th sign to their parents will achieve greater success than their parents, but this will only make the parents proud.

Our **2nd sign** should bring us financial or other benefits; we receive a lot from them in both our business and our family life. In married couples, the 2nd sign usually looks after the financial situation for the benefit of the family. Sexual attraction is strong.

Our **6th sign** is our 'slave'; we always benefit from working with them and it's very difficult for them to escape our influence. In the event of hostility, especially if they have provoked the conflict, they receive a powerful retaliatory strike. In personal relations, we can almost destroy them by making them dance to our tune. For example, if a husband doesn't allow his wife to work or there are other adverse family circumstances, she gradually becomes lost as an individual despite being surrounded by care. This is the best-case scenario; worse outcomes are possible. Our 6th sign has a strong sexual attraction to us because we are the fatal 8th sign for them; we cool down quickly, however, and often make all kinds of demands. If the relationship with our 6th sign is a long one, there is a danger that routine, boredom and stagnation will ultimately destroy the relationship. A child born under our 6th sign needs particularly careful handling as they can feel fear or embarrassment when communicating with us. Their health often needs increased attention and we should also remember that they are very different from us emotionally.

Finally, we turn to relations with **our own sign**. Scorpio with Scorpio and Cancer with Cancer get along well, but in most other cases, however, our own sign is of little interest to us as it has a similar energy. Sometimes, this relationship can develop as a rivalry, either in business or in love.

There is another interesting detail - we are often attracted to one particular sign. For example, a man's wife and mistress often have the same sign. If there is confrontation between the two, the stronger character displaces the weaker one. As an example, Prince Charles is a Scorpio, while both Princess Diana and Camilla Parker Bowles were born under the sign of Cancer. Camilla was the more assertive and became dominant.

Of course, in order to draw any definitive conclusions, we need an individually prepared horoscope, but the above always, one way or another, manifests itself.

Love Description of Zodiac Signs

We know that human sexual behavior has been studied at length. Entire libraries have been written about it, with the aim of helping us understand ourselves and our partners. But is that even possible? It may not be; no matter how smart we are, when it comes to love and sex, there is always an infinite amount to learn. But we have to strive for perfection, and astrology, with its millennia of research, twelve astrological types, and twelve zodiac signs, may hold the key. Below, you will find a brief and accurate description of each zodiac sign's characteristics in love, for both men and women.

Men

ARIES

Aries men are not particularly deep or wise, but they make up for it in sincerity and loyalty. They are active, even aggressive lovers, but a hopeless romantic may be lurking just below the surface. Aries are often monogamous and chivalrous men, for whom there is only one woman (of course, in her absence, they can sleep around with no remorse). If the object of your affection is an Aries, be sure to give him a lot of sex, and remember that for an Aries, when it comes to sex, anything goes. Aries cannot stand women who are negative or disheveled. They need someone energetic, lively, and to feel exciting feelings of romance.

The best partner for an Aries is Cancer, Sagittarius, or Leo. Aquarius can also be a good match, but the relationship will be rather friendly in nature. Partnering with a Scorpio or Taurus will be difficult, but they can be stimulating lovers for an Aries. Virgos are good business contacts, but a poor match as lovers or spouses.

TAURUS

A typical Taurean man is warm, friendly, gentle, and passionate, even if he doesn't always show it. He is utterly captivated by the beauty of the female body, and can find inspiration in any woman. A Taurus has such excess physical and sexual prowess, that to him, sex is a way to relax and calm down. He is the most passionate and emotional lover of the Zodiac, but he expects his partner to take the initiative, and if she doesn't, he will easily find someone else. Taureans rarely divorce, and are true to the end – if not sexually, at least spiritually. They are secretive, keep their cards close, and may have secret lovers. If a Taurus does not feel a deep emotional connection with someone, he won't be shy to ask her friends for their number. He prefers a voluptuous figure over an athletic or skinny woman.

The best partners for a Taurus are Cancer, Virgo, Pisces, or Scorpio. Sagittarius can show a Taurus real delights in both body and spirit, but they are unlikely to make it down the aisle. They can have an interesting relationship with an Aquarius – these signs are very different, but sometimes can spend their lives together. They might initially feel attracted to an Aries, before rejecting her.

GEMINI

The typical Gemini man is easygoing and polite. He is calm, collected, and analytical. For a Gemini, passion is closely linked to intellect, to the point that they will try to find an explanation for their actions before carrying them out. But passion cannot be explained, which scares a Gemini, and they begin jumping from one extreme to the other. This is why you will find more bigamists among Geminis than any other sign of the Zodiac. Sometimes, Gemini men even have two families, or divorce and marry several times throughout the course of their lives. This may be because they simply can't let new and interesting experiences pass them by. A Gemini's wife or lover needs to be smart, quick, and always looking ahead. If she isn't, he will find a new object for his affection.

Aquarians, Libras, and Aries make good partners for a Gemini. A Sagittarius can be fascinating for him, but they will not marry before he reaches middle age, as both partners will be fickle while they are younger. A Gemini and Scorpio are likely to be a difficult match, and the Gemini will try to wriggle out of the Scorpio's tight embrace. A Taurus will be an exciting sex partner, but their partnership won't be for long, and the Taurus is often at fault.

CANCER

Cancers tend to be deep, emotional individuals, who are both sensitive and highly sexual. Their charm is almost mystical, and they know how to use it. Cancers may be the most promiscuous sign of the Zodiac, and open to absolutely anything in bed. Younger Cancers look for women who are more mature, as they are skilled lovers. As they age, they look for someone young enough to be their own daughter, and delight in taking on the role of a teacher. Cancers are devoted to building a family and an inviting home, but once they achieve that goal, they are likely to have a wandering eye. They will not seek moral justification, as they sincerely believe it is simply something everyone does. Their charm works in such a way that women are deeply convinced they are the most important love in a Cancer's life, and that circumstances are the only thing preventing them from being together. Remember that a Cancer man is a master manipulator, and will not be yours unless he is sure you have throngs of admirers. He loves feminine curves, and is turned on by exquisite fragrances. Cancers don't end things with old lovers, and often go back for a visit after a breakup. Another type of Cancer is rarer – a faithful friend, and up for anything in order to provide for his wife and children. He is patriotic and a responsible worker.

Scorpios, Pisces, and other Cancers are a good match. A Taurus can make for a lasting relationship, as both signs place great value on family and are able to get along with one another. A Sagittarius will result in fights and blowouts from the very beginning, followed by conflicts and breakups. The Sagittarius will suffer the most. Marriage to an Aries isn't off the table, but it won't last very long.

LEO

A typical Leo is handsome, proud, and vain, with a need to be the center of attention at all times. They often pretend to be virtuous, until they are able to actually master it. They crave flattery, and prefer women who comply and cater to them. Leos demand unconditional obedience, and constant approval. When a Leo is in love, he is fairly sexual, and capable of being devoted and faithful. Cheap love affairs are not his thing, and Leos are highly aware of how expensive it is to divorce. They make excellent fathers. A Leo's partner needs to look polished and well-dressed, and he will not tolerate either frumpiness or nerds.

Aries, Sagittarius, and Gemini make for good matches. Leos are often very beguiling to Libras; this is the most infamous astrological "master-slave" pairing. Leos are also inexplicably drawn to Pisces – this is the only sign capable of taming them. A Leo and Virgo will face a host of problems sooner or later, and they might be material in nature. The Virgo will attempt to conquer him, and if she does, a breakup is inevitable.

VIRGO

Virgo is a highly intellectual sign, who likes to take a step back and spend his time studying the big picture. But love inherently does not lend itself to analysis, and this can leave Virgos feeling perplexed. While Virgo is taking his time, studying the object of his affection, someone else will swoop in and take her away, leaving him bitterly disappointed. Perhaps for that reason, Virgos tend to marry late, but once they are married, they remain true, and hardly ever initiate divorce. In bed, they are modest and reserved, as they see sex as some sort of quirk of nature, designed solely for procreation. Most Virgos have a gifted sense of taste, hearing, and smell. They cannot tolerate pungent odors and can be squeamish; they believe their partners should always take pains to be very clean. Virgos usually hate over-the-top expressions of love, and are immune to sex as a mean s of control. Many Virgos are stingy and more appropriate as husbands than lovers. Male Virgos tend to be monogamous, though if they are unhappy or disappointed with their partner, they may begin to look for comfort elsewhere and often give in to drunkenness.

Taurus, Capricorn, and Scorpio make the best partners for a Virgo. They may feel inexplicable attraction for Aquarians. They will form friendships with Aries, but rarely will this couple make it down the aisle. With Leos, be careful – this sign is best as a lover, not a spouse.

LIBRA

Libra is a very complex, wishy-washy sign. They are constantly seeking perfection, which often leaves them in discord with the reality around them. Libra men are elegant and refined, and expect no less from their partner. Many Libras treat their partners like a beautiful work of art, and have trouble holding onto the object of their affection. They view love itself as a very abstract concept, and can get tired of the physical aspect of their relationship. They are much more drawn to intrigue and the chase- dreams, candlelit evenings, and other symbols of romance. A high percentage of Libra men are gay, and they view sex with other men as the more elite option. Even when Libras are unhappy in their marriages, they never divorce willingly. Their wives might leave them, however, or they might be taken away by a more decisive partner.

Aquarius and Gemini make the best matches for Libras. Libra can also easily control an independent Sagittarius, and can easily fall under the influence of a powerful and determined Leo, before putting all his strength and effort into breaking free. Relationships with Scorpios are difficult; they may become lovers, but will rarely marry.

SCORPIO

Though it is common to perceive Scorpios as incredibly sexual, they are, in fact, very unassuming, and never brag about their exploits. They will, however, be faithful and devoted to the right woman. The Scorpio man is taciturn, and you can't expect any tender words from him, but he will defend those he loves to the very end. Despite his outward control, Scorpio is very emotional; he needs and craves love, and is willing to fight for it. Scorpios are incredible lovers, and rather than leaving them tired, sex leaves them feeling energized. They are always sexy, even if they aren't particularly handsome. They are unconcerned with the ceremony of wooing you, and more focused on the act of love itself.

Expressive Cancers and gentle, amenable Pisces make the best partners. A Scorpio might also fall under the spell of a Virgo, who is adept at taking the lead. Sparks might fly between two Scorpios, or with a Taurus, who is perfect for a Scorpio in bed. Relationships with Libras, Sagittarians, and Aries are difficult.

SAGITTARIUS

Sagittarian men are lucky, curious, and gregarious. Younger Sagittarians are romantic, passionate, and burning with desire to experience every type of love. Sagittarius is a very idealistic sign, and in that search for perfection, they tend to flit from one partner to another, eventually forgetting what they were even looking for in the first place. A negative Sagittarius might have two or three relationships going on at once, assigning each partner a different day of the week. On the other hand, a positive Sagittarius will channel his powerful sexual energy into creativity, and take his career to new heights. Generally speaking, after multiple relationships and divorces, the Sagittarian man will conclude that his ideal marriage is one where his partner is willing to look the other way.

Aries and Leo make the best matches for a Sagittarius. He might fall under the spell of a Cancer, but would not be happy being married to her. Gemini can be very intriguing, but will only make for a happy marriage after middle age, when both partners are older and wiser. Younger Sagittarians often marry Aquarian women, but things quickly fall apart. Scorpios can make for an interesting relationship, but if the Sagittarius fails to comply, divorce is inevitable.

CAPRICORN

Practical, reserved Capricorn is one of the least sexual signs of the Zodiac. He views sex as an idle way to pass the time, and something he can live without, until he wants to start a family. He tends to marry late, and almost never divorces. Young Capricorns are prone to suppressing their sexual desires, and only discover them later in life, when they have already achieved everything a real man needs – a career and money. We'll be frank – Capricorn is not the best lover, but he can compensate by being caring, attentive, and showering you with valuable gifts. Ever cautious, Capricorn loves to schedule his sexual relationships, and this is something partners will just have to accept. Women should understand that Capricorn needs some help relaxing – perhaps with alcohol. They prefer inconspicuous, unassuming women, and run away from a fashion plate.

The best partners for a Capricorn are Virgo, Taurus, or Scorpio. Cancers might catch his attention, and if they marry, it is likely to be for life. Capricorn is able to easily dominate Pisces, and Pisces-Capricorn is a well-known "slave and master" combination. Relationships with Leos tend to be erratic, and they are unlikely to wed. Aries might make for a cozy family at first, but things will cool off quickly, and often, the marriage only lasts as long as Capricorn is unwilling to make a change in his life.

AQUARIUS

Aquarian men are mercurial, and often come off as peculiar, unusual, or aloof, and detached. Aquarians are turned on by anything novel or strange, and they are constantly looking for new and interesting people. They are stimulated by having a variety of sexual partners, but they consider this to simply be normal life, rather than sexually immoral. Aquarians are unique – they are more abstract than realistic, and can be cold and incomprehensible, even in close relationships. Once an Aquarius gets married, he will try to remain within the realm of decency, but often fails. An Aquarian's partners need uncommon patience, as nothing they do can restrain him. Occasionally, one might encounter another kind of Aquarius – a responsible, hard worker, and exemplary family man.

The best matches for an Aquarius are female fellow Aquarians, Libras, and Sagittarians. When Aquarius seeks out yet another affair, he is not choosy, and will be happy with anyone.

PISCES

Pisces is the most eccentric sign of the Zodiac. This is reflected in his romantic tendencies and sex life. Pisces men become very dependent on those with whom they have a close relationship. Paradoxically, they are simultaneously crafty and childlike when it comes to playing games, and they are easily deceived. As a double bodied sign, Pisces rarely marry just once, as they are very sexual, easily fall in love, and are constantly seeking their ideal. Pisces are very warm people, who love to take care of others and are inclined toward "slave-master" relationships, in which they are the submissive partner. But after catering to so many lovers, Pisces will remain elusive. They are impossible to figure out ahead of time – today, they might be declaring their love for you, but tomorrow, they may disappear – possibly forever! To a Pisces, love is a fantasy, illusion, and dream, and they might spend their whole lives in pursuit of it. Pisces who are unhappy in love are vulnerable to alcoholism or drug addiction.

Cancer and Scorpio make the best partners for a Pisces. He is also easily dominated by Capricorn and Libra, but in turn will conquer even a queen-like Leo. Often, they are fascinated by Geminis – if they marry, it will last a long time, but likely not forever. Relationships with Aries and Sagittarians are erratic, though initially, things can seem almost perfect.

Women

ARIES

Aries women are leaders. They are decisive, bold, and very protective. An Aries can take initiative and is not afraid to make the first move. Her ideal man is strong, and someone she can admire. But remember, at the slightest whiff of weakness, she will knock him off his pedestal. She does not like dull, whiny men, and thinks that there is always a way out of any situation. If she loves someone, she will be faithful. Aries women are too honest to try leading a double life. They are possessive, jealous, and not only will they not forgive those who are unfaithful, their revenge may be brutal; they know no limits. If you can handle an Aries, don't try to put her in a cage; it is best to give her a long leash. Periodically give her some space – then she will seek you out herself. She is sexual, and believe that anything goes in bed.

Her best partners are a Sagittarius or Leo. A Libra can make a good match after middle age, once both partners have grown wiser and settled down a bit. Gemini and Aquarius are only good partners during the initial phase, when everything is still new, but soon enough, they will lose interest in each other. Scorpios are good matches in bed, but only suitable as lovers.

TAURUS

Taurean women possess qualities that men often dream about, but rarely find in the flesh – they are soft, charming, practical, and reliable – they are very caring and will support their partner in every way. A Taurus is highly sexual, affectionate, and can show a man how to take pleasure to new heights. She is also strong and intense. If she is in love, she will be faithful. But when love fades away, she might find someone else on the side, though she will still fight to save her marriage, particularly if her husband earns good money. A Taurus will not tolerate a man who is disheveled or disorganized, and anyone dating her needs to always be on his toes. She will expect gifts, and likes being taken to expensive restaurants, concerts, and other events. If you argue, try to make the first peace offering, because a Taurus finds it very hard to do so – she might withdraw and ruminate for a long time. Never air your dirty laundry; solve all your problems one-on-one.

Scorpio, Virgo, Capricorn, and Cancer make the best matches. A relationship with an Aries or Sagittarius would be difficult. There is little attraction between a Taurus and a Leo, and initially Libras can make for a good partner in bed, but things will quickly cool off and fall apart. A Taurus and Aquarius make an interesting match – despite the difference in signs, their relationships are often lasting, and almost lifelong.

GEMINI

Gemini women are social butterflies, outgoing, and they easily make friends, and then break off the friendship, if people do not hold their interest. A Gemini falls in love hard, is very creative, and often fantasizes about the object of her affection. She is uninterested in sex without any attachment, loves to flirt, and, for the most part, is not particularly affectionate. She dreams of a partner who is her friend, lover, and a romantic, all at once. A Gemini has no use for a man who brings nothing to the table intellectually. That is a tall order, so Geminis often divorce and marry several times. Others simply marry later in life. Once you have begun a life together, do not try to keep her inside – she needs to travel, explore, socialize, attend events and go to the theater. She cannot tolerate possessive men, so avoid giving her the third degree, and remember that despite her flirtatious and social nature, she is, in fact, faithful – as long as you keep her interested and she is in love. Astrologists believe that Geminis do not know what they need until age 29 or 30, so it is best to hold off on marriage until then.

Leo and Libra make the best matches. A relationship with a Cancer is likely, though complex, and depends solely on the Cancer's affection. A Gemini and Sagittarius can have an interesting, dynamic relationship, but these are two restless signs, which might only manage to get together after ages 40-45, once they have had enough thrills out of life and learned to be patient. Relationships with a Capricorn are very difficult, and almost never happen. The honeymoon stage can be wonderful with a Scorpio, but each partner will eventually go their own way, before ending things. A Gemini and Pisces union can also be very interesting – they are drawn to each other, and can have a wonderful relationship, but after a while, the cracks start to show and things will fall apart. An Aquarius is also not a bad match, but they will have little sexual chemistry.

CANCER

Cancers can be divided into two opposing groups. The first includes a sweet and gentle creature who is willing to dedicate her life to her husband and children. She is endlessly devoted to her husband, especially if he makes a decent living and remains faithful. She views all men as potential husbands, which means it is dangerous to strike up a relationship with her if your intentions are not serious; she can be anxious and clingy, sensitive and prone to crying. It is better to break things to her gently, rather than directly spitting out the cold, hard truth. She wants a man who can be a provider, though she often earns well herself. She puts money away for a rainy day, and knows how to be thrifty, for the sake of others around her, rather than only for herself. She is an excellent cook and capable of building an inviting home for her loved ones. She is enthusiastic in bed, a wonderful wife, and a caring mother.

The second type of Cancer is neurotic, and capable of creating a living hell for those around her. She believes that the world is her enemy, and manages to constantly find new intrigue and machinations.

Another Cancer, Virgo, Taurus, Scorpio, and Pisces make the best matches. A Cancer can often fall in love with a Gemini, but eventually, things will grow complicated, as she will be exhausted by a Gemini's constant mood swings and cheating. A Cancer and Sagittarius will initially have passionate sex, but things will quickly cool off. A relationship with a Capricorn is a real possibility, but only later in life, as while they are young, they are likely to fight and argue constantly. Cancer can also have a relationship with an Aries, but this will not be easy.

LEO

Leos are usually beautiful or charming, and outwardly sexual. And yet, appearances can be deceiving – they are not actually that interested in sex. Leo women want to be the center of attention and men running after them boosts their self-esteem, but they are more interested in their career, creating something new, and success than sex. They often have high-powered careers and are proud of their own achievements. Their partners need to be strong; if a Leo feels a man is weak, she can carry him herself for a while- before leaving him. It is difficult for her to find a partner for life, as chivalrous knights are a dying breed, and she is not willing to compromise. If you are interested in a Leo, take the initiative, admire her, and remember that even a queen is still a woman. Timid men or tightwads need not apply. Leos like to help others, but they don't need a walking disaster in their life. If they are married and in love, they are usually faithful, and petty gossip isn't their thing. Leo women make excellent mothers, and are ready to give their lives to their children. Their negative traits include vanity and a willingness to lie, in order to make themselves look better.

Sagittarius, Aries, and Libra make the best matches. Leos can also have an interesting relationship with a Virgo, though both partners will weaken each other. Life with a Taurus will lead to endless arguments – both signs are very stubborn, and unwilling to give in. Leos and Pisces are another difficult pair, as she will have to learn to be submissive if she wants to keep him around. A relationship with a Capricorn will work if there is a common denominator, but they will have little sexual chemistry. Life with a Scorpio will be turbulent to say the least, and they will usually break up later in life.

VIRGO

Virgo women are practical, clever, and often duplicitous. Marrying one isn't for everyone. She is a neat freak to the point of annoying those around her. She is also an excellent cook, and strives to ensure her children receive the very best by teaching them everything, and preparing them for a bright future. She is also thrifty – she won't throw money around, and, in fact, won't even give it to her husband. She has no time for rude, macho strongmen, and is suspicious of spendthrifts. She will not be offended if you take her to a cozy and modest café rather than an elegant restaurant. Virgos are masters of intrigue, and manage to outperform every other sign of the Zodiac in this regard. Virgos love to criticize everyone and everything; to listen to them, the entire world is simply a disaster and wrong, and only she is the exception to this rule. Virgos are not believed to be particularly sexual, but there are different variations when it comes to this. Rarely, one finds an open-minded Virgo willing to try anything, and who does it all on a grand scale – but she is rather the exception to this general rule.

The best matches for a Virgo are Cancer, Taurus, and Capricorn. She also can get along well with a Scorpio, but will find conflict with Sagittarius. A Pisces will strike her interest, but they will rarely make it down the aisle. She is often attracted to an Aquarius, but they would drive each other up the wall were they to actually marry. An Aries forces Virgo to see another side of life, but here, she will have to learn to conform and adapt.

LIBRA

Female Libras tend to be beautiful, glamorous, or very charming. They are practical, tactical, rational, though they are adept at hiding these qualities behind their romantic and elegant appearance. Libras are drawn to marriage, and are good at imagining the kind of partner they need. They seek out strong, well-off men and are often more interested in someone's social status and bank account than feelings. The object of their affection needs to be dashing, and have a good reputation in society. Libras love expensive things, jewelry, and finery. If they are feeling down, a beautiful gift will instantly cheer them up. They will not tolerate scandal or conflict, and will spend all their energy trying to keep the peace, or at least the appearance thereof. They do not like to air their dirty laundry, and will only divorce in extreme circumstances. They are always convinced they are right and react to any objections as though they have been insulted. Most Libras are not particularly sexual, except those with Venus or the Moon in Scorpio.

Leos, Geminis, and Aquarians make good matches. Libra women are highly attracted to Aries men - this is a real case of opposites attract. They can get along with a Sagittarius, though he will find that Libras are too proper and calm. Capricorn, Pisces, and Cancer are all difficult matches. Things will begin tumultuously with a Taurus, before each partner goes his or her own way.

SCORPIO

Scorpio women may appear outwardly restrained, but there is much more bubbling below the surface. They are ambitious with high self-esteem, but often wear a mask of unpretentiousness. They are the true power behind the scenes, the one who holds the family together, but never talk about it. Scorpios are strong-willed, resilient, and natural survivors. Often, Scorpios are brutally honest, and expect the same out of those around them. They do not like having to conform, and attempt to get others to adapt to them, as they honestly believe everyone will be better off that way. They are incredibly intuitive, and not easily deceived. They have an excellent memory, and can quickly figure out which of your buttons to push. They are passionate in bed, and their temperament will not diminish with age. When she is sexually frustrated, a Scorpio will throw all of her energy into her career or her loved ones. She is proud, categorical, and "if you don't do it right, don't do it at all" is her motto. Scorpio cannot be fooled, and she will not forgive any cheating. Will she cheat herself? Yes! But it will not break up her family, and she will attempt to keep it a secret. Scorpios are usually attractive to men, even if they are not particularly beautiful. They keep a low profile, though they always figure out their partner, and give them some invisible sign. There is also another, selfish type of Scorpio, who will use others for as long as they need them, before unceremoniously casting them aside.

Taurus is a good match; they will have excellent sexual chemistry and understand each other. Scorpio and Gemini are drawn to each other, but are unlikely to stay together long enough to actually get married. Cancer can be a good partner as well, but Cancers are possessive, while Scorpios do not like others meddling in their affairs, though they can later resolve their arguments in bed. Scorpio and Leo are often found together, but their relationship can also be very complicated. Leos are animated and chipper, while Scorpios, who are much deeper and more stubborn, see Leos as not particularly serious or reliable. One good example of this is Bill (a Leo) and Hillary (a Scorpio) Clinton. Virgo can also make a good partner, but when Scorpio seemingly lacks emotions, he will look for them elsewhere. Relationships with Lira are strange and very rare. Scorpio sees Libra as too insecure, and Libra does not appreciate Scorpio's rigidity. Two Scorpios together make an excellent marriage! Sagittarius and Scorpio are unlikely to get together, as she will think he is shallow and rude. If they do manage to get married, Scorpio's drive and persistence is the only thing that will make the marriage last. Capricorn is also not a bad match, and while Scorpio finds Aquarius attractive, they will rarely get married, as they are simply speaking different languages! Things are alright with a Pisces, as both signs are emotional, and Pisces can let Scorpio take the lead when necessary.

SAGITTARIUS

Sagittarius women are usually charming, bubbly, energetic, and have the gift of gab. They are kind, sincere, and love people. They are also straightforward, fair, and very ambitious, occasionally to the point of irritating those around them. But telling them something is easier than not telling them, and they often manage to win over their enemies. Sagittarius tends to have excellent intuition, and she loves to both learn and teach others. She is a natural leader, and loves taking charge at work and at home. Many Sagittarian women have itchy feet, and prefer all kinds of travel to sitting at home. They are not particularly good housewives – to be frank, cooking and cleaning is simply not for them. Their loved ones must learn to adapt to them, but Sagittarians themselves hate any pressure. They are not easy for men to handle, as Sagittarians want to be in charge. Sagittarius falls in love easily, is very sexual and temperamental, and may marry multiple times. Despite outward appearances, Sagittarius is a very lonely sign. Even after she is married with children, she may continue living as if she were alone; you might say she marches to the beat of her own drum. Younger

Sagittarians can be reckless, but as they mature, they can be drawn to religion, philosophy, and the occult.

Aries and Leo make the best matches, as Sagittarius is able to bend to Leo's ways, or at least pretend to. Sagittarians often end up with Aquarians, but their marriages do not tend to be for the long haul. They are attracted to Geminis, but are unlikely to marry one until middle age, when both signs have settled down. Sagittarius and Cancer have incredible sexual chemistry, but an actual relationship between them would be tumultuous and difficult. Capricorn can make a good partner- as long as they are able to respect each other's quirks. Sagittarius rarely ends up with a Virgo, and while she may often meet Pisces, things are unlikely to go very far.

CAPRICORN

Capricorn women are conscientious, reliable, organized, and hard-working. Many believe that life means nothing but work, and live accordingly. They are practical, and not particularly drawn to parties or loud groups of people. But if someone useful will be there, they are sure to make an appearance. Capricorn women are stingy, but not as much as their male counterparts. They are critical of others, but think highly of themselves. Generally, they take a difficult path in life, but thanks to their dedication, perseverance, and willingness to push their own limits, they are able to forge their own path, and by 45 or 50, they can provide themselves with anything they could want. Capricorn women have the peculiarity of looking older than their peers when they are young, and younger than everyone else once they have matured. They are not particularly sexual, and tend to be faithful partners. They rarely divorce, and even will fight until the end, even for a failed marriage. Many Capricorns have a pessimistic outlook of life, and have a tendency to be depressed. They are rarely at the center of any social circle, but are excellent organizers. They have a very rigid view of life and love, and are not interested in a fling, as marriage is the end goal. As a wife, Capricorn is simultaneously difficult and reliable. She is difficult because of her strict nature and difficulty adapting. But she will also take on all the household duties, and her husband can relax, knowing his children are in good hands.

Taurus, Pisces, and Scorpio make good matches. Aries is difficult, once things cool off after the initial honeymoon. When a Capricorn meets another Capricorn, they will be each other's first and last love. Sagittarius isn't a bad match, but they don't always pass the test of time. Aquarius and Capricorn are a difficult match, and rarely found together. Things are too dull with a Virgo, and while Leo can be exciting at first, things will fall apart when he begins showing off. Libra and Aquarius are both difficult partners for Capricorn, and she is rarely found with either of them.

AQUARIUS

A female Aquarius is very different from her male counterparts. She is calm and keeps a cool head, but she is also affectionate and open. She values loyalty above all else, and is unlikely to recover from any infidelity, though she will only divorce if this becomes a chronic trend, and she has truly been stabbed in the back. She is not interested in her partner's money, but rather, his professional success. She is unobtrusive and trusting, and will refrain from listening in on her partner's phone conversations or hacking into his email. With rare exceptions, Aquarian women make terrible housewives. But they are excellent partners in life – they are faithful, never boring, and will not reject a man, even in the most difficult circumstances. Most Aquarians are highly intuitive, and can easily tell the truth from a lie. They themselves only lie in extreme situations, which call for a "white lie" in order to avoid hurting someone's feelings.

Aquarius gets along well with Aries, Gemini, and Libra. She can also have a good relationship with a Sagittarius. Taurus often makes a successful match, though they are emotionally very different; the same goes for Virgo. Aquarius and Scorpio, Capricorn, or Cancer is a difficult match. Pisces can make a good partner as well, as both signs complement each other. Any relationship with a Leo will be tumultuous, but lasting, as Leo is selfish, and Aquarius will therefore have to be very forgiving.

PISCES

Pisces women are very adaptable, musically inclined, and erotic. They possess an innate earthly wisdom, and a good business sense. Pisces often reinvent themselves; they can be emotional, soft, and obstinate, as well as sentimental, at times. Their behavioral changes can be explained by frequent ups and downs. Pisces is charming, caring, and her outward malleability is very attractive to men. She is capable of loving selflessly, as long as the man has something to love. Even if he doesn't, she will try and take care of him until the very end. Pisces' greatest fear is poverty. They are intuitive, vulnerable, and always try to avoid conflict. They love to embellish the truth, and sometimes alcohol helps with this. Rarely, one finds extremely unbalanced, neurotic and dishonest Pisces, who are capable of turning their loved ones' lives into a living Hell!

Taurus, Capricorn, Cancer, and Scorpio make the best matches. She will be greatly attracted to a Virgo, but a lasting relationship is only likely if both partners are highly spiritual. Any union with a Libra is likely to be difficult and full of conflict. Pisces finds Gemini attractive, and they may have a very lively relationship – for a while. Occasionally, Pisces ends up with a Sagittarius, but she will have to fade into the background and entirely submit to him. If she ends up with an Aquarius, expect strong emotional outbursts, and a marriage that revolves around the need to raise their children.

Tatiana Borsch

Solid

Foundation

AN ORAL HISTORY OF REGGAE

REVISED AND EXPANDED EDITION **DAVID KATZ**

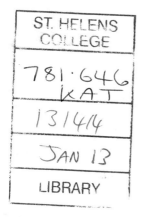
SOLID FOUNDATION

AN ORAL HISTORY OF REGGAE

DAVID KATZ

A Jawbone Book
Revised and expanded second edition, 2012
Published in the UK and the USA by Jawbone Press
2a Union Court,
20–22 Union Road,
London SW4 6JP,
England
www.jawbonepress.com

First edition published by Bloomsbury Publishing PLC, 2003

ISBN 978-1-908279-30-9

EDITOR Tom Seabrook
DESIGN Paul Cooper Design

Printed by Regent Publishing Services Limited, China

1 2 3 4 5 16 15 14 13 12

CONTENTS

"I'm going to tell you how reggae music really came about: our foreparents were taken from Africa and sold into slavery out here, that means them lower we down to some lower standard. They carry them to the Indian man's land and call we West Indians, but we know we is not Indians. The white man give we European names, and we know we is not European; we is African descendants, and we don't get African names. When my elders were before me, them try to use this reggae music to establish ourselves, establish a dignity and establish a music that could reach the world, and then the whole world would have to recognise we as a nation – a dreadlocks nation with that light shining upon our hilltop. Our light that we are supposed to shine with the reggae music, it is a light of righteousness, a light of dignity, because that is the only thing that can deliver us from the bondage we find ourselves in." – YABBY YOU

"Our goal is to have reggae music as exposed as any other music in the world, cause it's just as popular as any other music, maybe even more so, but we being a small Third World country, the money power no there behind it to move it. Me know each day the barriers are being broken down bit by bit. It still ain't come yet, but it going come. Right now we still an underground music, a rebel music, which is good, cause you have to be a rebel, but you want your work to reach the masses. Every Jamaican musician supposed to have that same hunger to see them work maximise. Not just from a financial standpoint, but from an artistic standpoint, you want your work to go to the widest possible audience." – LLOYD 'BREAD' MCDONALD

INTRODUCTION

Reggae has risen, against the odds, to wield tremendous influence. Despite being initially dismissed, even in its land of origin, its liberating message has inspired a broad spectrum of humanity: freedom fighters, dissidents, dignitaries, and, above all, ordinary people have rocked to its beat on every continent. And its distinct musical elements increasingly permeate other popular forms: the dub techniques of Jamaica's pioneering engineers have become the bedrock of modern dance remixes, and reggae's sub-genres of ska, roots, and dancehall are the basis of prevalent hybrids abroad. Most notably, the innovations of Jamaican toasters helped spawn rap and hip-hop culture, and vibrant cross-fertilisation continues. Despite detractors, it is evident that reggae remains a music of great importance; that such an innovation was fostered by the ghetto folk of a relatively small island, born with little more than natural creativity and musical sensibility at their disposal, makes reggae's unlikely rise all the more incredible.

My main motive in writing this book was to allow the people who built reggae's solid foundation to tell their stories. Rather than providing a slanted outsider's view, this book lets the pioneers of Jamaican popular music use their own voices to tell its tale. Who exactly created this remarkable music? Where did they come from, and how did they become the singers and players, the engineers and producers, the sound system operators and entrepreneurs who fashioned a distinctly Jamaican music? Why did the music take the shape it did, and how did it come to wield such a significant influence? What were the singers and players trying to express? How do they now feel about the music they created and the chain of events that brought it to the outside world?

As well as presenting as honest a portrait of the music as possible, an oral history captures the spontaneous circumstances of much reggae invention, and allows the wit and wisdom of its propagators to shine through. The cadence of Jamaica's patois lends itself more readily to this form than the dry monotone of a foreign observer. As the characters in this book all played important roles in reggae's complex history, they are surely the ones whose voices must guide it. I have been careful to present information as accurately as possible, though from time to time readers will notice conflicting accounts, notably when the songs in question concern a major shift in style, or were particularly popular hits.

In writing this book I wanted to give something back to the originators of a music that has been a constant and profoundly moving soundtrack for much of my life. I first became aware of reggae in my early teens, hearing tracks like Junior Murvin's 'Police And Thieves' on the progressive radio stations of the San Francisco Bay Area. The films *The Harder They Come* and *Rockers* drew me in deeper, as did the early books *Reggae Bloodlines*, *Catch A Fire*, and *Reggae International*, but experiencing the floor-shaking reality of Jack Ruby's 50,000-watt sound system in 1982 hooked me completely. Spending several months in London at the age of 17 was a further revelation: the city's Jamaican communities, vibrant pirate radio stations and the intense festivities of the Notting Hill Carnival brought the context of reggae into clearer focus. It was partly the prominence of reggae that made me base myself in London a few years later, and meeting Lee 'Scratch' Perry shortly after my return in 1987 had all kinds of repercussions on the life I have chosen to lead since then. Being in Scratch's private entourage for a number of years brought me into contact with all manner of reggae folk, yet all this seemed only a minor prelude to the dramatic assault on my senses of subsequent trips to Jamaica, where reggae music is everywhere and cultural revelations abound.

Reggae is all about connections, its sounds and styles shaped by select groups of musicians and singers interacting with a small number of producers. Finding the characters to speak to was a largely intuitive process, aided by the same connections that are so crucial to the music itself; this was particularly true in Jamaica, where the reggae fraternity is very much an extended family. And so, after taking me to meet producer Bunny Lee, who introduced me to the legendary singer

Dennis Brown by telephone, the singer Max Romeo could bring me to guitarist Earl 'Chinna' Smith, who knew where the percussionist Sticky was; Winston Jarrett knew where to find fellow singer Stranger Cole, who directed me to keyboardist Gladdy Anderson. Sometimes just hanging out at the right spot could work wonders: in an afternoon at Leggo studio on Orange Street I caught toasters U Brown and Tappa Zukie, percussionist Skully, and producer Linval Thompson after mingling with bassist Flabba Holt and trumpeter Johnny Moore next door; at Tuff Gong I encountered singers Albert Griffiths and Carl Dawkins, plus the toaster Dillinger and musicians such as Alva Lewis and Bongo Herman. Having the right connection could really be decisive; Clement 'Sir Coxsone' Dodd refused an interview when I first approached his record shop in New York, but after the Silvertones trio brought me to Studio One in Jamaica, he consented without the slightest hesitation.

The earliest interviews came from research for *People Funny Boy*, my biography of Lee 'Scratch' Perry. Scratch's insistence that I become his ghostwriter felt like both a blessing and a curse – a cumbersome burden, yet at the same time an honour that I could not refuse. Whether the end result was what either of us had in mind is another matter; nevertheless, the quest for knowledge initiated on Perry's behalf would ultimately lead me to write *Solid Foundation*.

Just as dub music teaches that what is absent from a mix is as important as what stays in, one of the hardest parts of assembling this book has been deciding what to leave out. I interviewed more than 300 of reggae's prime movers over 15 years. Naturally I have not been able to include all this material, so I can only apologise if favourite songs or artists are not represented. Sadly, certain performers died before I had the chance to meet them, others could not be located, and a few declined for reasons best known to themselves or their managers. And I am certainly grateful to the fellow journalists and friends who have allowed me to use extracts from their own interviews, each of which is indicated by a footnote.

This book does not claim to tell the 'complete' story of reggae music. The earliest testimony refers to Jamaica's 1920s jazz scene, with firsthand accounts of the post-war R&B, mento, and calypso that led directly to the reggae precursors of ska and rock steady; earlier styles from the colonial period receive only brief mention. Additionally, the original edition of the book ended in the mid 80s, when reggae was on the verge of going digital. This revised edition has continued the tale with extensive new material, to bring it much closer to the present, yet it is fair to say that the changes that have come since Jamaican music became computerised are too vast and varied to cover in their entirety.

I have attempted to highlight the most important songs and styles, but this book does not restrict itself to the Jamaican hit parade; equally, while I have never been wilfully obscure, certain lesser-known or forgotten figures are also given voice. And although the reggae of Britain and North America is touched on in places, the book focuses firmly on music made in Jamaica.

This book has taken me to places I surely would not have reached otherwise. Much of the journey has been truly wondrous. I have listened to Ken Boothe sing a chilling *a capella* in his uptown Kingston front room, eaten roast fish cooked by Congo Ashanti Roy in the ghetto of Independence City, and passed the chalice with several luminaries at the Freedom Sounds yard in Greenwich Farm. I have analysed the scriptures with Yabby You and Cocoa Tea, debated women's rights with Michael Rose and Junior Reid, and discussed the shortcomings of Western medicine with Augustus Pablo's personal herbalist. I shot the breeze in Gregory Isaacs' shop, swapped African travel stories with U Roy and Niney The Observer, and was regaled by tales of gang warfare from Prince Buster and Big Youth. I drank beer with Rico, sipped vodka with Rupie Edwards, had rum with LKJ, and gnawed sugar cane with Beres Hammond. I traded jazz anecdotes with The Skatalites, dissected rhythmic techniques with Sly & Robbie, learned that Glen Brown's culinary skills are on a par with his music productions, and was treated to the best Chinese meal I've ever eaten by Clive Chin. I have met Twelve Tribes, Ethiopian Orthodox, Bobo Dreads, Niyabinghi Theocracy, and adherents to other branches of the Rastafari faith. I have pulled the bronze eagle's claw that was the door handle of Edward Seaga's office in New Kingston, heard the frenzied beats of a Pukumina church meeting in Saint Thomas, and been transfixed by the pulsating heartbeat of Niyabinghi groundation drums in Saint Elizabeth. To hear

Winston Blake's Merritone sound system at the Turntable club was exquisite; to dance the rub-a-dub in the moonlight at a Sunday night session outside Rae Town's Capricorn Inn was positively heavenly.

Almost everyone I came in contact with treated me with the utmost kindness, not only being forthright with tales of their musical careers, but also welcoming me into their private homes and sometimes their personal lives. Of course, when things did not go according to plan that too became part of the experience. To reach a musician who lived in a remote village I had to drive on dirt roads though a flooded sugarcane estate, guided by an aspiring concert promoter who was apparently the resident 'bad man'. One singer, who lives uptown, insisted on bringing his loaded shotgun when I asked him to drop me at a local bus stop. Another artist invited me to the countryside, but neglected to tell me that on the return journey he would be transporting a consignment of counterfeit Gucci bags and the largest quantity of marijuana I have ever seen. As he rightly pointed out, such experiences helped me see aspects of life normally hidden from the average visitor, and thus understand better the tribulation the architects of reggae have often endured.

Overall, I hope this book will contribute to a greater understanding of reggae's complex history, so that the music's significance may be better appreciated. *Solid Foundation* is a testament to the greatness of reggae's originators, whose intense creativity brought forth such stunning, unique sounds. Reggae sprang from desperation, fashioned by those with little at hand as an expression of their predicament. Its rallying cry against injustice and its growing influence ensure that the music will remain a continual source of inspiration.

1

BOOGIE ROCK

Sound system culture and Jamaican R&B

"The two first sound system clashes in Jamaica was between Tom The Great Sebastian and Count Nick in 1952. Tom beat Nick, and the return was up at Nick's yard in Waltham Park Road – Tom beat him both times. Tom was great, man! Him friend send some big tune for him from New York and that night, if you see the crowd ..." – DUKE VIN

"We do rhythm & blues songs – all Jamaican artists in those days try to do rhythm & blues." – SKULLY SIMMS

Jamaica's popular music has undergone a series of labyrinthine changes, a transformation that mirrors the island's cultural and political growth. Born from the everyday struggles of the dispossessed in a seemingly peripheral island nation, reggae is infused with issues of identity and reactions to the centuries of colonialism that shaped modern Jamaican society. The music's progression charts a complex course, shadowing the growing pains of a developing nation.

When Jamaica achieved independence from Britain in 1962, the island celebrated with ska, a uniquely Jamaican hybrid. Ska is intimately connected to the independence movement and was the first Jamaican style to attract significant foreign interest; because of this, it is often seen as the starting point of contemporary reggae. But in order to understand the emergence of ska, certain earlier strands of musical culture must be traced. The most important include Jamaican R&B (ska's immediate predecessor), the thriving urban jazz scenes, the indigenous folk style called mento, and above all, the sound-system culture that since the 1940s has been the perpetual arbiter of Jamaican musical taste.

As the inhabitants of the 'Isle of Springs' all have ancestors from elsewhere, its popular culture has a wide range of influences. Although the British maintained the chief colonial presence for over 300 years, the music of black America provided the strongest model for Jamaica's urban musicians in the 40s and 50s – perhaps not surprising, given its proximity. The USA continues to exercise the greatest industrial, financial, and military power in the region, as well as cultural dominance: American radio and television programmes disproportionately fill Jamaican airwaves.

Although black American music had the strongest influence in the post-war years, other forms were also noteworthy. The *son* and *bolero* styles of Cuba, sandwiched between Jamaica and the USA, were highly influential, as was the music of nearby nations such as Haiti, the Dominican Republic, and Panama. But perhaps the most important elements came from the ancestral homeland: Jamaican slave descendants retained many more vestiges of African culture than their US counterparts. Sacred drumming techniques found in Pukumina church services or accompanying Junkanoo masquerade dances further evolved from the backbone of Jamaica's folk music and ultimately became defining elements of reggae. Other important folk elements developed during slavery days include the call-and-response chants of work songs and children's ring games, and the adaptation of 19th-century European dance music known as quadrille.

The fife and drum of quadrille was a particularly notable influence on mento, a style from the Jamaican countryside that has similarities to the calypso of other islands, but which is distinct, due to unique instrumentation. In the 40s, increased migration to Kingston brought mento bands with it. These roving groups of troubadours gave informal street performances offering social commentary and satirising current events. The bands typically featured hand drums, banjo, and the oversized kalimba or 'rumba box' (a distant relative of the *mbira*, used for bass), often with a fife or penny whistle, and perhaps a bamboo saxophone. From the early 50s, mento groups were regular features on the North Coast hotel circuit.

Among the savvier city-dwellers, jazz held greater currency. Since at least the 20s there was a thriving Jamaican jazz scene, and in the economically buoyant post-war years big-band jazz and swing remained most popular among the upper echelons. At high-class clubs and hotels, bands played American jazz standards and adapted pan-Caribbean forms like calypso and merengue, but the more creative players were forming new jazz variations through complex original compositions.

"Big band was also our pop music," says Winston Blake, operator of Merritone, the longest-running Jamaican sound system. "That was the swing era: Count Basie, Tommy Dorsey, Stan Kenton, Glenn Miller. The formative bands in Jamaica played that music as dance music."

13

Chief among the hotel groups were the Arawaks, featuring pianist Luther Williams, and saxophonist Val Bennett's band. Eric Deans' Orchestra became the most popular Kingston live act through a long residence at the Bournemouth Club at east Kingston's Bournemouth Beach; Deans was a multi-instrumentalist whose saxophone skills drew comparison to Glenn Miller. Redver Cook's band was a favourite of the light-skinned upper class and played regularly at a society spot called the Glass Bucket. John Weston's 12-piece band, Milton McPherson's group, the Baba Motta Quartet, Wilton Gaynair Quintet, and Foggy Mullins Trio were among the other popular acts of the period; trumpeter Sonny Bradshaw, who played in several, formed the Sonny Bradshaw Seven in 1950 after organising a landmark jazz concert at Kingston's Ward Theatre. Down on East Queen Street, where a venue with outdoor gambling tables was known as Coney Island, a hot house band with a shifting line-up was blowing jazz nearly every night of the week; its members would later emerge as the key set of session players once entrepreneurs began recording local talent.

But working-class Jamaicans could not afford the smart venues. Their entertainment was most often provided by the sound system. Inspired by Jamaicans who had visited the USA as casual farm labour and attended dance parties held by black Americans, restaurant owners and other aspiring businessmen had systems with powerful amplifiers sent down from the States, often with speaker boxes custom-built in Jamaica, with which to broadcast the sound. Their sheer power and volume inevitably drew large audiences when booming out at an open-air dance, and the advent of the sound system would be a defining element of the island's homegrown music industry.

Winston Blake's father, a civil servant, established the Mighty Merritone set in 1950 to earn extra pocket money. Though considerably smaller than the Kingston sound systems, it was the first in Saint Thomas parish. When Blake Senior died in 1956 aged just 41, Winston and older brother Trevor took over, moving the set to Kingston in 1962. Over 60 years after its creation, Merritone is still going strong. Seated under a portrait of Fidel Castro in his uptown Kingston home, the burly, grey-bearded Blake reminisces.

"The situation in Jamaica then was that schoolrooms or church halls was where you had social functions. Then you had the most important part of the Jamaican scenario called lawns, like Jubilee Tile Gardens and Chocomo Lawn, big places that were either concrete slab or wire fence, and you'd have a dance in that area, either at the back of a house or the side of a building

– a space where you could put up music. You had control, because there was an entrance gate. That's how the sound system started."

Low entry prices, the sound systems' mobility, and the fact that live musicians were not involved meant they could be set up at the most basic country venues. This kind of entertainment was thus accessible to a wide audience who were often barred from the elite live jazz venues.

"In Saint Thomas, you have three big dances a year with bands coming in: one for the police and two for the tennis club. It was like South Africa: only a certain clientele could attend, so 'proper' people would go to those dances and the little people were left out. In Kingston, there was the sound-system thing – no bands and people on the ballroom floor and others not getting an entertainment, so the sound system started a certain thing in those poorer areas."

Those who attended sound-system events were further inspired by virtuoso dancers and witty live commentary from the deejays attached to particular sets. Each sound was associated with a particular area – typically, a tough patch of the ghetto – with a set of fanatically loyal followers attached.

By the start of the 50s, sound systems made US rhythm & blues the music of the day. "Rhythm & blues probably crept in here about '49, and became an institution in the 50s," says Blake. Sound system competition has always been fierce, with exclusivity particularly important. In this early phase the sound system operators imported records from America, removing the labels from the most prized to stop the competition getting their hands on a copy.

"Those days, our records came into the country in two ways. When the ships came in, the guys would go to the whorehouses, and the touts of the sounds used to hang around the whorehouses – that's where they used to get the records to tout to various sound people. Then a lot of our people used to go up to do farm working and carry back records. Later on, there was a station [WLAC] sponsored by Randy's Record Shop of Tennessee, and you also had a station out of Miami, WINZ, and we could hear those stations just like we pick up the local station. We would listen to WINZ, because we only had one [Jamaican] radio station at that time, ZQI, and we would hear Cuban stations. Later in the night, after about one o'clock, the Tennessee stations would come in very clear and they would advertise specials, which would include ten records for a price. That's how a lot of records came into Jamaica. Later, one or two of the guys started to travel, started shopping for these records and carrying them back."

The idea of the sound clash quickly took hold. From at least as early as 1952, downtown venues such as King's Lawn or the Pioneer Club staged confrontations between two sets, based on exclusive discs. Sound-system battles were waged to establish dominance, with the public making clear which had the superior selection. The first to rise to prominence was Tom The Great Sebastian (initially known simply as Tom's Sound System), established by Tom Wong, proprietor of a downtown hardware store located at 51 Charles Street. Tom's father was a Chinese Jamaican, his mother of African descent. The professional name he eventually adopted stemmed from the moniker of a trapeze artist in the 1952 circus drama *The Greatest Show On Earth*.

"Tom was the number-one sound," insists the former Sebastian selector and sound system legend now known as Duke Vin. "He started in the early 40s. It was rhythm & blues: Louis Jordan, Coleman Hawkins. I used to stand up outside and listen to him play in Young Men's Progressive in Drummond Street: it was a club people hire to keep parties, not far from Tom's Hardware Store at Charles Street and Luke Lane."

In a West London basement lined with sheepskin rugs, Vin explains that Tom's popularity was partly due to the steady supply of records sent by a friend in New York. "He was a top-class tailor, we call him Won. He was along with Tom's sister."

Another reason for Tom's success was his custom hi-fi set, designed by electrical technician Headley Jones, who trained in the RAF during World War II; his speakers were hung from trees until more powerful freestanding units were constructed. That Tom sometimes strung up the sound at his store was also beneficial. "Some evening he hang up the box and play his music," Vin notes, "and people gather round and listen, Jamaica style."

Singer Derrick Morgan claims there were earlier sound systems. The son of a Presbyterian deacon, Morgan was born in rural Clarendon in 1940, but moved to Kingston three years later to obtain medical treatment, after a relative noticed vision problems. "I stay in Vineyard Town till I was about five and then I live in a big yard they call Orange Lane, downtown." Steeped in sound-system culture, and awarded the Order of Distinction in 2001 for his contributions to Jamaican popular music, he recalls Tom's predecessors. "The first set you have in Jamaica was called Waldron. Tom The Great Sebastian was more popular than Waldron, but Waldron have him sound long before. Waldron used to play just one place on Slipe Road; Orange Street runs into Slipe Road, and he was right at Torrington Bridge corner."

Although The Great Sebastian had plenty of competition in the early

16

50s, it remained the most popular set to the middle of the decade. The legendary singer and record producer Prince Buster, who insists that Tom was "the first dance hall sound system in Jamaica," recalls a number of his early rivals.

"The sounds at the time were Count Nick; Deans', a mighty sound system run by an Indian man at Maxfield Avenue and Spanish Town Road who had a bicycle shop; Doc's Thunderstorm at Brotherton Avenue; and Mellow Canary is from the beginning, he had a powerful sound in Saint Thomas. Waldron was a good sound and Buckram was off Lyndhurst Road, a little bit above Waldron's place. There was also Sherwood, but Sherwood wasn't a dancehall sound system: him make him sound to make people come in him shop."

Other notable early rivals included Lord Koos and the somewhat upmarket V-Rocket, who Morgan says was responsible for introducing the daring innovation of twin turntables in the early 60s. "V-Rocket spin the music better, but didn't carry that heavy beat. It was a more lighter sound, what we call hi-fi. He would play at a venue called Caterers' in Manchester Square, by Heroes Park. Caterers' and 1 Lissant Road, those are the two places those hi-fi play, like Billy's Hi-Fi, Thunderbird, El Suzy, and El Toro: those are the sounds that celebrity people go to, you don't have the ragamuffin dance there."

"I'd say Count Nick was the biggest competition," says Duke Vin, "because the two first sound system clashes in Jamaica was between Tom and Nick in 1952. Tom beat Nick, and the return was up at Nick's yard in Waltham Park Road – Tom beat him both times. Tom was great, man! Him friend send some big tune for him from New York and that night, if you see the crowd …"

Vin was born in Kingston in 1928 and raised on Wildman Street, "right beside the Success Club". Based in London since 1954, he continued to operate his sound until relatively recently, and says that his Christian upbringing kept him from smoking or drinking, but despite his advanced age, his smiling mouth often fills with swearwords. As a teenager in the 40s, when Tom was reaching the height of popularity and had three separate sound systems, Vin was just another local supporter. Then fate intervened in the form of a punctured tyre:

"I stand up outside Tom's Hardware Store one evening, him car get puncture and him was fighting to take off the tyre with a spring-blade. I come and press my foot on the spring-blade and him say: 'Thank you very much, Vinnie man.' When him done and fix up him thing, him say: 'You think you can handle a sound, play a party down on Princess Street? Come, we go set up the sound next week.' The Monday morning after, them come and pay Tom and say: 'Who's that likkle fella you send to play the sound? Everybody was clapping and praising him.' Tom say: 'From now on, you play the number-two sound.' It's three sets him have: when all three play, his brother play the number three, I play number two, and Tom play the number one. When people don't book the number two, I play the number one with Tom."

Tom The Great Sebastian reigned supreme by playing a varied selection, which included merengue and Latin music as well as rhythm & blues. Vin recalls that Tom varied his music to reach the upper-class sections of his audience, who were less enamoured with the rhythm & blues favoured by ghetto folk. "Tom play everything, because the uptown people like those things like [Russ Morgan's] 'Mockin' Bird Hill'. We also play calypso, like 'She 'Pon Top'."

"I enjoyed the way he played his music probably more than any other sound, because he was adventurous," confirms Winston Blake. "He used to play merengue and Spanish music. He played a repertoire, whereas most of the other sounds would play a hardcore of rhythm & blues, and drop in a few mentos and the slow type of New Orleans music. That was the music that was really dominant in the 50s."

Duke Reid The Trojan, who used strong-arm tactics to eliminate competition, eventually superseded Tom. The Duke, born Arthur Reid in Port Antonio in 1915, served for ten years in the Kingston police force, where he attained the rank of sergeant, leaving him with close connections to the criminal fraternity and a lasting love of guns. His Trojan sound system, operated with a man called Clifford and selector Leroy 'Cuttings' Cole from a spot on Pink Lane, was crowned King of Sounds and Blues at the Success Club in Wildman Street in 1956, '57, and '58. Reid then shifted base to larger premises at 33 Bond Street, the site of his Treasure Isle liquor store, restaurant, and dry cleaners. The Duke's fantastic success on the sound system circuit was largely due to the notorious henchmen from the nearby Back-O-Wall slum that launched regular attacks to sabotage rivals. However, any suggestion that Reid's wife won the lottery, enabling the purchase of 33 Bond Street, seems unfounded; after all, the building was nearly auctioned off in January 1962 following a default on the mortgage.

Some have suggested that Reid forced The Great Sebastian to flee from downtown Kingston, but Duke Vin refutes the notion. "Tom and Duke Reid were good friends. Duke Reid don't sabotage; the only persons who do that is him followers, the rough guys. They'll do it to other soundmen, but they never do that to Tom. Those rough guys know Tom very good, always come to the shop and say: 'Wha'ppen Tom, you all right?'"

In any case, Tom's fear of conflict made him move to the smart Silver Slipper club in Cross Roads, away from the downtown trouble spots and closer to the wealthier residences. "Tom used to play for the aristocratic, up-class people," Vin explains. "He never like to play for the rough guy; him can't take it, he's a coward. I have to face everything for him: when the police raid the dances, me have to go talk to the police. He don't like rough crowd, so he go and play in Slipper because the crowd is more selective."

Though Vin denies Reid used intimidation tactics against Tom, he admits Reid tried to lure him away from Tom's set with better pay. The pair first became acquainted when Reid was a policeman and Vin was still wearing short trousers. "Duke Reid know me as a little boy going to Calabar School; we likkle youth used to romp out of the Central Police Station, that was not far from the school. Him used to like me, so you find that when I play for Tom, he want to take me away to play for him. Tom used to give me 30 shillings a night to play and Duke offer me five pounds, but I never leave Tom. I dedicated to the man, because the man is a good man to me; it's not the money, it's the loyalty. I stick with Tom to the last, until I come to England."

It was only after establishing the first sound system in Britain, in 1955, that Tom's former selector became known as Duke Vin, a name chosen to remind the expatriate public of Duke Reid. Vin clarifies that during all the years he selected for Tom, The Great Sebastian never officially took part in a head-to-head clash with Reid's Trojan sound; the closest was when the two sounds were set up at separate parties in adjacent yards.

"It was in the late part down in 1953: we play next door to each other in Jones Town. Tom have a steel [speaker] and turn it to Reid, Reid have a steel and turn it to Tom, and the crowd come to our dance and Reid flopped. It was fun. We played R&B: Smiley Louis, Fats Domino, James Wayne's 'Tend To Your Business', 'Little Red Rooster' by The Griffin Brothers."

Jamaica's first commercial station, Radio Jamaica Rediffusion (RJR), was launched in 1950 after a British firm took over the former government station, ZQI; broadcasts were supplied to listeners by an inexpensive cable subscription service. By 1955, both Tom and Duke sponsored radio programmes to help keep their sound systems in the minds of the public.

"Duke Reid had a programme called *Treasure Isle Time*, and Tom The Sebastian had a programme called *Sebastian Time*," recalls Winston Blake.

"They would play all the new records and tell them where the sound system was playing over the weekend." But down in Kingston's slums, different kinds of battles were being waged.

The early onset of sound-system violence drew definite results, first as Duke Reid carved out a widening territory. Following the Duke's lead, King Edwards The Giant used bullying tactics to secure sound-system glory. The set was established in 1955 by Vincent Edwards, with selector Red Hopeton; Edwards built up a rough crew that was adept at spoiling dances held by rivals, greatly assisting his rise to the top by 1959. As for the pioneering Great Sebastian, it came to a tragic end in the late 60s when Tom Wong committed suicide, apparently due to relationship problems (and not financial difficulties, as some believed).

"He didn't have no debts," Duke Vin insists. "He got money, he loaded, but he kill himself because of his wife."

Before the rise of King Edwards, Sir Coxsone's Downbeat became Duke Reid's most notable challenger. The set was established by a young friend of Reid's named Clement Dodd, born in Kingston in 1932 and nicknamed Coxsone after an English cricketer. Dodd's selector, Count Machuki, was an innovative, jive-talking toaster who honed his microphone skills on Tom The Great Sebastian; his off-the-cuff wisecracks and Coxsone's supreme record collection made Downbeat a formidable contender.

Sir Coxsone died of a heart attack in 2004. Some years before, seated in the dishevelled Kingston office that was long his base of operations and flanked by deejay King Stitt and other associates, he detailed the family fondness for rhythm & blues.

"My father was a contractor mason, he built the Carib Theatre and other country theatres. My mother eventually ran a liquor store, but it started out from a little restaurant on Lawes Street and Ladd Lane called Nanny's Corner. This is going back to 1951. We used to play music in the place on a Morphy Richards radio, play Billy Eckstine, Sarah Vaughan, Lionel Hampton and Louis Jordan. My mother loved music, was a great dancer, and won many prizes."

In 1953, Dodd worked as a farm labourer in the USA and decided to enter the music business after seeing money being made at outdoor block parties. He thus sent funds to his mother from the USA for the construction of speaker boxes, and later sent down an amplifier. His family association with the Reids allowed him guest appearances on the Trojan set and he suggested this relationship kept their rivalry reasonably civilised.

"Duke was a close friend of the family. Mom and Dad knew him well, and his signature tune was given to him by my mother: 'My Mother's Eyes', an instrumental by [alto saxophonist] Tab Smith. I was a cabinetmaker and I did a course on automobile mechanics, used to train at the Ford garage on Church Street. I attended a lot of orchestra dances in the early days, but when the rhythm & blues came in about '53 or '54, I used to attend dances when Duke was playing and play some of my sides. His fans always look forward to seeing me coming with my little case of records, so I eventually went into the sound thing myself. My memories of the days of Duke and meself, it was like a musical challenge."

Duke Vin claims Tom The Great Sebastian sold Reid his treasured signature tune. "It was 1951. Reid come to him and ask if him have any old record to sell and Tom said: 'I have a few that I don't use.' Tom use [Billy Eckstine's] 'Blue Moon' as him sign-on tune. When him sell Duke Reid 'My Mother's Eyes', Duke Reid use it as a signature tune and it become a hit as a sign-on. That time Coxsone never have no sound at all. I was there when Tom was selling the record."

Further contradiction comes from another close associate, Prince Buster, who recalls the rivalry as anything but clean. Born Cecil Bustamante Campbell in downtown Kingston in 1938, Buster speaks of violence and sabotage as crucial determinants. Dodd, he says, recruited him from an area loyal to Duke Reid because of his tough reputation.

"I born and grow on Orange Street, right there in West Kingston. Coxsone grow in Saint Thomas, Duke Reid come from Port Antonio, so I am the only one born on Orange Street. My father work with the railroad, my mother work at the match factory and my parents grew me up with a strict principle of Christianity. How I came to work with Coxsone was that on Luke Lane and Charles Street corner, there was two sets of gangsters, and one night Noel Horse Jaw and them big men were gambling, playing Parapinto dice. I had some money, asked if I can join the game, and I broke the whole of them – lucky for me, the dice was rolling my way. When I start to scrape up the money, one of them named Mean Stick just fling up a foot and kick the felt hat offa me head. The whole of them draw them knife and I couldn't see where my money went. A week after, I was in my bathroom at Drummond Street and someone call me and say them 'pon the corner, so I just draw the clothes on my wet skin and come out and chase Mean Stick with me knife in me hand, and Coxsone and Count Machuki was coming down Luke Lane. Machuki told me later that as Coxsone was scared of people like Mean Stick, it shocked him. He said: 'Who's the little youth?' Machuki said: 'We grew him, that's who you want to have on your side to take the face off Duke Reid.' Then Machuki come to me and say Coxsone want to see me, so me and some youth go in him shop, have some nice drink, and him nice and friendly and say he would like me to move with him, but I wouldn't tell him yes. I went back on my corner at Luke Lane and Charles Street and have a meeting with the youths, and then I start to stay at Love Lane and Beeston Street – this was about '57, '58."

Though Buster knew changing allegiance was dangerous, he bore a lasting grudge against The Duke. "The only sound system I backed before was Tom The Great Sebastian, which is still the greatest sound system ever, and then Duke Reid ran him out of town. I had vengeance in my heart for Duke Reid, 'cos Tom was a nice, decent, calm, respectable man who just want to play music, but Duke Reid come with a band of Back-O-Wall bad man, they jump the fence and pull over the amplifier, mash up the boxes. Brother Baby Wire, who die the other day, him was the 'Don' of Back-O-Wall. When him and Rushy and Big Boy take off at night time, Coxsone haffe jump fence! When word reach Duke Reid's camp that I am at Coxsone's sound system, the problem that arise is that I grow with these men, but I'd have to oppose them now because them is Duke Reid's people."

The conflict rapidly escalated when Coxsone and Duke Reid fought each other in a sound system clash. Buster even resorted to breaking Reid's stylus. "The first night I went out with Coxsone is a drama, because when the time come for Duke Reid to come on, I tell Machuki: 'Don't sign off, continue to play more.' Machuki go to play and I scratch [Reid's] needle, and Duke Reid can't come on. I don't know why I do it, just that this is the thing wha' haffe do and I haffe do it." It took half an hour to replace the stylus, and when Reid's sound fired up again, Coxsone was still playing.

"Duke Reid had a song named 'Hey Mr Berry', and Coxsone couldn't find that tune in all his searches of America, so it was Duke Reid's top tune. When he put on the tune, that actually hurt Duke Reid, because the whole town thought Coxsone was playing it. Right there now, the charge of the Back-O-Wall brigade coming to the amplifier that we set up with Machuki, so that was the first forceful demonstration against the criminals. I was forced that night, for although it's them who grow me and them know me temperament, I flash my knife wild. This is how Coxsone get to become recognised, because the people who want to come to him dance didn't come 'cos them was afraid of getting hurt. But because them hear me and other Duke Reid youth now with Coxsone, his dances start to full."

Around this time there was a dramatic shift in the nascent Jamaican record industry: as a direct by-product of sound-system activity, the older sounds of calypso and mento, aimed largely at visiting tourists, were usurped by Jamaican rhythm & blues, which was far more popular with local record buyers.

The very first local music recordings were made in Jamaica on direct-to-disc machines as a 'novelty' venture. As early as July 1947, an entrepreneur at 76 West Street offered patrons the opportunity to record their own voice or instruments for a nominal fee. The following month, the public was invited to record their songs at special galas held at the Glass Bucket, backed by the resident Orchestra. Celebrated stage, radio and hotel pianist George Moxey, a Bahamas-born bandleader known as the King of the Ivories in Jamaica, then offered aspiring singers and musicians the chance to record their own songs at the Empire Building in Cross Roads, with free piano accompaniment. According to a 1948 *Gleaner* article, the pioneering Jamaican singer and guitarist Lord Flea (Byfield Norman Thomas) made use of such opportunities, but it must be emphasised that the resultant discs were never released commercially; the Jamaican direct-to-disc records of the 40s were simply one-off items made for personal use. In fact, they could only be played a few times on conventional record players, before wearing out. Noting the demand for Jamaican folk records from foreign visitors, as well as overseas music fans, Moxey published an editorial in the *Gleaner* in October 1948, calling for local music to be produced and sold commercially.

Jamaican businessmen, often of Middle Eastern or Asian origin, began releasing locally recorded mento and calypso in the early 50s. Exactly who was the first to take the plunge is contested, but newspaper advertisements indicate that, by August 1951, Jewish Jamaican businessman Stanley Motta had already issued a handful of 78 RPM discs by calypso singer and saxophonist, Lord Fly (Rupert Lyon), while his rival, Lebanese-Jamaican businessman Ken Khouri, had already issued material by the younger singer Lord Flea. Regardless of who was first, both Motta and Khouri are undeniable pioneers of the Jamaican music industry.

Motta's record label, MRS, was named for Motta's Recording Studio, the island's first official recording facility. In addition to the Lord Fly releases, backed by the Dan Williams Orchestra, other Motta acts included Harold Richardson & The Ticklers, Lord Composer & His Silver Seas Orchestra, and Monty Reynolds' Calypso Clippers, featuring singer Boysie Grant.[1]

Motta began selling imported radios at 10c East Street in 1932. After moving to larger premises at 5 Church Street, in March 1940, he unveiled a

23

soundproof listening booth where customers could hear the latest records prior to purchase. The following year he established a flagship appliance store at 109 Harbour Street ('Jamaica's House Of Quality'), which also had a record department. He later opened a woodwork factory at 43 Hanover Street, a few short blocks from the main store, and in September 1950, he opened a tiny, backroom recording studio there, with a piano, one microphone, and portable, direct-to-disc recording equipment, which was also available for external hire.

Motta's first known output comprised 14 Lord Fly songs, issued on five 78s, mixing traditional folk mentos such as 'Slide Mongoose' and 'Linstead Market' with humorous originals like 'Whai, Whai, Whai'.[2]

"In those days, there was only one recording studio in Jamaica, and that was Stanley Motta's," confirmed singer Laurel Aitken, a few years before his death in 2005. "In those days recording wasn't a business: it was more live music."

Resident in England since the early 60s, Aitken was still recording and performing in his late seventies. Born in Havana in 1927, he moved to Kingston at the age of 11. "My dad is Jamaican and my mom is Cuban, and my dad just wanted to go back home."

By the time the first Jamaican 78s had surfaced, Aitken was popular on talent shows. "I used to sing from when I was a little boy, and when I came to Jamaica there was nothing like ska; you had to sing jazz, and calypso, which comes from Trinidad. I sang [Rodgers and Hart's] 'Blue Moon', [George Gershwin's] 'Embraceable You', and I won three big contests in Kingston with [Bing Crosby's] 'Pennies From Heaven'. At the time, I used to work with the Jamaica Tourist Board, welcoming people with a big broad hat at the wharf when the ships come in, singing calypsos – 'Welcome To Jamaica', 'Jamaica Farewell', 'Coconut Woman' – and they fling money and give me."

He claimed his recording debut, captured at Motta's studio, was self-produced. "The first recording that I did, I did it for myself, that was a song called 'I Met A Señorita'. I used my own money and got my own musicians, nobody that's living now. The saxophonist went by the name of Number One; he was well known in those days. Then I did a merengue, 'Merenguito', and it was released by a man that had a record shop on King Street, by the name of Mr DePass."

Jewish Jamaican businessman L.R. DePass sold furniture, appliances, musical instruments, and records at 6a King Street from the 30s. He later moved to 68 King Street, from where he issued small quantities of mento and calypso records in the 50s, but his involvement in the music industry proved peripheral.

In contrast, Ken Khouri was a key figure. For his many contributions to Jamaican music, he was inducted at the Hall of Fame of the Caribbean Development for Arts & Culture in January 2001, a couple of years before his death, aged 86. Though Stanley Motta is most often cited as the first to release Jamaican recordings, Khouri energetically claimed the honour for himself. "He came in long after me and that was just a little voice recording setup he had. I am the complete pioneer of everything!"

At his uptown Kingston home, Khouri explained that he was born in rural Saint Mary in 1917, his parentage an unusual mix. "My father was born in Lebanon, came to Jamaica with his parents when he was 12; my mother was born here of Cuban parents. When I was growing up, my father had dry goods stores in the country and a furniture store in Kingston."

After moving to Kingston to work for the Issa Brothers' retail firm, and later running his own furniture business, Khouri became involved in the music business upon buying a second-hand direct-to-disc recorder from a man he met by chance in Florida in 1949. "It happened by accident in Miami: I took my father there for his illness and I met someone selling a recording machine – a disc recorder – so I bought it and came back to Jamaica."

The machine he bought came with 100 blank discs, which were soon filled with Jamaicans fascinated to hear the sound of their own voices. Then, Khouri began using the machine to record music. "I used to go around recording calypsos at different nightclubs; the first recording was with Lord Flea, 'Where Did The Little Flea Go?' [aka 'Naughty Little Flea']. The discs that I made, I send them as masters to Decca in England, and they made a record out of it and send it down to me."

Khouri then formed a partnership with Alec Durie, who ran the Times variety store on King Street: the output of their new joint venture, Times Records, would be sold exclusively at the store. By August 1951, Times issued ten Lord Flea songs on three 78s, beginning with 'Solas Market'; 'Naughty Little Flea' was not among them, and may have been issued considerably earlier.

A batch of Hubert Porter 78s, also manufactured by Decca, were then issued on Times by June 1953, including traditional favourites such as 'Ten Penny Nail' and 'Rum And Coconut Water', as well as less common numbers like 'Ugly Woman', all delivered in the 'urban' version of the mento style. As Khouri explained: "All the Hubert Porter, I record them in a studio that I built up myself, in 129 King Street: Records Limited. I brought down equipment from California, just one microphone, one track."

Records Limited was officially established by November 1954. After travelling to New York, Khouri consolidated his success by securing the Jamaican manufacturing and distribution rights for Mercury Records, later cutting similar deals with Decca, Brunswick, Capitol, Herald, Ember and Monogram. "I used to have franchises from the States, and the first records I put out were [Ralph Marterie's] 'Skokiaan', [The Chords'] 'Sh-Boom' and [The Gaylords'] 'The Little Shoemaker'."[3] Khouri was the first to bring record pressing equipment to Jamaica, and he did so partly to facilitate an easier distribution of American hits, which had previously suffered shipping delays of several months. But the pressing facility ultimately stimulated local music production.

Records Limited subsequently controlled the Kalypso label, on which Khouri released calypso 78s by artists such as Lord Lebby and Count Owen (Owen Emmanuel). The company also coordinated releases for concerns like Count Lasher's Lasher Disc, as well as Chin's label releases by the Calypso Sextet, featuring a certain Alerth Bedasse; Ivan Chin, owner of a radio repair service at 48 Church Street, recorded the group's output at his premises on a basic disc recorder.

As his empire grew, Khouri became the figure that sound system proprietors went to for their one-off acetates. He arranged the first Trojan and Hi-Lite 78s, featuring vocalist Lord Power and pressed exclusively for Duke Reid's sound system. As the island's recording industry blossomed, other sound systems were quick to take advantage, having realised that putting local talent on record was a sure-fire way of garnering exclusive material to impress patrons. The first Jamaican artists to record blues ballads and home-grown R&B were the duo of Noel Bartholomew 'Zoot' Simms and Arthur 'Bunny' Robinson, known first as Simms & Robinson and later as Bunny & Skully.

"We started off the first recording in Jamaica on soft wax [acetate] for Dada Tewari," the near-blind Skully wistfully recalls, perched on the kerb outside Kingston's Sonic Sounds. "We did the first recordings in 1953 at [Motta's] little demo studio at the corner of Hanover Street and Laws Street: he had a little matches box with quarter-inch tape."

Deonarine 'Dada' Tewari was another early entrepreneur to record local product. A Jamaican of Indian descent, whose father was a prominent planter and sportsman, Tewari was active in the family dry good business, and ran several downtown Kingston theatres. He formed the Caribbean

Recording Company by 1953 to release mento and calypso on the Caribou and Down Beat labels, as well as some of the earliest Jamaican R&B. Some claim Tewari was the first in Jamaica with mastering capabilities, but a fire at his Torrington Road premises brought an early departure from the music business.

Skully says Tewari's previous output was exclusively calypso, featuring Count Lasher [Terence Parkins], Count Owen, and Lord Tanamo [Joseph Gordon], but Skully and his partner changed the focus at their initial session: though they cut just two songs, 'End Of Time' and 'Another Chance', they were laying the foundations of a new Jamaican music. "That was the first tunes made apart from Calypsonians. That was the first R&B."

Skully was born in 1935 in Smith Village, which was renamed Denham Town after its swelling population made it another teeming West Kingston district. He and Bunny were school friends who launched their singing careers in the first Jamaican talent show, "which was [run by] Vere Johns – he used to write for the *Gleaner*. We was the champions for two years straight. We do rhythm & blues songs – all Jamaican artists in those days try to do rhythm & blues". The pair favoured slow ballads and were not averse to covering mainstream American hits, such as Bing Crosby's 'White Christmas,' and in these early days, the group concentrated more on live performances than on recording. "We keep going to shows on the North Coast, but we did not do much more recording, because it wasn't popular like now."

Skully says his neighbour Lord Flea was a big influence, naming Flea, who would later star in the 1957 Hollywood films *Bop Girl Goes Calypso* and *Calypso Joe*, as the first artist in Jamaica to score a big hit. "He start his career at the corner of Regent Street and North Street, where they had a little nightclub, the Esperanza. Then he go to Back-O-Wall and form a little band for himself, and go on the North Coast and sing at hotels before he did the films."

In May 1959, within a year of relocating to Miami, Flea tragically died of Hodgkin's Disease, aged just 25. Skully says Flea's main role models were Slim Beckford and Sam Blackwood, street singers active in Kingston in the 30s. "Slim and Sam were the two men who start music in Jamaica on the street-side of Spanish Town Road, one playing guitar and both of them sing in harmony. The songs that they sing, they have it on paper, printed out, and sell it for a penny; that was their livelihood for years. They used to sing songs like [local folk song] 'Man Piabba, Woman Piabba', and sometimes Negro spiritual songs."

Skully says Dada Tewari was not present during Simms & Robinson's debut session, which was arranged by the resident pianist. "Tewari really wasn't so much of a producer. He was an Indian who owned the Tivoli Theatre. Williams played keyboard and you had Lloyd Brevett's father [David Brevett] playing bass, a drummer by the name of Percy, and Val Bennett played the saxophone. We got £37 – 'nuff money for me and Bunny."

"Dada Tewari was well dressed all the time, with necktie and suit," Laurel Aitken added. "V-Rocket used to be a top sound: he heard me doing a rehearsal and said: 'I'll take you to see Dada.' I did quite a lot of songs, but the biggest one I did for him was 'Roll Jordan Roll', my first big hit in Jamaica."

By then, Ken Khouri had moved his base of operations to 220 Foreshore Road, an industrial area west of the wharf, to establish Federal, the first fully fledged recording studio and pressing facility on the island.[4] It was officially in use from October 1957. For his resident sound engineer, Khouri chose Graeme Goodall, an Australian radio technician trained in London who initially came to Jamaica to help set up RJR's cable service. Khouri's sons Richard and Paul also joined the business at an early age.

Federal's impressive facilities gave entrepreneurs greater scope to record local talent, while the monophonic studio at RJR was also occasionally used. Gradually, the leading sound system operators saw the benefits of recording rhythm & blues with local musicians. Coxsone Dodd said he was recording acts at Federal soon after it opened, as Skully confirmed: "After it start to develop, we did some more recording for Clement Dodd, otherwise known as Coxsone. We do a few originals and some foreign stuff."

In late 1957, when Caribou released 'Aitken's Boogie', it signalled a new direction. The song was a local variant of the type of rhythm & blues that originated in New Orleans, and its pronounced, shuffling beat was a template for much of what would follow. "That was done for Tewari as well, with the same band with Number One, and Crackers was the drummer," Aitken noted.

Since imported rhythm & blues had been the rage for the better part of a decade, and now that there was increasing scope for recordings, it was only natural that home-grown R&B would start to surface, and when Jamaican dance fans heard local artists belting out an obviously Jamaican version of rhythm & blues, it made the music sound that much sweeter, spurring dancers to wilder moves. The enthusiastic response shown by patrons at sound systems was thus a heavy catalyst for the prominent soundmen to begin issuing locally recorded R&B on a regular basis, using the sound system to boost a song's popularity prior to its official release.

Toward the end of the decade Duke Reid, Coxsone Dodd, King Edwards, and Lloyd 'The Matador' Daley were all issuing material on seven-inch 45rpm singles. They were followed shortly by a handful of others including Vincent 'Randy' Chin, a record shop owner whose carpenter father had left mainland China in the 20s to settle in Jamaica after a brief stay in Cuba; Chris Blackwell, the son of a Jamaican mother of Jewish extraction, born in Costa Rica, and an Irish military man; and Edward Seaga, a Harvard-educated anthropologist of Anglo-Syrian and part-African origin, whose father ran a lucrative travel agency.

Seaga, of course, is better known for his highly active role in the nation's politics, as he has been one of the most prominent members of the conservative Jamaica Labour Party (JLP) since the early 60s; he was Prime Minister from 1980 to 1989, and was leader of the opposition until his retirement in 2005. Though his involvement in Jamaica's music industry was brief, his contribution was important, and linked to his early political career.

At his office in New Kingston, the former JLP leader is surrounded by framed photographs of himself grinning in harmony with such right-wing luminaries as Ronald Reagan and Margaret Thatcher. Seaga explains that he entered the music business after conducting research into African-Jamaican religious practices; his field recordings of folk music were issued in 1956 as *Folk Music Of Jamaica* on the Smithsonian Folkways label. "It took three-and-a-half years, because I lived in the communities, was a part of the regular life of the communities, in one rural and one urban setting. I finished the research, but I never used it to get a PhD, because there were no postgrad degrees being given in Jamaica. Smithsonian Folkways were about the only one I knew of who would publish folk music, so I visited them, saw the mass of albums that they had done and this fitted right into that category."

An attempt to distribute the record in Jamaica brought him into the industry. "When the album was out in about '56, I was interested in having the material exposed to people. What's the use of doing research and nobody knows about it? I took it around to music stores – Stanley Motta's on Harbour Street, KG's at Cross Road, and Wonard's on Church Street – but they weren't too interested. It was a little bit too way out for them. Then they asked me if I could import other types of music for them, which I did. They wanted Pat Boone and Nat 'King' Cole, but there was also a very strong interest in rhythm & blues, like [Marvin & Johnny's] 'Cherry Pie', Professor Longhair. I found a source for that kind of music: Savoy Records, in the northern part of Manhattan, and I brought them in – artists like Fats solid foundation

Domino, Wilbert Harrison's 'Kansas City' – in lots of 50 or 100, or if it was a big hit, 250."

Before long, Seaga was pressing foreign material. "I became an agent for Columbia, Atlantic, ATCO, Epic – probably more labels than anybody else. I had a manufacturing operation and there was only one other manufacturer, Federal Records, but he was more interested in calypsos and mentos. He started two years before me, but they were manufacturing for the tourist market."

Seaga established his manufacturing base at 13 Bell Road, close to Federal. He soon began to produce local artists, issuing their work from 1958 on a label called WIRL – West Indies Records Limited. After hearing the duo Joe Higgs and Roy Wilson at a talent contest, Seaga brought them into the studio to cut 'Manny Oh', a landmark recording as one of the earliest hits by a Jamaican act.

"The popular music for the masses was rhythm & blues, and from that, young Jamaicans began to compose their own rhythm & blues-type music – not exactly the same beat, but that type of music. And I happened to be around at that time, importing and selling rhythm & blues and other types of music. Youngsters were now beginning to compose, but they didn't have an outlet other than to be able to sing on the radio or in live performance. The first popular hit song from those competitions was 'Manny Oh'. I went to one of the performances at Ward Theatre, because of my interest in the music. I didn't go there with the idea of looking for a song to produce, but when I heard it and heard the audience response, I thought: why not try producing it? I spoke with the writer, Jackie Edwards, and the singers Higgs and Wilson, about recording it, and we worked out a good arrangement."

Seaga says he actively supervised the recording session, but notes that the artists themselves selected the musicians. "That was done at RJR, that big studio they had there. It opened the door, because Jamaicans now realised that they could not only compose and sing their music, but they could get it reproduced on records; it could go on the air and they were on their way. That one effort really opened the door for what followed as Jamaican music, and from there it blossomed into different beats."

Though 'Manny Oh' made quite an impact, Seaga says sales figures have been exaggerated. "I've seen figures from other people writing about it, saying it sold 30,000 copies, but I doubt that. I don't think anything sold 30,000 copies until much later."

Despite working with other popular artists, such as the expressive young singer Slim Smith, Seaga's other commitments made him leave the music industry within a year or two of 'Manny Oh': "I didn't do too much after that, because I was moving away from commercial activities to political life."

Seaga was appointed to the Legislative Council in 1959 and shortly afterward purchased Chocomo Lawn, using it as a base to meet the public. "Chocomo Lawn was the first dancehall in Jamaica. Dances before that would take place in backyards with enough space that you could set up your sound and so on, but the first dedicated location that was a dancehall only was Chocomo Lawn. I bought it somewhere around the turning of that decade, because I needed space for the activities. I was using it as my political office, but that was just where I would see people who needed to see me."

And why, exactly, did Edward Seaga want to leave the academic and commercial worlds? "The research I had done had given me a whole range of new experiences that made me have the benefit of seeing life in a different way, from the point of view of the people in folk society. Politics is all about trying to better the life of people, especially the people who constitute the majority. And on that basis, I found myself being able to contribute. I gravitated to politics because that's where I could do things that would make a difference."

Entering the music business was hardly a serious ambition. "It was just something I got involved in out of interest. But when it became a commercial activity, it didn't replace the original interest that I had in folkways and wanting to do something for the betterment and improvement of the lives of the people. Chris Blackwell and I were at that time mostly doing the same thing; he started a little after I did. I could have continued along that route, and today I guess I would have been like him. But he chose the private life, I chose the public one."

Songs like 'Manny Oh' inspired Derrick Morgan to begin a recording career, though his early efforts were retained as sound-system exclusives. "I started on the Vere Johns' Opportunity Hour at the Palace Theatre; they had double-bill film shows on the night and a half-hour contest in between. I compete against Monty Morris, Owen Gray, Wilfred Edwards, Hortense Ellis, and I came in first imitating Little Richard. Bim & Bam, the comedians, they hear me at the show and took me on, and I used to go around with them doing stage shows.[5] I stay with them for two years; then '59, I start recording; after hearing Owen Gray, Wilfred Edwards, Higgs & Wilson coming over the radio, I asked them how them get through with it and they wouldn't tell. After a while, I heard of Duke Reid doing auditions, so I wrote 'Lover Boy' and 'Oh My' and take it by Duke; him say I must come to the rehearsal at Majestic Theatre with Drumbago and the All Star band. I went and rehearsed with them, that was a Wednesday, and we recorded it Thursday at Federal; Saturday I heard my song 'Oh My' on the radio, on Duke Reid's *Treasure Isle Time*, at four in the evening."

As was customary, Reid pressed these songs as one-off acetates, reserved for his sound system. "Now we call it dub plate, but we used to call it soft wax; the public couldn't get those songs in their home to play. Duke Reid give 'Lover Boy' to King Edwards to play on his sound as they were friends, and Edwards used to play on a corner they call S-corner: at Tewari Crescent, off Spanish Town Road, the road set like an 's'. This dancehall was right on S-corner, and 'Lover Boy' was the top sound on that corner. Edwards would be playing that song all the while."[6]

Meanwhile, developments on the Jamaican airwaves helped the music industry expand. In September 1959 a second radio station was opened, the government-owned Jamaica Broadcasting Corporation (JBC); its premises were quickly used to record Jamaican boogie-woogie. In the early 60s, Sonny Bradshaw established *Teenage Dance Party*, a weekday programme showcasing domestic product, but despite this show's extreme popularity, most radio airplay remained resolutely foreign.

It has been reported that the first locally made song aired on JBC was Laurel Aitken's 'Boogie Rock', but Aitken said the song in question was 'Boogie In My Bones', the first hit produced by Chris Blackwell. It entered the JBC chart in October 1959 and stayed at number one for 13 weeks.

"Chris came to see me one day, he say: 'You been doing quite a few things recently and I like them, I've got to do something with you.' And I say 'quite possible'. When Chris came the second time, we went to a bar with a piano and I played him a few of the things that I have written. He said: 'I've got a band I would like you to meet.' They was five white guys – I think they were Canadian. We went to JBC with a friend of mine, [saxophonist] Caroll McLaughlin, and I did 'Boogie In My Bones' and 'Little Sheila'."

The backing band was actually The Caribs, formed in Australia during the 50s with drummer Lowell Morris, pianist Peter Stoddart, saxophonist Max Wildman, and Haitian percussionist Albert La Guerre. By strange circumstances, in 1958, bandleader Wildman went to Haiti to help run a restaurant, and met a member of the Jamaican Tourist Board there, who was looking for someone to manage the Glass Bucket; Wildman took on the role on the proviso that The Caribs would be the resident band. Morris,

Stoddart, and Sindrey thus travelled to Kingston to fill the slot, drafting future Skatalite Lloyd Brevett on bass. The group was later resident at the Myrtlebank Hotel, and its members used on some of the earliest recording sessions arranged by Chris Blackwell and Clement Dodd, the latter helping them become resident session players at Federal, where they also cut material of their own.

'Little Sheila' also reached the Jamaican charts, but 'Boogie In My Bones' was the bigger hit. Aitken quickly tried to reproduce the formula with 'Boogie Rock', one of a handful of tunes cut with a group dubbed The Boogie Cats for aspiring producer Ruddy Abrahams, whose (Jamaican) RCA label releases were pressed by Tewari's Caribbean Recording Company; other numbers included 'Whole Lot Of Rock' and 'Edmarine'.

Though Jamaican boogie was little more than a crude attempt to emulate the music of the American South, these exciting early efforts retain a distinctly Jamaican feel. The Duke Reid Group's earliest instrumentals, such as 'What Makes Honey' and 'Joker', were fairly unadorned eight or twelve-bar blues numbers set to a loping beat; Laurel Aitken's 'More Whiskey' and 'Low Down Dirty Girl' (featuring saxophonist Trenton Spence) were much the same, though 'Daniel Saw The Stone' and 'Judgement Day' (backed by guitarist Ken Richards & His Harmonisers) drew from church music. Subsequent Duke Reid productions, such as 'Blackberry Brandy' and 'Yard Broom', used shuffling boogie blues beats as platforms for expressive soloing by saxophonist Roland Alphonso, while drummer Arkland 'Drumbago' Parks's 'Duck Soup' was somewhat more competent, augmented by vibrant African-styled hand-drumming.

Such releases reveal an emerging style, as Jamaicans grappling with African-American rhythms sowed the seeds of a national genre. In contrast to Reid's work, many early Coxsone productions consisted of slower, softer, American-styled R&B ballads, such as Alton & Eddie's 'Muriel' and Tony Gregory's 'Baby Come On Home', though numbers like Lascelles Perkins' 'Lonely Robin' were also shuffle mutations.

Simeon L. Smith was another early entrepreneur who found success with ballads and mutated blues in the late 50s. At his home in the Bronx, Smith explains that he found his way into the music business because he had a regular source of records from New Orleans. "I'm from Manchester, a little district called Harry Watch; I come to Kingston when I was 17, had a lot of family to welcome me there. Me and a friend named Delfos worked at the wharf together and he has a sound system called Deltone in Mountain View Avenue. I used to be more a businessperson, so I used to get records from a fellow who come on the SS America every two weeks: Fats Domino, Shirley & Lee. Then I opened a record shop, Hi-Lite Music Store, at the corner of Harris Street and Spanish Town Road. I had a haberdashery also, a hardware store and a wholesale liquor store."

Hi-Lite became a focal point for budding local talent, prompting Simeon to launch the Smith's label. "My place full of young people. I buy an old piano and have a place next door where everybody practise. I put on a lot of shows, helping the artists to make some money. I used to be in my shop every day, have a Grundig tape recorder, and several singers would come by and say them have a tune. I would take them in my car up to a man in Hagley Park Road that have an old piano, who can play good, practise with them, and it grows. First session was with Owen Gray, at JBC studio with Sonny Bradshaw. The first big hit was Keith & Enid, 'Worried Over You'. They went to Federal Records and Federal said they're singing too soft; nobody wanted to record them, because recording business was Laurel Aitken and heavy beats. But I love harmony and ballads, so I break with 'Worried Over You' and make everybody worried."

This soft duet, backed by tenor saxophonist Trenton Spence's group, topped the Jamaican charts in 1960. It was one of the first recordings licensed to Blue Beat, a subsidiary of Melodisc Records specifically designated for Jamaican product, in the UK; the label would later showcase Prince Buster's output. Emil Shalit, a Central European Jewish immigrant, founded Melodisc in 1949 as one of the first companies to issue black music in Britain; he was also involved in the pressing of the earliest Jamaican calypso. "Shalit used to do the calypso business with Khouri," says Simeon Smith. "He came out and heard about ['Worried Over You']; Sonny Bradshaw put him on to me and I gave him the rights to release the record in London. Then I start to do a whole lot."

Smith's next hit was Derrick Morgan's 'Fat Man', again backed by Trenton Spence, which blended the cadence of Cuban bolero with American rhythm & blues. Morgan says 'Fat Man' was his first recording to finally gain an official release. "After I do 'Lover Boy' and 'Oh My', I find Patsy, which is Millicent Todd. Her mum, Miss Kitty, meet me one day on Orange Street and asked me to come and listen to her daughter: she was living at Drummond Street, and I had to pass that street to reach where I live. Patsy start hum two lines of a gospel song and I like the voice I heard, so I sit right there and wrote a song, 'Love Not To Brag', and I take her to Duke, and him record that. Then we do 'Feel So Fine' off [Shirley & Lee's] 'Feel So Good'. Duke been playing these songs against Sir Coxsone Downbeat, play it for whosoever him come up against in contests, but it would be only on sound system. I also did 'Leave Earth' and 'Wigger Wee Shuffle' for Dodd in the early part, when we was just recording for sound systems. Then I hear about 'Little Wonder', Mr Smith: King Edwards and Mr Smith is two brothers. I went to Smith with 'Fat Man', and Monty Morris and myself do 'Now We Know', so Smith was the first person to release. He put out 'Fat Man' and people hark up the song; it pick up number one and Duke Reid was vexed about that. He sent some bad men to take me back to him, ask me why I do this, say I can't do that, and so on. I said I didn't know it would be offending to him, I don't under no contract with nobody, but I just stay back in his stable for a while."

'Album Of Memory' by The Magic Notes, a duo Smith recalls as "Victor & Cecil, two guys from over Maverley", was another notable Hi-Lite production, one of a handful Smith recorded with Drumbago. "His beat was getting very popular. Drumbago was really good on drums."

Diverted by other activities, Simeon Smith created very little music after 1963. Instead, he concentrated on his sound system, Little Wonder. "Sound system, I had about six sets. It was set up in '63 or '64." He also promoted live events, and even wrote popular plays such as *Two Time In Bed*, which starred the rumba dancer Esmarie.

In addition to Trenton Spence and Drumbago, Smith singled out pianist Theophilus Beckford for particular mention. Beckford's 'Easy Snappin' – said to have been recorded circa 1957 but not issued on vinyl until 1960 – shifted the standard blues blueprint by emphasising the after-beat of every measure. The song was a favourite on Coxsone's sound system, and was perhaps the most important precursor of the ska style.

Though Beckford's cadence was original, shuffle boogie was its most obvious root. Coxsone pointed out that Southern American music had the greatest influence: "At that time, my main emphasis was on rhythm & blues, boogie-woogie, rhythm with a shuffle, and some slow pop music."[7]

Once regular recording sessions were under way, musicians came together in various forms, the line-ups helping to impart a signature sound for each producer. Coxsone's earliest backing bands were Hersang & His City Slickers, led by pianist Herman Sang, and the Dew Droppers, led by pianist and organist Aubrey Adams. Clue J. & His Blues Blasters, a slightly later combo, featured guitarist Keith Stoddart, drummer Ken Williams, bassist Lloyd Mason, and Herman Sang, Aubrey Adams, or Theophilus Beckford on piano; the teenaged Monty Alexander also occasionally sat in. Duke Reid's early bands included The Duke Reid Group, Drumbago's

Orchestra, and trumpeter Baba Brooks's Band, which typically featured trombonist Don Drummond and his Cuban-born protégé, Emmanuel 'Rico' Rodriguez, saxophonist Roland Alphonso, drummer Aston 'Wackie' Henry, and players mentioned above. Popular music in Jamaica has always been communal, and these groups shared overlapping and constantly shifting memberships, recording in various conglomerations under different names.

Several pioneering musicians are largely forgotten, including pianist Herman Sang, although singer Cornell Campbell says Sang was key to Coxsone's operation, directly responsible for selecting him as a vocalist. "I started recording at 11 years of age, that was 1956, with a song named 'My Treasure'. In those days we didn't have reggae and ska – it was just rhythm & blues, not to mention the kind of boogie beat them had. A schoolmate urged me to be recorded. Someone told him Rico live somewhere on Gold Street, so we went to look for Rico and Rico tell us about Coxsone. I was in line for auditions, but Downbeat [Coxsone] was very embarrassing. He call everybody 'Jackson', and when Downbeat listen to the singer, he say: 'Jackson, which part you come from?' and the guy say he come from somewhere like Trelawny. Coxsone say: 'But Jackson, you mean to say you come from so far to mash up my business?'

"I think the guy sound good, so when Downbeat say that, I just walk out of the line. The other week me go back again. The pianist see me and say: 'Hold on, every week me see that little guy come up and he never sing a song yet. Come in, likkle youth, and let me hear what you have to do.' I start to get nervous, and when I sing the song 'My Treasure', my friend was supposed to harmonise with me, but him couldn't sing a note, so the pianist said my friend must stop. When Downbeat come down in the afternoon, he ask the musicians what's going on, and Hersang say: 'That little guy is bad.' Him say I must come back for the rehearsal Thursday."

Cornell's fragile soprano was featured on a number of other Coxsone sides in the late 50s and early 60s, but disputes over payment drove him elsewhere. "I did a sequence of songs for Coxsone, and I was taught printing, so I used to print the record labels for him, but through financial problems I leave Downbeat and went to King Edwards."

As the heated sound-system rivalries carried into the production sphere, aspiring producers fought over artists, particularly if an unsigned act was a talent-contest winner featured on a radio programme, or had created an impact on sound systems with a self-financed acetate. A case in point involves 'Lollipop Girl', The Jiving Juniors' debut.

One of the industry's enduring figures, founding member and group leader Derrick Harriott has been active as a singer, producer, record retailer, and exporter for several decades. Though perpetually busy, Harriott is a courteous host at his One Stop record, video, and shoe store in Half Way Tree, a major meeting point whose packed space has a pleasant atmosphere. Harriott says that before The Jiving Juniors there was Sang & Harriott, his singing career stemming largely from a love of sound systems. "That time, I'm always with the sound systems. If I'm at school, any sound that we picked up coming from far, sometimes maybe four miles down Mountain View Avenue, we would follow that sound just to stand up for a couple of hours and listen to music. Anywhere a sound was, we always go."

An important ally was a young man called Skitter, another of Bunny Robinson's singing partners. "I used to tour certain sound systems way downtown, High Holborn Street area, with Skitter of Bunny & Skitter. He was a type of friend in the music business that if you wanted to get the words for a song, he only needs to hear it once and he knows all the words."

In 1957, Harriott entered his first talent contest. "I used to go to the Palace Theatre, where they had Vere Johns' Opportunity Hour, and I'm thinking: I can do better than some of them guys, so I decided to enter and do a song by The Turbans, 'When You Dance'. I was about 15. Simms & Robinson, they had a big song in the earlies called 'End Of Time'. Maybe because of the inspiration of Simms & Robinson, I decided to go back with my partner that attended Excelsior High School, Claudie Sang Junior. The name was Sang & Harriott. We entered and that was it – we tear down everywhere you can think of, like Ambassador Theatre in the West. We sang a song called 'You're Mine, All Mine' by Bobby & Ronald, an R&B thing. That is a song I remember Admiral Cosmic playing at the Shady Grove all 15 times straight, so when we did that song the crowd went wild."

Not long afterward Harriot's partner went abroad. "Claudie Sang went on a Cable & Wireless course to Barbados. Then we formed The Jiving Juniors with myself as leader, Maurice Wynter tenor, Eugene Dwyer was baritone, and Herman Sang was the pianist – the same Hersang that played for Downbeat, brother of Claudie Sang Jr. He used to be around the piano like Little Richard, with him foot way out."

Shortly after forming, the group cut an acetate of an original song for sound system usage. "About '58, we decided we want to hear our voices, so we actually went down to Stanley Motta's: they had like a dub-cutting machine. We did a song called 'Lollipop Girl': Claudie Sang played the piano, we sang, and then we put in a handclap; that's all we had. While you're singing it, they're cutting it same time, straight on to acetate, so if you make any mistakes, you're in trouble. Carlyle Ho-Yun, he had the sound called Thunderbird. He used to play at some Friday evening sessions in Maxfield Avenue at Champagnie Lawn; it was an open-air thing. He played the song, couldn't take it off, big song just playing and playing. Finally, one day Coxsone swapped a foreign record for that record, 'cos it was making waves."

'Lollipop Girl' showed how intense sound-system competition had become. The one-off special became so popular that Duke Reid went to extreme lengths to acquire a copy, causing serious friction. "I heard there was a clash between Duke Reid and Sir Coxsone's Downbeat at a hall right beside the Gaiety Theatre, just off East Queen Street. The only person who was supposed to play was Coxsone, but then Duke Reid play too, and according to what them say, guns were drawn, because how the hell Duke Reid get it? [Maybe] it was one of the operators stole it out of Coxsone's box, went and make another dub plate and give it to Duke Reid, 'cos he was desperate for it."

By this time, Harriott made his first trip to New York to visit family. "I was in the States for about five months, but when it comes round to Christmas, my bones started tickling, so I had to find a way to come back to Jamaica to sing at the big Christmas morning show kept by Vere Johns at the Carib Theatre. When I came back to Jamaica, Claudie Sang also came back home, so he joined the group."

Within days of the performance, Reid ushered them into the studio. "When I come down, I heard that Duke Reid wanted to send a ticket for me to record 'Lollipop Girl' for him. He had me in the studio in late December 1959 and recorded it with 'My Heart's Desire' and 'Duke's Cookies'."

According to Harriott, Reid kept the material as a sound-system exclusive for a long period, boosting its popularity before it was officially released. "He had ['Lollipop Girl'] on his sound for one whole year before releasing it, and when he released it, it went straight to number one. And we [also] had the Number Four song, 'My Heart's Desire' – that was how big it was."

By then, Harriott had already formed the Crystal label, its first issue his cover of Donnie Elbert's 'What Can I Do (The Wedding)'. "I was the first artist-producer in Jamaica. Nobody ever thought about anything like that. Crystal started from 1960, same year we did 'Lollipop Girl'."

In 1961, not long after their hits for Reid were finally released, the group began recording for Coxsone, scoring their biggest number one hit with the spiritual 'Over The River', which benefited from an individual rhythmic pattern and expressive instrumental soloing. "Trombone solo was Rico Rodriguez, the guitar solo was Dennis Sindrey from Australia."

Sound-system battles continued to rage, with exclusivity being taken extremely seriously. On September 3 1961, Clement Dodd noticed three of his exclusive acetates missing; the following day, an employee heard rival sound-man Herman Moore playing the discs. Dodd had Moore arrested, being able to prove exclusive ownership, since he had not yet released the songs in question to the public.

Meanwhile, Derrick Harriott continued expanding his horizons. In 1962, he and Sang were back in New York, cutting material with an augmented Jiving Juniors line-up at Mirasound studio with soul arranger Teacher Wiltshire, from which the Frankie-Lymon styled hit 'Sugar Dandy' emerged. "We got the group together with Winston Service, who used to sing with The Downbeats, and Valman Burke, the son of Jamaican cricket umpire, Perry Burke. We did four songs in New York – that's where 'Sugar Dandy' was born. The back-up band was the band that used to back up The Shirelles and Chuck Jackson."

Harriott says the Jiving Juniors switched from Reid to Coxsone because they "just wanted to be a little flexible at the time", but it was typical that Dodd would score the bigger hit and bring out the best of the group's abilities. Dodd says he kept the edge over Reid by presenting stronger material to the people, both in the days when sound systems featured strictly imported tunes, as well as when locally recorded discs began to feature. "With importation, I had the stronger set of records, also when we started recording locally. But the rivalry was like this: you have weeks when I would be more successful at the places I played, much more than Duke. I remember really heading off Duke by myself."

As an integral part of Sir Coxsone's Downbeat in the late 50s, Prince Buster also claims credit for this success. Buster was often on the frontline for Coxsone, staving off physical attacks from Reid and King Edwards's henchmen. But it was not only his muscle that Dodd employed: Buster was also the one who identified the hottest records played by the competition.

After having his skull busted open numerous times without receiving promised financial compensation, Buster broke with Coxsone to establish himself on the sound-system circuit. "One of the main reasons I left Coxsone was that I was being stifled. I never work with Coxsone as a job, but I was the man who bring up his sound, because he didn't know nobody and I was a popular man. Coxsone used to bring records in from America and when Duke Reid had a record that he didn't have, people in the country put that record on pedestal. So Coxsone and Duke would go away and bring back a copy, and that became their own master recording – they would bootleg the thing on blank labels. I am the one who used to go to the dances when Duke Reid play and tell Coxsone who the artists are, try to discover the name through the lyrics. He had promised to recompense me in a certain way when he got the records, and every time the records come he always have a truck broke down or something, always short. I conscious that I am the man who carry the whole sound system and this don't make no sense, so I talk to Machuki 'bout it. Machuki was the number-one disc jockey, and Machuki was constantly leaving him for the same reason."

After choosing independence, Buster planned to travel to America to buy a stack of hot R&B, but despite government connections, his record-buying trip never came off. "A man named Zar and another one named Parker used to work at the Ministry Of Labour. After I tell them I set up my own sound, they arrange that I do farm working. I took test after test and pass everything, and the morning when we supposed to leave they did one more inspection, and the man look at my hands and say my hands can't cut cane and take me out of the line."

The reason, Buster explains, was that his badly mangled hands had taken "too much blows", according to the inspector, "so I can't get to America to buy rhythm & blues, but I didn't stop my intention to build up a sound, because I was going to overthrow them and show that I am the man". The source of the sabotage, according to Buster, was Clement Dodd's stepfather, Edgar Darlington, a prominent JLP-aligned trade unionist.

With his plan to use American exclusives foiled, Buster tried a different approach: recording original tunes with local musicians. He went to a popular uptown nightclub to discuss the situation with Drumbago and began rehearsing with musicians such as guitarist Jerome 'Jah Jerry' Haines, saxophonist Dennis 'Taste' Campbell, and trombonist Rico, with vocalist Teddy Charmers (aka Roy Willis) from the duo The Charmers assisting. "I went to Drumbago at the Baby Grand, a drummer who I know for a long time, tell him I would like to make some music. You did have an abundance of [Jamaican] rhythm & blues that I did buy from them and have as exclusives, so Drumbago and me talk, and then me and Charmers would go up in the early morning and rehearse with him, show him how we want it done. This is around '59."

It took a while for the musicians to catch on. "The musicians that were there didn't play the music that I wanted, because Baby Grand is a club where people sit down and eat, and then get up and dance with wife and girlfriend, so the music was somewhat different from what I intended. But, Drumbago being an instrumental man, it didn't take him long to understand what we were moving to. We went to JBC studio with Rico and make a tune called 'Little Honey'. That was the first tune I ever made on record."

By then, Prince Buster had established his Record Shack, and the attached Voice Of The People sound system, just around the corner from Coxsone. "I started at 49 Charles Street, but I was sharing that shop with a girl named Claudette and I needed more space, because she was doing hair and dressmaking." He eventually moved across the street, renting a larger space at number 36 from Winston Blake's aunt. "It was where Son The Junior Sebastian's sound system used to be. There was a baker there and a Chinese shop, and the sound system was in the shop. After Son left, I went across. Miss Blake say she was enjoying the music I was playing on the other side, so she rented me the place. That was where all them shocks came out of. I used to rehearse the band at the back of my record shop with different artists, and we went down to Federal records and recorded what we now call ska."

Ska was the excitement of the independence era personified, and its creation brought widespread changes to the Kingston music scene. Ska not only gave vast impetus to the fledgling music industry, it also increased the export and exposure of Jamaican culture. Perhaps most crucially, ska was a great creative stimulus to the island's musicians, as it allowed for less restrained and more honest musical expression. With the arrival of this uniquely Jamaican genre, the island's popular music had come of age.

2
CELEBRATION TIME
Authentic ska

"People who don't suffer like us can't perform that sound – it's a sufferer's sound. No middleclass Jamaicans can play the music we play; it's a ghetto sound that we play out of instruments, real suffering ghetto sound. It sound happy, yes, for it's relief!" – RICO RODRIGUEZ

"I didn't even know that the music was going to be serious. I didn't know it was going to go all over the world." – ROLAND ALPHONSO, OD

Ska differed from Jamaican rhythm & blues mainly in the accent of its beat. Instead of the fore-beat emphasis of boogie-woogie, ska used honking horns or staccato guitar chords to emphasise the after-beat – that is, the second and fourth beats of every measure, rather than the first and third. It was also faster than most R&B, with wild drum rolls accelerating the pace, while vibrant horn players used jazz techniques for expressive solos and melodic backing. Often, the defining honk of Dennis 'Taste' Campbell's sax gave ska its rhythmic delineation; other times, the raw rhythm of Jah Jerry's guitar divided the beat.

Many musicians and producers claim to have originated ska, and conflicting explanations have been given for its name. One of ska's most prominent musicians, saxophonist Tommy McCook, related the common tale that 'ska' derived from Clue J.'s use of 'Skavoovie' to address his fellow musicians – notably pianist Theophilus Beckford, who is often cited as changing the beat with 'Easy Snappin'.

"Skavoovie is a greeting. That's the way he used to greet you, even long before the ska came in. Instead of saying 'What's up, Jack?', 'Hello, Ronnie', 'What's cooking, John?' or whatever, he would say 'What happen, Skavoovie?' or 'Hail, Skavoovie!' Then, later on, I think Mr Dodd asked for a Jamaican music. He said to experiment and came with the ska thing, which was really the swing and the guitar playing the upbeat."[1]

Leading reggae producer Bunny Lee, who rose to prominence in the late 1960s and dominated much of the 70s, names Clue J., Dennis Campbell, Val Bennett, and Jah Jerry as some of ska's most noteworthy innovators. "Them don't talk about Clue J. When we make the American blues, Clue J. used to call [his group] Clue J. & The Blues Blasters; him and Rico did have a band. Him tell them: 'Make the guitar go ska! Ska!' If we did play the rhythm & blues guitar, it would be rhythm & blues. It's really Clue J. bring in the ska and nobody don't talk about him – him dead and gone and nobody don't remember is Clue J. say: 'Make it go ska.' Coxsone start call people 'Skavoovie' after you have a man named Taste Campbell, him play pure ska, him and Val Bennett hold the ska in a tune. The ska hold up the tempo of the tune when the drums fall down. Those horn man, them neck fat because them can't out of breath, and Jah Jerry do him thing, but them no talk about Jah Jerry neither. Those guys are some great guys who are the foundation."

Though numerous records from the period credit Clue J.'s band – including the pivotal 'Shufflin' Jug', a peculiar adaptation of Glenn Miller's 'Little Brown Jug', named by many as the first ska recording – guitarist Ernest Ranglin contradicts Lee's statement, insisting that he himself was the driving force behind the group and arranger of their recorded material. Ranglin was a leading player on the upper-class circuit, and as such remained incognito on downtown recordings associated with the poor. "It's my band, not Clue J.'s band," the amiable guitarist insists, with a slight trace of annoyance, at Chris Blackwell's London HQ. "Clue J. was my bass player, but at that time the music was like a rebel underground music. I used to play in the hotels and it wouldn't be too good for my reputation to really front a group like that."

Ranglin was born in Manchester in 1932 and raised by his grandmother. A gifted musician, he began teaching himself guitar aged five. After moving to Kingston and meeting his mentor, one Cecil Houdini, Ranglin joined Val Bennett's band at the ago of 15 and Eric Deans' Orchestra a year later. He then passed through Baba Motta's group, and began fronting a hotel quintet. By the late 50s, Ranglin's versatility and confidence with any number of styles, from Hawaiian music to merengue, mambo to boogie, set him in high demand as a session player. In 1959, when Chris Blackwell released the first album on Island Records, a live recording made with Lance Haywood, the blind Bermudan pianist resident at Montego Bay's Half Moon Hotel, Ernest Ranglin was featured on the B-side.[2] So began a long working relationship.

"I was the A&R man for Island Records, that was around 1958. During

43

that time, I did things for Coxsone, Buster, all of them. I did 38 tunes for Buster – any tune that you can think of that was done in that era."

Ranglin was featured on some of the earliest Jamaican recordings, from the days of manually operated direct-to-disc machines. "The first time I went into the studio, I was with seven guys. We used to play Hawaiian music in a little group when I was a young boy. We did this one record, and in those days they had to turn the vinyl – it has to keep turning. I don't think it was for a company – it was just a record that we did. This was long before studios were being built. It wasn't for commercial purposes."

By the time the ska era was underway, Ranglin was a prominent session musician. He was a part of the JBC studio orchestra when Prince Buster began recording there, and arranged some of Clement Dodd's biggest ska hits before travelling to London in 1964 for a nine-month residence at Ronnie Scott's jazz club.

Back on the island, Prince Buster really kick-started the shift in Jamaica's musical gears, once he was free to record his own productions. An early session yielded significant hits employing a markedly different beat, including Buster's own 'They Got To Go' and The Folkes Brothers' astounding 'Oh Carolina', which placed Count Ossie's burru drumming over a backbeat that inched away from boogie, despite the inclusion of an incongruous piano line, played by Owen Gray and adapted from Rufus & Carla Thomas's inaugural Stax hit, 'Cause I Love You'.

Count Ossie, aka Oswald Williams, had long been a creative catalyst. In the late 40s, Kingston's leading jazzmen often mingled with the drummers at Ossie's Salt Lane yard for late-night jams. After Hurricane Charlie destroyed this downtown space in 1951, the Count established a large Rasta camp at Adastra Road in Rennock Lodge, East Kingston, and the capital's leading jazz players congregated for regular sessions in the surrounding Wareika Hills, making music in praise of the 'Most High'. By placing Ossie's drums on 'Oh Carolina', Prince Buster brought the sound of Rastafari into Jamaica's popular consciousness.

The Rastafari movement had been slowly rising since 1930, when certain Jamaicans interpreted the coronation of Ethiopian emperor Haile Selassie I as the fulfilment of biblical prophecy. They held a statement said to have been uttered by Marcus Garvey, a Jamaican radical campaigning for black self-determination, as proof that Selassie was the true, living God, a black redeemer who would usher in an age of deliverance and repatriate black Jamaicans to Africa. The most significant Rastafari community was established in 1940 at Pinnacle, a commune headed by Leonard P. Howell

44

(aka Gangunguru Maragh) near Sligoville, in the hills above Spanish Town; in 1954, police destroyed it and Howell was forcibly detained at Bellevue mental hospital. Many followers dispersed to the West Kingston slums of Back-O-Wall and the Dungle, clustered on the edge of the city's garbage dump. It was here that the Rastafari are said to have encountered another group of social outcasts, the burru men, who migrated from Clarendon in the 30s. The burru propagated drumming traditions of their Ashanti ancestors, using a large bass drum (hit with a rounded, padded stick) and the smaller *funde* to hold the rhythm, with the repeater or *kette* taking the percussive lead. The two groups, who both venerated aspects of African culture that were rejected by Jamaica's Eurocentric mainstream, traded religious indoctrination for musical instruction. Count Ossie's mastery of the drum, learned from a burru man in Back-O-Wall, made the trio of burru drums the root of Rastafari music.

'Oh Carolina' was not the first Jamaican recording to make use of African percussion techniques. Laruel Aitken's 'Ghana Independence' and 'Nebuchanezer', released on Caribou 78s around 1957, had similar backing; the featured drummer, according to Aitken, was "a guy called Feely-Feely, from the same area we came from, the Greenwich Town-Maxfield Avenue area". Likewise, Lord Tanamo's Caribou 78s 'Call Calypso', 'Calypso Tango', and 'Give And Get' all featured Jerome Walter's Conga Drums, and a number of Count Lasher's 78s included prominent African-style hand-drumming. Lord Lebby's 'Ethiopia' took things a step further by using backing of this kind to emphasise longing for a utopian African homeland – probably the first Jamaican record to do so. But 'Oh Carolina' had a phenomenal effect on the Jamaican public. Demand for the tune was so intense that both radio stations were forced to play it often, despite initial bans. The song's spine-tingling arrangement has never gone out of fashion; in 1994, Shaggy's electric cover version was a worldwide smash. The repercussions of the particular combination of musical elements that came together in 'Oh Carolina' over 50 years ago are still rippling through Jamaica's popular music.

Incredibly, Buster says rival producer Ruddy Abrahams licensed 'Oh Carolina' to Blue Beat without his knowledge. "Abrahams used to sell calypso to Mr Shalit through Stanley Motta, and the man take my record and give Shalit, says is him own. If you look 'pon the original [Bluebeat] record, you will see the writer [credited as] Abrahams. I went to Eddie Seaga and him send me to his attorney, who write them, threatening to sue. Sonny Bradshaw and [accountant] Roy Hylton set up a meeting at the Myrtlebank Hotel, and this white man sit down and me and him talk. Mr Shalit said he didn't want to get into a fuss with me, him would prefer to work with me. Sonny Bradshaw and them advise, say it was good for me; after a while, me say me will go with him, and the man became one of me greatest teachers, me best friend. Mr Shalit is a man who know some ten-plus languages; he is a man who was an intelligence [officer] in the United States Army, jump out of airplanes in Germany 'cos him knew the dialect, so he is a very, very wise man. What I had at the time was a sort of village concept of things, and Mr Shalit internationalised my mind."

After the success of 'Carolina', music proclaiming an African identity became less taboo. Count Ossie made a series of recordings for Spanish Town-based sound-system proprietor Harry Mudie, though none repeated the success of 'Carolina', while Coxsone cut a number of discs with strong Rastafari undercurrents. For instance, Noel 'Zoot' Simms transformed the hymn 'Golden Pen' into a jumping Rasta ska, introducing it and a song called 'Press Along' in the Amharic language of Ethiopia, after learning its rudiments from Rasta leader Mortimer Planno in Trench Town. However, such material was still in the minority. A more popular Bunny & Skully single was a faithful cover of Bing Crosby's 'White Christmas' – doubly ironic in tropical Jamaica.

As a vocalist for Coxsone in 1960–61, Clancy Eccles helped to bridge the boogie and ska periods. His hit 'Freedom' was another early tune that proclaimed a longing for an African homeland. The son of a tailor and builder who often moved the family, Eccles was born in Dean Pen, Saint Mary in 1940. He began performing in his late teens in Ocho Rios.

"Higgs & Wilson, The Blues Busters, Busty Brown, and quite a number of us were on the North Coast," Eccles recalled at his home in Garvey Mead, Portmore, a number of years before suffering a fatal heart attack in 2005. "We all wanted to perform on various shows, and then I start producing my own thing by the White River Club – just myself and a fire dancer."

He began recording for Coxsone after impacting at a talent contest. "In early 1960, Coxsone had a talent hunt. It was 60 of us and I was a runner-up, but I was the first one that Coxsone recorded out of that crop.[3] I did 'Freedom' and 'I Live And I Love'. Around eight months later I did 'River Jordan', 'More Proof', and quite a lot of other tracks."

These numbers hover somewhere between Jamaican boogie and full-blown ska. 'Freedom' has a pronounced ska rhythm guitar, but its rolling bass sounds like American R&B; though recorded later, the booze-praising 'More Proof' has a jump-boogie beat and a ska-type horn solo.

Although these songs show the music in transition, Eccles jumped

Coxsone's ship before ska was really in full swing following arguments about payment. He reverting to tailoring and began promoting concerts, just as ska really came to the fore. "It was around late 1961. I signed a contract with Coxsone that would last for three years, so after I left Coxsone I didn't do any recording because I didn't want him to have anything on me that say I break the contract."

Ska's creation coincided with the Jamaican independence movement gathering steam, though the first concrete step toward self-sufficiency had been taken decades earlier. The Great Depression of the 1930s crippled the nation's economy: by 1938, the unemployment rate was at 20 per cent, and most in work were grossly underpaid. A series of strikes led to increased police brutality, which in turn sparked large-scale rioting and looting after police killed a number of workers at the West Indies Sugar Company's estate in Frome. In the aftermath, a charismatic middle-class moneylender called William Alexander Bustamante formed the Bustamante Industrial Trade Union (BITU), the first trade union in the Caribbean. In the same year, Bustamante's cousin, a lawyer and Oxford-educated Rhodes scholar, Norman Washington Manley, formed the nation's first political party, the People's National Party (PNP), which was originally aligned with BITU. When Bustamante was imprisoned during the struggles of 1938, Manley negotiated his release, but in 1943, Bustamante broke with Manley and formed the Jamaica Labour Party (JLP).

Many commentators have noted that Bustamante was an impressive extrovert, and his willingness to organise strikes and stand up to the nation's most powerful figures earned him great admiration, particularly among the poor masses. Hand in hand with such qualities came a tendency to self-mythologise. Bustamante was born William Alexander Clark; though his father was Irish and his mother from the Jamaican upper class, the JLP leader liked to imply a lineage unrelated to the British colonial rulers, and thus claim an in-born affinity with the downtrodden and oppressed.

When elections were held in 1944, the campaigns of both parties were sullied by stone-throwing and stabbing incidents, particularly in downtown ghetto areas; ultimately, Bustamante's call for higher wages gave the JLP a landslide victory. He remained in power until 1955, when Norman Manley was voted in, again after campaigns marred by ghetto violence. While initially there may have been little difference between the two parties, they would eventually become polar opposites. Manley's easy-going Fabian socialism gradually shifted toward the left, and Bustamante's liberal capitalism moved further right.

47

Once the PNP took power, Manley entered strident negotiations with the colonial rulers to determine the method of Jamaica's independence. In 1958, with Britain's approval, Jamaica joined the 12 other territories of the English-speaking Caribbean in the shortlived Federation Of The West Indies. These separate islands, united by language and similar histories, were due to gain independence from Britain as a single nation in 1962, with Trinidad awarded the seat of central government.

In 1960, Bustamante began a vociferous campaign against the Federation, arguing instead for Jamaica's direct, individual independence. To drive home this point, the JLP used Clancy Eccles's 'Freedom', despite the song's portrayal of African-Jamaican repatriation. It was the first of many instances of non-partisan songs being co-opted by a Jamaican political party. "The politicians used it as an escape route to bring their thing back to order, but we were thinking about a Rastafarian movement," Eccles explained. "It got to me by seeing the Rastamen out there preaching in different districts in Jamaica, trying to let the word reach people. They was talking about the Back-to-Africa movement, and my mother's side of the family is African."

When Manley called a referendum in September 1961 to resolve the question of the Federation, the people voted overwhelmingly for Jamaican independence. Bustamante won the April 1962 general election by a narrow margin; he thus became Jamaica's first Prime Minister when independence arrived on 6 August. In that same election, Edward Seaga won the notoriously volatile but strategically important Western Kingston constituency; he says his anthropological studies played a major role in his choice of seat. "Part of that study was in that very same area, West Kingston. That's the area that is richest in folk life and folk material."

When appointed Minister of Development and Welfare, Seaga was no longer able to oversee WIRL's operations, particularly the running of the recording studio that had been constructed at Bell Road. "Once I became a minister, I had no time to operate a business, so my father took it off my hands, along with Dora, a cousin of mine who was involved in it from the beginning. They ran it just long enough to be able to dispose of it, sold it to a man by the name of [George] Benson. He owned a studio which was destroyed by fire, so he bought this one."

While the island's inhabitants struggled to free themselves of colonial shackles, its musicians were striving to establish a popular music they could truly claim as their own. By the time of independence, ska had fully permeated Jamaica. The shuffling, American-based boogie hits of 1959 and 1960, like Laurel Aitken's 'Jeannie Is Back' (aka 'Come Back Jeannie'), 'Boogie In My Bones', and Derrick Morgan's 'Fat Man' gave way to the more clearly Jamaican ska of Chuck & Dobby's 'Do Du Wap', produced by Coxsone, as well as Derrick Morgan's 'Forward March' and Derrick & Patsy's 'Housewife's Choice', both produced by Leslie Kong, another highly significant producer.

Derrick Morgan says budding singer Jimmy Cliff got Kong involved in the music business. "One day this little youth come to me which was Jimmy Cliff, but he was James Chambers at the time. He said he meet a man named Leslie Kong that would like me to listen to his song. If it sound good, he should take me to Leslie. Beverley's was Leslie Kong's place, on the corner of Orange Street and North Street. It was a restaurant and ice cream parlour, with a real estate office in the back and upstairs. You have one brother named Fats, he was the head of it, then Leslie and Cecil used to do real estate together. Leslie was inspired to go into the music by Jimmy Cliff, because Jimmy go to him with a song named 'Dearest Beverley'. The place was called Beverley's restaurant, so he thought if he go in with that song, it would inspire them to do recording. When I listen to the song, it was a nice, slow ballad, but we was doing ska music, so him say him have another title, which was 'Hurricane Hattie', and I have a friend in the yard, a poet, who wrote 'King Of Kings'. We put a melody to it and go to Beverley's, and I told him about Drumbago and the All Star band. Drumbago take me and Jimmy to Greenwich Farm to rehearse, and we go to Federal the following day and recorded those songs. There I met Owen Gray – he do 'Darling Patricia', boasting on it – so I write a song named 'Be Still, I Am Your Superior'. I was throwing words at Owen. I record 'Be Still' and 'She's Gone', Owen did 'Darling Patricia', and Jimmy did 'Hurricane Hattie' and 'King Of Kings', and that was Leslie Kong starting off with a bang – all of them hit number one."

James Chambers took the stage name Jimmy Cliff to perform Fats Domino songs at 4-H Club singing contests held near his home of Somerton, a few miles from Montego Bay. Shortly after moving to Kingston in his teens to study radio and television engineering, Cliff made his debut recording, 'Daisy Got Me Crazy', for West Kingston sound-system operator Count Boysie The Monarch; the song was retained as a sound-system acetate, and Cliff offered one shilling for his labour. After forming the unsuccessful duo Cliff & Swift with a neighbourhood friend, Cliff cut 'I'm

Sorry' for sound-system operator Sir Cavalier, but the single failed to hit. Arrival at Beverley's put the singer firmly on the road to stardom.

"One night I was walking, frustrated, going back home in West Kingston, and I saw this place called Beverley's", confirms the soft-spoken Cliff by telephone in Paris. "I saw records in the shop, but it was also an ice cream parlour and a cosmetics shop, so I thought maybe if I write a song called 'Beverley's', I could probably get my foot through the door. I wrote the song just then and forced my way in: there were three Chinese brothers, and they said no, they're not recording, and I said: 'I think you can get into recording,' and I sang the song 'Dearest Beverley'. The two other Chinese brothers, they laughed, but [Leslie Kong] said: 'I think he has the best voice I've heard in Jamaica.'" Thus began one of the island's most consistently successful labels, as Cliff became a major star in ska.

In the years to follow, horn players would provide a defining musical element that elevated the ska genre through highly charged instrumental hits. These ranged from Baba Brooks's ska adaptation of the ring-game song 'Riverbank Cobberley' (recorded for Duke Reid as 'Bank To Bank') and Don Drummond's cheeky 'Schooling The Duke* (an instrumental dig at Reid recorded for Coxsone), to Roland Alphonso's ska adaptation of Mongo Santamaria's 'El Pussy Cat' and The Skatalites' adaptation of the 'Guns Of Navarone' film theme (both for Coxsone).

Prince Buster's early productions often made use of Rico's trombone talents. "I would say I did about a hundred records for Buster before I come to England in December 1961," Rico recalls. "He was a mentor for Duke Reid, so he used to come and say he wanted us to do some recording. Maybe he was doing it for Duke Reid, maybe for himself, but it didn't matter to us: we were young musicians and we wanted to go on the records. I was working for Coxsone, Duke Reid, the Kong brothers, and I used to play for every sound system; they have sound system contests, so they get you to make one instrumental for them."

Rico was very close to Count Ossie. He lived for long periods at the camp near Wareika Hills and was heavily involved in the early days of Ossie's Mystic Revelation Of Rastafari. "He is my brother, the only person in this society that really loved me. It's a lot of us, maybe 14 playing in the band, and if he got ten pounds, he want to give me five out of it. When I was coming to England, he didn't feel too good; you could see the sadness. When they looked around amongst the musicians after me, they didn't find no dedicated ones as myself and [Don] Drummond. We weren't playing for tourists in Montego Bay, Port Antonio, or Negril, we were just in Kingston, playing among the community – that is why we are so popular. Drummond maybe played with big bands, but I am one of the few musicians who have never played one iota with a band – that's how I got my popularity. I am always where the sufferers are and where the dangers are. I don't live out of it, I live into it. Maybe that's where I get my good musical buzz from, to see people suffering, and living it myself."

Rico says he learnt a great deal from Don Drummond, who was a fellow student at the Alpha School For Boys, a well-known Catholic charitable institution for underprivileged children that placed strong emphasis on musical tuition. "The most that I know on trombone is what he taught me. He was the only musician that I could sit and practise with every day. More than any other musician from Jamaica, he was my friend. I got a lot from Don Drummond."

Life at Alpha, Rico explains, was difficult, but rewarding. "As a junior, I listened to Drummond and great musicians like Vernon Muller, Ossie Hall, Tony Brown. Because they were so advanced, they were playing at clubs. All the juniors want to be as good as the seniors, but we didn't have much joy 'cos we didn't have an instrument. To get an instrument you got to be very excellent; the competition was high, and a lot of development comes through that. If you have ten trombone players, maybe you have four trombones, so to get a trombone you have to be better than two or three people. The upbringing was not really happy, but very hard. Listening to people like Clifford Brown, The Modern Jazz Quartet, and Charlie Parker at that early stage was like magic; to achieve this magic is one of the world's very hard things. We don't go to school all day, like the average person, we go to school half-day, music half-day. You didn't have a whole day to play music, so the little chance you get, you did as much as you could, and that have a lot to do with our style. We listen to a lot of Tommy Dorsey, Duke Ellington, Lionel Hampton. Our upbringing was very enlightening."

Several other ska horn players learned their craft at Alpha under the tutelage of bandmaster Lennie Hibbert, a multitalented musician who later recorded two excellent vibraphone albums for Coxsone, *Creation* (1969) and *More Creation* (1971). The long roll call includes trombonists Ron Wilson, Raymond Harper, and Vin Gordon, trumpeters Johnny 'Dizzy' Moore, Bobby Ellis, David Madden, and Jo Jo Bennett, and saxophonists Tommy McCook, Lester Sterling, Cedric 'Im' Brooks, Glen DaCosta, and 'Deadley' Headley Bennett. Besides the broken beat of ska and the lungpower of its vocalists, these horn players made crucial melodic contribution. The brass sections added a uniquely Jamaican take on jazz to give ska a particular feeling, be it in the big-band arrangements of a jumping tune or in the expressive soloing of horn-led instrumentals.

Another noticeable change in the ska treble section came on the piano. Instead of playing a strolling rhythm with the left hand and treble chords with the right (as heard on 'Jeannie Is Back' or 'Easy Snappin'), ska piano parts often had chord melodies played with both hands at the upper end of the keyboard (as heard on Don Drummond's 'Rain Or Shine' or The Skatalites' 'El Pussy Cat'). Gladstone Anderson, a session player and mainstay of Duke Reid's team, was one of the most notable performers to develop the style.

Anderson was born on the outskirts of Kingston in 1934. His father was a railway engineer, and his mother's brother, the respected keyboardist Aubrey Adams, taught the young Gladdy to play the family piano. Aubrey went to Panama when Gladdy was in his teens, but returned to Jamaica in time to play organ on the earliest sessions held by Duke Reid and Coxsone, introducing Gladdy to Reid in these early days: "I start with Duke Reid from around the middle 50s. My uncle used to play the organ, and we had many more keyboardists come around when he is not available, but I always have to be there in the rhythm. Those times we used to play sentimental tunes, rhythm & blues, and rock'n'roll."

As a session player, Gladdy helped increase ska's pace. "When we reach in the 60s, that vibes come to me for a change of rhythm; I used to play rhythm, bass, and treble [on the piano]. We was playing a rhythm in the studio with Don Drummond ['Tear Up'] and I was playing rhythm & blues to the music, but what I was playing with the left hand was clashing with what the bass was playing, and they say I must play the rhythm with both hands, instead of playing the rock'n'roll style. From I start play with both hands in the treble section, it change – it step up a little faster."

While the musicians were experimenting with such styles, the sound-system operators and music producers were struggling to maintain dominance. When Prince Buster left Sir Coxsone's sound system Count Machuki defected with him, leaving Coxsone to rely on his second-string deejay and sometime security man, King Stitt (aka Winston Spark), whose gruff and vigorous shouting style complemented a terribly disfigured face that earned him the nickname 'The Ugly One'. But if Coxsone was surprised that Buster's Voice Of The People gave his Downbeat set tough competition, he must have been truly shaken by the volley of hits that came from Buster's recorded ska works.

"Prince Buster, when he started his session, I help him with this song called 'They Got To Go'," says Derrick Morgan. "I record 'Shake A Leg', Monty Morris recorded 'Humpty Dumpty' and Basil Gabbidon do 'War Paint'. Buster get about 13 hit songs that day. One spoiled song, he gave it to Duke, which was 'Let George Do It' by Rico Rodriguez [mistakenly credited to Don Drummond]. The engineer didn't pick up the bass good, so you have mostly bass drum. That whole song, if you listen to it, the bass would be Drumbago's feet, but that was a number-one seller – every one of those songs was."

Buster's departure left a large gap in Coxsone's stable. As replacement, he eventually settled on a small and highly individual young man from Hanover named Lee Perry. Little Lee, as he was then known, was born Rainford Hugh Perry in the country town of Kendal in 1936. He was raised on the edge of a sugar plantation, but avoided such lowly toil by becoming a dance champion, amazing audiences with his mastery of wild American steps like the Mashed Potato and the Yank; subsequently he became a domino tournament winner. In the 50s, Perry helped build roads to develop the Negril area for tourism and married a woman of Indian descent in the town of Little London, but their relationship did not last long and Perry soon grew tired of roadwork. He was already writing songs and had a secret dream to make it as a singer, so when divine voices told him to go to Kingston at the start of the 60s, this deeply spiritual man heeded their call and went to offer his services to Duke Reid. However, Reid refused to record Perry and let more seasoned talent like Stranger Cole use the country youth's lyrics without permission. Perry thus went to work for Coxsone in 1961.

"He and Duke had some fuss at Federal studio over some song that was recording and he claimed that is his lyrics," Coxsone recalled. "I realised he was outnumbered, so I took him away from the crowd and whatever was happening. He told me where he's from, we spoke and I created a job for him. It was more like a handyman, because we used to be up and down and he'd run some errands, but he loved the studio so he stick by me in the studio, until we came up with the first song, 'Chicken Scratch'. I would say it was after about two months that we started recording him."

Inspired by Jimmy McCracklin's jump boogie tune 'Let's Do It (The Chicken Scratch)' that celebrated a popular dance, 'Chicken Scratch' was an exclusive acetate on the Downbeat sound. Despite never being given an official release as a single, it bestowed upon Perry his most lasting nickname. "Me never take it serious," says Perry, "but the people think it start, so that's where me get the name Scratch."

Though Perry would eventually cut dozens of vocal tunes for Dodd and play percussion on many sessions, his early role was more down-to-earth. He was chiefly a record plugger, delivery person, and general assistant, and an important task was to take over the spying previously handled by Buster, whom he began to attack in song on Coxsone's behalf. Perry co-wrote lyrics aimed at Buster for Jamaica's first child star, Delroy Wilson, who signed a contract with Coxsone at the tender age of 13 in 1961 while still attending Boy's Town Primary. The attacks included 'I Shall Not Remove', 'Spit In The Sky', and 'Joe Liges' – the latter reversing the themes of Buster's 'One Hand Wash The Other'. Then Perry started aiming volleys at the Prince himself, with 'Bad Minded People', countering Buster's smash 'Madness' with 'Mad Head', and providing further general denigration on 'Prince In The Back' and 'Prince And Duke', which decried Buster's alliance with Duke Reid. Buster says he took such vinyl assaults in his stride, noting that the parties remained on good terms. After all, Buster had initiated an earlier feud with Derrick Morgan, accusing him of being a 'Black Head Chinaman' after Morgan began recording for Leslie Kong.

"In '62, when Jamaica going independent, I did 'Forward March'," Morgan recalls. "Buster say the solo that Headley Bennett took sounded like one that Lester Sterling took for him in 'They Got To Come'. He said me stole his belongings and give it to the Chineyman in 'Black Head Chinaman', and I answer to him with 'Blazing Fire': he must walk the blazing fire and leave me alone. That cause a little rivalry, with the both of us singing off of one another."

The dispute continued with songs such as Buster's '30 Pieces Of Silver' and Morgan's 'No Raise No Praise', leading to commotion among supporters. "The government did have to intervene, because the fans were getting outraged; they would cause a war over it. Prime Minister Shearer had to come in and we had to take pictures in the paper, showing that we are the best of friends, just to cut down on the consequences.'

However, such intervention failed to stop the words from being thrown. As Morgan explains: "I see Desmond Dekker [aka Desmond Dacres] in the market for nearly two years before he record a song, and his first was 'Honour Your Mother And Father', the ska way. Bob Marley came to Kong in 1963 with 'Judge Not'; Jimmy Cliff brought him, just about the time when I was going to leave with Prince Buster and go to England – Buster bribe me back into him market, and we came and record for Blue Beat, and the blazing fire would never stop burn yet. I signed a contract with Melodisc Records – it was a binding contract, and I didn't like the idea after six months; I decide to come back home to Jamaica and I don't want to see Buster no more. Leslie Kong didn't want to record me, because he said I'm under a contract and he don't want to breach it, so I form a group called The Blues Blenders.[4] We were recording for Coxsone, but I still never comfortable there, because I really want to go back to Leslie; he treat us better as a promoter, pay us better, and he was a nice man to be with. I went to Eddie Seaga, he was Finance Minister at the time, and he get me out of that contract with Melodisc. Then I went back to Leslie Kong and did 'I'm A Blackhead Again'. Prince Buster, we're not cursing each other any more, but ... every time he do a song off me, somebody come tell me before I hear it. I used to swing around more as a freelancer; when I make 'Don't Call Me Daddy' for Duke, Prince write a song named 'Derrick, Ah Fi You Baby', so I write one and show it to him. Him wife, Blossom, we used to call her Bea, so I say: 'Prince Buster, while you were away at sea, I was along with Bea, all your children have the mark of this blackhead Chiney.' That's how he and I stop that one – he didn't put his out and I didn't record mine, I only give him the words in him shop."

Shenley Duffus, a baritone who was then one of Coxsone's prized hit-makers, also become involved in the feuding. Duffus suffered a fatal heart attack in 2002 at the age of 64. A few years earlier, on a street corner near his home in Ocho Rios, he spoke of his early musical career. "I were born at the border of two parishes, Saint Thomas and Portland, a place called Roland Field. My father worked with United Fruit Company and I grew up in Kingston and Spanish Town. Some Saint Jago High School girls was boarding in the yard where I lived. Every day they ask me to sing the blues, so I discover myself singing the blues at eight years old. One of my main songs was by Jackie Brenston, 'Independent Woman', a bad blues. Approaching 12, I make my stage debut at the Crystal Theatre in Spanish Town, then I move right into the Vere Johns' thing, went all over Jamaica singing rhythm & blues: Joe Turner, Louis Jordan, Ben E. King, James Brown. All the inspiration came definitely from the American music, but we were putting our own thing in."

His earliest work was made for Simeon Smith. "I did my first recordings for Hi-Lite on Spanish Town Road at Federal two-track studio, round about '58, with Trenton Spence and Sonny Bradshaw, top-class musicians."

Duffus was so steeped in R&B that his 'Million Dollar Baby', a duet with a certain Annette, was also a success in America. "I had a big impact with 'Million Dollar Baby' – it was a big song all over the States. Then Coxsone take me away from Smith. He said: 'This little man is going to be a star.'"

Coxsone's words were prophetic, as Duffus's Yankee-twanged baritone was featured on a subsequent series of popular songs, often with lyrics that insulted the competition. "I turned out nothing but hit songs for Coxsone. Every session is hit songs. My first for Coxsone was 'What A Disaster' – I wrote it off of Derrick Morgan and Prince Buster, stopped them from throwing words at each other. When they do 'Black Head Chiney' and 'Blazing Fire', the three of us were good friends, so I get right in the middle and write 'What A Disaster'."

More successful was the proto-ska 'Fret Man Fret', co-written by Lee Perry, of which Duffus said: "I dig it off Buster again."

Perry's quarrel with Duke Reid stemmed from Stranger Cole's hit 'Rough And Tough', which Perry claims to have written. The singer, born Wilburn Cole in Jones Town in 1945, explains that he had his nickname from birth. "I didn't resemble anybody in the family, so they said I was a stranger. But during my growth in life, they say that I more resemble my father."

Cole says music was a family preoccupation. "My father plays guitar and used to jam with people like Ernest Ranglin. My uncle, Gilbert Cole, is a more professional guitarist who also used to jam with Ernest Ranglin in the early days when the music wasn't so good, and I have an uncle called Roy Roachie, he used to be a great singer in Jamaica. You could say I'm coming out of a music family."

Stranger's brother Leroy introduced him to Duke Reid shortly after he won a singing competition at school. "In my very early teens, I was going to an evening institute in Denham Town, where I was learning chemistry, and they happens to have a function, and my friends put my name to sing at that function. One of my favourite singers was Wilfred 'Jackie' Edwards, so I sang 'Tell Me Darling' and 'I Know', and I got two ice creams that day. I decided to go to Duke Reid as my brother used to be there as the number-one disc jockey, and one of his big engineers. Duke Reid said I wasn't such a great singer like Eric 'Monty' Morris and Derrick Morgan, but I sang a song that he liked very much titled 'In And Out The Window'. He asked me to give Monty Morris that song, and after the song went number one, Mr Reid said that I was a good writer and I had a tone like Derrick Morgan. As Derrick Morgan was away in England, he said he was going to try me on a song in the studio. Patsy, who used to sing with Derrick Morgan, he said I should learn her one of my songs, so I teaches her 'When You Call My Name', and I rehearse 'Rough And Tough' for myself. On that first three outings, I did three number-one songs."

'When You Call My Name' still echoed the cadence of American R&B,

but the boastful 'Rough And Tough' was pure ska, with Cole's deep voice and grave delivery helping establish a reputation later enhanced by a series of hit records with Ken Boothe. As Cole recalls: "I was the first one to take Ken Boothe to the studio to make a record, and the very first [hit] we recorded was for Mr Reid, 'Uno Dos Tres'. It went way up in the charts, like number one, and then I and Ken Boothe went on to make many hit records, like 'Artibella' and 'World's Fair' for Coxsone."

Boothe says he came to know Stranger when the older singer's group used to congregate in Denham Town, near an establishment called Bar Twenty. "Leaving school every evening I would go to Boys Town, because that was the sports complex in those days where poor people could go freely," he explains at his uptown Kingston home. "On my way home I would pass a corner and hear people singing, and I want to sing so much that when they're singing, I fill in. Then the group drift apart and Stranger start recording for Duke Reid with people like Patsy and Millie Small. Stranger was one of the first ones who inspire me in every way, both creating and excelling into what I do, and I was always at the house waiting to sing with him, so one day he took me to Duke Reid to audition. I heard Duke Reid say: 'Who that likkle boy? Him can't sing.' But I don't pay him no mind."

According to Boothe, the duo auditioned with 'Mo Sen Wa', built on an imaginary phrase that an invented Chinese girlfriend was meant to have uttered to the song's protagonist. "Me and Stranger could write for all cultures – we could pick some words that sound like Chinese, we can pick some that sound American. It was me and Stranger who created those words. There isn't even a language that go like that, but we say we're going to write something like a Chinese song, and we say: 'Ah-mo-sen-wa, that's what she says to me.' We did it with Drumbago and Ribs [tenor saxophonist Stanley Notice] and it was playing in the dancehall. Duke Reid try us again, and me and Stranger make 'Uno Dos.' Then me and Stranger do songs for people like Mr [Linden] Pottinger, Edward Seaga, and Byron Lee. After 'Uno Dos', I didn't really so fond of Duke Reid – he's too rugged. My type of music that I truly love, it was Sir Coxsone who was doing it. Me and Stranger decide we're going to Sir Coxsone now, with 'World's Fair', 'Artibella', and 'My Marie'."

Eventually, Dodd suggested that Boothe go solo. "I don't know if he would remember this, but he said he would like me to sing on my own. I didn't consider that none at all, so I said to him: you're sure that I can sing on my own? Him say: 'You is the best.' It was an encouragement – it really make me feel good. The first song that Sir Coxsone let me do was a song named 'Prevention', by Federal. When I started growing up, he start to record me by Studio One."

The establishment of Dodd's Studio One by October 1963 (officially the Jamaica Recording & Publishing Studio), was one of the most significant moves in ska's solidification. It was housed in a former nightclub called the End, located at 13 Brentford Road in the Cross Roads area, its equipment installed by the supreme sound technician and session guitarist Headley Jones. It has been reported elsewhere that Studio One was the first Jamaican recording facility owned by a black man, but that honour goes to Linden O. Pottinger, an accountant who ventured into record production and distribution with the Gay Disc label, after working for a time supplying jukeboxes; his small but well-equipped studio, opened in a specially constructed annex of the family home at Sundown Crescent, off Molynes Road, was in use from 1961. However, Studio One quickly became the home of ska: many of the era's biggest hits were created here, despite technically inferior one-track equipment purchased from Federal when that studio upgraded to two-track. Coxsone's strong team of musically inspired individuals helped draw the best from the talent he located, notably keyboardist and arranger Donat Roy Mittoo, better known as Jackie Mittoo. Coxsone successfully groomed many ska artists after they made it through the crowd of hopefuls who turned up seeking to impress the producer at a Sunday audition, though hot talent could be snapped up on other days too.

Lee Perry, who was promoted to talent scout and auditions supervisor, says that talent could be recruited any time, any place. If a singer was located elsewhere, "we bring him in and then we arrest him – see him on the street and arrest him on the street". Perry has been credited with discovering some of Dodd's biggest acts, including the sensational Maytals trio.

The gospel-like intensity of lead singer Frederick 'Toots' Hibbert, nicely balanced by harmonies from Ralphus 'Raleigh' Gordon and Nathaniel Matthias (aka Jerry McCarthy), gave The Maytals its exciting difference. Toots, who was born in Treadlight on the outskirts of May Pen in 1942, says the near-religious fervour of his vocal style came from American soul and church choir influences. "I grew up in the church before I went to Kingston to do my music – Seventh Day Adventist and many other churches, where people would gather and singing so nice, praising God, so I always want to be there. I grow up in a spiritual way, as my father was a preacher and my mom was a preacher – it was a clapping church. I began in the church, therefore my music goes as a churchical order. I used to listen to Ray Charles, Mahalia Jackson, Wilson Pickett, and James Brown on the radio and I wanted to sing, so I went to Trench Town when I were about maybe 13. I used to do boxing in my youthful days, but people told me I could sing, so I stopped boxing. I stuck with some people who do barbering and I trim people's hair. Then I met Jerry and Raleigh, they was living in Trench Town. They say: 'I like the way you sing. I want you to teach me.' So I began to teach people in my youthful days, people who was elder than me."

Through early scorchers like 'Fever' and 'Never Grow Old' The Maytals helped keep Coxsone on top, but some overseas releases credited The Vikings, a popular live band that sometimes backed them on performances. In contrast, the apocalyptic 'Get Ready', later attributed to the group, was actually Toots in combination with another duo. "I sing the song with Bunny & Skitter," Toots confirms. "I was just the one who arrange it and do some slants in it. I never used to get credit, but from when I started in the business, I do my own arrangements."

'Six And Seven Books', The Maytals' first significant hit, was the trump card of a particularly noteworthy sound-system victory. "One Monday night, we actually disintegrated Duke Reid with it," says Lloyd Daley, founder of the Matador sound system and label. "Duke Reid and myself played at the Success club for a co-star of *Doctor No*, just after that movie was done. He's a very popular guy called Big Junior, an associate of Clement Dodd. Duke Reid wouldn't stop play and The Matador signed on and drowned him, couldn't hear him again. Coxsone had to come and seize the 'Six And Seven Books' that was lent to me, because I was killing Duke Reid with it. But it's not just the record, it's the sound – the weight I was dropping, the amount of bass. I was the first sound system to ever have signed on and completely over-powered Duke Reid, so that you couldn't hear him."

Born in 1939 and raised in central Kingston, Daley had an early fascination with electronics. "From the age of eight I used to make telephones, lights that would go on by remote control, alarm systems. I was very involved in anything intricate that involve electricity. Later, I built an RF [radio frequency] linear amplifier: it amplified the signal from a walkie-talkie, so I was able to speak to people overseas: I turned it into a sound-system amplifier and started to play at birthday parties. I met Coxsone Dodd and challenged him, about 1956 or '57, at 2h Windward Road. Coxsone played until 12 o'clock and I played until four in the morning. I didn't want a name like a king, a sir, a duke, a princess or anything like that. A matador really is a bullfighter, and I would actually take my opponent as a bull."

Although previous negative experiences have made him reluctant to be interviewed, Daley is resolutely courteous. "The whole music thing, it's like a barrel of crabs, that is why The Matador step aside. Most of the guys out there are still going through it, but I don't want to walk that road again. I am a electronic engineer and that is what I live off, because the money that I put into recording, I have not been repaid or compensated for it in any way."

Daley says he began producing around 1958 because his rivals refused to sell him their better tunes. Early sessions at Federal yielded Roland Alphonso's 'Bridgeview Shuffle', plus "some tunes with Neville Esson – he sang for Coxsone in the early days, even before Owen Gray. Owen Gray and Rico Rodriguez done several recordings for me in '59, '60, and I played at the send-off for Rico Rodriguez when he was leaving Jamaica, at 2a Water Lane, beside General Penitentiary".

Although hits were not forthcoming until the late 60s, The Matador's self-built set was one of the top sound systems of the ska years. "I started in 1956 and I was a small sound until about '59, '60, when I decided to get serious. My main dancehall was at Victoria Avenue, in front of the Machado cigarette factory – it was a Great House that was used strictly for dances, with a big palm tree in front of it. We had a disc jockey by the name of Icky Man, he used to play Lord Koos' sound, and after I demolish Lord Koos he came to me for a job.[5] Koos is a Chiney guy that had this restaurant called Sterling at the corner of East Street and East Queen Street, right across from the central police station. In '62, '63, a next big night was when The Matador alone played at the Gold Coast and five of Jamaica's top sounds were playing at Club Monaco, in very close proximity along the Saint Thomas Road: Duke Reid, Coxsone Downbeat, King Edwards The Giant, Sinclair The Lion from Central Kingston – that was a very good sound, he was even heavier than Sir Coxsone – and Count Boysie, a next good sound that came from Oxford Street. Five of them, and I destroyed them the night. I was playing my heavy KT88 amplifier and I shake the earth in such a way that everybody had to leave their dance and come to my dance, and they had to stop playing before nine o'clock. Gold Coast was overfilled; it was the sweetest victory I ever had. There is only six top sounds that the government recognised when we had independence: Duke, Coxsone, King Edwards, Prince Buster, Bells The President, and Lloyd The Matador. We played for the government on street dances and floats during the time of Edward Seaga and Sir Alexander Bustamante, right in independence, and it went on for around three or four years after."

The Matador also built amplifiers for several other leading sound systems, mostly during the late 50s and early 60s. Though most have been omitted from written reggae histories, those who were present recall their great importance. "Sir Percy was a very good sound from Regent Street, owned by Percival Tibby, who had gaming machines. His sound was very recognised and his deejay was Whitey, who was as popular as Machuki in his time. Admiral Chin was quite a large sound on Blake Road, at the back of Kingston College. Percel Chin owned it – they had Chin's Travel Service. Unitone was a very massive sound from Annotto Bay, from the 60s right back until the 80s, but he's dead now – his name was Joe Chin. Duke Hamilton from Saint Ann's Bay is owned by Ken Hamilton; he got an OD [Order Of Distinction] for contribution to sound system in 1999 or 2000, even before Buster – Buster got his own in November 2001. Count Muncey, that was built in 1959, went until about 1968, a very popular sound that played all over the Maxfield Avenue area and other places; it was owned by Roy Muncey, a machine repairman for Singer from Galloway Road, off Maxfield Avenue. He's a full Indian, and Tom The Great Sebastian's eldest son got married to his sister, some time in the 70s after Tom died. Cavaliers is a next sound based mostly in the Maxfield Avenue area, but he played in all of Jamaica. It was owned by Mr Chung, the manager of Lanneman's sweets factory. He was a prominent soundman, had a sound system before Duke Reid and Coxsone; I wasn't the first person who built his amplifier, but I built him a very large amplifier in the 50s. There was also King Prof of Spanish Town Road, he was a next older man. I also built an amplifier for Prince Buster and I've worked for Duke Reid and Coxsone, repairing their amplifiers."

As with the battles perpetually waged on the sound-system circuit, Kingston's ska producers continued to fight for dominance with record releases, and though Coxsone clearly kept the upper hand in ska, rivals also issued highly popular material. 'Carry Go Bring Come' by country trio Justin Hinds & The Dominoes was one of Duke Reid's most significant ska hits. Remaining exclusively with Reid into the 70s, they were ultimately his most loyal and prolific act. The soft-spoken Hinds, who died of cancer in 2005, lived most of his life in Steer Town, the Saint Ann's hillside community in which he was born in 1942. The son of a builder and quarryman, he began singing in the local Seventh Day Adventist church and formed The Dominoes with Dennis Sinclair and Egorton 'Junior' Dixon while the three were on the fringes of the tourist trade.

"Ernie Smatt started the water sports enterprise in Ocho Rios by doing skin diving, scuba diving, glass-bottom boat tour," Hinds explained, in the plumbing and air conditioning shop that acted as his office. "I become a part of it when I was 16, and I used to sing for tourists on the beach, sing B.B. King, Chuck Jackson, Louis Jordan, Smiley Lewis, Fats Domino – that's why I name my group The Dominoes – and I used to create my own sound in those days too. Dominoes group was from about '57 to '58, because all of us grew up in one village, go to one school. We started to sing young, all of us together, and all of us used to work for the water sports. At the Windsor Hotel in Saint Ann's Bay, close to where Marcus Garvey was born, we used to sing for these people. We don't have any pay, but the people love us and we realise we was going to be a star one day."

That stardom beckoned in late 1963, when the Dominoes found their way to Duke Reid's headquarters. "Charlie Babcock used to be a disc jockey on RJR – we call him C.B., the cool fool with the live jive. He came on the North Coast to work at the Arawak Hotel as the entertainment manager, and he said to me one day: 'We need you to sing for this party,' so I sing that night and the people love my show. Two days after, he said: 'You should go to see The Duke.' Before that, Carl Young was the first man I used to sing for on the North Coast. He's the guy that now own the radio station Irie FM and Grove recording studio. He was the only guy on the North Coast that was playing R&B music from the older days. He had a big sound system called Strand in Saint Ann's Bay and he was competing with Sir Coxsone and Duke Reid, so he was telling me about his good friend Sir Coxsone. I went to Kingston one day to see Coxsone, just by myself, but Coxsone don't have time to talk to me – he was driving away, leaving me standing on Orange Street. I walked and find Charles Street and I realise that was the street that Prince Buster have a little record shop on, and I find out that the Duke was further within Bond Street and Charles Street, so I went over to see The Duke and there comes the rest of Dominoes. We didn't plan to go together, but they realised that I was in Kingston and they realised the day they should be there too.

"Duke [was] having an audition, with about a hundred boys and girls that line up along the street. They say: 'You should go back to trade. Next!' I was shaking when it was my turn and I didn't want to sing on the street, so I went to Back-O-Wall where I meet Bongo Noel as the elder dread in Kingston – he was one of the first spiritual leaders for the Rastafari. They was chanting Niyabinghi and I was there chanting with them. A guy that used to stay by Duke come get me and I went up to see the Duke. He said: 'What's the name of your song?' and I said 'Carry Go Bring Come', so he said: 'Go upstairs.' I meet Baba Brooks, Tommy McCook, Lester Sterling, Lloyd Brevett, Roland Alphonso, Theophilus Beckford, Jackie Mittoo – all the greatest of the music. It was very impressive. The three of us went to Federal to record the song and 'The Stone That The Builder Refuse' [aka 'Cornerstone'] the next day."

Like much of the group's subsequent work, both songs were based on proverbs and folk sayings, incorporating gospel undertones. "'Carry Go Bring Come' is just an everyday system that people live within, where people double-back [gossip] on each other. The first time I hear it was at Forrester's Hall – it was a clash between The Duke and Sir Coxsone, and Cuttings was at the control. When Duke come at eleven o'clock, they play 'Carry Go Bring Come' for seven times straight. Then he put it on the street and it hit Jamaica like a storm: number one for eight weeks."

Although Justin Hinds & The Dominoes gave Duke Reid potent ammunition, Coxsone's secret weapon was The Wailers, a West Kingston harmony group that signed to Studio One as a five-piece in December 1963. Schooled in Trench Town by Joe Higgs, the group was then composed of Bob Marley, Neville 'Bunny' Livingston, Peter McIntosh (aka Peter Tosh), Junior Braithwaite, and Beverley Kelso. Their first release, 'Simmer Down', was Marley's call to the swaggering 'rude boys' of Kingston's street gangs to cool their terrorising attacks on innocent ghetto dwellers. It hit number one and remained in the charts during September and October 1964, a tantalising taste of the greater fame and glory that awaited the group's core in the future. 'It Hurts To Be Alone', a ballad led by Braithwaite, reached the charts soon after. Ernest Ranglin, who is rightly proud of his role in the group's rise, arranged this early material. "I did 'It Hurts To Be Alone', 'Simmer Down', and 'I'm Still Waiting'," he says.

Holding a privileged place in Coxsone's stable, The Wailers underwent a series of changes. Braithwaite's role diminished by the summer of 1964, and he left the group that September to immigrate to Chicago. Kelso and temporary member Cherry Green (aka Ermine Bramwell) would leave the following year, allowing the core of Marley, Tosh, and Livingston to tighten their harmonies and songwriting skills.

Like Lee Perry, The Wailers performed a number of tasks for Dodd in addition to their primary singing roles. Bob Marley was made musical arranger of The Soulettes, led by his future wife, Cuban-born Alvarita Anderson. Peter Tosh recruited other singers for Dodd and often provided guitar accompaniment at auditions, for which all three were typically present. One of the most notable singers whom Tosh brought to Studio One was baritone Leonard Dillon, founder of The Ethiopians, who first recorded as Jack Sparrow.

Dillon, who died of cancer in 2011 at the age of 68, said that his Seventh Day Adventist grandparents brought him up singing in the church during his childhood in Portland. He was active in local band The Playboys, covering tunes by Fats Domino and Wilson Pickett with his classmate, guitarist Hux Brown; after a change of management, the group became known as Ray & The Gladiators. Although Dillon made occasional trips to Kingston in an attempt to break into the music business, it was not until he had spent a year in the USA that he came to the capital to live. "I went in '63 on farm work, end up in Fellsmere, Florida – sugarcane, but I couldn't cut it. After two days, I tell them I can't make it and they send me to plant the cane."

His main ambition was to bring back enough fancy duds to convince record producers he had star potential. "It was a whole trunk of clothes I wanted to go back to Jamaica with, to see if I can achieve being a musician. I want to look good when I am going around the studios, as at shows I always see the artists them very smart."

Dillon returned from Florida in 1964 full of determination, and with the clothes to look the part, but no real money to speak of. King Sporty (Noel Williams), an old friend from Port Antonio, was then one of the top deejays on the Kingston sound-system scene; he had briefly replaced Machuki on Coxsone's set before settling into residence on Duke Reid's. Sporty arranged for Dillon to stay with a relative in the overflowing slum of Back-O-Wall. "Where I had to sleep some of the time, I had to go in there bent, 'cos if I stand up, my head going through the top. But I have to give thanks, especially to King Sporty's aunt, because she always prepare something for me to eat twice per day and always give me encouragement. I always be ashamed that I cannot finance the food, so I try to get home late, but don't care how late I get home, that woman always up and she going heat up food and give me, asking me if I got through today. If I try to leave the house without having breakfast, I can't, because she always prepare for me."

Through hanging out on street corners in the musical hotbed of Trench Town, Dillon eventually met Peter Tosh, who was impressed with his vocal talent. "I sang some songs for him and he took me to Second Street and introduce me to Bob and Bunny. Two days after they took me to Studio One."

Dodd liked what he heard at Dillon's audition, as the singer's country accent lent a near-mento feel, so he recorded four songs with the eager young man straight away. "I did 'Woman Wine And Money', harmonised by Delroy Wilson, 'Ice Water', 'What You Get You Must Take', and 'Bull Whip', harmonised by Peter, Bob, and Bunny."

The pick of the bunch was 'Ice Water', a tale of a simmering romance that was a fairly substantial local hit, but Dillon's initial stay at Studio One was brief. "The Wailers did not have enough time to spend with me, so I decided to see if I could get a group for myself. I'm a mason by trade and Coxsone gave me some money to buy some tools. I left Studio One, went to Waterhouse, and started to work on my trade in the day, the meantime rehearsing in the nights."

The Wailers enjoyed further hits at Studio One, but The Maytals quickly tired of the advantage they felt Dodd was taking and in 1964 began recording for other producers, including Vincent Chin and Leslie Kong. Another successful period followed with Prince Buster, for whom they cut notable works such as 'Judgement Day', 'Pain In My Belly', and 'Broadway Jungle' (aka 'Dog War'), the latter an electrifying stomp that celebrated their departure from Coxsone's stable. The song remained popular enough for Toots to revive it in 1998, and it was used in advertisements for the Euro 2000 football tournament. Unfortunately, the optimism of the original was shortlived. As Toots put it: "I went to record the song with Prince Buster when I was singing for Coxsone Downbeat. He treat me shabby, so I think Prince Buster would treat me better. When I went over to his place, he treat me the same shabby way: he let me down by not paying me well." The group's response was to move on again, recording the last of their ska works with producer and bass player Byron Lee.

Accounts of reggae music have often been unduly critical of Lee, partly because much of his music was middle-of-the-road material aimed at the Jamaican middle class and overseas pop markets. Much has also been made of his middle-class status and Chinese heritage, but those who focus on the latter seem unaware that Lee's mother was a black Jamaican from a rural area near the town of Balaclava and that he was raised in a family that actively upheld the surviving musical and cultural practices of their African ancestors.

"They were from a place called Auchtembeddie, that's way down in the depths," Lee explained, in his office, a number of years before succumbing to cancer in 2008. "They were up in the hills and they knew mento and Junkanoo and things called 'Brukins' [a celebration of emancipation by former slaves], and I broke in that too. I spend a lot of time down there, so the music was into my blood. I was born in Christiana, in the parish of Manchester, went to school there, and then when I was age eight or nine, come to the city – to Third Avenue in Mountain View Gardens."

Lee took a pragmatic view of his dual heritage. "My father is from Kowloon in Hong Kong and my mother is an African Jamaican. Whether I am called a half-Chinese or mixed blood, that's how it is. A lot of the Chinese who settled here came to finish the Panama Canal, as it was the Chinese who could withstand malaria. The boats going through the Canal to take them back to China went through the Caribbean, and they dispersed all over the Caribbean. My father came to teach the Chinese children here how to speak English. He was a teacher who only knew a little English, but he was able to translate from English to Chinese."

Lee learned to play piano at a convent school in Mandeville, but temporarily abandoned music when he became a member of the national football team. He later taught himself to play bass on a homemade instrument, and in 1957 founded The Dragonaires. According to Lee, the early line-up included guitarist Rupert Bent, trumpeter Frank Anderson, saxophonist Sam Ismay, trombonist Vernon 'Mullo' Muller, and veteran jazz bandleader and organist Granville Williams. The band began recording after being approached by Edward Seaga, following his success with Higgs & Wilson's 'Manny Oh'. "We didn't know each other then," said Lee of Seaga. "We met one day when the band was playing and he said: 'Would you like to make a record for us?'"

The resultant debut was an adaptation of Doc Bagby's late-period R&B sax shuffle, 'Dumplins', which kick-started a recording career that would span half a century. Seaga says 'Dumplins' was not a big seller, but it did receive significant airplay.

Shortly thereafter, Edward Seaga's quick departure from WIRL prompted Lee to conduct regular sessions at Federal. "Clifford Rae and George Benson took over West Indies Records, a joint company affiliated with West Indies Records Barbados. After Seaga left, I went across to Federal where we did all those ska music: Ahmet Ertegun from Atlantic Records came down and then we did Monty Morris's 'Oil In My Lamp', 'Sammy Dead', The Blues Busters – a lot of that stuff I play bass on. Jimmy Cliff, Stranger & Patsy, Prince Buster, Millie Small, Ken Lazarus, Keith Lyn – all these artists worked through the first couple of years of ska with us."

Some have protested that he was not a ska originator and merely cashed in on the music's popularity, but Lee always acknowledged that he was not directly involved in its creation. In fact, he was sent to the ghetto to study ska with mento bandleader Carlos Malcolm. "Eddie Seaga was the politician in whose constituency ska was. In 1962 he sent us down there to study the music, as he wanted to be the Minister of Culture who said: 'I have given you a music from the ghettos of Kingston to celebrate our sovereignty of independence.' We knew nothing about ska until Seaga sent us down there.

It was being played down in the western sound systems, but it was kept down in the ghetto and wasn't recognised by the people midtown and uptown who could afford to buy it and support it. It was not played on the radio stations, because they wouldn't accept the quality – the guitars were out of tune, the records were hop, skip, and jump. When I went down and learned ska, I didn't know about it before. We took it along – not with my band alone, but with the people who produced it – exposing them to the middle, uptown people who looked down, saying: that is music for the poor people, we don't want to be associated with it. But we crossed the barrier and brought it up, because Byron Lee was accepted by the middle, up-class. We helped to promote ska. I didn't find it, nor did I originate it, but by bringing it out we made it famous."

"I took Byron because he was somebody that I knew," Seaga confirms. "I said: you need to come and hear this beat. He came down, heard it, and tried it uptown, but it didn't work because uptown people are different from downtown people. It was when the ska left Jamaica and went to England as 'blue beat' that it became popular over there. After becoming popular in London, uptown people started to accept it."

In 1964, Prince Buster, Jimmy Cliff, Monty Morris, and Teddy Charmers (aka Roy Willis) of The Charmers duo appeared at the World's Fair in New York; the backing band was Byron Lee & The Dragonaires. Edward Seaga selected Lee's band, so that his uptown, mixed-race friend could be the presentable face of ska at a commercially oriented international event. Lee cut ska material aimed at US audiences, issued in the States by Atlantic; he was also awarded the licence to distribute Atlantic product in Jamaica. Adding to the irony is that Millie's 'My Boy Lollipop', delivered in a shrill teenage yelp, brought an awareness of ska to broader overseas audiences despite being a rhythmically faithful cover of an American record by teen singer Barbie Gaye. Millie's incredibly successful novelty hit was produced by Chris Blackwell in London and arranged by Ernest Ranglin, using London-based session musicians.

Much criticism has since been levelled at the choice of The Dragonaires over The Skatalites, since the latter are ska's true originators and Lee a mere pretender to their ghetto throne. But Seaga says he sent The Dragonaires to New York for purely practical reasons. "Byron Lee went because he had the experience in travelling; he had certain experience of touring and his music was more danceable. The Skatalites would have played The Skatalites' pieces, which were limited in number and not as danceable. Byron Lee would be playing the songs of the different artists, so it would have come at a much wider range." Winston Blake suggests that the fluid nature of The Skatalites was a factor. "I know for sure that it was a discipline problem. Those guys were great, talented, the best – but they were not disciplined."

Regardless of their absence from the World's Fair, the highly talented musicians that made up The Skatalites are definitely those most closely associated with ska. The group was officially together for only 14 months from June 1964, but most of the band had played together regularly since the late 40s. The nucleus included tenor saxophonist Roland Alphonso, alto saxophonist Lester Sterling, trombonist Don Drummond, trumpeter Johnny 'Dizzy' Moore, drummer Lloyd Knibb, bassist Lloyd Brevett, rhythm guitarist Jerry Haines (aka Jah Jerry), and pianist Jackie Mittoo. Despite being at first opposed to the idea, and wary of the ska form in general, the gifted tenor saxophonist and arranger Tommy McCook was eventually persuaded to lead the band by Coxsone Dodd following an eight-year stint leading a jazz group in the Bahamas.

Roland Alphonso said that several core members first played together on the Kingston Pier near the informal street fair and gambling area dubbed Coney Island, and also performed at night spots like the Orange Bowl. "We meet each other as teenagers," Alphonso revealed on a trip to London, shortly before his death in 1998. "Knibb was living at West Street, Brevett was living with his dad, and I was living in Jones Town. We were playing Coney Island six nights a week."

Like Tommy McCook and Rico Rodriguez, Alphonso was born in Cuba of mixed parentage. "I was born in Havana in 1931: my mother is Jamaican and my father is Cuban. My mother took me to Clarendon, where most of my family lives, in 1933, and afterward she took me to Kingston. I went to Saint Aloysius School and then I went to Stony Hill School at the age of ten – my mother was poor, that's why she sent me there. My father came to Jamaica, but though he speak Spanish, nobody couldn't understand him. They lock him up in a soldiers' camp and send him back to Cuba, but he didn't correspond with my mother. 1941, that's when I start to play music. I was too young to blow an instrument, so they put me on marching drums."

Alphonso progressed to trumpet at Stony Hill and learned saxophone at the age of 13; by the early 50s he was one of the island's leading players. "I was playing alto first of all. They rated Joe Harriott number-one alto sax, and I was a young player in my early twenties – they rated me number two. I was playing with Redver Cook for a start, and Eric Deans, up at Bournemouth Club: he claims that he's going to pay me £2 for six nights a week, but everything him get, he tell me: 'Boy, wait!'"

Alphonso said his first recording session came toward the end of the boogie period with the Cecil Lloyd Quintet, a jazz band led by Jamaica's top pianist, a graduate of the noted Juilliard School of Music. "I was working at a hotel, Cecil Lloyd lead the band. The band came in to do a session and Coxsone said: 'Rolie, cut a tune for me now!' So I said to them boys: 'Let's do a blues in C,' and them call it 'Four Corners Of The World'. I can't forget it at all – it was five of us."

Lester Sterling, the group's youngest member, recorded for Coxsone from the late 50s with Rico, Deadley Headley, and Johnny Moore. "Playing for Coxsone, it was Rico carry me there," says Sterling of his debut. "Rico was going to look for Coxsone with this song, he told me to come along, so I meet Coxsone and he had a session the following day. It was a vocal, I think with Lloyd Clarke."

Lloyd Knibb was born in Portland in 1931, but moved to downtown Kingston at a young age. In his early teens, he began observing rehearsal sessions of the Jump Sultans Orchestra, and was taught the rudiments of rhythm by the resident drummer, Donald Jarrett. While helping his aunt to sell her puddings and patties in Trench Town, he observed Rastafarian musicians playing goatskin hand drums on street corners, which was another source of early inspiration. Practising at home on tins cans and a wooden box, he began performing informally at various outdoor spaces at the age of 18, after a friend called Lionel built him a drum kit. He then gained valuable experience drumming at North Coast hotels in Val Bennett's band, Eric Deans' Orchestra, and other groups, as well as by attending Count Ossie's encampment. Knibb, who died of liver cancer in 2011, said that he started recording after hearing local players on the radio. "I was living in Montego Bay, playing in different hotels, and I hear a tune over the radio and go back in Kingston and present myself. Everything was cool, playing rhythm & blues." Knibb's individual rim-shots and drum rolls, along with Drumbago's rhythmic flourishes, gave the ska beat its particular character. As Knibb explained: "I changes the beat in 1964, so that's definitely my style."

Lloyd Brevett died in 2012, aged 80, after suffering from a long illness, his demise hastened by the murder of his son, who was slain the same day he collected Brevett's lifetime achievement award. Brevett said he learned his bouncing bass accompaniment from his father, David Brevett, a jazz bassist who fashioned his own instruments and founded the Count Brevett Band in 1950. Lloyd was also a member of Eric Deans' Orchestra. "My dad taught me to play bass, he play in a lot of groups. At this time, I play stand-up bass."

After their first performance as The Skatalites at the Hi Hat club in Rae Town, the group was soon in demand all over town. Their subsequent residence at the Bournemouth Club, where Lee Perry often joined them on percussion, is legendary for its electrifying performances. This intensity was captured on their studio recordings, mostly cut for Coxsone Dodd, many of which encapsulate the best of ska's musical possibilities.

Upbeat Skatalites numbers such as 'Tear Up' (based on Mongo Santamaria's 'Fat Back'), with Alphonso's fast solo flourishes, seemed to reflect the optimism of the newly independent island; others, like the raucous 'Ball Of Fire' and 'Guns Of Navarone', simply hold unbridled musical heat. McCook's compositions, such as 'Cow And Gate', tended toward the spacious, as did his understated solos, which often favoured the lower notes of the scale. When McCook and Alphonso traded solos on numbers like 'Black Sunday', 'Trotting In', and 'Hot Cargo', the contrast was always invigorating; Moore and Sterling, though more in the background, also contributed enthralling solos on songs such as 'Killer Diller' and 'Beardman Ska,' the latter an adaptation of 'Live It Up' by American boogie pianist, Ernie Freeman.

As with ska itself, The Skatalites' music was created from a pool of disparate influences. Group members explain that some of their biggest hits at Studio One were based on Latin tunes that Coxsone asked them to adapt. "'El Pussy Cat' come from Cuba," Roland noted, referring to the Mongo Santamaria original. "Coxsone give it to me and say: 'Rolie, write this tune now' – and I wrote it."

"Coxsone used to use a lot of Cuban tunes and we would write the tune in ska form," Lloyd Knibb recalled. "We would generally get those tunes, because a staccato thing was happening in ska."

Brevett mentioned Santamaria's *El Pussy Cat* album as particularly important, since it contained 'Hammer Head', which the Skatalites turned into the hit 'Phoenix City', as well as the title track, as noted above. In fact, for Coxsone, they adapted at least a dozen numbers by the Cuban-born, US-based percussionist.

"We play the songs as it had been played," Roland cut in, "but we arrange it and play the ska thing our style. We don't copy the solos."

Jazz was always the biggest source of inspiration for The Skatalites and the members covered songs that moved them, such as Roland's take on Horace Silver's 'Forest Flowers' or his adaptation of Duke Ellington's 'Caravan' as 'Skaravan'. Alphonso spoke of his joy at sharing the stage with Count Basie's band in Nassau, and gave John Coltrane his utmost admiration. "Coltrane is my man, and I respect him and honour him because his songs is on earth." Lester Sterling named Miles Davis, Dizzy Gillespie, Cannonball Adderley, and Sonny Stitt as musicians he was thrilled to see performing.

Although the bulk of their work was recorded at Studio One, The Skatalites also cut material for the other leading producers of the ska years. "We didn't sign any contracts with anyone, so we were free," Alphonso stated. "We work with Duke Reid and King Edwards also. We did some for Prince Buster too, but Coxsone get the most 'cos I sign contract with him."

"The songs we do with Buster was like 'Al Capone' and them tunes, with Val Bennett and Stanley Notice, Headley Bennett and Jah Jerry," adds Sterling.

Coxsone said he was powerless to stop Reid offering better money to these musicians. "Whatever it costs, Duke would find the money. Even if I had a contracted artist, Duke would still insist and use them, like Don Drummond and Roland was contracted to me, but after a while you realise the man is a musician and that's the only way he could really earn, so you let him play, which is different from vocalists."

Despite this protestation, Dodd says he and Reid exchanged two Skatalites songs: Dodd recorded Drummond's 'Green Island' but gave it to Reid to release, whilst Reid allowed Dodd to handle his recording of Drummond's 'Eastern Standard Time'. Shenley Duffus also revealed that Dodd gave Reid a helping hand when the former policeman was down on his luck: "When Duke Reid wasn't making any hit, Coxsone sent about a dozen of his artists, including me, on a session for Duke Reid. I did a song called 'Bitter Rose', which is on the flipside of 'Reload' with The Skatalites, a wicked instrumental for Duke Reid."

"Duke like to hear a certain kind of tune and Coxsone like to hear certain tunes," Knibb continued. "Duke would hear us sing a 'banton' by Coxsone, then he would do a repeat 'banton', that kind of throw word, cursing record. We also did a lot of instrumentals for [Top Deck records proprietor] Justin Yap, the 'Chiney Dread' down Barbican – a lot of tunes he get from Don Drummond."

Drummond was a major creative force in the group. According to official records, he left Alpha six weeks early to join Eric Deans' band; he also played with alto saxophonist Headley Bennett in tenor saxophonist Tony Brown's Orchestra, a band entirely composed of former Alpha students. Drummond's typically chilling compositions often employed unusual minor-key arrangements, perhaps reflecting the personal anguish of a man who voluntarily checked himself into Bellevue psychiatric hospital on several occasions. 'Confucius', 'Chinatown', 'Marcus Junior' (Top Deck), 'Away From It All' (Randy's), and 'Don Cosmic' (Studio One) are notable examples, their minor-chord changes and expressive solos tinged with shades of melancholy. Drummond also asked Knibb to emulate the burru style for the exquisite 'Dan De Lion' (Treasure Isle) and 'Addis Ababa' (Studio One), the African rhythmic root allowing for complex personal expression.

Don Drummond's vision gave his music a thrilling difference, but his idiosyncratic behaviour had a volatile side and his heavy medication probably exacerbated his drastic mood swings. Clancy Eccles recalled some of the trombone player's peculiar traits. "By working with Coxsone, I happen to meet Don Drummond on his first session. He did a song named 'That Man Is Back', and I worked eight months with Don Drummond on stage after that. While we were recording down by Khouri, they was digging out that piece of land, and Don used to go over and pick up this pretty piece of clay and put it in his Ovaltine. Don Drummond never eat anything hot – everything cold, lot of fruits and so on. One day Roland and Johnny looked in the bottle, it was clay and all those things mixed together, and Drummond said: 'People are supposed to live in an atomic energy, you are supposed to build atoms inside of you' – that's why he ate the clay. For a madman, Drummond was extraordinary – I wouldn't call Drummond mad. There's another story of Don Drummond performing in Port Antonio, and the MC said: 'Now we present Don Drummond!' and Drummond just came right out, in a suit, and just pull down the zip and just piss on them! Drummond was just something else. Drummond never wear a shoe – always wear his felt hat, him look beautiful, but he's not wearing a shoe. He was like one of those American jazz musicians, just a different type of person. Any time I hear Drummond play I hear something good."[6]

On New Year's Day 1965, Jamaica was rocked by the news that Don Drummond had murdered his common-law wife, the dancer Anita Mahfood (aka Maguerita). He was sent to Bellevue, where he remained until his death in 1969. The murder was a tragic moment in Jamaica's musical history, and Drummond's detention had other repercussions: it contributed to the demise of The Skatalites, ultimately signalling the end of ska.

The keen musicianship of The Skatalites meant that the group was really overloaded with talent. It was, in some ways, the first Jamaican supergroup. So it is not surprising that the group had difficulty sustaining itself as an entity after Drummond's death, especially since bust-ups had been threatened from the very first. As a result of internal rivalries, exacerbated by external pressures from competing producers, the band split into two after a final performance in August 1965. Roland Alphonso stayed at Studio One, first with a new version of his Orchestra that included Lloyd Brevett; later, with Jackie Mittoo, he led The Soul Brothers with drummer Joe Isaacs and bassist Brian Atkinson. Tommy McCook at first took over the horn arrangements of uptown club act Kes Chin & The Souvenirs, but later fronted The Supersonics with Johnny Moore and Lloyd Knibb and eventually became the leader of the house band at Duke Reid's newly constructed Treasure Isle studio, along with bassist Jackie Jackson, organist Winston Wright, and drummer Hugh Malcolm. Alphonso admitted there was "something near to" animosity between himself and McCook after the rupture, "but not on an all-out basis".

"Duke Reid started with Tommy and Roland was with Coxsone," Brevett summarised. "Roland was Coxsone's fancy and Tommy was Duke Reid's fancy" – hence their respective roles once The Skatalites split. The break-up of the band meant the ska era was over in Jamaica, but nearly 15 years later, a group of black and white musicians in the English Midlands revived the music of The Skatalites and Prince Buster for the 2-Tone movement; another decade on, white Americans brought in the 'third wave' of ska, and even Japanese groups later successfully re-created the genre. In addition, The Skatalites themselves re-formed on several occasions and McCook and Alphonso were blowing ska right up until their deaths in the late 90s.

Although ska has continued to enthral audiences outside Jamaica, it has all but disappeared in its homeland. Indeed, within a year of the initial break-up of The Skatalites, a new style swept the nation: the cool and spacious sound known as rock steady.

3
TAKE IT EASY

Cool rock steady

"The integral part of the rock steady beat is the background of the musicians. What is not well known is that a musician's type and style of play is governed by the section of the country he grew in. The intangible feel for words and music is part of the answer, and is difficult to explain. It is inborn, an inherent quality which comes from culture, heritage, and the tradition of the people of West Kingston." –
LINER NOTES TO KEN BOOTHE'S *MR ROCK STEADY* (STUDIO ONE)

"The musicians were very creative, and the dance has a lot to do with it – the dancing change the music a lot. In those times, when you make a song, you have to make a dance with it for it to sell." – LEONARD DILLON

If ska hit the newly independent Jamaica with the force of Hurricane Hattie, then rock steady arrived in the shape of a cool breeze, the calm after the storm. The division of The Skatalites into two self-contained units signalled an end to big-band jazz arrangements, and smaller, studio-based groups created rock steady with horns as complementary instruments rather than focal points. As with the shift from boogie to ska, the gradual ascendance of the slower, less-cluttered rock steady came largely from a change to the dominant beat. Instead of the after-beat emphasis of ska, rock steady made use of the 'one drop', encompassing a pronounced whack on the bass drum or floor toms on the third beat of every bar. The new rhythm, driven by chugging snare beats, was offset by strolling electric-bass patterns, full of rest stops and pushed to the fore to provide the melody line. The greater prominence and melodic importance of the bass allowed dancers to abandon the clenched fists swinging between splayed legs of ska in favour of a stationary pose with a rocking body, jerking shoulders, and snapping fingers.

As with the birth of ska, the shift to rock steady was accomplished by a handful of talented musicians working to fashion a new genre, but the new shift was more disparate and its exact creation is difficult to pinpoint,

74

especially since conflicting claims have further obscured its origin. Among the most notable contributors were saxophonist and bandleader Tommy McCook, pianist Gladdy Anderson, bassist Jackie Jackson, and drummer Hugh Malcolm of The Supersonics at Treasure Isle; guitarist/bassist and studio arranger Ernest Ranglin at Federal; saxophonist Roland Alphonso and keyboardist Jackie Mittoo at Studio One; drummer Winston Grennan and guitarist and bandleader Bobby Aitken of The Caribbeats; and freelance guitarist, arranger, and bandleader Lynn Taitt.

"It was the feel of the musicians," confirmed Leonard Dillon of The Ethiopians. "The musicians were very creative, and the dance have a lot to do with it – the dancing change the music a lot. In those times, when you make a song, you have to make a dance with it for it to sell."

Dillon formed The Ethiopians just prior to rock steady's emergence, while working as a stonemason.[1] One of their first recordings for Coxsone, issued in 1966, was 'Owe Me No Pay Me', a tune demanding fair recompense for one's efforts, cut in what would materialise as the rock steady style; 'Free Man', recorded later that year, has the faster pace and honking horns of the waning ska form. "That was just between the ska and rock steady. Ska didn't die, it was just in the middle: a little piece of ska would be on this, and a little piece of rock steady. Ska don't totally leave off when rock steady take it up. It was a transition period."

Dillon was the only one with earlier recording experience. After cutting his debut solo sides at Studio One, he teamed up with street-corner singers in Waterhouse, forming The Ethiopians with Stephen 'Tough Cock' Taylor and Aston 'Charlie' Morrison. "We rehearse for over a year. I introduce them to Studio One, because I've been there already. We sang four songs, but Coxsone did not give us much money for that and Charlie was making a lot of noise about I'm giving away him talent. Him leave the group and we went back, I and Stephen now, with 'I'm Gonna Take Over' and 'Free Man'."

Shortly thereafter, Dillon found a backer for the group's first self-productions. "By working on my trade, I met a man named Lee Robinson, he build house and sell it. I'm working and always singing, until one day he offered to finance a session and that session bring forth 'Train To Skaville', the one that really took off."

'Train To Skaville' had the strolling bass line and subtle horn accompaniment of classic rock steady, but retained the choppy guitar chords of ska; Dillon insisted the song is "a partway ska rock steady". When describing in retrospect the many stylistic shifts that have occurred in Jamaican pop, it is easy to overstate the way such changes were adopted, and a distorted picture often emerges. But just as mento songs such as 'Rukumbine' and 'Penny Reel' were adapted in ska, and The Wailers recorded the 'ska-quadrille' medley 'Rude Boy', even as rock steady was marching in, such changes have rarely been absolute or definite. Likewise, the conventional wisdom that fast ska gave way to slow rock steady, which in turn gave way to reggae, is not always how those involved in creating the music view things. "The music don't change, because in music, you have fast, middle, and slow," claimed Roland Alphonso. "From we start at school, we've been playing fast, medium, and slow, so it's nothing new to me."[2]

"Ska is not a matter of speed, ska is a matter of arrangement," Leonard Dillon insisted. "I can play you ska and it's slow: you have slow ska and fast ska, slow rock steady and fast rock steady." The defining element of ska, according to Dillon, is the relation of the drum to what he calls the 'riff', that is, the rhythmic bursts provided by the rhythm guitar or horns. "The snare drum and the bass drum, the way they drop on your riff, that's the main thing. The bass can be any way, the bass can be slow as ever." He saw rock steady, in contrast, as defined by the one-drop rhythm. "Rock steady is the one drop. It's the drum."

"I give a hard blow on the third," confirmed Winston Grennan, whom some credit with originating the one drop. "That would be a hard one drop, and it would cut the beat in half." Grennan died of cancer in 2000 at the age of 56. Speaking by telephone from his home in Massachusetts, some years before he encountered health problems, Grennan explained that he grew up in Duckinfield, Saint Thomas, where he played drums for Junkanoo dancers at Christmas. He drummed in jazz groups with Trenton Spence, trumpeter Raymond Harper, and trombonist Carl Masters in the early 60s, but the pay was so bad that he became a professional boxer. After eventually joining The Caribbeats on keyboards for a stage production, he subsequently became one of the leading rock steady drummers.

"We went to Mandeville to do a show and the drummer didn't show up. I didn't have any sticks, so I cut me a nice guava limb and make two pairs of sticks. When the show finish, Bobby says: 'You're great with keyboard, but stick with this.' They didn't know that I play drum because I don't tell people that."

"It's coming from calypso, with a bolero beat, then the ska came in from the blues," says Bobby Aitken, leader of The Caribbeats, as his home in Florida. "They double up on the blues and bring in ska, but rock steady is a different thing – the guitar just 'bop ... bop ... bop', and every two 'bop', you drop the drum."

Now known as the Reverend Robert Simmonds, Laurel Aitken's younger brother Bobby began his musical career after a youth marked by hardship. "My father was an A1 carpenter from Saint Ann's, my mother's from Saint Elizabeth. They got married and went to Cuba on honeymoon, started having kids and catch right there. I was born in Havana, 1933, went back to Jamaica maybe '39. We were living in the Whitfield Town area, Kingston 13, but my mother got sick and died, and my father had heart failure and died when I was about eight. We all grew on the streets – everybody scatter." Bobby was raised among strangers and ended up in the Eventide Home. "That's what you call the poor house. That's where they put me because I'm too big for little orphanage."

Aitken avoided a life of crime when an uncle took him out of a street gang to learn the masonry trade. He built his first banjo at the age of 11 from melted sardine cans, and eventually became proficient on a succession of borrowed and homemade guitars. "After a while, the mason work get slow and I decide to turn to music. I form The Caribbeats around '59, '60, but it was only three of us: me, Charlie Organaire [harmonica player Charles Cameron], and the third guy's name was something like Morgan – just bass, box guitar, and harmonica. We was playing calypso and a little ska, but that time ska was not too bright – everybody was mostly coming from calypso. We try to perform one night in Shortwood Road at Blue Ribbon Club, but the guys didn't show up, so we break up. I was discouraged and I went back in the masonry work."

In 1961, Aitken made his recording debut as a singer with 'Crackers Rush', which commented on a food shortage. "You had to line up to get crackers," he explains. Count P., operator of a sound system on Spanish Town Road, issued the single on a label called Blues. The following year Prince Buster produced Aitken's first big hit, 'Never Never', which joined elements of several American pop hits (including one by Louis Prima) with an irresistible horn line. "Duke Reid used to have rehearsals in the evening, and while I was coming to Duke, I met Prince Buster on a little Honda. Him say: 'Don't go down to no Duke, meet me at Federal on Tuesday.' And he gave me £8 without even knowing me. Those days, £8 was money. Because I had the money, I got drunk and I get hoarse, could hardly sing, but it work out to be the style of the song and nobody know it was spoiled."

After cutting further vocal sides for Coxsone, King Edwards, and Linden Pottinger, Aitken re-formed The Caribbeats and concentrated on guitar. Based at Aitken's home in Galloway Road, Whitfield Town, the group's shifting line-up began with Aitken, Charlie Organaire, and future Zap Pow bassist Mike Williams on drums. Other notable members included bassist Vincent White ("a country guy"), pianists Bobby Kalphat ("a clear-skinned guy from Tower Hill"), and Conroy Cooper (who later led show-band Fabulous Five), saxophonist Val Bennett, and keyboardist Ansel Collins, whom Aitken originally placed on drums. Drummer Carlton 'Santa' Davis also occasionally sat in.

Despite line-up changes, The Caribbeats soon became one of the leading rock steady acts. The rock steady dance craze seems to have arrived in earnest by the autumn of 1966, although the dance itself may have been prevalent from the spring of 1965. According to Aitken, a musical turning point came with the recording of Carl Dawkins's 'Baby I Love You', a grainy tale of disappointed romance with a proto-rock steady rhythm, issued on Carl Johnson's Sir J.J. label: "We tired of the ska, so me and Charlie get together and say we're going to change this thing, after we did 'Baby I Love You' for Pottinger."

Hopeton Lewis's 'Take It Easy', recorded at Federal with Lynn Taitt and The Jets, is more readily identified as the first rock steady, although it's unclear which one came first. The song is said to have taken its form because Lewis had difficulty fitting his lyrics into ska's rapid grooves.

"The first tune we do on the rock steady was with Hopeton Lewis, 'Take It Easy'," confirms session keyboardist Gladdy Anderson. "From there, the ska rhythm become slow. I was so glad, because the ska was beating me shoulder – whole heap of years playing this fast rhythm pain the shoulder. So when Hopeton Lewis come with that 'Take It Easy', it kind of give the hand a rest, because it was like going back to a kind of rock rhythm."

Though not present for the original session, the drummer on this record was Hugh Malcolm, whom many claim as the originator of the rock steady beat. "I was in Miami when they did the record," Malcolm explained. "I think it's Byron Lee's drummer back it up, but Ken Khouri didn't like it, so he says: 'OK, let's keep the rhythm. When Malcolm comes, we'll make him dub the drums in.' Then I dubbed the rock steady drums in it and turned it into the real 'Take It Easy'." Hopeton Lewis's follow-up, an even cooler tale of sound-system battles called 'Sounds And Pressure', helped to consolidate the popularity of this relaxed beat.

The bandleader and musical arranger of Lewis's Federal sessions, and of many of the best rock steady numbers to follow, was a talented guitarist and steel-pan player from Trinidad named Nearlin Taitt (better known as Lynn Taitt). Taitt played rhythm guitar on several of the most noteworthy ska numbers, but truly flourished as a lead player during rock steady.

78

Taitt discovered his innate musical abilities growing up in San Fernando. "I used to beat a rhythm on the edge of a barrel down at the standpipe, and a guy heard me and brought a steel pan for me," he explained, a number of years before he succumbed to cancer in 2010, aged 75. "I grew up with 24 boys in one area; we used to hang out together, and we built up a steel band when I was about ten years old. I entered the competition for the best soloist in Trinidad and came first in 1956." Eventually, Taitt acquired a guitar that a friend pilfered from a drunken sailor and joined The Dutchy Brothers, formed by the five sons of a Surinamese immigrant.

By 1960, Taitt's prodigious skills saw him leading the Nearlin Taitt Orchestra. Byron Lee brought him to Jamaica in 1962 to back calypso artists such as Lord Melody at the independence celebrations. When an unscrupulous manager disappeared with the money, Taitt stayed in Jamaica, playing in bands on the ska scene. "I ended up in The Sheikhs with [vocalist] Lloyd Wilks, [tenor saxophonist] Bobby Gaynair, [bassist] Lloyd Spence, Deadley Headley, and [vocalist] Honey Boy Martin. That is where I met Jackie Mittoo – he was on piano. The bassist get to know I could arrange, and he and I left The Sheikhs and formed The Cavaliers. The organist Winston Wright and Johnny Moore played in that group, and then when I meet Lloyd Knibb – he like how I play guitar." Knibb brought Taitt to Duke Reid, for whom Taitt played rhythm on some landmark ska recordings, including Baba Brooks' 'Shank I Sheck' (released by King Edwards), and Justin Hinds & The Dominoes' 'Carry Go Bring Come'. Taitt also became a substitute for Jerry Haines in The Skatalites at Studio One.[3]

By the start of the rock steady period, Taitt was fronting The Comets. "In 1967 I was with Prince Buster in England: we tour for about four months. At that time I changed platform and had a group called The Comets: Lloyd Wilks, Honey Boy, [vocalist] Glen Miller, trombonist Ron Wilson, and Lloyd Knibb used to play stage shows in my group. Then I formed The Jets with Headley Bennett, Brian Atkinson on bass, a trumpet, tenor and alto saxophones, and a second guitarist named Jerry." Taitt said the unique picking style he developed on his Hofner, which helped define many a rock steady tune, was inspired by the cadence of steel-pan music. "The bubbling of the guitar comes from the steel drum – I try to imitate that."

When not making one of his regular appearances on Supersonics sessions, Taitt was essentially a freelancer whose skills were put to optimum use by others. For Federal, he arranged Hopeton Lewis's debut hits, work by the Paragons, and casually expressive instrumentals. The Jets were also the backing band at WIRL for much of the rock steady period, including the brief but crucial phase when Lee Perry was in-house producer. They also backed the earliest material produced by Joe Gibbs (aka Joel Gibson), a record salesman who ran the Amalgamated television repair shop on Beeston Street. Gibbs hailed from Montego Bay, but worked on the US naval base at Guantanamo Bay in Cuba in his teens. He returned to Kingston at the end of the ska period, and rose to prominence as a producer with Roy Shirley's 'Hold Them', another of rock steady's defining moments perceptively arranged by Taitt.

Shirley, who died of a heart attack in 2008, aged 63, drew heavily from American soul. He explained that, as with 'Take It Easy', the peculiar timing of 'Hold Them' stemmed from his inability to adapt soul music to a ska beat. "The first thing that came on the scene was ska. Ska was a very powerful music, ruled by a band named The Skatalites. I don't know how they get that ska thing, but I think it was built up between them, Sir Coxsone, and some jazz thing from America, because most of those guys was away abroad, and when they come back, they just form that thing into their era. I find out that it was difficult: I couldn't score into the ska, because I was still into that kind of soul vibes, and it was difficult to cross over. I remember I went to Sir Coxsone and I manage to get 'round the piano. I start to sing 'Hold Them' and him say: 'No man, that youth there, come back and check me in three years' time.' I check out Coxsone because he put on a lot of big shows, have artists like Theophilus Beckford and tunes like 'Four Corners Of The World' with The Skatalites, 'Freedom' by Clancy Eccles, and the man Owen Gray, some tune named 'On The Beach' – that's real influence to bring any young singer with ambition forward. I think I was too small for him, because their beat was more up-tempo and I was coming with a slow thing, so it was too new."

Coxsone's refusal was a humiliating response for a singer who already had recording experience under his belt, but Shirley said it only strengthened his resolve to make the song hit. He was raised in Trench Town as Ainsworth Roy Rushton, with his mother and stepfather, part of a community centred on a Revivalist church. Like many of Jamaica's foundation singers, he got his start on talent contests. Early recordings for Simeon Smith failed to gain release, but 'Oh Shirley', his debut issue on the Beverley's label, co-arranged by Jimmy Cliff, was a hit in 1965. He then formed The Leaders with Ken Boothe, Joe White, and Chuck Josephs (aka Chuck Berry Jr), but recordings for Federal failed to be of much consequence. Subsequently, with Slim Smith and Franklyn White, Shirley joined the first incarnation of The Uniques, a spin-off of the frequently changing Techniques vocal group. "We are the original Uniques," Shirley clarified. "Out of Techniques or Uniques come the same set of man, them fall out and form different name. Me and The Uniques sang tune for J.J., but he was always a little guy in the production field." The Uniques also recorded for Caltone, a label established by former Skatalites manager Blondel Calnek (known professionally as Ken Lack), but the material was equally unsuccessful and the group temporarily disbanded.

Left on his own, Shirley crafted the unique and influential 'Hold Them.' "I always sing a lot of soul, like Sam Cooke, but I could only play two chords on the guitar, so that's how 'Hold Them' start to come up. I said: 'Get in the groove and move those feet,' and everywhere I go, people love the tune, so I just keep singing it, but I couldn't start a beat, or a bass line, to get it going. One day I was standing just opposite Beverley's and I happens to see some Salvation Army people coming down Orange Street. The man was beating the drum and cymbal, and the thing just come into me."

A mutual friend brought Shirley to the attention of Joe Gibbs. "I used to sing with Slim Smith, because we were very close friends. There was a tailor friend of ours who was impressed by how me and Slim Smith sing, and him and Joe Gibbs was friends because they was in Guantanamo Bay together, but Slim Smith's guys never really want to know, because them sing for Duke Reid and them no want fi mash up them group. When I find I couldn't get nobody else from Slim Smith's group, I go to Ken Boothe and we go to a rehearsal place at Cross Roads with Drumbago. We start to rehearse the song, but for some reason, Slim Smith and Ken Boothe couldn't manage that part that I am singing. They are still singing the ska, because the ska was stealing everybody; them start to war and quarrel until the producer say: 'A good tune, that.' Then Gladstone Anderson call the producer and say: 'You have to make Roy sing the tune, him write it, make him alone sing it.' And from me start go 'pon the mic, everybody start dance. We go to Federal about a week after with Lynn Taitt, Drumbago, Jackie Jackson, and Jerry on [rhythm] guitar."

When Gibbs aired the song at his shop, it was obvious that 'Hold Them' was something special. Its augmented marching-drum beat, given further demarcation by a choppy piano line and embellished by off-beat bursts of Taitt's guitar, is a thrilling backdrop to Shirley's individual delivery, his quavering voice exhorting his audience to let the music take hold. 'Hold Them' was a massive hit that helped the music shift further from ska. As Shirley recalled: "Joe Gibbs cut a dub to test it out, and as the man put on the dub, the youth left the corner and come in the shop: 'Play back that tune there!' In the evening, I go carry it over east, to Dunkirk. At the time, [singer] Maxie Romeo was a deejay playing with a sound at Longstone Road, and I remember that he played it 17 times that night."

The immediate success was so great that Coxsone had Ken Boothe cover the tune in an effort to capture the overseas market. Boothe scored a number of solo hits for Coxsone in ska, including 'You're No Good', backed by The Sharks, and 'Come Running Back,' but only began to be recognised internationally in rock steady. "'Train Is Coming', that is the hit that make me big all over Jamaica," Boothe recalls. "During that period, Downbeat was going to foreign and bringing back songs that he think me can sing over, like [Kenny Lynch's] 'Moving Away', and 'Come Tomorrow' by Manfred Mann – that song was a big hit. Me was a big household name in Jamaica and start to get big in Nassau, but the song that take me abroad is 'Puppet On A String' that won the Eurovision with Sandie Shaw."

Studio One transformed the pop song into something akin to rock steady. As Boothe pointed out, Coxsone's recently upgraded equipment now allowed for multi-track recording and separate overdubs: "You could do the rhythm without the singer present, so Jackie Mittoo made the rhythm of 'Puppet On A String' without even I knowing about it. It take off in the dancehall, and then Downbeat release it in England and it took off there too."

Meanwhile, Joe Gibbs followed 'Hold Them' with rock steady hits by Errol Dunkley, a pubescent West Kingston vocalist, born in 1951, who emerged as the next child star. "The music business were about in its second generation when I started singing," he explains. "I started at the tail end of ska, then it change to rock steady and I was really popular in Jamaica in the rock steady era. As a kid, I was mostly a dancer, and this is how I used to hustle at my mum's bar: people used to pay me to dance, then I develop singing from that. I started singing at churches and talent concerts, and my gate on Woodrow Street was a hangout point for the kids in the evening, because there was a lamppost. Night-time we'd be under the light post, singing and writing songs."

Dunkley soon joined a street-corner group with Junior English, who later became a popular solo artist in London. "Junior English come and see me and ask me if I want to form a group. I was about 11, Junior was about 14." The duo answered an ad placed in the *Gleaner* by Prince Buster, who was looking for new talent and would produce Dunkley's first inconsequential sides. Eventually, a chance encounter with future producer Bunny Lee led to the link with Gibbs that brought Dunkley to the top of the Jamaican charts.

"I was a member of a youth club and I had a letter to see Vic Sampson, one of the owners of West Indies studio, to do an audition. When I went there, Bunny Lee was outside the gate, and he say: 'I know you, don't I? You sing some tunes already for Prince Buster. What you do around here?' He wasn't a producer then, he was trying to be a singer, moving around the circuit. He tell me he know this man who is just coming in the recording business and is looking for artists, and took me to Joe Gibbs's on Beeston Street, just the other street from Prince Buster. He had a shop fixing TV, radio, and amplifiers, and was selling records, but he had done 'Hold Them' with Roy Shirley."

Gibbs liked Dunkley's singing voice but thought he would be more successful with cover tunes. "He was living in Guantanamo Bay for a long time and had a lot of songs that he brought back, so he gave me this seven-inch by Gloria Lynn, 'You're Gonna Need Me'. I did like that song, so I said: 'All right, we're going to work on this one.' It was Slim Smith and I, because Slim Smith and Bunny Lee was friends. I did 'You're Gonna Need Me' for Joe Gibbs and it was a hit – my first hit song. We recorded it at West Indies with Lynn Taitt, Hugh Malcolm, Jackie Jackson, Gladstone Anderson, and Winston Wright – some classic musicians we had at the time."

As rock steady solidified, Treasure Isle emerged as its leading proponent. Although Gibbs and Federal may have released the genre's first efforts, Duke Reid ruled the sound, reversing disappointments during ska, when he was largely in the shadow of Coxsone and Buster. Reid's Treasure Isle studio, located above his liquor store at 33 Bond Street, had a wooden interior that leant added warmth and richness of tone. Much of its equipment was purchased from the defunct studio of Linden Pottinger, who continued to produce music for a few years after selling the equipment to Reid in 1964.

Pottinger's wife, born Sonia Eloise Durrant in 1931 in the country town of Leith Hall, Saint Thomas, became an unexpected production force in rock steady following the couple's separation in 1965. She had helped run her husband's Record Distributors outfit, initially at 107 Orange Street, and later at 103, where it was renamed Tip Top; left with three children to feed, she moved Tip Top to 37 Orange Street and launched labels such as Gay Feet, Excel, and Rainbow, with the Glory imprint reserved for gospel. A devout Christian who avoided Kingston's tumultuous dancehalls, Mrs Pottinger used instinct to guide her recording sessions, scoring an instant hit at one of the first with the ballad 'Every Night' by Joe White & Chuck, which remained in the Jamaican charts for several months. Further impressive sides by Baba Brooks, Count Ossie, and Stranger & Patsy followed, as well as huge hits with The Ethiopians, Ken Boothe, The Melodians, and The Gaylads. In addition to being the sole female record producer active in Jamaica, Mrs Pottinger's early training in the accountancy and secretarial fields sharpened her no-nonsense approach. She later emerged as an important record manufacturer, while her skills as a distributor meant that rivals sometimes licensed hit-bound material to her to allow for greater market permeation. She also retained strong ties with Duke Reid, ultimately reviving his dormant studio and label in the mid 70s, following Reid's health-related retirement.

Reid's chief engineer during rock steady, Byron Smith, had a perceptive ear for recording and was respected for his expertise in balancing sound. Most crucially, The Supersonics provided the perfect backdrop for the love songs, dance tunes, and 'rude boy' commentaries that comprised the rock steady genre. Bandleader Tommy McCook played a central role in the definition of the Supersonics sound, especially where horn arrangements were concerned, while the combined efforts of bassist Jackie Jackson and pianist Gladdy Anderson gave their recordings greater texture, augmented by scintillating organ from Winston Wright, complex beats from Hugh Malcolm, and steady rhythm guitar from Ronnie 'Bop' Williams.

Bop was born Lorraine Williams in Spanish Town in 1942 and joined The Supersonics after a spell on the North Coast hotel circuit. "When I reach 19 or 20, I started to play music and travel. I was discovered by Tommy McCook in Ocho Rios, playing at the Maracas club – he told me he wanted me to play in Kingston with his band as a rhythm player. I think the first tune I played on was 'Expo 67' [a huge rock steady smash for The Melodians] and I stayed at Treasure Isle until I went to England in 1970."

Clifton 'Jackie' Jackson was born in 1947 and grew in various parts of downtown Kingston. His uncle, pianist Luther Williams, led one of Jamaica's first big jazz bands. Jackson studied piano in his youth, but switched to bass after encountering Lloyd Brevett's artistry; Stax session player Duck Dunn was another major influence. Like Brevett, Jackson had a tall frame perfectly suited to playing the bass. He adapted well to the instrument, and eventually switched from upright to electric to play in small live bands. "I didn't get into a band until four or five years after. In those days, the big bands were Carlos Malcolm, Byron Lee, Kes Chin & The Souvenirs, and The Vagabonds. Then you had the little bands, like The Cavaliers and Ty & The Titans. I play with Ty & The Titans by accident: I knew the drummer and followed him to a rehearsal, and the bass player and the bandleader got into a fight. I was in that band for three years. By that time, The Skatalites had disbanded. Lester Sterling formed this band called The Cavaliers, and I became the bass player for two or three years."

Then Jackson received a surprise visit from one of his idols, resulting in his installation at Treasure Isle. "My mother said somebody's at the gate for me. When I went out there, this gentleman said his name was Tommy McCook, and he was forming this band called Tommy McCook & The Supersonics, and he's here to put me in the band as the bass player. That was it – I was in university now, being in that band: the rest of the stuff I was doing was just comprehensive school. After about a month, I started recording. My first song was 'Girl I've Got A Date', and that became like an anthem in Jamaica. I was the resident bass player for Treasure Isle for years."

'Girl I've Got A Date' was the first of many substantial hits by Alton Ellis & The Flames that really worked to establish rock steady as Jamaica's dominant music. 'Rock Steady', a later smash, is the song most associated with the genre itself. Drummer Hugh Malcolm claimed this as the first rock steady recording. "The type of drums that I play on that rhythm was the very first anywhere in the world," he said.

Before he died of a heart attack in his mid sixties, circa 2005, Malcolm lived in an isolated village in the depths of rural Jamaica. Cutlass in hand, he said he was born in a small town in Hanover, raised in Westmoreland by farming parents, and brought into a big jazz band in 1955, a year after moving to Kingston to study woodwork. "From baby days in the country, I used to go where the big bands are playing in the Christmas party, and I used to request playing the drums, so from those days, I know about drums. When I was 17, a bandmaster placed me in the Jocelyn Trott Orchestra – that was the biggest orchestra in the West. We work at the Montego Beach Hotel and the Half Moon for a long likkle period. Those days I didn't start to read music yet, just play by ear."

After living with an uncle in Port Antonio, where he attended high school, Malcolm returned to Kingston to study music at Alpha under bandmasters Alfred Delgado and Vincent Tullo. He started playing in small live bands, undertaking building work during the day, and appeared on sporadic recordings for Coxsone and Duke Reid during the late 50s.

"I didn't earn money from recording, but bandleaders took me out and I get 30 shilling per night. I played with Trenton Spence, Percy Myers from Allman Town, a good saxophonist, and myself and Jackie Mittoo played with Ansel Smart & The Rivals.[4] Then the university formed this band, Kes

85

Chin & The Souvenirs[5], and then another band form, The Cavaliers: Lester Sterling was the bandleader and a little youth called Jackie Jackson was the bass man. We elect Rita Marley as the singer and go round the island advertising Dragon Stout for Desnoes & Geddes – no big money, but we enjoy it. When Vere Johns started *Opportunity Knocks*, they elect me for most of the shows, 'cos I was a drummer that plays every beat. Skatalites go on for a while; I do one and two hits with them, such as 'Simmer Down' with Bob Marley, and Jackie Opel, 'Cry Me A River', and I back other artists like Doreen Schaffer for Coxsone."

When The Skatalites split, Malcolm declined an offer to play with The Soul Brothers and instead joined The Supersonics. "Roland Alphonso wanted me to come and play drums with him, but he was a kind of ignorant bandleader and we couldn't wrap too tough – I got some ways he didn't like, and he got some ways I didn't like. Those days I used to rent house, so I go down to Bournemouth Gardens to look at this apartment; I saw a car driving behind me, and I noticed it was Kes Chin, my former bandleader, running me down. He say: 'Some instruments we put together, and Tommy say he elect you as his drummer.' I drove behind him and go out to Club Havana, owned by Matthew Chin in those days – he was also one of the band's managers, of which Duke Reid was the founder; he spend his money to buy these instruments. When we get there, [McCook] names that he wants me on drums, and who and who on other instruments."

The Supersonics, Malcolm insisted, originated rock steady. "I've heard a lot of people say they make this, they make that, but Hux Brown and Lynn Taitt, we make that beat with Jackie Jackson, Winston Wright, Gladstone Anderson. We make the beat, rock steady." Malcolm defined the beat as complex: "I play a galloping, like a horse, on my snare, and on the bass drum, I play funky and one drop in between, so it's very tricky – funky sometimes, because the one drop is the beat, but the accents sometimes are funky. When the space is there, we just put the double in it. Then I used to get a lot of fight from musicians to play 16 on my hi-hat – that's the spice on the rock steady: you play triplet, but as soon as you go in like a horse, riding and put in the 16, then you gotta get up and *wind* to this thing."

Despite his acknowledgement of 'Take It Easy' as an early rock steady, Malcolm named Alton Ellis's 'Rock Steady' as the first recording built on a rock steady drumbeat. "That time, ska was raising Cain and there was no beat named rock steady yet, so we do that rhythm, 'Get Ready, Let's Do Rock Steady', with Alton Ellis."

Ellis succumbed to cancer in 2008 at the age of 70. Born and raised in

CLOCKWISE FROM TOP: Fats Domino live in Jamaica, February 1961; Noel 'Zoot' Simms, aka Skully; 'Lover Boy' Derrick Morgan; keyboard king Jackie Mittoo.

THIS PAGE: The Skatalites, ska's authenticators;
Stranger 'Soul' Cole.
OPPOSITE PAGE, CLOCKWISE FROM TOP LEFT: bass
player Jackie Jackson; rock steady guitar genius Lyn
Taitt; Marcia Griffiths.

CLOCKWISE FROM TOP: Soul Syndicate; Crown Prince of Reggae, Dennis Brown; Johnny Osbourne.

Trench Town, he and his singing partner Eddie Perkins hit big in 1961 with the ballad 'Muriel,' recorded for Coxsone Dodd. Further work followed with Dodd and Vincent Chin. When Perkins went to the USA, where he appeared on *The Ed Sullivan Show*, Ellis teamed briefly with John Holt before the latter joined The Paragons. Then Ellis formed The Flames with neighbours Winston Jarrett and Eggar Gordon; Ellis's brother Leslie and a friend named Ronnie were temporary members. As Jarrett recalls: "After Eddie go to the States, Alton was vexed, 'cos they singing so long. I came by and say we could form a group, and him say he's going to think it over. We start practice every night, write lyrics like 'Girl I've Got A Date', 'Cry Tough', and 'The Preacher', the first song we recorded at Treasure Isle. Jackie Jackson was there and Lynn Taitt, Tommy McCook, Drumbago, Gladstone Anderson, Winston Wright. We was the first man who christen Duke Reid's studio."

Winston Jarrett is one of the few artists I did not have to search for in Jamaica. Within days of my arrival he turned up at my doorstep, then effectively homeless since his downtown living quarters had recently burned up. Jarrett says his early inspiration stemmed from spiritual singing and American soul. "I born 1940 and grow in Saint Ann, Lime Tree Gardens. I came to Kingston at an early age with my mother and father. My mother came to Kingston to work with white people in the colonial days. My bigger brothers was living in Trench Town, so I grow up at 24 Fourth Street, Kingston 12. I really grow up in a Christian family, Church of God, where everybody clap hands and praise God, read your Bible two times a day to drive vampire away. My father was a deacon in the church, but Sundays in the dining room, he would put those 78s on the gramophone, and that's where I get all my ideas from. Many songs inspired me by the great Impressions with Curtis Mayfield, and I love Sam Cooke, Dinah Washington, Chuck Berry. In those days I get my little sardine pan and lay a flat piece of board across. I made a little guitar, put that puss-gut fishing line on it and made three strings that you could pick like a banjo, and I have that little bamboo drumstick underneath my arm. That's where I started from."

Jarrett says that Trench Town, one of the least privileged places on the island, was fertile ground for vocalists. "Bob Marley, Peter Tosh, Bunny Wailer, Ken Boothe, Jimmy Cliff, Alton Ellis, Hortense Ellis, Higgs & Wilson, The Richards Brothers – so many singers in the same little district." He says The Flames had a shifting line-up, with Skully Simms or Lloyd Charmers occasionally taking the place of Eggar Gordon. They took the name The Flames, he explains, "because I was on a show with James Brown & The Flames, we perform together at the Carib Theatre".[6]

91

The Flames' earliest material warned of the excesses of rude-boy life: their 1965 ska smash 'Dance Crasher' detailed the exploits of a thug named Busby who caused mayhem at sound system events. The following year saw slower rock steady numbers with a similar message, including 'The Preacher', 'Blessings Of Love', and the popular 'Cry Tough', another tune inspired by Busby's brutality and given melodic structure by the violin of a player known as White Rum Raymond.

That such songs would become hits in 1966 is understandable, as the rudie violence that began in the late 50s had intensified to such an extent that the government was forced to call a State of Emergency that lasted a month. Violence was not only more commonplace but had rapidly taken on a political dimension. In the early 60s a number of street gangs were formed: some overtly criminal like the Denham Town Park Gang, others based more on kinship and support in fragmented communities that lacked basic amenities. The Spanglers, originally formed downtown on Regent Street, were loyal followers of Duke Reid's sound, which was also frequented by notorious criminals such as Whoppi King; the gang was based in the slums of Back-O-Wall and Lizard Town, until Edward Seaga had the tenements bulldozed in the summer of 1966 in order to build Tivoli Gardens, Jamaica's first government-backed housing scheme. However, this new concrete estate was populated not by those whose dwellings had been destroyed but by JLP supporters, and the area was then kept loyal to the ruling party by the heavily armed 'enforcers' of the Tivoli Gang.

Seaga is unrepentant about the way Tivoli was created. "Back-O-Wall was the worst criminal den in the entire country," he says. "Police couldn't go there. It wasn't a community – it was just a collection of shacks, and part of it was on what is now Marcus Garvey Drive, which was in full sight of everyone travelling by. We had to do something to remove that type of unsightly community, so the intention was really to remove the shacks and to bring a community with proper housing."

Was it true that the residents were not given warning before the slum clearance, as has often been stated? "We always give prior warning, even unto today, but no matter how much warning you give, persons who are squatters on land, they don't go, they are there right at the end. You rarely find a community where warning is given and the people take warning and go. Some might, but the bulk of them stay to the end."

What about the fact that Tivoli was housed by JLP supporters who had not been living in the area? "People who were housed there were people who wanted to go there. It was open to everyone, but I guess because the government that I was a part of bulldozed the area, the people who were then there, who had by that time taken up residence in other areas of western Kingston, didn't see themselves as wanting to go back there, because they have not felt comfortable, so they weren't making applications – but somebody did."

Could Seaga confirm whether the original Spanglers were supporters of Duke Reid's sound? "That's correct, but they had nothing to do with Duke Reid. Duke Reid wasn't involved with any group known as a gang. Duke Reid had a number of fellows who were always around with him, because if his sound system was going out to be played, you need people, and some of them were deejays for the sound system. But that didn't make them into a gang. Matter of fact, one of his top deejays was someone who was very helpful to me, a man called Dapper Dan.[7] He became involved at the very beginning when we were building up a constituency. You'd have to build up your support from all levels and he was from that sort of working-class level of vendors and higglers and so on, one of those who worked with us."

Before 1966, most rudie battles were waged with knives, bottles, or fists, but now the Tivoli Gang had handguns and Molotov cocktails, so the Spanglers moved to Matthews Lane and accepted arms from the PNP. Likewise, the previously independent Vikings, based on the Kingston waterfront, threw in their lot with the PNP when the Phoenix gang tried to gain control of the area, allegedly at the JLP's instigation. By the following year, the violence had gotten so out of hand that thugs raped a schoolgirl and assaulted a teacher at Denham Town School, prompting Prince Buster to record the best-known anti-rude boy song, 'Judge Dread', following Derrick Morgan's 'Tougher Than Tough'. Although his peers warned that the recording could have repercussions, Buster knew he could count on support should any backlash arise: "I have my likkle youth ah Luke Lane ready fi face anything." Buster says he appeared in the song as an Ethiopian judge to stop those who participated in wickedness despite claiming to be Rastafarian. "A lot of the people who was doing the act was wearing long dreads and calling themselves Rasta. The authority to them is Ethiopia, so I had to come as an Ethiopian for them to understand what I was saying."

Although the rudie feuds were intensifying, soothing love songs made up most of the rock steady idiom. Alton Ellis's emotive tenor, backed by the Flames' choral harmonies, proved the perfect vehicle for the romantic themes of 'Baby I Love You', 'Breaking Up', 'Remember That Sunday', and

'I'm Just A Guy' – all serious, long-lasting hits. In addition to the captivating harmonies, the high quality of The Supersonics' backing helped these songs retain an individual flair; 'Breaking Up', for instance, has a wonderful flute from Tommy McCook, while 'Remember That Sunday' is marked by Winston Wright's percolating organ. McCook and Wright also cut instrumental versions of many rock steady hits for Treasure Isle B-sides.

While Ellis gave Duke Reid some of his biggest rock steady hits, the singer's flawless deliveries ensured that he was in demand to moonlight for the competition: several songs cut for Reid were recorded again for Coxsone Dodd, along with original material and individualised covers of American soul. When Dodd sent Ellis on a UK tour with Jackie Mittoo and The Soul Brothers, it signalled the break-up of The Flames and Alton's departure from Treasure Isle.[8] Nevertheless Reid stayed at the top with a number of other strong rock steady harmony groups, including The Paragons, The Jamaicans, The Melodians, The Silvertones, and The Techniques.

The Paragons first recorded for Coxsone around 1965. Original group member Keith Anderson, better known as Bob Andy, recounts their formation: "The group started out with Tyrone Evans and myself as a duo, Andy & Ronnie; we went to the same church downtown and were members of the same scout troop. 1957–58 is when we really started: we were only about 14 or so. We actually recorded a song for Duke Reid, 'I'm In Love'. It was so good that it was a dub plate – they just kept it for competitive purposes when the sound played out." Anderson says the greater success of better-established duos made the pair seek to expand the group. "We started looking for other guys in the church club that we had, that was just about the time of the dance called the hully gully. We changed three or four names and seven or eight guys. Funnily enough, the group that we patterned ourselves after vocally was The Drifters, and somehow our group ended up with a history like theirs, because the guys drifted in and out."

Eventually, The Paragons became Anderson, Evans, and Howard Barrett, with John Holt drafted in as lead singer. "We had this other guy called Leroy Stamp who we got rid of. Someone told us about John Holt and he worked out perfectly. That quartet is actually what went to record with Studio One firstly. Coxsone loved us because we were very organised – we were a neat bunch of guys and knew what we were about. The songs we did for Coxsone were ballads: we did a cover of The Drifters' 'Follow Me' and the other three songs were originals. 'In Love At Last' was number one on both radio stations."

Anderson says internal friction followed. "We were having ego problems with John Holt, so we tried Vic Taylor when we were nominated for the first Festival song contest, held to commemorate Jamaica's independence in '66. Vic Taylor and myself, we grew up at the same children's home. He was with Lynn Taitt & The Comets, but he started out with a group called The Monarchs. After the Festival, Barrett and Evans quite rightly said that while Vic is a great singer, he wasn't as suited to Paragons as John was, so they were going to bring him back. So I said I will step if John comes back, because he's not going to change. John is still my brethren until this day, but I felt overshadowed in the group." Anderson went back to Studio One, where he "did odd jobs around the studio to make a living" before launching a solo singer-songwriter career.

Holt continued to model the group after The Drifters. Reaching Treasure Isle in late 1966, The Paragons' blissful harmony was responsible for 12 number one hit singles in a row, including 'Happy Go Lucky Girl', 'Only A Smile', 'On The Beach', 'Wear You To The Ball', and 'The Tide Is High' (the last of which was later adapted into a major international hit by Blondie).

Tommy Cowan led The Jamaicans, a vocal quartet. They hit big in 1967 with the close harmony of 'Things You Say' and 'Ba Ba Boom', the nonsensical winner of the annual Festival song competition.

What set The Melodians apart was that two of their three vocalists sang lead: Brent Dowe's deeper tones were sometimes supplanted by the higher, tremulous voice of founder Tony Brevett, nephew of Skatalites bassist Lloyd. In the back room of Alton Ellis's All Tone record shop in South London, a jittery Brevett tries to explain the group's evolution. "Melodians was like more than one group, because we all sing together from Ebenezer School on Darling Street, and at the school football team sports club. About 1962, it was me, a guy named George Allison, and Bob Marley, we used to sing at the club. Bob say he hear about a white boy on Slipe Road, we have an audition, so we harmonise some foreign tune, for we have to sound like foreign singers. Another guy named Eddie Fraser, after a while them call him a murderer, but him is the man who always used to give you the key to go into the church so that we ah go play the pipe organ. A next man, him get two guns – it's pure bad man involved – but him give me a ukulele, and we start learn that one-finger G, a one-finger D, and two-finger, three-finger D. We start rehearsing at Back-O-Wall, so we ready to form a group."

After Marley made his recording debut for Leslie Kong, he tried to assist Brevett by schooling his evolving group. "We still gwan ah school, me 13 now, and Bob come for me, say: Tony, come around Beverley's fi sing one

95

tune. He gwan ah studio, so me ah beg teacher to let me out. After a while we had a guy named Bradfield Brown in the group, he was the bass man, sing tunes like [Frankie Lymon's] 'Juvenile Delinquent' at Trench Town in the night. Bob said him want me to sing in me natural tone of voice, so me have to sing falsetto on top of the harmony. Me find Trevor McNaughton, go ah Greenwich Farm and a man say Brent Dowe is one of him school friends, a brother who can sing."

"Tony Brevett met me in Greenwich Town in 1962 and we becomes friends," Brent Dowe confirmed to me at his home in Portmore. "We started singing in clubs all over the place, sing every Friday night at Kittymat Club." Known as Porky because he was fat as a child, Dowe was born in Point District, Saint James, in 1946 and died of a heart attack in 2006. His mother, who worked for the Coffee Industry Board, brought him to Greenwich Town, more commonly known by its earlier appellation, Greenwich Farm, in 1953. This sprawling ghetto lies to the west of downtown Kingston, below Spanish Town Road, squeezed between industrial areas and May Pen Cemetery. Like nearby Trench Town, Greenwich Town/Farm was a breeding-ground for vocal groups.

Brevett says The Melodians first recorded as a quartet for Prince Buster, but the material may have been reserved for sound-system specials. Bradfield Brown subsequently left the group, and some of their best material was later co-written by silent partner Renford Cogle.

The group passed their audition before B.B. Seaton and Ken Boothe at Studio One, and Dodd issued a handful of Melodians discs in 1966. The group then moved to higher wages at Treasure Isle, where they became one of the leading acts through hits like 'You Have Caught Me', 'You Don't Need Me', and 'Expo 67'. "It was a money thing – who was paying more money," said Dowe of the move. "Coxsone was giving £6 for one shot, down at Duke we got £10 for one shot."

Like The Paragons, The Silvertones made their name at Treasure Isle adapting American hits, led by the baritone of Delroy Denton. "The group started with me and Keith Coley," recalls founding member Gilmour Grant. "After a while we meet Denton, and through he could play the guitar most, he really get to be lead singer. Duke Reid used to have auditions on Sunday, so we take a try, but we didn't get through the first time. When we make our first song it was a lucky time for us, because they record eight songs that night and our song was the last. In those days it was only two tracks, one for the music and one for the voice. The musicians was Tommy McCook & The Supersonics; he said to us if we can make one cut he will record, but if you spoil it you don't have another chance. So that's the one chance that we get, and we take it. [Brook Benton's] 'True Confession', that was the only hit song out of the eight. Then we made [Wilson Pickett's] 'Midnight Hour'. We was around with Duke Reid, and in between that we sing 'Guns Fever' with Miss Pottinger."

The Techniques, one of West Kingston's constantly changing street-corner groups, was another act that helped keep Reid far above the competition. At his record shop on Orange Street (which burned to the ground in an arson attack in 2009, two years before his terrible murder), founding member Winston Riley said it all started in late 1964 at a neighbourhood youth club established by Edward Seaga. "I grow up in West Kingston, in the ghetto, between Milk Lane and North Street, Tivoli and them place there. I used to sing in contests with Vere Johns and on school concerts, sing on the street and all type of things. While we were singing at school, Edward Seaga form a club on Wellington Street, near by Tivoli Gardens, and I come and join the band as a singer and bass player, with Slim Smith, Frederick Waite, Franklyn White, and The Richards Brothers. We were friends, because we used to sing at the same school, Kingston Senior School."

"None of them could play music," notes Seaga, "but I gave them instruments and they practise. A lot of the top artists would come there and sing with the band: Jimmy Cliff, Ken Boothe, Stranger Cole, Marcia Griffiths, Prince Buster, Toots & The Maytals."

"We go on concerts and back them up," Riley continued. "Then our first recording was organised by Edward Seaga at Federal records. Major Lance came to Jamaica, an American singer, and we did the first recording, 'No One'. Major Lance record the whole group: we get musicians and we were just the singers. Then Ken Boothe and Stranger Cole carry we to Duke Reid. 'Little Did You Know', that was a number-one hit."

Keith 'Slim' Smith, The Techniques' original lead singer, was an emotional individual with a powerful tenor-alto range. Fellow singer Jimmy Riley was a close friend of Smith and followed the group's many permutations. Perched on a chair in the back room of Derrick Harriott's shop, Riley tries to make plain the interwoven strands between The Techniques, Uniques, and Sensations. "I used to go to Kingston Senior School where a lot of singers used to go: Alton Ellis, Slim Smith, Carl Dawkins; Slim Smith and myself was in the same class. Me and Dadum [Frederick Waite] used to live at Waterhouse, so we used to ride together on the bus, and he used to tell me about the group they had formed. I wasn't

97

paying him no mind, then one evening I turned the radio on and heard this ska record, 'Little Did You Know', an original Duke Reid record. They said [it was] by the Techniques. I said: 'But that's my group in my school! This thing is for real!' So I started hanging – I was like the fifth member of The Techniques. I wanted to be in the group so bad, but all groups was four members, so I used to carry Slim Smith's clothes [to performances] to go in for free. I rehearse with them downtown in West Street and teach Winston the harmonies, but I wasn't officially in the group."

Riley decided to form his own group with other singers from the neighbourhood. "I said since I can't get into Techniques, I'm going to form my own group, The Sensations, along with Cornell Campbell and Buster Riley, Winston's brother, and a big guy, Aaron Davis, we call him Bobby [aka 'Dego']. Then The Techniques took us to Duke Reid, right at that point of late ska going into rock steady, and we started recording for Duke Reid – Gladdy auditioned us. King Sporty came there, he had been in America and heard 'Juvenile Delinquent' by Frankie Lymon & The Teenagers, and he brought it to us and we start rehearsing. That was the first song we recorded as The Sensations, and it was a hit in the dancehall."

Cornell Campbell adds a few particulars: "I started to develop myself as a printer and I forget about singing. Then Jimmy Riley, he grow in my neighbourhood, he said: 'Cornell, make we form a group?' I wasn't interested, but him was demanding and always focus on me to form a group, so him get two other guys, Buster Riley and Dego, and we form The Sensations, but Jimmy Riley had the name Dynamics. I said: 'I don't like the name Dynamics, it too silly. You have to name Sensations or something.' We do several recordings for Treasure Isle. Earlier, I took Slim Smith to Coxsone Downbeat, but Coxsone never record him, say: 'Keith, you no ready yet,' so he went to Treasure Isle and formed The Techniques. Then, when I split up The Sensations, my group went with Slim Smith. All of us did form the group together, but I drop out, said so much bull can't reign in one pen, because everybody wanted to be leader."

After previous collaboration with Roy Shirley and Ken Boothe, Slim Smith recruited Jimmy Riley to form a modified Uniques after The Techniques and Sensations shifted membership. "I love Slim Smith like my own brother," Riley says, with obvious sincerity. "Me and him was closer than brothers, because he was close to my age and we used to hang out – not just singing, but with girls at night, we go parties, we go dance, we play cricket … we just had a bond. He and Winston Riley had a falling out over some money, and the original Techniques broke up, so we formed The Uniques, which was a spin-off of The Techniques. I left The Sensations and Jackie Parris came after, and they was again four. Uniques was me, Slim Smith, and then we found Lloyd Charmers, and the first song we record, 'Let Me Go Girl', was a number one."

Backed by The Caribbeats and cut for fresh producer Bunny Lee, 'Let Me Go Girl' was the first of many hits for The Uniques, now a challenge to better-established groups. "Uniques was the most popular group, the only group that ever give Bob Marley & The Wailers a run for the money. They had a show called the Battle of the Groups at Ward Theatre, and Uniques won. Bob Marley draw his knife and create a scene. It was war downtown and our posse said nobody can fight Uniques, so it was just a stand-off."

The Uniques and the re-formed Techniques kept the hits flying, notably with modified covers of Impressions hits, such as The Uniques' version of 'Gypsy Woman' and The Techniques' 'You Don't Care' and 'Queen Majesty'.

"Curtis Mayfield was a major influence," says Pat Kelly, whose cool, wounded lead is featured on 'You Don't Care'. "We grew up in that era: Curtis Mayfield, The Temptations, Smokey Robinson, Jerry Butler." Kelly is on the veranda of his home in the Kingston suburb of Patrick City, close to the homes of John Holt and Bunny Lee. A quiet, unassuming man, he says he was born Horatious Kelly in Kingston in 1944 and raised the ghetto of Maxfield Avenue by his mother, a housewife, and father, a builder who became a church minister when Pat was 17. He became a temporary Techniques member when he returned to Jamaica on vacation while studying electronics in America. "I had no intention of singing," he insists. "I went to school and studied as an electronic engineer. Firstly I went to Kingston Technical, and then I did three years in electronics at the Massachusetts College of Technology. It was during semester [break] in 1967 that I came and did these things. Winston Riley asked me if I could join the group; he saw me first sing when I was at Kingston Technical. The group was Winston Riley, Junior Menz, and myself, just the three of us. It took me about three months before we record 'You Don't Care'. Directly it went to number one."

Kelly returned to the States to continue his studies and was therefore not available to record further, but later re-joined the group for other recordings with Duke Reid. "Junior Menz became leader of 'My Girl' and 'Queen Majesty' because I left back for college. Junior Menz left, and then I end up with Winston Riley and Bruce Ruffin; they call him Bruce Ruffin [after American soul star David Ruffin], but I know him as Bruce Downer. We did 'Day Oh' and 'Run Come Celebrate', which was the Festival song." When

Kelly broke away shortly afterward to pursue a solo career, a modified Techniques remained aligned to Treasure Isle. Bruce Ruffin would later enjoy solo popularity in Britain.

○

As rock steady continued to rise, other less prominent producers, including Derrick Harriott, enjoyed considerable hits. After acquiring his first record shop in 1966, Harriott's biggest production successes came with Rudy Mills's 'A Long Story' and Keith & Tex's 'Stop That Train' and 'Tonight'. A later hit version of The Temptations' 'Don't Look Back' was recorded at the tail end of rock steady, but Keith Rowe's subsequent immigration to New York and Texas Dixon's to Canada cut short the duo's rise.[9]

Ever in tune with the sounds of black America, Harriott also found success with rock steady numbers that drew from soul and jazz. His sensitive rendering of 'The Loser', arranged by bassist Boris Gardiner and boosted by thrilling drum rolls from Joe Isaacs, had an uncommon piano solo that made it all the more irresistible, probably inspired by Bob Haymes' standard, 'That's All'. "The piano man, Lloyd Delprat, was like a concert pianist," Harriott emphasises. "He used to play with Boris's band, but he had that concert touch."

Other hits came with material written by Junior 'Soul' Murvin, including the sensual 'Solomon'. "That time you had things like 'Baby Be True', The Heptones, 'Penny For Your Song', The Federals, and my 'Solomon'. 'Solomon' was going for number one like a non-stop train, but Toots went in jail for a little while and was just coming out with this '54–46', which went straight to number one."

I asked Toots if it was true that, as has often been reported, he was busted for ganja in 1967. "I didn't," he insists. "Not for ganja. I get arrested because people wish me bad. I was just bailing a friend who got arrested, and I get arrested for nothing, because it was planned. That's why I sing about it." Is it true, I wondered, that '54–46' was his actual number while in jail? "No, I just make it up." Was the rhythm of this song borrowed from Marcia Griffiths's Coxsone-produced 'Feel Like Jumping', or vice versa? "They come after me. A lot of people in Jamaica copy my rhythm – and all over the world."

Although Duke Reid's stable ultimately overshadowed Coxsone's in rock steady, Studio One had formidable hits by popular artists including Marcia Griffiths, Ken Boothe, The Gaylads, and The Heptones. Griffiths says she started singing professionally "at the age of 13, in 1964". Her ghetto

100

upbringing was financially poor but spiritually rich. "I was born and raised in western Kingston. We were a family full of love and godliness. My father was a carpenter: he made furniture. We had sweet parents: even when we didn't have food to eat, we had love – love was always on our table. I usually sing on the choir at Saint John's Presbyterian Church and participate in concerts at school. Philip James of The Blues Busters was the boyfriend of my friend; she lived next door to us, and he heard me singing one night and was overwhelmed. I was 12, still in school, and he was just knocked out, said he travelled all over the States and he's never heard anybody like me. There was a show planning at the Carib Theatre, Easter Monday morning, with Byron Lee & The Dragonaires; Blues Busters were appearing and he insisted that I appear on the show. I did Carla Thomas's 'No Time To Lose', and I can honestly say that I brought the house down. Ronnie Nasrallah, the manager for Byron Lee and The Blues Busters, he immediately offered to manage me and I went on TV and did two Nancy Wilson songs. From that time, I guess it was green light all the way. Then another friend who worked at RJR, Linford Anderson, took me to Studio One; I didn't even do an audition, because they had already heard that I had performed at the Carib Theatre. Studio One is like Jamaica's Motown: that's where all the great artists pass through, where we all graduate. That's where I do my first recording, 'Wall Of Love', in 1964. I was accompanied by my father, 'cos I'm still under-age."

Griffiths says Coxsone wanted her to form a male-female duo, but it was not until Bob Andy began writing and arranging her material that her career took off. "When Mr Dodd found me, he coupled me with almost every male singer, seeking a hit. Bob Marley and myself did a love song, 'Oh My Darling', Bob Andy and myself did 'Really Together', and the late Free-I, Jeff Dixon, we did 'Words', a cover version of The Bee Gees. I did a duet with Tony Gregory, 'You're Mine', and one with another brother named Owen Boyce ['Don't Cry Baby']. So I did five duets with five different male singers, and then Bob Andy started writing songs for me: I did 'Feel Like Jumping', 'Melody Life', 'Mark My Word', 'Tell Me Now'."

Andy's sensitive vocal arrangements and visually oriented lyrics drew the best from Griffiths's vocal capabilities. She says their relationship was blessed by divine properties. "Bob Andy and myself had an intimate relationship, and I can honestly say that all of this was ordained by the Most High God, 'cos Bob Andy was like a father figure. He was like a big brother – he was my guide, my everything. I met him at a rehearsal at Rockfort with The Paragons. After I went to Studio One, we hook up back, and it wasn't

101

an accident, it was ordained, because he was a man with a lot of experience and wisdom and knowledge, and he was like a guide for me, because I was just a young girl then. For a young female singer in a male-dominated business with men surrounding you, God knows what could have happened, so I think God placed him there. He guided me through all the years, writing songs for me."

The abstract vocalising of 'Feel Like Jumping' and romantic optimism of 'Melody Life' gave Dodd two of his biggest rock steady hits. Both are musically complex, with strong horn arrangements featuring Lester Sterling, Vin Gordon and trumpeter Bobby Ellis. Griffiths says Jackie Mittoo, who also provided backing vocals, determined the song's overall shape.

While Duke Reid had his greatest rock steady successes with vocal groups, Dodd tended to fare better with solo artists. The most successful Studio One rock steady vocal groups were The Gaylads, who were mainstays of the era, and The Heptones, who appeared at the tail end.

The core of The Gaylads was inspired songwriter Harris 'B.B.' Seaton and his talented singing partner, Winston Delano Stewart. They first sang together in The Rhythm Aces, a Vineyard Town harmony quartet led by Boris Gardiner. Seaton began recording solo for Coxsone in 1959, linking back with Stewart in 1962. They joined with Maurice Roberts to form The Gaylads, but disbanded when they failed to produce a hit during the first wave of ska. Seaton passed through The Carousels on the North Coast and fronted The Astronauts in 1964–65, before The Gaylads finally re-formed and broke through with Seaton's 'Lady In The Red Dress'.

"One night I was visiting a friend who live close to a cemetery," Seaton explains, in his busy Northwest London office. "While waiting for him, I sat on a tombstone and this melody came to me, the lyrics and everything. The next day, I saw Winston and Maurice, and we rehearse it and went back to Coxsone." The near-American feel of 'Lady In The Red Dress' was hugely successful, and in addition to subsequent hits 'No Good Girl', 'Peculiar Man', and 'Love Me With All Your Heart', on which the group played their own instruments, Seaton was also an important member of Coxsone's team, co-writing hit material for others and supervising auditions. "We had about 12 hits in that period, and the Gaylads period was when I used to audition artists for Coxsone. I used to get three different salaries from Coxsone every week: being a backing singer, being an A&R man, and just being a friend." He recalls with fondness auditioning "some incredible guys like The Heptones, Melodians, Lloyd Parks, who came as The Termites, and Fred Locks, who used to sing in a group called The Bassies".

The group subsequently switched allegiance to Leslie Kong, for whom they cut more successful material. "We did 'There's A Fire' – it was number one in Jamaica for a good while. We did 'My Love' and an album called *Fire And Rain*." Seaton also co-wrote some of Ken Boothe's biggest hits for Kong, including the self-determined 'Freedom Street'.

The Gaylads later enjoyed some of their biggest hits as part of Sonia Pottinger's growing stable, but internal friction saw Delano Stewart leave the group in March 1968 to cut a series of strong solo sides, before ultimately immigrating to America. "We went to Pottinger and did 'Hard To Confess' and 'ABC Rock Steady', and I wrote some serious songs for artists in that period, like 'Say You' and 'Lady With The Starlight' by Ken Boothe. Delano left the group and then went to the States; it was Maurice and myself alone that did 'ABC Rock Steady'."

Seaton says the void left by Stewart's departure was never filled satisfactorily. Although he continued to lead The Gaylads into the early reggae period, Seaton went solo in the early 70s. "We brought in Kesto Oakley, who did a song with us called 'Little Girl'. He wasn't totally committed, so we brought in Ricky Grant, a dreadlocks who used to hang around Franklyn Town with all of us; he used to do electrician work, and he sang on 'Soul Sister' that we did at Beverley's.[10] He went away too, and then I got disillusioned with the whole thing because the sound wasn't there any more. Delano Stewart, he's a pedigree. So that's when I went on my own."

Though The Gaylads' departure from Studio One spelt a notable loss, The Heptones brought considerable gains from the success of the suggestive 'Fattie Fattie'. Leroy Sibbles, Barry Llewellyn, and Earl Morgan were blessed with unrivalled harmonic abilities, and although Sibbles led the group, he was the last to join it. "Heptones is not a one-man thing, Heptones is a three-man thing," says Earl Morgan. "From when we get together, the three of we is like magic and that's what make we domineer the 60s and 70s."

Morgan is seated on the bonnet of a dilapidated Jaguar at his home in Duhaney Park as he recounts The Heptones' formative days. "The group really started about 1958, but we never start recording until about the end of '66. A whole heap of people always did in there, man come and go. Glen Adams was part of the group at one time."

Morgan says that the group came together as teenagers on a street corner in western Kingston. "I was born in 1945 at 12d Benbow Street in Jones Town, and I go by Trench Town when I was about four year old. Early on, I was listening to people on the Rediffusion, and in the evening everyone just go 'pon the corner and hang out and talk. You don't see that nowadays, because in the evening time everybody look 'pon the television. Barry grow up in my area, so me and Barry always rehearse as a duet, and people come and join up. One time Leroy have a group over Newland Town, [near] Trench Town, with a girl named Claire and a brother named Winston, so me and Barry go there one day for a street contest and we dethrone them. It's from then on Leroy join our group."

Sidney 'Luddy' Crooks of The Pioneers arranged for The Heptones to audition for Ken Lack in 1966. "Luddy Pioneers was in Trench Town, he did have a band down Crooks Street. We was rehearsing one evening and he say we must come down tomorrow evening. Them always had this likkle band going round the island, do likkle shows and t'ing. We go down there and them say Ken Lack going to have a session Monday coming. From that session, Ken Lack released 'Gun Man Coming To Town'. It was going good on the charts, until Delroy Wilson come with [a cover of The Tams'] 'Dancing Mood'."

"That was the first time we heard ourselves on the Reddifusion, the only radio we had back then. That got our interest really tight on music and I started writing like hell," says Leroy Sibbles, swinging in a hammock at his uptown Kingston home. Sibbles exudes a determined confidence that borders on arrogance, making it easy to picture him emerging as leader in The Heptones' early days. "Barry was doing mechanics and Earl were doing some *Star* newspaper selling," he continues, "so when we got together at night I would always be introducing new songs to them. I was writing like hell, because I had so much inspiration."

Moving on from Caltone, the group signed a five-year contract at Studio One. "We check Beverleys, Duke Reid, until we decided to check Coxsone, when all those people like The Wailers, most of them was leaving," says Morgan. "We go there one Sunday, and Ken Boothe and B.B. Seaton take audition of 'A Change Is Going To Come', 'Fattie Fattie'. and 'Nobody Knows'. 'Nobody Knows' and 'A Change Is Going To Come', people like it in the dancehall, but the big break come when they release 'Fattie Fattie'. From when they release, everybody need it. They ban it on the radio, but it was a number-one seller."

'Fattie Fattie' was built on a tremulous bass line from Wallin Cameron of The Soul Vendors; a sparse guitar riff from Hux Brown, who had been playing at Studio One for several years, accentuated the incorrigible rhythm.[11] The continued popularity of 'Fattie Fattie' sparked several instrumental re-cuts, as would many other Heptones Studio One creations. The first, Jackie Mittoo's 'Ram Jam', was almost as popular as the original.

"It's the 'Fattie Fattie' rhythm that really start Jackie Mittoo as a solo artist," says Morgan, who names Mittoo as the key figure at Studio One. "When you're there in Trench Town and you hear all these artists over the Reddifusion, like Bob Andy, The Wailers, Toots & The Maytals, then you're at the studio and you see them in person, it was wild. But the icon of all of the musicians who ever go through Coxsone for me is Jackie Mittoo, because he sing, him play organ, him do everything."

The Heptones ultimately recorded the most influential hits in rock steady, and since then people have returned to the rhythms behind their voices time and time again. Songs like 'Love Won't Come Easy', 'Heptones Gonna Fight', and the life-affirming 'Party Time' have become part of the canon of Jamaican pop – surrogate folk songs perpetually recycled over generations. Though Sibbles says 'Party Time' was inspired by "some song that I heard the Wailers do", songs like 'Heptones Gonna Fight' and 'Equal Rights' came from observing the injustices suffered by black people in America. "I was always involved in the black movement and in black history on a whole, so I was reading a lot of magazines about the way blacks were being treated down South. I even tore out pictures from articles and had them in my little room, of black people being tarred and feathered and hung on trees. That's where the lyrics 'Don't hang him on a tree / Every man have an equal right to live and be free / No matter what colour, class, or race he may be' came from: I was bearing my pain and anger from those things."

This shift in subject matter was one of the many changes that came to the fore once rock steady began to wane. The reggae style that followed may have begun as another sound to fit a dance pattern, but socially conscious and politically aware lyrics would increasingly become reggae's focus. As with the shift from ska to rock steady, the most immediate differences involved particular instrumentation and melodic arrangement, with the bass retaining its crucial role.

4
FEEL THE RHYTHM
Ribald early reggae

"Ska music, that's where we start. We feel the energy and we start to ska, then we feel the energy change and we start to rock steady, then the energy change again ... we say that we want reggae." – LEE PERRY[1]

"Reggae music was taken from Poco music and calypso music. Poco was the African man's religion – we never know the European way of life. Their music was these carnival types of thing, and we bring the two in one to establish ourselves with the rest of the world." – YABBY YOU

As with ska and rock steady, the precise birth of reggae is greatly contested. While some name Larry & Alvin's Studio One single 'Nanny Goat' as the first example of the new genre, others say it was The Beltones' 'No More Heartaches', produced by former insurance salesman Harry Johnson. On 'Nanny Goat', Boris Gardiner's tight bass patterns and added rest stops simply made the strolling of rock steady seem passé; a choppy organ break and intricate cymbal patters also help to move the rhythm forward. Though slower and more in tune with traditional rock steady choral and horn arrangements, 'No More Heartaches' had a pronounced organ rhythm that would come to dominate the reggae form.

Many observers feel that reggae did not arrive properly until late 1968, when a handful of smaller producers brought the new sound forward. Though 'Nanny Goat' may have been the first to show that rock steady was on the wane, the efforts of the upcoming 'ghetto promoters' really brought in the reggae sound with full force. Among the most notable were Lee 'Scratch' Perry, Clancy Eccles, Bunny Lee, and Linford Anderson, as well as Joe Gibbs, Derrick Harriott, Alvin 'G.G.' Ranglin, and Winston 'Niney' Holness, close associates who formed shifting allegiances and rivalries, in the process steering the music in a new direction. At Studio One, further melodic and technical developments also helped shape the new style.

Like ska and rock steady, reggae had a dance that came with it, most famously celebrated on The Maytals' 'Do The Reggay', often cited as the first record to name the genre. Although Toots claims to be "the inventor for the word reggae, the one who say our music called reggae", Bunny Lee, Clancy Eccles, Niney, and others say the name is derived from 'streggae', a derogatory term connoting a woman of low morals, just as 'rock'n'roll' is said to stem from black American slang for the sexual act. "There's a lot of things me do inna this business," Lee says. "All reggae, our name that again. It was streggae, and the radio station wouldn't play streggae, so we change it to reggae."

The first tune to use the name reggae, according to Bunny, was one recorded by his brother, Don Tony Lee. "Don used to work at WIRL records and he did radio business; him and [announcer] Jeff Barnes grow up together. Him do the first reggae song, 'Come Do The Reggae Now' [aka 'It's Reggae Time']."

Regardless of who was the first to name the new style, the faster, dance-oriented sound was typically built around a rhythmic, two-chord organ shuffle that almost seemed to echo the word 'reggae' in sound. "The reggae thing that time have some mad shuffle," Lee continues. "The reggae is the organ, so when man talk 'bout reggae, they don't even know how it come in."

Relaxing at his suburban home in Patrick City, the man born Edward O'Sullivan Lee has a bottle of beer clenched in each fist as he recounts how he entered the record business in the early 60s. "I was born in Kingston in 1941 – it's Greenwich Town now, but it was Greenwich Farm then. My father was a shoemaker and my mother was an ordinary housewife. Nine children follow me, but only six of us survive. After I leave school, I used to do electrical work, then I went into the parts department at United Motors, then I go to Kingston Industrial Garage. From there, I been in the music business. I used to go round with Derrick Morgan, Max Romeo, Laurel Aitken, Jackie Edwards, Owen Gray, and Slim Smith."[2]

Lee was first famed as an able dancer of the Mashed Potato. He soon built strong contacts in the industry and was known to insist with some force that certain music was regularly played. "I used to go 'round Duke Reid a lot, and sometimes up by Coxsone, used to plug records for them and Leslie Kong on *Teenage Dance Party* at the radio station. Sometimes Prince Buster and myself used to be very close too. Then when Roy Shirley come around, Roy Shirley bring Joe Gibbs to me."

Lee was instrumental in ensuring the success of 'Hold Them', but spent so much time promoting records that he was fired from his garage job in

1967. Given free studio time by Duke Reid, Lee cut his first session with Lynn Taitt & The Jets, hitting with Roy Shirley's surreal 'Music Field' and Lloyd & The Groovers' 'Do It To Me Baby'. He then went to work for WIRL, replacing Lee Perry as in-house producer. "Them fire Scratch because Scratch never make no hit, and it's Scratch cause himself to fire. I doing a session with Slim Smith and Scratch was the producer for WIRL at the time, but he didn't know Mr Rae did give me permission to run the session, and Scratch tell the musicians the session shouldn't go on. When them stop, I carry them up to the office and Mr Rae pay them, and so Scratch lose him work. The tune come out and was a big hit: 'Let Me Go Girl' with Slim Smith & The Uniques."

Perry then went to work for Joe Gibbs, just as Errol Dunkley was voicing his second hit, 'Please Stop Your Lying'. He remained with Gibbs for several months, cutting his own witty vocal sides, often with startling sound effects, and arranging hits by groups like The Versatiles, The Overtakers, and The Pioneers. Perry also arranged for Gibbs to handle Stranger Cole and Gladdy Anderson's self-produced 'Just Like A River', a sizeable post-rock steady hit, but eventually left the partnership after disputes over pay, his shoes temporarily filled by Niney. Perry then returned to WIRL and forged an alliance with engineer Linford Anderson – aka Andy Capp – then just entering the production field himself.

Anderson now lives in New York, where he is a sound engineer for the United Nations. When asked how he came to work in music production, he responds: "That's something I can't figure out myself. All I know is we used to have a record player and a little radio attached to it, so I used to imitate things I hear on the radio, play parties with one turntable. From there I was an accountant, and I went to RJR as a log keeper in 1959. They took me back later as a trainee engineer. I worked there for a couple of years, and then Mr Nasrallah asked me if I wanted a job at West Indies Records – Nasrallah took it over and built a new studio." Anderson learned his mixing craft from WIRL's resident engineer. "Graeme Goodall was the engineer when they opened, he's the one that taught me most of what I know. It was only a little console they had then, a portable Ampex two-track."

Anderson says he founded the Upset label in conjunction with Lee Perry and Barrington Lambert, WIRL's trainee engineer, in 1967, working at first with female harmony trio The Gaylets, featuring a young Judy Mowatt. Though such early material failed to gain favour, some later Upset creations truly upset the predominant beat.

Around the same time, Perry was also collaborating with Clancy Eccles, who had recently returned to recording after concentrating on concert promotion.[3] When Eccles moved into record production he retained Perry in an A&R capacity, and converted part of his tailoring premises at 121a Orange Street to handle record sales. Eccles cut the rock steady love song 'What Will Your Mama Say' in conjunction with Perry, using Lynn Taitt's band at WIRL, followed by 'Darling Don't Do That'. The songs from their partnership that most impacted were Monty Morris's 'Say What You're Saying' and Eccles's 'Feel The Rhythm'. Ernest Ranglin, who played guitar and provided arrangements on the session at Treasure Isle that produced both tunes, names these as the first reggae records. Both have a bouncing pace, with 'Feel The Rhythm' in particular pointing to the style that would soon storm in.

Perry's 'People Funny Boy', recorded at WIRL with Eccles's assistance and released on the Upset label, was another monumental record. "I helped Scratch with 'People Funny Boy'," Eccles noted. "I was the man who set the music, and I do the ghost vocal in the studio while Scratch was the man on the mixing desk. I set the rhythm for it at West Indies, late '68."

The highly charged intensity of 'People Funny Boy' was Perry's attempt to capture the rhythm of a Pukumina church service that he and Linford Anderson had stumbled upon the night before. With vocals that lashed out against former employer Joe Gibbs, and a melody that parodied The Pioneers' 'Longshot', one of Gibbs's biggest production successes, Scratch used the cries of a wailing baby, lifted from a sound effects record, to drive home the message of an underpaid man's frustrations. The song's popularity launched Perry as an independent producer, enabling him to form the Upsetter label and commandeer Prince Buster's former record shop at 36 Charles Street. It also sparked replies from The Pioneers and Joe Gibbs, including 'People Grudgeful' and 'Pan Yu Machete'.

The Pioneers, then the duo of Sidney Crooks and Jackie Robinson, gave Gibbs some of his biggest hits in the days when reggae was first blossoming. They would subsequently score bigger hits for Leslie Kong and then emigrate, but after nearly 30 years in Britain, Crooks returned to Kingston in 1996 to become in-house arranger at Joe Gibbs's studio. He later settled permanently in Brazil. Crooks says he came to Trench Town from the countryside at the age of 17, met future session player Earl 'Bagga' Walker, and started singing with him at a neighbourhood roundabout. At Crooks Street in Jones Town, his group gradually took shape: various members passed through what was initially called The Spectaculars and later The Counts. The first version of The Pioneers to enter a recording studio

109

consisted of Crooks, his brother Derrick (aka Joe) and Winston Hewitt. Though self-produced, the material was issued on Ken Lack's Caltone label. "I get a little money from my mom, so we rented Duke Reid's studio with a band called Al & The Vibrators and made a song called 'Good Nannie'. We funded it ourselves cause we couldn't get recorded. We go to Duke Reid, we go to Coxsone, they push their head out and say: 'Time finish, you have to come back again and you have to practise hard.' The song started to get one and two little plays on the radio, but it's nothing to speak about. We did [Johnnie Morisette's] 'Never Come Running Back', an American song done over, and that one started showing a little bit better. After that, I started keeping stage shows around the country."[4]

Crooks says things began falling into place after he linked with Joe Gibbs and reformed The Pioneers with Jackie Robinson, a stranger in the right place at the right time. "Winston Hewitt went to Canada and my brother went to work with the Alcoa bauxite company, so I was left alone. I met Joe Gibbs, bumped into him on Beeston Street, and I started working for him, carrying out records. I tell him that I want to make a record, so we went to WIRL one night with Hux Brown, Jackie Jackson, Gladstone Anderson, Winston Wright – the top of the line – and we made a song called 'Give Me Little Loving'. Outside the studio I saw a boy, so I said: 'Me want you to sing a harmony.' Jackie Robinson then became the lead singer of The Pioneers, and me and him started singing for Joe Gibbs: 'Longshot', 'Jackpot', 'Catch The Beat'."

On some of these songs the group's humour really shines. 'Longshot', their biggest hit for Gibbs, was about a losing racehorse that left a punter broke when it failed to break the tape at the finishing post; 'Pan Yu Machete', a retaliatory swipe at Lee Perry, mocked the producer with a yapping puppy atop a slurring violin. These and the celebratory 'Catch The Beat' all helped to move Jamaican music into the reggae dimension.

Bunny Lee, who helped consolidate the reggae beat in late 1968, says his link with the British Pama label indirectly led to the new sound's emergence. The Palmer brothers – three Jamaican immigrants who owned rental properties in Northwest London – established Pama in 1967 as competition to Island, the main UK issuer of Jamaican product after Chris Blackwell moved the company to London in 1962. Other concerns such as Sonny Roberts's Planetone, Emil Shalit's Melodisc, and Rita and Benny Izons's R&B/Ska Beat were also issuing Jamaican music. One of Island's subsidiary labels, Trojan, was established in 1967 to handle Duke Reid's product; the following year, Lee Gopthal, a Jamaican of Indian descent and Island's initial landlord, relaunched Trojan to handle reggae from any producer.

Gopthal was also the man behind the Muzik City chain of London record shops, and had founded the B&C distribution company. Though Pama initially beat Island in terms of reggae popularity, Trojan would shortly emerge as the most prominent reggae label in Britain.

Harry Palmer was initially in charge of Pama's record production. At his real estate office in Mandeville, I note a close resemblance to his younger brother Carl, longstanding head of the massive Jet Star record label and distribution company in London; both have Semitic features derived from their Jewish grandmother. Harry says the family lived in Thompson Town, Clarendon, where his father was a Baptist deacon and Justice of the Peace with links to PNP founder Norman Manley. Harry's older brother Jeff left Jamaica for London in the mid 50s, Harry and Carl following a few years later. "Young people always looking for adventure, and underdeveloped Jamaica didn't offer a lot of adventure. Jeffrey went in '55 to Willesden Polytechnic, where he did engineering."

When Harry arrived in Willesden, he got a menial factory job, packing parcels, and eventually qualified in business administration; Carl came in the early 60s and studied engineering. Though Harry worked chiefly in insurance and Carl was later concerned with real estate, the brothers were involved in the music business as early as 1962. "We opened our first record shop, Happy Sounds, at 827 Harrow Road, with a partner from the insurance business, but he was an electrician originally, so we stocked electrical fittings as well as records. By then Jeff had opened Club 31, at 31 Harrow Road; it was a basement club, but it was very popular. All the great Tamla-Motown artists used to appear there: Stevie Wonder, The Jackson Five, Diana Ross, Martha & The Vandellas." In 1968 Jeff opened the larger London Apollo Club on Willesden High Road, which he still controls today.

Harry says Happy Sounds stocked rock and pop, and later carried Jamaican music, selling a phenomenal quantity of 'My Boy Lollipop'. "We sold some four thousand copies of 'My Boy Lollipop' in that little shop. We put a speaker outside, and it was on a bus route, so people would come from all over."

Around 1966, a fire destroyed Happy Sounds. Jeff continued running his night club, while Harry and Carl set up an estate agency across the road from their former record shop. The brothers also began managing local bands, which led to a few tentative productions issued by Island in 1967; Harry says the first was Joyce Bond's 'Do The Teasy', backed by a band of young Jamaicans based in Kensal Rise called The Shadrocks, featuring singer Tim Chandell.

Although the Palmers thought Bond had commercial potential, major labels showed no interest. "We used to go to Phillips and Pye simply because Chris Blackwell went to them. They did Steve Winwood and The Spencer Davis Group, so we thought we could get in. We started thinking about putting it out ourselves, but then Island agreed to put it out."

Island issued Bond's 'Tell Me What It's All About', written by Jackie Edwards, and some Shadrocks material such as 'Go Go Special', but nothing hit. Then Harry Palmer travelled to Jamaica in search of undiscovered talent, the resultant licensing deals leading to the foundation of Pama Records. "By this time we had fallen out with Joyce Bond, and I had come down to find a replacement female singer. I stayed in Kingston for two weeks, put an ad in the paper for female singers, and I went back to London with three mailbags full of applications." He also attracted the attention of Jamaica's leading record producers: "Coxsone Dodd, Bunny Lee, Scratch, everybody. We got this record by Clancy Eccles, 'What Will Your Mama Say', went back with it and nobody wanted to put it out, so we formed Pama Records and that was our first tune. We had to pay him a decent advance, maybe a couple of thousand pounds, which was a lot of money then. And we were new into the business, so he got a large percentage – larger than what we learned to pay later on."

Palmer also licensed material from Alton Ellis and brought an unknown singer called Beverley Simmons to London to record. "When we took her back to London, Otis Redding died, so we decided to make a tribute album. Same recording session we made an instrumental called 'The Champ', based on a US soul thing [Lowell Fulsom's 'Tramp', covered by Redding]. Although we put out the album, *Tribute To Otis Redding*, the instrumental just took off. Atlantic licensed it and it was a hit in America – that was the first release on Cotillion." Harry also reveals that 'The Champ', credited to The Mohawks on release in 1968, was played by "all white guys, session people", with Alan Hawkshaw on organ.

Pama Records was formed in a branch of their estate agency in Peterborough Road, Harrow, but moved shortly afterward to a permanent base at 17 Craven Park Road, Harlesden, a larger building with space for proper offices and distribution stock. Harry says their association with Bunny Lee placed Pama above the competition. "Christmas '68 was really when it started to happen. Both Island and Trojan conceded that we had the Christmas – we had all the big things through Bunny Lee. In Harrow I had a phone call from Bunny Lee, but he was dealing with Island: he thought he wasn't getting such a good deal, so he wanted a little switch. He had tapes of his own, but we didn't want those, because they were already offered to Island. He asked us to come and see him and played us 'Hold You Jack' by Derrick Morgan, but we knew [Island A&R man] David Betteridge and Blackwell and everybody, so we weren't about to take what they had. We gave him £2,400 to come down and make records, and he did extremely well, but Bunny also wanted to outdo Clancy, because he realised that Clancy had a good deal, so he wanted to be in on it as well. Matter of fact, when he went back to Jamaica, I think there was some scuffling between them."

Lee remembers things differently, claiming his link with the company was forged after a dispute arose about an album by London-based singer Dandy Livingstone [aka Robert Livingstone Thompson], then enjoying a big hit with the anti-rude boy song 'Rudy A Message To You'. "I go to England the first time in February 1968, and I used to deal with Island. Dandy Livingstone used to work for Rita Izons in Stamford Hill, she used to pay him £20 a week as a producer. Me and Dandy meet and we turn good friends. I take Dandy 'round ah Jackie Edwards's house and them start to be good brethren. Pama give Dandy some money to make an LP, but Dandy and me go to Island and me introduce him to Dave Betteridge. Dandy say him have an LP coming named *Dandy Returns*, so Dave Betteridge stay 'pon the phone and sell about 25,000 right there and then, 'cos Dandy said him would give it to them. When the three Pama brothers find me over my yard in the East End, they start to talk about the Dandy thing. Them say they don't really want to lock up Dandy for we all are black men ... them say Harry Palmer did come to Jamaica and give Clancy and Alton money, and it didn't work out neither. Beverley Simmons was at the Sheraton and him carry her up and do a whole LP with some Otis Redding tunes, but nothing didn't come of it. Them say them down 'pon them face and them no have no money, but he would give me three hundred pounds cash, that's all them can afford. I say: 'I will give you some tune, we can work together.' I say we have to make a label with a black hand and a white hand shake 'cross a mountain named Unity. I go back to Jamaica and Pama and Bunny Lee now amalgamated."

Unity was the first of several Pama subsidiaries created to specifically showcase the efforts of one producer. A session Lee ran in October 1968 resulted in several early reggae hits for the label, the most noteworthy of which were 'Bangarang' by Stranger Cole & Lester Sterling and 'Everybody Needs Love' by Slim Smith. "'Bangarang' is the first reggae record make in Jamaica," insists Cole. "I was passing by Treasure Isle one day and I was told that Bunny Lee is making records, so I went up to see him because he's a

113

good friend of mine, we go to Denham Town School together. He said: 'I have a song here called 'Bongo Chant' [by Kenny Graham's Afro Cubists]. I would love to put some words to it, could you come up with some words?' I think for five minutes and come up with 'Muma no want bangarang', and we went in the studio, and it was a hit instantly. You could say that the melody belongs to somebody else, and the words belong to me."

Lee agrees this was the first reggae song, naming the shuffling organ as its defining element. Slim Smith's 'Everybody Needs Love', inspired by Mary Wells/Gladys Knight's Motown soul hit, was also marked by a livid organ shuffle, played on both tunes by Glen Adams, then chiefly known as an auditions assistant and arranger at Treasure Isle; Adams began as a singer and came to play organ on the session almost accidentally. "It all started from my mother, she was a dancer and a singer. She put on a show around 1957; it was the Jiving Juniors with Derrick Harriott, so I saw them young men singing and it motivate me. I form a group when I was around 12 with some friends and I went to Palace Theatre where I auditioned for Vere Johns' Opportunity Hour. They didn't pick our song that time, so I went back by myself and I got selected."

Adams suffered from the degenerative muscle disease Polymiositis for many years, which contributed to his death from kidney failure, following a stroke, in 2010, when he was 65. I met him some years earlier in his unofficial office: the local Dunkin' Donuts in his corner of New York's Flatbush. Despite a mentally disturbed woman at the table behind yelling at the top of her lungs about God's punishments, Adams readily dug deep into memories. "I usually do cabaret, places like Club Havana, Bungalow, Penguin Club. I used to do the show circuit alongside The Blues Busters and The Indian Rubber Boy. Mr Dodd had a talent show and during the rehearsal he heard this original song, 'Wonder Thirst', and wanted to record it; it's a love lyric, written by my sister. I did that song for Mr Dodd. It never released, but I was popularly known for that song, because I got the dub and I gave it to a popular sound system selector, Lord Comic. I just do one song for Studio One, but I was always a fan of Mr Dodd, and I have maximum respect for him for giving me the opportunity. Even until this day, Mr Dodd will remain my best friend."

Through his friendship with Ken Boothe, Adams was present at the recording of Stranger Cole's 'Uno Dos Tres', sowing the seeds of a long association with Duke Reid. "Me and Ken Boothe started practising and we did a couple of songs with Stranger Cole – some harmonies on 'Uno Dos Tres'. Me and Ken used to sing as Ken & Glen. We came second in the first

Festival Song Competition in Ward Theatre with 'I Remember' [in 1966]."

Glen then went to work in tailoring, but still passed through The Heptones and joined The Pioneers in time for some of their earliest recordings. "Heptones was myself, Joseph Forrester, Jackson Jones, Earl Morgan, and Barry Llewelyn; Jackson was the guitarist. Then we split up the group, and I go with The Pioneers; that time Winston Hewitt went to Canada, and I fill in for him about a year or so. I did 'Shake It Up', 'Good Nannie', and a couple more for Joe Gibbs and Ken Lack. Anywhere we travel, The Heptones would travel too. After Pioneers, I took Heptones to Studio One. Ken Boothe was there, he had 'The Train Is Coming', and Jackie Mittoo was there, who I knew; I knew most of the guys because my sister Yvonne was a popular singer.[5] I have a nice sister, so naturally the guys want to be my friend!"

Glen began playing piano on rehearsals for Duke Reid in the late ska era. "I usually practise down by Duke Reid – I actually rehearse and shape the song 'Woman A Come' with Marguerita. I selected artists for Mr Reid like Joe White, and [Reid] is the one who gave me the incentive to play. After The Pioneers, I was doing a lot of stuff for Bunny Lee, singing 'Silent Lover', a song named 'She' [aka 'I'm Shocking, I'm Electric', recorded at Lee's inaugural session], 'Taking Over Orange Street', 'Hold Down Miss Winey'. I sang harmony with The Uniques with Slim Smith on 'Hooray' and 'Give Me A Love'."

Gladdy's band had refused to play on Bunny Lee's October 1968 session because they were still owed money from a previous session, so Duke sent Adams to play piano. "Bunny Lee didn't know I play. I tried to play the piano on 'Bangarang' but it didn't work out, so Lester Sterling asked us to switch, make Lester Sterling play the piano and let me play the organ. I'd never played the organ before." On the same session, Lloyd Charmers gave Glen some pointers for the organ chops he supplied on 'Everybody Needs Love', with Charmers himself providing the exciting lead lines. After the immediate and far-reaching success of 'Bangarang' and 'Everybody Needs Love', Adams stuck to the organ.

Adams's singing partner Alva Lewis also made his recording debut as a guitarist at this session. Known as Reggie Carter, due to his resemblance to a local comedian, Lewis was born in Manchester in 1949. Sitting in the waiting room at Tuff Gong studio, Lewis nowadays looks decidedly worse for wear. He had a long period of alcohol dependency and walks with a limp; though still occasionally recording, he is often out of work. Like many of his peers, Lewis came into music in the Greenwich Farm community. "When I was 16 I left Manchester, come to Kingston and stayed with my brother in West Avenue, Greenwich Farm. They wanted me to get educated, send me to college, but something is inside of me: me want to play music. My bigger brother was in America and he send a semi-acoustic Gibson, an electric Fender guitar and a small amplifier. You have a bar downstairs, but through I no hear the guitar so much, my guitar never properly tuned. Derrick Morgan was living over by Bunny Lee, and The Melodians, they come one Sunday and Derrick asked one of The Melodians to tune my guitar. Them play the guitar and me observe them. Bunny Lee and Slim Smith carry me down to Duke Reid's studio one day and the first tunes me lick, 'Everybody Needs Love' and 'Bangarang', the songs was two number ones. The backing band was Reggie, Family Man, Carly, Glen Adams, and Lloyd Charmers play the solo with the organ."

It was this backing band – usually without Lloyd Charmers, and often with lead guitarist Ronny Bop – that became one of the crucial studio combos that developed the reggae sound, first as the Bunny Lee All Stars, later as The Upsetters, and ultimately as backing to The Wailers. An earlier version had been established on the live scene as The Hippy Boys, which Family Man and Carly joined before this pivotal session for Bunny Lee.

Aston 'Family Man' Barrett had already played on hits for The Uniques. His recording debut adapted two American hits for one single, Buffalo Springfield's anti-Vietnam War anthem 'For What It's Worth' (as 'Watch This Sound') and The Manhattans' 'I'm The One That Love Forgot' (as 'Out Of Love'). The session was arranged by Lloyd Charmers for Winston Lowe, a smaller producer of Chinese descent whose Tramp label was based in Greenwich Farm. Jimmy Riley explains that the refrain from 'For What It's Worth' was transformed into "watch this sound" because he misunderstood the lyrics. "I was sleeping one night and I heard the phrase 'watch this sound'. I couldn't make out all the words they was saying, so I just make 'watch this sound' as the chorus. That was the first song Family Man played bass on. He was playing with a little band, and then we decided we were going to use him on the session. The drummer was Winston Grennan, Bobby Aitken on guitar, Ansel Collins on piano. We did 'Watch This Sound' and 'Out Of Love'. Both sides hit, but 'Watch This Sound' hit first."

Aston Barrett and his younger brother Carlton grew up at 26 Beeston Street, sharing a downtown Kingston yard with saxophonist Val Bennett. Nicknamed 'Family Man' (or 'Fams' for short) because of the children he fathered with different partners at an early age, Aston was an unruly teenager, sent to the Jamaica Youth Corps' Cobbla Camp for discipline.

There he led a harmony quintet which influenced his approach to bass. "I love singing," he declares in a deep, slow drawl, "so when I'm playing bass, I always imagine that I am singing. I try to play a kind of melodic bass." Barrett names Lloyd Brevett, Lloyd Spence, and Jackie Jackson as his most immediate influences, stressing that "one good artist always inspire from another".

The greater prominence of Family Man's beefy bass, which emphasised offbeat cadences through audible rest stops, would greatly elevate the emerging reggae sound. By the time of his debut session, he and Carly were playing in The Hippy Boys, a live band that emerged after the demise of The Gaylads. Web Stewart was the group's lead guitarist when the Barretts were drafted in for a regular engagement at the Baby Grand. Their lead vocalist was then Maxwell Livingston Smith, former leader of The Emotions trio and better known as Max Romeo.

In the late 80s, Max Romeo was a short-haired Buddhist living with a white woman in New York, but he later returned to Jamaica sporting dreadlocks again. He spent most of the 90s living on West Avenue in Greenwich Farm, back on the same block where Bunny Lee was based when the new sound was coming together in 1968.

Romeo smiles as he recounts his early days. "I was born in the parish of Saint Ann in Alexandria, about four miles out of Browns Town. My mother had to migrate to England in 1954; I was ten years old, so I was taken to Kingston to live with my father, but me and my father's wife couldn't get along, so I had to run away from home. After drifting around for years, trying to find myself, when I was about 17, I followed a friend to a place and saw this man looking at me. He called me over and said: 'A brown man like you, brown complexion …' Those days in Jamaica, high-complexion people were looked upon to live a certain standard, and I was suffering then: pants all torn, shirt without sleeves, shoes with hole in the sole and the heel leaning. He gave me a piece of paper and a pencil and said: 'I want you to write 20 things in life you think you would want to be.' I wrote from mechanic, electrician, painter, carpenter, pastor, singer. I gave him the paper and he said: 'I want you to narrow it down to two.' I was trying to find the easiest of them, so it came down to preacher and singer. He said: 'Now I want you to choose one of the two,' so I choose singer. He said: 'From now on, you're a singer. Don't let nobody call you anything other than a singer.'

"I left with that in my mind and then I started working with Ken Lack, taking records to the record shop. He heard me singing one day and said: 'Hey, give it a try.' The first song I did was 'A Rainbow', and it went to

117

number two on the charts. I started with two other guys singing harmony – Lloyd Shakespeare, the brother of [bassist] Robbie Shakespeare, and Kenneth Knight – and we called the group Emotions. After a little while, there was disagreements in the group. I decided to work on my own, and I met Bunny Lee then. At that time, he was working as a desk clerk at Kingston Industrial Garage. He wasn't yet really in the music business, but he used to be around Duke Reid, take the records to the radio station, see to it that they play it by any means necessary. Duke Reid gave him some studio time, and Ken Lack and myself put together some money to buy the tapes. Tommy McCook & The Supersonics played for him and he came up with a hit: Roy Shirley's 'Music Field'. That was the starting point for Bunny Lee, 'Striker'. He did 'Get On The Ball' with Roy Shirley. A set of songs was recorded then, and that launched the whole Bunny Lee era. I was around, but I wasn't actually singing because I had to find a name."

His debut hit as a solo singer – once his determined courtship of a local girl earned him the name Max Romeo – came after Lee asked him to write a rude song for the rhythm of Derrick Morgan's 'Hold You Jack', itself already laden with minor innuendo. "I started moving with Striker – that's how 'Wet Dream' come into play, the first song with Bunny Lee. He came with this idea about doing this dirty song."

When Romeo wrote something suitably suggestive, he found that Slim Smith, Roy Shirley, John Holt, and Derrick Morgan all refused to sing it, forcing Romeo to do the honours on a session at Studio One. The resultant song, issued on Unity, stayed in the UK charts a full six months despite a radio ban, and brought Romeo to Britain for live performances. It also led the Palmer brothers to open a record shop in Kingston, above music producer and goods trader H. Robinson's Caribbean Distributing company. "Bunny Lee said we should open a branch of Pama Records in Jamaica, which we did, at 118 Orange Street," notes Harry Palmer. "It lasted for a couple of years, then Bunny Lee took it over as Bunny Lee Records, because we can't manage Bunny for too long."

Before Romeo's UK performances, a booking agency called Commercial Entertainment, run by former rock musicians Bruce White and Tony Cousins (aka Anthony Bautista), brought The Ethiopians to Britain in 1968. It was the first of many tours for Jamaican artists arranged by the company, and the pair would subsequently be involved in record production and artist management.

"'Train To Skaville' went off in England, was on the chart, and Bruce White and Tony Cousins – who later becomes Rhino Records – they request me up there," Leonard Dillon recalled. "We play all over England, three months this year and two months the other year. The audiences were mixed. I worked some places in Kent and in the audience is one black I see."

Other popular Ethiopians songs surfaced on Doctor Bird, the label established by Graeme Goodall when he immigrated to Britain. "Graeme Goodall engineered 'The Whip', 'Stay Loose Mama', and 'Cool It Amigo' at West Indies with Linford Anderson. At that time, Lynn Taitt & The Jets was the star band at the studio, and I always hire the horns, like Trommy [trombonist Vin Gordon]. Doctor Bird Records was the sole distributor."

Back in Jamaica, The Ethiopians began recording with Sir J.J., the producer who drew the best of their abilities. "When I got back from the first tour, I met J.J. at his record shop at 136 Orange Street. As an artist, you walk through these places, because some nice girls used to be in them places, and you have to go nice with them and buy them lunch; when people come in to buy records, they'll introduce people to your record, so you have to be around, niceing the people. J.J. wasn't really in the business too tough, but he was a great man, my best producer. He just look upon me and say: 'Write a song about everything crash.' We went in WIRL studio and did it with Bobby Aitken's band, The Caribbeats. At that time, all essential services in Jamaica was on strike – it's between them and them governmental system where pay is concerned. My politics is Africa, Rasta, and I don't go into them political business. I beat them every time musically, that's all I can do: when I see them doing a likkle thing, I write a song about it."

'Everything Crash' commented on the growing social unrest that reflected increasing dissatisfaction with the ruling party. Jamaica had been independent for over five years, yet for the majority of its citizens, little had improved. The general strike was one of a series of widespread protests to grip the nation that year, and Dillon's song captured the public's frustrated indignation.

Melvin Reid provided harmony on 'Everything Crash', as well as on subsequent hits such as 'Hong Kong Flu' and 'Woman Capture Man'. The latter pair (and songs like 'Well Red') also had vibrant hand drumming, evidence of Dillon's longstanding awareness of his African origin and a coded signifier of his Rastafari faith. "I never leave the conga drum, as I was taught about Africa by my grandmother and grandfather. They taught me the tribe that I'm from, Ashanti, and the name of my ancient African ancestor, the first man that reach Jamaica: Quao."

119

He was drawn to the wisdom of Rastafari in the ghetto. "It's an in-born thing, but there was a place in Waterhouse called the Ethiopian Reorganization Centre, run by two elder Rastas, Nasser King and Daddy King, and that's where we really spring from. We learnt a lot from them where Ethiopia is concerned, and that's where we used to be, before I start sing as Ethiopians, but after the Jack Sparrow days."

Enjoying a strong working relationship, The Ethiopians stayed with Sir J.J. until he stopped making records. As Dillon recalled: "He's not a man who's really into a whole lot of competition and he could not take the fight. The radio stations never used to play the songs and you have to let go a lot of money. Everything becomes corrupt after a while and he just ease up out of it and start meditating on his jukeboxes – he was a jukebox agent."

Dillon noted the producer's wealthy origins but praised his business practices and personality. "His father is one of the biggest bus company magnates in Jamaica, and his brother had Johnson's drive-in restaurant and club up the top of Maxfield Avenue. He was a conscious black man, with a sensible manner, an *irie* man, cool. My best producer, and me wasn't on no contract. He say: 'You no have to sign a contract, me live up to my word, you just have to live up to yours.' That's what happened, so that's why I sticked with him so long – no producer had me that long."

Roy Shirley, who recorded for J.J. with The Uniques, offered an alternate view. "He was always a little guy in the production field. You couldn't put them man against Beverleys, Federal, Coxsone. J.J. had a lot of money and his father had some bus company before that, but the guy look so simple – he always dress like them way-out cowboy and walk that way, but him was a money guy, so he could pay his way to promote his tune on the radio."

The sad postscript to Sir J.J.'s career is that he was robbed and murdered in his Kingston home in 1972. "It's just something intending, because it's three times them shot him, and he was living with shot in him," Dillon stated gravely. "The fourth time, they shot him, and then they cut him throat."

Rival producer Rupie Edwards opened his Success record shop on Orange Street just as the reggae beat was rising up in 1968. Early one cold Sunday morning, at the record shop in East London's Ridley Road Market that he has occupied since the mid 70s, he and a young niece are gulping shots of vodka from polystyrene cups while gospel music blares at top volume. Edwards says he began his career as a singer and piano player. "I used to sing in school, started beating drums and make a few little instruments out of bamboo and pumpkin vine, anything I can blow or beat and do a sound; I had a little band from them times. From there, I went on Vere Johns' Opportunity Knocks. After I left school at 15, I started training as a mechanic. I started recording in 1961 for Hi-Lite, Little Wonder. 'Guilty Convict' was the first record I did, and 'Just Because' was the other side. I played piano in a nightclub during the same time: Kittymat, on Maxfield Avenue near Spanish Town Road."

Edwards says his next recording was a sound-system special for Count Bells that earned him "seven quid". In the mid 60s he formed The Ambassadors with Junior Menz, but the duo was shortlived. "We made [The Impressions'] 'Amen' and 'The Choice' [aka 'Your Wife And Your Mother'] for Harry J. and got 15 quid.[6] Then I just started producing for myself, in 1966 at Coxsone, but I wasn't going to make a living from that. I recorded four songs on that first session, me and Junior as the same Ambassadors, live with The Virtues. Graeme Goodall was the engineer, along with Coxsone himself. I released the first on a little label I called Diamond. Then, by about '68, I toured Canada with The Virtues."

Edwards met Coxsone and other producers while working in downtown Kingston garages. "I was a motor mechanic and I used to work on his car and Duke's car; I started learning the trade at KIG [Kingston Industrial Garage], but I finished over United Motors – Bunny Lee was there."

Edwards recorded 'Falling In Love' (aka 'Let Me Love You') and 'If You Can't Beat Them' for Studio One, but ended up releasing the songs himself. "Coxsone wasn't releasing them quick enough for me, so he sold them back to me for 20 quid. He actually wanted an album out of me, but then I was also headed in his direction: to run my own company" – hence the formation of the Success record shop and label, which took time to live up to its name.

The Concords vocal trio, one of Edwards's most notable acts, was fronted for a time by Gregory Isaacs, one of reggae's most legendary figures. "Gregory came to me as lead singer with The Concords. The first song he did was 'Don't Let Me Suffer'. He was the lead singer in that, then The Concords went back and did 'Buttoo' – or it could have been 'Buttoo' first."

As Edwards could not recall the details, I went to the African Museum record shop to ask Isaacs himself. From the late 70s, Isaacs was the best-known reggae singer after Bob Marley and Dennis Brown, but subsequent problems with firearms and substance abuse resulted in an uneven career marked by spells in jail. Isaacs died of cancer in October 2010 at the age of 59, his early demise hastened by his lifestyle. His best-known shop was downtown on Chancery Lane, a meeting point for musicians popularly known as the Idler's Rest; later, his shop and Poor People's Recording Studio were located on one of the rougher patches of Red Hills Road, an area marred since the late 90s by gang violence linked to the local drug trade.

At the crumbling and nearly abandoned complex that housed African Museum, a group of intimidating young men were gathered on the staircase, scowling with menacing contempt. When the jittery Isaacs eventually arrived, his attention span was short, but his recollections frank and informative. "I was born 1951 in western Kingston, grown in Denham Town by my mother. From early childhood, my friends used to tell me that I am good, like at school concerts. Sam Cooke, Otis Redding – those were my favourites."

His recording debut came in the late 60s. "I started out single, with a song called 'Another Heartache', produced by me and Winston Sinclair, a youth that I grow up with that like the music business too; he sing the next side, and we put it out on a blank. I did one song for Prince Buster, 'Dancing Floor'. He asked me to do it, because my friend was a close friend of his, Jim Brown" – the same Jim Brown who was a political 'enforcer' and notorious gunman for the JLP. "We grew in the same western Kingston. After 'Dancing Floor', I start singing for Rupie Edwards – that's where The Concords come in. We did songs like 'Don't Let Me Suffer' – quite a few." Isaacs named the other two members as "a brethren called Bramwell and one named Pengro, they came from western Kingston".

Although Edwards first travelled to England in 1969, licensing Concords material to Trojan's Blue Cat subsidiary and establishing the Escort label with Pama, he did not have a substantial Jamaican hit until 1970, when Dobbie Dobson's rendition of Tom Jones' sugary ballad 'That Wonderful Sound' reached the charts. Greater fame followed later in the decade.

Like Edwards's ironically named Success imprint, Alvin Ranglin's GG label took time to land a major hit. Ranglin's current base is near Kingston's Heroes' Circle, at the recording studio he bought from executive George Benson some years ago. The busy premises also house his pressing plant and offices, and, as Ranglin used to run a bakery from an adjacent building, the whole place smells of yeast. He is obviously an astute businessman – he owns property around the island and often cruises town in a crisp utility vehicle, blasting gospel on a high-powered stereo. The short, portly man often breaks into a hoarse laugh as he speaks of growing up in the countryside. "I was born in 1942 in a small district known as Eden in Clarendon. In that area, most people does farming and cattle-rearing, and raising chicks has always been good for feeding people. Myself, I had to go and milk the cows in the morning. I leave from there to May Pen at age 13, because there was a better school in the higher part of the city."

Ranglin began performing in his teens, although his introduction to music came far earlier. "In 1958 I started to sing on concerts, but from age three or four I was sent by my mother to a lady a few blocks from me that always play piano and organ for the church. I was brought up in the Adventist church, so from age four or five I sing in the choir."

When Ranglin came of age, he studied a number of unsatisfying trades before venturing into music. "I wanted to learn carpenter, then I started to get fed up, because the teaching from the elder gentleman was not up to date. Then I remove to mason, but I wanted to do something else because I believed I could do better. My mother put me into welding, and I get eye-flash [an injury], and I decided again not to go back. Those times, people from here usually migrate to London. My mother said she's going to send me there, but I decided that I don't want to go. I decided that I would be an electrician, then I start learning at Yarmouth Estate in the south coast of Clarendon, attend different schools and took course from National Technology, and I work as a radio and television technician. I used to build tube amplifiers, the KT88; those used to get the music more to the people, so I always try to own a discotheque for myself, called GG. GG was a business name coming from family members, like Gloria and her sister, and another cousin, 'Girlfriend', so we just formulate it like that."

Having a sound system made it easy to enter record production, especially as Ranglin was also involved in the jukebox industry. "We start with The Maytones and we had Trevor Brown from Linstead: he used to sing some Christmas songs like 'Every Day Is Like A Holiday'. I usually sing with another gentleman, Emmanuel Flowers, as Flowers & Alvin: 'Howdy & Tenky' was number one for many months. The jukebox business helped me to promote the songs; only the middle class or the wealthy could buy a radio, but the poor persons could go and play those jukebox with the shilling and ten cents, so I bought a few jukeboxes by the help of my mother, and I was in the game-machine business as well."

By this point Ranglin had already opened his first record store at 47 Main Street in May Pen, as well as a TV repair shop. His first Kingston store was at 45 Slipe Road, with later branches in Half Way Tree and Old Harbour, as well as satellite establishments in Brooklyn and East London. GG produced the first recordings by The Maytones in late 1968 or early 1969; as both lead singer Vernon Buckley and partner Gladstone Grant are natives of May Pen, their style is infused with provincial elements.

"I grow up with my grandmother, and I was compelled to go to a Seventh Day Adventist church every Saturday," says Buckley at his home in Montreal. "I never really active in choir, but I used to do a lot of observation. A block down the road there was a Church of God. Sundays, they would clap hands, so sometimes you get some good vibes. I used to do the bookwork for my dad, a government contractor. Gladstone Grant was driving a mini-bus. The town that I live in is May Pen, so we just give the group the name Mighty Maytones. Someone tell us about GG in our early days and we went down for an audition at his shop in May Pen. My first song never been released – we went into town, recording at Studio One, did 'A Little Bit Of This' and 'Land Of Music'. A few months later we went to Dynamic, did 'Loving Reggae' – wow, that was a hit. The next big hit was 'Funny Man'. We go in the studio more regular and songs keep coming, like 'Bowee Wowee', 'Serious Love'." The Maytones continued to supply Ranglin with hits until Buckley moved to Canada in 1980; he also assisted with the running of Ranglin's May Pen shop from 1971.

Another notable record label, formed in 1968, was Techniques, established by Winston Riley at his home on West Street, initially as a vehicle for his group The Techniques. Riley began licensing material to Trojan and Pama shortly thereafter; his first hit production was 'Warrior' by Johnny Osbourne & The Sensations, a song decrying the nation's growing polarity. "That was the early time when this Jamaican political uprising was in its baby stage, and the people just starting to have political warfare," Osbourne says, relaxing at a Boston hotel after a performance. "Guns wasn't so prevalent, but the people were taking sides politically, and then it becomes a two-sided thing."

Osbourne says time spent at Alpha set him on a musical path. "I was born in 1947, grew up all over Kingston, but in the latter years it was more western Kingston. I went to Alpha Boys' School in my teens and even join the Alpha band, learning to play the trumpet four or five years. Alpha was always teaching you all kinds of things: we have school choir, church choir, and the music teacher, Mrs Hall, always motivated us. I get to understand music some more, and I was really interested in music from then."

Osbourne subsequently began to record after mingling with local street-corner groups. "There was a band called The Wildcats I used to sing with – Earl 'Bagga' Walker used to be around that band. We used to come together in the evening time, practise these American songs and learn the harmony. The first tune that I recorded was 'All I Have Is Love'. That was for the band, but I guess the manager figure that he was just an independent producer, so seeing how it was done at Studio One, he gave it back to Mr Dodd and it was released on Studio One."

Osbourne subsequently began recording for Winston Riley with The Sensations, then composed of Jackie Parris, Buster Riley, and Bobby Davis. "Me and The Sensations, Techniques, Noel 'Bunny' Brown, Tinga Stewart, we always run into each other somewhere, or somebody may say 'Come here, sing this harmony', and then you just get involved. The Sensations was going on, so if they're making a record and I would be around, if I can sing a particular harmony, I might just chip in and sing that harmony, and if I'm recording a song, they do that. In 1968–69 I recorded 'Come Back Darling' for Winston Riley, 'See And Blind', 'Warrior', 'Fish Mouth', and by the summer of 1969 he compiled the first album, *Come Back Darling*."

The album's title track was a particularly big hit. "'Come Back Darling' was about one of my little girlfriends when I was young. She moved to another area, I couldn't see her for a time, so I sit down with my guitar and the words just came up. But I happened to migrate to Canada right in that same month that I did the album, so I never even see that girl again."

Despite Osbourne's departure, Riley's productions continued to gain prestige. In 1970, Trojan launched a Techniques imprint after the incredible success of Dave & Ansel Collins' 'Double Barrel'. Although the song itself was never popular in Jamaica, its success allowed Riley to open a record shop on Orange Street.

While the smaller, ghetto-based promoters made their entry-level smashes in reggae, changes at Studio One were also bringing important elements to the new style. The most notable involved Leroy Sibbles's mastery of the bass guitar and engineer Sylvan Morris's special effects, many born from budgetary restraints. The Heptones' early Studio One work featured bassist Wally Cameron, while Boris Gardiner, a veteran of bands such as Kes Chin's Souvenirs and Carlos Malcolm's Afro-Jamaicans, played on noteworthy hits such as 'Party Time'. But when Jackie Mittoo introduced Sibbles to the bass, the course of reggae history was radically altered.

"Jackie said he wanted to put a trio together to do a weekend gig at the Tit For Tat club on Red Hills Road," Sibbles explains. "He said he had the drummer, Billy Wade, but he didn't have the bass man and he wanted me to play bass. I said: 'Me? I never play bass!' He said: 'Grab the bass guitar there,' because the studio had a Fender Jazz, and he hummed the line of one of the songs that he had out, and I find the line and start playing it. We

125

start practising, played the gig and tore the goddam place up for weeks in and weeks out."

Sibbles played memorable and lasting bass parts at Studio One, creating several of reggae's best-loved bass lines. "The first song that I recorded, [The Cables'] 'Baby Why', and the next side, 'What Kind Of World' – those are two of the biggest bass lines ever recorded in Jamaica. I realised from that time on, the most-revived bass lines in Jamaica is the ones that I play."[7]

The bass of ska was an acoustic stand-up, frantically pumping to the beat; rock steady was a more prominent electric sound, with melodic strolling lines. As the early reggae bass is even more to the fore, its melodic features take heightened emphasis, particularly at Studio One, where augmented equipment boosted bass frequencies. In the hands of Leroy Sibbles, the bass took on a quality of gravity; instead of the bright bounce of 'Nanny Goat', the patterns of 'What Kind Of World' and 'Baby Why' seem emotionally laden, the sense of movement contrasted by subtle moments of rest.

Cornell Campbell notes that Sibbles played bass on 'Stars' and 'Queen Of The Minstrel', two landmark early reggae hits featuring Campbell's chilling falsetto, cut while he was leading the Eternals group. According to Campbell, the tunes were originally earmarked for a smaller producer, but changed shape when he brought them to Studio One. "I formed Eternals with Ken Price and Errol Wisdom as a rival to The Uniques and The Sensations. 'Queen Of The Minstrel', 'Stars', and 'Just Can't Find Loving' were three songs which I wrote. I went to Phil Pratt on Orange Street, but I tired out all the while. When I come to him for the recording, it's like he wasn't prepared – 'Come back next week' – so I went to Sir Coxsone Downbeat again. The session was going to cancel, because [Eric] Frater was supposed to play guitar, but him never turn up. [Pianist and arranger] Richard Ace said: 'Cornell Campbell can play guitar – play the guitar now, man.' So I grab the guitar and show the man them what to play. I write them to sing as a soul-beat music, a foreign music thing, but Richard Ace say: 'Why don't we do it in rock steady?' The Eternals say: 'Cornell, rock it now, man.' So when we rock it in rock steady, everybody jump up in the studio."

'Queen Of The Minstrel' was given a dreamy quality through the application of an echo effect devised by engineer Sylvan Morris. "Echo wasn't that prevalent as now," Morris explains, seated behind the mixing desk at Dynamics, the studio originally known as WIRL. "Being a technician, I take the playback head and feed it back into the record head, feed it into a track on the board, so you had this echo on the voices."

A gifted engineer from Trench Town, Morris had been interested in electronics since his boyhood. After formal training at a telecommunications firm and technical school, he came to WIRL in the ska era at the age of 17. "A gentleman by the name of Abrahams was working here; they wanted a technician to help with the installation of a three-track. Graeme Goodall, a very good engineer, was here and wanted an assistant, so they bring me in. He taught me the practical work of mastering and the sense of the board. We did work on some of them tunes with Linford Anderson, but I didn't stay that long. Once I was in the studio and Byron Lee came in and push up some controls, trouble the monitors and everything, and when him hear the sound, him say: 'What kind of noise is that?' Being young at the time, I said: 'If you don't know what you're doing, don't touch it,' so I was fired! Within about two days, they sent back for me, but I was down by Duke Reid. Byron Smith was the main man at that time. Because of my knowledge of electronics, the word that Duke used was that he needed somebody like me to really boost the thing. I didn't really do a lot down there, stayed about five months, but I remember 'Ba Ba Boom', the Festival tune by The Jamaicans. Smithy had mixed some of the versions but didn't like it, so I did the final mix. Once I was making a suggestion to Duke, and he said: 'Whenever you see me doing anything, you don't have nothing to say.' I don't think it's appropriate, so I told him a few weeks after that I'm leaving. I went to Coxsone immediately and Duke wanted me to come back, call me twice a week for years after that, never stop calling me until he died!"

Morris applied electronics expertise and musical intuition to get the best from Coxsone's low-fidelity set-up, joining the establishment just before Sid Bucknor, Coxsone's cousin, moved on. "He had Ampex two-tracks and a Lang board, and I sort of revolutionised the sound, because whenever a session is being done I never used to sit down at the board. I used to stand up, because I have to dance while I feel the music. If the musicians see me don't dance, they stop play, say: 'What's wrong?' I say I don't like the bass line, so they change it. I noticed that from the back of a speaker you usually get a very heavy bass sound; it is a lot louder in the back than at the front, so I created a box where I left two holes and put the mic at the back. Then there was an Electro-Voice mic that Coxsone had which create a lot of those bass sounds. It was a ribbon mic and the ribbon had broken, but the two-track tapes used to have a silver piece at the beginning and I created a ribbon out of it, but because this ribbon is not created for the mic all it did was pick up a certain range of frequency – mostly bass – so you got a rounder bass penetrating. A lot of Coxsone's mics was selective because they've dropped them – you find that they're not picking up the right frequencies, so I have to try to equalise it."

Morris says that Sibbles became the key musician at Studio One. "When I went there, Jackie Mittoo was there, a very professional individual. He did a lot of the work, but he left shortly after to Canada, so myself and Leroy Sibbles did most of the producing. Coxsone used to do auditions, sometimes Leroy Sibbles, Enid from Keith & Enid, also Larry Marshall. They select the individuals they want and we had sessions three times per week. After Jackie Mittoo left, Leroy Sibbles was one of the main man."

Al Campbell, who then led vocal group The Thrillers, notes that a female bassist also played on select sessions for Coxsone. "A girl from Trinidad, she was playing bass as well. I don't remember her name, but she play a portion of tunes and went back to Trinidad."

Campbell's Studio One debut came when he was 13, after a youth of sacred songs in western Kingston. "My father was a preacher in the Church of God at Oakland Road, between Three Mile and Two Mile," he explains, at the counter of the West London restaurant he uses for business meetings. "I used to sing at rallies, collecting money to build the church fund, and at school we used to have concerts every Friday. With my friend Michael Black, a youth named Sweet Pea, and one named Buzzer, we form a group called Al Campbell & The Thrillers and audition for J.J. on Orange Street. He say we could record, but he didn't have his own studio, so we go to Coxsone and record 'Heart For Sale', 'Don't Run Away', and 'Last Dance' – I think it's '67. The group split up after and Mr Dodd said I could sing solo."[8]

Campbell remained at Studio One until 1973 as part of The Freedom Singers and Underground Vegetable harmony groups, backing luminaries such as Alton Ellis, Freddy McGregor, Horace Andy, Burning Spear, and Dennis Brown. He was also present for the creation of 'Nanny Goat', and says that rhythm was originally laid for the pre-pubescent Jacob Miller. "I took Jacob Miller to Mr Dodd," Campbell emphasises. "It's me who take him from school and say: 'Come sing.' We record 'Love Is A Message' and the original 'Nanny Goat' – the original tune is 'My Girl Has Left Me'."

"Coxsone came around and said he don't like the song," adds Boris Gardiner. "He call in brother Marshall and say: 'Sing a tune on this rhythm, make we hear what it sound like.' And it fit it perfectly. That's how that tune really got on the market."

Preparing a family barbecue at his home in Miami, a chuckling Larry Marshall says Coxsone was reluctant to issue the version that he and Alvin sang. "When me do 'Nanny Goat', Downbeat said: 'This don't sound like it could go out, Larry, because this sound empty.' I said to him: 'No, man – empty? The people ah wait 'pon this,' and me just take a dub from him and go to a soundman in Barbican named Duke Anjo, and the man want to buy away the dub from me. Alvin Leslie play a little set named King Victor at Stanley Park [in Papine, East Kingston], and it's there 'Nanny Goat' bust out of – all roads lead to Papine off of 'Nanny Goat'. Fi five months him crash every set, and then people start to ask all about – Duke Reid and everyone – where they can get it. When you look at Tommy's Lawn inna Papine Square, they're so ram with people, yet me in one corner with one little piece of boot 'pon me foot, all the bottom broke, and Alvin and me have number-one tune named 'Nanny Goat'."

Having hit tunes but no money was all too familiar. Born Fitzroy Marshall in Lawrence Hall, Saint Ann, in 1941, he had spent part of his childhood with his father in downtown Kingston. In 1957 he joined a cousin in Graham Heights, near the uptown Barbican neighbourhood, where he worked as a gardener. He made his performing debut at the Ward Theatre in 1960, backed by The Rhythm Aces, and won five shillings. Word of his skills spread to other local singers, who brought Marshall to local entrepreneur Philip 'Justin' Yap in 1962. "Two cousins in Barbican, Ferdie Nelson and Joe Henry, we becomes friends, and when they heard me they encourage me, and the word go to Philip Yap. Down by Federal studio, that's where we do our first recording, a song named 'Too Young To Love' [based on the melody of Ben E. King's 'Stand By Me']. The people just go wild, and the guy sell it to some people in Trinidad."

In 1963, Marshall passed an audition at Studio One and scored a minor hit with the original 'Please Stay'. He returned to Yap's stable in November 1964 to record a duet with Ferdie Nelson, 'A Promise Is A Comfort To A Fool'. Marshall's first big hit came with a cover of Paul Martin's 'Snake In The Grass', recorded as a duet with Jackie Opel and issued by Yap in 1965. However, he parted company with Yap after being disappointed financially.

Around 1967 Coxsone tried to persuade Marshall to join The Checkmates, but the singer began to record for Prince Buster instead, yielding the popular 'Find A New Baby'. Marshall also sang harmony for Buster, but says money matters were also unsatisfactory, causing him to record a handful of tunes for Clancy Eccles, including a re-cut of 'Please Stay'.[9] "I owe rent inna Barbican them times – you rent a place, and the people sit in the doorway and wait for you to pass, so you can't pass where you live, you can't sleep in, and sometimes me have to walk from downtown Kingston go ah Barbican … so Clancy pick me round one corner."

He then settled into a long period of engagement at Studio One, where his recorded material, harmony vocals and assistant engineering helped consolidate the emerging reggae genre. Marshall and Alvin Leslie followed the popularity of 'Nanny Goat' with further outstanding singles in 1968–69, including the intensely emotional songs 'Mean Girl' and 'Your Love', while the rhythm of the equally proverbial 'Throw Me Corn' proved as infectious as that of 'Nanny Goat'. Marshall also had a hand in shaping 'Hello Carol', the first hit by harmony trio The Gladiators and one of Coxsone's biggest in the early reggae style.

Standing in the hallway of Tuff Gong studio, a serious and thoughtful Albert Griffiths scowls as he details the history of The Gladiators. "I was born in Saint Elizabeth in '46, grow from Kingston 11 to Trench Town. My mother die, so I was raised by me father and myself, because father didn't have anything. Me is a mason and me used to grow 'mongst The Ethiopians, because they used to do the same mason work. My boss named Leebert Robinson book a session and me do 'You Are The Girl', the flipside of The Ethiopians' 'Train To Skaville'. After that, me start The Gladiators when me sing 'Train Is Coming Back' for the same Leebert Robinson. The first Gladiators was me, David Webber, and Errol Grandison: we were all in the neighbourhood at Kingston 11. David Webber used to sing with his sisters named The Webber Sisters, but he's a guy who kind of go and come – we call him 'madman'. We go to Treasure Isle where we do 'Sweet Soul Music' – Hopeton Lewis give it some background vocals – and another one named 'Live Wire'. Then we go ah Studio One and do 'Free Reggae' and 'Soul Music' [aka 'Mr Sweet'], but Coxsone didn't really release those songs."[10]

The group's breakthrough came in December 1968. "Me and Nicky Thomas go to Studio One to sing this song named 'Hello My Love', and Coxsone run him out of the studio with it. He was doing the lead vocals and I was doing the background. Larry Marshall say: 'Gladiators, why you don't just call an individual name?' Jacob Miller say: 'You could say, Sonia, Sandra, or …' and Larry Marshall say: 'You could even say Carol.' Me just say: 'True, people would think it's a Christmas carol if it named "Hello Carol"' – and it get a number one!"

"'Hello Carol' was my first number one," says session keyboardist Robbie Lyn, who played on several principal early reggae numbers at Studio One. Largely self-taught, Lyn was given early coaching by his mother, a popular pianist known as Bobby Lyn ("she did light jazz and cocktail music in hotels in the 60s and 70s"). He came to Studio One at the suggestion of half-Panamanian drummer Filberto Callender, a neighbourhood friend with whom he would later form The In Crowd. "He was the drummer for the Virtues and Studio One drummer at the same time. Jackie Mittoo was the musical director for Studio One, but he migrated, so Studio One basically locked down production on a whole, but there was a cigarette about to come on the market called Embassy, and the company wanted to take a live band around Jamaica, so they ended up going to Coxsone for assistance and Fil recommended me.[11] At Studio One I play on a lot of Alton Ellis, like [Tyrone Davis's] 'Can I Change My Mind', a lot of Ken Boothe songs, and some Ken Parker stuff. Richard Ace was the lead keyboard player: he would be playing mostly organ and I'd be playing piano, but if he came late or didn't come at all I'd move to the organ, which is how I ended up doing 'Full Up'. While we were getting the idea together, he came and played the piano on the song. The organ was more important at that time – that kind of dominated the reggae sound for the shuffling. Plus Eric Frater played a very heavy strum on his guitar, so sometimes you would miss the piano."

With such ace session players and a keen engineer in his studio, Coxsone had something of a self-contained hit factory in the early reggae period. Outside of Studio One, Randy's four-track studio, located upstairs from the landmark record shop at 17 North Parade, was the most significant. It was operational from late 1968, just as reggae came into being. Although it would take a while to establish itself, Randy's became the studio of choice for reggae in the early 70s; its sparse, clean sound was particularly fitting for the rebellious lyrics and organ breaks that reggae embodied, and its downtown location made it popular with the upcoming producers based nearby. Vincent Chin's eldest son Clive describes the gradual process that led to its foundation, starting from when his father worked for the Issa family.

"The job that my father had was to go and clear the money from jukeboxes around the island every fortnight and apply fresh music for the boxes, and he started to collect all these old records. Rather than disposing of them, he would stock them up in his garage, and that's how he started Randy's Record Store down on East Street – he obtained the name through a radio programme that was sponsored by Randy's of Tennessee. The first was just a tiny store he obtained from a friend, but he wanted to expand and moved in the early sixties to 17 North Parade – it was an ice cream parlour run by a Chinese immigrant, and my father rented just a small section, probably about eight by ten feet. A few years after, he was offered to purchase 17 North Parade. He continued to run the ice cream parlour until around '66 to '67. Before that time, he was also doing recordings with The

131

Skatalites, Lord Creator, John Holt, Alton Ellis, Ken Boothe. Desmond Dekker and Jimmy Cliff used to pass through."

Randy's biggest early hits were by Lord Creator, including the under-age romance 'Don't Stay Out Late' and the sentimental 'Evening News', but when the Trinidadian singer ran into trouble with the law in February 1967, Vincent Chin turned his attention to building a studio. "The foundation of the studio started during the rock steady era, that's one of the reasons you never come across any rock steady tunes on the Randy's label," Clive explains, sipping tea at a friend's apartment in New York's Lower East Side. "Lord Creator was arrested for ganja, so he went to prison for about a year. Upon his release in '68, the studio was about finished." Sentenced to 18 months imprisonment with hard labour in May 1967, Creator was a free man by July 1968.

WIRL's technical engineer, Bill Garnett, who had worked at Federal during Graeme Goodall's tenure, set up the studio, rushing its completion in order to house The Wailers, who had been recording at WIRL for Johnny Nash's label, JAD. He then moved to New York to work at Harry Belafonte's Impact studio, the name of which was subsequently adopted for one of Randy's labels. "Bill Garnett brought in Johnny Nash's people, who brought in Bob and Peter and Bunny. They had booked the studio solid, but we would use time in between for our own purposes, and that's how Peter started collaborating and doing some work like 'You Can't Fool Me Again', projects funded by my father." Recorded in the spring of 1969, 'You Can't Fool Me Again' had an overtly antiauthoritarian message that railed against the myths of Christianity – one of the first reggae songs with such a directly rebellious message, and one that prefigured the hard-hitting material of the 70s.

Among the first songs with a Rasta theme to reach number one on the Jamaican charts was The Little Roys' 'Bongo Nyah', recorded with The Hippy Boys for Lloyd 'Matador' Daley in May 1969. Earl Lowe, otherwise known as Little Roy, was lead vocalist, with his schoolmate, Donovan Carless, on harmonies alongside him. This gently lilting song, which cloaked Rasta sentiment in a nursery rhyme, pointed the way toward the direct expression of Rasta beliefs. As the singer explains: "I was just starting to get conscious toward Rastafari, although I wasn't really seeing Emperor Haile Selassie I as the First."

Lowe scored further solo hits for Matador, including the forlorn 'Without My Love' and determined 'Hard Fighter', before breaking away to form the Tafari label. He started out recording for Coxsone and Prince

132

Buster in rock steady. "Buster was the one who gave me the name Little Roy, as I grow up with a small structure. Then I move on to Matador."

Daley was then in his most successful period as a producer, but had dismantled his sound system in 1966, due to hostile police action. "It was partially destroyed at Center on Shortwood Road – some malicious reason why they did it," Daley laments. "I sold my sound system that same year. It was so large, I had to sell it in three different lots."

In 1968, Daley moved his radio and television-repair service and record shop to 43 Waltham Park Road, the site of a noteworthy dancehall; his wife Deanna, daughter of noted band leader Eric Deans, ran a beauty parlour upstairs. 'Dark Of The Sun' by Jackie Mittoo (his first significant hit) was the only song Daley recorded at Studio One, although 'Ugly Man', sung by The Scorchers in October that year, was even bigger. "They came to my shop, singing a kind of sentimental tune, and we realised that people didn't like those music, so we gave them a few words. The next day, in the studio, they were the last set of guys we dealt with, and it was the only hit we made that day."

Daley says the biggest hits he ever produced were 'Bongo Nyah' and Alton Ellis's 'Lord Deliver Us', released in 1970. The 1969 session that yielded 'Bongo Nyah' also resulted in Lloyd Charmers's 'Zylon', an instrumental counterpart to Lloyd Robinson's 'Death A Come'. Although it was conceived of as filler, the organ piece actually topped the Jamaican charts. "We were counting on 'Death A Come' to be the A-side, but we had to flick it because the people liked "Zylon" more. It became the number-one hit."

That 'Zylon' would be issued as a chart-topping A-side, instead of an incidental B-side, evidenced a notable shift in style in 1969: instrumentals, usually led by an aggressive organ, were enjoying a popularity seldom seen since the days of The Skatalites, as The Upsetters' 'Clint Eastwood', The Hippy Boys' 'Dr No Go' (issued by Sonia Pottinger), and Harry J. All Stars' 'Liquidator' were all highly popular in Jamaica. What made these different from most ska instrumentals was that each was an altered version of a previously issued song with the vocal removed, and all but 'Eastwood' had an organ overdubbed on the rhythm. It was partly the success of these abstract instrumentals, and of others such as The Upsetters' 'Return Of Django' and 'Man From MI5', that would enable Jamaican music to enjoy an unprecedented popularity in Britain, once white working-class youth adopted the rude boy style.

The year 1969 was when reggae really broke in the UK. Toward the end of 1967, Desmond Dekker's late rock steady hit '007' (aka 'Shanty Town') had made an impact. Then, after the success of The Ethiopians' first tour, Commercial Entertainment brought Dekker to Britain in December 1968, just as his Leslie Kong-produced 'Israelites' reached number one; his follow-up, 'A It Mek', entered the charts in April 1969. Pat Kelly's 'How Long Will It Take' (produced by Bunny Lee with Lee Perry's involvement) had hit the charts by July, largely supported by airplay from offshore station Radio Caroline, and its popularity brought the singer to London for his first overseas performances. Prince Buster made another British tour in August, and at the end of September the first Caribbean Music Festival was held at the Empire Pool in Wembley, featuring Max Romeo, Desmond Dekker, and Johnny Nash. By the following month the charts were full of reggae tunes, with The Upsetters' instrumental recasting of Chris Kenner's 'Sick And Tired' as 'Return Of Django' beginning its ascent, followed quickly by The Harry J. All Stars' 'Liquidator', an instrumental cut of a love song called 'What Am I To Do' by upcoming unknown Noel Bailey (mis-credited to Tony Scott, who funded the recording), led by a stunning organ melody from Winston Wright.

In November 1969, Lee Perry and The Upsetters came to Britain with The Pioneers, who were in the charts with 'Long Shot Kick The Bucket'. By now The Pioneers had shifted their allegiance to Leslie Kong following disputes with Joe Gibbs. "The Pioneers was getting real popular," Sidney Crooks explains. "Then me and Joe Gibbs had a little argument, so we decided that we're going to leave. We was walking up Orange Street the following day and I saw Leslie Kong and his brother Fats. He said: 'Wha'ppen, Pioneer? Whey you ah do?' I said: 'I ain't doing nothing now I leave Joe Gibbs.' He said: 'Come sing some songs for us now.' The first song we did for Kong was 'Samfie Man' and that went to number one straightaway – we were an instant success with Kong. Then we did 'Easy Come Easy Go', which was another hit."

While working for Kong, the group drafted in Desmond Dekker's brother George Agard as a third member, despite initial resistance from their producer. "While we were at Beverley's George Dekker used to be there, singing harmonies with Desmond Dekker & The Aces. He even sang with Derrick Morgan – his alias at that time was Johnny Melody.[12] He joined us when we got to Beverley's because we wanted to strengthen the group, but Leslie Kong only want the two of us that was The Pioneers originally. Straightaway we had a number one with him leading it, because the country folks love his kind of singing."

Their biggest hit – and the one that brought them to England – was 'Long Shot Kick The Bucket', a continuation of the 'Longshot' saga, cut when the dud racehorse bit the dust. "One morning we were sitting out at Beverley's, and Mr Kong came in and said: 'Why are you guys sitting out here? You don't hear that the horse Longshot dead? Go around the back and make a tune!' There was a piano round the back where Derrick Morgan, Desmond Dekker, all the guys clown around and rehearse. At that time, Derrick Morgan used to control Beverley's; whatever he says would go. We went round the back and about an hour after that we said: 'Boss, we finished the song.' He listened to the song and said: 'I have to go to England, so Luddy, you go to the studio and do the song.' I don't want to take nothing from Kong, because he is a good guy – one of the best guys I've met in the business – but he wasn't there when that song was produced. We did the song and when I bring it up to let Fats hear it, he say: 'Let's release it straightaway.' It was an instant success in Jamaica. We get popular now, so the kids want us to come and play at their schools. Desmond Dekker was to appear on a show with the singer Joe Simon, but Desmond had to go to England because 'Israelites' was in the charts, and Mr Kong went down to see Byron Lee to put us on the show in Desmond's place – as Chinese to Chinese, they work it out together. We did 14 shows with Joe Simon, and Bruce White and Tony Cousins saw us and went to Kong and said they want us to go to England, and there comes the call from England that 'Long Shot Kick The Bucket' was number 14 in the charts. At the end of that tour, we came back to Jamaica, but our minds were set on going back to England." (They did indeed leave Jamaica shortly afterward, joining Dekker for long-term residence abroad.)

Along with Derrick Morgan, bandleader Roland Alphonso played a key role in the arrangement of Leslie Kong's product, ensuring that the hits kept rolling by drafting in the core of the rival Supersonics band as the Beverley's All Stars. As Jackie Jackson recalls: "Roland Alphonso was the musical arranger for Beverley's Records. When there was going to be a session, he went and found all the musicians and said: 'We have a session this morning at West Indies Records. You can do it?' I said: 'Yeah!' He said: 'You sure Tommy won't vex?' I think that first session could have been 'Poor Me Israelites' – that was the first session for Beverley Kong. Them days it was Desmond Dekker & The Aces, The Maytals, and The Pioneers."

This same core of musicians played on most of the biggest hits of the era, including those that broke big in England. "Jamaican producers, they are so traditional – all of them," Jackson explains. "If a set of musicians plays a song and it becomes a hit, everybody wants to use that set of musicians. From Leslie Kong it went Tip Top, Mrs Pottinger, then Clancy Eccles, then Derrick Harriott, then everybody else. When Scratch formed his Upsetter label, we did all of his recordings and all of Joe Gibbs's stuff. Gladdy was always on the piano, but after a while, sometimes it was Gladdy and sometimes it would be Snapping [Theophilus Beckford]. Organ was always Winston Wright. On guitar was different people: Ronny Bop, Douggie Bryan, Lynn Taitt, and Hux Brown. There were many drummers: Paul Douglas, Hugh Malcolm, Drumbago."

According to Derrick Harriott, Wright's organ playing often gave a reggae tune its defining character. "Winston Wright was a man that I rate very big. When you leave him out of a session, it's like something is missing." Alvin Ranglin, who made use of Wright's talents on an instrumental re-cut of 'Oh Carolina' called 'Man From Carolina', also sang Wright's praises. "He taught me a lot and I respect that, 'cos in the early stage, he was there on bandstand. Me and him is from the same area in Clarendon, so we live quite good." Credited to G.G.'s All Stars, 'Man From Carolina' was the first of Ranglin's productions to sell widely in Britain.

Ansel Collins was another organist responsible for early reggae instrumentals that were major hits in the UK. At his home in Portmore, Collins says he started his musical career as a singer. "I was born in Kingston in 1948, raised in Maxfield Avenue. In 1960 I was singing with Sonny Bradshaw, do [Mark Dinning's] 'A Star Is Born' at Carib Theatre, Vere Johns' Opportunity Hour. My first recording was with Coxsone, 'I Tried', with Bobby Aitken, backed up by Jackie Mittoo. I was a vocalist in Bobby Aitken's band with Winston Grennan."

Collins confirms that Grennan taught him to play drums. "Drums, I play on a couple of Delroy Wilson songs, like [The Isley Brothers'] 'This Old Heart Of Mine'." Eventually he learned to play the piano. "I was doing nothing in the days, so Bobby Aitken said: 'Why don't you practise the piano?' – because Conroy Cooper, he could play so good, but he didn't have the time to play in Bobby Aitken's little band, so I just becomes self-taught. The first session I play on is a Bunny Lee session with Max Romeo, Roy Shirley, and Slim Smith, 'Never Let Go' and 'Blessed Are The Poor' [aka 'The Beatitude']. That's where I learn from, right in the Bunny Lee stable."

The first record to feature Collins's organ skills was 'Night Doctor', a song produced by Collins himself at Randy's in 1968 but issued by Lee Perry as an Upsetters single in 1969. Collins was then leading the RHT Invincibles, a club band based at the Rainbow Healing Temple bakery, run by a Rasta on Spanish Town Road; the band featured bassist and former Termites vocalist Lloyd Parks, guitarist Bertram 'Ranchie' McLean, and drummer Lowell 'Sly' Dunbar. "The first recording, I did four songs," Collins recalls. "Lloyd Parks sing one for me and another one I gave to Coxsone. Sly was on drums.[13] It was his first session, but I took him to the studio to sing a song called 'Diplomat'. In those days, I could only record and wait for somebody else to do the releasing. You have to have money to deal with those things. For one year I had 'Night Doctor' on dub plate, and I give it to Scratch to listen to and somebody took it away from Scratch. When Scratch found it back, he get back to me and I give him the tape, and it went in the British chart, sell like hot bread."

Perry subsequently scored another melodic Collins organ hit with 'Man From MI5', while Collins says the massive 'Double Barrel', issued by Winston Riley in 1970, began as a freelance project. "'Double Barrel' was really arranged by me and Sly Dunbar. I make it and give it to Winston Riley to release. It was his idea to put on Dave Barker."

Barker, born David Crooks in Franklyn Town, now lives on a sprawling housing estate in North London. He says he started singing in street-corner groups before teaming with Glen Brown in the late 60s. "I first met Glen Brown on Cable Street in Franklyn Town. We were rehearsing in this yard, and I didn't know Glen Brown visit next door. Him say he would like to team up together as Glen & Dave. We approached Harry J. with 'Lucky Boy', which played a lot on the airwaves."

Brown introduced Crooks to Lee Perry, who renamed him Dave Barker after he delivered a James Brown-styled vocal for Perry's 'Prisoner Of Love', a big hit in both Jamaica and Britain in 1969. Scratch also had Barker shout a wild introduction to 'Shocks Of Mighty', the first of many such numbers that Barker voiced in the style of an American radio announcer. "The whole buzz about me is that I am an American star. We would go to bars where you have jukeboxes – people would punch 'Prisoner Of Love' or 'Shocks Of Mighty' and my fellow Jamaicans say: 'Boy, is who sing that tune there?' And a next one say: 'Ah, some Yankee.'"

This Yankee-styled disc-jockey talk is what Winston Riley asked Barker to voice on 'Double Barrel' at Joe Gibbs's studio, then located on Burns Avenue in Duhaney Park. "Winston came by me at an earlier time and asked me to join The Techniques, because Pat Kelly had left and they wanted a lead singer. I did two tracks: it was me, Bruce Ruffin, and Winston Riley. Also, I used to rehearse with The Sensations. One day I was home and Winston came and said that he has got this particular track that he would like me to try a thing on. At that time, I must say that I was skint. I went to Joe Gibbs's recording studio: him and his brother, Buster Riley, played this track and I could not really get into that track. Buster Riley was encouraging me to try and find a vibe: 'Make it sound like something big, like them James Bond movie thing, 007.' Once I start, the flow automatically comes: 'I am the magnificent, I'm back with a shock of a soul boss, the most thundering, storming, sounds of soul! I am double 0–0–0 …' When I finish, Winston gave me 20 dollars to do that track. I left that place, not thinking of that track any more, because I must deal with my family, and the next thing I know is that it is raising Cain here."

After 'Double Barrel' entered the British charts, Dave and Ansel Collins toured the UK for three months and appeared on *Top Of The Pops*. Unfortunately, conditions on the tour were less than satisfactory, according to Barker. "I must say, the plenty clothes, the heap of money, and the nice place we didn't really get." The follow-up, 'Monkey Spanner', was also highly popular in the UK, and after they went back for more performances, Barker remained in Britain, while Collins returned to Jamaica to craft more inspired instrumentals.

Although the raw sound of organ-based reggae shook up Britain to a great extent in 1969–70, the music was rapidly evolving back home, and the new decade would see all kinds of further changes. In the increasingly turbulent 70s, reggae would undergo shifts in tempo, pace, subject matter, and composition, and its creators would make further innovations to keep their music perpetually unique.

5

BLOOD & FIRE

The prophetic sound of early roots

"Soul Syndicate was my band because they understand everything about me." –
NINEY THE OBSERVER

"Studio One was good elementary, high school, college, university: that's where I
learn everything." – HORACE ANDY

The 60s ended with reggae still trying to find its feet. It had arrived as a
startling burst of energy, but by mid 1970, the music had slowed again. The
new style that began to dominate was generally slower, heavier, thicker, and
more complex, a meditative and naturalistic sound equally suitable for
ballads or songs of social protest. Several important developments took
place in the early 70s, altering and strengthening the foundations laid in the
preceding decade. As before, some of the most significant changes came
from the ghettos of West Kingston.

In the late 60s, the former Supersonics, now known as The All Stars,
were the most in-demand session band; their fruitful association with the
Beverley's label was ended only by Leslie Kong's fatal heart attack in August
1971, and they continued to work for other producers. However, in the early
70s there were challenges from other quarters, notably the former Hippy
Boys, now identified as The Upsetters, and smaller outfits based at
nightclubs. Soul Syndicate, a group of talented young musicians from the
Greenwich Farm ghetto that had a way of conjuring a sparse, eerie sound,
was the most significant new band to emerge in the early reggae period.

Most of the group have lived in California since the early 80s, and
currently perform as The Fully Fullwood Band. Before taking the stage at an
open-air event in the Oakland hills, bassist George 'Fully' Fullwood and
rhythm guitarist Tony Chin recount the band's genesis. "I was raised in Rae
Town in 1950, then when I was about five or six, we moved to Greenwich
Farm," Fully begins. "My parents was very supportive of me in terms of

139

music. I used to make a lot of sardine-can guitars, and then my father get involved when he realised that I was very serious. He was a sheet-metal worker at the Public Works at Industrial Terrace, beside Tivoli Gardens, and he brought a friend to teach me to play guitar. Tony was living on Spanish Town Road, but I was one of the only youth around that time that could play guitar. I started showing Tony a couple notes, and then he call me one day when someone was looking for a bass player, but I didn't play bass – I use the guitar to play bass with the E-string."

"Soul Syndicate formed when I was living in Spanish Town Road, near to Greenwich Farm, about '67 or '68, as a club band playing around Jamaica," adds Chin, whose heritage reflects the Jamaican motto 'out of many, one people'. "My father is half-Chinese, half-black, my mother is half-Indian, half-black, so I get that mixture. Greenwich Farm is where I grew up, but I spent some time in Trench Town too, maybe about two years. Then when I was about nine [in 1957], I grew up with my grandmother in Westmoreland and Saint Andrew. My father was working as a salesman, ride bike and sell school books, and he was a fisherman, and my mom was a domestic worker, wash clothes and iron." Chin says he came to know Fully in the mid 60s through a mutual friend. "My father bought an acoustic guitar from a drunkard and I start practise. A friend of mine show me a few chords – he and Fully was schoolmates. We heard that this shoemaker named Meggy up Maxfield Avenue have some guitars and a drum set and wanted to put a band together. When the band did form, it named Rhythm Raiders: me, Fully, a drummer named Elgin, and Meggy – he was the leader, he played guitar. That's how the band start, and then Fully's father took the band."

Chin says the band kept this line-up for "about a year", backing artists at live shows, but Fully says they did not perform live until later. "We play a club named VIP Lounge," Chin insists, "and we play on one and two stage shows, back up Roy Shirley and Stranger Cole in May Pen and Spanish Town. Them was the rock steady days. After that, the band get different members."

Fully says the membership changed because of musical deficiency. "Elgin and Meggy come from the country and they couldn't play that well. Those guys was older and they couldn't really keep up with us, so a next guy came in, Cleon Douglas. He used to play guitar and sing, and he was in the same area of the ghetto in Kingston. Then [drummer] Leroy 'Horsemouth' Wallace, he used to be around us because he was from Alpha Boys' School; he was a poor bad boy in the ghetto and he used to live at my house. My mother and father like him very much and he used to sleep on my couch –

he was like a half-brother to me. That's how the band started as Rhythm Raiders. Later on, we started adding keyboards."

"Then you have a next drummer, a brother named Max Edwards," Chin continues. "We go through some different drummers, but Santa [Carlton Davis] was the last drummer."

"Santa used to be in the area, because Santa's father and my father used to work at the same place, and I used to kind of baby-sit Santa," Fully adds. "He was playing in a little boys' club."

"That was late 1969," Santa confirms by telephone in Los Angeles. "It was Tony, Fully, Cleon Douglas, and the keyboard player – his last name was Scott." Santa's nickname dates from childhood. "It was close to Christmas, and I used to be on the street, make skates and run around. There was a tar patch I used to ride through, and this day the sun was so hot, the tar patch melted, and I fell off the skates and scrape my face up bad. At the clinic, they use iodine, so my face was red and blue. This guy said: 'Carlton, how you look like Santa Claus?' and it just stuck."

Santa first played drums in church. "I grew up in the ska era, just before it start to turn into rock steady. I used to hear a lot of that and a lot of American music, like The Impressions, The Platters, Brook Benton. When I was a kid I was fascinated with the military, and I used to like to see these guys march around the place, so I think that was one of my main influences. At 11 years old, I used to leave school every evening and pass a church at Saint Joseph's Road and Waltham Park Road – I hear music playing, and it sounds good. One day they were recruiting for the junior group, and I was so into the thing that I was recruited into the senior group – I had that interest to learn fast. I was playing snare drums, and then I became an all-rounder, so I started excelling. I stayed with those guys for about five years. Bobby Aitken was giving a couple of the guys guitar lessons, so he was passing by the band room one day while I was inside, trying to play a rock steady beat, and you know those guys [The Caribbeats] were the kings of rock steady. He said: 'Make the bass drum and snare drum drop together, and then you play an eight beat on the hi-hat.' He was the first man who gave me some kind of instruction. Basically I was self-taught.

"I left the group when I was about 14. One thing lead to another, and I run into this guy Kofi, he used to live in the New York area – Jamaican, but got through – and those guys were into jazz, the Coltrane kind of stuff. He came back to Jamaica and started a band, Kofi Kali & The Graduates, so that is how I met Ken Boothe, Joe Higgs, Alton Ellis, Hortense Ellis.[1] We used to play rock steady, ska, calypso, play different clubs like the Blue Mist on Slipe Road, and we did gigs on the North Coast. We used to do functions in the ghetto, but back then the ghetto was sweet – it wasn't like now, when you're afraid to go some place. In the early 70s you could go to Trench Town any hours of the night or day, and you wouldn't have to worry about: 'Oh, they're going to shoot you.' Those were the days when ghetto was the place all the singers used to hang out."

Santa says he surprised Fully's camp at his audition. "One day somebody told me that Fully want a drummer – he was asking about me. Then I used to play in the Drum Corps, and Fully's father said: 'You just play marching drums, you don't know how to play drums.' At audition time, I played, and everybody's mouth went open wide."

"These guys were very talented, and he learnt pretty fast," says Fully. "I change the name to Soul Syndicate, then we brought in Chinna [lead guitarist Earl Smith]. Chinna used to come as a young boy from school, watching us and said he could sing. Then Tony start show him some stuff on his guitar."

At his Kingston home, near Half Way Tree, where a guitar is never far from hand, Chinna explains that Greenwich Town/Farm, Kingston 13, attracted singers and ghetto toughs from the neighbouring district of Trench Town, Kingston 12, and beyond. "I was born at Moore Street in 1955. I grew up with my godfather and godmother in Greenwich Town, place named Kingston 13, but Moore Street is right round-ah Trench Town, so it's like 12 and 13. Everyone 'fraid of the number, but 13 carry the vibe, because 13 have the beach, so all of them 12 man would have to come down Greenwich Town to get red snapper and doctor fish and all of them substance there to keep them voice and everything bubbling – and the herb too, because we used to have one of greatest herbsman in the world, George Croucher.[2] People from all over the island come to buy herb on East Avenue, because him sell herb the cheapest and him always have the wickedest herb."

Chinna says family sound-system connections drew his interest in guitar. "My old man, a roofing specialist, used to have a sound named Smith's, and Bunny Lee used to operate my old man's sound. In other words, Bunny hold me as a likkle baby; Bunny's mother and my mother was close, so it's a whole family thing. My godfather have a sound, Down South The President; Prince Buster and Snapping used to sell him soft wax inna them days, £14 for seven, what the man them now call dub plates. My old man used to love music so much that he just had the wickedest sound. He didn't care about whe' him play, used to string up every day and play music and just dance to it. I remember a DJ them time there, the early 60s, come by the house with a guitar and it's the most fascinating thing. Me just see this thing and it haunt me, but as a youth, you're never allowed to touch things due to respect, so me just look 'pon this thing and me never see nothing that fascinate me so much. Me try to make something look like it out of sardine can and use fish line, nylon strings; through we inna the fisherman area, Greenwich Town, we get fishing line easy. We realise we're not getting that kind of melodic sound, but at least we're getting the feel of the instrument."

Chinna also received his nickname from sound systems, derived from a form of stereo amplifier commonly known as a tuner. "Through my father have a sound, as a little youth I always have my little toy sound made out of broken records, and through its patois, rather than 'Tuner' it's 'Chuner', and then it come out more popular as Chinna."

As a neighbourhood music fan, Chinna was often around Soul Syndicate, and officially came into the group when Cleon Douglas was preparing to relocate to New York. "Greenwich Town was an area where 'nuff musicians used to hang out. We have The Melodians, Slim Smith; Wailers used to pass through, and The Gaylads; and then you have Bunny Lee as a man who in the business and him live next door to me. Sunday him used to have auditions and him used to have Glen Adams audition the artists. I remember the first time I hear Jacob Miller, him come with a group named The Schoolboys. I lived on East Avenue and I hear a band up Ninth Street named Soul Syndicate, they rehearse every night, so we used to go up there, hear some wicked music. They used to play top-ten, reggae, and certain other things, so it's just fun to go up there and hear the music play – a full band with horns and drum and bass and keyboard.

"Me and a next youth named Earl Zero start singing and we have a little group with my brethren named Rush-It. Then there was a brethren who used to work over the sawmill named Eastman: he was a cabinetmaker and he just love the vibes, so he buy a guitar, but him no really so much into playing it, so me and Earl, it was like a rat race to see who could get that instrument. We don't know no chord or nothing, just have this instrument out of tune, so we go for this rehearsal and watch the guys playing every rehearsal night, and start looking on the shape. When them finish all the songs and you strum the same thing, it don't sound like how his sound, and you say something wrong, so I asked the guitarist, Cleon Douglas – wicked singer and guitarist: 'How's it my guitar don't sound like yours?' and him take the guitar and say: 'No man! This no tune.' So me figure out the tuning, and me go up there every night again, and me know all the songs, because me understand the shape and the position. Cleon did have to leave and go to the States, so the band need a guitarist, so Fully's father say: 'We have to try that little big-eyed boy – it look like him can do a thing.' Me know all the songs because me don't miss no rehearsal. It's fun now to get a real guitar – an electric guitar – and start play."

Before Douglas emigrated, the band had already cut their teeth in the studio; as Chinna was still at school, he missed several early recording sessions. "The first guy who brought us into the studio to do recording was Bunny Lee," recalls Fully. "I think it was with Slim Smith, but I can't remember the exact tune."

"Bunny is a man who don't go to the studio and do one song – he do many songs, many, many rhythms, over and over," Tony Chin adds. "He's the one that bring us to the studio to do recording first. I think Slim Smith was one of the first, with The Uniques." According to Santa, the vocal group The Twinkle Brothers featured on the session. "Bunny came and hired the band, took us to the studio and work our ass for 200 dollars, but we didn't know the difference. We treated it like it was a gig: 200 dollars was a lot of money, but not for the type of work we were doing."

Santa says these early sessions quickly established Soul Syndicate on the recording circuit. "Back then it was Jackie Jackson, Hux Brown, Gladstone Anderson ruling the studio. We were just young kids who started playing, and we used to rehearse every day, week after week, just for the love of it. Then there was a couple of others for Phil Pratt and Niney, and Keith Hudson – we used to do a lot of stuff for him too. It's cool when guys come together from different directions. We were a band that had a very tight sound, so people got attracted to that."

"Bunny Lee was from the same area, Greenwich Town, and he used to come by and hear us playing," Fully adds. "Then all these promoters came by. Everybody wants us because we were putting out a lot of hit songs."

"Soul Syndicate, me and Bunny Lee take them from day one," says the man known as Phil Pratt. "We are the first people them record for. They was young and have fresh, nice ideas, so when you go ah studio it's easier to get a hit record from them than the older heads, who would tend to repeat themselves."

Pratt is an elusive character who tries to avoid interviews. At the Jamaican take-away restaurant he operates in Northwest London, he nearly expels me when I ask his date of birth, but eventually explains how he got involved in music. "My name is George Phillips – that's a musical name, Phil Pratt," he begins, though he is sometimes called George Chukoe. "I was born in Milk Lane, left Milk Lane when I was about 17, came to England in

1960 to join my dad, but I didn't know my dad until 1959, so it never work out – we couldn't get on. I came into music when I go back home, that was 1965. I start to sing for Coxsone, but the tune never came out.[3] I start to do my own thing in '66. Ken Lack, that's where I was first, at 15 Mark Lane. We was partner: I have John Tom label, he have Wiggle Spoon and Caltone. I did 'Reach Out', a wicked tune, and 'Sweet Song For My Baby' – that was pirated in England."

Pratt says his failure to break through as a singer made him move into production, but bigger producers blocked his early efforts. "There's a song by Ken Boothe called 'The One I Love'. It's a magnificent song, but why it didn't sell, I was having problems with Coxsone and Beverley's. The other people who have songs for him, they boycott me, because I was a new man coming in the business; they was stronger 'pon the radio station and everything, so I have to take my beating until people came to know me."

Pratt's link with Soul Syndicate brought forth 'My Heart Is Gone', John Holt's first big hit as a solo artist and one of the defining songs of 1970.[4] The partnership hit in 1971 with Holt's 'Strange Things', a forlorn love song that showed the emotive brilliance the Syndicate was capable of generating, although it was overshadowed by Holt's version of Shane Sheppard & The Limelights' 'Stick By Me', named by producer Bunny Lee as "the longest-selling number one in Jamaica". Pratt and Soul Syndicate also scored with Pat Kelly's 'Talk About Love', an adaptation of The Main Ingredient's thoughtful 'Brotherly Love', on which Kelly's delivery was ably supported by the group's musical abilities and vocal harmonies.[5]

By then, Soul Syndicate had drawn Lee Perry's attention. He had spent the latter half of 1970 reshaping The Wailers' sound with his Upsetters, creating what many feel are the best recordings of their entire career, among them 'Soul Rebel', '400 Years', and 'Don't Rock My Boat'. Working with Soul Syndicate, Perry crafted the Wailers classics 'Sun Is Shining' and 'Mr Brown'; indeed, 'Sun Is Shining' greatly benefited from the Syndicate's languorous backing, making it an immediate success. Tony Chin also pointed out that The Wailers and Soul Syndicate had deeper links, since Glen Adams and Alva 'Reggie' Lewis were temporary Syndicate members. 'Glen Adams used to make our uniforms – we used to wear some red coats. When Cleon Douglas migrated to America, Reggie came in, and then Wailers and Bob Marley come around with us. We used to back them up at different clubs, like the Psychedelic Lounge in Greenwich Farm, and the VIP Club, and we did play the King's Theatre in Harbour View. That's the first time I saw Ziggy Marley and his brother Stephen, little boys dancing on stage."

145

Despite such well-forged links, Perry was unhappy with the results when he tried to fashion Marley's boastful 'Duppy Conqueror' with Soul Syndicate. It was ultimately re-recorded by The Upsetters, leaving the original Syndicate rhythm to be transformed into 'Mr Brown', a song that related the widely reported sighting of a three-wheeled coffin driven around the island by buzzards.

"The 'Mr Brown' rhythm track is actually the first rhythm track we did for 'Duppy Conqueror'," Glen Adams confirmed. "We had a money problem, so Scratch get upset and went for a group that we were training named Soul Syndicate; I was the singer at that time for the group, 'cos I was training them, so I would just go around and jive with them. I would practise Chinna, tune him guitar, and give him the rhythm. Scratch went for them and do this track, so when Bob heard the track, he never like it. It was a really good track, but it's just the stigma to say we didn't do it. We know the song, because we already had rehearsed it as well, so Scratch come back and get us and we went back and do it."

As Chin recalls: "We record 'Duppy Conqueror', but I don't think Scratch like the rhythm, so he get Family Man them and re-record 'Duppy Conqueror', but then Glen Adams write lyrics and put them on that song and call it 'Mr Brown'."

"I wrote 'Mr Brown'," Adams confirmed. "I was about to sing that song, and Scratch asked me to let Bob do it, because he think he was the best for the song. Matter of fact, I'm glad he did it."

"I tried to get them to play 'Duppy Conqueror' and they couldn't do it neither," Perry adds. "Bunny Lee's band couldn't do it. Me have to take them to the studio to start together, but they couldn't perform, that's why me have to use Family Man them to do it. Bob did realise that the band could not do it, and if Fams them could do it, then this is the band!"

Marley was so taken with the skills of Family Man and Carly that he stole them away from The Upsetters when The Wailers broke free from Scratch in late 1971 and made them his permanent rhythm section. The Wailers then shocked the charts with 'Trench Town Rock', their self-produced debut that proclaimed how far-reaching and influential reggae music would become, rising from the ghetto of Kingston 12 to conquer the world.

Another problematic situation involving Soul Syndicate and The Wailers arose from Niney The Observer's 'Blood & Fire', released to great commotion on Christmas Eve, 1970. The apocalyptic song, featuring Hux Brown and Chinna Smith on guitar, with vocal backing by Lloyd Charmers and organ from Cleon Douglas, had a keyboard line that Marley & co felt

146

resembled one of the tunes they crafted earlier. Niney got into a fracas with Glen Adams, who drew blood from the aspiring producer and vocalist. "A likkle terror go down between brethren and brethren," Niney says at Bunny's Lee small studio in Duhaney Park, the Burns Avenue premises originally established by Joe Gibbs. "Me and Bob have a little problem, me and Glen Adams have a little problem, like a fighting. My blood come up, a lot of shit go down – I have to end up in the hospital, and it's like the song become a prophecy. People never want to buy the song, because they say the song is dreadful and they don't know what it's all about. Charlie Babcock, the top announcer at RJR, he get laid off to play the song."

Despite such rocky beginnings, 'Blood & Fire' is a true classic. Named as 'song of the year' in 1971, it launched Niney as one of Jamaica's most individual producers and marked the start of a long and fruitful relationship with Soul Syndicate. "I always use Soul Syndicate. They was my band because they understand everything about me and I used to give them a lot of inspiration."

Niney was born George Boswell in Montego Bay in 1944, but was raised as Winston Holness when his parents split up. An industrial accident severed a thumb, hence his enduring nickname. Niney was a record plugger and salesman for leading producers, entering the production field after a long freelance period. "I grow between Montego Bay and Kingston, where my auntie live in the suburb part of town, and when I come of age, I decide that I'm going to stay with my family in town. I start to move with Derrick Morgan and Monty Morris, then me and Bunny Lee hook up, and me and Lee Perry. Andy Capp is a man who I get a lot of experience from – he was the greatest engineer at those times, and he was a genius in the business. Night 'pon nights I used to be around Andy: we sleep at the studio and he make songs, and I'm the salesman for them. I work with him on 'Pop A Top', 'Fat Man' by Derrick Morgan [issued as 'Top The Pop'], and [The Race Fans'] 'Bookie Man'. I work with every single producer in the business: Beverley's, Coxsone. I used to go to studio with them and used to sell songs for them. I record a lot of songs at Coxsone like 'Music Police' and 'Cocaine Doctor' – all those rhythms with Family Man and Carly before they played with Bob Marley. After I work for Bunny Lee, at night I do freelance. I just go and make rhythms and any guy want a cut, I just sell him a cut. Joe Gibbs liked my rhythms, but he never really want me to sell, he want me to be with him, 'cos I used to make a lot of songs and give him, like Ken Parker, 'Only Yesterday'."

Niney says the circumstances of Max Romeo's 'Macabee Version' convinced him to issue his own product. The song was a Rasta refutation of

147

the King James Version of the Bible, and one of the first tunes with a conscious theme recorded by the singer, but as Romeo licensed it to producer Willie Francis, he failed to reap when the song took off. "I was still working for Bunny, and me and Maxie Romeo live together in one house. We used to work together and whatever hit, we share. He make 'Macabee' and I don't know if he never think the song was going to hit, but he sell it and the song hit. I decide I'm going to leave everything and do my own shit, so I just break off everything, cut everybody loose, come with 'Blood & Fire' and open up the road."

Although Soul Syndicate greatly changed the dominant sound by working with producers based in their vicinity, numerous other hits were created elsewhere. Carl Dawkins, an emotional vocalist who drew on Otis Redding's style, topped the charts in 1970 with the determined 'Satisfaction', recorded with the All Stars for Sir J.J., the producer who first recorded him in rock steady.

At Tuff Gong studio, Dawkins displays a restless, agitated energy as he briefly describes his career. "I was born in 1948 in Spanish Town, grew up in East Kingston, Allman Town. I come from a musical family. My daddy, Joe Dawkins, was one of the first drummers in this country – he used to drum with Sonny Bradshaw and Baba Motta. Myself, Slim Smith, and Jimmy Riley used to go to school together, and me and The Techniques were rehearsing. We was coming from the beach one day – matter of fact, we was going to smoke some herb behind Steel's Vehicle garage – go up Greenwich Farm and come up Orange Street, whole heap of crowd in this shop doorway at Orange Street and North Street, JJ Records. I go in and sing the two tunes, 'Baby I Love You' and 'Hard Times'. Both sides hit, but them times money never pay, but me go through anyway, 'cos me love pretty clothes and 'nuff girls. After that, I stopped for a little while, because police hold me for herb. When me come back, it's like the music gwan all over the place, but me have some idea with the sound – me call it the heartbeat – so this song 'Satisfaction' came about with the heartbeat. It was the shortest song in Jamaica, two-and-a-half minutes. Jackie Jackson play the bass – earth-shaking. Ken Boothe was on the road with 'Freedom Street' and me bumped him off and take the whole thing over. I do 'Get Together' – it take off, too. All the while me no have no money, but me still singing."

Derrick Harriott also reached number one in 1970 with the wah-wah-laden 'Psychedelic Train', featuring vocal quartet The Chosen Few and backed by an emerging set of musicians called Now Generation.[6] "We used to do all the Derrick Harriott stuff," bassist Val Douglas says in his adopted home of New York. A tall, light-skinned, courteous man, Douglas says the group was formed in the late 60s while its members were still at school. A number of musicians drifted in and out, including Augustus Pablo on keyboards, Ernest Wilson on guitar, singers William 'Bunny Rugs' Clarke and Keith & Tex, and drummer Lloyd 'Tin Legs' Adams. "Before Tin Legs left, he was the first person who took me into the studio, about late '69. Ernest was still playing too. I don't remember the name of the singer, but I know it was a redo of a Lloyd Price tune called 'Just Because'."

Now Generation were resident at the Stables Club on Kingston's bustling Red Hills Road. The group eventually centred on Douglas and guitarist Mikey Chung, with Chung's brother Geoffrey handling arrangements and some keyboard parts; Earl 'Wire' Lindo was often on organ. "Now Gen was another part of the Jamaica legacy, because Now Gen had a unique sound in reggae music, made a lot of hit songs," says Robbie Lyn, who moonlighted with the group during his time in rival club act The In Crowd. "The funny thing about the Now Generation arrangement was that their drummer, who played in the night-times, had a day job he didn't want to give up, so for recordings they used Mikey Boo, who was In Crowd's drummer. Myself and Mikey Boo would be In Crowd, but we were with Now Gen in the studio."

Now Generation's calm yet confident studio sound – centred on Douglas's solid bass lines, Richards's understated drumming, and Mikey Chung's rock-inspired guitar – graced many of Derrick Harriott's biggest hits in the early 70s, including The Chosen Few's take on Isaac Hayes's 'Shaft'. They were also responsible for some of the most noteworthy numbers produced by Joe Gibbs, Lee Perry, and Harry J. In 1972, they backed Dennis Brown's smash 'Baby Don't Do It' and the popular 'Things In Life' for Lloyd Daley, but because of disputes, they were dismissed as the 'John Crow Generation' on one of Daley's instrumentals.[7]

Dennis Brown began his recording career in the late 60s. He had been groomed for stardom by Harriott but ended up coming to prominence at Studio One. "I'm the first one who recorded Dennis Brown," Harriott states with pride. "The song was 'Lips Of Wine', but it was called 'Obsession' before. Around the same time he did 'Changing Times' for me, the original was by Roman Stewart and Dave Robinson. Dennis used to rehearse at the back of my shop at King Street with Junior Murvin and sometimes Horace Andy – he was one of my artists, too, with 'Lonely Woman'. I brought back

[The Van Dykes'] 'No Man Is An Island' from America, teach Dennis Brown the words and everything, but I left to America for a little while and when I came back, he went and did it for Coxsone." The hit featured The Soul Defenders, a group from the country town of Linstead who recorded sporadically at Studio One. Their leader, a guitarist known as Jah Privy, imparted a country feel to their sound through a particular picking style.

Dennis Brown and Horace Andy were two of the most significant Studio One artists in the early 70s. Brown was a child star whose father, Arthur, was a popular actor of some social standing, but his mother raised him in the ghetto. In 1966, at the age of ten, he appeared at the West Kingston Charity Ball at the National Arena, and supported Miriam Makeba and Adam Wade shortly afterward; he also appeared at the Smashville 68 concert with King Curtis, Johnny Nash, and The Sweet Inspirations. Brown passed through The Falcons before fronting Soul Syndicate on live performances around the time of his Studio One debut. "Falcons was a group with Dennis Brown, Cynthia Richards, Noel Brown, and Pat Satchmo," Fully recalls. "They call me to play bass for them, and Horsemouth was the drummer."

"Dennis Brown was our main vocalist," Tony Chin adds. "The first vocalist we have in Syndicate was Cleon Douglas, then we have Donovan Carless and a guy named Ferris [Fitzgerald] – two lead vocalists to go round the clubs and do cover songs. Donovan Carless used to sing in The Little Roys: we'd say he was an uptown guy. Donovan fall out after about two or three years. Dennis Brown was just a little youth, he did have 'No Man Is An Island' out, then he came as lead vocalist."

Despite his youth, Brown had an incredibly rich vocal tone. At Studio One he recorded mostly cover versions and love songs but began to cut socially conscious material after returning to Derrick Harriott in 1972. Songs like 'Concentration,' 'He Can't Spell', and 'Changing Times' from the *Super Reggae And Soul Hits* album evidence a new maturity.

Horace Andy has a very individual style, a quavering soprano that once heard can never be forgotten. He was born Horace Hinds but renamed Andy by Coxsone in deference to Bob Andy. At the offices of his management in London, Horace says his mother, a store clerk, raised him in East Kingston's Allman Town, but he also spent time with his carpenter father in Jones Town. He cut his debut recording, 'Black Man's Country', for Phil Pratt around 1966. Andy says a friend named Ever, who wrote the song, heard him singing on the street, liked his voice, and took him to Pratt, who recalls that the pair first tried to sing it as a duet. Although Pratt says the song "had a little impact", Andy felt he needed to improve his skills. "I couldn't sing, so I had to start to learn to play the guitar and start to learn to sing. I practise for four years, then I decided to go to Studio One in 1970, because Studio One was the best.[8] I record my first two songs, 'Got To Be Sure' and 'Something On My Mind'. Leroy Sibbles was the head musician."

'Skylarking', which condemned the begging practised by Jamaica's youth, established Andy as a major star. "Living as a Rastafarian, you're going to be doing political songs all the time. Being a young man and being a Rastafarian, looking at the surroundings and what's happening, that's why I sing that song." He first became conscious of Rastafari in his teens. "From before I start sing, from I was 18 years old, I'm a Rastafarian. I used to go over Jones Town where you have Charter 15 of the Ethiopian World Federation, so from a young age I start to learn about consciousness, about the Father."

Andy had significant hits for other producers in the early 70s, including 'I'm Alright' for Keith Hudson, 'Lonely Woman' for Derrick Harriott, and 'You Are My Angel' for Bunny Lee.[9] He spent most of his time at Studio One, however, and it was there that he gained his most valuable experience. "The time was good. I learn a lot. I say Studio One was good elementary, high school, college, university: that's where I learn everything."

The Abyssinians, a trio who favoured minor-key arrangements, also cut outstanding spiritual and social material at Studio One in the late 60s and early 70s. Lead singer Bernard Collins returned to Kingston some years ago after a long period abroad; he was raised in the capital, but spent six years in Saint Catherine as a young man while his mother was working in London. Collins formed The Abyssinians in 1968 with Donald Manning, adding Donald's brother Lynford shortly afterward. Lynford was then a member of Carlton & The Shoes, a popular Studio One act led by his older brother Carlton.

Collins says he joined forces with Donald after the encouragement of a mentor. "Lloyd Thompson, he's more than just a friend: he's like a brother and sometimes even a father. He knew Donald Manning always wanted to sing and strum his guitar, so he introduce me to Donald, and I and Donald started to learn together. We sit together at nights and try to create something, until 'Satta Massa Ganna' came out. Lynford already sing before with Carlton & The Shoes on songs like 'Love Me Forever', and Lynford came in and sang the harmony of 'Satta Massa Ganna' and decided he would sing with us from there on. But the whole vibes of The Abyssinians was really between me and Donald."

'Satta Massa Ganna' was a momentous debut, recorded at Studio One in

151

1969 with plenty of Rasta burru drumming from Bongo Herman and Bongo Les.[10] Thematically related to a Carlton & The Shoes number called 'Happy Land' (the B-side of hit ballad 'Love Me Forever'), 'Satta Massa Ganna' spoke of a utopian resting-place for the black faithful and used Amharic salutations to the Almighty to drive home its Rastafarian ideals. "In those days we used to be closely involved with the Ethiopian Orthodox Church," Collins explains. "My brethren Donald was a foundation man of the Church, he used to communicate with Ethiopia and actually get books from Ethiopia with Amharic language and interpretation back into English. The whole concept is from the Ethiopian Orthodox Church, coming up in caves, climbing up on rocks, to go there and worship and pray."

Although Studio One declined to issue the recording, when 'Satta Massa Ganna' was released in 1971 on the group's Clinch label it began to pick up steam. It has since become one of the most versioned songs ever recorded in Jamaica, and an all-time Rasta anthem. That same year Coxsone issued the anthem-like 'Declaration Of Rights', which called for self-determination in the black populace. It was another oft-versioned number with a great Sibbles bass line, for which Collins says they were paid '17 bucks'. Determined to concentrate on their own productions, but typically short of finance, The Abyssinians continued sporadically cutting spiritual and cultural sides in the early reggae period. 'Yin Mas Gan', recorded for Lloyd Daley in late 1972, was a notable example.[11]

The Wailing Souls, one of West Kingston's finest harmony groups, was another significant Studio One act of the period. Although known by different names as its membership fluctuated, the partnership of Winston 'Pipe' Matthews and Lloyd 'Bread' McDonald remained at the core. "Growing up in the ghetto of Trench Town, there was so much music round us," says Pipe at home in Los Angeles. "I born in Trench Town, 1949, grew up at 6 First Street. My grandmother was an office maid at the Ministry of Supplies and my uncles were port workers. As a youth I used to do a lot of singing, like in the evening the older guys would have a talent parade in the yard, and I would win the dollar every evening. Them time I was around eight, nine, ten. I used to sing foreign songs mostly, like [The Drifters'] 'Mexican Divorce'. This guy said: 'You're really the Pied Piper, 'cos people have to listen to you when they hear your voice'. So from that they call I Pipe."

"Growing up in Trench Town, you can't get away from music," adds Bread. "I was born in Trench Town inna the early 50s. When I was about three years old my parents migrated, so I was raised by my grandmother and some uncles and aunts. My grandmother came from Westmoreland, so she had her skills: she would make starch and sell it. At a very early age I fell in love with music, couldn't sleep unless I was hearing music; sometimes I even used to go and wash my face so I could listen to the top ten. My grandfather used to have a mento band in those days, and they used to play at bars and likkle public functions. As far back as I can remember, a guitar was always in the home. Listening to the music on the radio, I start mimicking singers like The Temptations, The Impressions, Sam Cooke. You also used to get Elvis Presley and even country & western." Bread's nickname came about "'cos we inna the ghetto, we change everything around: you have an English saying, it's 'a piece of cake', so if something is easy we say it's 'a piece of bread'."

As a singer with an easily identified high-C tenor, Pipe made a natural group leader. He was also the first to gain concrete experience, having made his recording debut before reaching adolescence. "'Little Dilly', that was my first song. At the age of ten-and-a-half to eleven, I did that as The Schoolboys with another Trench Town youth, Colin Johnson. I wrote the song and used to sing in class every Friday. A friend was living downtown, and he said: 'You supposed to can record that song – I know a man I can carry you to.' So one evening me and him went down by Prince Buster's record shop, and two days after, we did the song at Federal. We did a couple more tunes with him, but after 'Little Dilly' get popular, my partner's father said that he had other things for him to do. We had done a couple shows together in the city, but in Montego Bay at the Palladium Theatre I did that show by myself and that was when I really proved myself. Jimmy Cliff, The Blues Busters, a lot of the top guys were on the bill, and they all congratulated me afterward. After my partner fell out I wasn't doing any singing, I was just dealing with school. But at evening time, we would sit down amongst the rest of the guys and practise. Then we form the group.'

"Trench Town is a place that is really known for singers," Bread continues, "and in those days you had people like Joe Higgs, Alton Ellis, Lascelles Perkins, and young groups coming up, like The Wailers. Coming from school in the evening, we naturally go play cricket and soccer, 'cos we had a park right by where we live on First Street. And most of the time, Ken Boothe and most of the other professional singers in the area who were coming up, they would gather right in front of the park, so when we finish playing soccer or cricket we younger guys used to just go right into the government yard, into the kitchen where those guys would be rehearsing, and pretty soon we start join in the background, like a choir. Trench Town is a place like that: when somebody start sing, pretty soon you see all ten people gather round and start singing too, provide background vocal for an established singer. So we started doing that – me, Pipe, George 'Buddy' Haye, and 'Saboo', who is Oswald Downer, and 'Fats', Norman Davis – he sing in The Tennors before he came to us – and then you have Vision Walker, a cousin of Rita Marley who in and out of The Wailers. It's just like one big family. People start to recognise us, and then it got to the point wherein people couldn't even tell when the professional guys were there from when we were there."

Bread says the group's first official incarnation was sparked by unexpected session work in 1966. "Ainsley Folder, one of these elder guys that always hear us singing, he worked at Federal records as an accountant. They know he's from Trench Town, and that's where the singers are from, so if they need any background vocals they usually contact him. Federal was the biggest recording studio in the Caribbean at that time, had all the latest equipment. It so happens that this Englishwoman called Pam Blythe – in those days one of Jamaica's top female vocalists – was doing some songs and she wanted some singers, but at that time we never even had a name. Ainsley came and say: 'Guys, I got a job for you.' We went and did two songs with her: one was 'Somewhere My Love', the title song from the movie *Doctor Zhivago*. It was me, Pipe, Buddy, and Rupert Edwards – he wasn't a professional singer, but he lived in Trench Town. We did those songs in the morning, and by the next day the song was on the radio because Federal was so big. It was a number-one song, so they said: 'You guys need a name.' We consider ourselves rebels, so we came up with the name The Renegades. Right after that, Ainsley came and say: 'Ernest Ranglin's doing an album [*A Mod A Mod Ranglin*] and they want you guys to do the background vocals.' So we went as The Renegades, but this time it was just myself, Pipe, and Buddy. That was how we, as a group, really get started."

The group then cut a handful of sides for Federal. "Because they were so impressed with us we did a little recording contract, but there wasn't no lawyer involved. Not even our parents were there, and all of us was under-age." Most of the resultant material, like 'You've Lost The Love', 'Why Make Me Cry', and 'You're Too Young To Love', consisted of heartache and young romance ballads, delivered in a soul-influenced style; 'Mr Hops' was a depiction of the street toughs' preference for warm beer.

Generally wary of the music business, the Renegades disbanded when other commitments took precedence. "We grow up under all those artists and we sit down and listen to their horror stories, so we say we nah go make any producer exploit we. About the same time Buddy started going to art school; that was one of the main reasons why we take a break. He said he's not going to have too much time for rehearsal and he want to penetrate him art. Then I was a great cricketer, play for the Jamaica Schoolboy All-Schools cricket team, and that used to take up a lot of my time."

As the 1970s approached and the reggae sound began to consolidate, however, Pipe and Bread felt an urge to re-form their group. "Me and Pipe wanted to find a third singer to make up for Buddy's spot," Bread recalls, "so we actually was using Delroy Wilson's younger brother Errol – everybody call him Batman. He was a great singer and songwriter, and he could play drums. Bob [Marley] was even thinking of him being his drummer before Bob had his musicians together. We started rehearsing as a trio, but in Trench Town you have a lot of bad; you have a lot of gun play and it's a thin line." Such unsavoury ways led to Batman being ejected from the group; shortly afterward, he immortalised himself in song on The Slickers' 'Johnny Too Bad' – the ultimate rude-boy homage.

Soon the group became a quartet, and a renewed closeness with The Wailers saw them christened The Wailing Souls. "When we find that it wasn't happening with Batman, we get Saboo and Fats, and that's how the original Wailing Souls were really born. Fats sing almost a baritone, Saboo the falsetto. We were always close friends with Bob and Peter and Bunny, we were like their younger brothers, so you find we move with them real tight. Spiritually we check the Bible, and we like the character John The Baptist, who they say was the soul crying in the wilderness. Then when we see that The Wailers was there and The Soulettes, we were thinking of just one family, so we figure say The Wailing Souls. We went to The Matador, because him was a soundman, come from the ghetto, like some roots man – a young guy too, and he start to do some nice shots, like 'Bongo Nyah'."

'Gold Digger', their debut for Matador, caused controversy due to its street-slang reference to women's private parts. "It was banned in Jamaica because we use a term, 'nusney'," laughs Bread. "We only end up doing one song for Lloyd, 'cos the other song was 'Back Out With It', but them days we say 'Back Out Wicked', and every word come like them so dangerous: 'You say you love when you know say your heart is like a poison dart / Back out wicked, your days are numbered.' So he figure it too heavy."

"His wife didn't like the words," Pipe adds, "so I change it and we went to Mr Dodd. Mr Dodd was the most current producer, put out shots after shots, so we did an audition and Mr Dodd wanted us to come record. We went back and did 'Row Fisherman Row', 'Back Out With It', and 'Mr Fire

Coal Man', those three songs first." All were significant hits in Jamaica, with 'Mr Fire Coal Man' particularly notable for its original lyrics and unique sound effects.

"The first song that I really sing lead on was 'Mr Fire Coal Man'," Bread notes. "Growing up in Trench Town, there's always a lot of emergency vehicles going by, fire truck and ambulance, 'cos things always happening bad and fire always burn. Inna them days, we deal with consciousness of black people. From an early age we know about Rasta, we know about black solidarity and oppression and righteousness, so we always try and make songs to reflect them type of things. We always look 'pon things in a certain way, 'cos them say Jesus Christ speak in parables, and I-and-I make songs whe' you have to read between the lines, 'cos in 'Mr Fire Coal Man' we talk about the black man – we figure the black man rise up and come and do him work, 'cos fire coal is black. Although you hear the sound of a siren, a fire engine type of thing, if you check the lyrics it's not about that." Bread further notes that responsibility for the siren lay with Errol Dunkley, who pressed the session guitarist's effects pedal at specific intervals; he also says Jackie Mittoo was featured on much of their Studio One material. "He was in Canada, but Jackie used to come to Jamaica regular still."

In their brief period at Studio One, The Wailing Souls cut dozens of originals, typically credited to The Classics. Pipe has also spoken of cover tunes that Dodd asked him to record, including his sensitive rendition of The Wailers' 'Sun Is Shining'. Although Pipe's voice held echoes of Bob Marley's style, the cover also hinted at the intense closeness between the two groups. When The Wailers and their manager, noted footballer Alan 'Skill' Cole, established the independent Tuff Gong in 1971, The Wailing Souls were part of it; their songs 'Harbour Shark' and 'Back Biter', which both attacked self-centred greed, were issued on the label and credited to Pipe & The Pipers.

"The first two records that come on Tuff Gong was 'Trench Town Rock' and 'Harbour Shark' – that was the same session at Dynamics," Bread notes. "We let go of Studio One now, and then we and Bob start record and really get tighter than we were before. Saboo got one of the government houses, right there on First Street in Trench Town, and that became the rehearsal house, and that's the house that 'Trench Town Rock' was made in. We sung on the song in the studio and 'Back Biter' was done at the same session. Bob later did 'Baby We've Got A Date' on the same rhythm. Me and Pipe do background vocals for Bob on a lot of them tunes there, like 'Redder Than Red' and 'Lick Samba', along with Peter and Bunny. Peter Tosh used to do some separate works with Joe Gibbs, like 'Here Comes The Judge' – that's me and Peter and Pipe and Vision. In Saboo's house, Bob them started getting instruments, but police raid the house one day and we run, and they took out the equipment and we never got them back. Sometimes police raid, because we smoke weed, and Peter lose a lot of guitars like that – we have to throw the guitar over the wall and the neck break. Whole heap of things we have to go through them days."

Although their music was somewhat out of step with the love songs that still dominated the charts, the rise of groups like The Abyssinians, The Wailing Souls, and Burning Spear pointed the way toward the spiritual and political focus of the approaching roots reggae period. Winston Rodney, the man who became Jamaica's Burning Spear after adopting the moniker of Kenyan freedom fighter Jomo Kenyatta, wrote some of the era's most outstanding material. His unblemished career has lasted to the present; he maintains a growing international popularity based on an impressive body of recorded work and arresting live performances.

Rodney was born in the small coastal town of Saint Ann's Bay in 1948. "My mother was in the food business," he explains at his present base in Queens, New York. "She was doing food for people on construction jobs, and my father was a man who believe in his little farming, raising chickens."

Rodney had a variety of unsatisfying jobs before being directed to Studio One by Bob Marley in 1969. "At one time I was learning mechanic trade, another time I was cleaning clothes. I happened to meet Bob in Saint Ann's, cause Bob is from Saint Ann's too, and he told I I should check Studio One. I went there and sing my song – I think Heptones did involve in the audition. The following day we start to record."

The fiery 'Door Peep', Burning Spear's debut, created an immediate impact through its melodic individuality, with shifts from major to minor keys adding an ominous feel. "I think 'Door Peep' create a newness musically in Studio One. When I went there and do my thing, the music wasn't in that flavour or arrangement."

Rupert Willington, an aspiring baritone singer, travelled to Kingston with Rodney to sing harmony on 'Door Peep' and a handful of other early works. "He was a young man who grow up in the same town where I'm coming from. We never used to associate until after I was singing, and sometimes he's going by and he involve in what I was doing, and I happens to like his tone, so we did those few singles together for Studio One, and that was about it with me and him."

In the early 70s, Burning Spear recorded a series of stupendous singles for Studio One, mostly with historical and religious themes. He also issued two excellent albums, *Burning Spear* and *Rocking Time*, before he left the label in late 1974. Spear's Studio One material is rightly regarded as classic, and its individuality is highly inspiring. The military snare rolls, bubbling organ, and jazzy vocal arrangements of 'New Civilization', for instance, sound very different from the work of his contemporaries. Rodney describes the song's lyrics as prophetic: "Sometimes you feel the things what going to take place before it even take place; sometimes you see things ahead of time. So what I was singing about, that is exactly what is taking place now: a new civilisation."

Of equal importance were the songs that worked to heighten the profile of the Rastafari faith, such as the chugging 'Ethiopians Live It Out' and the prayer-like 'Zion Higher'. "We all born as Rasta, and it was a good experience, knowing that I could identify myself within the roots and culture and the history and the *livity*. You hear it in the music: all of us was free to express that, and I wasn't the only one expressing that. After a while, everyone was expressing Rastafari within the music and through the music, and that became a strong part of Jamaica's music also – nobody didn't present no form of opposition to that."

Leroy 'Horsemouth' Wallace, then the resident drummer at Studio One, provided the beat behind such work. He once lived in an odd property development on the outskirts of Spanish Town, where our interview took place; though described as a 'gated' community with 24-hour security, the contractors never completed the gate, so the security was non-existent. Horsemouth's dwelling had no visible number, but the sound of Burning Spear blasting from a row of speaker boxes advertised his presence. He says his playing style was greatly influenced by African-Jamaican folk rhythms. "I was born in Three Mile in 1947. My grandmother lived in Trench Town at 7 White Street, which is walking distance. She was a healer, sees inside of your soul. Where I'm from, we've got a lot of culture, like Junkanoo, Pocomania, and I was already playing Pocomania drums for my grandmother when I was very young. Drumming was a very deeply inflicted thing in me."

Wallace says he joined the Alpha school band at the age of six. "My mother sell fish on the street. She was very poor and couldn't afford me, and my father wasn't interested. Alpha Boys' School, it was different. Coming from a poor family in the ghetto, you move to this big dormitory of 600 kids. They give you a white people's God and you see statues of Mary. I go out with Alpha band in the space of two weeks." But he ran into trouble with the disciplinarian regime and was expelled. "I leave Alpha when I was maybe 14. Sister [Ignacious] run me out of the school because I was not getting conformed to the system. Sister give me a recommendation to go into the army, but I left straight down to where I'm from, 'cos I was tired of conforming with colonisation. My mother live at 202 Spanish Town Road, right beside Excelsior biscuit factory, but it was very hard for me the first two years I leave Alpha. I didn't know how to cope with the outside world after spending almost 12 years in an institution. My mother chased me out right away, so I used to stay at the Silver Dollar Club, where they gamble 24 hours. That's on East Queen Street, past the Central Police Station, and there's a whorehouse there at High Holborn Street."

He found his way into recording studios because of printing skills rather than musical talent. "I learn three trades at Alpha: printing, music, and tile making. I used to work at West Indies Records before it become Dynamic Sounds to print labels, leave and go to Coxsone and do printing. They didn't know I'm a drummer." At the time Fil Callender was still Studio One's resident drummer. "He had a good Latin beat. He plays on some of the songs on *Heptones On Top*, but there was a lot of good drummers like Bunny Williams, and Joe Isaacs – he was there before Fil. One day Fil didn't turn up and it was a blessing for me. I went in the drum booth and Sylvan Morris, the engineer, didn't see me go inside. I start to play and it sound so good, everybody think Fil is there. When I come out: 'Horsemouth, you was playing drums?' Coxsone comes in the evening and the engineer tell him: 'Horsemouth play drums on those songs – the printer play better than Fil,' so he make Fil play guitar and I becomes the resident drummer from that day, play on Wailing Souls, Larry Marshall, and I'm the one who take Dennis Brown to the studio. All this Burning Spear, three persons play: Fil [guitar], Bagga [bass], and Horsemouth play the drums."

Horsemouth was also building a reputation on the live scene, though his gravitation toward conflict sometimes got in the way. After he joined Soul Syndicate, he was jailed for protesting against the Shearer government's banning of Walter Rodney, a lecturer at the University of the West Indies' Mona campus. Rodney, a Guyanese Marxist who stressed the potential of Rastafari to aid the struggle against imperialism in the Caribbean, was deemed a security threat and was therefore refused entry to Jamaica on his way back from a black writers' conference in Montreal.

"On 28 October 1968, there was a big riot in Kingston," Wallace recalls. "Dr Rodney and Mohammed Ali was supposed to come to Jamaica, but they banned him at the airport, and everybody make a protest. It was a black demonstration, and they start to burn Kingston. I get charged for stone throwing, and Mr Fullwood come bail me – I really appreciate that. Then Santa went with Mr Fullwood's band and I went to The Mighty Vikings, but those jobs were like ten dollars a night."

He quit another hotel gig because of perceived prejudice. "I was travelling with Byron Lee's band one time, Kes Chin was talking about 'blacks from the ghetto', and I didn't like that. I figure I didn't fit in and I wait till they reach Ocho Rios, just opt out, give them back their shirts for the band uniform, and I sit down at Jack Ruby's and smoke a draw, eat fish, and went back to Kingston."

Ruby, aka Lawrence Lindo, operated a highly popular sound system in Ocho Rios. "He was real roots," Horsemouth says. "He would play in the ghetto for roots people, bringing up Jamaican music. He used to live in Greenwich Farm, with Jack Ruby's Hi-Fi, but after the mid 60s Greenwich Farm, Jones Town, and all those areas get real violent. People start to come from country and the environment start to get spoiled. It got broken down by bad people from evil areas – that goes on from the city all over the world."

Part of what made Burning Spear's 'Door Peep' so striking was its spectacular horn riff provided by saxophonist Cedric Brooks and trumpeter David Madden, the duo otherwise known as Im & David. Previously, the Studio One horn section had featured saxophonist Glen DaCosta and trombonist Vin 'Don Drummond Junior' Gordon (aka Trommy). All but Brooks would eventually be active in the experimental jazz-reggae group Zap Pow, and all four were ex-Alpha boys.

"I was raised in Gordon Town," says Madden at his home in a quiet uptown cul-de-sac. "There was a storm in 1951 and my mother couldn't manage things, so she sent me to Alpha Boys'. Me and Im went to Alpha together: he went to the military band, I came in after. When he left the military band, he went to a hotel on the North Coast, and then he went to the States and started to go into jazz. During that time I left the army, played in several bands.[12] In [October] 1969 I was playing at this little place in New Kingston with Nancy Wilson. Jesse Ferguson & The Outer Limits, a group from the States – they had one song on the charts, 'Putting It On, Putting It Off', one of them American Gospel spiritual things – they came to Jamaica and heard me playing. Their trumpet player would be drafted into the army, so they invited me to Las Vegas for four months. Reggae was just about budding now, and Cedric came home. I hear everybody talking about Cedric Brooks, so we got linked up and started to go down to

Coxsone, because Glen and Trommy had left – that regular thing with Coxsone had broken up. Coxsone started to give us some tracks to play on: we play on Burning Spear's first time, with Ernest Ranglin playing guitar."

In addition to backing other Studio One stars like The Heptones, Brooks and Madden cut several inspired instrumentals for Coxsone, including the vibrant 'Money Maker', which rose high in the Jamaican charts in 1970. Shortly afterward Brooks joined Count Ossie's Mystic Revelation of Rastafari and Madden formed the first incarnation of Zap Pow. "Me and Cedric put a group together called The Mystics," he says.[13] "The group was going on fine, but Cedric was going off on his religious thing. He had gone to a couple of groundations with Count Ossie, playing saxophone. [Drummer] Danny Mowatt decided to come with me, and that was the birth of Zap Pow. We found [bassist] Mikey [Williams] and [guitarist] Dwight Pinkney, starting this little piece of group together. There was one song that me and Cedric were introducing to Coxsone, which was 'Mystic Mood'. Coxsone had wanted to record it, but not the way that we had it. I think Mikey had had an experience with Coxsone that he didn't like, so we just went to Joe Gibbs's little house studio in Duhaney Park.[14] The song became a hit: that is what catapult the group Zap Pow into anything."

Albert Griffiths of The Gladiators also remembers playing on some of Burning Spear's Studio One material. "I play with Burning Spear, back up Stranger Cole – Bagga was the bass man, me was the rhythm guitarist, Benbow [aka Anthony Creary] was the drummer, and Pablove Black [aka Paul Dixon] was the keyboard player."

In the early 70s, The Gladiators were in a state of flux. By 1972 David Webber had been replaced by Clinton Fearon, a tall young man with a deep voice who wrote convincing religious material. "I was playin' my guitar on my veranda one day, and Errol Grandison passed by and heard me playin' and singin'," Fearon states by e-mail from Seattle. "We sing a few songs together and he informed me that they had lost a member and he think I would be perfect for the slot. A few days later he brought Albert by, and musically it was magical. The first songs I recorded with the group was 'Freedom Train' and 'Rock A Man Soul' for Lloyd Daley. At that time it was Albert Griffiths, Errol Grandison, and myself."

Grandison was next to leave. "Errol tell me that I was doing foolishness," Griffiths recalls, "because inna those days you sing and you're not getting any money, and he have him woman and pickney [children] to mind. Me and Clinton get it going with 'Sonia' and all them songs there."

"We did a song named 'Sonia' for Coxsone," Fearon continues. "It was

Albert, myself, and this girl. I seem to remember her name was Beverley, and we did maybe one or two more songs together."

"After, it was me and Clinton Fearon, but we decide that two of us kind of unbalanced," says Griffiths. "Gallimore Sutherland was with me all the time doing building work, so we bring in Gallimore to be the third man." Sutherland's command of the upper register completed the picture, giving the trio a warm, harmonic whole.

Griffiths and Fearon were regular Studio One session musicians in the early 70s. Fearon began on guitar but turned out to be a great bass player. "Gladiators did employ as the backing band for Studio One artists," Griffiths notes. "We go to Studio One to record a song named 'Selassie Bandman' by a group named The Manchesters. I was playing the bass and Clinton Fearon was playing the lead guitar, but he couldn't manage it, so I give him the bass, and from that day he begin to play him bass." The group remained solidly at Studio One as vocalists and backing musicians until late 1974, when they branched off to work for other producers.

Although the Gladiators had an unseen hand in shaping the music emanating from Brentford Road in the early 70s, their greatest contribution, like that of Burning Spear and The Abyssinians, was aiding the shift of focus at Studio One. On songs that spoke of the spiritual devotion blossoming in a land plagued by social injustice, these artists helped to usher in the format later designated as 'roots', while Soul Syndicate and Now Generation were responsible for the dominant musical backing utilised by other producers. In the same era, a number of significant changes to the reggae form arose from experimentation in the camp of Coxsone's traditional rival on Bond Street.

6
MERRY UP
Deejay, dub, and other innovations

"A deejay is just a person who talks over the mic, puts records on, and reads the invitation where the next dance is going to keep. Who could ever tell that this thing would ever reach like this, people having number one on the chart!" – U ROY

"The bass and drum is the key to any music, and the rest of the stuff is just spice." – FULLY FULLWOOD

Duke Reid may have ruled rock steady, but he was largely in Coxsone's shadow with reggae. Left behind by the changes that swept Jamaican music, he was unable to get his head around the new style and gradually lost touch with his audience as the form evolved. The mutation of The Supersonics to The All Stars made matters worse, and Reid had to borrow the talents of other producers to find a hit. Lee Perry assisted him with 'Lock Jaw', a 1969 organ instrumental with a shouted introduction by Dave Barker, but Perry says that Reid was already in decline then.

A major reversal of Duke's downturn came in the early 70s, after he achieved an unprecedented success with U Roy's amazing deejay discs. U Roy at Treasure Isle simply redefined the role of the deejay, with major consequences. Not only did the deejay's increased status inordinately change the shape of Jamaican music, but the revolution started by U Roy's innovations at Treasure Isle would ultimately help spawn rap in America, and rap is now one of the most popular music genres in the world.

U Roy was not, however, the first Jamaican deejay to appear on record.[1] There had been instances of deejays breaking the monotony of ska instrumentals with exciting, Africanised whelps and peculiar vocal interjections, most notably Cool Sticky [Uziah Thompson] on The Skatalites' 'Guns Of Navarone' and 'Ball Of Fire'. In 1967, Sir Lord Comic went one step further with slowly drawling toasts on 'Ska-ing West' and 'The Great Wuga Wuga'. However, although these highly popular songs were pioneering

163

attempts to extend a deejay's chatter throughout an entire rhythm, in truth Comic sounds awkward and out of time, his delivery little more than a series of proverbs and gimmicky quotations carelessly thrown together.

More substantial deejay hits came with reggae's 1968 arrival, although the vocal input was always fairly limited. The first to gain popularity was King Stitt's wild 'Fire Corner' for Clancy Eccles; 'Herbman Shuffle', recorded for Linford Anderson, also had a shouted introduction and plenty of vocal sound effects to emphasise the song's pro-ganja message.[2] "I was the one who put King Stitt on 'Herbman Shuffle'," Anderson states proudly. "If you listen to the record, I'm also talking on there. You can hear my voice along with King Stitt."

Similarly, the wacky 'Pop A Top', voiced by Anderson under the alias Andy Capp, was another early quirky deejay disc. On this one Anderson attempted to mimic the bubbling sound featured on an advertisement for Canada Dry ginger ale over an adaptation of a popular New Orleans R&B number. As he explains: "I did 'Pop A Top', the first talking record in Jamaica – you can put that in any book. I heard the commercial – the guy said 'Pop A Top'. Then I had this rhythm, 'South Parkway Mambo', a very old song by Dave Bartholomew. The instrumental version I was trying to re-create didn't work, so we didn't touch that tape for years. One day I got it out, Lloyd Charmers started playing 'pup pup pup, pup pup pup' [on the organ], so I said: 'Oh, Pop A Top!' That's how that song came about. The tune became a big hit, so eventually we had about 13 different versions of it."

These discs all hinted at the broader potential of toasting as deejays gradually made longer appearances on record, but the true limits of the form were not realised until Daddy U Roy stepped up to the microphone at Treasure Isle. In 1970, U Roy achieved the seemingly impossible hat-trick of scoring the top three records on both Jamaican radio charts. All three featured his fluid, continuous toasting over Reid's rock steady rhythms. The deejay daddy, who remains entirely humble despite his great achievements, was keen to point out that no one was more surprised by the success of the discs than himself: "I didn't think that something like this would ever happen, and that it would still be going on until now. At the time it was like a joke! A deejay is just a person who comes to a dance, he talks over the mic and puts records on and reads the invitation where the next dance is going to keep. Who could ever tell that this thing would ever reach like this, people having number one on the chart!"

U Roy's love of music hit him early, making him a regular fixture at Kingston's sound-system events by the age of 11. In the mid 60s he began chatting on Sir Dickie's Dynamic, later switching to Sir George The Atomic and eventually settling by 1968 on the famed King Tubby's Home Town Hi-Fi, operated by electronics technician and sometime Treasure Isle mastering engineer Osbourne Ruddock in the Penwood area of the Waterhouse ghetto.

Ruddock's nickname stemmed from Tubman, his mother's maiden name. He founded his sound system in 1958 at 17, and was crowned 'King of the Dancehall' at a neighbourhood event in the early 60s, but Niney suggests that his set was initially a small concern affiliated to uptown venues. "King Tubby used to have a likkle hi-fi that he played up Red Hills, play all about. There is certain little people follow him – not the rebel people those days – cause he have a hi-fi. Tubby used to tape songs off the radio, like certain time of night he plug in the radio station and play it back into his sound. I used to go when he's playing at Rockall: he have a crown on his head and his amplifier was a little baby amplifier."

Fellow deejay Dennis Alcapone notes that U Roy's presence on Tubby's sound greatly established the toaster's reputation, partly because of the impact of the King's custom-built effects. "King Tubby's was definitely the greatest sound ever to come out of Jamaica. You wouldn't listen to the other sounds, because they was just bringing out normal voices with normal bass. Duke Reid and Coxsone, their bass was heavy, but Tubby's bass was just so solid, and then he brought in reverb, which wasn't introduced to the public before – it was mind-blowing."

Lloyd The Matador adds details of Tubby's sound-system reverb. "Number 3 Tiverton Road was one of the most popular dancehalls in East Kingston. It was owned by Brown's Funeral Parlour – the owner would build and store coffins there and rent it out for dances. Some time in 1960, when my sound system was playing there, King Tubby came to the dance as an admirer of my sound. He asked if I could give him a circuit diagram for the reverb my sound was using, so I sat on one of the coffins that was in the yard, draw the circuit and gave Tubby. That was the reverb that Tubbs built from my circuit diagram and used on his sound system for a long time."

Bunny Lee says hearing U Roy live on Tubby's sound was astounding because he toasted over exclusive mixes of hit songs with the vocals removed; Lee names this as the start of the 'version' phenomenon in which remixed instrumental B-sides began to appear in the late 60s. He credits Rudolph 'Ruddy' Redwood, the financially solvent owner of sound system Supreme Ruler of Sound (SRS), as the developer of this form. Lee likes to say that Ruddy's development was a "mistake", but the way he describes it the experimentation seems quite deliberate. Ruddy, he says, was "another wealthy man who can help himself. Him inna racehorses and have him record shop and a big club 'cross Fort Henderson, so when him come ah Duke Reid and Coxsone, them give him any tape him want. One evening them ah cut dub plate, and when them cut, it's difficult to put in the voice, and Smithy ah go stop it and Ruddy say: 'No, make it run.' When it done, him say it art, and me and Tubby stand up right there, me look 'pon Tubby and Tubby look 'pon me.

"Saturday night him drop the singing cut first and the deejay name Wassy said: 'I'm going to play part two!' and the whole dancehall start to sing the song 'pon the pure rhythm. Him have to play it about ten, fifteen times because it's something new. I say: 'Boy Tubbs, you see the mistake whe' Smithy make? A serious thing! The people ah Spanish Town love it! You have to start do something like that.' Tubby just bang onto U Roy, U Roy come in and say: 'Part two, another version' on 'Too Proud To Beg' with Slim Smith, ah so the name version come in. When it start, you hear Slim Smith start to sing and then you hear the voice gone! Then you hear him come in again, and you hear U Roy talk: 'Love the life you live and live the life you love, here come the brother Slim Smith again, tell them,' and a man say: 'Boy, Tubby have amplifier that can take out the voice and play pure rhythm.' Little did them know that's how the dub make out. There goes version now, and everybody wants it 'pon them record."

It is worth noting that rhythm tracks had already been used for more than one purpose. At Studio One in 1965, Roland Alphonso blew sax on a song called 'Rinky Dink', using the rhythm of Lee Perry & The Dynamites' 'Hold Down' with the vocals removed. However, the standard practice of 'version' B-sides being constructed from customised rhythm tracks clearly follows from the legendary 1968 session described above. The rise of version would ultimately pave the way for the experimental contours of dub, in which previously recorded songs would be remixed to emphasise drum and bass, making greater space for deejays to appear on record, particularly after U Roy showed what could be done with the form.

By late 1969 U Roy's verbal prowess saw him lured to the studio by dental technician and aspiring producer Keith Hudson, who was then on the verge of success with Ken Boothe's broken-hearted love song 'Old Fashioned Way'. The producer cut U Roy over this rhythm, but test pressings bewildered radio station personnel, causing Hudson to delay the song's issue. U Roy's next recording, 'Rightful Ruler', cut under Lee Perry's direction, was a radical religious toast that celebrated Roy's Rastafari faith. Set to Niyabinghi drumming by Count Ossie, with the toaster's grave chanting of Psalm One spurred on by fervent shouts from Peter Tosh, the disc failed to capture the public's imagination. These tunes, says U Roy, "didn't get very far", selling only "a couple hundred" copies.

Success was finally achieved when Duke Reid placed the toaster over older material, resulting in new mutations of rock steady classics. "When I started working for Duke, my first songs were 'Wake The Town', 'Rule The Nation', and 'Wear You To The Ball'. From 'Wear You To The Ball', it just broke the place right up: I had number one, two, and three on the chart, on two radio stations for six weeks, and I had one tune at number one for twelve weeks. I just couldn't believe it."

'Wake The Town' and 'Rule The Nation' were little more than invitations for dancers to strut their stuff, with the previous vocal tracks removed to make way for the toaster's reverb-laden chat. But 'Wear You To The Ball' set a precedent by retaining fragments of The Paragons' vocals; this allowed U Roy to frame his toast around the message of the original hit, drawing deeper recognition from those who loved the original. This format would be most lasting in Jamaica, and would find greater resonance in the construction of American rap in the late 70s.

Despite Reid's blanket ban on lyrics expressing Rasta sentiment, U Roy stayed with Treasure Isle for the next couple of years, building up a strong working relationship that culminated in the voicing of nearly three dozen tracks, the best of which were compiled as album releases. Roy continues to speak highly of the Duke: "He was giving me some money all right at that time and we have an agreement that, when everything is kind of crapping up, I'm going to want a little house out of my royalty, and he did do that. I used to go to him for any money I want during the weekend for running my house. I never really have no problem getting some money from him, but I still used to know that I wasn't getting what I really supposed to get. When you're just young in this, you don't understand. It's just fun for you to know that you've been in the limelight and things been good for you. But the vibes was really with Duke Reid, definitely. Duke was a man who used to deal with me all right."

One of the earliest hits U Roy scored away from Duke was 'Scandal' for Lloyd Daley. As he explains: "After the incident with the police damaging my sound system, my wife wrote a tune, 'Born To Lose', meaning that we always lose a lot of money. She teamed up with Lloyd Robinson and sang it in 1968 at Federal. It came out on blank label pre-release and didn't go very far, so we went back into the studio with some horns men, including Tommy McCook, and U Roy, and made it into 'Scandal', a big hit."

The way U Roy shifted the status of the deejay from that of a peripheral fixture to a recording star whose microphone rhymes were as important as any singer's lyrics earned him the apt title of 'The Originator', and it was only natural that younger toasters would try to emulate his success. Dennis Alcapone, star toaster with the small but popular El Paso sound system, based in the Waltham Park area, was next to excel at the form. Born Dennis Smith in the rural district of Culloden in 1946, he was also attracted to the sound system at an early age. "When I went to Kingston I was living on Waltham Park Road, where there was a dancehall at number 28. That's where all the big sounds come: Duke Reid, Coxsone, King Edwards The Giant, Sir Percy, Count Bells The President, and Thunderstorm. There was also a place quite close by in Oakland Crescent; Lord Comic would be there, playing."

After spinning records at parties, Dennis formed his own set with two friends. "We started borrowing speakers from people in the area, playing in the yard. We play one and two places until we started to establish ourselves, buy our own speakers and a 72 steel amp, and start buying dub plates from Duke Reid. Our first had [The Melodians'] 'Everybody Bawling', John Holt's 'Ali Baba', and The Techniques' 'Travelling Man'; it cost about ten dollars. We didn't actually have a name at that time. There was a sound in the neighbourhood that was very good: El Toro, down by Greenwich Farm, run by Vivian Blake. His deejay was Cry Cry [later known as Prince Fari] and this guy named Bunny Remus, who was more or less his upfront deejay, because Cry Cry used to go to prison. El Toro had a tune that we used to love listening to, [Marty Robbins's] 'El Paso', so that's how the name born."

A deejay called Pompadoo also inspired. "I was not great then. More or less them times we used to just introduce the songs. When I really get fascinated about deejay is when a sound named Kentone came to Waltham Avenue to play at a dance. Pompadoo was the deejay and he said: 'My name is Kentone, I come from the other side of town.' He was a very stylish deejay. Those days playing sound was not like now, when you have a selector and all kind of different people operating the sound. In those days it was just the deejay that do every damn thing, including lifting up the box and setting up the sound! When Pompadoo was deejaying, he was so stylish that I was just fascinated by him. Then we decided to take it a bit further lyrically."

As with U Roy's recording debut, the imaginative producer Keith Hudson first brought Alcapone into the studio. "In those days, El Paso was carrying the swing. Everybody used to come and listen to El Paso: producers, singers, rude boys. Everybody used to come for one reason: that was to hear me. Obviously the word go around that I'm expeditious, so Keith Hudson said he want me to do the 'El Paso' song for him, but the rhythm that he had wasn't the rhythm that I did 'El Paso' on for the sound system. I used to work on The Techniques' song 'You Don't Care', but he had a different rhythm that just didn't fit."

Despite this uncertain start, Alcapone is full of praise for the producer. "Hudson was a 'soul man' with a big Afro. He was a handsome guy and he give me good encouragement; for instance, he opened my first bank account and get stage gear." It was difficult for either of them to break into the big time. "I did several other songs for him, including 'Spanish Amigo', which went into the charts, but people wasn't accustomed to deejay music in those days so it didn't make that amount of impact until later. Keith Hudson was more or less what you'd call a new man in the business: he didn't have influence to get radio promotion. Duke Reid was more established, so whatever Duke Reid does, the public hears, because he had a half-hour programme each week on RJR."

'Spanish Amigo', an alternative cut of 'Old Fashioned Way', was also ahead of its time because it had Alcapone toasting through a false start of the record. "That was Keith Hudson's idea, because Keith Hudson is a man who's always trying something new. When I did the intro he made Errol Thompson, the engineer at Randy's, splice back the intro so it would repeat."

Although Alcapone drew much inspiration from U Roy, adapting a higher shriek of "Yeah yeah *yeah!*" as a trademark, he tended to make use of more rhymes than The Originator and was not averse to adapting nursery rhymes. With a few popular tunes under his belt and continued appearances on El Paso, demand grew rapidly. "U Roy was at Duke Reid and I decided that Coxsone has some prime rhythms, so I'll just go to Studio One. I went and did 'Nanny Version' [over Larry & Alvin's 'Nanny Goat']. When I was recording for Keith Hudson I was recording under my right name, Dennis Smith, so to make it sound a bit more interesting I tell Coxsone, "Put Dennis Alcapone." After 'Nanny Version' hit, I did 'Home Version' over Ken Boothe's 'Home'. One day Duke Reid send for me and said: 'That tune that you did, "Nanny Goat", didn't U Roy help you on the tune?' I said: 'No, it's just me did it.' Then Byron Smith asked me to do 'Mosquito One', and he called me 'El Paso' because at the time I was with Coxsone."

When Reid finally caught up with Alcapone, the result was another series of hits. "I think Duke Reid was impressed by the whole thing, and though I went back to Coxsone and did a few other songs, one day Duke Reid call me again and say he wanted me to do a song for him. I went down and did

'Teach The Children', which was a hit song, though I didn't think for a minute that tune would be so big. We did 'Wake Up Jamaica' after that and 'Number One Station', and then I bring in Lizzy for 'Big Beat'."

The duet deejay discs created by Alcapone and Lizzy scored hits like 'Big Beat' and the nonsensical 'Ba Ba Ri Ba Skank'. The team established a combination formula that prefaced the internationally popular Jamaican acts of the 80s and 90s, such as Michigan & Smiley and Chaka Demus & Pliers, as well as the superstar US rap combos of the late 70s such as Run DMC, Dr Jeckyll & Mr Hyde, and Double Trouble.

Lizzy was then the star deejay on Prince Jammy's sound system, established in Waterhouse by Lloyd James in 1962; the set was out of action from 1969, because James went to live in Canada. Although Lizzy was popular when recording with Alcapone, he failed to maintain the momentum with solo material, and his own eventual emigration to Canada marked a permanent departure from music. In contrast, Alcapone continued to churn out hits, distinguishing himself by unusual vocal elements such as his imitation of a cockerel on 'Wake Up Jamaica', 'Power Version', and 'Rasta Dub' (the latter a cut of Bob Marley's 'Keep On Moving' recorded for Lee Perry).

"In Jamaica, when you wake up in the morning there's a lot of cock crowing," the toaster explains. "It's a sound that you hear early in the morning and sometimes in the night when the little bastard them dropping off the roof. Cock crowing is a thing that we live with day by day, and when you're making a tune you try to make an impact, so you think of everything that will attract attention." As a result of such efforts he was awarded the first-ever deejay cup, presented by Rupie Edwards's *Record Retailer* magazine for 1971–72.

While the deejay continued to climb the musical ladder, Jamaica was set for major political change. In the 1972 general election, Michael Manley defeated the JLP incumbent, Hugh Shearer, striding into office on a platform of elevating the poor, and it was partly reggae music and symbolic, Rasta-sympathetic rhetoric that got him there. Delroy Wilson's determined 'Better Must Come' topped the charts in 1971; Manley co-opted the tune as his campaign song. He made public appearances with a staff he said had been given to him by Haile Selassie – it was dubbed the Rod Of Correction by his followers, who saw Manley as 'Joshua' and Shearer as 'Pharaoh' – and got Clancy Eccles to organise political bandwagons featuring The Wailers and other artists performing around the island in his support. "I have a belief in socialism," Eccles explained, "because capitalism, one set get rich while one set go poor, and if it was equally divided, half would be rich and half would be poor. But you're going find that two per cent get rich and 90 per cent live under the poverty line, and there is eight per cent that we would say lives off the cream of the rich. That part, I feel it's not proper. I believe that the distribution of the wealth of the world should be given to everyone equally for their amount of work."

Although they were never officially part of the PNP government, Eccles said he and his peers were given a chance to express their feelings once Manley took office. "We were the non-paid advisers to Manley. We could call him any time and say: 'Hey, we feel that that no right.'" Bunny Lee says Jamaica clearly needed a concrete change in political outlook, speaking of food shortages and other difficulties that affected the poor most of all.

Manley did implement a number of policies aimed at improving conditions for the poor majority, but most of the promised changes were slow to arrive, and artists that supported his campaign soon voiced dissent. Junior Byles recorded 'Pharaoh Hiding' in praise of Manley in 1972, but the following year he cut 'When Will Better Come' in scathing reference to the party's campaign song. Both were recorded by Lee Perry, the producer that drew the best results from the sensitive singer, and who scored one of the biggest hits of 1972 with Byles's defiant 'Beat Down Babylon', his best-known hit. "You know why most people can't record Byles?" asks Perry. "He's really a confusing artist if you don't know how to get with it. He's one of the best artists to come, he has a sweet voice, but he's not easy to control. He had good thoughts, very good ideas, but you have to have patience. Junior Byles is something different, very different – something special."

Rising session band Now Generation provided the musical backing for the hit, and Val Douglas says the link was down to Tin Legs. "Tin Legs used to record for Scratch and Bunny Lee, but Bunny Lee used to use Family Man strictly, so I did one and two little things, like 'Beat Down Babylon'. At that time Mikey Chung and Wire was in the band."

Now Generation hit big in 1971 with Peter Tosh's drawling 'Maga Dog', produced by Joe Gibbs, this version far exceeding the popularity of the original Wailers ska recording for Coxsone. In 1972, Now Gen was working at Harry J.'s 16-track studio on Roosevelt Avenue, near the National Stadium; like Joe Gibbs's Duhaney Park facility, the studio was set up by Bill Garnett on one of his weekend visits to Jamaica, and it was here that the band backed their biggest international hit: Lorna Bennett's rendition of

Baby Washington's 'Breakfast In Bed', now centred on Douglas's bouncing bass notes and released abroad on Island's Blue Mountain subsidiary. As Douglas explains, "'Breakfast In Bed' is probably my best bass line, and I never forget what happened after I played that line: Geoffrey [Chung] was producing and arranging at Harry J. We had done a redo of Cat Stevens's 'Morning Has Broken', and the next song we did was 'Breakfast In Bed'. Harry J. came in and said: 'I don't like this rhythm.' Right then, he had a hit out there with Joe Higgs, 'World Upside Down', Jackie Jackson there 'pon it. That was the other session group that was happening: Jackie Jackson, Hux Brown, Winston Wright. Harry J. said: 'Give me a bass line something like that.' I was like: 'Boss, this is the line for the tune.'"

Around the same time, Zap Pow achieved their first overseas hit at Harry J., their breakthrough partly assisted by Chris Blackwell's intervention. "Zap Pow was known for 'Mystic Mood'," David Madden recalls. "Then we found ourselves with a second hit, 'Scandal Corner', which was more a comedy side. Harry J. wanted to have the group record an album, so he gave us studio time to do some more songs and Mikey got this idea one rehearsal evening, which was 'This Is Reggae Music'. Harry J. had a contact with Chris Blackwell. It sounded to him like the record wasn't finished, because Mikey didn't really sing the words, so Chris call Jim Capaldi [of the group Traffic] to ask him to finish writing the words. He brought it back down, Mikey do whatsoever we was supposed to do and send it back up to Chris who put strings on it." Blackwell was so taken with the end result that he subsequently titled Island's reggae compilation series *This Is Reggae Music*.

Then, in 1973, Soul Syndicate was back on top in Jamaica with Niney's sterling production of Ken Boothe's 'Silver Words' (originally by Detroit soul artist Rodriquez) and Dennis Brown's 'Westbound Train' – the first of many hits created by the electrifying combination of Niney, Dennis and Soul Syndicate. Niney says this made him a fully fledged producer.

"I was singing and wasn't so interested in other singers. I just use my own rhythms that I make, never used to give people them because I find a new trend, so I just hold them and sing on them myself. The only people who would share it was Maxie Romeo. Lloyd Charmers told me he love my type of rhythms and asked me to make some rhythms like that for him too, although he was a great keyboardist and a great arranger himself. I decide to shift, because a lot of singers like Ken Boothe, they always come to me and say: 'I like your rhythms, I would like some rhythms like that.' So I decide to cool off with the singing and just go into producing. When I was working with Bunny Lee, me and Slim Smith used to write songs at this yard up Orange Street, the same place Dennis Brown born, and we meet Dennis as a likkle youth who want to sing, but Dennis was so likkle that we couldn't bring him in the camp. Slim Smith take him down to Derrick Harriott and he make a headway, then I think Alton Ellis take him up to Coxsone. After I do 'Silver Words' my name start to call differently – I in a different league. I meet Dennis Brown and we say we want to work, then me and him start to move so close that the two of we live together in one house up Pembroke Hall. Me and Dennis start to go to parties and dances, and we drive uptown one night to New Kingston and I hear a song play, Al Green's 'Love And Happiness'. After I drop him home, it was four o'clock in the morning and I never go and sleep. I just go to Chinna and Fully, wake them up and say: 'I'm going to run a session tomorrow,' because they play for Joe Gibbs every Sunday, and me operate Joe Gibbs's session every Sunday – I was still helping out with Joe Gibbs. As they come, I lick the song first. Joe Gibbs was the engineer – a very good engineer in those days."

"I invent that 'flyers' guitar on 'Westbound Train'," adds Tony Chin. "We were doing some songs for Niney up at Joe Gibbs's studio, and Niney said he wanted one more rhythm. That time Dennis Brown wasn't even in the studio. I said: 'Let's do the Al Green song as an instrumental,' and Chinna started to play it. A month after, I hear a vocal on the rhythm, call it 'Westbound Train'."

"I did bring Dennis round there to do an album for Joe Gibbs," Niney continues, talking about the set of new songs ironically issued as *The Best Of Dennis Brown*. "Joe Gibbs said: 'I want a cut of this song to put on the album,' so from there me and Dennis very tight. It's all a new vibe, because this is the first time me and Dennis working. Before the first song come out, I know it was a hit. One day we go to the beach and we drive in town, on Orange Street and North Street, and it's right at that corner he born and grow, so he decide to take a prip at his home. He have a likkle cough, and he said: 'Come here, Skipper, I cough and spit blood.' I take him to a chest clinic and they say I must take him to the hospital – a lungs problem. He in the hospital for four or five months, and meanwhile the song becomes number one. We need the follow-up, so I take him out of the hospital one night, take him to Randy's, and we do 'Cassandra' at four o'clock in the morning. From there, we have that relationship coming down."

Niney says King Tubby was responsible for breaking this material. "When we make a song, we take it to him and when he mix off the song, he keep that cut for his sound system, and then he make different cuts and sell dubs to other sounds. He promoted the song so that when the song come to street, it hit. Tubby's was Jamaica's dancehall radio station: wherever he play the sound, people talk about what Tubby's play the next morning, so that be a demand on the street. We would give Tubby a song and he play it like two or three months, and whenever the song reach a demands we release it. We go to him and he says: 'Don't release it yet, release it two weeks' time.' And then he makes U Roy boost that song. The word go round, so when it release it's a hit."

Bernard 'Touter' Harvey, later keyboardist with Inner Circle, brought a particular sound to much of this material. As Niney explains: "Sometimes we bring in certain guys like Ossie Hibbert, Ansel Collins, but Touter was the most important piano man, the one that play the great part of Dennis Brown's career."

Ultimately, Soul Syndicate's exquisite backing gave this music its unique definition. Niney says he was always keenly aware of the group's abilities. "I have Soul Syndicate working from them time when nobody know them. People laughed after me, say all these guys play is pure slash-chord note, they can't read, till I shame them when I drop the Ken Boothe 'Silver Words'. Then everybody want part of them."

While Soul Syndicate, The All Stars, and Now Generation were fighting to maintain dominance, a handful of creative producers and engineers were shifting instrumentals into the realm of dub. In the late 60s Lee Perry was one of the most prolific creators of instrumental versions, but once he hooked up with Bob Marley, he concentrated on vocal material. When The Wailers branched out on their own in late 1971, Perry celebrated the rupture by issuing an entirely instrumental version of their *Soul Revolution* album as *Soul Revolution II*. Stripped of the voices, these songs were transformed to emphasize different elements of their musical composition: 'Kaya' focussed on a lively acoustic guitar melody; 'Duppy Conqueror Version 4' highlighted the song's choppy organ; 'Keep On Moving', 'Put It On', and others placed greatest emphasis on drum and bass, foreshadowing standard dub practices.

Herman Chin-Loy was also stretching the contours of the instrumental in 1971, often using rhythms played by The Upsetters' core, through work credited to Augustus Pablo. At his home in Miami, Chin-Loy describes his mixed heritage. "I was born in Duncans, Trelawny, then I move up to Clarendon. My father, who died when I was a babe, had a shop there; he was strictly Chinese, and my mother is half-Chinese, and the other part of me is black. My great-grandparents, I don't think they came as indentured labour, maybe they came as merchants, but certainly the black part of me would have been in slavery, which is where I need to expound on more precisely. I have come to find out that these people taken to the Caribbean as slaves are actually Israelites. If you read the Bible, it say Abraham's seed shall be in a strange land for 400 years of affliction, and that is the trans-Atlantic slave trade."

After arriving in Kingston at the age of ten in 1958, Chin-Loy gradually entered the retail record business. "I went to live at Princess Street and that address was Kong, Beverley's Records; we are related, maybe through my mother's side. I just stopped there for a while in passing through to go and live with my half-brother up by Waltham Park Road. Then I went back to my mother, she was living downtown at Hanover Street, working as a clerk at one of those stores in King Street. Then I move to Spanish Town, to the blacker side of my family, for about three or four years. One of my aunts, her boyfriend used to be at Spotlight, a family-owned business; they fix radios, sell tubes and amplifiers, and they had a recognized sound system in Spanish Town, so I was around the music there. Then my brother came by one day and I went to live with him again."

So much moving around meant that Herman got a poor education, ending up at a reformatory institution. "Me and people like Family Man used to go to Saint Aloysius, but I used to skulk more than go to school. My last time in school I came last, that was in the sixth grade, the reason being that I was going back and forth and I wasn't focussing. Matter of fact, the people who were teaching me, they needed to be taught." These experiences later inspired him to record 'Dunce Cap', for which he took the name Teacher.

After leaving school, Herman ran a downtown record shop. "When I was going to school I used to work with Beverley's, like Christmas holidays. My older brother Keith was working there. He used to live with the Kongs, and I would go there because I really loved the music. When my brother came for me in Spanish Town, he saw me selling records in the Spotlight shop, so he knew that I loved music. He and another friend found a shop for me on King Street at the corner of Beeston Street: One Stop Record Shop, they finance it, but the shop really belongs to me. That was the early 60s."

Herman says his chief supplier was Neville Chow-Fong at KG, a record shop and commercial distribution service. "We used to get all the American music from KG, and I used to buy most of my stock from him. He opened a shop up by Half Way Tree, then I used to work there too. I left my shop downtown, gave it to Derrick Harriott, because KG had a club around the back called Lotus A Go-Go, the first stationary discotheque in Jamaica, so I would deejay the disco in the night and work around the record shop in the day. While working there, I went up to Northside Plaza to the Tunnel club. Inner Circle used to play there, and I used to MC the band and do a little singing, as they used to come to KG's to buy. That was the place to come, so that's where I met everybody."

Around 1969, Herman set up the Aquarius record shop and label in Half Way Tree, issuing material crediting the imaginary Augustus Pablo on Aquarius and a related imprint called Scorpio. "It was the Age of Aquarius when I opened the store. That was the time when the movie *Hair* came out, so a friend of mine said it would be a good thing. I was just using the Zodiac, but was born in July and that would be Cancer, and nobody would want to come to a place that have cancer! By that time I had produced 'Shang I', 'African Zulu', and 'Black Coffee' by Augustus Pablo. Those songs were actually done by Lloyd Charmers at Dynamic Sounds, with Val Douglas, Mikey Chung, Wire Lindo, and Ranny Bop. The name Augustus Pablo, I just thought of something that would sound mysterious. Movies was a lot of influence to us: sometimes we would watch Clint Eastwood movies and I would watch the Bible stories, and in my mind Augustus sounds like a big name. I realise later on that the name Pablo means Paul, but neither one of them has nothing to do with nothing."

Other material to bear the name Augustus Pablo came about through collaboration with aspiring producer Pete Weston, again with Lloyd Charmers on organ. "They would bring their music," says Herman. "That's how I get to meet Lee Perry, Bunny Lee, Clancy Eccles, Lloyd Charmers, and Pete Weston. Weston was working in the insurance industry, and then he wanted to produce, so I just afforded him a place for what he could do. 'Jug Head' was done by Pete Weston – that again was Lloyd Charmers, to set the record straight. Alton Ellis's 'Rise Blackman' was done by Pete Weston, but I actually got a cut of the rhythm, a dub which I name '62636', the telephone number for my shop. 'Invasion' is my production with Lloyd Charmers."

To confuse matters further, other songs credited to Augustus Pablo featured Glen Adams. "Family Man, Glen Adams, and Reggie would bring a rhythm for me to buy," Herman explains. "'Reggae In The Fields' was one of those rhythms, but I put the piano on it with Lloyd Charmers."

On one such rhythm, the mantle of Augustus Pablo was finally assigned to Horace Swaby, a resident of the lower middle-class Havendale district whose father, a man of Indian descent, was an accountant. Horace and his brother established the Rockers sound system in Havendale in the late 60s, and Horace often bought records at Aquarius. One fateful day in 1971 he went there with a melodica, and the producer had enough curiosity about the instrument to take him into the studio. In so doing, Herman launched the career of a highly talented individual with a unique take on instrumental sound whose work would bring great changes to reggae.

"It all started when someone lent me a melodica – a sister, I can't really remember her name," Swaby explained. "Her father was a big important lawyer and her brother is a lawyer – the whole lawyer family. She went to a girls' school and they used the instrument in the school, and I didn't have any, so she lent me her instrument and I used to practise it every day. I went down to Herman Chin-Loy to buy some records for my sound, Rockers. He asked me if I could play that instrument, I say yeah, and he carried me to the studio."

This first session yielded 'Iggy Iggy', an oblique, chord-strewn instrumental loosely based on The Heptones' 'Why Did You Leave'. "That was another cut of Glen Adams and Family Man," Herman notes. "I do the talking, which was youthful exuberance, more like an MC than a deejay."

More invigorating was the original 'East Of The River Nile', on which Swaby blew an inspired melody over the song's jazzy beat, relying mostly on the black keys and hinting at the 'Far East' sound he would later develop. "I was looking for a new sound," Herman insists. "I didn't want to produce everything that everybody else is producing. When he came, he wanted to play piano. The story goes that I saw him with this melodica and I said: 'That's exactly what I want,' so we went into the studio – I didn't even know if he could play very well. We got this rhythm, 'East Of The River Nile' – Family Man, Glen Adams, and Reggie are responsible for that – so he went on it and I said: 'That's exactly the sound that I want,' because to me it had a Middle East sound. That's why the name 'East Of The River Nile' came."

On his final visit to London, a frail and nearly bedridden Swaby was in the care of Rastafarian herbalist Owen 'Bagga' Forrester, having suffered from the nerve disorder myasthenia gravis for many years. Swaby only agreed to be interviewed on the condition that Bagga was interviewed first, and the ensuing discussion was a surreal exchange about the herbalist's methods of treating lymphatic disorders. Afterward, the man known the world over as Augustus Pablo revealed that Glen Adams's departure from Jamaica to Brooklyn transferred the alias permanently to him.

"Glen Adams did 'Aquarius One' for Herman as Augustus Pablo. A lot of people think it's me, but it's not, because Herman is the one that created that name. Anyone could name Augustus Pablo – he just take it out to use gimmicks to rule the people. Glen played that organ on 'River Nile' with me too, but he went to America the next day."

Adams's emigration had direct consequences on the Kingston music scene: The Wailers had no regular keyboardist and would eventually draft Tyrone Downey as replacement, while The Upsetters and the Treasure Isle house band were also short of an organist. Horace Swaby was able to partially fill the gap as Augustus Pablo, working as a session keyboardist for some of the better-established producers after Herman Chin-Loy spent a period abroad. "I used to play studio musician for Treasure Isle, Bunny Lee and a few other producers. I play back-up music because they didn't have an organist any more, and Family Man used to help me a lot. I passed through Now Generation – wasn't really in the band, but I played studio musician with them through Herman."

While Pablo's early melodica efforts breathed new life into the reggae instrumental, in 1972 engineers such as King Tubby and Errol Thompson took things a step further. Dub version B-sides, and the odd instrumental A-side, began to elevate drum and bass to the fore, with heavily modulated rhythms transformed through the application of effects such as reverb and echo, applied either to instruments or to snatches of vocals that drifted in and out of the mix. "The drum and bass part now, Tubbys strike out," says Bunny Lee. "One of the first drum and bass tunes that come out was 'Merry Up' with Glen Brown. That reverb, watery sound, that ah one of the first."

Credited to The God Sons, 'Merry Up' is a very peculiar record. The song opens with a heavily reverberating noise, courtesy of Tubby, which gives way to a plodding, bass-heavy rhythm over which the singer Joe White blows a minimal melodica, accentuated by saxophone and trombone notes. Midway through, the music cuts and a voice proclaims: "Hold it Mr T! This daughter can't keep up to this rhythm. Ask me questions, I tell you no lie; ask me no questions, I play music." Then the plodding beat starts up again. An unlikely combination for a hit, perhaps, but 'Merry Up' scored big in the Jamaica charts.

Brown is another reggae enigma who sometimes dislikes having his photograph taken and prefers to engage in "reasoning" as opposed to formal interviews. At Don One studio, in the depths of Brooklyn's East Flatbush, he seems frazzled, but his comments are still insightful. He says 'Merry Up' began as a totally different entity.

"In Jamaica, there's some songs that didn't properly done. 'Merry Up' was the spoiled cut, and it hit the same way. 'Merry Up' is a song made vocally, which I wrote, named 'Welcome To My Land', sung by me, B.B. Seaton, and Ken Boothe. We voice it at the bottom studio at Dynamic; Karl Pitterson was the engineer. When I ready to pay for my studio time, I can't find the tape. Byron Lee was in the studio and Bunny Lee and other producers, so I can't blame no one [in particular], but somebody snatched my tape – they stole the vocal cut, so I said: 'Anybody thief this music here can't put it out.' I went home and go for my melodica and I blow the melody of 'Merry Up'. Joe White had the same instrument, like Augustus Pablo – it's the three of us blow it. I keep showing Joe White for about one whole day, because I have to pay for studio time. Every minute Joe White blowing till he get close to it. I still have the rhythm, and Merritone did have a two-track studio in Half Way Tree, so we record there. I put the instrumental out, and it take Ernie Smith's 'Pitta Patta' off the charts. 'Pitta Patta' be the number two for six months, can't reach number one because of 'Merry Up'. God just make the instrumental turn out to be a hit song, kill everybody tune."

As a young producer in the early 70s, Brown was often low on finance but high on ideas. His product, issued in small quantity on shortlived labels such as South East Music, Pantomine and Dwyer, was usually driven by a full brass section informed by jazz; Brown says his musicality was sparked by Jamaica's finest horn players. "I was born in downtown Kingston at 14 Wildman Street, 1944, and I moved throughout the community. I always spend a little time listening to Tommy McCook, Roland Alphonso, and various musicians, so it put me in the vibes of trying to be part of it."

In the mid 60s Brown formed his first singing duo with Lloyd Robinson while doing casual work at a department store. "I had a guitar given to me by a gentleman who fix TVs: Mr Wong at Wong Brothers, one of the big stores at Cross Roads. I always go by Mr Wong and play my guitar and he accept me, even though he's a Chiney man, so sometimes he had me behind the counter, selling. Sometimes I go downtown and Lloyd Robinson play the piano, off Spanish Town Road, behind the theatre. Tony Brevett live down that street; if Lloydie get the piano before Tony, Lloydie play for the whole day. When me and Lloydie sing, we make a harmony that people say sound like Sam & Dave. We went by Duke Reid's studio, about '66, started doing a few songs like 'Oh Little Girl' – we change the Sam Cooke lyrically, use his melody with our lyrics. We do a few tracks for Mr Pottinger and everybody start accept our harmony. At the Ward Theatre, sometime we perform with Byron Lee as guest artists. We do some tracks for Derrick Harriott also, like 'That Girl', and 'The Loser' – me and Lloyd Robinson do [harmony] on that. Then I started to sing with a band at Sheraton Hotel Ballroom."

After Brown became lead singer with the Cecil Lloyd Quintet, then the island's leading hotel jazz band, he and Robinson went their separate ways.[3] Brown subsequently sang with The Sonny Bradshaw Seven and formed duos with Hopeton Lewis and Dave Barker in 1968–69, cutting a number of solo sides before finding a way to production. "As Cecil Lloyd take a holiday, I join Sonny Bradshaw Seven at Sheraton. Jackie Jackson was the bass player, but he leave and start to play with Winston Wright and Gladdy, so it move to be a street band. Me and Hopeton Lewis met at Wong Brothers and we do a few songs like 'Girl You're Cold', that's produced by Mr Wong."

M.G. Mahtani, proprietor of a downtown jewellery shop called Shalimar on King Street, was another entrepreneur who assisted Brown. "Shalimar have a likkle shop – he's a nice Indian guy, talk Amharic and various languages, so being a nice person he accept me. I was in Derrick Harriott's shop, and Shalimar have artists like Stranger Cole & Gladdy, so we do some songs for Shalimar. I always be in the shop and sell my product, even though they selling gold there."

When Brown finally started producing, a shop of his own contributed to his success. "I have a label, I up and down, and going to Mr Wong Brothers and say I'd like to get a shop, so him say: 'Why don't you try to get a shop across the street, beside Carib?' I build a shop and put it right round the Post Office side of Cross Roads, Caledonia Place. You have The Abyssinians' record shop right across the street. Immediately as I build the shop, I come with this song named 'Mr Harry Skank'."

'Mr Harry Skank' was one of the first hits to bring deejay Prince Jazzbo wider recognition. It was voiced on an instrumental featuring young tenor saxophonist Richard Hall, who adopted Dirty Harry for his moniker, playing in tandem with Tommy McCook. The rhythm track was originally recorded for 'Realise', which paired Glen Brown with Ritchie MacDonald from The Chosen Few. Brown says most of his rhythms, including Roman Stewart's debut 'Never Too Young To Learn', were shaped by his time in the jazz band. "Being in the jazz, it makes I more musically, so 'Never Too Young To Learn', that's jazz, and that's what I write. I make Roman Stewart voice it and everybody say it's Dennis Brown. The song played by Now Generation band, we record that at Harry J.'s studio."

The lyrics, Brown adds, were inspired by singing with a jazz band:

> *When we gather around*
> *We meditate a way of life*
> *The more we go*

Is the more we learn
We're never too young to learn
Even an old man gets his turn …

When running such sessions, Brown often allowed his collaborators to cut their own creations. "I been helping singers coming up along the way, recording Lloyd Parks with the song 'Slaving'; I'm one of the [backing] vocal, and he did 'Officially' for himself on the session. Prince Jazzbo, when I record him, I pay for a song and let him record a song for himself, 'cos I love to see artists survive. I would pay for the band and pay the studio time, but him would just deal with it."

Another popular rhythm, known as 'Tubbys At The Control', made reference to the prominent role King Tubby played in mixing most of Glen's material. "King Tubby was from the South, just in my same area. He was right at High Holborn Street in the early days, and I below Barrow Street on High Holborn Street. King Tubby always build some little speaker, he always have a little bike, so King Tubby build a little thing on the bike. Sometimes you're talking to him and he'll record you. I love music going up, so I always go to Tubby's. If I have a music, the first person hear it is Tubby and the first person I would leave my tape with is Tubby. After me and Tubby link up, a lot of producers and singers start going by Tubby's. At that time, I leave Tubby and gone 'pon the North Coast, sing backup with Cecil Lloyd. Every six months I come in with a nice money, run another recording session."

Like most of Brown's productions, King Tubby mixed 'Tubbys At The Control' at his home studio at 18 Dromilly Avenue, Waterhouse. The tiny space was not a studio in the conventional sense, nor was Tubby an actual producer until the late 80s. His bedroom studio was never large enough for rhythms to be created in full, but the space was gradually converted into a sound manipulation unit complete with a machine to cut acetates.

"Tubbs is an innovator," says 'Prince' Philip Smart, engineer at the studio for much of the mid 70s. "He didn't buy his first console, he built it – built the chassis and everything, put all the components together. That's what he used first, until he bought the MCI console from Dynamics, their studio B. It was just that room he had at first. You have a carport, and then the carport is a bedroom and a bathroom, so him turn the bathroom into the voice room and the bedroom into the control room, and he had his repair shop in another little house in the back. His main income was building amplifiers and winding transformers, because he had contracts for hotels that needed transformers for stabilising the current. The music was an addition, because he had the sound and he always wanted to make his own dubs, so that's how he started: he bought the dub machine to cut his own dubs."

"The home amplifiers like Pioneer, Marantz, it's them amplifiers him started with," says singer and producer Roy Cousins. "He did have about three of them transistor amplifiers, one of them old cutter, and them likkle two-track reel-to-reel that come in a suitcase, him did have one like that him used to put on a stool. Then when Byron Lee decided him going cut stampers, him decided to sell [the equipment in] studio two, which was four-track. It's through Bunny Lee that Tubby get the mixing desk: Byron wanted cash and everybody just want to leave a deposit, but Tubby go down there with the whole of it."

At a South London restaurant, Cousins supplied further information about Tubby's domestic set-up: "His house was owned by Miss Sissy, that's Tubbs's mother. The studio was him bedroom, and him used to have a board thing at the back where him used to make amps. Tubby had two four-track machines and a two-track. That time he didn't even have a car yet – he used to ride one of them Honda, big M50. It's three brothers. Stagga, the biggest brother, is a better engineer than Tubby; Stagga build the sound. Lloyd Ruddock, Tubby's younger brother [a sometime vocalist also known as Scuner] was a tailor, but him and Tubby never get on."

After Tubby installed the equipment purchased from Dynamics, he held rudimentary voicing and mixing sessions, partly at Bunny Lee's instigation. Pat Kelly was an early engineering assistant, hired for his knowledge of electronics. "I started engineering from '69 at King Tubby's," he recalls. "We used to do mixing and voicing, as early as that, with a two-track machine. When I first recorded with Bunny Lee I used to go there and voice, and it was King Tubby himself who was operating the board."

In the early 70s, the most creative Kingston producers were beating a path to Tubby's door, with Cousins among the first to make use of Dynamic's former mixing desk.

Cousins was born in downtown Kingston in 1949. He formed his first harmony group in 1962 to attend the Junior Festival competition, and by 1965 was part of the first incarnation of The Royals, then called The Tempests, along with neighbourhood friends Bertram 'Harry' Johnson and Errol 'Tralla' Green.

"We did quite a few tunes for Duke. I remember we did a track on the session with the first song Melodians do for Treasure Isle. We did about five tunes for Duke Reid, but none of them release. Errol Green then left the group; he was the one that sing lead on all them tracks."

182

Cousins then took the lead, writing the group's material and coaching other members in harmony. Errol Wilson, whom Cousins came to know through his job at the Post Office, replaced Green and the group went to work with Lloyd Daley. In 1967, Coxsone selected The Tempests to record the electrifying 'Pick Up The Pieces', which highlighted their harmonic excellence. But somehow Coxsone held back its release, so Cousins re-cut it himself in 1971 as The Royals, with fellow postal worker and future Jays member Lloyd Forrest temporarily taking Errol Wilson's place. The success of the new number, issued on Cousins's Uhuru label, prompted Coxsone to release the original and led Cousins to have premier deejay I Roy voice 'Monkey Fashion' on the new rhythm at Tubby's studio. "It's in King Tubby's we voice it, 'cos I used to live down the road from Tubbys," Cousins explains, adding that great songs like 'Ghetto Man' and 'Sufferer In The Ghetto' were also voiced and mixed there.

"We start voice tunes up at Tubby's," continues Bunny Lee. "The first set of tunes, we go for Scratch again. Scratch do 'Bathroom Skank' and all them tunes. We do the rhythm at Dynamic and voice it at Tubby's." The sound-effects clutter of 'Bathroom Skank' – a rude duet voiced with Perry's common-law wife, Pauline Morrison – was one of a series of heavily modified discs that Perry cut at Tubby's studio in 1972–73. Other notable examples include 'Black IPA', on which the horn parts were subjected to extreme phasing, and 'Flashing Echo', a drum-and-bass cut of Leo Graham's 'News Flash' given heavy doses of delay. Other producers drew equally exciting results: Derrick Harriott transformed The Ethiopians' 'No Baptism' into the spooky sounds of 'Blacula' at Tubby's, while Keith Hudson, Glen Brown, and upcoming producer Carlton Patterson all mixed the bulk of their dubs there.

Tubby's studio was also a magnet for those from the very poorest levels of society who were seeking to break into the music business. Vivian Jackson, an impoverished youth who was then scraping a living by giving betting tips at the racetrack, was a notable example. Jackson died in 2010, after suffering from serious health conditions for much of his life, following an early bout of malnutrition. Obviously a deeply religious man, his conversation was littered with biblical references; though his dreadlocks were long and matted, his rejection of Selassie and veneration of Jesus made him doubly ostracised, resulting in the ironic sobriquet, Jesus Dread. Jackson said he was so poor in 1971, when he founded the Prophets group and record label, that he had to convince musicians to record for free: "The original Prophets was Chinna, Family Man, Horsemouth, and myself."

Horsemouth says friends whom Jackson lived and worked with supplied finance. "There was a big Rastaman on the gully bank in Waterhouse: Solomon Wolfe, the first man that lead the Rasta delegation with Mortimer Planno. These Rastas, Alric, and Cleo, they have a furnace, gather aluminium from all over the streets, melt it, and make pots. On the weekend they go to Ocho Rios, Montego Bay, and sell pots to make the sessions. Karl Pitterson was the engineer, a very roots guy, even though he was uptown. He knows we are from the ghetto, respects me and Family Man as good musicians, and just give us extra time."

The following year, King Tubby gave Jackson free studio time when he was ready to voice the material with his harmony group. "It was in 1972," Jackson confirmed. "Alric Forbes and a brother who come sing as Bobby Melody carry harmony with me." Tubby gave Jackson his peculiar stage name of Yabby You, stemming from the onomatopoeic chorus of his debut single, 'Conquering Lion'. "When me start doing music, I say me ah go do it privately, and if it flop, me just take me losses and nobody won't know. I never know it would sell. I said I would just go around all of the Rastaman and beg them to buy one. When it did start to sell, here comes one of Tubbs's number-one dubs. Me tell them it's Tubby me sell the record for, so them always wonder who this group is. Then me do a song name 'Love Of Jah', and it came up the same way. When me do 'Warn The Nation', Tubbs tell them ah me – him used to tell them the group is an American group named Yabby You."

By 1974, Tubby's mixing artistry was officially acknowledged on version B-sides, notably on material cut for Carlton Patterson's Black & White label by artists such as Larry Marshall and Lizzy. Upcoming producer 'Prince' Tony Robinson also name-checked the soundman and mixer on an early disc called 'Tubby's In Full Swing', credited to Lloyd & Kerry (toasters Lloyd Young and Carey 'Wildman' Johnson). The song was a bizarre cut-up blending the opening bars of the Staple Singers' 'I'll Take You There' with a trombone instrumental.

The partnership formed by Clive Chin and Errol Thompson at Randy's was another important element in the development of dub. "Them time there, Tubby try and experiment more fi dub, but me and Errol start dub music," says Chin. "When I say start it, I'm not saying we going to take credit for any other man that put out a dub album, but we really experiment, because we had the time and the facility to do it. Another man like Phil Pratt or Niney, time was so important that you have to run in and run out – that's how studio used to run."

As the son of the burgeoning studio's proprietor, Chin naturally spent a great deal of time at 17 North Parade, becoming more actively involved in record production at Randy's by the end of the 60s. "My first personal self-production was a tune called 'Young Love', but I always had disappointments with vocal tunes in the early beginnings, because the artists never seem like they could sing. 'Young Love' was cut with a schoolmate of mine, Douglas Boothe – he took that name because him always trying to come off Ken's styling. Him just couldn't cut it, so we did it as an instrumental with Soul Syndicate – that was around '69. I was basically brought in as an auditioner, because my uncle Keith was more in charge of production, but me used to do some wickeder tune than him, and him used to take credit fi it and me never used to like that. A whole heap of tune, my uncle Victor press them up and put 'produced by Keith Chin', and it's really me do it!"

Among the tunes was the wonderful Augustus Pablo instrumental 'Java', produced by Clive with Errol Thompson at the mixing desk in 1971. "My uncle take credit for 'Java' up here, and put The Chosen Few as the artist – it was called 'East Of The Rio Cobre' by The Chosen Few on the New York Impact label. That really did get Pablo upset – Pablo didn't even get credit on that, and Chosen Few only said the intro and did the likkle chorus, but at the time Chosen Few had a name and nobody don't know Pablo."

Chin says 'Java' was intended as a vocal, but when the vocalist could not supply what he had in mind he got Pablo to reach for his melodica, resulting in his first big hit, named 'best instrumental' of 1972. "The rhythm was a vocal tune that was not successful. The artist was another schoolmate of mine called Dennis Wright. It was some little love song, but him just couldn't cut it. Pablo was around, so I get Errol to cut a dub plate and he carry it home and work on it, come up with two melody lines, one for the version and one for the A-side."

Chin added The Chosen Few to counteract the novelty of Pablo's melodica playing. "It was a new instrument on the scene, so I have to build around it and make it attractive, make people interested in it. I get the idea to throw in The Chosen Few because I had a tune with The Impressions called 'East Of Java', and I wanted that song to be on a reggae rhythm, so I just have them come in saying: 'From the east of the Rio Cobre to the west of the Rio Cobre hails the hottest Java.' The Rio Cobre is a river in Jamaica where there are bamboo rafters. Again I just throw that in, just a spice, like when you're cooking food and you want to flavour it up."

The song's tremendous success naturally spawned further versions, including Tommy McCook's 'Jaro', Dennis Alcapone's 'Mava', and I Roy's surreal 'Hospital Trolley'. It also saw Pablo, Clive Chin, and Errol Thompson spending many a Sunday at Studio 17 with Family Man and Tin Legs, creating the 1973 release *This Is Augustus Pablo*, a stunning debut LP for the young melodica master. "The album was really something that me and Pablo sit down and talk about, cause doing work as a musician and doing work as an artist is two different things. Weeks we've been there mixing. There wasn't even a Sunday that I had to go out and mingle with my friends or check my girlfriend. We decided to dedicate to this mix, because I wanted it to sound so good."

Two of the album's tracks, 'Lover's Mood' and the popular 'Pablo In Dub', were produced by Leonard 'Santic' Chin, a relative of Clive's that sang with The Graduates. Santic often subsequently made use of Pablo's keyboard and arranging skills, before moving to Britain in 1974.

Errol Thompson was an old school friend of Clive's, and he became the chief engineer at Randy's following a brief apprenticeship at Studio One. "We had Bill Garnett, and then we had this other engineer from one of the radio stations, I think his name was Neville. A man named Mr Galbraith used to come to fix the organ: he brought Errol down as an apprentice, because my father told him he was seeking an engineer. I knew him before that from Choir School out by South Camp Road and North Street. I had a good relationship with Errol, a very innovative relationship where we wouldn't just idle talk about things on the street or girlfriend business. We would talk more like how we could further the music, how we can do a different kind of fixture to it, spice it, rather than have the same old pattern of just Tommy [McCook] blowing a horn, Bobby [Aitken] playing a guitar, Winston [Wright] playing an organ."

Java Java Java Java was one of the first dub albums, issued in a limited pressing of 1,000 copies in 1973. Thompson keeps the bass at the top of the mix for the whole of the disc, shuffling in reverb-treated keyboards, guitar, horns, and the odd snatch of vocals or melodica. The final track, a version of Lloyd Parks's 'Ordinary Man' retitled 'Forward The Bass', incorporates a hilarious argument between studio personnel and an aspiring session musician in which the song's individual musical elements are highlighted. The album's concentration on drum and bass was a radical departure, and underlines the creative interaction between Chin and Thompson at the mixing desk.

"It was works done between me and Errol, and it was something new at the time," Chin says. "There wasn't an album out there that wasn't mento, calypso, or one of them uptown reggae albums by Byron Lee or Tomorrow's Children, so we wanted to do something different and say: 'We ah go give them a wicked dub album.' We didn't commercialise it, we do it more like a dub-plate special, so the market at that time wasn't great enough to keep the dub flow. People was just starting to listen to this new music, so we didn't consider it was going to be a big hit."

A few other dub albums appeared around the same time, all vying for the title of first dub LP. Lee Perry's groundbreaking *Upsetters 14 Dub Blackboard Jungle* (aka *Blackboard Jungle Dub*) was mixed in true stereo with channel separation; Perry kept the drums and percussion upfront, and made greater use of reverb, echo, and tape effects at King Tubby's studio. Studio One's *Dub Store Special*, mixed by Clement Dodd, highlighted the stable's minimal, lo-fi production values. Prince Buster's *The Message*, mixed by Carlton Lee at Dynamics, kept reverb-laden horns and organ rolling over driving drum and bass; Joe Gibbs's *Dub Serial* highlighted the strength of its minimal rhythms, as did Herman Chin-Loy's *Aquarius Dub*, which mixed cuts of Chin-Loy's strongest productions (including Pablo's 'East Of The River Nile' and 'Cassava Piece') with raw rhythms rapidly laid by Now Generation.

"That was the first dub album, as far as I know," insists Chin-Loy. "Anybody that has a set always wanted a dub plate, and the dub plates those days were more or less just rhythm. Then the deejay would play the rhythm and talk on it, so I get Val Douglas, Michael Richards, and Mikey Chung, about three or four musicians there, and about half an hour it take to do that in Dynamics' second studio. 'Drum Song' and a couple others, 'Home' by Ken Boothe – they were done there immediately. Whatever rhythms I had, like the Alton Ellis thing ['Alton's Official Daughter'], I just put on that too. Carlton Lee mixed the album – that's half an hour too."

Another innovation from that period was displayed in Rupie Edwards's *Yamaha Skank*, the first album entirely composed of different cuts of the same rhythm. In 1973, Edwards used a cut of The Uniques' 'My Conversation' to score two big chart successes with Shorty The President, a deejay who was born Derrick Thompson in the rural parish of Trelawny in 1949, but who now lives in New Jersey, where he works as a telecommunications engineer. During a visit to London, he explains how he came to record for Edwards.

"In the country where I come from is plenty of farming: yam, bananas, Irish potatoes, cow, goat, so we always have something to eat. I leave the country and go to Kingston when I was 19. I was doing mechanic trade, but

I didn't like too much of the mechanic work, because it's so dirty. I moved to Newhaven when Duhaney Park was just built up. I was there with my sister, but I didn't like the vibes, because she was living with a policeman, he throw down his gun everywhere. I find a friend name Bongo George, he have a small sound named Conquering Lion, so I always go down there and stay with him and make a little voice business live on the set. Rupie living over Duhaney Park, near the border, so he always come around. He is a rebel, he did have a girlfriend that live right beside us, so he hear me deejaying on the little set. One day we was under a tree, chanting, knocking some little pans, smoking a draw. They call me Stumpy them times, so he just come up and say: 'Stumpy, I'm going to record you today.'"

His debut related the circumstances of a recent sound clash. "How I get the lyrics for 'President Mash Up The Resident', about three days before, we went to a dance with the sound named President, and that dance was crazy. The President mash up the other sound, Stereo from Spanish Town – the front of the amplifier was like a jukebox, so they called it Stereo – and every man was talking about it. Rupie did carry U Roy Junior to studio to voice that track, but he couldn't manage it, so he have on the track: 'Here comes the pick of the past and this one's going to be the cream of the heart.' After I hear that, I just come in and say: 'Uh oh, you know, the President ah mash up the resident, you rock so you come so you move so you go so …' The lyrics was off of sound. You did have Bingy Bunny [guitarist Eric Lamont] and Bongo Herman in the studio. Rupie said: 'What you could do [is] whistle something in there,' so after I do it everybody go in for the second cut. After 'President' it was 'Yamaha Skank'. Those two tunes: it's the same rhythm, and I make it a number one, two of them in the one year. Me is the first deejay to do that."

The popularity of Shorty's homage to the Japanese motorcycle made Edwards assemble the *Yamaha Skank* album the following year, treating listeners to an endless succession of deejay, instrumental, and dub cuts. The disc highlighted the infinite versatility of a good rhythm, and showed how any song has the potential to be endlessly transformed. "He start to make a lot of version with the harmonica sound blowing, dubbing on," Shorty recalls. "Everybody always like to laugh after him: 'You version too much, you do too much version!' But some of those version sell just like the original tune, because those times every soundman need version."

Edwards says it was easy then to get a cut of a rhythm produced by someone else, and notes that a popular rhythm could have a prolonged shelf life when reshaped by various hands. "Jimmy Riley sold me the 'My

Conversation' backing track, and then I did 'Yamaha Skank' on that backing track. Then Bunny Lee come in and say he is the owner of the rhythm, and then I understand that Phil Pratt produced it, then I understand that Lloyd Charmers produced it ... Bunny Lee sold me 'Bangarang', then he sold me 'Everybody Needs Love' and 'Out Of Love' and some others, then I just do the versions. But that didn't stop Bunny Lee from using them afterward."

The appearance of dub and version albums greatly elevated the status of these Jamaican innovations, and they have both since remained constant features. As with the deejay innovations that were so closely allied to dub, in time dub techniques would be adapted by producers in other countries, greatly influencing various dance music genres including house, garage, trip-hop, trance, ambient, and most recently, dubstep. Dub proved to be one of the most significant of reggae's early 70s innovations, and the version phenomenon would help usher the music into other territories as the decade progressed.

7

DEEJAY'S CHOICE

The further ascent of the toaster

"You have other people that run the sound that don't want to give you the privilege cause them see that you have the power, but we bad boy offa the road so you have to demand." – BIG YOUTH

"Working with Tubby was a pleasure." – PRINCE JAZZBO

As Jamaican popular music continued to wind its peculiar course, the status of the deejay was elevated further by a series of hit singles and album releases in 1973–74. Dennis Alcapone led the way, although he had recorded so much material for so many different producers by the end of 1972 that a glut of Alcapone albums crowded the market.

"While I was at Duke Reid, me and Bunny Lee was friends, because Bunny Lee is not that serious a producer, like Duke Reid and Coxsone, who is just business. Bunny would give you all two gal too – he is a man about town, if you understand," Alcapone explains. "Me and Bunny get together and did 'Ripe Cherry' off Eric Donaldson's 'Cherry Oh Baby', 'Alcapone Guns Don't Argue', and 'It Must Come', a version of 'Better Must Come'. Bunny said Byron Lee was interested in an album, because Dynamic Sounds put out the singles. Word got around that I was working on that album, so Duke Reid wanted me to do an album, then Coxsone hear about it and wanted his own as well, and everybody was in a competition to get the first album out. I think Coxsone was first with the *Forever Version* album, then Dynamics with *Guns Don't Argue*, then Duke put out *Soul To Soul: Deejay's Choice*; in fact, when I came up to England on my first tour in 1973, Duke Reid actually gave me the tape to carry to Trojan Records."

'Deejay's Choice' was the first of many songs to celebrate the unexpected rise of the deejay, and on this song Alcapone duly saluted contemporaries such as Big Youth, I Roy, Lizzy, and U Roy by relating their distinguishing vocal traits, an idea borrowed from a rival deejay. "When our sound system wasn't playing we used to go to Spanish Town to listen to Ruddy's, because Ruddy could afford whatever dub plates he wants. When Ruddy comes to Studio One or Treasure Isle, he would just tell them: 'Put on plate what you made today.' Ruddy's used to have a deejay named Mango, and Mango used to have that 'Deejay's Choice' kind of thing going on the 'Sidewalk Doctor' rhythm, so that's where I get the idea from."

Soul To Soul: Deejay's Choice has plenty of rapping momentum, with Alcapone and Lizzy alternating on the mic. In contrast, *King Of The Track*, cut for Bunny Lee, was done too hastily to be of much significance. "When I was leaving Jamaica in 1973 Bunny Lee said: 'Dennis, as you're going to England, I think you should walk with some material so that you can make some money. We'll go by Tubby's tomorrow and make an album.' He just run the track down and keep on running. When I said to him: 'Striker, that's just a run-down,' he said: 'That tune there done, man. Next tune.'"

By the time Alcapone arrived in Britain, I Roy was firmly in the ascendancy back home. Born Roy Samuel Reid in Saint Thomas in 1944, I Roy was one of Jamaica's all-time greatest toasters, yet wound up homeless, with mental health problems, before suffering a fatal heart attack in 1999. During the mid 60s, Reid worked at Customs and Excise, which gave him more ready cash than some of his peers, so he made a point of always being immaculately dressed. He first operated a set called Soul Bunnies in the rock steady era, playing Friday nights at Rose Lane in downtown Kingston, but in 1968 moved to Son's Junior, a sound system with an extensive selection of Studio One dub plates based at the New Yorker club in Spanish Town. After Son's proprietor moved abroad, I Roy became the star deejay of Supreme Ruler Of Sound, and when U Roy hit with 'Wake The Town', I Roy moved to the rival Stereo set. His verbal skills drew the attention of producer Harry Mudie, who cut the toaster's debut, 'Hearts Don't Leap', in late 1970. I Roy voiced more for Mudie, including a version of Dennis Walks's chilling 'Drifter', and helped distribute Mudie's product on a Honda motorcycle. While recordings for other producers, the quick-witted toaster began chatting on the Clarendon sound V-Rocket, and ended up temporarily filling U Roy's shoes on King Tubby's Hi-Fi in 1972. That same year, he voiced the arresting 'Sidewalk Killer' for Ruddy Redwood, making optimum use of Tommy McCook's sax-and-flute reworking of Phyllis Dillon's haunting cover of Marlena Shaw's soul hit 'Woman Of The Ghetto'. The disc was so popular that Roy voiced an alternative version, the atmospheric 'Dr Phibbs'.

I Roy's debut album, *Presenting I Roy*, captured the deejay at his best.

Gussie Clarke, then a young record importer, oversaw its creation. Clarke now presides over Anchor, the biggest recording studio on the island, complete with CD duplication and other facilities. As with many peers, he came to record production through sound systems.

"I grew up downtown, at Beeston Street and Church Street, with an adoptive mother who work with the government – an ordinary poor lady, nothing unique about her except her heart. Music was one of those things that was within you, and I just love music. In those days an amplifier was made by buying parts, so I usually buy the parts from lunch money. I was a born entrepreneur: I used to have a bicycle and sell rides to the school gates, and I usually ask for foreign records from the States and sell them to all the sound systems. I graduated from Kingston College in '71, so I was actually involved in having the sound system King Gussie's Hi-Fi prior to '71. After that, I had this dub cutting machine – I think we bought it from Treasure Isle – get it working downtown at a home studio in a wooden building, upstairs at 79 Church Street – that's where we started the first productions, cutting dubs for all these sound systems. I swapped an old amplifier to Errol Dunkley for the use of a rhythm ['Baby I Love You'] and we used the rhythm to voice U Roy's 'The Higher The Mountain', that was the first thing."

The close links he formed cutting dub plate exclusives enabled Gussie to hand pick the choice rhythms used for I Roy's debut. Touching on a range of subjects, from the Rastafari-praising 'Red Gold And Green' to the social realism of 'Pusher Man' and 'Peace', Roy's delivery was consistently relaxed. Even when proffering a lyrical deluge, as in his forceful castigation of freeloaders on 'Black Man Time' (a witty reworking of 'Slaving'), the toaster made it seem effortless. The same laid-back confidence characterised the follow-up, *Hell And Sorrow*, which compiled work cut for various producers. On songs like 'Black And Proud', Roy demonstrated the influence of American black power movements, and on 'Buck And The Preacher' an enduring love of popular films. The album also had a noteworthy level of echo and delay, courtesy of King Tubby. The popularity of these albums in Britain encouraged I Roy to follow Alcapone to London in late 1973, where he remained for the better part of a year. He made several live appearances backed by rising local band Matumbi, and became a star feature of Lloydie Coxsone's sound system residency at the Roaring Twenties club in the West End.

In Jamaica, an upstart rival, Big Youth, matched I Roy's composure. This tall, lanky dread with a deeper voice became a sensation through recordings cut in 1972–73. Manley Augustus Buchanan was born in a Southeast

Kingston ghetto in 1949, and regards his religious upbringing as formative. "My mother is a Revivalist preacher and my mother was my father also, because she have to take care of everything, including my three sisters and one brother. I was born at 1a Water Street in Rae Town, and I move to 132 Matches Lane [aka Matthews Lane] in the heart of the city, because my mother always have to be moving to get somewhere she can keep her church and preach. That wasn't the road I take, but that teach me Rastafari, because I was so biblical that the love was already in me. But I wasn't ready for Christianity and the condition of Christ."

Before launching himself into music, Big Youth repaired and maintained machines. "I was a mechanic at Harvey's Cab Company in Rae Town, that's where I learn trade. Then when the Kinston Sheraton was building, I used to do diesel mechanic work on the site. That was the last time I work."

Although he had deejay aspirations from the time of U Roy's success, he met resistance when approaching sound systems, and had to use intimidating tactics to reach the mic around 1971. "You have other people that run the sound that don't want to give you the privilege cause them see that you have the power, but we a bad boy offa the road, so you have to demand. One night you have a sound named Down South The President. [Fellow deejay] Errol Scorcher and my brethren keep the dance and them say it's me going to have to go mash it. I go to the dance and just use the one song, 'Satta Massa Ganna' – 'A wiggle wiggle wiggle wonna, you no on-yah but you born-yah' – and mash up the whole place the night. We nice it up, and it was a new star born."

Big Youth came to the limelight on Lord Tippertone, a downtown set initially called Finger Tone that was based at Princess Street, and his popularity enabled him to supersede fellow neighbourhood tough Jah Stitch as regular boss of the microphone. Big Youth consciously strove to bring the spirituality of Rastafari into his microphone chants, a direct reaction to the apolitical lyrics set as standard by U Roy at Treasure Isle. "It just happened that I start to run the Tipper thing a spiritual way, and tell people must make love and not war, because war ugly and love lovely, cause me have a whole heap of brethren that me see just dead. Babylon or them friend or a next gang kill them through differences where they can't agree, so all those things teach me knowledge, and Jah himself. We used to hear about 'hit me back' and 'chick a bow, chick a bow, chick a bow wow wow', but I wasn't into the 'hit me back' and 'bow' thing. I see where we need to say: 'Live it up Jah,' 'Hit me front and never hit me back,' 'cos we're moving forward. We're not into no bend down – we're getting up."

193

West Kingston-based producer Ivan Radway – known as 'One Foot Jimmy' because he lost a leg in the infamous Kendal train crash[1] – first approached him to record in early 1972 after finding success with Errol Dunkley's 'Black Cinderella', but Gregory Isaacs beat Radway to the draw and captured the toaster's talent first, placing Big Youth over Dunkley's 'Movie Star'. "Jimmy Radway wanted me to come and toast on 'Black Cinderella', but he was joking, and Gregory Isaacs already hear me working the sound, so Gregory just jump the gun, and that's where I do 'Movie Man': 'If you're coming from far in a bus or a car / Man I'm begging you make love and not war / I'm so sad to say that when you deal with war you have to stay far / Makes things right to do things right in the middle of the night / And promise me you would do that.' The same day I did the 'Black Cinderella'."

Isaacs said he approached Big Youth because of "the vibes of how I circulate in the ghetto. I see Big Youth as a youth with a lot of talent. Him come and blast off differently, seen? Everyone start take onto him – he's a very great deejay. We were friends, because him used to cook food for me".

Dunkley says 'Movie Star' marked the formation of the African Museum label. "I was at Coxsone – me, Dennis Brown, Horace Andy – until Wailing Souls started recording for Coxsone. I feel down all the time, because nothing ain't happening. Me and Dennis, sometimes we deh-deh and have no money, eat no food. I decide to move on after Coxsone and I fall out over something. I left Studio One with tears in my eyes, even asked Dennis if he's coming with me. Gregory Isaacs was singing for Rupie Edwards, but nothing wasn't really happening for him; he never really had a hit song. Gregory took me to Rupie Edwards and I did a medley of all my hit songs, because at the time it was a medley thing happening, but it was only a few that really hit, and mine was a hit. Then Gregory and I start working together. We form this African Museum label and we did three songs: we did over [Freddy McKay's] 'Picture On The Wall' rhythm and Winston Wright do a little keyboard. We did that instrumental song ['Jah Picture'], then I did 'Movie Star', then Gregory did 'Look Before You Leap'. We were working like half and half: we rent the studio and hire the musicians, and any money that will come we split it down the middle. We did another session, and I did 'Darling Ooh' and Gregory did 'My Only Lover'. After I did 'Movie Star', I did 'Black Cinderella' for Jimmy Radway, a good writer – he born and grow in the west of the city, same like us. He was a businessman, but he write songs like 'Mother Liza' that Leroy Smart sing. I was supposed to sing that song, and another song called 'Hell And Sorrow', [recorded by] Hortense Ellis.'

As Dunkley had licensed 'Darling Ooh' to Rupie Edwards, Edwards reaped the lion's share of its proceeds. "Me sell it to Rupie Edwards and regretted it, because the song was number one for 14 weeks in Jamaica, and it sell a lot on export. But I used to sell Sonia Pottinger 'Movie Star' – that's how she get to know me. She said: 'Let's do a thing,' and that's how I did my first album."

The LP, *Presenting Errol Dunkley*, had the first cut of 'A Little Way Different', one of Dunkley's most popular tunes; he says the song was inspired by rivalry with Dennis Brown. "Delroy Wilson was the first kid in Jamaica doing recording, then I was the second kid. I was like Delroy's rival, then Dennis come, and Dennis was like my rival. They used to compare us together. Sometimes they say me and Dennis sound alike, and this is how this song come up. If you sing the song I sing, you can still hear the difference."

Such work signalled the end of Dunkley's involvement in African Museum. "We had an office in Orange Street, but them time Gregory were really short-tempered. Him and the landlord couldn't get on, so we had to pack the office up, and I get so downhearted with him that I form my own label called Silver Ring. I had a store in Honour Town and a couple of jukeboxes, cause I wanted to go into the jukebox business. All my equipment was from money made from that album."

Isaacs continued with African Museum, but the song that brought him widespread fame in Jamaica was 'All I Have Is Love', one of the first hits recorded at Channel One, a studio opened by local entrepreneur Joseph Hoo-Kim in the heart of the Maxfield Park ghetto. As producer Phil Pratt recalls: "Joe Hoo-Kim call me one day and said: 'The studio just done. Come and test out the studio – you are free.' So I brought my musicians with me, and Gregory Isaacs. He arranged the horn section and the bass line and wrote the song as well. 'All I Have Is Love', that was Gregory Isaacs's first number one."

"We gave everybody a free try, because I didn't understand anything about running a session and I want to get experience," Hoo-Kim confirms at his Brooklyn pressing plant. "Any producer that was in the business, it was a day we usually give them, just to let them experience it and maybe get their business."

Joseph was the oldest of four brothers, all of whom would eventually be involved in running the studio. "I was born in 1942," he explains. "Paul comes after me, then Kenneth and Ernie." The Hoo-Kims are typically described as Chinese, but turn out to have a mixed heritage. "My father is from China. He was going to Panama in '26, stopped off in Jamaica and never go to Panama. My mother, born in Jamaica, was half-Jew and half-Chinese – her surname was Solomon. They were running an ice cream parlour and rum bar at the corner of Maxfield Avenue and Spanish Town Road, and then we moved to 29 Maxfield Avenue in '66. It was an ice cream parlour and a wholesale liquor store, and the property belongs to us. My brother-in-law usually work with a company that operate jukeboxes, which was Issa's, and sometimes when he's going to the country, he usually pick me up. Then Issa begin to sell out the boxes and I acquired some, and that is where I started from. I think the jukebox business started about 1960."

A fateful visit to Dynamic Sound inspired Joseph to build Channel One. "John Holt and I grew up together – we know each other from we was small. He takes me to Dynamic one day and I was fascinated with the sound in the studio – the sound just hold me right there, and I said: 'This is what I want to be in.' Bill Garnett is the one that select the equipment. I paid $38,000 for an API console, one of the most expensive on the market, maybe $60,000 for the console and the two tape machines. The studio opened 1972, with just four tracks. Bunny Lee run the first session: it was [Tyrone Davis's] 'Can I Change My Mind' with Delroy Wilson and Soul Syndicate – that was a trial session really. I started the studio myself, but Ernest came into it after we had an engineer problem. He usually fix jukeboxes and operate one-armed bandits. The original engineer was Sid Bucknor, he was there for about a year. During the period when we start up, Bunny Lee said: 'The studio doesn't sound good,' and I have in the most expensive console. I did an LP with Alton Ellis that I couldn't release. The bass was tied with the drum – it wasn't recorded properly. Then we make sessions and they were all flops, and I decided to lay back and see what we are doing wrong. But the main thing was about the sound. After Sid Bucknor, we decided to go into the studio ourselves. The first record that we put out was 'Don't Give Up The Fight' [by Stranger & Gladdy]. Then we came out with hits: [Delroy Wilson's] 'It's A Shame', 'Call On Me', [Horace Andy's] 'Girl I Love You'."

While Channel One was in the process of establishing itself, Big Youth was gaining popularity on vinyl. His second recording, 'Tell It Black', voiced on the emotive rendition of Peter Green's 'Black Magic Woman' recorded by Dennis Brown and Soul Syndicate for Phil Pratt (patterned after Santana's reworking of the song) was the first of many to make an impact. "'Tell It Black' and 'Phil Pratt Thing', those start to create a little heat," he recalls.

"Then the other producers want me – they all start coming. People have to wake me up out of my bed and we took a bike in the studio. We did 'S 90 Skank' the same day we did 'Chi Chi Run'. The two of them went to number one. I did things for Glen Brown too that same day – some great things happen that Friday."

'S 90 Skank' really showed the best of Big Youth's abilities on record, aided by perceptive production from Keith Hudson. Youth spoke of personal experiences on the record, warning about the consequences of excessive speed. "Me was riding a bike and crash at 12:20 in the afternoon, wake up at about 7:30 in the night. While they pronounce me dead, I was there visioning how I'm singing and Jah tell me me must go round the world and sing 'Jah'. So I say: 'If you ride like lightning, you will crash like thunder.' I get some bad crash. I used to ride wild, you know."

The success of that disc, and of the Prince Buster-produced 'Chi Chi Run', made Big Youth in high demand. "Everybody hearing this 'Jah Jah Jah, Jah wah wah rock', so everybody want a piece, cause it's the science – is that open the key to reggae music. Then Joe Gibbs want me, Miss Pottinger and Derrick Harriott, and I had seven tunes in the chart at the same time, with five in the two top tens."

For Gibbs, Youth scored high with the boxing commentary 'Foreman Versus Frazier'; 'Cool Breeze', for Derrick Harriott, was a popular cut of Keith & Tex's 'Stop That Train'. Even The Wailers got in on the act, voicing Youth on their self-produced 'Craven Choke Puppy', although the toaster failed to earn much from it. "Them times [The Wailers] do bad," he explains. "Them never have nothing! Me do 'Craven A Go Choke Puppy' [issued as 'Craven Version'] so Rita can buy some food, but them no treat me good."

After a steady stream of successful singles, a strong album consolidated his popularity both at home and abroad. As with I Roy's debut set, Big Youth's *Screaming Target* was released by Gussie Clarke in 1973. Youth makes full use of the disc's impeccably chosen rhythms, perpetuating the dejected message of Leroy Smart's 'Shame And Ambition' on 'Pride And Joy Rock', continuing the mournful determination of Gregory Isaacs's 'One One Cocoa' on 'One Of These Fine Days', and subverting K.C. White's re-cut of the oft-versioned 'No No No' [based on Willie Cobb's 'You Don't Love Me'] for both the ghetto description of 'Concrete Jungle' and the more famous gangster-movie commentary 'Screaming Target'. "This guy was firing his gun wilder than Clint Eastwood, so I said this one was ranker than Dirty Harry," says Youth of the title track's cryptic introduction.

Soon Big Youth launched the Negusa Negast and Augustus Buchanan labels for self-produced work; later imprints included Tanasha and Nichola Delita, the latter named after one of his daughters. In 1974 he issued the double album *Reggae Phenomenon*, on which the toaster controversially sang. "That is when me get good, get conscious and start defend the African daughters. Me take War's 'The World Is A Ghetto' and turn it 'round and call it 'Streets In Africa' with D. Brown – it give me much strength. Me do 'Love Me Forever', 'Hot Stock', 'Downtown Kingston Pollution', 'Hell Is For Heroes', 'African Daughter', and [The Temptations'] 'Papa Was A Rolling Stone', so that is when I start get versatile, but some of the fools, them say me can't sing. That was the better part where I was achieving and seeing my career looking progressive."

And why, exactly, was Big Youth inspired to sing? "Because in a lot of audiences, it's not everyone could understand the 'dee dee dah dah dee dee dey', so you have to show them that Big Youth have something inna him; me can sing, so me ah go touch some big song all of them know. When me come with [Dionne Warwick's] 'Touch Me In The Morning', God cry. Seeing the women, them love me more, me have to start hide from girls. Me show them me versatility because me creative, me have a force to generate."

Although Big Youth's singing technique was inspired by the jazz tradition, he took his greatest inspiration from female soul vocalists. "Me practise off of the woman them, like Diana Ross, and Dionne Warwick was my favourite, from early until now. Lady D now have the edge, because she take some wider notes."

Doctor Alimantado was another deejay to rise from live appearances on Tippertone. Born Winston Thompson in the early 50s and initially known as Winston Cool or Prince Winston, Tado is a good-natured Rasta with a sharp sense of humour. Widely travelled and with a Ghanaian grandfather, he is currently based in the Gambia, West Africa.

Tado says he ran away from his comfortable Kingston home at the age of eight to live with rough people in the slums. His experiences of hardship caused him to gravitate toward Rastafari, bringing conflict with his strongly Christian grandmother. His main deejay inspiration was Prince Rough of Sir George The Atomic, a toaster who always drew large crowds before he died in the early 70s; U Roy was another role model. 'No Go On So', recorded for small producer H. 'Bussa' Marston, was one of Thompson's earliest records, but work for Lee Perry in 1971–72 brought wider recognition. "I was on Tippertone, the sound that made Big Youth famous, and The Upsetter came to one of the dances and said I should come and do some songs for him. Jah Stitch used to be around my sound, and Jah Stitch

THIS PAGE, CLOCKWISE FROM LEFT: Winston Riley at Techniques Records; Aston 'Family Man' Barrett; melodica master Augustus Pablo. **FOLLOWING PAGE**: spiritual rootsman Burning Spear; King Tubby, the dub master.

THIS PAGE, CLOCKWISE FROM LEFT:
U Roy, the originator; I Roy, drifter
at the microphone; The Mighty
Diamonds At Channel One.
FOLLOWING PAGE: Dr Alimantado
at Prince Buster's shop.

used to play Upsetter's sound, so that's how it really came about. I did songs like 'Macabee The Third', 'Piece Of My Heart', 'Tip Of My Tongue'."[2]

Thompson's artistry really shone when paired with the work of Junior Byles. Not only did he mutter ominous Rasta proclamations on 'Ital Version', the flipside of Junior's anthem-like 'Beat Down Babylon', but the thoughtful meditation on his African homeland delivered on Byles's heartfelt 'Place Called Africa' fully captured the reverence the Rastafari accorded their ancestral continent.

In 1973 Thompson founded the Vital Food label, renaming himself Doctor Alimantado 'The Ital Surgeon', with the self-produced 'Just The Other Day', a woeful comment on Jamaica's crippling inflation, voiced at King Tubby's studio over The Flames' great 'Zion' rhythm obtained from Lee Perry. From his base at 40 Beeston Street, Alimantado issued further stunners, sometimes on the Ital Sounds label, including the half-sung pledge for unity, 'Ride On'. Setting up his own label was partly a reaction to the negative attitude of larger entrepreneurs. While the bulk of his subsequent work was self-produced, he occasionally voiced material for smaller producers.[3]

Then the constantly echoing voice bouncing through 'Best Dressed Chicken In Town' caused a storm in 1974, sparking interest in the UK.[4] According to Alimantado, the rhythm track for 'Best Dressed Chicken' resulted from a jam session at Dynamics funded by producer Lenroy Moffatt and a number of other individuals; it loosely emulated Bill Withers's 'Ain't No Sunshine', previously covered by Ken Boothe. Many cuts of Moffatt's rhythm later surfaced, and Tado himself used the rhythm for alternative cuts such as the religious 'Plead I Cause', the topical 'Oil Crisis' and the nonsensical 'She Wreng Up', but 'Best Dressed Chicken' is definitely the most inspiring. Tado's closeness with Lee Perry at the Black Ark determined the shape of the tune. "I've got an innovative mind where music is concerned, and so has Mr Perry. Put the two of us together and the result is 'Best Dressed Chicken'. It was an innovation I had in Randy's studio, but if you go to Mr Perry with an idea he doesn't just handle it as though he's an engineer, he handles it as though it's his thing – he puts his initiative behind it."

By the time Doctor Alimantado recorded 'Best Dressed Chicken In Town', Dennis Alcapone was already spending most of his time in Britain, but returned briefly to Jamaica to record. "When I came to London in 1973, I met up with The Pioneers. Luddy Crooks used to take me to the Q Club in Praed Street, Paddington, quite regularly, because at that time Q Club was swinging. Pioneers and Nicky Thomas was living the high life, because they

203

had tunes in the charts, so it was more or less the jet set that would go to that club. They used to take me down there and introduce me to some top-class whores. When I go back to Jamaica, Harry J. just built up his studio, so Luddy and I went to Harry J. and did the album *Belch It Off*. I don't have fond memories of that album. It is a strange album, because that wasn't something that was planned."

Negative circumstances later saw him shift base to London permanently. "After my first trip to London I went back home and had a terrible bike accident, and it's like I lose something out of that accident. I lose two of my front teeth, because my head went inna this van, and I had a girl on the back of the bike and she drop inna the middle of the road. After I get better, I come back up to England with the Jamaica Showcase, which was Dennis Brown, Toots & The Maytals, Cynthia Richards, and Skin Flesh & Bones with Al Brown. That's when I didn't have roots any more in Jamaica, cause from '74 I overstayed my time here. My father died, and I couldn't go back to Jamaica because my papers wasn't sorted, and the government said if I leave the country I wouldn't be able to come back in. So I got married, and that's how I really get caught up in the England thing. In Jamaica the violence was going on and the dance was being shot down, a whole heap of shooting going on. The runnings was quite different here; it was a cool operation compared to down there. Dance couldn't go on, because if the police didn't shoot it down the rude boy did, so that's one of the reasons that swing me a bit."

Away from Jamaica for extended periods, Alcapone's influence naturally dropped, but before leaving the island he passed the deejay baton to Lester Bullocks, a protégé who would gain greater fame as Dillinger. Born in 1953, he was raised by his grandmother on the outskirts of Kingston. "My mother was living in America, so I was living with my grandma. She used to sell in the market on Friday," he says, leaning against an oil drum outside Tuff Gong studio. "Down the years I've been inspired by U Roy, Alcapone, King Stitt – deejays before my time."

Alcapone distinctly remembers his early enthusiasm. "Dillinger was living just across the way, so whenever the sound is playing he always come right beside the amplifier. One night him ask me fi give him a talk over the mike. He wasn't brilliant, but you could hear that there was something. Him used to come more often when I'm playing and work himself in."

Dillinger subsequently became the leading deejay on Smith The Weapon, based on Payne Avenue, off Spanish Town Road. Anxious to record, he began doing the rounds of Kingston's studios, but encountered little interest until Lee Perry decided to give him a chance at Dynamics in 1973. "I remember Scratch voice him for about two days straight, just in case the man bust out," Alcapone recalls. "But really and truly Dillinger wasn't in his peak yet, so those tracks didn't make an impact."

As something of an apprentice to Dennis Alcapone, Lester Bullocks originally called himself Alcapone Junior, but Perry deemed the name Dillinger more suitable. Although singles such as the topical 'Middle East Rock' and rebel-praising 'Headquarters' were taken from his initial session, much remained in the can. His first big hit, 'Platt Skank', which decried the vanity of men who plait their hair, was for upcoming producer Phil Pratt. Dillinger then cut a few sides for Augustus Pablo, including 'Brace A Boy', recorded in combination with a certain Clive, apparently about the braces that hold up little boys' short pants. He continued to record on a freelance basis. "I was campaigning," he says. "I do a couple songs for Abyssinians, a version of 'Satta Massa Ganna' ['I Saw E Saw'] and 'Crashie Project', and a couple for Bunny Lee and GG Records." Dillinger also recorded extensively for Coxsone Dodd, who eventually issued the compelling *Ready Natty Dreadie* album.

Prince Jazzbo, a toaster whose deep voice bordered on the menacing, was another deejay to reach the Jamaican charts in 1973. Face to face with the toaster at Kingston's Countryside Club, the former street urchin, born Linval Carter in 1951, has prominent facial scars and an intimidating manner. In his largely unsupervised youth, Jazzbo gravitated to the downtown Kingston music scene, gaining valuable contacts in the industry. As he explains: "Me know Lee Perry, from boy days, and Bob Marley and The Upsetters."

Jazzbo's deejay apprenticeship came on the Whip sound system in Spanish Town. In 1972 he talked his way into Studio One, where 'Crab Walking', voiced in one take on Horace Andy's 'Skylarking', resulted in a major hit that mixed dance-craze motivation with snatches of proverbs and Rastafari intonation, all delivered in a charged, low growl. Other intense singles followed, including the stern 'Crime Don't Pay' and the devoted 'Imperial I', but Coxsone held back the bulk. His debut album, *Choice Of Version*, was not issued until 1990.

Coxsone's hesitancy led Jazzbo to the competition, with 'Mr Harry Skank', 'Meaning Of One', and 'Mr Want All' surfacing through Glen Brown. As Jazzbo explains: "Inna the 70s, Glen Brown is the man who give me a lot of encouragement. He get me to be self-reliant."

Despite Coxsone's reluctance, Jazzbo insists he holds no grudge.

205

"Coxsone is a nice producer and I respect him very much. Coxsone Downbeat's the best producer inna the whole reggae industry. Me never have nothing bad fi say about Coxsone, because Coxsone make me popular and make the music industry get so established that millions of people are eating food out of it."

Upon linking with Brown, Jazzbo made crude attempts at self-production by cutting further versions of the 'At The Cross Roads' rhythm: 'Plum Plum' had sexually suggestive imagery, incongruously introduced by a religious phrase, while 'Crankibine' decried the negative tendencies of loose females, its instrumental B-side utilising peculiar, out-of-time instrumentation. "The off-beat piano is me, and I'm playing a melodica on it as well," Jazzbo reveals. "It's just a natural mystic: music is a thing where you just see it before you even make it – you just put it together and put it out." The work was voiced at King Tubby's studio. "Working with Tubby was a pleasure. I work with Tubby from 1972."

After releasing sporadic singles on the Count 123, Mr Funny, and Brisco labels, Jazzbo voiced two songs for Lee Perry at the producer's recently inaugurated Black Ark studio in early 1974. 'Penny Reel' had a cool stream of proverbs, and 'Good Things' warned of the dangers of truancy, although Jazzbo lost his train of thought and fell silent after the latter's opening lines.

Jazzbo's international fame stemmed from his infamous feud with I Roy, charted on a series of clashing discs produced by Bunny Lee in 1975, instigated by the owner of a record shop in Toronto. The pair's first sorties were built around insults: on 'Straight To Jazzbo's Head', I Roy accused Jazzbo of ugliness, while on 'Straight To I Roy's Head', Jazzbo claimed I Roy was an imitator of U Roy. The next round contained more serious allegations: in 'Jazzbo Have Fe Run', I Roy made reference to an incident that took place near Kincaid Pharmacy, in which Jazzbo was attacked by music promoter Trevor 'Leggo Beast' Douglas for plagiarising Big Youth's lyrics.

Jazzbo's retort on 'Gal Boy I Roy' had bite, but was ultimately weaker; his insistence that "If deejay was your trade, you wouldn't talk about Kincaid" only emphasised the conflict with Douglas, and his claim that "If I wasn't ugly, you couldn't call my name in your record to get promotion" hardly asserted superiority. When I Roy struck back with 'Padlock' Jazzbo dropped out of the contest, and Bunny Lee had to convince singer Derrick Morgan to aim a volley at I Roy with 'I Roy The Chiney Come Round', but Roy swiftly eliminated the competition with the gloating 'Straight To Derrick Morgan's Head'.

The feud between Jazzbo and I Roy recalls the earlier vinyl battles of Derrick Morgan and Prince Buster, but even though the records had a nasty edge, privately the parties remained friendly, and I Roy would later record for Jazzbo. These battles prefaced the recorded jousts of American hip-hop, such as those waged by LL Cool J against Kool Moe Dee and Roxanne Shanté versus UTFO, as well as later Jamaican deejay battles between Beenie Man and Bounty Killer; a coffin was even paraded on stage when those two toasters clashed in the late 90s. But such rivalry was not always symbolic. In 1975 Jah Stitch, who had switched his allegiances to the new Black Harmony set, was wrongly blamed for the death of a Tippertone employee; since the two sounds were scheduled to clash, some said Stitch must have been responsible. He was subsequently shot in the face at point-blank range, but miraculously survived.

The deejay experimentation recounted in this chapter was one of the most important elements of the evolving reggae continuum. The album successes of U Roy, Big Youth, and I Roy showed that the art of toasting had reached a new high in the mid 70s, and since then, the status of the deejay has never slipped.

8
NONE SHALL ESCAPE THE JUDGEMENT

The flyers and rockers styles

"He pioneered the 'deejay' records through Hugh Roy, then brought in the 'version' flipside styling. His own unique engineering skills produced the almighty 'dub', which has now evolved into the very latest – the now sound – 'styling symbols' or simply 'flyers' ... Tubby will always be at the roots of Jamaican sounds."
– LINER NOTES TO *DUB FROM THE ROOTS*, TOTAL SOUNDS LP, 1974

"Channel One have a time when it used to run things." – TABBY DIAMOND

As the deejays were bringing more rants and chants onto vinyl, the dominant sound was shifting again, a momentous change resulting from the rhythmic innovations of The Aggrovators, a Soul Syndicate spin-off utilised by Bunny Lee. The name came from an expression used by Eddy Grant, the Guyanese singer then leading mixed crossover group The Equals. As Lee explains: "Me used to have the Bunny Lee All Stars, till Joe Gibbs come with the Joe Gibbs All Stars, and it never fair to the musicians, because me or Joe Gibbs can't play a note. Me and Eddy Grant start spar from inna the 60s, and every time you say something, Eddy say: 'That's aggro, man! You're causing me aggro!', because you're aggravating him. Me start call my musicians The Aggrovators, and The Aggrovators tear up some music inna the 70s right back to inna the 80s."

The Aggrovators' loose line-up typically featured Chinna and Tony Chin on guitar and Bernard 'Touter' Harvey on organ. Santa was the mainstay on drums, but Carlton Barrett and 'Benbow' Creary sometimes took his place. On bass, Family Man gave way to George Fullwood, occasionally supplanted by Earl 'Bagga' Walker, who in turn was replaced by Robbie Shakespeare, a young protégé of Family Man from an East Kingston ghetto who had a tough reputation. Shakespeare's heavy bass lines gave The Aggrovators' material its solid anchorage, and he eventually became the bandleader.

"Growing up from school, what I really like was drums," Shakespeare says, relaxing on the balcony at Sonic Sounds studio. "I used to have drumsticks and play on a bench, and then guitar got my attention – rock'n'roll lead guitar. When I hear the bass, the bass sound powerful and it make a difference. Jackie Jackson had an album where he stand up with a bass [The Supersonics' *Greater Jamaica: Moonwalk Reggae*, Treasure Isle, 1969], and it always fascinate me – he was one of my greatest inspirations. Coming from school, I used to hear Jackie Jackson on [John Holt's] 'Ali Baba'; every one of them Treasure Isle stuff. My older brother Lloyd, that time he had a group named The Emotions: he have an acoustic guitar, and I used to trouble it. My first real encounter with a bass guitar was when Hippy Boys was doing some rehearsal – Family Man was playing. At that time, I didn't know it was really bass. Family Man started showing me the songs, so when Family Man left Hippy Boys I was the lad to come in. They didn't like to pay money, but I didn't care about the money then."

The rhythmic style most associated with The Aggrovators was a 1974 innovation called 'flyers'. This was the 'flying cymbal' sound built on a mechanised hi-hat adapted from the 'Philly Bump' soul beat developed by Philadelphia studio ensemble MFSB, whose song 'The Sound Of Philadelphia' (aka 'TSOP') was the theme of popular American television show *Soul Train*. According to Santa, the beat was first used on Johnny Clarke's 1974 single, 'None Shall Escape The Judgement'. "MFSB, with 'The Sound Of Philadelphia', they use a lot of that. The drummer [Earl Young] was a favourite drummer of mine, and I said: 'Damn, let's try that in a reggae sound.' 'None Shall Escape The Judgement' came up, and I started the song with that. Bunny Lee wanted that in every song. He was the one who name it 'flying cymbal', which is an open-and-closed hi-hat. Then the whole thing started ballooning."

According to renowned drummer Sly Dunbar, the 'flying cymbal' was actually first used on Joya Landis's rock steady classic 'Moonlight Lover,' cut with The Supersonics in 1968, but 'None Shall Escape The Judgement' was certainly the song to bring the style into widespread use. Earl Zero, who wrote the song, first voiced it for Bunny Lee with Chinna Smith (with a couple of other Greenwich Farm amateurs and Johnny Clarke sitting in on harmony), but Clarke's own rendition was the version to make the final cut.

"Chinna was one of my best friends – he lived a couple blocks from me," Zero says at his home in Northern California. "His dad had a sound system, so every day we meet, play some songs and lick chalice. Bunny Lee have a bar right there at Fifth Street, and the empty lot, we used to go round there and sing. Bunny Lee come and hear us all the time and say: 'Me want to take you to studio to do something.'"

The singer was born Earl Anthony Johnson on East Avenue in 1953, but Lee dubbed him Earl Zero. "My dad is a fisherman who always dock at a wharf called Zero Wharf, so them call him Fisherman Zero. When me and Chinna do the song, Bunny Lee just use the name Earl Zero. Me do 'None Shall Escape', but he never like my version, so he go in the studio with Johnny Clarke."

'None Shall Escape The Judgement' gave Clarke his major breakthrough. "Singing started from school days," the tall, burly singer says in the lobby of a London hotel. "I was born in Kingston in 1955, grow up in Waltham Park Road, and I was in Trench Town for many years. I get a scholarship to Jamaica College. With Ibo Cooper from Third World, and Roger and Ian Lewis from Inner Circle, we had a school band together."

Clarke nearly recorded as a schoolboy. "Me and Jacob Miller were close friends, and we used to go to Studio One and buy drinks for Leroy Sibbles and them man. Bob Andy was supposed to write some songs for me, because Downbeat loved my voice, but because my parents wanted me to concentrate on school, I never had the time to go to the studio regularly, like Jacob. After school I started taking it more serious, trying to get some recording done, but it wasn't happening, so I started doing talent shows with Barry Brown, Mighty Diamonds, and Sugar Minott, who had The African Brothers, but we were young and nobody had any name yet."

Clarke began recording in 1973, but his debut, recorded at Federal for pianist/engineer Glen Stair, was not released, while an early effort for Clancy Eccles, 'God Made The Sea And Sun', was not promoted sufficiently. 'Everyday Wondering', produced by Rupie Edwards and released in 1974, was the first to impact. "I was at the bus stop, wondering from which angle something's going to happen, so me just bring forth the song," Clarke explains. "It's all about me wanting to be successful. It was a hit in the dance, but it wasn't popularised countrywide among the population. That was my first time in King Tubby's studio – Rupie took me round there to voice. I made the rhythm at Channel One with Jackie Jackson and Hux Brown."

'Wondering' was relatively popular in London and New York, but Edwards's recasting of the rhythm as the abstract 'Skanga' – in which the producer imitated the sound of instruments with his voice – was such a big hit that Edwards appeared on *Top Of The Pops* and soon relocated to London. Although 'Wondering' never brought Clarke that level of fame, it attracted the attention of other downtown promoters including Keith 'Stamma' Hobson (aka Derrick Hobson), an associate of Keith Hudson for whom Clarke cut the unusual 'Golden Snake'. "He was more like a bad man – the first kind of man there who have them knife and ratchet," laughs Clarke. "That's the reason he was around Hudson, because he was there like a protector."

After covering Smokey Robinson's 'You Really Got A Hold On Me' for Glen Brown, Clarke finally broke through by linking with Bunny Lee. "Striker was on the corner at Chancery Lane, right beside Salvation Army, where we all used to hang out: me, Gregory Isaacs, Stamma, Dirty Harry. Bunny Lee usually go to England a lot, so one day he came around and just create an excitement: 'I hear a tune you do for Rupie in England, mash up the dance up there!' He wanted me to do a cover, 'My Desire', one of those old type of Shirley & Lee songs, so I went to Treasure Isle studio. Earl Zero and some other guys from Greenwich Farm came there with this song, 'None Shall Escape The Judgement'; Bunny now want me to go with the group, because he had different ideas.

"When there was a session about to get underway, the musicians would have a little workout, so there was Santa just playing the cymbal, and Bunny came in and heard it – 'Oh boy! That's what we want' – so he translate the little workout straight onto the real thing. Normally Santa was just doing it as a joke. It was a new sound, because that is the thing that really tip me now. We went to voice 'My Desire' at Tubby's, and [Lee] said I should try to do back 'None Shall Escape' in my way different than Earl Zero. I develop the vibes and run down the place, because it was all about that new sound and a new youth. From that it was strictly Bunny Lee right along, because Bunny Lee had the sound and everybody wanted to go to Duke Reid's studio. Gregory Isaacs and G.G. went there after to do 'Love Is Overdue'."

Clarke stuck solidly with Lee for the next few years, "through the cymbal, because that was the hit way, that was what the people needed". The sound proved the perfect platform for Clarke's vocal style, which was punctuated with undulating slurs. Along with singers such as Al Campbell, Clarke was one of the first to record the forerunner of what would later emerge as the dancehall style. His lyrics alternated between love songs and 'reality' themes, and he was equally adept at cover tunes.

Clarke says his strongest influences were sound systems and Rastafari. "I grow up with a sound system next door to me, Vee Jay The Dub Master, that was at 31c Waltham Park Road. He's the type of soundman that get up at four o'clock in the morning, and those days we have some steel horns up in the trees and you hear some wicked Alton Ellis; it usually wake me up to go to school. Vee Jay focus 'pon Rasta. We're really from the ghetto, and Rasta was a focus from them times. My mom was a Christian, but I grow up with my bigger brother 'Obadiah', James Clarke, a Rastaman, so after a while me start focussing on Rastafari."

Obadiah founded the shortlived Clarke's label and produced some unsuccessful sides with Johnny; another brother, well-known drummer Eric 'Fish' Clarke, also helped direct Johnny to music. "He has a lot to do with my career too, but he never grow up with us. He ended up at Maxfield Park Children's Home, then he move on to Alpha Boys' School. When he usually come home for holidays, he always deal with music, so I was more clinging to that."

Clarke's partnership with Bunny Lee brought the singer into the big time. After 'None Shall Escape The Judgement', 'Move Out Of Babylon Rastaman', 'Peace And Love In The Ghetto', and 'Rock With Me Baby' were substantial hits built on the flyers sound.

Cornell Campbell, who moved to Lee's stable from Studio One by 1972, emerged as Clarke's most consistent rival from the success of 'Natty Dread In Greenwich Town' (aka 'Natty Dread In A Greenwich Farm'). "I became frustrated when I went to Randy's record shop and hear songs like [The Bassies'] 'Things A Come Up To Bump'," Campbell explains. "The music sell, and my good tunes, them nah sell. I write 'Natty Dread In A Greenwich Farm' because me say: 'Let me sing pure reality tune, pure tune whe the people on the street them like.' I went to Bunny Lee with that song, because I had a band named Don Cornell & The Eternals. Robert Shakespeare used to play in my band with Carly [Barrett], so Bunny Lee came one night to hear the band play at Greenwich Town – that's the first time I know Bunny Lee, and him love how me sing. Him came to Robert Shakespeare and ask if him can play on sessions. I never like the idea, because if Robert Shakespeare leave, the band going go down. Robert Shakespeare left the band and go to Bunny Lee, so I use one of my singer partners, Ken Price, to play bass, but the band never up to the prestige of how we did have it. After a while me automatically start to sing for Bunny Lee, backup artists with guitar and piano, and I play the bass with artists like Derrick Morgan. I said to Bunny Lee: 'What you think about "Natty Dread In A Greenwich Farm"? You think it going to do anything?' Him said: 'Yes, man, that is a bad tune.' King Tubby tell me: 'Boy Cornell, I went ah East Kingston the other night and hear the song play, and somebody tell me police want to raid the place and shoot up the sound, because the way the song bad, whole heap of man get mad up there' – every time a song going to hit, some disaster happen. 'Natty Dread In A Greenwich Farm' start to run the place big time."

Campbell explains how his rivalry with Clarke took root. "Johnny Clarke came before with a song named 'None Shall Escape The Judgement'. A brother named Earl write the song, and Bunny Lee give me the song to sing first, but Bunny Lee owe me some money, [so] me draw away a little bit, and Bunny Lee give it to Johnny Clarke to sing. That was him first big record. When me come back ah town, Bunny Lee say: 'You see if you sing the tune what would happen? Johnny Clarke sing it over and it gone.' The tune start sell, so that's why I sing another version of it named 'Gun Court Law'."

That song referred to Michael Manley's drastic response to Jamaica's escalating firearms problem. Opened in April 1974 at Camp Road, the barbed-wire-encased fortress serves as a court of law and detention centre for those caught with unlicensed guns. Trials are conducted without juries, and with no opportunity for bail or appeals; the maximum sentence was initially indefinite detention, later changed to mandatory life imprisonment, and guilt could be established by the possession of a single bullet shell. Although it was generally welcomed at its inception, the Gun Court was a surprisingly repressive creation from a man elected on a human rights platform.

When Clarke addressed similar themes on another cut of the rhythm for 'Joshua's Word', the rivalry with Campbell was in full swing. "It become a competition," Campbell observes. "Every man feel him bad, so I go write a song named 'The Gorgon', and then Johnny Clarke come with 'Move Out Of Babylon', and me come with 'Dance In A Greenwich Farm', and Johnny Clarke come with [Barbara Lynn's] 'You'll Lose A Good Thing', and me come with [Gene Chandler's] 'Duke Of Earl'."

Much of this material was mixed by Philip Smart, then resident engineer at King Tubby's. "The Bunny Lee era, that's when I came in the picture," the portly engineer says at HC&F, the studio he currently runs in Long Island. "All the Johnny Clarke, like 'None Shall Escape The Judgement' – I convinced Bunny to put out Johnny's version. Bunny wasn't really too hot on the tune, but after Johnny sing it I tell him: 'That tune there hot.' He say: 'If you feel it, mix it' – just like that."

Smart came to music through the sound-system circuit, and recalls early studio experience via Errol Thompson. "My mother says I was born with some turntable in me hand," he laughs. "I was always into music and collect records as a youth, used to play at birthday parties, keep coming up until I play at dances and clubs. I used to live at Harbour View, and Errol was living in Harbour View with his relative named Goff, an electronic engineer who usually repairs and builds amplifiers. He had a set named El Don, and all who was interested in electronics used to hang out over there. At that time, Errol was working at Studio One, used to bring home exclusives like 'Nanny Goat'. When him leave Studio One and go to Randy's, I start going to Randy's after school to watch him work."

Then Smart moved to Havendale and became friendly with Augustus Pablo. "Myself and Augustus Pablo put together lunch money, book a studio session, and recorded some tracks with a band that we brought in, Reckless Breed, like six rhythm tracks to a two-track tape. Pablo was playing piano. Those tracks weren't hardcore enough, so we went back and did 'Skanking Easy' [a melodica re-cut of The Soul Brothers' 'Swing Easy', based on the theme of *Fiddler On The Roof*]. Myself, Pablo, and another friend put our money together and produced that record, pressed it, and put it out on the Hot Stuff label. I was still in high school, but we use the top musicians at that time: Family Man, Carly, Tyrone Downey, and Reggie. We did that on four-track at Randy's – that was my first real production."

Soon Smart was working with Tubby. "I had my own sound called Sound Of Distinction, just a little neighbourhood set. We used to go to King Tubby's and cut dubs – that's how I first met him, with rhythms that Pablo would record, like Pablo and myself did 'Cassava Piece' originally at Dynamics. I always was at Tubbs's and Tubbs was more receptive, he let me hang out there every night, until one day he just say: 'Jackson, go and take that voice' – probably about a year and a half from I was first going there."

The flyers sound, with its uncanny hi-hat emphasis, provided Tubby with ample opportunity for exciting dub experimentation, as heard on the classic albums *Dub From The Roots* and *The Roots Of Dub*. Similarly, Smart created a new dub technique, heard on certain single B-sides, by subjecting the tape machine test-tone to short bursts of repeated delay. "I put it on John Holt's 'The Clock'," he says. "When it starts, you hear 'beep-beep-beep-beep-beep-beep-beep-beep-beep' – you had to find stuff to be innovative, as people always looking out for something new."

Stereo mixing was another 1974 innovation. "Those days, everything was mono. Pablo did [a melodica version of Ken Boothe's] 'When I Fall In

Love' [issued as 'Forever Love', aka 'Jah Light'], that was done in stereo, and 'Black Is Our Colour', by Wayne Wade – that was Yabby You's production, recorded at Lee Perry's studio." The overseas popularity of such experiments saw Smart mixing his first dub album. "England was very hot on some of the mixes I was doing, so after Bunny go to England, him say: 'Philip, you are the man!' That's how me get to do the LP *Creation Of Dub*, the one with Bunny Lee's picture on the front, but them no want to tell Tubbs that I did a dub LP."

Tubby pioneered other innovations during this period, despite the police raids that would ultimately close down his sound system. Smart mentions one particular event that took place in late 1973 or early 1974, after police had already once destroyed Tubby's sound. "It was twice them have it," says Smart. "The first time them shot up him sound, they had mashed up the amp and he decided he wasn't going to play any more – he was just going to do the studio thing – but everybody said Tubbs have to bring back the sound, and him rebuild. The first dance that play was at Up Park Camp where they have the Gun Court right now, but Gun Court didn't exist then. Around midnight, U Roy ride in on him bike and tune up the sound. Nobody know that Tubbs put a secret thing in the amp: when they put on the mic, U Roy say: 'You're now entertained by the number-one sound in the land-land-land-land-land-land.' [It was] the first time people hear echo: 'King Tubby's Hi-Fi-fi-fi-fi-fi …' A man fire a shot inside the dance! That was the first time him unveil echo in an amp and you can't see it, because he have it incorporated inside the amplifier."

Not only was this the first time that echo had been unleashed on the nation at a dance, it also marked the debut airing of Ansel Collins's 'Stalag', created for producer Winston Riley. The song's forceful bass and vibrant horns have remained consistently popular, with the original rhythm used in new creations for decades to come. "Riley brought 'Stalag' and give it to Tubby," Smart recalls. "That was the first time it played and that was the first tune that play that night, play for about half an hour."

Soon after, Smart relocated to New York to further his education in engineering and broadcasting. Then Tubby's sound was destroyed again. "The second one was some politics dance. Police spray the amps [with bullets] and took away the amps. Tubby was suing the police because them mash up his sound, shoot up the dub plates. Him was very upset."

With Smart overseas, Pat Kelly returned to Dromilly Avenue for another stint of engineering. "I work in Tubby's in three different sessions – left and come back," he explains. "I did about three years of mixing at various studios, like Tubby's, Dynamic, Joe Gibbs, Randy's." Some months later, when Prince Jammy returned from Canada in January 1976, he took over most of the engineering duties, becoming a highly valued member of Tubby's team.

○

While King Tubby and his crew continued their dub explorations, Sly Dunbar dissipated the flying cymbal with a new style called 'rockers', developed at Channel One with his house band, The Revolutionaries. Rockers revolved around the improved Channel One drum sound, which obtained a better depth of clarity once the studio upgraded to 16 tracks in 1975.

Sly made the most of these enhanced capabilities on a number of new beats. Often, his precision timing marked a 'militant' time on the snare; sometimes he doubled the rhythm to make better use of the bass drum and tom-toms. "Sly would play for a whole day when we were just trying things out," says Joseph Hoo-Kim. "He was very helpful in that way. You wouldn't get another drummer who would want to do that."

The Revolutionaries often made something new out of an old standard by re-cutting a Studio One hit, giving old favourites a thoroughly contemporary make-over driven by Sly's modern rhythms. I Roy's residency at the studio, along with keyboardist and arranger Ossie Hibbert, also assured heavy measures of sonic excellence. "He usually play sound, and we wanted somebody that have a sound knowledge," says Hoo-Kim of I Roy. "We figure that he knows the most popular rhythm that is being played in the dancehall."

Dunbar says The Revolutionaries evolved from various club bands of the early 70s. "Ansel Collins was the one who really taught me to do floorshows; he was playing in the RHT Invincibles and I was playing in The Yardbrooms. Ansel ask me to come on 'Night Doctor', and he called me again to do 'Double Barrel'. I start doing some sessions, and then I was a member of RHT Invincibles, playing at Tit For Tat, and then we play with Supersonics for a little while. Ranchie used to play in Volcanoes, with Al Brown. They were seeking a new drummer, and that was a steady job: every Wednesday I play with the band, because [Supersonics] was every weekend.'

Although most back then knew him as Charlie, he received the nickname Sly while in The Volcanoes. "The owner of the band, Mr Harvey – every time he see me I'm talking about Sly, because I was a great fanatic of Sly & The Family Stone. Mr Harvey look at me and say: 'Everything you say is Sly.' If I do something he would say 'just like Sly', so the name just stuck."

Eventually, The Volcanoes became Skin Flesh & Bones. "We used to play in Discovery Bay at the Calypso Colony hotel; the hotel went under receivership and we came back in town. Ranchie and myself went back to Tit For Tat and spoke to Dickie Wong, the owner of the club, about getting back the band. We were trying to do a name like Earth Wind & Fire, then we call it Skin Flesh & Bones. We played the club for like five weeks, and we record Al Brown's version of Al Green ['Here I Am Baby'], and then a lot of recordings start coming in. We used to play at the club every Wednesday to Saturday. We had a weekly salary, so we never really have to depend on sessions, but we love to play on sessions, so when Ranchie or Ansel or Lloyd Parks get sessions they would call – that's how I end up playing on Tubby's 'Psalms Of Dub' [the version B-side of Carlton & Leroy's 'Not Responsible'], through Ansel for Black & White."

By 1975, the bulk of Skin Flesh & Bones became The Revolutionaries. As usual, the membership fluctuated. Keyboardists Ossie Hibbert and Robbie Lyn were sometimes featured. The horn section usually included Tommy McCook on tenor saxophone, Herman Marquis on alto, and Vin Gordon on trombone. Robbie Shakespeare played bass on some of the later material, but the core members were normally Sly, Ansel Collins, Ranchie, and Lloyd Parks. When Joe Gibbs opened a new studio that year at 24 Retirement Crescent in an industrial area near Cross Roads, with Errol Thompson as engineer, this same core of musicians most often provided the backing, though Maurice 'Blacka Morwell' Wellington and Eric 'Bingy Bunny' Lamont of The Morwells also had prominent positions there, and members of Soul Syndicate and other musicians sometimes held court. Parks eventually became the resident bassist, after Robbie Shakespeare became more prominent in The Revolutionaries.

"When Skin Flesh & Bone start playing Tit For Tat again, Robbie was playing at a club next door," says Sly. "So when we get a break, we would go and check every band and they would go check us."

"First time I see Sly was on Red Hills Road where there was clubs named Tit For Tat, Stables, and Evil People," Robbie confirms. "At Evil People, Fab Five used to be their resident band, but Fab Five had some overseas engagement. The band I was playing with at the time was Big Relation from Spanish Town. Benbow was playing drums and the keyboard player left, which was Tyrone Downey; Touter Harvey, who later play with Inner Circle, was originally a singer with Hippy Boys, and only knew two chords, but we say him better play keyboards. He said he's going to check this band with Sly and Ranchie and [Cynthia] Richards, Sly's band named Skin Flesh &

Bones. I go over there and see Sly, and the way him sit down 'pon the drums, the drum set was way out here and it sound wicked. At that time, we was doing a lot of recording. We just finished Burning Spear's *Marcus Garvey*, and Johnny Clarke and Slim Smith material, and I was one of the main Peter Tosh bass players, because I finish 'Concrete Jungle' and 'Stir It Up' for The Wailers – I play on those tracks. I was one of the main men with The Aggrovators, so me say: 'Bunny Lee, blood clot, see this little drummer here wicked? We have to do a session with him.' So Bunny just call in Sly and we build a lot of tracks."

"I always like Robbie's bass, because when we start meet in sessions down by Randy's, we talk and ask questions," Sly continues. "In those times, every musician used to respect each and every one, so we go and check one another, sit down and work out some music, design a few chords and things. That was then in Jamaica – it doesn't exist no more. After I hooked up with Robbie we started some sessions for Bunny Lee, but a little before that Robbie and me was playing in The Revolutionaries, 'cos the first song he played on, he played piano on 'MPLA' [a Channel One re-make of 'Freedom Blues']. He play a lot of guitars too, cause Ranchie was playing bass when Robbie came in. Because Lloyd Parks didn't turn up for a session Ranchie would play bass, but when Robbie came in and played a few guitars they change over: Ranchie play guitar and Robbie play bass."

"The real Revolutionaries was me, because that was part of Skin Flesh & Bones – we moved to Channel One and they call it The Revolutionaries," Lloyd Parks says on the veranda of his home in New Kingston. "After that, Robbie came in as the bass player, but we started it: me, Sly, and Ansel Collins."

Parks started his career as a vocalist in The Termites during rock steady. "Wentworth Vernon, he had a band in Waterhouse called The Termites; Bobby Kalphat plays keyboards. I never really like the name, but I wanted to record, so I join him. Termites lasted about three years; we made this album called *Do The Rock Steady* for Studio One. Then I join RHT Invincibles – it was a Rastaman who get it together for us, his organisation was called Rainbow Healing Temple. That's where I really get my goal where I can go on an instrument and play as a guitar player. At that point, I played on a million-seller for Ansel Collins called 'Double Barrel'.

"About a year after, I switch to bass. I was playing in a band called The Thoroughbreds at the Stables.[1] The bass player didn't show up one night and I tell Bobby Aitken, the bandleader: "I can play that, you know." That night, first time I play a bass on a stage, a lot of people crowd around me, like you have the Go-Go dancers that used to be there, everybody crowd and say: "Hey, hey, hey! It's a new thing." From that night, I never stop playing bass. Because of the sound I had, I play 'Nebuchadnezzer' [aka 'King Of Babylon'] by Junior Byles, and the man say: 'What's making that sound? It's just something different.' In other words, when a Lloyd Parks song is playing, you can tell it's Lloyd Parks on bass." In those days, Parks used to break up his low bass patterns with cascading spirals of rapidly plucked high notes, pointing to his proficiency on guitar.

Parks became the in-house bassist at Randy's, playing with the core of the future Revolutionaries. "I used to do songs for Randy's Impact label, like a studio band. Whenever anybody recording, they call me, Ansel Collins, Sly, and so on." He also began cutting self-produced vocal work, including the autobiographical 'Slaving'. "As a youth growing up, my parents migrate to England when I was 13, so I end up with my aunt in the country, Port Antonio, and I had a hard time. When I come back to town I just get that inspiration – 'I'm slaving every day for my living' – because I was really trying to make it. Tyrone Downey played on 'Slaving'; he was a little schoolboy in khaki uniform, used to leave school and go to the studio, he was so young. Even today, when I listen to what he played, I can't believe it."

Parks then joined Skin Flesh & Bones. "We were in the same neighbourhood, Waterhouse. They produce a song with Al Brown, who sang over an Al Green song. It was a massive hit and I get a lot of raises for that bass line – even UB40 did a version using the same bass line."

At Channel One, Skin Flesh & Bones became The Revolutionaries. With their new 'rockers' sound, the group backed the biggest hits of the mid 70s, including The Mighty Diamonds' 'I Need A Roof', Leroy Smart's 'Ballistic Affair', and The Meditations' 'Woman Is Like A Shadow'.

The Diamonds' strong vocal harmony was equally suited to politically relevant and romantic material: whether singing of Marcus Garvey or heartache, the soaring harmonies created a lasting impression. Their different tones are exciting when intermingling in unison, and lead singer Donald 'Tabby' Shaw's clear tenor is given pride of place when answered by call-and-response choruses from Fitzroy 'Bunny' Simpson and Lloyd 'Judge' Ferguson. Judge is the group's main lyricist, and his Garveyite upbringing ensures plenty of references to the Jamaican hero; his falsetto has also been put to good use on numbers such as 'Go Seek Your Rights'.

On a brief visit to London, where he always makes sure to visit his dentist, Tabby says that when the group came together its members were doing welding and carpentry jobs, while Bunny ran a small sound called

Soul Pack. "We start out late 1969, come together in a full-force trinity in mid December. When Bunny Diamond was a youth he used to sing with Jah Lloyd's group named Meditators, and he used to check me, 'cos we used to live in the same street. We say we want a next man, search and search, and it takes about two years. We buck up on some different youths, but they weren't ready yet, until December '69 we buck up on Judge and the vibes start. Me know Judge from long time, but me never did see the music between me and him, because we used to go to the same school, but different age group. The first song we recorded as a group was 'Girl You're Too Young' for Rupie Edwards."

After cutting 'Oh No Baby' for Stranger Cole, they issued the self-produced 'Got To Live Some Life' and a cover of The Stylistics' 'Betcha By Golly Wow' before landing at Lee Perry's Black Ark, where they recorded 'Talk About It' and provided harmony on Susan Cadogan's 'Hurt So Good', the latter a chart hit in England in 1975 but not particularly popular in Jamaica. 'Jah Jah Bless The Dreadlocks' and 'Carefree Girl' followed for Bunny Lee, but their true breakthrough came from their association with Jah Lloyd, a singer and deejay who had worked as a record salesman for Edwards and Perry.

A few months before his untimely death in June 1999, the man born Patrick Lloyd Francis was at his regular hangout, one of the rougher street corners in the Kingston suburb of Washington Gardens; his matted beard reached his grimy T-shirt, and a miasma of stale rum surrounded him. Lloyd was proud of the role he had played in bringing the group to prominence.

"I was born in 1947 in Saint Catherine, a place named Point Hill," he said. "My dad used to love farming. At the age of 12, I left school and come to town, because my mum die and I have to grow with a stepmother, which was not very smooth. I meet up on man like Theophilus Beckford, Eric 'Monty' Morris, Toots & The Maytals, and trod on to Success Records where I do 'Look Who A Bust Style' as Meditators, Paul Aston Jennings and myself; we meet in Trench Town. I was a salesman for Rupie Edwards, selling tunes like 'This Wonderful Sound' with Dobby Dobson, 'Burning Fire' with Joe Higgs, and The Gaylads' 'My Jamaican Girl'. Me and the youth rehearse together, people like Ansel [Cridland, later of The Meditations] and Roland Burrell, and along Diamonds come. They was very good, and I take them to Coxsone, but Downbeat say them not ready: 'Two months' time.' Come to Rupie Edwards, they do 'Girl You're Too Young', and I select that song there."

Francis scored his first hit as a deejay at the Black Ark in 1974 with the self-produced 'Soldier Round The Corner', which described the tense feelings in the street brought on by emergency curfews. Its success allowed him to bring The Mighty Diamonds into the studio. "I go back for them and do 'Shame And Pride': Robbie Shakespeare on bass, Horsemouth on drum, Reggie on guitar, and Errol Thompson, the engineer. That is the song that give them the go. After doing that, I take them to Channel One, telling Joe Hoo-Kim that he should record them. I couldn't manage them much more, because I was getting penalised by selling the record: people buying three or six copies, sabotaging, victimising and jeopardising, so this is when I have to carry them to Joe-Joe, who tell them it's time fi do them album."

"My best experience was Channel One, because it's the first cut, the foundation," Tabby emphasises. "Channel One have a time when it used to run things." They started at Channel One in 1975 with two more Stylistics covers, 'Hey Girl' and 'Country Living', the latter of which was a hit in Britain. 'Right Time', a symbolic number relating Garvey's prophetic vision as a signal for black retribution, was even bigger. Other strong singles followed, including 'Back Weh', 'I Need A Roof' (on a re-cut of Larry & Alvin's 'Mean Girl'), and 'Have Mercy' (on a re-cut of The Cables' 'Baby Why'). The Diamonds were among the first reggae acts signed to Virgin Records, who issued the acclaimed *Right Time* in a gatefold sleeve.

The Meditations were another of the classic harmony trios to rise to prominence. In the depths of Flatbush at Sir Tommy's studio, I found leader Ansel Cridland and fellow member Winston Watson adding harmony to a Glen Washington track. The friendly Cridland describes the hardships that led to his chosen career: "Them say I-man were born in '51 in Westmoreland, a little place they call Lambeth Pen. My father leave Jamaica when I was seven years old and my mother was in Kingston, so it was just me and my gran. After my father leave, a stepmother took me to a country town named Darliston, and they was mistreating me. Some lady next door see that and take I back to my people, and then my uncle take me to my mother in the Mountain View area. My father was a horse trainer and he had to live on the premises in Red Hills. I want to be a jockey, but I used to listen to Delroy Wilson, and the man who really inspirate I was the guy that used to fix the tractors. I hear those guys singing one day, that amaze I so much, I say: 'No, I'm going to sing.' One of our brethren, a horse kill him. From there, things never look bright, so I told my friend: 'We're going back to town. I'm gonna sing, you know.' Back in the Kingston 11 area, as a youth, I say I want to be a mechanic; I want to be a barber. But that wasn't the way, for all I wanted to do was sing."

Cridland made his first recordings in the late 60s as part of harmony group The Linkers.[2] By 1972 he was collaborating with Danny Clarke, with whom he would subsequently form The Meditations. "I do 'Sitting On The Sidewalk', that was when I just met Danny; I produced that song, I sing it, and Danny blowing the melodica on it. I give it to Sir J.J. to put out and him send it to Creole [for UK release]. Danny was with The Righteous Flames, doing back-up harmony."

At home in Arizona, Danny Clarke picks up the tale. "I was born in Trench Town in '53; my mom went to England in 1960 and I went to stay with my step-dad in Clarendon. At 11, I went back to Trench Town with my biological dad. I start singing with Winston Jarrett, had the pleasure of singing with Alton Ellis in Alton & The Flames. After they stop singing with Alton, I was one of The Righteous Flames. The first session I did was with Coxsone Downbeat, 'Free Angela Davis' and 'Working Time', but I don't know if it come out. Then I did two songs for Scratch: 'Zion' and 'You Can Run'.[3] Things wasn't going too right, so I leave The Righteous Flames and start out for myself. The first song I recorded was 'Great Messiah' for GG, that was as Danny Clarke & The Meditations. Then I live in Majesty Gardens [a West Kingston ghetto known as Back-To] – I met Ansel down there in '72, and Ansel teach me a few guitar chords. Me and him started to become good friends, so we started trying a thing together. Like when I'm rehearsing, Ansel would come around and help me out harmony-wise, and when he's rehearsing I would go around and help him. We used to hang in a group called The Hombres, one of the first groups in Majesty Gardens."

"Winston Heywood & The Hombres, they asked me to follow them for an audition to play guitar," Cridland recalls. "They was doing 'I'll Never Fall In Love Again', singing it in ska, and I change it to the one-drop. I do the harmony in it also. I do 'Bongo Man' on the same session, but my group never maintaining the harmony."

"We wanted to form our own little group," Clarke explains. "Winston was a good singer, he's got a good voice, but he couldn't control it. Whenever I would go check Lloyd Forrest, I would bring him with me. We were going to use him, but Lloyd couldn't wait; he was going to go with the Jays. So me and Winston start walk together, teach him more and more. We come back up by Ansel, so all of we just sing. We start to rehearse together, not as a group, but if Winston find somebody who wanted to record him, he can rely on me and Ansel to give him harmony, and if Ansel wanted to record, me and Winston would do backing vocals."

Winston Watson's soprano provided a strong contrast to the deeper tones of Cridland and Clarke. He says his inspiration came from soul singers of both sexes. "I was born in Trench Town in '54, mostly grow in Kingston 11. My daddy was a writer and performer and I think I get the inspiration from him; he used to perform magic, turn newspaper into an ice cream. Along that journey I used to go to Opportunity Knocks and win, not even near my mind being in a group. Ansel was a 'face-boy' with bell-foot pants and soul hair; I guess I was about the same. I hear a lot of singers and everything I heard I sing – female singers too, like Diana Ross."

"I see the potential in him," Cridland continues. "Him say him want to be a singer, so when we sing The Impressions' harmony it sound good. At the time, I was about to do 'Woman Is Like A Shadow'. This brethren named Calvin was to come and sing the harmony for us; we waiting on him and he didn't come, so Winston come along and say: 'I will sing that tune.' When I hear Winston come with the harmony, I say: 'Winston remind me of Bunny Wailer's harmony, and this is the harmony we want.'"

The group recorded the song in late 1974, but Joseph Hoo-Kim did not release it for over a year. When he finally did, the song was a major hit. "I went to see if I could get somebody to do it good, so I went to Channel One," Clarke explains. "Ossie Hibbert used to be up there taking auditions, and I know him from way back with The Righteous Flames. I said: 'Ossie, we have some tunes,' and sing a couple of songs. He said: 'Come back Friday,' and when I went back I carry Ansel. As he opened his mouth, Ossie said: 'Don't sing no more. Come back Monday!' After we did that, Joe-Joe said he didn't like the lyrics, so we had to change it about three times and he still didn't put it out."

"I didn't like the lyrics," confirms Hoo-Kim. "I didn't like 'A woman is like a shadow and a man is like an arrow' – it never sound practical to me. We sell a lot of it on dub, but I didn't like the song."

"I was on Marcus Garvey Drive at Federal and met Dobby Dobson," Cridland continues. "I know him from long time in Flames days. He said he's the one taking the auditions over there, so I went there and the first song I sing he likes it, second song he likes it. I saw Winston coming down the road, so I said: 'This guy have some good songs too. I want you to listen to him.' Dobby say we have to come back, so we went to Dobby Dobson and it was 'Babylon Trap Them', 'Longest Liver', and Winston did 'Man Piabba, Woman Piabba', and Dobby loved those songs. After he released those songs, he said he wanted to do an album. 'Longest Liver' was the first song that came out as Meditations. After that, Joe-Joe released 'Woman Is Like A

Shadow', and that was the song that really break the name Meditations." It was also one of the biggest songs to boost the Channel One rockers sound.

○

Although the advent of rockers stole the fire from the flying cymbal, The Revolutionaries' habit of adapting Studio One rhythms naturally caused offence at Brentford Road, particularly after many artists defected to Channel One. Sugar Minott, a man with his ear constantly on the pulse of Jamaica's dancehall scene, became Coxsone's greatest weapon in the war of styles.

"It was a living war with Channel One," he said. "They used to call me 'Coxsone's Boy'. When they made 'I Need A Roof' for Channel One, I immediately know what it was [copying], because I'm an expert in music and rhythm from when I was a kid, so I went to Coxsone and said: 'Look, it's "Mean Girl".' We went to buy a flask of rum, so I was hyped up, did over 'I Need A Roof'. Me and Tabby them was friends, but I didn't care because I was like: 'Channel One? I hate Chinese.' That was my thing in them times: 'I'm not singing for no Chinese.'

"There was a next one called 'Woman Is Like A Shadow'. Coxsone called me and said: 'I want you to sing this music, listen that tune,' so I thought it was an old song that never came out and he wanted me to do it over, but I didn't know it was a Meditations song that never even came out yet. I did over 'Woman Is Like A Shadow' and it came out before the original, because the original used to play on the sound. When my version drop in, the whole of Back-To was looking for me – it was a war with Channel One. Every time they try to do a Coxsone song, I go and tell him, so they came and fling bottle and stone to mash Coxsone's studio up. They had the force – everybody was following the Chinese. Somehow Coxsone and Joe-Joe got in some fight and that was that." (Perhaps unsurprisingly, Hoo-Kim contests Minott's version of events.)

Minott's untimely and unexpected death came in 2010, when he was just 54, following a heart complaint. On a trip to the UK some years earlier, he explained that, as he grew up next door to one of Kingston's most popular dancehalls, music was always a central element of his life. "My house was right beside Champagnie Lawn, at 82 Chisholm Avenue, run by a man called Champagnie. We get to know the music from them days, like Delroy Wilson, Derrick Morgan, and you used to see man like King Stitch. As small kids we couldn't go in this dancehall legally, so we have to make holes in the fence, and we used to imitate the dance, keep our own dance afterward, with cardboard box and condensed milk can. I grow up with my mom, four brothers and three sisters. My father was a man that sells salt beef in the ghetto on the street, but he had a rough time. He couldn't take the pressure, so he went back to the country where his family was and start to do some farming."

Lincoln Minott had a sweet voice, but the nickname Sugar stems from another source. "Chisholm Avenue was a rough ghetto, 'nuff bad things was happening, so my mother was trying to take us to a better life. She save up a little money and rent this house in this middleclass area, Waltham Gardens. That's where I got the name Sugar, from my friends as a little boy in the street. I was a fat kid, porky, so they always say: 'You must have eaten all your mother's sugar, Sugar Belly!' After a while they just say 'Sugar'."

Like many of his peers, Minott got his start in an amateur group. "There was two big girls, Beverley and Trudy, and we try to form a group with some likkle boys, named Telstar. That wasn't working out so good, so these two big girls, they said they wanted to sing with me, but they didn't know harmony, and I didn't know nothing about that myself. We were trying to be in the Festival competition, but it was rubbish! We didn't even pass the first level.

"My mother was struggling. She used to sell at the market, go with all these big loads on her head, so she had it rough with eight kids. Then she had to move from that area, because we couldn't afford the rent and the landlord didn't like us, because we were people from the ghetto trying to live in a posh area. So we end up back in Kingston 11, where we came from, and that was a good thing. At Delamere Avenue there was a big yard where all of us used to meet and burn herb, learning to build a spliff as a little kid, in time to go to school. That's where we meet Tony Tuff, a likkle man on an old car, playing a guitar – he's our godfather. He was singing with people like Bop & The Beltones, trying to carry two harmonies, around 1969–70. I was like 14, going to first form in school, and we meet a youth called Derrick Howard from the country. He say his group was The African Brothers, say he want us to join in it. He took us to Rupie Edwards and Micron Music, but it was Dessie Young, Tony Tuff, and that youth first, because I was just a little kid in beanies. They did one song, 'Behold I Live' – I think that was for Micron Music – and somehow it wasn't happening. Dessie Young wanted to sing by himself, so I was in the group officially.

"We enter the Festival at the Ward Theatre, and in the second run we dropped off. Tony Tuff did write the song, saying we're not going to follow the English no more, so I guess that was too heavy. We started recording for people like One Foot Jimmy. The group did 'Lead Us Father', this came on our own label called Ital through Micron Music. We did a couple songs for Rupie Edwards, like 'Mysterious Nature' and 'Party Night', and I did a song called 'Youths Of Today' – the first song I get to lead – and 'Righteous Kingdom' for Micron Music. We used to hang out at Randy's Records – that's how I get to know Clive Chin, Gussie Clarke, Leonard Chin, they were the king of the road for selling records. For Clive we did 'Hold Tight', and we do 'Torturing' for some man on our street named Duke Thelwell, but he never gave us no money. That was one of the first songs that made an impression for us."

The group passed through much tribulation before splitting, at which point Minott aligned himself with Coxsone. "First of all, Derrick Howard was the leader for the group; we was going to stage shows and people boo, because this guy couldn't lead. Tony Tuff start to lead, so the songs start to get better; then he was giving problems in the harmonies, but all of it was experience. Ronnie Burke and Mike Johnson, they were Micron Music. They had Pete Weston working there, they had Merritone, and Merritone didn't like my music. We were singing Rasta, we sound like The Abyssinians, that's our kind of sound – real cultural roots, and they didn't like it. It was American style music they was promoting – Beres Hammond, Cynthia Schloss, Ruddy Thomas – and they was all singing Stylistics. They always say our music was no good, and then the company somehow wasn't working right, so Mike Johnson just gave us back our tapes, and Merritone went to do Turntable club, Ronnie Burke went to do Sunsplash, Pete Weston went to Canada.

"On Delamere Avenue, in the rough ghetto where we used to meet, there was a big bar in a backyard, play sound system; Coxsone used to pass there and take a drink. One time he came and listened to us and say: 'Yeah, it sound good.' We did a song at Studio One, 'No Cup No Broke', but them say: 'Coxsone's thieving.' I'm saying: 'Don't you hear the music, man? That's where I want to be. I don't care if I get no money, because that's the music I want to sing to.' We decided this group's not working out, 'cos we make an impression but the music not going anywhere."

Heavily involved in sound systems, Minott knew exactly which Studio One rhythms he wanted to sing on, and approached Coxsone with the idea of updating earlier hits. "I used to be a selector, play sound from when I was likkle – that was my first job. First sound I played was my brother-in-law's sound, and in Maxfield Park there was Sounds Of Silence and Keytone, and I used to play those sounds. I end up having a sound called Jah Live, so it was always sound – I was a sound-system man. Many people say they start singing at the church, but I start singing in the dance. I was born in the dance – I was raggamuffin style, so sound system was my beginning. That's how we got to be singing on the Studio One records, because we only had to play the version from a Studio One record and make up our own song. That's how it started, and nobody was doing that before us.

"When I went to Coxsone, I already know what I wanted to sing because I taped off 'Love Me Girl' with Leroy & Rocky, and I taped off 'Going Home' with Bob Andy, and I made my own song to it, because I figured these rhythms are so bad I don't need to make new rhythms. I could make a song to this, and if I go to Coxsone and do it quick he doesn't need to get no musicians. I went to this audition – it was a long line of people, and I was the last. It was Coxsone himself, say: 'Man, what you used to do before?' 'I was just in the country, planting some food.' 'I think you should go back there … You, come back next year.'

"I say: 'Look, sir, I know you've got this rhythm already, I can make a song for it.' When he heard he don't have to go and make no music, he took me 'round there same time. He said: 'Come back tomorrow,' and that was it. I signed a contract to be at Studio One for one year, and I was there for six years without no contract, voicing every day, doing back-up, shaking tambourines and whatever."

Together with Johnny Osbourne and Freddy McGregor, Minott played an influential role in shifting Studio One toward the evolving genre that would be known as dancehall by the end of the decade. In the election year of 1976, however, Studio One had to fight hard to counter the exciting developments coming from Channel One and Joe Gibbs, where musicians and vocalists were best able to translate the feeling of ghetto suffering into music.

9
NATTY DREAD
TAKING OVER
The ultimate rise of roots reggae

"If you listen to reggae music, you don't need to buy the paper. Reggae music tell you everything wha' happen in Jamaica." – ROY COUSINS

"I eat, sing, sleep, drink, live red-green-and-gold music." – JOSEPH HILL

The late 70s were particularly turbulent as Jamaica became ensnared in the opposing ideology and rampant demagoguery of the Cold War. Michael Manley embarked on a series of ambitious projects to better the underprivileged, but which ultimately weakened the Jamaican economy, crippling the poor and alienating middle-class supporters. He was also vociferously attacking neo-colonialism with rhetoric that dismayed the conservative United States government.

In September 1974 Manley announced a dramatic shift in policy, steering the nation further left through 'Democratic Socialism'. Although the concept seems an ill-defined marriage of the free market to Marxist values, much of Manley's new campaign was clearly against capitalism. He nationalised most of the bauxite industry, which was central to the island's economy, and proposed an international alliance by which the industry's electricity would be generated by Mexico and Venezuela. Most importantly, in May that year he changed the way that fees were paid by the multinational corporations that purchased Jamaica's bauxite. By replacing the low fixed rate with a percentage levy, he aimed to ensure that these fees would be in keeping with the actual price of the mineral. The result, unfortunately, was that the multinationals turned to other Third World nations for a cheaper supply, greatly reducing Jamaica's annual income.

Henry Kissinger, Secretary of State in the right-wing government Gerald Ford inherited from Richard Nixon, was displeased by the new

228

bauxite levy; more troubling were Manley's growing links with Cuba and his support for Cuban soldiers in Angola, who were helping the Marxist MPLA government fight off an invading South African army backed by the CIA. Kissinger came to Jamaica in December 1975 to pressurise the leader into silence, threatening to cancel a billion-dollar trade agreement if Manley voiced support for the Cuban intervention; as a prominent member of the Non-Aligned Nations group, Manley refused to be dissuaded, and the trade deal evaporated.

Naturally Kissinger found an ally in Edward Seaga, who assumed leadership of the JLP in November 1974. In February 1975 Seaga began an offensive against Democratic Socialism by requesting a State of Emergency. The number of politically motivated murders had increased in recent months, and Seaga aimed to show that Manley was not in control. Unsurprisingly, the request was denied, and the violence escalated. The following month one of Manley's bodyguards, PNP heavy Winston 'Bury Boy' Blake, was killed; during his ostentatious state funeral, eight people were injured by sniper fire as the coffin passed the JLP stronghold of Tivoli Gardens.

In January 1976 the violence significantly worsened when JLP gangs started a gunfight in Trench Town, which culminated in the firebombing of 20 homes. The following day a PNP picket of an International Monetary Fund convention in New Kingston was infiltrated by JLP saboteurs, who started a riot. Dozens were killed, including four policemen, and shops were looted and burned. Then, in May, further politically motivated violence resulted in dozens of deaths, notably when a JLP gang firebombed a West Kingston slum yard. Apart from the dead, over 500 people were left homeless.

By June there had been 163 known murders, including those of 19 policemen. Manley had no choice but to call a State of Emergency, the first since 1966; this time the levels of violence were so high, with automatic weapons and firebombs used, that the Emergency would be in place for a full ten months. Mindful of the way the progressive Allende government in Chile had been obliterated by a military coup in 1973, with scores of human rights abuses and terrorist activities orchestrated by the CIA, Manley feared a destabilisation campaign was aimed at toppling his leadership. Such ideas were given credence by ex-CIA officer Philip Agee, who visited Jamaica in September 1976 to speak out about the Agency's destructive presence and overall control of the region.

When asked about what role the CIA played in the political power struggles of the era, Seaga gives an ambiguous response. "It's much of a myth to say that the CIA played any great role," he insists. "I think they may have done certain things in the background, but out front we never saw them. If they were here, they surely never introduced themselves to me, and I can't tell you of anybody that we knew who was invited abroad to be trained in anything. Maybe people were here who were agents who I have been introduced to, but not as operatives. I just don't know where they would have participated. Certainly we wouldn't have needed their help anyway, because people were reacting in an extraordinary way. They just didn't want to have anything of Manley's concept of Jamaica being socialistic. [The PNP] were doing a wonderful job stumbling over themselves, telling people they are not wanted in Jamaica – 'There are flights leaving every day for Miami', that sort of thing. [Manley] did everything that was wrong to do, destabilising himself."

Although Seaga is unwilling to identify any concrete CIA intervention, he suggests that Manley's 1975 *brigadista* programme, in which unemployed Jamaicans were sent to Cuba for a year's training in construction techniques, had sinister undertones. "Manley was having Jamaicans trained in Cuba as *brigadistas*, and they were very active in making the country far more militant – dress militant, act militant – so they put the country on almost a wartime footing." Additionally, senior Jamaican police officers were training in Cuba and PNP ministers were meeting with the Castro government. Cubans also came to Jamaica to build the Jose Marti Technical School in Spanish Town, opened shortly before the general election of December 1976.

The election campaign was resolutely violent: in October, gunmen sheltering in a local PNP office fired at Seaga and former Prime Minister Shearer in the settlement of York Town; after a lengthy gunfight, in which ten people were shot, the office was burned to the ground. Then, 12 days before the elections were due to be held, an attempt was made on Bob Marley's life. By then, Marley was an international star: while he was certainly not the most popular singer at home, he was definitely the best-known Jamaican artist worldwide, and one seen as wielding significant financial and political power.

After signing with Island for the *Catch A Fire* album in 1972, The Wailers underwent massive changes. They were marketed as a Jamaican rock band led by Marley, whose 'rebel' image was further cultivated, and their material was subjected to overdubs by Island's rock musicians and remixed for foreign audiences. Peter Tosh and Bunny Wailer left the group after the 1973 set *Burnin'* to pursue solo careers; they were replaced by The I-Three

(Rita Marley, Marcia Griffiths, and Judy Mowatt) for the acclaimed *Natty Dread*, which they cut with Sylvan Morris at Harry J. Then Marley recruited American guitarists Al Anderson and Donald Kinsey to broaden the group's overall sound. Despite such personnel changes, Marley's message was still rooted in the rebelliousness of Rastafari. When it was reported that Emperor Haile Selassie of Ethiopia had met his physical death in August 1975, Marley refuted the notion with 'Jah Live', expressing eternal devotion.

Although The Wailers often toured abroad and based their Tuff Gong organisation in Chris Blackwell's former property at 56 Hope Road, close by the Governor General's residence, they had not lost touch with their Jamaican audience or the ghetto communities they came from. In October 1976 the group proposed a concert for the people, due to take place in December, called Smile Jamaica, which became a government-sponsored event. Soon The Wailers found themselves pawns in a political game: Manley set the election date for a few days after the concert, linking the two events in people's minds and insinuating that the group were tacitly endorsing the PNP.

"That was a crazy time," remembers Family Man. "They was going around with the campaigning for who wanna be in position, and who's going to be opposition, and not everybody was really into that change, but that's how our country is run. We were getting a lot of rumours that things were happening, both sides at the warpath, a lot of gun smoke. Shortly after we get our date, the campaign was set for the same time, so people looking at the thing differently. In the middle of one of the rehearsals, it was ambush in the night!"

The band had received telephone threats not to appear at the event, but Marley insisted. An armed group of PNP supporters, known as the Echo Squad, were despatched to guard 56 Hope Road around the clock. Marcia Griffiths wisely chose not to stick around, using the pretext of a non-existent concert engagement to retreat to her sister's home in New York. "I told [Marley] that I didn't get the vibes to stay back and do it, because I was just so sure that something was going to happen and because sister Judy had a vision plain-plain," she recalls. "I told him: 'Please don't do it – something terrible is going to happen.' I begged him. The same day that I left Jamaica, they had the shooting."

Seven gunmen, allegedly from a downtown ghetto, stormed 56 Hope Road on the night of December 3 1976. Amazingly no one died in the attack, although Marley's manager, Don Taylor, took several bullets and had to be airlifted to Miami for emergency surgery. A bullet grazed Marley's chest and lodged in his arm; another penetrated Rita's head. Despite their wounds, the Marleys and most of their band, supported by members of Third World, went through with the performance, sending a message of defiance to whoever was behind the attack.

Various theories have been put forward as to who organised the shooting. The most widely held belief is that the orders came straight from the top of the JLP; others have suggested PNP involvement, because of Marley's links with JLP enforcers, while some say it was merely due to a racetrack scam gone wrong, or a mishandled drug deal carried out by people who based themselves in Bob's camp. "Nobody has ever found out who the gunmen were. We don't really know," says Seaga. "People at the Bob Marley level would always have a string of hangers-on who are close to them. In that sort of mix any souring of relationship may take place, causing that kind of reaction."

If the JLP was behind the attack they miscalculated badly, as Manley won a second term of office and his PNP acquired a comfortable majority when the election finally took place on 16 December.

The events that culminated in the 1976 general election were widely commented on in song: Pablo Moses recorded 'We Should Be In Angola', The Meditations cut 'Running From Jamaica', Max Romeo sang of 'War In A Babylon'. Even the instrumentals of the day spoke of Cold War politics: alto saxophonist Herman Marquis and trombonist Vin 'Trommie' Gordon created 'IMF'; Ossie Hibbert arranged 'Kissinger' at Channel One, where an instrumental remake of 'Freedom Blues' was titled 'MPLA'; over at Joe Gibbs, house band The Professionals, led by Lloyd Parks and Sly, cut an album called *State Of Emergency*.

A headline declaring the imposition of the 1976 State of Emergency was also used for the front cover of The Gladiators' debut album, *Trench Town Mix Up*, produced by 'Prince' Tony Robinson and released internationally by Virgin. "Them time was when we were going to give up," remembers Albert Griffiths. "[Producer] Enos McLeod get me in to play on a session, but didn't have any money to pay us, so I lay a little rhythm that I didn't even finish plan, and when things split up I go to Ossie at Channel One and say: 'Beg you a little time,' and we voice it as 'Know Yourself Mankind'. When we go down there, Prince Tony say: 'Who really write for The Gladiators? It's a long time me want to find the man.' I said: 'What you mean? Ah me named Albert Griffiths,' but him say him no believe me, because he look to see man who look more fussy. That's how me and Prince Tony get linked up. We signed to Virgin, do *Trench Town Mix Up*, then *Proverbial Reggae*."

Recorded at Joe Gibbs's with Lloyd Parks, Sly, and Sticky, *Trench Town Mix Up* was a stunning debut. Although the title track had originally been cut at Studio One as 'Bongo Red', the Prince Tony version had a palpable tension mirroring that which engulfed the Kingston slums as Natty Dread made an increasingly visible stance against 'Babylon'. Aside from a couple of gratuitous Wailers covers – cut to make the most of vocal similarity between Griffiths and Marley – the rest of the disc, and virtually all of The Gladiators' subsequent work, used proverbs and folk sayings to describe the everyday reality of ghetto life.

"They used to call me the parable man," Griffiths explains. "Me sing songs that teach you to be wise and clever. Me have a thing that says 'Looks Is Deceiving', because you don't judge a book by the cover. It was that kind of thing that me sing: songs that say don't underrate people, mind what you talk, don't talk too much and chat bad things about people. Me no really sing no song yet that doesn't have a meaning."

When asked about the line "Cow never know the use of him tail till the butcher cut it off" in 'Looks Is Deceiving', a slight smile passes Griffiths's lips. "The cow use him tail to swat flies, mosquito, anything that will bite him; when him lose it, mosquito and flies start to bite him and him no have nothing more to fight it. Him have to sit down in a ground and rub them off, so him never realise his tail was so important. I have another one where I say 'A sailor-man never know the value of his piece of knife till it break'. Those things teach you to be wise and think twice. That is mainly what we grew up on, old-time proverbs, things whe' your grandparents teach you."

While The Gladiators' Virgin releases drew critical acclaim in Britain, Griffiths and Clinton Fearon continued to back Yabby You, notably singing harmony on his album, *Deliver Me From My Enemies*, issued in the UK on singer and promoter King Sounds' label, Grove Music. "A whole heap of songs me have with Yabby You," Griffiths confirms. "King Sounds set up Yabby for money to produce and we used to play most of them songs."

The dominant overseas labels, Island and Virgin, were battling to control the best of Jamaica's new music. Island spearheaded the international marketing of reggae through Bob Marley; Third World signed with Island in 1975, and eventually became the second most successful reggae act on the label. The original Inner Circle group, active since the late 60s, included Third World's future core: guitarist Stephen 'Cat' Coore, keyboardist Michael 'Ibo' Cooper, vocalist Milton 'Prilly' Hamilton, and percussionist

Irvin 'Carrot' Jarrett. William 'Bunny Rugs' Clark, who has been Third World's lead singer since 1976, first performed with these musicians in Inner Circle when he returned to Jamaica in late 1969, following a year spent in New York with his parents.

Clark was raised in harsh streets in the heart of downtown Kingston, but met Inner Circle closer to their base in a more genteel area uptown. "I went to this night club, the Tunnel, off Hope Road above Matilda's Corner, and I heard this band and told them that I wanted to do a number with them. Their singer was Bruce Ruffin, and Bruce Ruffin went to England, so I took his place." Clark stayed with Inner Circle until 1971 when he returned for a longer stint in New York, where he worked with expatriate bands Hugh Hendricks & The Buccaneers and The Bluegrass Experience.[1]

Meanwhile, Inner Circle continued to evolve. Cat Coore had joined the group in 1967 at the tender age of 12. In 1973 exam pressures forced him to leave, and in July of that year he formed the first incarnation of Third World with bassist Colin Leslie, who would later be the group's business manager. Jacob Miller began fronting Inner Circle, and his stammering vocals brought a contract with Capitol.

Coore has said his group's original name was Sons Of The Third World, and its underlying concept directly related to Manley's Democratic Socialism – perhaps an unsurprising sentiment from a musician whose father was then party chairman and Minister of Finance in Manley's government. Although Coore was musical director from Third World's inception, members drifted in and out in its early years.

Ibo, Prilly, and Carrot also found their way into Third World from Inner Circle. Drummer Carl Barovier, also ex-Inner Circle, was briefly a member, with former Tomorrow's Children and future Zap Pow drummer Cornel Marshall filling his shoes for a period. Bassist Richard Daley also joined after the disbanding of Tomorrow's Children, a group also associated with the uptown section of Kingston society (yet competent enough to back Toots & The Maytals on their 1972 North American tour). In the early 70s Daley was a member of the Hell's Angels house band at the VIP club, with multi-instrumentalist and future producer Clive 'Lizard' Hunt, plus Wayne Armond and Ervin 'Allah' Lloyd, who would later found the group Chalice. Before that, Daley played in The Astronauts with keyboardist Earl 'Wire' Lindo and drummer Mikey 'Boo' Richards; his recording debut came on Ken Boothe material in the late 60s.

In 1975, a stabilised Third World played some gigs in England. They caught the attention of Chris Blackwell and signed to Island for their self-titled debut, a strong collection of roots reggae songs flavoured with rock, jazz, and soul. The following year Clark joined Third World. The singer began recording as a solo artist in 1974–75, after being brought to the Black Ark by Glen Adams. Clark subsequently returned to New York, hoping to land a contract with Atlantic; instead, he unexpectedly joined his old Inner Circle bandmates in a truly professional Third World that had already supported Bob Marley at the famed Lyceum concert in London.

"I knew this Jamaican who was working for the Vice President of Atlantic Records, and I spoke with her several times," Clark explains. "Then I went to New York and started to write songs, trying to put together a demo tape to present to Atlantic. Third World was on their first United States tour – that was 1976. They were already signed to Island and they were playing in the Village at the Bottom Line. I went to the concert, and I've been with them from that day until now."

With Clark as lead vocalist, the group's sound grew markedly stronger. Willie 'Roots' Stewart, a solid drummer tutored by Winston Grennan, also joined the band at the same time. The resultant second album, *96 Degrees In The Shade*, is considered by many to be Third World's best. The emotive 'Human Market Place' showed their awareness of social injustice; 'Jah Glory' expressed a deeply felt spirituality; '1865' was a slice of Jamaican history that was a major hit abroad. "That is strictly about Paul Bogle, who was hanged in Jamaica for leading a revolution against the English for equal rights and justice for his people," says Clark. "That was a true story, and the year for that was 1865. Paul Bogle is one of Jamaica's national heroes, so the same way Burning Spear sings about Marcus Garvey, we sing about Paul Bogle." The band would remain with Island to the end of the decade, scoring their biggest hit in 1978 with a cover of The O'Jays' 'Now That We Found Love'.

Once Winston Rodney teamed up with Jack Ruby in 1975, a contract with Island brought Burning Spear to the attention of overseas audiences with the release of *Marcus Garvey* the following year. "Jack heard about me, and he happen to check me out," Rodney recalls. "We were talking musically, but Jack was more like a sound system man, he never get involved in recording business before. His argument did sound strong and constructive to me at that time, so he we did two albums, *Marcus Garvey* and *Man In The Hills*." For these recordings, Burning Spear took the form of a trio. "When dealing with Jack Ruby, I need some harmonies, so I draw for Delroy Hines and happens to give back Rupert Willington some work, use both of them to do background vocals."

In this phase Rodney began the veneration of Garvey that has marked the bulk of his work. "Marcus Garvey is from the town where I-man is from. There were elderly people who knew a lot about Marcus Garvey, but not so much of the young people. I go around, listen to various people saying different things about Garvey, and each person know something different. Then I start to run a research, musically, to see if anyone were there singing about Marcus Garvey, but no one was really hitting that point musically, so I decided to get into that. I think the message from Garvey really stands out, not only for me, but for a lot of other people. I think Garvey did have a strong plan, and if more people did pay attention to Garvey and his work it's possible things would be easier for folks like we today. More people has forgotten Marcus and his philosophy and his doctrine, cause people get carried away."

Equally moving were songs that examined the legacies of slavery, such as 'The Invasion', 'Tradition', and 'Slavery Days'. "Those songs was part of my history, part of my heritage, the struggling of my people," Rodney says. "Knowing that I am an African descendant, an African-Jamaican, those songs based upon the struggling of black people overall – not only in Africa. Those songs carrying a different concept, sending a different message."

Similar ideals – but with more overtly religious overtones – were explored on *Blackheart Man*, Bunny Wailer's debut solo set; also issued by Island in 1976, the album was an artistic triumph but less successful in terms of sales. It was also partly through the Marley/Wailers connection that Chris Blackwell made a licensing agreement with Lee Perry, issuing a series of adventurous albums in 1976–77, most of which rapidly achieved cult status. Perry was in the midst of what many feel was his most creative phase, and the new equipment that Island's funding enabled allowed him to expand his sonic horizons, particularly on his superb 1976 creation *Super Ape*, a disc rivalled only by Augustus Pablo's *King Tubbys Meets Rockers Uptown* for sheer dub brilliance.

Richard Branson's Virgin company entered the reggae arena at a particularly opportune time. When Virgin began to sign artists connected to Channel One, Trojan was experiencing severe financial problems which ultimately resulted in voluntary liquidation. Smaller labels such as Klik and Vulcan spun off from Trojan's demise. Klik's first release, the highly successful *Dread Locks Dread*, was a Big Youth set put together by Prince Tony in 1975, but Virgin eventually took control of the disc after Klik failed to maintain momentum. The album's outstanding tracks include 'Marcus Garvey Dread', a powerful recasting of Burning Spear's monumental

'Marcus Garvey' that highlighted prophecies attributed to the Jamaican hero of black self-determination.[2]

The Pama group also ceased producing in 1975, within a year of Harry Palmer's return to Jamaica, where he began farming and preaching to a congregation in Mandeville. "It was a blood-and-sweat business," Palmer says of the music scene. "I think I suffered a lot dealing with the artists." He recalls being physically attacked by singers and producers: "One broke a bottle and said that he's going to cut me up with it. He just want money – his royalty's not enough. Then one of them got me and bucked me with his head. They made up their minds that the records sold millions, and nothing didn't go like that. When they were finished I said: 'I'm going to give you guys this, but I don't want anything more to do with you.' I wrote out a cheque, but the bank said they can't change it, because I had called. I wasn't going to give them that money. They came back and threatened me, said Mr Seaga told him they'll take it up. I said: 'I don't have to be afraid of anybody, because I'm straight.'"

Palmer ultimately reaffirmed his religious commitment. "My wife being a devout church lady, I had to keep dropping her at church and picking her up, so one day they persuaded me to come in. I thought, gosh, I'm driving a Rolls Royce, and I sat where I could see the car. Then something came to me: 'Why are you worshipping a bit of tin? Don't ever look out there again! Change your seat and listen to what the preacher is saying. These material things won't get you anywhere.' I went to Nottingham and got baptised, and that's when I went into agriculture. The reggae thing was conflicting with my religious thing, because by then the records were getting really rude."

Pama had typically aimed their releases at Britain's black population, while Trojan targeted the white working class; instead of reaching for either group, Virgin followed Island's lead by going for university students and rock hipsters. The Channel One connection brought Virgin successful albums by The Diamonds and I Roy, plus dub works featuring The Revolutionaries; with Prince Tony, Virgin scored The Gladiators and U Roy. However, some have suggested that Virgin had a tendency to place too much emphasis on appearances. "I heard that Virgin never sign us because I never carried a Rasta image," says Vernon Buckley of The Maytones, whose finest and most spiritually oriented work was handled outside Jamaica by Burning Sounds, a smaller independent. "Those days we used to sell a lot, but we never really saying 'Rastafari'."

In contrast, Keith Hudson had the right look when signed to Virgin in 1976, but the poor response to the soul mode of *Too Expensive* caused his contract to be terminated early, forcing Hudson to issue the excellent dub set *Brand* on his Joint label in New York; its vocal companion, *Rasta Communication*, was released by UK independent Greensleeves. Virgin fared better with Peter Tosh's 1976 solo landmark *Legalize It* and its strong follow-up, *Equal Rights* (both handled by CBS in the USA and Europe), but Tosh was later lured to Rolling Stones Records by Mick Jagger, whose attempt to bring pop stardom to the reggae firebrand drew predictably inconsistent results.

Although these companies' involvement in reggae has sometimes been viewed with scepticism, certain acts clearly drew artistic benefit from the patronage of major labels. Sly Dunbar says the live tours that Virgin organised brought dub into the performance arena, as heard on a U Roy 12-inch recorded in London in August 1976. "The Lyceum Ballroom with The Diamonds and U Roy, I think this was the breaking point that the drum became such a dominant figure within reggae. They said that dubwise couldn't be played live, they said it was the engineer doing all these tricks, so when we went to drum and bass and work it the people said: 'No, I can't believe they're really playing it!' One time there was a cue that somebody missed and I was playing the drum alone, and I start rolling the tom-toms around and the band came in. It was really a miscue, but we work it out and the place went in a frenzy."

The Channel One sound was a perfect platform for deejays, and Dillinger was the one to hit the biggest on rhythms cut there by Sly and company. 'Ragnumpiza' utilised the bare rhythm of a hard Channel One re-cut of Bob Andy's 'Unchained', with Sly's militant drumming and vibrant horn breaks providing a solid backdrop for Dillinger's jargon-filled lyrics and lengthy rolling 'r's. 'CB 200' was a major hit that shifted Gregory Isaacs's uplifting cut of Bob Andy's 'Sunshine For Me' into a tale of dreadlocked motorcycle bravado. The atmospheric 'Caymanas Park' (aka 'Race Day') was a further success that captured the excitement of an afternoon at the island's racetrack, saluting champion jockeys Emilio Rodriguez and George HoSang.

Ultimately, the Yankee-styled tale of substance abuse, 'Cokane In My Brain', launched Dillinger to international stardom. "I used to be on the North Coast at the Playboy Hotel in Saint Mary where a lot of hippies used to hang out, and we used to jam in the moonlight," Dillinger explains. "I used to watch them get high, and they sing 'I've got cocaine in my brain', so I get the inspiration from there." The rhythm track of 'Cokane' was adapted from B.T. Express's American funk hit 'Do It 'Til You're Satisfied', its bouncing grooves allowing Dillinger to better explore what life was like on the streets of New York City. His half-sung delivery and clever, rhyming lyrics brought the greatest success a deejay had ever achieved when the record was chosen for overseas promotion by Island and promptly became a smash in the UK, USA, and Europe.

The rising popularity of 'Cokane' and the *CB 200* album in 1976 somewhat overshadowed another creative deejay work released by Island, the densely textured and esoteric *Colombia Collie* by Jah Lion, the toaster better known as Jah Lloyd. It was the first Island-issued album produced by Lee Perry, with whom he worked solidly for much of the mid 70s, but financial disagreements led to a rupture by 1977 and the toaster subsequently signed to Virgin. "I move away because there was a dispute between me and him," Lloyd explained. "Perry wanted to take me on a tour after we done *Colombia Collie* – never get much happiness from it. We start another album, do quite a lot of songs, but I left and do *The Humble One* for Morwell as Jah Lloyd The Black Lion, and I do *Black Moses* for myself."

Perry had better success with Max Romeo's *War Ina Babylon* and Junior Murvin's *Police & Thieves*. Murvin is a singer with a wide vocal range, but is best known for a searing falsetto patterned after Curtis Mayfield's. In person he is a distinctly humble, still living in the modestly furnished home of his youth in Port Antonio. "I was born in Swift River and my mother took me up here to my great-grandmother when I was one week old, so I grew up in this same house. From six years old I usually imitate Billy Eckstine, Wilfred Edwards, Nat 'King' Cole, Louis Armstrong, Sam Cooke. I sing in every voice, but I mostly use the treble voice they call falsetto. When I was 13 my great-grandmother died and I went to live with my grandmother in Montego Bay, pursuing a career in mechanics. After I left school, my auntie sent me a guitar from the States. The first band I sang with was The Hippy Boys – that time I usually sing as Junior Soul. About three times I sang with the band. After I left Hippy Boys, I went to sing with Derrick Harriott and Miss Pottinger. The first song I wrote was 'Solomon', a hit for Derrick Harriott."

While living in Trench Town, Murvin cut further material for Harriott and Pottinger before Noel Brown of The Chosen Few brought him into The Falcons.[3] Frustrated by a lack of concrete success, Murvin spent a few years back in Portland. "I was singing in a band named Young Experience in Port Antonio; Bobby Ellis was the arranger. We went to Cuba, play right round Jamaica, play at National Arena for the Prime Minister's wife's birthday, Beverley Manley. When the band went defunct, I wrote 'Police & Thieves'."

The song captured the tense feeling of a Kingston riven by political and social differences and translated perfectly well to London, where the 1976

Notting Hill Carnival erupted into a riot following the attempted arrest of a pickpocket. It stayed at the top of the British reggae charts for nearly six months and was named 'Reggae Single of the Year' by *Melody Maker* and *Black Echoes*. 'Police & Thieves' was also covered by The Clash, offering direct evidence of the way the British punk movement was influenced by reggae's rebellious spirit and musical individuality.

Island issued the acclaimed *Police & Thieves* album in April 1977. Much of the disc – and other recordings like 'Cool Out Son', a 1979 single cut for Joe Gibbs – made use of folk wisdom and parables. "I never know that I was singing in proverbs until [disc jockey] Winston Barnes from RJR started calling me 'Proverbs'," laughs Murvin. "That means I'm spiritually oriented, along with the line of David."

Although British record companies were spreading reggae's liberating message, artistic compromise was sometimes involved. For instance, Virgin executives tried to steer The Mighty Diamonds into crossover territory, cutting the bland *Ice On Fire* in 1977 with Allen Toussaint and American session players in New Orleans, followed by the marginally less commercial *Planet Earth*. As Tabby recalls: "Virgin Records, we sign with them in 1975 with *Right Time*. *Right Time* was a four-track album, and them say them need a 24-track recording, and through we sign with the company we no have no option, so we went to Nassau, Compass Point studio; it finish decorating and fix up, but we were the first to record in that studio, and we did an album named *Planet Earth*. *Planet Earth* come in a different kind of vibes, 'nuff things a gwan with it through Virgin that we never bargain for. We have the blame, but the album was like a test. The company want a crossover thing, so there was a little bit of contrast with this album."

Similarly, after the long gap caused by Leroy Sibbles's emigration to Canada, The Heptones sprang back into action with *Night Food*, released by Island in early 1976. The disc coupled classic singles from 1973–74 with re-cut Studio One material and other new songs, all cut at Harry J. and assembled under the direction of Island staff member and music columnist Danny Holloway. Unfortunately, the album was altered overseas, with cheesy overdubs and gratuitous strings added to certain tracks. While such elements were theoretically included to bolster mass-market appeal, the end result was a throwback to the late 60s, when pop-oriented reggae was given a philharmonic sprinkling in the hope of reaching *Top Of The Pops*.

"We have some good songs on that, but I don't like the production – it too watered-down," says Sibbles. "But I was willing to do whatever necessary to get a breakthrough. I was hoping that these guys know what they were doing and were capable of getting the right sound – I was hoping that they know what it took to break, but I was wrong again." The follow-up, *Party Time*, was artistically more successful, having been created without foreign input at the Black Ark, but its release marked Sibbles's return to Canada and his ultimate departure from the group.

Geoffrey Chung made some of the more challenging productions of the period for Tropical Sound Tracks, often in conjunction with Clive Hunt. Taking a break from a Tuff Gong session with Ivorian reggae star Alpha Blondy, Hunt says the company had high-ranking connections. "It was a communications office where they do advertisements for the government, and they were involved with the government. They hired people like Geoffrey Chung, Bob Andy, and some of the guys from Corporation Of Love – these were talented people who were university graduates on the edge of the music business. Geoffrey Chung tell them they need me, because me and Geoffrey Chung were always a team: in our day we used to be Psyche & Trim, Bonnie & Clyde."

Like many of Jamaica's great horn players, Hunt first learnt music in reform school. "I born in 1952 in Linstead. My father was a cane farmer and herb farmer – he was a Rastaman. I have 18 brothers and sisters, and I'm the oldest one. I was a real bad boy at school: they took me to family court and I end up going to Stony Hill Approved School, a reformatory. Everyone had to do a trade: I was a tailor, and I was at the top at 13. They said they was going to send me home for Christmas, but I felt really bad going back to the community cause you made your parents feel like you were a disgrace, so I didn't feel good enough going home with the surprise of being the first in tailoring. With the music class I wasn't involved, but I stay outside and watched through the windows. One day I went inside to join. The teacher, Joe Moore, one of the man who involved with putting together the national anthem, he say: 'Today is the day they are taking the test,' so I start tell him all the notes, the bass and the treble clef, and the position of the trombone, fingering on the trumpet – I learn all of that from outside. We went and did the test, and I came first – went home with both prizes. When I came back, he decided that I wouldn't do anything else – no more tailoring, just music – and it's been like that from that day."

When Hunt graduated, a lack of employment opportunities brought him into the army, and he began recording as a solider. "My first session, I was a trumpeter – Fabulous Five asked me to do something. The first real session I

did was Lorna Bennett, that album she had with 'Breakfast In Bed', at Harry
J. Studio [*This Is Lorna*]. I remember I thief some time and go over the fence,
as the studio is next door to the military camp, and Geoffrey Chung was the
one who asked me to come to play. I remember I was sitting and reading: I
wasn't really interested – I didn't know that these were the top musicians in
Jamaica. I was helping out the musicians, so they discovered that I knew a lot
about music and asked me to come back the next day."

Hunt's partnership with Chung shaped the most notable Sound Tracks
productions, including Max Romeo's challenging concept album *Revelation
Time* and The Abyssinians' *Forward On To Zion*; Hunt also arranged prime
material elsewhere. "Whenever Geoffrey Chung would sign some project, I
would get to do it. When I was working on Abyssinians, I was doing overdubs
at Joe Gibbs's and it sounded so good that I just started to work a thing with
Joe Gibbs. I said: 'I work on your stuff and then you give me studio time.'"

At the same time, Hunt was cutting solo work credited to Lizard, Azul,
or occasionally The In Crowd. "Me is the first man in the studio making
things by meself with no other musicians. Me did 'Satta I', do everything
almost, and 'Milk And Honey Bees', me did all of that. The original credited
In Crowd band, but it was just me."

Hunt has a keen sense of musical arrangement, as heard on the
Legendary Skatalites album (aka *African Roots*), a 1975 reunion set of
Niyabinghi instrumentals instigated by Lloyd Brevett. "I start a group with
Ras Michael on vocals, but he take the tunes that we write, go behind our
back, and start to sell them, so I just back out and start my own thing. Then
I make an LP out of that named *African Roots* with Brother Jack, Sidney
Wolfe, I Marts. I use them for the Rasta drum and it end up with Skatalites
play on it: Lester Sterling, Tommy McCook, Ernest Ranglin." The album
was cut between Lee Perry's Black Ark and Herman Chin-Loy's recently
opened 24-track Aquarius studio in Half Way Tree.

Some of the most politically relevant music to benefit from the
Chung/Hunt association came from Pablo Moses, a highly inspired singer
with a wide range and very individual approach. "From when I was a kid,
singing was a thing that was in me," he says, after an enthusiastic
performance. "I was born in a little district in Manchester named Culloden
in 1948. My mom was a singer in the church choir and I went to church
choir too. My mom usually have a shop, and when I was five they put me on
the counter to sing for everybody that come in. It just happened that from
when I was a kid I can sing falsetto in a certain way, and I can sing natural
baritone, so I usually practise along with Ray Charles and Sam Cooke. My

mom migrated and I was raised by my aunt, and then my mom brought us out to Vineyard Town. I went to Excelsior High School on Mountain View Avenue, then I went to Jamaica School of Music for two-and-a-half years, did guitar and theory of music."

After an unsatisfactory period in singing groups, he became a solo artist with 'I Man A Grasshopper', an unusual number relating the conflict he experienced when smoking herb. "Most of the guys I formed a group with, they don't want to stick to being original. Maybe they would make a quicker money [copying others], but I was telling them it's not just the money, you have to establish a foundation. All the groups got broken up, so I became a soloist. The name that them give me is Pablito Henry and you know that not an African name, so it couldn't be my name: it's a slave-master name, so that's why I call myself Pablo Moses.

"In 1975 I did my first song, 'I Man A Grasshopper', at the Black Ark studio, with Lee Perry as the engineer and Geoffrey Chung as the producer. In Vineyard Town I met up with Geoffrey Chung's brother Mikey, he was the first one that introduce me to some chords on guitar. We usually hang out together and he was an accomplished musician, so being around him was an honour. Seeing him playing, and listening to the music and observing how they do things, I just adopt those principles. Then I get introduced to Geoffrey Chung, we start to move together and he liked the song. He said: 'This is something new, it's unique.' Mikey Chung played rhythm guitar, Michael Murray from In Crowd played the lead guitar, Clive Hunt played bass, Robbie Lyn and Geoffrey Chung was on the keyboards. We had synthesizer, organ, and piano. Everyone had a jam session – they all enjoy that type of chord change in that song, so immediately in the studio it was a buzz."

The song made an impact on both sides of the Atlantic and led to further recordings. His exquisite debut album has a very particular sound, marked by rock guitar, synth lines, and jazzy horns. "Sound Tracks wanted an album, so I started to write songs. Every set of new chords that I learn I write new lyrics, and that's how *Revolutionary Dream* came about. 'We Should Be In Angola' was done at Aquarius, and we did the rest of the songs, 'Give I Fe I Name' and 'Blood Money', at Joe Gibbs's studio."

Although Moses's material gained kudos overseas, rockers and the sound of Channel One really ruled Jamaica in the mid 70s, reigning largely unchallenged, until a tragic incident caused temporarily disruption. "What really get us down is when my brother Paul got killed, that's '77," says Joseph Hoo-Kim remorsefully. "He usually sell motorcycles and parts from the same premises, and the Channel One sound system, he get involved with it; Kenneth, the next brother, was involved in the motorcycle thing too. We was playing dominoes, three o'clock in the morning, on the beach in Greenwich Town; it was a robbery – they rob him for his gun. I get a bit down when Paul got killed – we weren't doing anything for a long little while. That was the main thing why I came abroad, went to Brooklyn and opened a record store: J&L, at Utica Avenue, with a fellow by the name of Lowell."

Back in Kingston, Joe Gibbs's 16-track studio in Retirement Crescent was the next to lead the field. Gibbs followed Channel One's lead by revamping Studio One and Treasure Isle rock steady rhythms for hits with a pool of singers and deejays, plus a series of sublime dub albums. Different sets of musicians, typically composed of members of The Morwells and Soul Syndicate, built rhythms for Gibbs; regulars such as Sly Dunbar, Ossie Hibbert, Vin Gordon, Herman Marquis, Tommy McCook, and Richard 'Dirty Harry' Hall brought stylistic similarities to Channel One's sound. By late 1976 The Professionals were the in-house band, featuring Lloyd Parks on bass; on keyboards, Franklyn 'Bubbler' Waul diversified the sound with bubbling clavinet and synthesizer licks, augmented by players such as Errol 'Tarzan' Nelson. Gibbs's product was given international issue from 1977 on Lightning, a subsidiary of the Warner-Electra-Atlantic group. Later material surfaced on Laser, another sub-label of WEA. Gibbs's dub albums, expertly mixed by Errol Thompson, were also highly popular in Britain. *African Dub Chapter Three* was particularly successful; the first two chapters in the series were fairly sedate Soul Syndicate dubs, but the third had ringing doorbells, banging gongs, and myriad other '3D' effects.

Culture, a trio that favoured religious material, was the most exciting vocal group to break at Joe Gibbs's. Joseph Hill, the group's leader and composer of most of their material, used his distinct soprano to shape lyrics in the vernacular of the countryside, the songs made fuller by the able harmony of the other two members. During his impressive career, Hill was driven by uncommon energy and displayed refreshing enthusiasm, although his red-gold-and-green false tooth and lazy left eye were visibly peculiar. He died in 2006 at the age of 57, while on tour in Europe – doubly shocking, as the cause of death was cirrhosis of the liver, even though many Rastas shun alcohol.

On a visit to London several years earlier, Hill said everything started at Studio One. "Myself was part of the band Soul Defenders, and in the early days of Freddy McKay I helped arrange a lot of his harmony, like 'Picture On The Wall'. I did a lot of percussion in Coxsone's studio as well, and I did my first song, 'Behold The Land'. That was back in 1972. Three years went by, then I start doing my own thing."

He formed Culture, originally known as The African Disciples, with his cousin, Albert Walker, and Kenneth Paley (aka Lloyd Dayes) in 1976. "It was during the season of Easter – I used to play instruments in other bands on the North Coast, and I came home to catch a little rest. I was at my uncle's house and I saw Albert appear. He proposed we do something in the studio. That same Friday, we saw the politicians came with a band. I ask one of the band-members what's happening in town, so I say: 'I'm going to the studio on Monday morning.' We went there and a lot of adventurous things take place, visible or invisible, wherever we went. It was a joy to be there, because we gain acceptance."

Before the group's successful audition at Joe Gibbs's, Jah Lloyd gave Hill a helping hand. "I buck up on Joseph Hill," Lloyd proudly related. "Him carry me way down in the bush and say: 'Hear this, Jah Lloyd. Me can sing, you know.' Him come ah town for me to record him a couple times, at Chancery Lane corner where Gregory Isaacs's shop is, and I financially embarrassed, couldn't afford to produce them, because the business taking up more cash. Blacka Morwell was up at Joe Gibbs's doing a thing for Gibbo, so I said: 'Go to Morwell, and tell him Jah Lloyd sent you.' When them go there, they wasn't named Culture, they was named something like The Israelites – it was four of them. When we select them, we lay the rhythms like 'See Them A Come' on 'State Of Emergency'."

The song to bring the group widespread attention, particularly among a punk audience in Britain, was the apocalyptic 'Two Sevens Clash', recounting Garvey's many prophecies. "It was a Saturday morning when lightning and thunder, which is a natural disaster, chopped down a cotton tree right before the police station at Ferry," Hill explained. "That was a bad sign, but they take no heed of brutality. Marcus Garvey was imprisoned at Spanish Town by the Jamaican government, and on his way out of the prison, when the sentence was over, he prophesised and said: 'That gate that I walk through, no other one shall use it again.' It has been pasted up, locked, and if they wished to speak the truth about cell number 18 in that prison, for a number of years it could not be locked, because that was the one that Marcus Garvey was in."

Hill was inspired to sing about Garvey because the leader's message remained relevant. "When they see their back is going up against the wall, that was the time we reminded them to remember what Marcus Garvey say. That was the time they start getting awake. If I and Burning Spear and Mighty Diamonds did not start making suggestion of Marcus Garvey, and keep making suggestion of Marcus Garvey, they would be there still sittin' on their same butts, making their same mistakes all over again."

Along with Dennis Brown, Culture was one of the key acts that boosted the popularity of Gibbs's stable, but although a number of other hits followed, such as the triumphant 'Natty Dread Taking Over' and faithful 'Zion Gate', their time with the producer was brief. By 1978 they had begun a relationship with Sonia Pottinger, who took over Treasure Isle on Duke Reid's death, in September 1976, following a long battle with cancer. The resultant material, including songs first recorded at Gibbs's and cut afresh at Treasure Isle, was issued abroad on Front Line, Virgin's reggae subsidiary.

Much of the Front Line roster was selected after former Sex Pistol John 'Johnny Rotten' Lydon flew to Kingston in February 1978 with his disc jockey/filmmaker friend, Don Letts, to seek out artists on the label's behalf. One of the most important acts to sign to the label – independent of this process – were The Twinkle Brothers, a group from the dusty country town of Falmouth, east of Montego Bay.

The group began as a vocal duo in the ska years. "My brother Ralston and myself, from '62, we actually got the name," says lead singer Norman Grant, taking a break from rehearsals at a dingy South London studio. "We make our instrument out of cans and fishing line, and people always gather around and listen, so one night a Rastaman named So-Mi-Say say: 'I'm going to give you guys a name – The Twinkle Brothers.' It was in the evening, so I guess he see the stars. When Jamaica got independence, they came with this pop and mento Festival song contest, so we enter at our parish level and won every year from '62 to '68."

"We are from the ghetto area of Falmouth, and we started very young: Norman was about six, I was about eight," adds the soft-spoken Ralston, harmony specialist of the group. "Inna them early days, we tune into the American music on the radio – Otis Redding, James Brown, Aretha Franklin. We get a little from the R&B, blend it with a spiritual, gospel thing."

"We usually took part in church concerts," says Norman, who has a slight cockney accent after decades in London. "We used to go to the Anglican and other churches. You had the Pocomania church in the week where they play drums."

From 1960, when he was ten, Norman was performing in North Coast hotel bands such as Schubert & The Miracles and The Cardinals; he cut his debut single in the mid 60s. "My aunt was in Kingston, close to the university hospital. She said: 'You guys are talented, come to Kingston and go to the studios,' but it wasn't easy, 'cos it's far. Me and my brother were going to Prince Buster, Treasure Isle, J.J., when we get school holidays. The day we went to Coxsone they were just packing up. They said: 'Youth, if you guys came earlier, we would record you.' Then my brother went away to a camp where they teach you skills, so I went to Kingston on my own and made my first record for Leslie Kong, 'Somebody Please Help me'."

"My mother is a higgler," adds Ralston, "so that day, Norman went to Kingston to buy some stuff for her to sell and went to Beverley's, and Roland Alphonso tell Beverley's: 'This youth have a nice tune.' Then we bring in another guy that live in the same yard with us, Eric Bernard, and go on for a while. Eric went to Montego Bay, and we bring in my brother-in-law, Karl Hyatt, then we do the first group song on the Treasure Isle label with Duke Reid." The song, 'Matthew Mark', made reference to the apostles. "From when I was 16, I was putting on stage shows," Norman adds, "bringing down all the top guys from Kingston: Desmond Dekker & The Aces, John Holt, Ken Boothe." Both he and Ralston gained further live experience on the North Coast. [4]

During this period, The Twinkle Brothers were augmented by the various additions of Karl Hyatt, Eric Bernard, and Derrick Brown. "When one guy wasn't around, we'd use another," Norman notes, "so it was from two to three, then to four." Meanwhile, the group progressed to higher levels of the Festival contest. "In '68 we won a gold medal in the group section, and I won a gold medal as a solo artist. In '69 we won again, and 1970 we took part in the professional side and came third, got a bronze medal, with 'You Can Do It Too'. Being in the Festival, we were getting more exposed, so we met up with Bunny Lee. He recorded the Festival song and 'It's Not Who You Know', 'Miss Labba Labba', 'Sweet Young Thing', 'Miss World', 'Too Late'. Soul Syndicate, the first session they played on as a band, it was Twinkle Brothers they backed. We also do some songs for Phil Pratt, like 'Do Your Own Thing'; 'No Big Thing' was a hit in Jamaica." [5]

By 1973, The Twinkle Brothers were a fully self-contained unit. "Norman said: 'This group is too big, we have to learn to play some instruments,' so he buy some second-hand," Ralston laughs. Ralston handled guitar, Eric Bernard keyboards, Derrick Brown bass, and Karl Hyatt percussion. "Nobody would play the drums," Norman chuckles, "so I end up playing them." Norman continued to be employed by hotel bands and toured Mexico and Guatemala with Sonny Bradshaw in 1975, but was chiefly concerned with Twinkle self-productions. "We were recording with other producers, but about '75, I stop singing for other people. That's where we came with the first album, *Rasta 'Pon Top*."[6]

Rasta 'Pon Top addressed liberation struggles and Rastafarian identity. It was a notable shift of focus. "All over the world, there were changes," says Norman. "You have groups like The Temptations singing some heavy lyrics, so myself as a writer, I decided I'm going to do things like that. Plus, with humanity, I sing what I believe. It's not even a matter of the sales, 'cos the music take us around different people, and you hear of countries that you thought weren't even in the world. When I was growing up, the spiritual part of the Bible tell me about Jerusalem, and I used to believe it was somewhere in the sky, but being in music opened my eyes very early to know that these things was on earth, that it wasn't a dream thing."

"Most of our songs say something about Africa," Ralston adds. "We have the love side too, but we're more into the deeper roots, what's going on around the world. Things that we feel from the ghetto, that's what we put out. We like to go in some chords that nobody else touch – that's how we feel it. We're from the countryside and we feel it more spiritual. We are not the city person, we are more laid back and with God."

With the band now on solid footing, Norman opened a record shop in Falmouth's Water Square and began producing material with local talent. "One of the guys in the band was a cabinetmaker. He build me a shop: 'the little shop with the big stock'. When we started producing ourselves, if we have five songs for The Twinkle Brothers to record on a session, I would carry five other artists, and record one-one song with them."[7]

Rasta 'Pon Top and the accompanying singles surfaced in Britain on Grounation, a roots subsidiary of Vulcan Records. "I was putting out lots of stuff in Jamaica on my label and it was very hard," Norman recalls. "We were doing everything ourselves, driving 'round the island. Every other week you go to a shop and they tell you: 'We have that one. You have a new one?' I couldn't be putting out new songs that often, so I say I have to find a new market. A lawyer friend of mine was going to England and he said: 'You could stay where's I'm staying,' so that's how I came. I went to Vulcan and they was interested in all those material."

When Vulcan folded, executive Chips Richards set up Carib Gems with former Pama employee Joe Farquarson and his colleague Adrian Sherwood, who had previously run the J&A distribution service together. Sherwood would shortly go into production, notably working with Prince Fari on his splendid *Message From The King* set and mixing the *Cry Tough Dub Encounter* series. The Twinkle Brothers' second album, a less-focussed set called *Do Your Own Thing*, was licensed to Carib Gems in 1977, and a couple of singles, including a re-cut of 'It's Not Who You Know', surfaced on the Tops label, based at a record shop in Brixton's Acre Lane.[8]

The disc that gave The Twinkle Brothers the broader recognition they deserved was *Love*, initially issued as a ten-inch mini-LP on Virgin Front Line; half the material was cut with Sly & The Revolutionaries at Channel One. "The ending of '77, I did a session in Jamaica and came up with five songs. I went to Island and they told me to come back in two weeks, but them time I come to England only for four weeks, so you have to do things quick. Chips Richards told me that Virgin is looking for artists, so I went down there with 'Solid As A Rock', 'Free Africa', 'Watch The Hypocrites', and the version to 'Free Africa' with Sir Lee. I had this other track, 'I Love You So', which I recorded at Treasure Isle, but I didn't think it was up to standard because the volume was very low. When I play it to them, they say: 'Yeah, we like that,' so they got the six tracks and they came out with it as a ten-inch."

The strong harmony arrangements and pertinent message of *Love* brought The Twinkle Brothers into the overseas major league; at home in Jamaica, they continued to run their grassroots record shop and label. Similarly, although Dennis Brown's material for Joe Gibbs was given major-label promotion from 1978, the singer remained strongly aligned with his core roots audience on self-produced work. Brown also played a major role in raising the profile of Junior Delgado, an old friend whose deep, rough voice carried spine-tingling portents of anguish. "I know Dennis Brown from I was a kid," the burly singer revealed, some years before his sudden death in 2005, apparently precipitated by a diabetic coma. "I and D. Brown have around two decades tied up in music, because Dennis Brown was like a whiz kid. Everybody used to love him – they even used to love him more than Bob Marley."

Delgado was born Oscar Hibbert in Kingston in 1954. "48 Luke Lane, I grew up there until the city was getting combustible and my people move out to Rockfort. The first time I was singing is at Ward Theatre. Me and my mother went to watch the movies, and I went up on the stage and they throw money at me. My mother was a dressmaker, a merchant tailor also. My dad used to work on tower cranes and heavy-duty equipment like JCBs and E25 Caterpillar. It's really singing that take me away from that area."

He started with the group Time Unlimited. "I and Orville Smith and Junior Marshall was Time Unlimited, but this guy that was bigger than us, Glasford Manning, he used to sing for Coxsone Downbeat and he used to

249

live over in Trench Town. Then they was evacuating some people to Callalloo Bed, near to Washington Boulevard, so we meet up Glasford Manning in that swamp over there with a lot of mosquitoes. We were rehearsing and Trevor Douglas take the group to Scratch to do an audition. Scratch says: 'We have to record him right now.' He wanted to do it right there, same night, because he's a genius."

A few crucial singles surfaced from these early sessions. "He and Joe Gibbs release 'Reaction' on a label called Reflection," Delgado recalled. "'African Sound', Glasford Manning was doing lead, and '23rd Psalms', I was doing the lead." Because Scratch held back additional material, the group cut sides for Rupie Edwards as The Heaven Singers; they then cut some tunes for Tommy Cowan that remain unreleased.[9]

In 1975 Delgado went solo, re-cutting 'Reaction' for Larry Lawrence with The Wailers at Harry J.; this was followed by 'Thinking' and 'Every Natty' for Niney The Observer, which re-established close contact with Dennis Brown. "Niney used to have us in his hand, me and D. Brown. We lived together, move up and down together. Me and Dennis Brown went away and recorded [a version of The Heptones'] 'Party Time'. He did put it out on DEB first and we did sell 40,000 out of a car back, just like that. We start making songs like 'Trickster'. A lot of hits keep coming."

The earliest Delgado hit to surface on Brown's DEB Music label was 'Tition', a critique of politicians set to an infectious rhythm. "It was me and Chinna who do that song in Channel One studio. Chinna was playing bass, Keith Sterling was playing keyboards, and Santa Davis was on drums – only three instruments." A later hit, 'Devil's Throne', was subsequently licensed to Joe Gibbs. "Those tunes was done in Channel One, it was Ossie Hibbert done that song with me. He gave it to Joe Gibbs and they gave him a car, a Ford Cortina L."

Delgado's debut album, the 1978 set *Taste Of The Young Heart*, was highly popular in Jamaica and the UK. Tastefully assembled by Dennis Brown, the album was issued on DEB Music and distributed in the UK by EMI. One of its outstanding tracks is the fearsome 'Storm Is Coming', an apocalyptic number produced by Augustus Pablo. "I and Pablo go back from kid days, like Dennis Brown. We didn't come in this business as big people. I remember when we used to go to a club to sing, they were hiding us from the naked women because we were little."

While DEB Music helped Delgado's rise, Pablo was gaining international prestige through the overseas issue of ethereal productions on the Hawkeye label, some of which had been recorded several years earlier. "Everything in

250

Pablo's camp happens very slowly," says Carlton Hines, founder of the group Tetrack. "Money was always in short supply."

Although only a backing vocalist in the group, Hines wrote and arranged their material. Over an excellent lunch of steamed fish at the restaurant he runs in Queens, Hines recalls the group's rise. "I spent my formative years in east Kingston. In Mountain View there was a sound system called Tetrack, run by Owen Archer. Tetrack is really the title of a provincial ruler in the Roman Empire.[10] That set was one of the baddest sets in the East – many artists would come by and leave dub plates. With Paul Mangaroo and Dave Harvey, we form a group as Tetrack. They were guys in the neighbourhood; we used to meet under a mango tree. A guy called Denzil would sit in on the rehearsals sometimes; he used to go to KC with Pablo. He said: 'I'll introduce you to Pablo,' and we were in awe of Pablo because of 'Java'.

"The group started '72, so we had been rehearsing for almost two years. We went uptown, check out Pablo and discover Pablo always wanted a group, because Pablo love group singing. We went to Black Ants Lane, off Red Hills Road – a have-not community. Pablo's playing some tracks and he picked up 'Let's Get Together' [a 1968 recording by Johnny & The Attractions] – an obscure song, and he gave it to us to rehearse."

This debut recording was executed at the Black Ark with the assistance of Lee 'Scratch' Perry.[11] "When we went into Black Ark studio, it's like three scaredy-cats – they had to turn off the lights in the studio," Hines recalls. "We ended up positioning ourselves in such a way that Scratch could not see anybody's face."

Tetrack came to the attention of the outside world a few years later, when Hawkeye picked up an original number called 'Let's Get Started'; the label later issued a remixed 'Let's Get Together' on a 12-inch EP with Jacob Miller's 'Each One Teach One'. "We did a couple of other nondescript songs, then we did 'Let's Get Started'," Hines recalls.[12] "That song did not include all three Tetracks, because Dave wasn't there. We went to Tubby's to record that, and a number of Rockers people were to record that day, like Ricky Grant, Locksley Castell, Hugh Mundell. Pat Kelly happened to come along and Pablo said: 'Come sing a harmony.' We look in [British music newspaper] *Black Echoes* and saw it at number ten [in the charts]. When I looked back later it was at number one, so Pablo said: 'Let's do an album,' but because of finances the album came much later than it should." The bulk of Pablo's work never made it onto a major label, but it is among the most moving and individually spiritual music ever recorded.

The Phase One catalogue, which also remained outside the majors, was similarly composed of enthralling roots material. Roy Francis, the label's founder, is on the balcony of Mixing Lab, the perpetually buzzing studio he currently runs near Half Way Tree. Despite the hectic atmosphere, with his two cell phones constantly ringing, the moustachioed Francis is relaxed and cheerful. "I was born in Trench Town, 1945. My dad used to sell things on the street like mangoes, all kind of hustling he used to do, and my mom used to sell downtown on the sidewalk. When I was around ten I went to Spanish Town, and I go to America when I was around 17. My dad went on farm work, hook up with some woman, get his green card, and sponsor me up there in Brooklyn. I go to Peterborough School of Aeronautics in New Jersey. I'm a certified airline mechanic, work for Delta and Pan Am."

Francis's job enabled him to make frequent visits to Jamaica, where he went into record production in 1977. "As I used to work with the airline and fly free, I used to be in Jamaica every week. I met Derrick Smith, alias Gurr, who used to work for Jimmy Radway, selling his records. I was fooling around with his cousin, so he say: 'You want to invest in some music?' I decide I'm going to put some money into it, so he bring this group to me named The Chantells, tell me that they're wicked singers. They record a couple songs with Duke Reid before I met them. I don't know nothing about producing, so Gurr was the one. We went to Randy's downtown and he do the rhythms, produced four tracks with the group: 'Children Of Jah', 'Natty Supper', 'Blood River', and 'Stumbling Block', with Horsemouth Wallace, Robbie Shakespeare, Ansel Collins. How I get the name Phase One, I copy it from Channel One. Channel One at those times was having nothing but big hits."

Phase One rapidly became noted for its quality, with the work of The Chantells outstanding. The group styled themselves after the soul acts of Philadelphia and Chicago, with lead singer Samuel Bramwell's soaring falsetto backed by responsive harmonies from Tommy Thomas and Lloyd Forrest, but much of their repertoire dealt with Rastafarian retribution, as is evident from the titles named above, which Francis says initially failed to hit. "They wasn't being successful, so I left Gurr in Jamaica to be doing the business and I went back in the States. The first four recordings sold maybe a thousand, two thousand, and that was like a drop in the bucket; I barely make back my money. Those days you could sell 30–40,000 records in Jamaica as a hit song, because then you didn't have much cassette player, no CDs, so everybody have a little turntable in their house. It's not like now, when a hit song in Jamaica is maybe 2,000."

The Chantells' 'Waiting In The Park' finally established the group and the Phase One label in 1978. "That's when I said I'm going to do this on my own. We went to Joe Gibbs's and did 'Waiting In The Park' and 'Man In Love', and 'Waiting In The Park' was a huge success. The group was really big in England. I fly to London and stay at my sister's house in Walthamstow, and Pama [back in business since 1977 as the Jet Star distribution company] used to send a taxi to my house to buy those records. Then I was spending so much time in Jamaica I get fired from my job, but the job was only paying me $500 a week, and I could make that in a hour, so I didn't mind losing my job – the only thing I miss is my flying benefits. I decide I'm going to be a producer full time, and I start recording all kind of tracks by Keith Boswell and Lopez Walker. I was at Channel One doing sessions and saw [Walker] standing outside; he say he want to do something for me, start to sing 'Jah Jah New Garden', so I take him right in the studio and record the rhythm, voice him a week after and put it out."

'Jah Jah New Garden', cut in the vibrant, danceable style known as 'steppers', was a vision of Rastafarian utopia. Francis also used the rhythm for a fine deejay cut by Jah Berry, another hopeful from his growing stable of unknowns. "I met him at Joe Gibbs's when we do 'Waiting In The Park' – he's a guy who come from somewhere down Maxfield Avenue," Francis recalls. "I had The Terrors, Leroy King who did 'Mash Down Babylon', The Untouchables with 'Sea Of Love' [a cover of The Twillights' Cajun pop song, previously cut in reggae by The Heptones], and I dig out some of the wickedest rhythms I had for *Phase One Dubwise*."

Although Francis allowed a second dub album and some singles to be issued by an associate in the UK, he essentially kept Phase One as an independent, resisting offers from established reggae companies that wanted to license his material. Unfortunately, the untimely demise of The Chantells led Francis to leave the music business for a considerable period. "Some company in England wanted them on a tour, singing some little clubs like Palm Beach; I don't know who give them some weed, but the three of them went to jail. After they got bail, they had to stay in the country until they went on trial. Two of them got away and one of them do time. Because they were my main group and I was feeling so goddamn disgusted over what happened, I decide I'm not going to mess around with this damn recording no more. I went to America, working for this firm that build aeroplane parts. I left my tapes in a friend's basement, and the guy's basement flood out."

JA Man, a West Kingston outfit formed by Dudley 'Manzie' Swaby and Leroy Hollett, was another entirely independent label issuing quality roots. "The record thing started about '73–'74, but I really influenced from youth

253

days," says the dreadlocked Swaby at Capo studio in Flatbush. "The school that we used to go to was right behind Studio One, so I used to go inna the studio before Mr Dodd come run we out. Don Drummond's mother used to live inna the same yard 'pon Love Lane with my grandmother, so more time him used to come round with him horn. '73, me live round ah Craig Town, and Junior Byles used to live up the road, right near to gully bank, so more time we used to go down there and smoke herb, play a little guitar, until we just say: 'Cho, let's go do two tunes.' Blacka Morwell ah the first man that carry me down at Randy's, through him used to know the runnings. The first tune that me do was 'See The Dread There' with Rupert Reid – he used to be there inna the yard with me. The next tune was a version of 'Drum Song' with Bobby Ellis [The Rebels' 'Rhodesia']. We do four tunes, but me just give Morwell two: 'Bit By Bit', and I don't remember the next one. Jah Whoosh used to deejay 'pon one sound over Jones Town, so Jah Whoosh did a tune named 'Free Up Me Ganja' and me get a fight fi that tune because of the lyrics: 'Babylon sell it, the lawyer love it, the doctor recommend it,' all long before Peter Tosh do him tune ['Legalize It']. 'Take A Set' was the biggest seller that come out of that session."

In late 1975 JA Man moved from Manzie's Love Lane home to 129 Orange Street, site of the House Of Music record shop. By then, the outfit had already recorded 'Remember Me' with Junior Byles, the first of a handful of prime singles cut before the singer succumbed to mental illness. "Then me no do no more tune ah Randy's again," Manzie recalls. "Me gone ah Channel One and do over 'Movie Star' with Hortense Ellis as 'Super Star', and do 'Remember Me' and 'Chant Down Babylon' with Junior Byles. When Junior start get kinky is really the tune named 'Pitchy Patchy', that's a little after him do 'Fade Away'."

One of the label's finest singles is Dave Robinson's 'My Homeland', given an optimistic backing by The Revolutionaries. "Dave Robinson and D. Brown used to live in a big yard together, so all the while me say: 'D. Brown, let me do two tunes.' It's really him who say: 'Do two tunes with Dave.'"

After cutting further works with various singers and deejays, JA Man issued an untitled dub album in 1977. Swaby subsequently set up the Manzie label on Slipe Road in 1978, leaving the House Of Music to became the Roots & Roots Shoe House.

Beres Hammond's debut album, *Soul Reggae*, was one of the most commercially successful local releases of 1977–78. Recorded while

Hammond was singing with Zap Pow, *Soul Reggae* was the first hit album to surface from Aquarius studio, but was somehow never issued overseas; ironically, the esoteric Zap Pow had the benefit of a contract with Island. Hammond is at present one of the most in-demand of reggae singers, and his sensitive musical arrangements have earned him widespread respect as a producer. At his Sileckshan recording studio, chewing on some freshly cut sugarcane, he relates the details of his long and varied career.

"I was born in Annotto Bay, where my father was a councillor for the area, a politician for the JLP. Those days politics was much better in Jamaica; they never used to have these guns. My mother, I never knew her as anything but a person around the house, taking care of all of us, because she had ten children. From when I was about nine, I used to come to Kingston on the weekends. I had sisters here, scattered all over, so I used to just go between all of them. Then I took the opportunity to go downtown and see the different record stores and studios. The voice that I really used to like was Alton Ellis and Ken Boothe – I thought they were exceptional. The Heptones, Melodians, I used to love their harmonies. On the radio stations here we were flooded with foreign music – The Beatles, Engelbert Humperdinck, and Gilbert O'Sullivan – and I used to try to imitate them. Marvin Gaye, he stood out in my mind. Stevie Wonder, I thought he was brilliant. My American inspiration was shared too between Sam Cooke and Otis Redding. I used them to test out how well I could sing."

Hammond moved to Kingston full-time "in my last year in primary school. I was doing the same juggling between the sisters, because then the dollars was very few". His singing career began in the capital city: "I did one recording when I was about 11 or 12 with Clancy Eccles ['Wanderer'], because Clancy was a friend of the family, but it was never released until a few years ago. One day when I was passing on Eastwood Park Road, an audition was taking place: Merritone was running an amateur talent series, and my brethren forced me to write my name down. I did four ballads and he asked me if I know any reggae, and at the time Delroy Wilson had 'Rain From The Skies'. I did that one and he said: 'Yeah, everything all right.' Wednesday night, the crowd was with me – this was VIP, a club in Half Way Tree. The response was overwhelming."

About two years later, in 1975, Beres Hammond was drawn into Zap Pow. "I was performing as a solo person, still doing amateur shows, and then there was Cynthia Schloss. We teamed up as a duet, went right up to Jamaica House quite often. I was also a member of a group called Tuesday's Children.[13] One night, when the group got a gig in one of the hotels, Zap

Pow was the backing band. After the show Dwight Pinkney checked me and said: 'Youth, you can sing. Come join we.'"

Hammond's rich timbre and expressive delivery brought Zap Pow new scope, freeing its members to concentrate on their instruments and injecting an essence of soul into the group's intriguing combination of roots reggae and jazz. His talents helped the band score an album contract with Island in 1978, but he left the group the following year. "I wanted to get a feel of what outside of Jamaica was, so Zap Pow provided that. We went up to USA and Canada, so I was with them from '75 until '79. Chris Blackwell signed us, but I thought if we got signed we'd be on billboards. I thought we would have been in Australia and New Zealand, Malaysia, but that didn't work out, so that's when I thought I should be doing something else, and I started working with [guitarist and arranger] Willie Lindo. Zap Pow was some political-motivated kind of music. Zap Pow would just tell it like it is, different issues from my love thing. I had some songs that was burning up inside me, which was more a line between people – a family type of thing.

"When my album came out, it took less than a month for it to blow out all over the place. I released a single, 'One Step Ahead' – it went like a bolt to number one, stayed there for three and a half months, stayed on the chart itself for maybe two years. We figured we would work with Aquarius because Herman Chin-Loy was always down our necks, plus he had a big studio there, not doing anything, because there was no hit songs coming from there. It was kind of a big graveyard, so working by Aquarius we would be undisturbed."

"When I was in the studio, I didn't even want a person to come in and peek or walk through the door," confirms Chin-Loy. "It breaks your concentration." The studio was often used for radio advertising. "A lot of commercials was done there by Boris Gardiner and Peter Ashbourne. Fabulous Five had a thing with my brother going on there." Chin-Loy agrees that the studio lacked a roots sound, but says this was not his intention. "I always wanted a roots sound, it's just that the studio was not capable. It had a better quality in terms of the top end, like for voicing, but for the bass and drum, which I really needed – because bass and drum is reggae to me – it didn't have it, no doubt about that. That's the reason I went down to Channel One and did some bass and drum, and came back to my studio and finished it."

Aquarius may not have achieved the ghetto bass-and-drum sound, but as the only 24-track studio on the island it was the perfect setting for the complex, big-band brass arrangements of Cedric Brooks's *United Africa*.

Brooks's multi-layered score brought instrumental reggae to another level in 1978. Likewise, Rico's *Man From Wareika*, recorded at Joe Gibbs's, Randy's, and Island's Hammersmith studio under Karl Pitterson's direction, was such a well-constructed set of reggae jazz that the esteemed Blue Note label licensed it from Island in 1977.

"I would say that was the first album I was able to perform to the best of my ability," says Rico. "[Pitterson] got the best musicians to do this album. In Jamaica, we had Robbie and Sly and Ansel Collins. The first things that came to me were the things that I family used to play in Wareika Hills, with Count Ossie and Don Drummond. I'd say that was my first album with a lot of jazz in it, and creative elements. If you notice, I don't solo a lot, I put more melodies into the thing than solos.' One of the album's outstanding tracks, 'Africa', was cut with session players in London. Its rhythm was also used by Ijahman Levi for a song on his acclaimed Island debut, *Haile I Hymn*.

Blue Note was then a subsidiary of United Artists, who made further tenuous dips into the reggae market with material acquired from secondary sources. First, the company took over the catalogue of Tropical Sound Tracks after that label went bust. The result was the haphazard *Anthology Of Reggae* series, issued in 1978; these ranged from the concept albums co-produced by Clive Hunt and Geoffrey Chung to older Studio One compilations. The Magnum label, which issued reggae in the UK from 1977, was connected to Pye (though initially aligned with Philips); in 1978 it was relaunched as Ballistic, another UA subsidiary. Mo Claridge, who had broken away from Creole Records to form the Mojo distribution company, licensed the Magnum and Ballistic material. To start with, Claridge issued singles by artists such as The Meditations on an independent label called Bam Bam; concurrent with Ballistic, he also issued roots material on Warrior.

Claridge promoted The Royals' compilation album *Pick Up The Pieces*, which led to their breakthrough in Britain. However, according to Roy Cousins, Claridge acquired this material from Militant Barry (aka Barry Dunn), a deejay who worked with Keith Hudson and ran the Kiss record label in London, but Barry had himself received the material from a secondary source. "When I was living at Grassquit Glade [in Cockburn Pen, West Kingston], David Mohammed's grandfather was the owner of the yard" Cousins explains. "He came up to England and become my link. I send the tape to him, and him took the tape to Militant Barry, and Barry take the album to Mojo." After Cousins presented himself in England, Claridge cut out the middlemen and further material was licensed directly. "When I come it was Pye who had *Pick Up The Pieces*; I went back to Jamaica and send up *Ten Years After*. I was closely associated with [South London sound system operator] Lloyd Coxsone [aka Lloyd Blackwood], so Coxsone get a whole lot of dubs from *Ten Years After*, play it all round London. John Telford was Mojo's publisher, so through Telford, he set up a deal with United Artists. They send a first-class ticket and I bring up *Israel Be Wise*. United Artists take *Freedom Fighters Dub*, *Liberation Dub*; them take over *Ten Years After* and *Pick Up The Pieces*."

Similarly, 'Conscious Man', a radio-friendly song of romantic conduct recorded at the Black Ark by harmony trio The Jolly Brothers, first surfaced in 1977 on Seven Leaves, a label founded by Jamaican expatriate Tony Owens; Mo Claridge quickly licensed the song from Owens and issued it on Magnum. When re-released on Ballistic in 1978 it turned out to be the label's biggest success, skirting the lower regions of the UK pop charts and hitting further in Europe when issued on an extended 'disco mix' EP by United Artists the following year. Unfortunately, the anticipated Jolly Brothers album did not live up to expectations. After Cousins introduced Claridge to the group, the uneven *Consciousness* was recorded with Prince Jammy; further Black Ark material cut for Owens, which retained a similar feel to the hit single, remained unreleased for many years following protracted disputes.

At the Black Ark, Lee Perry was inches away from toppling into an abyss: although the popularity of *Police & Thieves* was matched by that accorded the psychedelic soul of George Faith's *To Be A Lover*, by the end of 1978 Scratch and Island were in conflict over Blackwell's refusal to issue *Heart Of The Congos*, the stunning debut by the harmony group The Congos. Island also failed to issue an experimental set by two Congolese singers and a pop-reggae album by Candy McKenzie, plus early work by deejay Mikey Dread and singer Earl Sixteen. After succumbing to various financial and personal pressures, Perry concentrated on an individual spiritual quest, and by early 1979 had shut the doors of his studio.

The Congos' lead vocalist, Cedric Myton, was also involved in Prince Lincoln Thompson's Royal Rasses, another group that scored a contract with Ballistic through Cousins. Thompson and Myton first sang together in The Tartans with Devon Russell and Lindburgh 'Preps' Lewis. The group scored big with the rock steady hit 'Dance All Night' for Federal, moved on to work for Caltone and Treasure Isle, and cut some self-produced numbers at Studio One before pursuing solo careers. By 1975 Thompson had formed the Royal Rasses with Keith Peterkin and Clinton Hall, ghetto toughs known as 'Cap' and 'Johnny Kool'; Jennifer Lara also occasionally contributed. The group's piercing harmony, led by Thompson's anguished voice, caused interest in British reggae circles when singles such as the uplifting 'Love The Way It Should Be' and the haunting 'Kingston 11' were issued in small quantity by London sound system operator Neville King.

As is alluded to on 'Kingston 11', Cousins recalls that such sweet harmony was fostered in conditions of extreme hardship, where toughness becomes essential to survival. "Prince Lincoln was a member of the Pigeon gang, like Devon Russell. Cedric was a saint out of the four of them. Prince pass his scholarship and went to Excelsior School, which is a top school in Jamaica, but because him always have him knife, he was expelled. Him mother kick him out of the house, so Prince Lincoln was living down Hunts Bay Road in a likkle board shack, planting greens for a living, never wear shirt nor shoes. When I take Mojo down there, him never have on a shirt. Prince did have the *Humanity* album them time, produced by Errol Thompson, Marcia Griffiths's baby father, a deejay at JBC."

Given major promotion overseas, *Humanity* was a sweeping success. As with The Royals' material, Brixton-based sound system Coxsone Outernational stoked up interest among the black population, while quality album packaging and a major 1979 European tour won progressive student fans. Unfortunately, subsequent albums aimed at the crossover market failed to reach either audience, signalling the demise of Ballistic in the early 80s.

In an effort to match the superstardom of Bob Marley, the major overseas promotion of singers and vocal groups such as Prince Lincoln, The Gladiators, The Mighty Diamonds, Culture, and Dennis Brown brought the reggae message to increasingly wider audiences. Concurrently, though typically less polished, the hottest deejays of the period were also playing a crucial role in the international acceptance of Jamaican music.

10
OH LORD

Deejays and the international pinnacle of roots

"Trench Town, that's where Jah pick me up and put me, so when I sign with Virgin I build a community centre and that Golden Age home, to give back to the people and show my appreciation ... a lot of things could have happened to me, but God take care of my reward." – TAPPA ZUKIE

"I become like an overnight hero ... because reggae was not regarded as no substantial or enlightening art form." – MIKEY DREAD

In the late 70s the deejay retained a crucial role in reggae's international dissemination. As the roots style made an indelible impact overseas, deejays had a particular bearing on the shape of popular music in Jamaica, and were accorded an elevated status in Britain, where major labels helped the form to achieve unprecedented popularity.

Virgin ultimately had the greatest success with deejays, but by the time they tried to sign Doctor Alimantado, the toaster had largely reinvented himself as a singer after disaster took the form of a speeding bus that nearly killed him in December 1976. "It was a very traumatic time in my life," he recalls with a shudder, "when many people start to realise that what I was saying all these years is something that mean a lot to the world, so everybody seems to be zooming in on me, trying to take a bit. I was supposed to do a rehearsal for my first show at the Carib Theatre, and my friend invite me to the sea that morning, and I went in the water and nearly drowned. I took in a lot of water – someone had to stand on my stomach and pump it out. Then I leave the sea, and I was going to the road and the bus hit me down, and I believe it wasn't an accident: because my dreads was flying, that's why the guy just swing around and hit me; the bus run me over and some people have to be shouting, go in front of the bus and stop it. In the hospital, a few things happen to me, like food poisoning. My recuperation stage was very, very traumatic."

Fortunately, these traumas would bear wonderful fruit in Tado's biggest hit, the life-affirming 'Born For A Purpose' (which he sang), and its attendant toast, 'Life All Over'. "When I came out of the hospital, I was lying on my bed at home and an idea came to me. I started to sing it and I needed to get a paper and pen to write it down, but I wasn't able to move. I pull myself off the bed, which was very painful, and get on my knees – you don't know the beauty of your foot until you're in that stage. It took me nearly half an hour to get a pen and paper, and I didn't know how to write music, but I tried to write it so that I know how to fall into a rhythm pattern so I could get the remembrance of it. When I was able to walk on crutches, I went to the studio and said to the musicians: 'I've got this song to do and I haven't got any money.' They say: 'Cho, no worry,' and Joseph Hoo-Kim said: 'You working in the studio all the while. Just come.' Really and truly, I didn't pay any money to get that song recorded. The musicians and the studio was free.[1]

"When the song was recorded, Mighty Diamonds and everybody was going crazy over it. I went to Channel One and said: 'I can't put it out now. Would you put it out for me?' I told them the song named 'Reason For Living' but Joe-Joe said: 'No, this tune should name "Born For A Purpose",' so that's how it was originally on his label. I put it on my label later, when I was able to move around." The record's fame spread far and wide, finding a champion abroad in Johnny Rotten, who voiced approval of the song's defiant stance on London's Capital Radio.

After he recovered from his injuries, Alimantado performed to a capacity audience at the National Arena – a definite high point of his career. He immigrated to London in the latter half of 1977 with the intention of setting up a UK branch of his label. Discussions with Island proved mutually unsatisfactory, however, and although Virgin licensed the sung 12-inch 'Find The One', they were unable to establish a long-term agreement.

"I came to England to set up a company, and [retailers] Dub Vendor and Daddy Kool was supposed to be the managers, but negotiations break down. We had to go our separate ways, with me owing them some plane fare and a bit of money. At the time, companies like Virgin were willing to put half a million pounds on Doctor Alimantado, but Greensleeves offered to help me set up my own company, which was more important to me. Greensleeves' offer wasn't financially viable, but it offered me the best in a stable company." Alimantado's *Best Dressed Chicken In Town* became the company's inaugural album release in 1978.

After U Roy and I Roy, Tappa Zukie was one of Virgin's most prominent deejays, although his relationship with the company was turbulent and much of his best material was issued elsewhere. At Mixing Lab, I found Tappa swaying on his feet, the sweat on his brow caused by rum, rather than the afternoon heat. In West Kingston, where he was born David Sinclair in 1955, he endured a rough upbringing. "I grew up between Greenwich Town and Trench Town, the hardcore town. Most people know me as the 'cork and tar': a cork and tar is a ball that you beat till it becomes likkle. It is so tough that when it hit you, it's like a bomb. The leather ball, if you're beating it, it bust wide open, but a cork and tar, it never bust, and the smaller it get is the hotter it make. My parents, pressure reach them, and they didn't have time to think about we, so I have to go 'pon the road from I was 12. When I run away from home, the people of Trench Town take to me; they say: 'When your mother and your father forsake you, the lord God Jah will pick you up.'"

In these youthful days, Tappa deejayed on the I-Oses and Maccabees sets, prefiguring the fame of youngsters like Little John and Beenie Man. "I was the dancehall crave, the first little-boy deejay, and I used to hear people saying I greater than U Roy, Big Youth and Dennis Alcapone." Along with this early fame came wildness. "I used to play sound and everybody rate me, and they say that I was a hyped youth. People say crazy things and I'll do crazy things, so Bunny Lee, my brother and my mother decide to send me to England to escape these crazy things I do. I was 17 years old."

The move brought Tappa even greater exposure. "I had never recorded, never appeared on a show, and Bunny Lee introduced me on this show U Roy had at Woodlands Hall in Ladbroke Grove. They played the rhythm for Slim Smith's 'The Time Has Come' and I toast over it. At the time, everybody had me as a warrior. People was scared of me – for what, I don't know! I'm just a guy who stand up for my rights and don't let nobody push me around, so I figured the man is a warrior, so that's when I made that album *Man Ah Warrior.*" The album, produced by Clement Bushay and issued circa 1974 by Klik records, caused quite a stir overseas. American new-wave singer Patti Smith professed her admiration of it, and later brought the disc greater acclaim by facilitating a significant reissue on her Mer label.

Although Tappa's voice had yet to break when the album was cut, he sounds surprisingly confident. On the title track, he translates the hardships of street existence into calmly charged defiance. Other tracks seem rather juvenile, particularly 'Archie The Red Nosed Reindeer', a barb apparently aimed at one of the neighbourhood toughs. "Archie was one of my friends," Tappa explains. "He used to live in White Street. Those guys was the big guys on the corner, but I was a shooter – I was a hit-man, so I was just troubling him, because Archie was a bad guy."

262

When Tappa returned to Jamaica toward the end of 1974 he was chiefly employed as muscle. "I was actually a bodyguard for Bunny Lee and I enforce artists to record for him. Bunny Lee is like a father to me. Me and my brother Blackbeard [aka Rodguel Sinclair] used to go to the studio with him." Lee was at first reluctant to record the young man, so Tappa cut the strong 'Judge I Oh Lord' for an associate, Lloydie Slim. He then began voicing the odd tune for Lee, who subsequently gave the toaster cuts of a number of hit rhythms. These backing tracks and others obtained from Channel One gave Tappa the platform for further material, with driving rockers-style beats allowing for more zestful and energetic performances.

Tappa then founded the Stars label, moving into the producer's chair with ease. In addition to producing his own vocal and dub material, he recorded exceptional work with Greenwich Farm vocalists such as Junior Ross & The Spears (notably 'Judgement Time') and Prince Allah ('Bosrah' and 'Heaven Is My Roof'). In the summer of 1976 Zukie returned to the UK to license more material to Klik, hitting with the singles 'MPLA' and 'Pick Up The Rockers'. Tappa's dynamic stage shows, where his vocal skills were matched by limber kung-fu moves, complemented the esteem that the *Man Ah Warrior* album brought; Klik thus quickly issued the popular *MPLA* album. "A lot of things could have happened to me, but God take care of my reward," he insists. "The people nominate me to be a star, though I came to England to promote Junior Ross and Prince Allah."

Virgin enjoyed great success with *MPLA* after picking it up from Klik. As Tappa's star continued to rise, a Virgin contract for the *Peace In The Ghetto* album enabled him to offer tangible assistance to the underprivileged Trench Town community that had given him support when he most needed it. "Trench Town, that's where Jah pick me up and put me, so when I sign with Virgin I build a community centre and that Golden Age home, to give back to the people and show my appreciation."

The subsequent *Tappa Roots* album included the suggestive 'She Want A Phensic', one of the biggest reggae hits in England in 1978, but Tappa withdrew his allegiance from Virgin for political reasons. "Virgin write me up as a Mafioso because I demands back my contract from them. No disrespect intended, but I heard they was selling a lot of records in South Africa, but those monies wasn't coming back to England. Some people tell me they was investing in guns to use against my people in South Africa, so I confront Mr Branson, say: 'I'm a black man and I don't support such things.' He said: 'Tappa Zukie, I'm surprised at you. What are you talking about?' I said: 'That's the argument on the street, so I don't want to be a part of this,' and that's how me and Virgin mash up. At the time U Roy was going for them in Africa, and Culture and I was going for Virgin in England; I had 'Phensic', so I was happening for them. From there, no big company would deal with me, so that's how I decide to come back to Jamaica and establish my own thing."

Released around the same time, 'Living In The Ghetto' was a firsthand account of life on the street that could only have come from someone who had spent most of their days in such surroundings. "That's after me decide to make the community centre, so it's exposing the lifestyle. I was living deep in the ghetto then."

More hits followed, including the boastful 'Oh Lord', which swept the island more than any previous Zukie hit. Then, his duet with Horace Andy on a re-cut of Soul Syndicate's 'Natty Dread She Want' drew a strong response on both sides of the Atlantic when issued independently by Tappa; Jet Star's distribution of the extended 12-inch was particularly successful in the UK.

The half-sung 'Raggy Joey Boy' was another poignant description of ghetto life, but Tappa avoided the trend set by older deejays and never made the full shift from toaster to singer. "That's when everybody say that Tappa Zukie was a terrorist," he suggests, "but I was just tired of seeing people taking advantage of poor people. *Raggy Joey Boy* is the only album with a little singing on it, because the way I take it with music is from one extreme to the other: I don't see myself just like a dancehall artist, I just see myself as a musician, so I'll make jazz, funk, reggae, anything – just the frame of mind and vibes to really hit me at that moment."

Of all the deejays signed to Virgin's Front Line, Prince Fari is perhaps the most legendary. The self-styled 'Voice Of Thunder' hailed from Spanish Town and was originally known as King Cry Cry until producer Enos McLeod renamed him. His recording debut came at Studio One, where he was previously employed as security; his smooth yet charged delivery on 'Natty Farmyard' gave a hint of things to come. Fari's debut album, *Psalms For I*, was a stunning religious concept disc cut for Lloydie Slim around 1975; the following year *Under Heavy Manners* made good use of hit rhythms from Joe Gibbs, while the *Message From The King* and *Long Life* albums subsequently issued on Virgin's Front Line brought him to a wider overseas audience.

U Brown also had two albums issued on Front Line: the excellent *Mr Brown Something* and *Can't Keep A Good Man Down*. Hughford Brown became U Brown on the sound-system circuit because he patterned his style after U Roy, whom he regularly heard when growing up. As the tall, bald toaster explains: "I live at 35 Bond Street, and Duke Reid was next door, and in life, each one teach one."

At Leggo studio, about eight blocks from his former home, Brown details his career genesis. "I started with Silver Bullet from Tower Hill, mess around with that sound for over a year, and then a friend was keeping a dance with Sounds Of Music, based in Waterhouse, so I mess around with them for another 15 months. I get my real big break when U Roy met with a motorbike accident, fracture his leg; I Roy wasn't around much to fill in, 'cos he was travelling very often. There was a dance keeping in Sunrise Crescent, and Dillinger was the one that they requested to deejay, but a guy that work with Tubby's sound recommend me to Tubby, and on the night Tubby say he really want me round the sound. Each night I go, it's always more inspiration; Tubby's was the number-one sound in the world that time, play everywhere in Jamaica, from Negril Point to Portland."

U Brown's fame on King Tubby's sound led to his debut recording in 1975, produced by Joe Gibbs's cousin, Winston Edwards, then a law student, based in London. "I first went into the studio with Winston Edwards and the first two songs were 'Jamaican Tobacco' and 'Wet Up Your Pants Foot' – I record those at Tubby's. My next was for Yabby You, 'Dem A Wolf'; Yabby You sing a song on [the rhythm] named 'Anti Christ'. At that time, Tubby's was *the* studio. Although it wasn't a studio where you lay rhythm tracks, most man always come to Tubby's to get a mix, because Tubby's have the spice. Yabby come there, Niney come there, and Bunny Lee come like him ah the resident man there."

After his time on Tubby's sound, U Brown had a number of other significant residencies, most notably on King Attorney, the sound system owned by PNP 'enforcer' Tony Welch, later known as Socialist Roots.[2] When that sound encountered problems, U Brown found himself on the mic at Jack Ruby's Hi-Power in Ocho Rios. "Jack Ruby take me from Kingston when politics was getting hot, because one time Socialist Roots did have to stop play – too much pressure from the people and the police, and in those days police don't respect entertainers." Ruby then had a supremely powerful sound system that gained island-wide appeal.[3]

Around 1977, through Bunny Lee, U Brown started releasing self-produced material on the Hit Sound label. "Bunny Lee is like another Coxsone," he emphasises. "When you 'round Bunny Lee, you must learn something 'bout the business. Bunny Lee give me the first rhythm: a version of a Barry Brown song ['Youths Of Today']. That's where I started my first production, 'Badness A Madness' – I gave it to Federal to distribute." Brown's biggest hit was 'Weather Balloon', a flight of fancy inspired by his wife June and narrated with gusto at a Channel One session supervised by engineer Crucial Bunny. Another high point came with his toast on the extended mix of Linval Thompson's 'Train To Zion', cut in 1977 for Socialist Roots.

At this point, Thompson himself was reaching full stride as a singer and producer, following a series of false starts. "I was born in Kingston in 1954 and grew up in the Three Mile area," he explains. "My mother and father had their own business, like grocery stores; I was singing at school when Jacob Miller started recording for Coxsone, and I was trying to record, just like Johnny Clarke. We was living in the same area, Kingston 13."

In the early 70s Thompson's parents relocated to Brooklyn, where they took domestic work. Linval joined them and subsequently settled in Queens, where he remained for roughly two years; in order to further his singing career, he often mingled with expatriate musicians. "Buccaneers was one of the first reggae bands in New York. Bunny Ruggs was there, before he turned Third World, and Rick Frater. Me never perform with them, but I was trying to, and Horace Andy used to come around also."

Although progress was slow with live performance, Thompson made his debut recording within a year of arriving stateside. "I went to a studio in Brooklyn named Art Craft with Patrick Alley, a singer that sound like John Holt; I spend the money and do 'There's No Other Woman In This World'. I come back to Jamaica maybe '74, and the first thing I do is for 'Stamma', K. Hobson – I know him from Orange Street. He hear the first song that I recorded and he liked that sound, near like how Dennis Brown sound, so we do an original song named 'Westbound Plane'. I voice it on a rhythm track at Randy's studio. Then I do two songs for Phil Pratt [the superb 'Jah Jah Redder Than Red' and 'Girl You've Got To Run', both recorded at the Black Ark]. He hear the sound and everybody say that this new artist comes around, has that Dennis Brown sound. I do two for Scratch too, 'Kung Fu Man,' and the other one I can't remember." Another number called 'Kung Fu', again celebrating martial arts, was cut the same year in Jamaica for Kass Harris, "a guy that have a record shop".

These early efforts formed steppingstones to success, which Linval achieved by 1975, upon teaming up with Bunny Lee. "They create a little buzz that make Bunny Lee get interested in me and that's where the hits come – hit after hit." His first recording for Lee was the highly popular 'Don't Cut Off Your Dreadlocks', which led to an album of the same name. Afterward, Thompson gradually took charge of his own creations, a process he describes as intuitive. "I never plan it, it just happened. A guy will come and say he want me to do some songs; I say: 'All right, I'll sing some for you and some for myself, so I can get a cut of the rhythm tracks.' That's the way I start, exchanging. The first song what I do, 'I Love Marijuana', I use Family Man at Randy's; Socialist Roots hear the sound. I was the youngest artist in Jamaica on my own, so they ask if I could sing a song for them, play this instrumental track in the dance and I listen to it, never write no song, never have no idea, but I say: 'Yes, I will voice it.'[4] Then we go to Channel One and the lyrics come to me. 'Train To Zion' was the biggest hit after 'Don't Cut Off Your Dreadlocks'. It mash up the whole of Jamaica."

Not long afterward, Thompson began licensing albums to the revitalised Trojan label (now controlled by Marcel Rodd of Saga, specialists in low-budget classical LPs), and Clocktower Records in New York. "I do my first album, *I Love Marijuana*, I do a dub album [*Negrea Love Dub*], and I do a Big Joe deejay album, *African Princess*. I know him from Three Mile; he was on some likkle sound at that time."

In addition to crafting further hits such as 'Six Babylon', a tale of police brutality, Thompson was also working with upcoming neighbourhood singers such as Al Campbell and Wayne Jarrett, and deejays such as Trinity and Ranking Trevor, each of whom was helping to shift the focus of the local scene toward what would eventually be identified as the dancehall style. The deejays arguably made the most important stylistic changes, and several of the most notably innovative were based around Waltham Park Road, a broadly snaking thoroughfare that winds through significant ghetto hamlets of western Kingston. The road is a key route that cuts through communities on either side of the political divide, and although most artists seek to rise above such internecine conflicts, it is worth remembering that the political dimension is never far from the realities of sound system culture, especially as each sound has its base in a particular patch of the ghetto, with its own distinct history of allegiance.

Prior to his emigration to Britain in 1973, Dennis Alcapone's El Paso set was based at Brotherton Avenue, near the bottom end of Waltham Park Road, situated in Whitfield Town, a sprawling ghetto loosely affiliated with the PNP (known colloquially as Two Mile because its southern border lies two miles along Spanish Town Road from the centre of downtown Kingston). One of the most popular sets of its day, El Paso helped launch the career of Dillinger, who became the star deejay of Smith The Weapon in Payne Avenue, a dilapidated road forming the heart of the neighbouring ghetto, a PNP district officially named Tavares Gardens (known locally as

Payneland). Dillinger subsequently brought his friend Trinity onto Smith The Weapon and helped him launch a recording career at the nearby Channel One studio, where Dillinger already had a foothold; in the latter half of the 70s, they were two of the island's most noteworthy deejays, their stylistic flourishes and 'reality' lyrics, inspired by the harshness of ghetto life, helping steer Jamaican music closer to dancehall. And although Dillinger had greater success internationally through hits like 'Cokane In My Brain,' 'Cornbread,' 'Funky Punk', and 'Woody Woodpecker', Trinity had greater impact in Jamaica.

"It's strictly dancehall me come from," he says, seated under a large mango tree in the yard of the modest home he occupies uptown. "Me and Dillinger usually up and down as two youths together, strictly ghetto youths who usually hang around sound systems whenever we hear it." Born Wade Brammer in 1954, Trinity is a lean, affable man seemingly at odds with the prominent scar that marks the length of one cheek. Growing up in the rough confines of Two Mile, music was an early focus that kept him from going astray. "It easy fi get inna badness and take up gun, and a lot of guys that I know died in those days, so me just deal with music. U Roy played King Tubby's sound, Big Youth play Tippertone, and they usually pass through in my area. As a little boy I look at them the whole night, then me have to sneak home and sleep underneath the cellar. Big Youth was my deejay because Big Youth was a more of a messenger; U Roy was a toaster that free-talk, so I usually like Big Youth more, and if you listen to my songs, I sound more like Big Youth."

Trinity's first record, 'Believe In It,' was produced by upcoming producer Enos McLeod at Dynamic Sounds studio circa 1974, and credited on release to Prince Charming. "Enos McLeod know my stepmom, he was licking chalice in the lane that I lived on and him hear me. Him give me the name Prince Charming and I didn't like it." When the tune sank without trace, the toaster reverted to the moniker Prince Glen, a pet name applied by his stepmother in reference to a local drummer who had fascinated him in his youth. Other inconsequential numbers were then voiced for producers Lloydie Slim, Joe Gibbs, and Winston Edwards, including a couple cut in combination with Dillinger, who ultimately facilitated Brammer's breakthrough as Trinity at Channel One.

"Me and Dillinger was good friends because the two of we smoke chalice together, so when Dillinger was playing Smith The Weapon, one night him call me up to the mic and the crowd start to go wild. A little after, Dillinger took me to Channel One where Joe-Joe Hoo-Kim say him don't like the name Prince Glen, so him look inna the Bible and choose Trinity. Them times there, every song I made was a hit."

The rockers style was perfectly suited to deejay tales of ghetto life, so Trinity scored local hits with the mournful 'Jailhouse' (voiced on harmony duo Earth & Stone's minor hit of the same name), and the determined 'All Gone' (voiced on The Mighty Diamonds' popular 'Have Mercy'). Such material fared well, according to Trinity, because the toasters were so active on sound systems that crafting spontaneous lyrics was second nature. "It was head-top, because we usually practice at the dancehall before going to the studio, so we know exactly what we want to do. Sometimes I go to the studio and take one cut. All deejays in them days usually imitate me and Dillinger, because me and Dillinger was the cream of the crop. In those days, Soul Hombre was a little community sound in Payne Avenue, so when we left the studio, we usually come up Payne Avenue, lick pipe, and sing in the evening time to get our practice: me, Dillinger, U Brown, Leroy Smart, Barrington Levy, and Clint Eastwood – that's my brother." Each member of this crew played a significant part in dancehall's evolution, with singer Barrington Levy being particularly important.

Trinity cut inspired material with religious roots producer Yabby You, and then launched the Flag Man label as a vehicle for his own productions; 'DJ Jamboree' was probably the first record to salute the contribution of deejays to Jamaican music. In 1977, he achieved a spectacular international breakthrough with 'Three Piece Suit' for the hit-making production team of Joe Gibbs and Errol Thompson (voiced on a re-cut of Alton Ellis's 'I'm Still In Love' recorded by one-hit wonder Marcia Aitken). Although the song reputedly sold 10,000 copies within a week of release, it was ultimately eclipsed by the alternate cut, 'Uptown Top Ranking,' a novelty record by uptown schoolgirls Althea & Donna. Trinity later made the typically shortlived shift to a singing career, but remained an important part of Jamaica's deejay culture to the mid 80s.

Ranking Joe was another important deejay to pass through El Paso and Smith The Weapon. He rose to greater prominence by changing the focus of the nearby Ray Symbolic set, one of the leading roots sound systems of the late 70s. "That sound used to play disco music and reggae," he explains. "Certain venues would request soul music. Then, after a while, it become strictly rub-a-dub, through I became the permanent deejay."

Born Joe Jackson in 1959, the portly dread says he was captivated by sound systems at an early age. "I was raised in western Kingston and my father love the sound-system thing: he play the music on sound system and

269

actually take part in selecting on the sound, and I get inspiration from seeing him doing those things."

With a preponderance of sound-system activity in his neighbourhood, it was natural for Joe to pick up the mic in his teens. "The first sound system was Soul Shot, up the lane that I lived on, near Waltham Park Road; you would catch a little talk on the mic and people would gather round. Apart from that, the first sound system I used to really deejay round is El Paso, and then Smith The Weapon. When I came on El Paso, Dennis Alcapone was already in England, so anybody could deejay; it was a freestyle thing, but I became a main deejay after a likkle while."

He soon took the stage name Little Joe, partly in contrast to Big Joe, a better-established rival. "Big Joe used to deejay a sound named Small Axe, from Payne Avenue, so through he's Big Joe, I say I'll just come as Likkle Joe, 'cos I used to influence by *Bonanza* [television series]; most deejays used to have them name from a movie, cause you have to make a deejay name sound extravagant."

After graduating to Smith The Weapon, Little Joe made his recording debut at Studio One in 1974. "Studio One is a famous studio, like Motown, so when you want to make you name, you try to go for the best. I leave school and go there, beg my way to do a song, and the first song I do is 'Gun Court'; I did three or four more songs at Studio One, but I never hear some of them come out. From there, I emerge to different producers like Watty Burnett from The Congos, Lloydie Slim, and Bunny Lee."

In addition to launching his recording career before his voice had fully broken, the Studio One connection also brought Joe onto Ray Symbolic, a set he names as "a champion sound that go 'round the world". As he explains: "I run into Ray, through he's getting dub plates from Studio One; one night he was playing at Cross Roads, I do a bit of toasting, and the crowd went wild. That sound based 'pon the Waltham Park Road area at Chisholm Avenue, then it end up on Hagley Park Road at a club named Bionic, which he built. Him have an automobile store, sell car parts, but that sound used to play disco music and reggae music, and me alone used to deejay 'pon it. Jah Screw was the main selector, so that's where Ranking Joe and Jah Screw come about as a team."

Joe was respected for his longevity, being able to deejay all night without a break, riding the heavy beats deftly selected by Jah Screw. By the time he was crowned Ranking Joe in 1977, his engaging style, well-suited to heavy roots rhythms, brought him and Screw onto the mighty King Sturgav, the highly influential sound system established by U Roy in the adjoining district of Cockburn Pen, an expansive, down-at-heel conglomeration of twisting streets located just north of the traffic-clogged Three Mile roundabout and noted as a JLP stronghold. It was here that Joe developed the trademark 'bong-diddly-bong' phrasing, a stylistic flourish later adapted by many other toasters in the dancehall style.

U Roy says he started the sound system as 'King Stereograph', but through the convoluted street vernacular of Kingston, it ended up with the name 'King Sturgav'. Within a year of Ranking Joe and Jah Screw joining the set, Sturgav's warm-up man was Charlie Chaplin, a brawny young deejay who often brought humour into his toasts – another important element of the emerging dancehall style. "From school days I always give a lot of jokes and drama," the dreadlocked Chaplin confirms in a rasping baritone, holding court at Kingston's Sheraton hotel, where he obviously has many friends. "You don't want to keep people sad at all times or keep reminding them of how dangerous life is. Sometimes you have to give them a break and make them laugh."

Chaplin was born Richard Bennett and raised in the Red Ponds district of Spanish Town, a tough portion of Jamaica's second-largest city, located 12 miles west of Kingston. He picked up the nickname Charlie Chaplin at school, because of his walk. In 1973, at the age of 14, he moved to Olympic Way in the politically volatile ghetto of Tower Hill – another JLP flashpoint located just a few streets up from Sturgav's base camp. "Sturgav was a sound for the people," he says. "Gemini and Echo Tone was like a society sound, but Sturgav was for everyone: U Roy's concept as a Rastaman was, if poor people want to buy a stove, they go check Sturgav, keep a dance and make them money, so it was for all kinds of entity. From school days we used to listen to Sturgav and I always say I would like to deejay like Ranking Joe, because he used to deejay from eight o'clock in the night until six in the morning; he doesn't move, just goes straight through, so that inspired me, 'cos every other deejay go for two, three hours, and that's it. When Ranking Joe finish deejaying and the dancehall empty, then I would deejay for one hour; the box man and the workers talk to Mr Roy, so I start go ah Sturgav and warm up the mic for Ranking Joe, but they suspend me from school, so I forgot school and just deal with sound."

As with Trinity, Chaplin says that music kept him from taking the wrong path. "Tower Hill is a garrison community, one of the roughest sets of garrisons in Kingston, and for you to survive, you have to move like them, but because of my status as a young, upcoming deejay, I have people who look out for me, so I didn't have to walk certain roads. I was the warm-up deejay for Sturgav for about one-and-a-half years; they call me in at 12 o'clock and I get to do four songs, and if Ranking Joe didn't come to work, I would run the dance. Those days I just freestyle: you speak your mind and you rhyme a little and try fi keep the crowd happy – no written lyrics, just something spontaneous that you build on the spot: you see a girl pass and she have a beer, you build something off of that and people would appreciate it."

Although many producers wanted to record him during the late 70s, Chaplin preferred to concentrate on sound-system appearances, and did not reach the studio until significantly later. "All I want to do is be on the sound system. You're young and you just want this big crowd following you everywhere, and you don't really have time for no studio, as we play every night except Tuesdays; no monetary reward were in it, because that was not our motive at that time – we just do it because we love it." He would later impact strongly as a recording artist through hits for Roy Cousins and other astute producers.

Meanwhile, on the other side of Spanish Town Road, heavier and more deeply religious roots music was being constructed by a core of committed artists in Greenwich Farm, a few streets south of the Three Mile home ground of proto-dancehall stars Johnny Clarke, Linval Thompson, and Al Campbell. Bertram Brown's Freedom Sounds label, based at Brown's home at 14 East Avenue, next to the family's wholesale liquor store, was a focal point for local singers concerned with truth, rights, and justice.

"I was born right here in 1950 – right here so, me navel string cut," Brown explained in the Freedom Sounds yard, some years before he disappeared at sea in 2008 after getting into difficulty during a night-time swim. "Me father was a cooper, they make barrels to store rum in, and my mother was a housewife, because it's ten pickney and me ah the last one. Me grow up round here through '51 storm, all them bad elections, the wars and peace, and me still here with the youth."

Bertram was a short man with a ruddy complexion who seemed always to be on the go. Freedom Sounds was reactivated during the 90s as a base of operations for veteran Rasta singers based nearby, and Brown spent most of the day on the telephone. He had a dour countenance and seldom smiled, despite giving a friendly welcome to the roots fans that made pilgrimages to his workplace. The bustling headquarters was a dilapidated concrete shell, badly needing a lick of paint and new furniture, with records stacked haphazardly against the crumbling walls, yet it retained a homely character, obviously operating on a grassroots level.

Brown said the area's dominant dancehall had long been a great inspiration. "Right beside my yard was the biggest dancehall inna western Kingston, the New Style Lawn. Coxsone usually play there, Duke Reid, Sir George The Atomic. I grow up attending these dances, listening to all this good music, getting the inspiration and vibes." Bunny Lee, who lived two doors away, also acted as a role model for record production. "Slim Smith usually pass through, Ken Boothe, and Cornell Campbell."

Working chiefly with Soul Syndicate and cutting dubs at King Tubby's studio, Brown oversaw some of the heaviest roots music of the late 70s, his artists' indignant lyrics matched by fearsome rhythm tracks and dubs that emphasised the songs' foreboding and menacing qualities. The Freedom Sounds label was officially inaugurated in 1975, although Brown said he began producing at the start of that decade, conscious that local talent creating message music was being ignored. "Me get the inspiration from Prince Allah and Milton Henry. When me come from school, me see them play them box guitar, and Prince Allah always chant biblical songs 'bout 'Lot's Wife' and 'Great Stone', and me no see nobody record him. The first job me father get for me was in the same barrel place, and we save up our money and go by Randy's, there so me lay me first rhythms: 'Thank You Lord' and 'Judgement Time' with Prince Allah, and 'Cornbread And Butter' with Milton Henry. Then we include Philip Fraser, Earl Zero, Rod Taylor, Frankie Jones, Sylvan White; we cook and eat and live together. I say the youth have talent, and them have the message to really show the people truth and rights, because where there's no truth, there can't be a kingdom and a proper government, so it's that we seek within the music to make the people understand. Freedom Sounds is here, from those days, to give the people good music which portrays love and harmony at all times, and discipline within mankind as a whole, show how mankind fi live with one another. I deal with who the people reject, who the people nah listen to. I always have a notion that the stone that the builder refuse always come back to be the headstone."

The man called Prince Allah, born Keith Blake, is also known as the Gentle Giant, and the latter epithet seems entirely appropriate: his hefty frame is often crowned by a radiant smile, he is courteous and helpful, and seems governed by a peaceful religiosity. It was in church, in fact, that the quality of Blake's voice was first noted. "My mother and father used to love go to church, so when I was about seven them carry me to Hope Methodist

273

Chapel, and I sang 'Our Father', and everybody said: 'Yes!' After I leave school, I had a friend by the name of Soft [aka Roy Palmer] and one by the name of Milton Henry. They love music and Milton could play the guitar, so we used to sing together. We met Joe Gibbs when he just come from Guantanamo Bay. Him carry we to studio and we did two songs for him, 'Hope Someday' and 'Fay,' as The Leaders."

After recording a handful of other sides for Gibbs, at the start of the 70s Blake renounced all things worldly to join the followers of Prince Emmanuel Edwards at the 'Bobo Dread' camp in Bull Bay, Saint Thomas. The Bobo branch of Rastafari has come to be associated with fundamentalism, particularly after a dramatic expansion in the 90s, following Emmanuel's death; some of the faithful have suggested that Edwards was another manifestation of Selassie, and drumming and chanting have always been central to their worship. "I was up at the Bobo Camp about six years, just chanting, so when I leave, I start dealing with record. Up at Emmanuel we used to read about Melchizedek, this High Priest that have no mother or father, no beginning nor no days at the ending of time. So when I leave there and come home on Seaview Avenue, Tappa Zukie, used to run likkle weed as a likkle youth, but him with Bunny Lee now, and Bunny Lee decide fi help him get a little studio time. We went to the Black Ark: Lee Scratch Perry does the arrangements, and the harmony, it's Soft and Tony Brevett of The Melodians."

The result was the arresting 'Bosrah', a 1976 single credited to Ras Allah & The Spears. "When I small, I used to love Mohammed Ali, the boxer, so everybody just call me Allah," the singer explains. "After Tappa Zukie went to England with that tune, we do an LP at Channel One [*Heaven Is My Roof*] with 'Funeral' and 'Daniel In The Lion's Den'."

The outstanding 'Funeral' was a symbolic rejection of society. "When I was up at the Bobo, we used to read the Bible every day. Him say: 'Let the dead bury them dead,' so it's just that likkle vibes. When I look inna myself, I say it's not just a physical funeral, because even the system round you is like a funeral. So I say I nah gonna follow them system, that mean I'm not going go to them funeral. I wasn't really dealing with a physical dead, like my father and mother, because if them dead, me going go to them funeral. I looking at the system: it's like a funeral, just lead to destruction the same way."

He also cut strong material for Freedom Sounds, such as 'Lot's Wife' and 'Bucket Bottom', the latter using a proverb to illustrate Allah's disappointments within the music industry. "It was just a thing I was going through with some of the promoters," he explains. "I say: 'Every day them bucket go ah well, one day the bottom must drop out.' You use me, one day it's going to stop." Another outstanding track was the 1977 single 'Great Stone', again inspired by Bible readings at the Bobo camp. Bertram Brown noted that King Tubby greatly shaped this record by adding a custom sound effect to illustrate Allah's message of a "great great stone just ah come to mash down Rome": "King Tubby mixed that, and I think that is one of the wickedest mix we have ever made with that rumbling – you *hear* the stone coming in that song. We get the rumbling from some thunder sound we get out of a movie [soundtrack] – get it and stretch it, put it 'pon a two-track tape. We usually work with King Tubby because King Tubby inspire we a lot. The greater portion of work was done by King Tubby: Scientist did things, but him was just an assistant, because Jammy used to mix in between. Even before Jammy become a producer, we work with them man as the engineer. All of them is Tubby's understudy, so King Tubby really do a lot for music business."

After his return to Jamaica and installation as Tubby's assistant engineer, Jammy rapidly established a reputation as a skilled mixer. He had already inched into production before returning to Kingston. "I produce one record I released in Canada with Nana McLean, a do-over song, [Sandy Posey's] 'Single Girl'; when I came back to Jamaica in 1976, I redid it in a better fashion with the same artist." Jammy was subsequently instrumental in shaping what would be known as the Waterhouse style, working largely with neighbourhood singers who favoured a particular vocal slurring. "All of those artists that I used to work with grew with us in the Waterhouse area: Black Uhuru, Locksley Castell, The Travellers. I was the young producer coming up in the area. Everybody think about supporting me, and I used to cater for them. We were just experimenting in those days, but some of those songs became legendary."

Black Uhuru, a vocal trio with an ever-shifting line-up, was the Waterhouse act to become most famous. The group was initially formed as Uhuru, the Swahili word for unity, with Garth Dennis as lead singer and Don Carlos and Derrick 'Duckie' Simpson providing harmony. At home in Los Angeles, Dennis says Uhuru came together when he carried the vibes of Trench Town singing groups to Waterhouse, after the building of the Olympic Gardens housing scheme brought a massive influx of people from Kingston 12. "I grew up in different parts of Kingston as my dad travelled all around doing carpentry. My sister Joan is the famous Joey from the duo Andy & Joey. She did that early recording 'You're Wondering Now', and it was a monster hit.[5] When we relocated to Trench Town, that happens to be the same yard that Joe Higgs was living in, and I'm a twin brother-in-law to Joe Higgs: one of his brothers and one of my sisters had a son, and one of my brothers and one of his sisters had a son. Myself, Junior Braithwaite and a guy named Ricardo Scott, we had the first little trio around there.

"After we left Trench Town and moved to Waterhouse, I still used to come back to Trench Town to do rehearsal with Bob and The Wailers, and with The Wailing Souls. Waterhouse, that's where I met Duckie and Don Carlos – since they know I was from Trench Town and they know my sister is a singer, they used to come by my house to attend rehearsal with me. Our home at 14 Balcombe Drive was like a community centre, because my parents used to travel to London from a very early time. We was left alone for a while, so we could invite friends in without being hassled. I decided we needed a trio, 'cos I love groups because of Joe Higgs, and we always listen to The Impressions and The Temptations. Me and my sister left Trench Town and bring the musical vibration to Waterhouse, to the youth. Before that, you have Yabby You and them people from up top, but the youth, the vibrancy, Duckie and the whole of them, it's right through we them come."

Uhuru's recording debut resulted from their incidental discovery. "In Waterhouse there was an elder by the name of Brother Junie. He has a place on Henley Road that we used to go and recreate weselves, just jam there during the days. Sometimes he would cook lunch and sell it, and these guys from Dynamic Sounds came to have lunch one day: George Philpotts, an engineer, and Paul Fuller, another producer. We sang a couple of songs for them and they liked 'Folk Song'. I get the idea from Curtis Mayfield, but I put some melody to it and add some words. They arranged a session for us at Dynamics, and Karl Pitterson was there. I already know Karl from a younger days, because I had a girlfriend who was a cousin to his girlfriend, and then here he is, this engineer."[6]

Dennis says this initial recording did not run smoothly. "After I put my lead voice down, there was problem putting the harmony together. Boris Gardiner had a session after us, and our time was running into his, so he asks if we wanted him to assist, and Boris lend his voice. That's how 'Folk Song' was completed. It come out on the Top Cat label, distributed by Dynamics, but this was Karl's project – between Karl, George, and Paul Fuller. A couple months after that we did 'Time Is On Our Side' [aka 'Jah Is My Guide'] at Randy's for Clive Chin, but the same thing happened: the harmony's lacking."[7]

The third and final single featuring this initial line-up was 'Slow Coach', a song that addressed conflicts in Jamaica and the Middle East. "That war

276

there with Golda Meir in '66, and the Prime Minister who came to power shortly after that, Michael Manley: those two persons inspire that song a lot." It was recorded for Andy's, a label established in New York by record shop owner Raymond 'Benno' Anderson. "He grow up in Waterhouse and migrated to the States from a very early age, come down and hold an audition and chose that song. We lay the rhythm at Randy's, and when we come to Tubby's to do the vocal, it was the same thing with the harmony – couldn't nail it. Andy went back in New York and put out that song as a single [with the backing vocals removed]. Instead of putting the group name, he just used my name. We become ... not really inactive, but after those songs I hardly see Duckie."

Uhuru's temporary inactivity coincided with the reactivation of The Wailing Souls, after original member George 'Buddy' Haye re-joined founders Winston 'Pipe' Matthews and Lloyd 'Bread' MacDonald, who had been singing with Joe Higgs as Atarra the previous year, following the departure of Oswald 'Saboo' Downer and Norman 'Fats' Davis. "We did some background work with Jimmy Cliff on a song called 'Dear Mother' that Joe Higgs wrote, and he re-did [Bob Marley's] 'No Woman, No Cry' also," Bread notes. "Joe say him have some songs fi record and he need us to do the background vocal, and in return he's going to teach us how to really knit-up the group. Fats and Saboo were much older than us, big men with kids to support, and you never make no money from singing, so Fats started working on a ship and Saboo got some kind of deal with the government, wherein they went into the country and start doing some farming. So it was me and Pipe and Buddy along with Joe Higgs. Garth Dennis wasn't a member of that foursome, but he used to always be around and drop inna the harmony sometimes.

"Channel One start to crack over all the Studio One hits, and Channel One had a track for one of our songs, which is 'Back Out', so Joseph Hoo-Kim say him would like if Wailing Souls sing 'pon the rhythm as the original guys to sing 'Back Out', but 'cos Atarra was our own business and we start spend our own money, we say: 'We nah sing for nobody else, so no bother call we.' For about a year he was trying to get us. Eventually he send one of our brethren named Kaiso who live inna the neighbourhood, he was working up there as an all-rounder. Kaiso come and preach and say him figure if him could get us fi come, it would be a feather in his cap, so we go up to Channel One, but instead of 'Back Out' we did 'Things & Time'. We build new lyrics, 'cos from our early days we always say we no like to sing over songs. 'Things & Time' was our first official number one inna Jamaica."

277

Garth Dennis was then drafted in, giving the group the greater harmonic depth for which they had been noted at Studio One. "Because we had started singing with Fats and Saboo, when we did 'Things & Time' we never feel right," Bread recalls. "We said we need a next man, and Garth is the man."

"Buddy Haye was there in Trench Town, and then he come to live in Waterhouse," says Dennis. "He was still in communication with Pipe and Bread, and they went to record 'Things & Time'. They asked me to work out some harmonies on a couple of songs for them, and the songs that we did became instant hits: 'Jah Give Us Life', 'Very Well', 'Joy Within Your Heart'. There was a programme, *Where It's At*, run by Alphonso Walker at JBC every Saturday, so I start appearing there with Wailing Souls."

As The Wailing Souls gained top chart positions, Black Uhuru began to solidify. "By then, a young Michael Rose used to come amongst us in Waterhouse," notes Garth Dennis. "Michael had a brother, Joseph Rose, who was a good friend of Sly; Sly wanted to record some songs with Michael, because he's a good singer. Michael find Duckie, and they start going to Channel One to visit Sly. 'Shine Eyed Gal' and 'General Penitentiary' – I used to rehearse those songs with them while I was with The Wailing Souls."

"When me start sing with Uhuru, it was me, Duckie and Garth Dennis," confirms Rose at his Miami home. "We used to rehearse at one schoolyard and at Garth Dennis's yard." Dennis says that Rose – then often called Tony – was previously active in The Jays, another aspiring neighbourhood vocal trio. "Ruddy [Rudolph Reid], Errol Wilson, and Scuner [Lloyd Ruddock], the brother of King Tubby, that was The Jays. Scuner left for the States, so Ruddy and Errol continue singing, and they use Michael Rose. I saw them on *Where It's At*, and I saw them doing a couple of shows as well. That was before he joins Black Uhuru as the lead singer."

Rose states that the first Black Uhuru recordings with himself, Duckie Simpson and Errol Wilson yielded the powerful 'Wood For My Fire' and 'Rent Man', both portraying the hardships of ghetto life. "Ah Dennis Brown we did record it for," Rose notes, "but 'Rent Man' end up on Joe Gibbs's label for some reason." Before joining Black Uhuru, Rose cut a number of strong singles as a solo artist, making him a natural choice for group leader. He says his brothers and Sly Dunbar played an important part in his musical development. "I grow up a Waterhouse. My father used to work at a chocolate factory, then he work at a glass company, make all kind of different glass and drinks bottles. My brother Joseph used to sing around the house, that's how I get enthusiastic about singing. The other one, Rap

278

CLOCKWISE FROM TOP LEFT: Sugar Minott; the cool ruler, Gregory Isaacs; the Rhythm Twins, Sly & Robbie, at Channel One; reggae phenomenon Big Youth.

THIS PAGE: Third World, roots with quality; Junior Murvin and friend. **OPPOSITE**: Tappa Zukie, watering the garden.

Mikey Dread on the roof of Treasure Isle; The
Wailing Souls.

Rose, used to do harmony. Joseph used to work at the Ministry of Works, and when holiday time come they used to sing at company functions. So they recorded 'We Three Kings', that Christmas carol, at a little studio in Waterhouse named SRS – it's Newton Simmons's studio, a little two-track thing. Newton used to work at the airport, maybe inna the lookout tower. Sly was the one who recorded the track – Sly knew my brother very good."

Rose made his recording debut for the same outfit as a deejay, toasting on a song by Andell Forgie, a founding staff member of *Reggae Swing* magazine. "We used to fool around with a sound system named Sammy's, sing 'pon the mic and deejay. Them come up with a tune named 'Woman A Ginal Fi True' and asked me to just do something on it."

In 1974–75, Rose cut more notable work with Niney The Observer and Soul Syndicate. "I start sing like Dennis Brown and then people start hear 'bout me. Niney want to do a track, so we did 'Freedom Over Me', 'Clap The Barber'." The latter was reworked as 'Guess Who's Coming For Dinner' (aka 'Dreadlocks Coming For Dinner'), giving vent to the frustrations of the young dread; a further re-cut was later a major hit for Black Uhuru. "A Rastaman would see a girl and can't follow her home, because he's a man who grow him hair," Rose explains. "Other people can't see through that." Rose also cut the arresting 'Observe Life' for Lee Perry, before gaining broader experience by performing on the North Coast hotel circuit.[8]

In 1976 Rose cut the exhilarating 'Running Round' for another neighbourhood entrepreneur, and of all his solo work, it is this song that provides the most evidence of Dennis Brown's influence. The rhythm track, as usual, featured Sly Dunbar, who also had Rose voice a cover of Ken Boothe's 'Artibella' for an early release on Sly's Taxi label.[9]

Rose's strong link with Sly would yield particularly fine results in Black Uhuru; the singer says that the group's debut album, recorded in 1977, was originally conceived as a Taxi disc. "*Love Crisis* was supposed to record for Sly, but it never happen because Sly go 'pon tour with Peter Tosh. We did so anxious to record the tunes that when Jammy say him would do the album, we just did it for Jammy." The album did much to establish their reputation as a hard roots trio, with lyrics focussing on Rastafari values and pertinent social issues; it also established Jammy as a formidable producer.

Dubs of many of these tracks appeared on *Prince Jammy In Lion Dub Style*, an album that highlighted Jammy's individual remixing skills, which contrasted Tubby's approach by placing a greater emphasis on cymbal crashes and keyboard sounds, with the treble sphere typically well represented and equalisation implemented with greater subtlety. Jammy's stark and moody dub of Horace Andy's sublime *In The Light*, recorded at Harry J. in 1977 for New York-based producer Everton DaSilva in conjunction with Augustus Pablo and bassist Michael 'Myrie' Taylor, was another forceful disc. Jammy would later mix minimal, echoing dubs of some of Pablo's best works, including the dub counterpart to Hugh Mundell's *Africa Must Be Free*.

○

Tubby and Jammy also helped give shape to the mind-bending dubs dreamed up by Michael Campbell, the man who transformed Jamaican radio through his night-time show *Dread At The Controls*. The towering Campbell, better known as Mikey Dread, succumbed to a brain tumour in 2008 at the age of 54, but had remained active as a performer and recording artist right up until the tumour's unexpected onset.

From his final home base in Miami, Dread revealed that his interest in radio and electronics began when he was a boy. "I live between Port Antonio and Negril, and in Negril I become aware about the power of electricity and communication. Me and my likkle friends take a generator from a bicycle wheel and rub it and spin it until we get light. We take a battery and connect it to a bicycle bulb and it lights up. When I was 12, I came again to Port Antonio. At Titchfield High School, where I did my O-levels, I was always into mathematics and physics."

At the same time, the lure of the dancehall was irresistible. "Me inna me teens when me a play sound called Safari, play some dangerous tune: 'Satisfaction' by Carl Dawkins, and 'You'll Be Sorry' by Freddy McKay. We play the sound anywhere – I don't see my house for weeks. Me play another sound as well named Sound Of Music, later in the years. Me develop a certain love for broadcasting later on in life with the sound-system thing.

"Eventually me and some friends create a radio station at my high school called Radio Titchfield. We may be the only school in Jamaica who ever had a licence to broadcast. We had a five-mile radius for the radio station, and we used to jam the radio, because the rich people who carry their kids to school in the car listen to RJR, so me just change [Radio Titchfield's] frequency to RJR: they come within five miles of the radio station, the radio just switch to me. When you ride into school and you hear some rub-a-dub inna the morning, you wonder what's going on. Me have a deejay friend and the two of us used to MC the events at the school, plus me always perform a tune, like Big Youth's 'S 90 Skank,' or something else that's current."

Once Campbell saw the inside of a real radio station, his desire to enter broadcasting intensified. "One of the main things every school does is carry you to the Gleaner company to see how the newspaper is done, and take a tour of the radio stations and King's House. I see the man talk at the radio station and I was fascinated by it, and years later me come back to the same job. Me go to town when I-man go to the College of Arts Science & Technology: for a couple years, me study electrical engineering. I wanted to do electronics engineering, but they never offer that – them do three-phase power building, like how to install an elevator, something me no really into, so me leave from there and start working. In Jamaica, within them time, there was a lot of [prejudice] because of how black your skin is, so that force man like me who is well-black to really excel inna whatever I-man doing in terms of academics, because me can see a next youth who, through his father is Chinese, they will say he can get a job at the airport, but me must work inna one sugar factory. Me still have that vibes about me and me no like how life treat certain people."

Despite such hurdles, Campbell scored an internship at JBC. "RJR turn me down, saying I was too qualified, so me go ah JBC and learn from some of the pros, like Ossie Harvey, he was a popular technical operator. Back in the days, radio in Jamaica was not like one man spinning the music, playing commercials, reading the news and the weather and talking. Radio was divided up into different departments, with a booth for the announcer, who faces the operator through a glass. I sit at the control, and I control him: if I turn the board on 'audition' and I'm playing strictly rub-a-dub on the next side, he don't even know. It was supposed to be six months before I go into the field as a transmitter engineer, but within six months I realised that I can take this to a next level: JBC sign off at midnight and the kids from school were up studying until late, so we wanted something to keep us company. Me tell Ossie Harvey and another man named Mr Linton why them never go 24 hours and them say: 'Nobody listen to the radio after 12 o'clock,' so through me's a country man, me tell them I would like to do a little thing at night-time and them say: 'We're going to give you this, because we like what you're doing, but you would have to work Saturday night too' – I normally work Monday to Friday."

The *Dread At The Controls* show was thus born in 1976, but with certain restrictions: Campbell, as an engineer and not a 'radio personality' as such, was not allowed to speak on air. "A girl named Freddy Rodriguez used to be the announcer – a nice, sexy announcer," said Campbell of the show's early phase. "Me and her would select from what the library had, but when she left, I just bring in my record box and dub plates. At school, I have to write certain research papers in English, and I did mine on reggae, so me interview every man 'pon Idler's Rest and every artist, and me start to know all the producers through Watty Burnett from The Congos, who's also from Port Antonio. From I did my research for college, me already knew all of the man who saying anything in reggae – me know where to locate every man and me know what them deal with. I was moved by Tubby, Coxsone, and Lee Perry. Me did know Joe Gibbs too, Rupie Edwards, I Roy, Keith Poppin, Freddy McKay, Gregory Isaacs, Dennis Brown, Augustus Pablo. I was moved by a lot of people, but Tubby teach me the most, 'cos Tubby always respect the fact that me into the sound thing, take it to the broadcast level and still deal with the street people."

Unlike other Jamaican programmes, which relied heavily on foreign pop music, *Dread At The Controls* presented pure, authentic, indigenous Jamaican roots music from midnight to 4:30am, every night of the week except Sunday. Since Campbell was unable to speak, he built an impressive battery of complex sound effects and customised 'jingles' that turned his broadcasts into seamless blends of exciting sounds. Campbell's airing of exclusive dub plates meant his show was always ahead, presenting the latest sounds even before they caught on in the dancehall. In addition to captivating Jamaica, the programme gained cult followings in Cuba and Trinidad as well as in the USA and UK. But some of his superiors were displeased by its success. "Within JBC, there's a lot of jealousy. Everywhere people talk about the show and I become like a overnight hero, and them people never see me as a hero, them see me more or less as a country man. Them get mad, because reggae was not regarded as no substantial, culturally enlightened or enlightening art form. I start make some tunes, because the people give me a fight fi make a tune that say: 'The dread you have to love.' Me make Dread At The Controls company, and me put out whatever I feel."

Campbell says his debut recording, 'Love The Dread', was instigated by King Tubby. "When me go to town and meet Tubby, me start read a whole heap of books 'bout sound recording that me never have access to before, specific books 'bout the mixing console. He know me is a man who love to read, so Tubby make me read textbooks and magazines, and him could answer me questions. Then me would go Sundays with Tubby and Carlton Patterson, and him show me some little things about multi-track recording and dub. I recorded my first song because of my involvement with Tubby: I was making a jingle for my radio show and me and Tubbs talk about [the concept of 'Love The Dread']. Tubbs like it, so Tubbs say: 'Do the whole tune and just make it a record.' Tubbs show me how fi get me label and how to get into the business, and here I am today – no other man ever show me nothing about how fi start a label, or how fi get me tune recorded, and how fi mix it right, and how fi lay the rhythm ... Tubbs teach me everything. Other people, me just end up working with them."

Mikey Dread sometimes appeared on Socialist Roots with U Brown and Ranking Trevor during this period, while the first producer to benefit from his vocal input was Joe Gibbs with 'Friend And Money', a cut of Dennis Brown's biggest-ever hit, the rockers-style re-cut of 'Money In My Pocket'.[10] He was asked to voice the tune partly because of how his ceaseless promotion of Althea & Donna's 'Uptown Top Ranking' had helped the novelty groove become a substantial hit.

"Me always there ah studio ah look fi dub," Dread said. "Me said me want to listen to some tunes whe never released and them play 'Uptown Top Ranking'. Me ask them why them don't release it, and them never like the tune. From me start rinse it, that blow up the place, and them call me back, and then me start give them ideas. Me tell them me need to do a tune and them put on Dennis Brown's rhythm, and me just take one take and lick it and then me move on. Them days me just build my label, and me just do one-one tune for certain man. Scratch was the luckiest, because me do more than one tune fi him – Scratch get the best of Mikey Dread. Scratch check me one time and say that him want me to do a tune. I think I did 'Dread At The Mantrol' first. Me make some tune when me really fresh, because every morning me leave JBC and reach home by six o'clock; Lee Perry's there, and him gone with me for the whole day, until it's time for me to go back and work the night. We do a lot of tracks, like 'Sun Is Shining' with Bob Marley. Him always have some great ideas and me and him never had a problem, because the man is a genius and I could recognise it, because I come from a different academic school. It's just before 'Barber Saloon' Scratch come."

'Barber Saloon', the humorous tale of a dread who chops off his locks, was another single to surface from Dread's link with King Tubby and Carlton Patterson. Although U Brown had bowed out of voicing the rhythm for Patterson, creating 'Weather Balloon' on his own instead, Dread's spontaneous cut proved equally successful. "Due to how certain things did gwan, and me did get the rhythm [for 'Love The Dread'] from Patterson, then me owe Patterson a favour. We never plan fi do 'Barber Saloon' on the rhythm, it just happen that we go inna the studio and me just remember something that me see, and me just joking around to say: 'What a rude little dread like that,' and by the time me ready fi do the tune, they say: 'We take it already' – them already voice it and me couldn't put what me wanted to put on the rhythm."

Another strong one-off collaboration was 'Proper Education', a track voiced for producer Witty Reid. Like 'Barber Saloon' and 'Love The Dread', the song was eventually included on Mikey Dread's debut album, *Evolutionary Rockers*. "Witty was a good producer," Dread consented. "He was a policeman, and him produce 'Just Like A Sea' with David Isaacs, a tune that me always push 'pon the radio. It became a number one, and me said: 'Me want a cut of this tune.'"

As his radio show increased in popularity, Mike Dread began voicing a series of hard-hitting singles by upcoming artists. The first was 'Molly Collie', sung by Edi Fitzroy and written by radio and television producer Pam Hickling, wife of well-known psychiatrist Dr Fred Hickling. "I produce it and created the rhythm with Sly them, but the lyrics were written by Pam Hickling, one of the greatest unknown writers out of Jamaica. Because we always working with JBC at the same time, I always have Edi doing some jingles for me, because Edi was one of my main supporters at JBC. Me end up taking him to Mona where me live – him never have to worry about rent or nothing. Me take Edi Fitzroy and certain other man under my wings and move them out of the ghetto. We just have a bonding where we really take reggae to a certain level. We start making proper tunes: a lot of people were promising to start producing him, like [comedian] Ranny Williams. Me and Pam became very close friends and we have a company [40 Leg] – the three of we own everything equally."

Although his tone is high and bright on record, face-to-face the dreadlocked singer's speaking voice is definitely at the lower end of the scale. At his box-like home across from the imposing Gun Court, Edi, born Fitzroy Edwards, navigates the twisting path that led to the unlikely circumstances of his first recordings. Born in the town of Chapleton, Clarendon, he spent his early years in Montego Bay where his father, a cane farmer and grocery store manager, ran the Vasco sound system, "one of the first sound systems inna the West".

When his parents split in 1969, Edi went with his mother to downtown Kingston, where she found domestic work. "Those days, downtown Kingston was the place to be – not like now, when you have war and crime," he explains. "I start going to Westminster Commercial Institute with my brother. We pursue accounts and after I graduated, my first job was at JBC, where I reach the level of Accountant Payable. Coming from a musical family, where my father used to deal with music, I know that fire was in I. I love Jacob

Miller, because we both live in the same community, Kingston 13, and I feel he's one of the strongest voices out of Jamaica. Him have a long range, so he had a great influence on me. I usually go by Joe Gibbs's 'pon Saturdays – fi years me go there, but all me can hear is: 'Come back tomorrow.'

"One day me there at JBC and sing inna the studio, and Pam Hickling just pass and hear that voice and say: 'I'm going to record you.' The next day she go and draw the money, about 300 dollars, to do a rhythm: that time Michael Campbell, the Dread At The Controls, usually work at JBC. Him know a likkle about engineering, so he took me and she to Channel One, and Sly & The Revolutionaries, them lay the first track entitled 'Molly Collie' – it was number nine in the top 40 charts in Jamaica. About four months after that, my second song was 'Country Man' – that was even bigger. 'The Gun' was also a monster hit.

"If you listen to my early songs, I don't see myself singing fantasy, or making up something which is not real, because you can't put people on a dream trip. When I look around the city, seeing so much sufferation – people not working, some people cannot even pay them rent, so they can send them kids to school – and being fortunate that my mother could work and support my education, seeing the vibes, me say my music haffe have depth."

Fitzroy's 'Country Man' had a captivating dub, incorporating various hard-to- identify sound effects and highlighting a driving drum pattern. Like much of Mikey Dread's early work, the dub was mixed by King Tubby. "It's just a DATC [Dread At The Controls] thing," Dread explained. "We were trying something and it works. It's like in the lab: you're testing formulas, some of them work and some of them have side effects that make people sick. That's how me look 'pon life and look 'pon me music: we have to create, but when we find a formula, we keep it."

Other strong material came with singers like Rod Taylor and Michael Israel. "Rod Taylor had done a song [for Freedom Sounds] which I used to play on the radio called 'Ethiopian Kings', so me make him come audition at my house fi play 'His Imperial Majesty' and 'Behold HIM'," Dread continued. "He wrote the lyrics for 'Behold HIM', but 'His Imperial Majesty' was my song. We recorded it and we used to get it played on both radio stations heavily. Wayne Chin always play it 'pon RJR – he don't really play strictly reggae, but we always in a competition thing. Michael Israel is a champion singer. Both of us come from Port Antonio, and we're still friends up till now. From when we were kids, he was a guy who always win a lot of song competitions. Him named Michael Brown, but me call him Michael Israel."

Meanwhile, the *Dread At The Controls* radio show had such prestige that

Mikey Dread received some tempting offers of employment. "Chris Blackwell came to bring me to Nassau, and I had to tell him no. I think I had found a formula and it was working for me. How would I be at the height of my career and go and jump on a bandwagon that is uncertain? Him want me fi leave radio to do sound engineering in Compass Point, because he see me as a great engineer-to-be; Tyrone Downey had brought me to him. Them days there, me no really know who the hell Chris Blackwell is. Them man there never really come ah JBC to give me no music."

When things eventually turned sour at JBC, Mikey Dread took over Errol Brown's engineering position at Treasure Isle studio because Brown was preparing to move to Tuff Gong, the new studio that Bob Marley built at 56 Hope Road. "Me and Errol were friends, and I'm about to leave JBC because me couldn't take the bullshit, so Errol come down and show me a few things, and when him leave, I-man just take it over. Me do some Culture t'ing, maybe 'Natty Never Get Weary' LP [*Cumbolo*] and some other likkle Treasure Isle tunes. I was there for maybe a year. After that time, things start happen for me and me start travel."

Photographer Dave Hendley, who was then working for the rejuvenated Trojan company as well as running his own Sufferer's Heights label, brought Dread to the UK after meeting him on a trip to Jamaica in early 1979. "Dave Hendley was the one responsible for getting Mikey Dread to London to help me to launch Dread At The Controls in England, as well as Sugar Minott's label. Trojan signed me and Sugar Minott that same year, and part of the deal was to come to England to promote. I give Trojan *Dread At The Controls* [a remixed *Evolutionary Rockers*] and I was going to set up a company, do all my productions through there, and we were going to start with *African Anthem*." The album, a thrilling dub set mixed to parallel a *Dread At The Controls* radio session, was issued on Cruise, a label that Hendley established with fellow Trojan staff member Paul Wateridge. The partnership was shortlived, however, and Dread subsequently issued his material in conjunction with other fledgling UK independents.

When he returned to Jamaica after his first brief visit to the UK, Mikey Dread was approached by The Clash, with whom he furthered the reggae-punk alliance by producing and toasting on their 'Bank Robber' single. "The Clash sent for me the second time around," he explained. "Them say they try a lot of producers – Lee Perry and a whole heap a guy – and they never have no hits. Them ask if me want to work with them, but I didn't want to. I didn't know who they were and I didn't want to go back to England – England too cold."

Eventually Dread was persuaded to return to Britain, where he went on the road with the group; Edi Fitzroy also joined them on certain performances. "For me to produce them, I wanted to hear or see what it was," Dread laughed. "Me come from Jamaica where no man no play some punk music. I didn't even know which beat I'm on, or where is the start of this damn note! In order for me to take a job, I need to know which sort of fans you have and how does your music go across. We do the work and it was good. They were cool with me and we got some good stuff accomplished."

By the time Mikey Dread and Edi Fitzroy toured Britain, roots reggae had reached the pinnacle of its international popularity. In the years that followed, the status of Jamaican sounds would become devalued. This was partly in response to a shift in the ruling style: the classic harmony trios, who sang of suffering while praising Jah, were giving way to the spiky edges of early dancehall, in which a solo singer or deejay would typically address less weighty matters. But as with previous stylistic shifts, such changes were not absolute; a few harmony trios survived, and several artists composed songs of sensuality as well as 'sufferers' lyrics, but in general the mood was becoming less heavy and more geared towards dancing feet.

As the major overseas labels gradually lessened their commitment to reggae, the faddish British music press denounced the music as passé and most publications ceased covering it. In retrospect, it seems this attitude was motivated by financial concerns. The collapse of lucrative markets in West Africa had a decisively negative impact, and Jamaica's worsening political situation drove companies to seek material elsewhere. As the appetite for exoticism intensified, executives discovered an alternative means of peddling it by adulterating the music of Africa for a so-called 'World Music' category. Such factors isolated reggae once more, causing most Jamaican artists to concentrate on their home audience. This would ultimately bring a refreshing rawness and authenticity to the predominant sound that arose as the 70s gave way to the 80s.

11
NICE UP THE DANCE
Dub poetry and dancehall rub-a-dub

"Most of what I write is what I feel and what I see. I learned that the pen is sometimes mightier than the sword and people can write things and motivate people to think; that is what my work is all about, to make you think."
– MUTABARUKA

"Some so-called producers, when you start playing something for them, them say them don't like it, so we were saying we would take all of those rejected stuff and play them for ourselves, and all the rejected things started running."
– ROBBIE SHAKESPEARE

At the end of the 70s, Jamaica was gripped by dramatic social upheaval. With the new decade came a change of government, the result of a transformation that was anything but smooth. If the 1976 general election had seen plenty of bloodshed, it was but a prelude to the extreme violence unleashed in the run-up to voting in 1980.

Despite Michael Manley's grand idealism and willingness to challenge the policies of world powers, shortages of food and basic goods, frequent power cuts, runaway inflation, and escalating unemployment made it increasingly clear that Democratic Socialism was not working. Additionally, grotesque acts of violence and politically motivated murders were becoming more commonplace, and certain incidents suggested that Manley was not fully in control.

The most notorious was the Green Bay Massacre, which took place on January 5 1978. Twelve JLP gunmen from the Southside ghetto, close to the wharf, were lured to the Green Bay firing range, believing they could access automatic firearms, but soldiers from the specialist Military Intelligence Unit were waiting to ambush. Five JLP men were killed in the ensuing shootout, and several others were wounded. Manley claimed the action was part of a determined effort to rid the streets of violent crime, and refused to make the soldiers appear in court; the reputedly radical National Security Minister, Dudley Thompson, even went so far as to say: 'No angels died in Green Bay.' However, widespread rumour indicated that the action was the work of MIU renegades, suggesting that Manley was not in charge of the nation's armed forces. The notorious event was widely commented on in song, the most direct criticism coming from deejays such as Tappa Zukie, with 'Murder', and Lord Sassafras, on 'Green Bay Incident'.

In the wake of this violence came an unexpected peace treaty between the downtown gangs, brokered on January 10 by PNP 'Don' Bucky Marshall and senior JLP man Claudie Massop, with assistance from fellow toughs Tony Welch and Carl 'Baya' Mitchell, plus members of a Rasta organisation known as the Niyabinghi Theocracy. Again, the peace was widely referenced on disc: Jacob Miller scored a chart hit with 'Peace Treaty Special'; Dillinger impacted with 'War Is Over'; George Nooks revived Little Roy's 'Tribal War'; and Oku Onoura surveyed the situation on 'Reflections In Red', one of the first songs recorded at Marley's Tuff Gong studio and one of the earliest examples of Jamaican 'dub poetry' committed to vinyl.

Dub poetry stems from the experimental setting of verse to music: the politically challenging poems, often expounding a Rastafari world view, are typically recited in heavy patois, while the rhythmic emphasis is provided by straightforward reggae or a backdrop of jazzy instrumentals and Niyabinghi beats. Although others would find greater fame with dub poetry, Onoura is the true pioneer of the genre in Jamaica.

Onoura was born Orlando Wong in Franklyn Town; he was of mixed Chinese and African ancestry but eventually took the name Igbo name Oku Onoura, (meaning 'Light' and 'Voice of the People'), to signify an African identity. In the late 60s he set up a school and first-aid centre for underprivileged youth in the eastern Kingston ghetto of Dunkirk, but was sent to prison for armed robbery in 1970. Four years later, Cedric Brooks's Light Of Saba group performed at the prison, and prisoner Wong recited his poems to their musical backing; he was given an early release in September 1977, after a campaign supported by the academic Poets, Essayists & Novelists (PEN) organisation. Then, in February 1978, the re-named Onoura and his fellow poets Mutabaruka and Michael Smith aired poetry set to music at a Rastafarian rally at Kingston's Heroes Circle as part of the peace treaty festivities, and to mark the 50th anniversary of Marcus Garvey's Universal Negro Improvement Association.

Mutabaruka, an outspoken individualist, is the best-known Jamaican dub poet. His late-night *Cutting Edge* broadcasts on Irie FM currently have the ear of the nation, and Muta never fears to speak his mind. Perpetually barefoot and with a grey widow's peak in his forelocks, he cuts a striking figure. After a charged live performance, in which he appeared in chains to emphasise the inhumanity of slavery, the poet spoke of the way he came to harness the power of the word.

He was born Allan Hope in Rae Town, but left at a young age to spend 15 years in the countryside. After returning to the capital in the 60s he began to publish poems under the name Mutabaruka, having been inspired by the work of the Rwandan poet Jean-Baptiste Mutabaruka. His vibrant poetry, which embraced Rastafarian philosophy and the political activism of black power, was highly critical of mainstream Jamaica. In the 70s his work was published widely on the island, especially in *Reggae Swing* magazine. "I was doing poetry from the late 60s, in books and magazines," he explains. "Then a book came about [*Outcry*], and I started to perform them in different literary circles. Most of what I write is what I feel and what I see. I learned that the pen is sometimes mightier than the sword and people can write things and motivate people to think. That is what my work is all about: to make you think. When you listen to my poems, when you read my poems, it must motivate you to find solutions for your problems. I cannot guarantee to have all the solutions, but I can make you think of these problems and be motivated towards a constructive solution."

Michael Smith cut 'Word' with Light Of Saba in 1978. He came to prominence through the Jamaican School of Drama, where the Poets In Unity collective was formed in 1979. Smith's strong command of street vernacular, often delivered rapid-fire, gave his poems a gripping realism. "Michael Smith was one of those extraordinarily gifted people that the Third World just throws up every so often that has a tremendous way with words, that was able to use the ordinary spoken language of Jamaicans in a way that was both entertaining and spine-chilling," says London's foremost reggae poet, Linton Kwesi Johnson, producer of Smith's album *Mi Cyaan Believe It*. "He was totally committed to ordinary people, to the struggles and the plight of the sufferers of Kingston, the peasants. As a performer, he was electric on stage. He brought so-called 'dub poetry' to a level of acceptability which hadn't been there for it before and has since had a lot of imitators."

Johnson has a well-groomed beard and is always smartly dressed, often crowned with a pork-pie hat. He is typically short of time and reluctant to be interviewed, but we have enjoyed several informal discussions about music, literature, politics, and emigration – all elements that inform his work. In addition to his razor-sharp mind, grounded political beliefs, and ongoing commitment to facilitating social change, the well-read poet's penchant for debate reveals a refreshing openness. For instance, I have seen him engage in a lengthy, lucid exchange in the small hours on the relative merits of social order with a tattooed Spanish anarchist, one of a group of squatters that occupied a building in Johnson's South London neighbourhood.

Johnson was born in Clarendon, but migrated to the UK at the age of 11 in 1963. "My parents were peasants: my father was working in the Four Paths bakery, my mother did domestic work," he revealed in a now-defunct bar that once served as his unofficial office. "I was born and raised in Chapleton, then when my mother came to work I was living in Sandy River at the foot of the Bull Head mountains, not far from James Hill, where the poet and novelist Claude McKay came from. I spent some holidays in Kingston with my mother – she was living at Slipe Road, near Torrington Bridge. I spent a lot of time in Hope Gardens, because I had three uncles and an aunt working there. My grandparents were farmers; my grandmother raised me for three years when my mother came here."

Johnson says his teenage membership of the Black Panthers first inspired him to write. "The Black Panthers were a militant black organisation in England that took the name from the American Panthers, but it was completely separate. There were no political ties in that sense, although we used to read the Panther papers from America, read Bobby Seale's *Seize The Time*, Eldridge Cleaver's book [*Soul On Ice*]; we followed the teachings of Huey P. Newton and so on, but we were an organisation which was tackling racism in Britain and organising around issues dealing with the police and the courts, because those were the burning issues of the day. That was where I first learned about black literature and began to become interested in poetry."

After being awarded a sociology degree by Goldsmith's College in 1973, Johnson wrote the play *Voices Of The Living And The Dead*, examining the legacies of colonialism. He was also actively involved with the *Race Today* collective. "*Race Today* was a combative journal that not only reported on the struggles and burning issues of the day, as far as the black community was concerned, but was also involved in helping to build organisations, working in close alignment with the Black Panthers movement and other organisations like the Northern Collectives in Bradford and Leeds. We were involved in several important campaigns that helped to transform the political and cultural lives of black people in Britain."

In the mid 70s, when Johnson was writing about reggae in the British music press, he coined the phrase 'dub poetry' in reference to the verbal artistry of deejays such as U Roy and Big Youth. The tag was later applied to his own work after he cut the first full-length album of poetry set to reggae rhythms, *Dread Beat And Blood*, released by Virgin in 1977 and credited to Poet & The Roots. Johnson is an erudite man and his careful choice of words gives his poetry a particular cadence; when set to the complex arrangements of the multi-talented Barbados-born musician Dennis Bovell, its emotional content acquired greater emphasis, rendering the medium accessible to audiences which might normally be turned off by politically oriented verse.

In Britain, poets such as Johnson and Benjamin Zephaniah gave dub poetry a worthy status; in Jamaica, Oku Onoura, Mutabaruka, Michael Smith, Jean Binta Breeze, and others associated with the Jamaican School of Drama were using the power of the word to ferment change. However, leading lights in both countries have tried to distance their work from the term, with Onoura the only one among them who is really comfortable with it.

The dub poets' performance at Heroes Circle in February 1978 marked the end of Bob Marley's 16-month overseas exile, following the attempt on his life at Hope Road. He returned to Jamaica that same night after being approached by peace treaty intermediaries from the Twelve Tribes of Israel to headline the One Love Peace Concert at the National Stadium on 22 April, with all proceeds to benefit ghetto communities. During his performance, Marley famously called Seaga and Manley on stage to join hands. "That was a very special event," Edward Seaga earnestly remembers. "The peace had been established already and people looked at it as something that would endure, so they arranged the peace concert and asked Marley to come. By that time, things had become quite harmonious: [the concert] happened in April and the peace process had started in January, so the parties had a much smoother relationship – on a leadership level as well. There was no aspect of that initiative that would have caused me to say: 'I don't want to get involved in this.' It was something I wanted to see as a natural extension of what was happening." When I suggest it is surprising that he and Manley shook hands at a time when they were bitter enemies, he insists: "In the system you don't have bitter enemies. You have strong opposition."

In either case, the sad fact is that the peace treaty was derailed in February 1979, when police killed Claudie Massop and two of his colleagues. Massop's body was found to contain over 40 bullet wounds. His death followed a spate of riots instigated by the National Patriotic Movement – a group said to have been backed by the JLP – after an IMF-instigated currency devaluation and the shortfall of projected finance brought huge increases to the price of petrol. Kingston's power station was temporarily shut down, as were banks, schools and other civic institutions; tourists were detained at unofficial roadblocks; shops were looted and destroyed. The 'tribalist' violence that had been the norm gradually returned and reached its climax during the 1980 election campaign, which was akin to a civil war.

In April, snipers fired on Manley when he appealed for votes in Southside; in retaliation, nearly 100 PNP activists, some armed with machine guns, invaded a JLP fundraising dance on Gold Street, killing five and injuring ten. In June, a military coup planned by Vietnam veteran H. Charles Johnson, leader of the far-right Jamaica United Front, was discovered and prevented by the army; some spoke of a supposed destabilisation campaign devised by the US National Security Council. In July, an American magazine named Richard Kinsman as being in charge of 15 CIA operatives in Jamaica; shortly thereafter, Kinsman told the *Gleaner* that his home had been bombed, but never reported the alleged attack to the police. By mid July the number killed was estimated at 350 and rising; hundreds more would be slaughtered in the months of mayhem to come. In October, three weeks before the election, PNP Member of Parliament Roy McGann was murdered; on polling day there were major fires in Jones Town, and citizens were shot while attempting to vote. By the end of the year, more than 1,000 Jamaicans were said to have been killed, most in election-related violence.

The election resulted in a crushing defeat for the PNP, which won a mere nine of the sixty seats in Parliament. When Seaga took up the reigns, there was rejoicing in Washington as Jamaica turned its ideals away from Cuba and back to the free market; most observers saw Manley's defeat as inevitable. "He destabilised the economy," says Edward Seaga. "We were the only country in the entire world to have lost eight consecutive years in negative growth: he made the people 20 per cent poorer at the end of his term of office than they were at the beginning, lost 20 per cent of the GDP. Unemployment was at a record high; the cost of living was at a record high; there was a scarcity of foodstuffs, until some 14,000 small shops closed – there was nothing to put in there. Motor vehicles had to be parked at the roadside, factories had to close, because they couldn't get simple spare parts. He totally destabilised himself by wrecking the economy, which in later years he admitted – in the early 80s, he admitted that socialism was dead and that it was a mistake."

○

Musically, there were also great changes afoot as the old decade gave way to the new. On March 23 1980 Jacob Miller was killed in a road accident. At the time the most popular roots singer in Jamaica, despite overseas releases aimed at the disco market, he was given an impressive state funeral. Then, the death of Bob Marley from cancer on May 11 1981 was followed by the best-attended funeral in Jamaican history. Marley's passing is sometimes regarded by foreign commentators as a reference point for the symbolic death of roots music, but it is worth remembering that Marley's status outside Jamaica is disproportionate; he is certainly the best-known reggae artist internationally, but the albums for Island that made his name abroad were less highly regarded at home.

In any case, the early dancehall style had already gained considerable ground by 1979. The duo of Sly & Robbie was one of the most significant new production outfits to bring about the stylistic change. They had increasingly joined forces on recording sessions in the late 70s, and when Peter Tosh was assembling a band for an international tour, Robbie made sure Sly was included. The pair subsequently entered the production arena in early 1979, despite initial apathy from their peers.

"Sly got some free time at Channel One and nobody didn't want to play at first," Robbie recalls. "I remember I even stand up and cry and Sly said: 'Cool, Robbie man, everything will work out.' One day Gregory Isaacs came and give us six songs, and in those six songs was 'Soon Forward', our first Taxi hit."

Often working with keyboardists Ansel Collins and Robbie Lyn, plus guitarists Douggie Bryan, Ranchie MacLean, and Geoffrey Chung, Sly & Robbie's Taxi productions naturally emphasised drums and bass. Sly had been the backbone of Channel One, and needless to say his mechanised beats were pivotal to the new style they were forging. Robbie's driving, spacious bass melodies provided the perfect foil. Sly says his 1978 contract with Virgin brought the badly needed financial backing that enabled the duo to forge ahead with rhythmic experimentation. "I made *Simple Sly Man* with some rhythm from Joe-Joe, and I got some money from Virgin and put it into Taxi. That's where the whole Taxi label start growing and everybody start running back to us."

It is fortunate that Sly made use of this money when he did; a year or so after the 1979 release of *Sly, Wicked & Slick*, Virgin wound up the Front Line label, reportedly because their export revenue had been curtailed by a change of government in Nigeria. "Their biggest market was in Nigeria, South Africa, places like that," says Norman Grant, "so when those markets fell, they pulled out." The Twinkle Brothers' *Countryman* was one of the last Front Line releases. It contained dread anthems like 'Never Get Burn' and 'Since I Throw The Comb', and according to Grant had been heavily tampered with for the overseas market. "We record it on eight-track at Harry J.," he says. "At the time the big companies want you to go 24, so I run it off to a 24-track tape and Virgin went into their studio and do a bit of overdubbing with [bassist and dub mixer] Paul Smykle when we weren't around. Some of the guys wasn't too pleased, because they even roll off one of the bass lines."

As Front Line closed down, Gregory Isaacs, Prince Fari, and Ashanti Roy from The Congos were signed to Pre, a subsidiary of Charisma, but despite considerable success with Isaacs in 1980–81, the label soon ceased promoting reggae. Of the Jamaican acts transferred to Virgin's parent label, both I Roy and The Gladiators made their least appealing and most commercial sets to date before being dropped by the company – just as Sly & Robbie's instinctive feel for future trends landed them a deal with Island.

Part of what made the Taxi sound so appealing was Sly's adventurous approach to rhythm. He was the first Jamaican drummer to experiment with Syndrums, which he used to build a number of furious post-rockers styles. "I'd heard the Syndrum on some electronic song, but I thought that was the only sound you could get: 'doop doop'. Then I heard M's 'Pop Music', and I said: 'How can I get that sound, but still in a groove that could fit in reggae?' On *Sly, Wicked & Slick*, 'Queen Of The Minstrel', that was the first song I played it on, then the next song was 'General Penitentiary' by Black Uhuru. After that, I tried to experiment in 'Guess Who's Coming To Dinner'."

Such experiments are partly what make Black Uhuru's 1979 release *Showcase* such a brilliant record. Like the Gregory Isaacs album of the same name, it had six songs, all presented with extended mixes, placing Uhuru's chilling vocals over Sly & Robbie's unbeatable rhythms and strong production values. As ever, Michael Rose's lyrics were sharply to the point on songs like 'Abortion' and 'Plastic Smile'. "I have to enlighten my sisters that abortion is dangerous, because woman take abortion and lose them lives. Why not be cautious, that's what the song is saying. 'Plastic Smile' is like, someone smiles with you, but when you turn your back they say: 'He's a piece of shit.' When you're a Rasta, you find 'nuff discrimination. These

299

things have to enlighten you – you have to tell the world about it."

The trio now had greater harmonic symmetry with Sandra 'Puma' Jones, a black American drafted into the group when Errol Wilson re-joined The Jays. "Puma do some social work inna Jamaica and she used to dance for Ras Michael," Rose recalls. "We went up Hope Road to visit an elder knots and run into Puma, heard her singing to Bob Marley's *Kaya* album. We ask her if she did interested, she said she would try it out."

Although she had been an official group member since *Showcase*, Puma was absent for *Sinsemilla* (originally issued as *Stalk Of Sensimenia* in Jamaica), the album that brought a contract with Island in 1980. "When we record *Sinsemilla*, she wasn't there for some reason and me have to sing the harmony," Rose reveals. "We just put her face 'pon it, and the album run away."

Along with the herb-anthem title track, *Sinsemilla* offered poetic reasoning on various topics, including the human race's unnecessary division on 'The Whole World Is Africa'. "The whole inspiration with that is how earth set up, and the everyday life of the Rastaman, the fighting, and Babylon at war fi land. An earthquake separate the land: if you look at the world and see how it was one [landmass], but because people fight so much, it have so much negative vibes that the earth move. If people more 'pon a neutral level, where everything free and people just live natural life, that mean you have a different vibe, but you have to pay for land, you have war, man capture, take away. That just push off a whole negative thing inna earth, so some place stable and some place move."

The sound that Sly & Robbie created on Black Uhuru's *Showcase* and *Sinsemilla* was so captivating that Island subsequently promoted the 'Rhythm Twins' as members of the group. The duo was also the anchor of their live touring band, and Island harnessed the pair for other high-profile projects such as those recorded by hard-edged singer Ini Kamoze, and androgynous funk chanteuse Grace Jones. "A lot of people don't know that Grace Jones record was actually a Black Uhuru sound," says Sly of 'Pull Up To The Bumper', her first big hit. "We brought the master tape of 'Sinsemilla' to Nassau, and we're playing it for Chris Blackwell, and he said this is wickedest thing he heard, and [producer/engineer] Alex Sadkin was saying they need to get the drum sound for Grace. That's the way the sound was born."

While Island helped raise the Rhythm Twins' profile abroad, their Taxi label was picking up steam in Jamaica. By 1980 they had a hot stable of artists, scoring big hits with Jimmy Riley's re-cut of The Uniques' 'Love &

Devotion', The Tamlins' version of Randy Newman's 'Baltimore' (based on Nina Simone's restructured rendition), deejay General Echo's humorous kung-fu epic 'Drunken Master', and two from the gruff-voiced Junior Delgado: 'Merry Go Round', a plea for fidelity, and 'Fort Augustus', which warned of the perils of prison. "From I was a kid, I don't know if it's because my mommy went to America to work, but I used to always feel like I'm caged up, like I'm in prison," Delgado said of the latter. "Plus, when I was driving past that prison in the middle of the sea called Fort Augusta, that's how the song came. Sly & Robbie did love it, they want to record it, and we did 'Merry Go Round' also, same session."

Although Black Uhuru continued to sing of Selassie's glory, the rise of Sly & Robbie as a production force, with Sly's mechanised, modernistic drum and Syndrum patterns, ultimately pointed away from roots and further into dancehall. As the predominant sound began to show a harder edge, The Roots Radics emerged as the most crucial backing band in defining its form. They were an amalgamation of session players created after Sly & Robbie's rise spelt the demise of The Revolutionaries.

The Radics started as an offshoot of the fading Morwells, with bassist Flabba Holt and rhythm guitarist Bingy Bunny forming the nucleus. On Orange Street, at the offices of Leggo Records, Flabba speaks of the Radics' gradual formation. "The band wasn't really that tight, because I use Winston Wright, Santa, Bo-Pee [guitarist Winston Bowen], and Tarzan [keyboardist Errol Nelson]; like The Revolutionaries, man just come in. We play and play, until we find Steelie [keyboardist Wycliffe Johnson] and say that little youth sound more wicked than anything – me and the drummer, 'Style' Scott [aka Lincoln Scott] say: 'Sound like him could come in.' Long time me and Bingy Bunny juggle before at Randy's, did 'nuff sessions. Radics no really come yet at the time."

According to Flabba, the first recording session to feature an early version of the Radics yielded "a song with Earl Zero – the first Earl Zero sound. After that we get Steelie. We use Santa until we buck up on Style Scott, then we just form the band Radics officially, because them man there dedicated: me, Steelie, Style Scott, and Bingy Bunny. We did play and play until we get the guitarist named Sowell [Noel Bailey, a former Youth Professionals member who began his career as a singer], bring him in as a lead. He come with a different sound, like him put a pipe inna him mouth [due to liberal use of wah-wah and fuzz-box effects]. It sound different and people like that."

With a string vest exposing his hefty frame, Flabba is running through a

301

rumbling bass line, reclining in an easy chair, his feet pressed against a table. A friendly and welcoming gentleman, Flabba says his stage name was acquired during his youth. "My full name is Errol Alexander Carter. When I sing, people say I sound like John Holt, so they call me Flabba Holt. I used to have a brother who make some big dumpling, him tell me if I don't eat that dumpling I'm going to get beaten, so I eat the whole pile of dumpling. Flabba just stick 'pon me from youthman days, original name. I born in Trench Town, but I really come from Denham Town. Most of the man like Alton Ellis, Heptones come from Trench Town, but Ken Boothe, Flabba Holt, Johnny Osbourne come from Denham Town. My birth date is 1950. I really raised by my mother, because my father meet in some kind of accident and die when I'm small. I used to dance 'pon stage, Opportunity Hour, and I win 'nuff prize at Majestic Theatre. I really dance to one special song, 'Ball Of Fire' by The Skatalites. Any time that song's on, man try to contest me. As a youth me used to follow Coxsone, because Coxsone had the better sound. Duke Reid was a bad sound, but King Stitt – that deejay wicked."

By the early 70s, Flabba was associated with Rupie Edwards's Success label. "I did some songs with him like 'Yamaha Skank' with Shorty The President and Earl 'Chinna' Smith. I really move with Rupie Edwards when Gregory Isaacs come in a group them call The Concords. Johnny Clarke, me rehearse them youth there and build them into perfection." In this period, Flabba also voiced a song called 'Girl From Manchester' as a deejay, but the record flopped. "It was really Rupie Edwards's idea. We go in Randy's and just do a little thing, but it never took off because the rhythm wasn't right."

Flabba subsequently cut songs as a singer, of which the most notable is the 1976 sound-system favourite 'A You Lick Me First'. By 1975 his bass skills brought him into The Morwells. "In Trench Town I play the guitar, and someone said: 'Try the bass,' so me take up the bass and play something wicked. Theophilus Beckford, that man give me 'nuff encouragement. Them time, a little band form up. My bass guitar had no name on it, but me get the real thing from Big Youth, a Fender Jazz."

By 1979 The Roots Radics were making their presence heavily felt, often with tightly wound, slowed-down versions of classic rhythms. In the band's early days, when they were still relying on Santa and Bo-Pee, pivotal releases were cut with a teenage dancehall crooner called Barrington Levy. The singer started in the relatively unknown Mighty Multitudes, who signed a contract with Byron Lee in 1977 but later disbanded. As a solo artist Levy made his Radics-backed debut with 'A Yah We Deh', but it was 'Collie Weed', voiced on a rollicking cut of the 'Conversation' rhythm, that first brought him to the top of the Jamaican charts, followed quickly by 'Looking My Love' (on a hesitant remake of 'Real Rock'), and the censorious original, 'Shine Eye Girl'. Levy's poignantly poetic lyrics always retained a sense of humour; for instance, in 'Many Changes In Life,' his descriptive powers named youthful days as 'Long time ago when my eyes was at my knees'. His vocal trademark is a stretching of vowels, elongating words for greater emphasis, and a frequent exclamation of 'Whoah!' in the upper register.

Levy has maintained a high profile ever since, rendering him perpetually busy; despite reluctance to be interviewed, following an appearance on TVJ's breakfast show, a popular programme that greets much of the Jamaican nation each morning, the singer provides particulars on his crucial role in the birthing of the dancehall style, achieved after a few false starts. "I grew up in Kingston 11, then I go to Clarendon when I was eight years old; the quietness of country really give me the energy to sit down and put lyrics together and the excitement of Kingston help me to go out there and do it. Music is everything from day one: I decided that I want to be a singer when I see Michael Jackson on television, that really bring a buzz as a young kid; Dennis Brown and John Holt uplift me the same way. I come back to Kingston 11 when I was 13 years old and started out with my cousin; we do two songs together as The Mighty Multitudes. I was still going to school, but I was more focussed on getting my songs on the radio."

Levy was then living in the West Kingston slum of Majesty Gardens, home to notable harmony groups, and it was here that Ansel Cridland, leader of The Meditations, first noted young Barrington's talents. "Meditations used to sit on the gully bank and play their guitar, and as a kid I used to just stand by and watch them. Then I get a chance to go up to Ansel and say: 'I can sing, you know, I have a song'; I sing it and he strum the guitar." Cridland brought Levy and his cousin, Everton Dacres, to balladeer-turned-producer Dobby Dobson, who recorded their debut, 'My Black Girl', which the producer released overseas; some time later, a second song, 'Been A Long Time,' was produced by Barry Biggs at Dynamic Sounds after a musician from the 'Black Girl' session alerted Biggs to Levy's vocal skill.

"After that, it was struggling again," Levy continues. "Me and my cousin started to argue about money, so I take to the dancehall, the sound system, as a solo act, and that's where it all started: there was a sound called Burning Spear and one called Tape Tone, they were based in Kingston 11, at Payne Avenue; one night, Leroy Smart was singing on the sound and Trinity said: 'Come here youth! You can sing,' and just give me the mic. I sing 'Shine Eye Girl' and 'Collie Weed' and that place was going crazy!"

As news of an original singing talent spread throughout the music fraternity, it did not take long for upcoming producer Henry 'Junjo' Lawes to hear of Barrington Levy's invigorating style, but Levy says Junjo was not well established when he first approached the singer; in fact, each found that their collaboration was precisely what the other needed to make a significant breakthrough. "One day I went to a talent show and Junjo Lawes send somebody, so I went to see Junjo and he's saying he has a track that he would like me to go on. I went to the studio and did 'A Yah We Deh,' giving thanks and praise, and then I did 'Collie Weed' and 'Collie Weed' becomes huge in Jamaica. I used to walk to the established studios like Joe Gibbs's and they used to give me the run-around – 'come back next week' – but Junjo believed in me."

Junjo was a tough character from Waterhouse with a stick-thin frame, whose harnessing of The Roots Radics as a platform for new dancehall artists saw him rapidly emerge as the leading producer of day. Linval Thompson, a close associate and one of the first producers to work with the Radics, says Junjo came to music from an entirely different arena. "I really brought Junjo in the business. He just see me in the road and want to follow me around, want to come with me to the studio. He wasn't no musician, he was a guy on the street, working for the politician, if you understand what I'm trying to say. Then I was *the* singer, so everybody want to go up there with me."

The combination of Barrington Levy and Junjo Lawes brought the kind of aural dynamite that Jamaica had been waiting for: the humorous 'Collie Weed', which adapted a folk rhyme to praise the "wisdom weed", was followed by other chart toppers such as the female-friendly '21 Gal Salute' and the broadly salutary 'Reggae Music'. Such hits led to the album *Shaolin Temple*, released overseas as *Bounty Hunter*, a landmark disc in reggae evolution.

"When that voice came, it was like a whole new era had started in Jamaica," says Chris Cracknell of Greensleeves, the label that released Levy's follow-up albums *Robin Hood* and *Englishman* in Britain, along with the majority of Junjo Lawes's productions. "We sold thousands of 'Shine Eye Girl' in the shop – we just could not get enough copies, and we could not keep the *Bounty Hunter* album in stock. It was just unbelievable. Suddenly, people wanted that new sound, that new flavour. Times were changing and in Jamaica, the roots and culture and the whole Rasta thing was changing, and there was a change in producers as well: just before Junjo came, we were in the days of Island Records putting out Black Uhuru with Sly & Robbie, but because Black Uhuru got so popular, Sly & Robbie were off the island touring; there was this void in Jamaica and Junjo filled that void. There was an opportunity for him to be working at Channel One, as Channel One were hiring out the studio as opposed to just using it for themselves and their house band; things were changing and it was a revelation."

Greensleeves began as a specialist record shop in Acton in November 1975, servicing West London's Polish community, but soon shifted focus to Jamaican music, moved to Shepherd's Bush (an epicentre of Jamaican emigration), and began releasing material in 1977 by artists such as Doctor Alimantado and The Wailing Souls. Word got around that the company was paying proper advances and actual royalties, leading several producers to their doorstep, but Junjo was the one with which they really bonded.

"I remember the first time Junjo turned up," laughs Cracknell, "he'd been around to some other labels and turned up at our store. We said: 'Oh, Barrington Levy, *Bounty Hunter* ...' and he said: 'I'm afraid you can't have that album, I've already licensed it,' and he had some things with him that hadn't been licensed that we listened to. Junjo was a real character and we really warmed to him, so we said: 'We don't really want the leftovers, but on your next trip up here, make sure we're the first stop.' On his next trip up, he'd done the *Englishman* album, and *How The West Was Won*, with Toyan, was voiced about an hour before they left Jamaica. These were the sort of things we really liked, so on his second trip up, we got a lot of material off him."

As with Linval Thompson's productions, Junjo Lawes typically had The Roots Radics build their rhythms at Channel One, aided by a fresher crew of engineers who understood the needs of dancehall audiences. Those who shaped the sound included Lancelot 'Maxie' McKenzie, who cut material with The Revolutionaries from 1978; drummer Stanley 'Barnabas' Bryan, who worked on material for GG and others from 1977; and 'Crucial' Bunny Graham (aka Bunny Tom-Tom).[1]

Anthony 'Soljie' Hamilton, a former Jamaica Defence Force conscript who had worked on the Echo Vibrations sound system, was another to get his start at the studio as an engineer, later becoming a leading producer. He started hanging out at Channel One in the late 70s, making his way to the mixing desk by 1980. After building their basic rhythms with some of these engineers at Channel One, Lawes and Thompson would usually voice and mix their productions at King Tubby's, initially using Prince Jammy and later Scientist for the bulk of their creations.

Scientist, the teenage electronics wizard and apprentice amplifier repairman at Tubby's, otherwise known as Overton H. Brown, became part of Junjo Lawes's team one fateful day in 1979. His knowledge of electronics and innovative approach to dub subsequently made him the top remix engineer of the early 80s. He says he was born in 1960 and raised in Harbour View, close to Kingston's international airport. "I been living with my grandparents from days old – it was the thing to do back in them times. My grandfather was a policeman and he went into accounting. My dad, he was into electronics professionally, so I kind of picked it up from him. I was repairing televisions, building sound system amplifiers at 16. I would build one and test it with instruments and everything would read normal, but when I test it with one of the mixes from Tubby with that 'flying cymbal' and that crisp high-hat, the amplifiers go crazy. Every time you play reggae through this thing it start freaking out.

"That kind of interest me to meet Tubby, because he was doing all those sound effects. I had this friend who was doing this welding job for him, and he introduced me to Tubby. I buy a couple hard-to-get transformers that he would wind himself; it was a regular place to get hard-to-find parts. After Tubby saw what I could do, he had me there repairing amplifiers and televisions. Before I went to Tubby's I had a vision about building a recording studio and building a console. I was running jokes with Tubby about making consoles with moving, motorised faders back in the 70s – I envision the whole automated thing. When I started to talk about console with automation, they say: 'It must be a scientist.'"

○

Although Scientist was Tubby's electronics apprentice, he secretly wanted to try his hand at recording, and did his best to observe the techniques of resident engineers. "Jammy was the main engineer there and Pat Kelly used to engineer on and off," he recalls. "I was going in there just to look over somebody's shoulder, but the main thing was to get back inside to wind some transformers and fix something. I was telling Tubby I can go in there and do that thing [sound engineering], but it was like a joke, because he didn't have anybody my age doing that type of work."

Differing accounts of his engineering debut have been printed. Scientist himself says that smaller producers such as Errol 'Don' Mais, proprietor of the Greenwich Farm label Roots Tradition, had encouraged Tubby to give him a try at the mixing desk, but that it was Junjo who eventually gave the youth the go-ahead. "One day Junjo Lawes came there with Barrington Levy, waiting on Jammy. He get frustrated, it getting late, and he ask King Tubby to go and mix for him; he begging Tubby to do it, but the King tell

306

them: 'Send the kid in there – let him do it.' Everybody was reluctant because I was just a kid – I had no history. Junjo didn't want me to – he just do it because there was nobody else to work. I apply my electronic experience and powered up the console, get the mic to work, figured out how to string up the tape. He sang 'Collie Weed' and that song went to number one! I didn't do much electronics after that … [instead], it was most of Junjo's sessions: Barrington Levy, Johnny Osbourne."

Scientist's creative mixing was partly what brought Sammy Dread to the attention of British audiences; his second recording, 'African Girl', was issued as an extended 12-inch single by the Lovelinch label in England, with seamless editing and a particularly inspired dub. Dread was one of the first dancehall singers from Greenwich Farm to gain popularity in the late 70s; he names Linval Thompson and Sugar Minott as influences, but Michael Prophet's style, drawn from the techniques of Bob Andy and Dennis Brown, was his most obvious inspiration.

"I grow up in Kingston 13 with Michael Palmer, Ranking Joe, Ranking Trevor, Nicodeemus," he says. "In Greenwich Farm it was me, Rod Taylor, Michael Prophet, Philip Fraser, Sylvan White, Barrington Levy. I know Earl 'Chinna' Smith and Earl Zero. They used to play the guitar, and I was humming and they said: 'You going to sing one of these days.' I was a forklift driver, working at the Kingston wharf. Then Bertram Brown from Freedom Sounds, I come with this tune 'Reggae On The Move' for him, but that never release in Jamaica. Don Mais, he do this recording with me, 'African Girl', whe Leroy Smart do the back-up vocal. That 45 was a big hit for me in London, with Peter Ranking."

"Don Mais give me a try," notes Michael Prophet, "because he try to make himself be a producer with Sammy Dread and Peter Ranking." Michael has lived in London since the mid 80s. When he rolls up to a meeting in a silver Mercedes, wearing a crisp suit and lots of gold, it is evident that life is treating him well. Born Michael Haynes, he got his stage name by working with Yabby You, but says Don Mais was the first to produce him. "I did a few songs for Don Mais with Soul Syndicate even before I sing anything for Yabby You, but them tune never get no publicity." As with Sammy Dread's early shots, this material surfaced abroad on Lovelinch releases, after Prophet came to prominence with Yabby You.

Although Scientist became a leading light by shaping the material that Junjo Lawes and Don Mais were forging with the Radics and Soul Syndicate at King Tubby's, at the same time he made an important contribution by helping to rejuvenate Studio One in 1979–80. The Studio One renaissance

307

began partly as a result of the vinyl 'war' against Channel One, instigated by Sugar Minott; formidable hits followed from a loyal set of singers, including Minott, Freddy McGregor, Johnny Osbourne, and Willie Williams, plus deejay duo Michigan & Smiley. The upgraded musical texture came largely from session keyboardist Pablove Black and bassist Bagga Walker, both prominent members of the Twelve Tribes Of Israel organisation; with Scientist often at the mixing desk, their creations had intensified brightness, particularly in the treble spectrum.

"A few months after [the 'Collie Weed' session] I went and checked Studio One, because I wanted to learn how to do live recording," Scientist recalls. "Hanging out at Randy's corner, 'Idler's Rest', I got to know [singer] Peter Broggs. He was recording there and encouraged me to go. Mr Dodd is a type of a man who would give anybody the break, but you have to go through a screening process. Me, Sugar Minott, Michigan & Smiley, Freddy McGregor – all of us would wait outside. Mr Dodd would say: 'Jackson, check me tomorrow'; you come back the next day and go through a couple more days like that. By that time, he was up to 24 tracks. The engineer – I knew him as Bim-Bim – showed me the basics: this is this mic and this is the drum room, but I had an electronics background, so everything just came second nature to me.

"The first session I did there was Peter Broggs, then Michigan & Smiley's 'Nice Up The Dance', Willie Williams, some of the Johnny Osbourne, Sugar Minott, and we did a bunch of overdubs with Bagga Walker and Pablove Black. Dodd had the old rhythms on two-track. We would run those into the 24-track and he would have Bagga play over the bass lines and Freddy McGregor played a lot of those drum overdubs. I was at Studio One close to a year, on and off, because my main thing was to try and gain experience recording live music. I missed Tubby's environment because it had a mix of electronics, so I was kind of in between both of them, but Mr Dodd didn't feel too comfortable about that."

Sugar Minott's 'Oh Mr DC', which transformed The Tennors' rock steady classic 'Pressure & Slide' into a herb dealer's plea for mercy from the police, was one of the biggest hits of 1979. "You have people in Maxfield Park that live off herb business," Minott explained, "and when people go to the country to get herb in Jamaica, it's like you've gone to rob a bank, so your kids are waiting and fretting. The song came to me, like people just trying to live – can't you give us a chance? That time was a hard time for me and I had to sell the song for $50, 'cos I have two children, very young, and no food. Scientist was the engineer on that song. He'd just left Tubby's and came to Studio One, but Coxsone run him away: 'Tubby send you here to mash up me business, what kind of thing you doing?' Him used to do some experimenting and Coxsone couldn't understand it."

"After a time, Mr Dodd brought up this scenario that they send you down here to spy," Scientist confirms. "Mr Dodd figured that everybody wanted to steal the secret of his sound. Until now, he trusts no one. When I went down there I started to point out a lot of problems with the equipment, and how Mr Dodd wanted us to record, it didn't really sound right. Everybody was trained to record flat; it was taught that you EQ afterward, so I invented my own style where we recorded with EQ. The sound with Sugar Minott and Michigan & Smiley, you started to get a crispness to it, and Mr Dodd would go crazy! He thought we was trying to sabotage something. Bagga Walker and the rest of the musicians convinced Mr Dodd that them rather [have] that sound, so everybody started to do away with the flat recording."

Eventually, Scientist tired of repeated conflicts with Dodd and returned to Dromilly Avenue. "After Mr Dodd's paranoia, I start doing more stuff at Tubby's, because Tubby was more technically inclined. Mr Dodd was not, and when we make recommendations to him he always think we are trying to sabotage. I'm a kid, telling this big icon: 'This is outdated, and you need to calibrate the machines.' He don't want to hear that. It becomes like a waste of talent after a while, so I just continue working at Tubby's."

Lee Perry had pioneered live equalisation at the Black Ark, with instruments also subjected to heavy phasing and echo effects while they were being recorded. At Studio One, Scientist's application of live EQ brought an increased sense of high fidelity to Coxsone's tracks, with Freddy McGregor's overdubbed drumbeats, Syndrums, and cymbals given enhanced treble emphasis. The technique is particularly noticeable on tracks like 'Nice Up The Dance', a number-one chart hit by Michigan & Smiley that celebrated the culture of the dancehall on an updated 'Real Rock' rhythm; Willie Williams's apocalyptic 'Armagideon Time' also made use of a less-embellished cut of 'Real Rock' that left greater space for his subdued vocal.

In the corridor of an anonymous hotel on the outskirts of London, Williams recalls that his Studio One link dates to the rock steady period. "The artist that brought me to Studio One was Bob Andy. I live close to where he and Marcia Griffiths was living in Washington Gardens. We became friends and started checking each other out music-wise. On Sundays they would always go to Tyrone Evans's home, bang around with the piano and sing along."

Williams's debut session yielded 'Calling', issued on Studio One's *Party Time In Jamaica* album, plus an original called 'Prisoner Of Love' that was not released; the session also yielded The Gladiators' hit 'Hello Carol'. Williams was still attending school then, but music was always his primary focus. "Where I was born is not far from where Bob Marley come from. My dad was a carpenter, but passed away at an early age. I was seven when I came to town, about 1960, and ended up in Trench Town with my brother and his wife. At Trench Town Comprehensive, Sly Dunbar and myself were in the same class. I had a sound system at an early age called Triple Tone, with two brethren in Duhaney Park; that love for the music drive me to want to make my own songs to play on the set. The songs that I was singing, most people didn't want to record those songs, said they were too revolutionary, so I went into Harry J. about '69 and produced 'Prisoner Of Loneliness' on the Soul Sounds label, with Bobby Kalphat, Benbow, and Albert Griffiths playing guitar and singing."

After a few more inconsequential tunes, in the early 70s Williams began to produce other artists, including Delroy Wilson and a later incarnation of The Versatiles, reformed after Junior Byles and Louis Davis left the group.[2] After subsequently gaining important live experience in Toronto, Williams cut his most memorable work toward the end of the 70s. "I went to Canada about '74, met up with Jackie Mittoo and forge a friendship, and we start working together. I was the singer for his band, along with Lord Tanamo on hotel gigs. I get tired of that after a while, because I wanted to express my own thing: that is when I started going back to the studio with Lloyd Parks, Benbow, and Bobby Kalphat, do 'Messenger Man' and 'Unity'. We do the rhythm at Channel One and voice and mix at Tubby's. 'Messenger Man' became an album. The song was being played on a regular basis in New York, so Coxsone heard the song and wanted to start something again – this was '79. Jackie Mittoo and myself went back to Jamaica and started doing an album, which eventually became *Armagideon Time*."

Like Yabby You, who later became a close associate, Williams is a dread who worships Jesus Christ and does not recognise the divinity of Selassie. 'Armagideon Time', another song that captivated the punk audience, eventually covered by The Clash, is partly a depiction of the fulfilment of biblical prophecy.

The perpetually devout Freddy McGregor sought to emphasise the general unity at Brentford Road in this period, partly fostered by shared religious faith. "Myself, Sugar Minott, Johnny Osbourne, Jennifer Lara, we do most of the harmony tracks at Studio One since after Ken Boothe. We are responsible for about everything that goes on there, because we pretty much run the studio. We all sing harmonies together on each other's stuff. Bagga and Pablove, these were the musicians at the time and we are all very, very close, because we are all members of Twelve Tribes of Israel, so we were really locked in. We just hold a vibe together and share ideas."

McGregor's reputation had increased after touring with popular show bands Generation Gap and Soul Syndicate, but the struggle for recognition was long. "In 1972 I was living at Al Campbell's house on Delacree Lane: it's in the ghetto, and that's another experience for me. I was always a youth with Afro, my bell-foot pants and my soul comb, 'cos I wasn't in for badness – I was in for music. Being a ghetto, it was so tough as a country boy: you have no place in terms of getting by. I was depressed, because every song you release, you're hoping it's going to be the one, and it was never the one. Sometimes me think about getting another job, take up the newspaper, but I wasn't really qualified for any job, so it always revert back to the music. It was really frustrating, searching for the next hope, but don't want to go back to country. My goal was really to help my family.

"One evening I heard a horn blow outside. Horsemouth say: 'Me have some uptown boy, them have band, and ah you me come for, because you are my little grassroots ghetto singer.' Me jump in the van with him, and this is my audition with some uptown youths who are really university – that's a different scene for me again. Me do some Stylistics, 'Black Magic', [Billy Paul's] 'Me & Mrs Jones', Lou Rawls – anything within the top 40. My first salary was $13.50 a week. We play every place across Jamaica, uptown, downtown, midtown. We became the most famous band performing on nightclubs, office parties, school graduations. Singing in the dance band was creating a difference for me, 'cos I was becoming more versatile, singing soca, soul, calypso, you name it, but I still had to carve out a sound for myself, and that sound would only come through recording. I was always conscious of that."

Another skill he learned in Generation Gap was mastery of the drums. "One New Year's Eve, we were playing in Saint Elizabeth at a hotel called Treasure Beach. When the band took a break, Horsemouth took a boat with a fisherman to Savannah La Mar to get some smokes. That's how I got to play the drums. For about two months I had to play drums and sing and it turned out nicely, until the manager decided they needed me back out front, so we got another drummer."

After Generation Gap disbanded, Freddy fronted Soul Syndicate from 1975, finally achieving concerted success with a series of anti-establishment hits at Studio One; he says the shift of focus that helped facilitate his breakthrough was directly related to his membership of Twelve Tribes. "The whole of us start to see Rasta, read the Bible 'nuff, and it's purely them inspiration we nah see before, so the trend of my music start to move: 'Africa Here I Come', 'Bobby Babylon', 'Rastaman Camp', 'Wine Of Violence', 'cos the Bible me a read, and me start to get deeper into things."

In addition to singing harmony on Sugar Minott's material, Freddy McGregor added new drum parts as well, as Coxsone was keen to give his older rhythms a more contemporary sound. "I do loads of drum tracks at Studio One. Most of the Sugar Minott era I overdubbed, cause Mr Dodd was just getting into updating, and that became another earner for me. I would sing harmony every day, but there was always something else to do, so that Friday you would ensure yourself of a salary."

However, by the time he cut the atmospheric 'Rastaman Camp', most of his peers had moved on from Brentford Road. "Them time we have the studio all to weself, cause Sugar gone out to Channel One, Johnny Osbourne start move. I was the last one to leave Studio One."

Sugar Minott began crafting his own productions at Channel One in 1979, bartering studio time and getting musicians to lay rhythms for free. "Some guy give me $800 and I just beg my friends, the musicians, so they all chipped in. First songs I put out were all hits: 'Man Hungry', 'River Jordan'. Then we start producing and all the kids start following us. I had my van marked Black Roots maybe a month after leaving Studio One and I was dropping off records at Coxsone, trying to sell them. The first song I did was 'In The Resident' with Stepping King Miguel, a youth from the country who used to take us everywhere on his bike. Me carry it to Coxsone, but me never realise it was Coxsone's rhythm still.[3] I was trying to help Barry Brown, 'cos me and him was close, so we record 'Not So Lucky', and then Tristan Palmer, 'Spliff Tail' – all number-one songs, just out of the blue, from nowhere."

Freddy McGregor also began recording outside Studio One in 1979, at the instigation of Niney The Observer. "Niney come for me and say: 'Youth, your name big ah England; song there popular, so we have to do some other things, as Studio One hold you down.' Me really worried about it too, because Sugar had left and the Channel One sound clean, sound wicked, and me really have to take a deep breath and think about it seriously, in terms of leaving Mr Dodd. That was probably the most pressure I had gone through as a youth, not knowing whether that was the right move, but I wanted to take my chances, because I wanted it to happen for me any which way.

"We walked into Channel One and we whacked off all the rhythm tracks in one day, and it took me another two days to write all the songs. This was something we been doing at Studio One every day, so writing songs for a rhythm was like a joke to me and Johnny Osbourne – we could wrap up 20 songs in no time. That was how that album [*Mr McGregor*] came together, but I think the beauty with the album was that I used some of my Studio One experiences. It was the norm for most artists to just voice a rhythm track, but we always said some harmony can make it nice, some horns here and there.

"He promised me he would make me go to England, and I have so much respect for Niney from that day onward. I never realised those were people with such good heart until I actually get a chance to work with them. Bunny Lee too – I used to spend a lot of time with Bunny Lee and his family in Greenwich Farm. Those are people I have enough love, regard, and respect for. I like to look at every single aspect of my career as a blessing: everyone who has contributed in any way, I really look at it as a blessing."

McGregor also scored a substantial hit in 1979 with the self-produced 'Jogging', a song that benefited not only from his drumming skills but also from finely balanced harmonics and skilled musical arrangement. It was created with former members of Generation Gap, including bassist Howard 'Spread' Bedasse, keyboardist Mikey Hewlitt, and guitarist Dalton Browne, who remains his bandleader today. McGregor also produced Judy Mowatt's *Black Woman* album, as he was romantically involved with her at this time. "I was living at Bull Bay, Saint Thomas, out by sister Judy's house, and myself and Dave Gad, our fitness guru, we used to go down to the beach every morning and run, swim, exercise, then go to sister Judy's house, get on the piano. We were getting the *Black Woman* album together, so we spent lots of nights out there, so we could be at the beach early morning, working out. After running one morning, it's just a concept: we're jogging on the sands in a Babylon, feeling fit fi conquer creation, crisp track shoes and ah big bobby socks – that's what people wear when them ah jog. Every morning we used to see people run: people have on them track shoes and run at Mona Reservoir, so seeing people getting into physical fitness, I thought it was a good idea to create a song like this."

The song ultimately benefited from Island's overseas distribution. "The first time I produced a track was 'Jogging', thanks to Bob Marley for allowing me the opportunity to use his studio. Chris Blackwell walked into the studio that day, asked me if I am interested to go to Nassau to do a remix of a track, 'Jagged'. He licensed that track from me in 1980 and released it with a Michigan & Smiley on the other side – has it on a few compilations too. That was the beginning of real production for me."

Johnny Osbourne was happy to be accepted at Studio One after a decade of living abroad. "Studio One was where I wanted to be all the time, but I didn't get a chance to do anything before 1979. I was singing in Canada with a group called Ishan People – we did two albums, produced by David Clayton-Thomas from Blood Sweat & Tears, with a Canadian company called GRT.[4] But I wasn't a solo artist – my name wasn't upfront – so I decide to build back my name. When I came back to Jamaica, 1979–80, I start singing for Studio One. The first song was 'Water More Than Flour', and I did this album, *Truths And Rights*."

The album is one of Studio One's most outstanding recordings. Its emotionally charged vocals are delivered with great depth of feeling, yet Johnny insists his lyrics were spontaneous. "Most of these songs just come in my mind and I sing them – I don't even write them up. Sometimes I might have to sing a song today and I don't know what I'm going to sing about, but by the time I reach the studio a song just come right in me. These are not songs that I sit and write. It's more like an inspiration."

Many of these songs addressed topical social issues and spiritual matters. 'Forgive Them', a Studio One single delivered in searing falsetto, asked the Almighty to forgive those engaged in political violence. "That time I used to love to sing Earth Wind & Fire, The Delfonics, The Temptations, The Miracles, and The Stylistics, so I had to learn that sort of falsetto. I went back to Jamaica ten years after I left and I saw that politics get to be a bigger thing, the order of the day. People are killing each other who grew up together, taking different sides like they didn't know each other, so I'm saying: 'Forgive them, they know not what they do.'"

In addition to providing backing vocals on Studio One material, Osbourne played harmonica on notable tracks, including the extended mix of 'Mr DC'. He had previously played harmonica on Black Uhuru's 'Love Crisis', as he was friendly with Prince Jammy in Canada; the pair would later create the strong *Folly Ranking* album after Osbourne left Studio One in late 1980. "When I come back to Jamaica, I *had* to be with Jammy, so we just started making some music."

The departure of Sugar, Freddy, and Johnny from Dodd's camp made way for the arrival of Earl 'Sixteen' Daley, a mellifluous tenor that had already cut much inspired material. "I started out at Waltham Park Road, where I grew up on the street corner, hanging out at night," he says with a grin. "At the age of 13 I started getting into The Chi-Lites and James Brown. Dennis Brown was a role model for us."

After singing in various talent contests, he formed The Flaming Phonics with some school friends. "Sundays was audition day at Treasure Isle; Duke liked one of the songs. We tried to start recording and Duke started letting off gunshots – we didn't get round to voicing it, because we didn't want to go back. With Herman Chin-Loy we did 'Hey Baby', but Jamaica wasn't really ready for a Four Tops kind of thing – they were into U Roy and King Stitt."

When the group split, Earl Sixteen went solo. "The first solo recording that I did was for Phonso [Alphonso Bailey]; his label is Globe International. I had this schoolmate, Winston MacAnuff – he wrote 'Malcolm X'. He asked me to follow him into the studio one day, me and Franklyn Waul, 'Bubbler'. Winston had already laid some tracks at Joe Gibbs's, so we did 'Malcolm X' first there – the first song that Franklyn actually recorded. A couple months afterward, we didn't hear it come out, so we went to Derrick Harriott and did [a version of] it for him as well with a couple of other songs. When Derrick went to press 'Malcolm X', we find out that Joe Gibbs was actually pressing 'Malcolm X' on a white label for export, so it kind of cramped our thing."

Around the same time, in 1975, Earl replaced Tinga Stewart as lead singer in the Boris Gardiner Happening. "It was really strenuous. You had to do all the current songs in the charts – calypso, soul, reggae – because a road band is like cabaret. Boris was a proper musician ... I was really impressed with him and I kind of fell in love with the whole scene. Me, Boris Gardiner, and Errol Walker was the three main singers. Keith Sterling was playing keyboards, we had Willie Lindo on guitar, Paul Douglas on drums. I was so thrilled being involved – these guys were stalwart musicians – but I started getting influenced into Rastafarianism, started growing my locks, and Boris fired me. They had a big nurses' ball at the Oceana Hotel and Boris goes: 'You have to trim your hair, you have to be clean for this gig.' I just went up there with my stretch-foot trousers and my Clarke's shoes, looking good with my tam on my head and a couple of locks hanging out. Everybody was dressed up in long floral gowns as it was a proper, formal ball, and I was in my roughneck pants. After that gig, Boris went: 'I'm sorry, you have to go. We probably won't get this job again.' Then I started working for Scratch."

Following a handful of sides for Lee Scratch Perry, including the heartbroken 'Cheating' and declaratory 'Freedom', Earl Sixteen became more spiritually oriented, which drew him toward Augustus Pablo. "After working with Perry I got really into smoking the raw weed, going really *ital*.[5] That's when I starting hanging out with Pablo, 'cos Pablo was really into the ital stuff. He was busy working with Hugh Mundell, Delroy Williams, Norris

315

Reid, Tetrack, so I had to wait. I've only done two songs for Augustus Pablo, 'Changing World', and 'The Rastaman' – we did it for a guy called Maxwell Lynch. I met Pablo through Hugh Mundell, but everything that I did was through Boris. Boris Gardiner's really a great person. Mundell and all these guys lived around him and there was all these producers coming up to get him to do sessions, because he was one of the best. Apart from Lloyd Parks, Boris could write music, so he was essential."

Earl Sixteen's debut album, the hastily voiced *Shining Star*, was produced by Earl Morgan of The Heptones. "I met Heptones through Perry at the studio. He got some rhythms which he'd acquired from Lloyd Parks and a couple people, and he was coming to England and said: 'If we do a couple songs, we could try to get a deal for you and make some money.'"

Sixteen's second set, the Mikey Dread production *Reggae Sounds*, also drew mixed results. "I got involved with Mikey about 1980 when I used to hang out at Aquarius. He put out a couple singles in Jamaica which didn't really come out too good, because they weren't really ready for Mikey Dread's stuff. He was working at Tubby's, trying to update it, using soul with a lot of guitars. It wasn't really ready for Jamaica, but it was working in England."

A chain of events eventually led to Studio One. "I started working between Pablo and Yabby You, because I was doing backing vocals for Yabby. I wanted to do some tunes for Junjo, because Junjo was kicking in '82, '83 – he was really stinging. I used to go to Channel One, even ended up doing a few songs for Joe-Joe Hoo-Kim. I didn't really do any songs for Junjo, but I was there with him. Then Linval Thompson came along and I did a few songs for Linval. After that, I thought: I'm going to go and do some work with Studio One, because I got to find out that all the tracks that Channel One do was Studio One's tracks; they made them over, so I don't think I should really work on a copy when I can work on the actual stuff."

His most significant Jamaican work was thus recorded at Studio One. "Donald Hossack, my schoolmate from long time, wrote a song for me and goes: 'Let's go down to Coxsone one Sunday and see if he would be interested in it.' We waited around a couple of Sundays, until Coxsone noticed us sitting under the tree. I reach about three verses and he goes: 'Where's the chorus in the song? You haven't got a punch line. You have to rewrite that song, you're wasting my time … I'll tell you what, I like your voice,' and he gave me about ten seven-inches. 'What you should do, listen to these versions and write some songs, because you could sing on the rhythm.' I practised up: 'Fight It To The Top' [aka 'Heptones Gonna Fight'] was one of the famous rhythms in Jamaica, but nobody really had any other covers of it at the time."

The end result was 'Love Is A Feeling', a song written by Calaman Scott, who actually sang lead on the original version, which had been recorded earlier at Harry J. with The Wailers, featuring Earl Sixteen and Richie MacDonald on backing vocals. Unfortunately, this original was never released, due to conflict between Scott and MacDonald, but rather than let a great work go to waste, Sixteen decided to voice it himself at Studio One, yielding another bestselling anthem. "Coxsone goes: 'Earl, I've never told anybody this, but that song "Love Is A Feeling", I pressed it till my hands were weak. I run out of labels trying to press that tune.'" Also highly popular on sound systems was 'No Mash Up The Dance', voiced on the 'Peanut Vendor' rhythm, itself based on the Cuban hit 'El Manisero'. Both hits helped maintain Coxsone's profile in the early 80s.

On the international scene, Island continued to issue inspired reggae. A deal with King Sounds brought Grove Music material produced by Yabby You to Island, distributed by EMI in 1979–80, including Tony Tuff's self-titled debut LP, Yabby's own *Jah Jah Way*, and, best of all, Michael Prophet's *Serious Reasoning*. "Yabby You is in a class by himself," Prophet says. "That Ras there a very strong Ras, and you have to be strong to deal with man like Yabby You: headstrong, rootically strong, biblically strong, physically strong. When I meet up with Yabby You, it's like all hell break loose. It was actually three of us: we grew up together and were going to deal with a group, but when Yabby You hear my voice he know I don't need no backing. I usually at all of the studios in Jamaica, seeing if I can meet a producer, and I get a lot of let down. One day I was coming from Sonic Sounds and, passing Channel One, I see Zebby – he control Channel One gate – and Zebby tell me: 'Yabby You ah work with Wayne Wade, Patrick Andy, and Alric Forbes.' Yabby You have 'nuff music out there. 'Conquering Lion' ah wicked sound; his bass line is just different from any other producer's, so me go in there and confront him.

"The first lyrics that I ever write was 'Praise You Jah Jah'. He say: 'Yeah, you have any more?' and me just continue singing. Him say I must pass by him yard up Waltham Park Road and we start to do rehearsals. The first time we go to the studio we voice 'Fight It To The Top', but to me, 'Praise You Jah Jah' is bigger, because it's a self-contained tune. It's from the belly, the heart, the earth." The album's other outstanding tracks include 'Love & Unity' (aka 'Mash Down Rome') and 'Turn Me Loose', the latter also notable for appearing on the soundtrack of the film *Babylon*, a London sound system drama starring Aswad's Brinsley Forde.

Similarly, The Wailing Souls' *Wild Suspense*, released by Island in 1979, brought the group to wider overseas audiences. After their success at Channel One, the quartet sought greater independence by forming the Massive label, scoring further self-produced hits with The Revolutionaries. "We went to collect some funds off of a previous song, but feel we weren't dealt with justifiable," says Garth Dennis, "so we decide to get some studio time for the money, and we produced 'Bredda Gravalicious'."

"The big man keep getting bigger, the poor man keep getting poorer," says Bread. "Him have everything and him still want more, so that is 'Bredda Gravalicious'. We did that for ourselves, then two guys from Island offered us a proposition, and that was *Wild Suspense*. Some of the horns was done in Jamaica, with Dean Fraser, and another set of the horns was done in England with Rico Rodriguez, Vin Gordon, Bobby Ellis." The overdubbed horns gave the album a strong contrast to the original Massive single releases. Its rhythmic cohesion came courtesy of Sly Dunbar, who developed a number of notable new beats around 1978: the introduction of 'Bredda Gravalicious', for instance, had an augmented military drumroll known as 'Sly Tackle', whilst the drumming of 'Row Fisherman' imitated a dribbling basketball.

The extended hit singles 'Old Broom' and 'Sugar Plum Plum', issued by Island in the UK in 1980, were hits produced by Sly & Robbie, but Pipe recalls the mixed reaction to such ballads. "'Sugar Plum Plum' was number-one all over, but when I write love songs, people say Wailing Souls gone soft, that's why I always write about protesting. With the name Wailing Souls, we were thinking about lost souls crying out in the wilderness, so those kinds of music make people recognise Wailing Souls, but whenever we do a love song, it build a boom too." A planned album, produced by Sly & Robbie, was unfortunately left unfinished after disputes arose.

Pablo Moses also had forward-facing roots material issued by Island in this period. Moses's second album, the 1980 set *A Song*, was as contemplative as his debut. *Pave The Way*, released the following year, had a futuristic sound built on metallic bass and drum from Val Douglas and Mikey Boo, spiced by synthesizer licks from Peter Ashbourne. "'A Song' itself was partially a vision, a dream," says Moses of the title track. "The rest I put together in a yard, under this pear tree; I put a bench underneath it and I would sit there and practise, and people from the street couldn't see me. It was like a little hideout, so I would smoke my herb round there. That corner gave me three albums: *Revolutionary Dream*, *A Song*, and *Pave The Way*. *Revolutionary Dream* was more aggressive, pretty, and *A Song* was more of a spiritual connection within a cultural way. *Pave The Way* was a combination of both, with aggression and a spiritual, cultural connection. I try to name each album making a statement along the way, like *Revolutionary Dream*: 'I'm a revolutionary dream that came'; in order to deal with the revolution, I bring *A Song* with many songs; in order to get through the revolution, you have to *Pave The Way*." Later arguments between Island and Geoffrey Chung led to Pablo Moses being dropped by the label, however, despite the critical acclaim awarded *A Song* and *Pave The Way*.

Meanwhile, The Roots Radics were gaining a higher profile abroad. Junjo's agreement with Greensleeves saw his releases widely distributed in the UK and USA (the latter via folk label Shanachie), introducing the Radics and the evolving Jamaican dancehall style to a whole new audience from 1980. Certain elements of the Roots Radics sound remained constant from the band's inception: their material was always constructed to make the most of Flabba's meaty bass lines and Bingy Bunny's reliable rhythm guitar. Early on, percussionist Christopher 'Sky Juice' Blake helped form a readily identifiable sound through accentuated wood-block and cow-bell beats, in contrast to Sticky's preference for graters and shakers and Skully's reliance on the conga drum and tambourine. Occasional horns from saxophonist Dean Fraser, trombonist Ronald 'Nambo' Robinson, and trumpeter Chico Chin helped build a fuller sound; the three were taught their craft by Babe O'Brian of the National Volunteers' Youth Organization, and were an integral part of Lloyd Parks's We The People band at Joe Gibbs's studio. Once The Roots Radics' line-up solidified in the early 80s, Style Scott's tight drumming – often on Syndrums – helped propel the sound forward, given a modern complement by Sowell's effects-laden guitar and offset by Steelie's trilling organ and piano (greatly inspired by Jackie Mittoo's style at Studio One).

Sugar Minott was among the first to make use of this crew on 'Hard Time Pressure', a blistering re-cut of Hopeton Lewis's 'Sounds And Pressure': "'Hard Time Pressure' was just growing up in Maxfield Park: I live amongst people who used to rob banks and betting shops just to feed people, not because they want to rob. I used to run from police every day of my life, duck from gunshot every day of my life, so these were the things coming out in the music. I record that at Channel One, the first time that Style Rotterdam played drums. Jammy mixed it."

Mikey Dread, who worked solidly with the Radics from 1980, was one of the first to showcase Steelie's piano skills on an instrumental cut of 'Jumping Master' that proved highly influential on the ruling style of the day. "Me built 'nuff of me original t'ing with Sly, Horsemouth, Bagga Walker, 'nuff Studio One musicians, and later on me just work with the Radics, because me and Style were very close friends, as well as me and Sowell. That time those guys want recognition, because Sly & Robbie was the only 'name' people. Nobody know Flabba Holt nor Style, but they had played on 'Just Like A Sea', and I asked the producer who the musicians were, and him introduce me to them man there. Them guys would come to my house and hear the songs we wanted to make, and we were waiting on the right time; one night we go to a dance and we say: 'We going to lick some tunes right now.' Sly had this 'Drunken Master', and me say me going to do something wickeder than that, and me just go inna the studio and try something, and it just magic, it just wicked. Me say that one there ah the 'Jumping Master', and me voice it like that. Me run into Bunny Wailer at the mastering lab and him say: 'Who play them rhythm there?' The next thing me know, it's 'Rock And Groove' – Bunny gone jump 'pon the same vibes."

Like Dread's 'Jumping Master' and 'Break Down The Walls', Sowell Radics's 'All Night Jammin' also surfaced on the UK branch of DATC, distributed in 1981 by independent punk company Rough Trade and boosted by airplay on the Northwest London sound system Jah Observer. "Sugar Minott was supposed to help him get it out, but Sugar never do it," Dread explained. "So me just do it and make sure Sowell have some money."

Sowell left The Roots Radics shortly after, opting to stay in England after the band's first tour with Gregory Isaacs, whom they backed on a series of exceptionally successful early-80s LPs, including *The Lonely Lover*, *Night Nurse*, and *Out Deh!*. He was replaced by Dwight Pinkney of Zap Pow, whose lead licks gave subsequent material a more aggressive edge. "We went to England two times with Gregory Isaacs," Flabba explains. "The first time, in 1981, we bring Sowell for some show at the Rainbow; we leave him there because he say him not ready to go home. We used to rehearse up by Zinc Fence at Ripon Road, and Dwight come in and say: 'You want a lead guitarist.'"

As with much early dancehall work, Junjo's Radics-backed material was a mixture of love songs and protest. Junjo was the next to make material of consequence with Michael Prophet after the singer broke away from Yabby You; although 'Gunman' was their biggest collaboration, 'Here Comes The Bride' was also highly popular. "After leaving Yabby You, I start to jump around, because you have to eat food as artists," Prophet explains. "I do tunes for Niney, Sugar Minott, and Winston Riley, and I produce myself as well, me and a next guy [Denzel Bowford], with [Minnie Ripperton's] 'Loving You'. Through Junjo is a ghetto man – the ghetto king – Junjo just started producing, so he draw for me: 'Hold On To What You Got' was the first tune, and then me do 'Here Comes The Bride'. 'Gunman' is a thing whe really happen to me – they robbed me, and that's why 'Gunman' never die, because it's a history song."

Similarly, younger singers like Little John and Barry Brown, taken in from Sugar Minott's Youth Promotion concern, mixed romance with tales of 'sufferation'; some of Johnny Osbourne's biggest hits were songs of failed romance, such as 'Ice Cream Love' in 1981 and 'Yo Yo' the following year, but he was also cutting material that reflected the hard realities of ghetto life. "Sometimes you're recording for a producer and maybe he's channelling his music for a particular area," Osbourne notes, "trying to make songs that suit where he thinks his market is. He's going to send these songs to some company in England, and England always love a lover's tune, so 'Ice Cream Love' was the first song I made for Junjo, hoping that he wanted a direct lover's song for the winter."

Junjo also coaxed the best from Yellowman (aka Winston Foster), the phenomenally successful albino deejay, and Eek A Mouse (aka Ripton Hilton), an inordinately tall man who developed an individual take on the sing-jay style by interjecting scat-vocal nonsense between verses. Greensleeves became the hot label for reggae in the early 80s, and Junjo their top producer. The label also brought the mixing skill of Scientist the broader attention it deserved.

Scientist took dub into a whole other dimension. He had a way of isolating Flabba's Holt's bass, as heard on albums such as *Scientist Meets The Roots Radics*, and he also made use of the test-tone in a highly creative manner, as heard on *Scientist Meets The Space Invaders*. "If you watch *Voyage To The Bottom Of The Sea*, you hear that kind of a test-tone, and you hear a echo behind it," Scientist explains. "That's where I got that from." *Scientist Rids The World Of The Evil Curse Of The Vampires*, supposedly mixed at Midnight one Friday the 13th in 1981, not only had plenty of EQ manipulation, ghostly echoes of drumbeats, and squealing tape-winding effects, but was also given a liberal dose of shrieking zombie sounds.

On the wonderful series of dub LPs he mixed for Junjo, Linval Thompson, Roy Cousins, Al Campbell, Mikey Dread, deejay-turned-producer Jah Thomas, Blacka Morwell, and others, Scientist created what many believe are the last true 'classical' dub albums cut in Jamaica. Most of them made use of The Roots Radics. "I was doing a lot of unorthodox things," he recalls. "Things that a lot of people didn't approve of. Junjo had gotten lucky with me, so he allowed me to explore whatever's in my head. I did improve the sound in Tubby's studio and I started to do a lot of stuff Tubby didn't even do on his own console. Then everybody started to ride the bandwagon. Bunny Lee used to record at Channel One and come to Tubby's to mix, and I did quite a few Pablo tracks with Hugh Mundell. I got very close with his family; the whole neighbourhood thought I was Tubby's son. Tubby had given me my own set of keys to open and close the studio and he would barely come around himself. I was the person running the whole business."

Although Scientist continued to mix at Tubby's as late as 1983, by 1981 he was engineering live recordings at Channel One – despite a familiar reluctance to employ him. "I wanted to get experience in live sessions, because Tubby's was only a four-track place to do voice-overs. The same thing followed me everywhere: when I went to Channel One they thought I was a spy for Tubby's, because a little after I went there, Tubby started building his 24-track. I could barely get a session; you had Soljie, Bunny Tom-Tom, and Barnabas. Ernest Hoo-Kim was running the studio. Joe-Joe was in New York, and he wanted that sound for himself, so Joe-Joe would come down and he was pretty much the only one using me. I start engineering Yellowman [the *Mad Over Me* LP] and all that stuff that Joe-Joe produced. I tightened up things at Channel One. I was the one who pioneered that type of a drum-and-bass sound down there with Viceroys [the *We Must Unite* LP] and Michigan & Smiley, the 'Diseases' rhythm. I did some Gladiators down there, and Don Carlos, too."

Up in New York, Joseph Hoo-Kim opened the Hit Bound manufacturing plant in Long Island City in 1982; his J&L record shop closed the following year. When in Jamaica, he continued to shape the sound at Channel One. "When Scientist mix down, we begin to re-echo the tapes," Hoo-Kim explains. "After he mix, we run the four tape machines, echoing right along with the master tape." The technique can be heard on albums such as *Showdown Volume 3*, featuring Don Carlos and The Gladiators.

Soljie Hamilton helped keep Channel One material hot in the dancehall. After mixing an early dub album for Sly & Robbie, he instigated what was easily Sammy Dread's biggest hit, the dancehall anthem 'M16' (aka 'Bushmaster'). "'M16' wasn't a tune that really voice for a record," the singer reveals. "It was a dub plate: Soljie come to me one day in the studio and said: 'I'm going to Oracabessa, a dancehall four-sound clash.' He tell me he want a tune to go and kill some sound in the dance. He was playing a lot of rhythm, but when I hear the rhythm named 'Scandal', I was thinking nobody never sing on that rhythm before – the only man who was on that was U Roy. When Soljie run the rhythm, I say: 'Bad boy ah fire M16, policeman ah fire AK47 …' That's how 'M16' really come."

'M16' related the frightening array of firearms displayed on Kingston's streets; 'Roadblock', his other big hit for Channel One, drew on Marley's description of being stopped for herb. "When police and soldier blocking the place and you can't come out, curfew, Bob Marley did a tune named 'Three O'clock Roadblock'. I say I could go around this tune, because this is what's going on, so I just said: 'They call me Sammy Dreadlocks, and me no want fi run up in a roadblock.' And it was a number-one tune." The eventual *Roadblock* album, issued in 1982, had a forceful dancehall-style Soljie mix that emphasised the drums and bass.

With the grassroots producers of Greenwich Farm, Waterhouse, and Three Mile doing their best to usurp the popularity of Joe Gibbs and Channel One, more deejays began recording at Studio One as part of a general trend, making way for new styles and youthful talent. Increasingly, deejays came to wield more important roles in determining the fashion of the moment.

The rough edges of Tappa Zukie's dancehall-oriented early work held some of the first portents of a significant shift in the dominant deejay style. As the 70s gave way to the 80s, such stylistic shifts were becoming more dramatically pronounced through the emergence of a younger set of dancehall performers that included Welton Irie, Prince Mohammed, and Lui Lepke. Lone Ranger was among those making the biggest impact. Born Anthony Waldron in 1958, he lived in Whitfield Town until he was five, when he joined his parents in Tottenham, North London, where his mother worked as a nurse. He returned to Jamaica in 1971 and attended the Vauxhall Drama School, after which he became heavily involved in various Kingston sound systems. "You have Merry Soul first, and Yard Sound," Ranger explains. "Then I step up to Soul Express in Franklyn Town, and from that, I went to Soul To Soul, a big uptown sound. Being on that sound, I was more in the limelight than down the ghetto."

Through chatting on the mic at sound system events, Ranger voiced his first records as part of a harmony group called The I-fenders, formed with future promoter Chester Synmoie and another friend. "The first song I sung was 'Anne Marie', we voice it at Treasure Isle. But the deejay thing was stronger, so about '77 I was doing one and two deejay tunes." His style developed through a constant exposure to sound system events: "Going to school, my favourite deejays were U Roy, Jah Youth, Jazzbo. When I get my lunch money from my mum, instead of going to buy lunch, we go downtown and buy records, so the latest records hide in my school bag. With deejay lyrics, I was very well adapted. I play the sound, hold the mic and I can deejay 12 different records straight. Them say it sound good, so me take it serious."

His big breakthrough came in 1979, with a song about a vampire portrayed in a popular television series. "I was at my peak with Soul To Soul, and I did a tune named 'Barnabas Collins' – I grow up in England and used to watch *Dark Shadows*, so me just write something off of it. It was my first international hit: that tune gave me a tour throughout Europe two times as within the space of one month, they request me back again. Then I went back into the studio and did another number-one tune named 'Love Bump'."

'Love Bump' is a typical example of Lone Ranger's dancehall-oriented style; to keep the momentum flowing, he spices things up with exclamations such as "ribbit" and "oink" as though imitating frogs or pigs. The style would be adapted by other deejays, most notably by Yellowman, perhaps the most successful deejay of all time; it was specifically the use of such exclamations and other nonsense words that contributed to his early rise on hits like 'Mad Over Me', 'Jack Sprat', and 'Zungguzungguguzungguezeng'.

A series of further hits resulted from Lone Ranger's fertile association with Studio One; most of the material was cut before 'Love Bump', but Dodd was slow to issue it. "Me have a friend named Tony Walcott, a good friend of Coxsone who have a whole heap of dub plates. Every Sunday him come from church and put on this rhythm ['Heavenless'] and tell me fi deejay. One Sunday he told me we have to meet somebody, and that person happens to be Mr Dodd. We went up to Studio One and voice tunes like 'Three Mile Skank' and 'Answer Me Question', then we do the *Other Side Of Dub* album and *Badda Dan Dem.*" The latter is more representative of Ranger's talent, with outstanding examples including 'Automatic', relating the tale of Garvey's betrayal over Johnny Osbourne's magnificent 'Truth And Rights', and the boastful 'Badda Dan Dem', cut on the 'Shank I Sheck' rhythm.

While Lone Ranger's style was increasingly being adapted by upcoming dancehall deejays, after moving to the popular Virgo sound, he maintained his top position by a further string of hits for other producers, beginning with the Jamaican chart smash 'Rosemarie', a loose adaptation of Ray

Charles's 'Girl Next Door' cut for Winston Riley. "Back in them days, there was a stiff competition," he explains. "You had a lot of deejays around, like General Echo, Michigan & Smiley, and Eek A Mouse, and each one was in the chart, so I do 'Rosemarie' for Techniques. Then I was with Channel One with 'The Big Fight', a tune by me and Welton Irie, then we did 'Johnny Too Bad' and 'Loving Arms', and all these tunes went into the chart. A couple other tunes from Coxsone start to come out, like 'Strictly Rub A Dub', so I had one tune at number one, one at number two, one at number seven, about five tunes in the charts. That's when I did a show in the States at Madison Square Gardens."

That Lone Ranger would appear at such a prestigious venue showed that dancehall was set to run things in the early 80s, as the international roots fervour began to wane. When major record labels ceased to promote reggae abroad, Jamaican musicians and producers became somewhat less fixated with the outside world and the music entered another introspective phase.

12
UNDER MI SLENG TENG

Bringing dancehall to the brink of digital

"You have to go with the time if you want to eat food. If you want to earn a living from the music, you have to do whatever is going on today. In the early 70s we used to do live music. Then we just want to experiment, so we did something with 'Sleng Teng' and it changed the whole scene ... 'Sleng Teng' was the big hit that made everybody switch over." – PRINCE JAMMY

"Reggae music is the only music in the world that every nation relates to. If them don't understand the lyrics, at least the rhythm gets to their mind, their heart – it penetrates." – COCOA TEA

At the start of the 80s, the emerging dancehall style gave Jamaican music a bold new focus. As dancehall rapidly captivated the island, a host of new stars began to appear. The more versatile roots artists adapted. Although the form was largely about fresh blood, a number of veterans regained significant glory by rolling with the changes, even if such transitions were not always smooth.

For instance, Junjo successfully rejuvenated The Wailing Souls when 'Firehouse Rock' was a huge hit on both sides of the Atlantic in 1981, but Bread says the group was initially reluctant to work with him. "Them time Junjo just come, and most of the product wasn't all that professional. We say: 'You put ten man on one track, we no deal with that – ah creativity we deal with.' We had an association with Greensleeves, which is one reason why we even did things with Junjo. We said: 'If anything, Junjo can't play any tricks 'pon we,' and it work out to be one of the best associations we ever have with a producer. Junjo was the first producer we could check any time, night or day. He has good ideas and would make good recommendations. We ended up doing five albums together."

326

John Holt also benefited from an association: 'Sweetie Come Brush Me' was a big hit in 1982, and 'Police In Helicopter', which described the drastic anti-ganja measures enacted by Prime Minister Edward Seaga in conjunction with US President Ronald Reagan's War on Drugs, was an international smash in 1983. That same year, Junjo established the Volcano sound system at his base in Myrie Avenue, a busy patch of the ghetto near Three Mile, which kept Junjo and The Roots Radics at the height of popularity.

"Music started to pour in, but Junjo was our main key man," recalls Chris Cracknell. "Junjo was a street man, a ghetto man, and he went to all the dances. He was very instrumental to how a lot of the rhythms sounded; he'd hear somebody in the dance chatting their lyric, go and tell that guy: 'I need you at the studio, I need that lyric.' He wanted his tracks to work in the dance, 'cos if they worked in the dance then they were going to work anywhere. We were coming out of roots and culture and I suppose there was artists that didn't want anything serious, they just wanted a bit of fun, just wanted to nice up the dance, so we got all those new artists. And because of Junjo's success, everybody wanted to voice for him. He was at Channel One all the time, and when I went down there in 1982, the whole studio control room was full of people, and loads of people outside wanted to get in on the session. It was just very vibrant."

The vibrancy was evident in fresh material from Junjo's sound-system discoveries, including the earliest recording by Josey Wales, one of the most stylistic toasters of the period. "That youth was a brilliant youth," says Josey of Junjo. "I don't know about his educational background, and he wasn't a person who went to any music school either, but he had a good ear and could put things together to make it work. Junjo built Yellowman and revived John Holt; the truth is, he made a great contribution."

In 1980, after Ranking Joe left Sturgav to return to Ray Symbolic, Charlie Chaplin's status increased on Sturgav, but the 'outlaw' Josey Wales became the real star. Known for his involvement in a street gang affiliated with the JLP, the 'Colonel,' as he is also known, had undeniable street credentials, even taking seven bullets in a politically motivated shooting in 1977. "I used to admire U Roy and I used to admire Claudie Massop, a gangster," he explains, sipping rum at a bar on Waltham Park Road. "I wanted to be like him, 'cos I like his style of gangsterism, badness and leadership, but people start liking me in the music, and I figure to be good is better than to be bad."

He was born Joseph Sterling in 1959 in rural St Mary, but moved to the capital in his teens, just as Jamaican entered a terribly fractious period. "Most of my life is between Kingston 11, 12, and 13, from right here at Waltham Park Road to Tower Hill, Cockburn Pen, Lizard Town. In those days, things were not as fruitful as it is now by ways of finance, so life wasn't all about what you have, it was about how you live and how you enjoy your life; the crime rate wasn't this high, but the politicians mash up Jamaica with their guns and hand-outs, so people lose the sense of self-reliance. Back then, the PNP and Labourite used to link together in unity, and when election comes around, we just say: 'Your people lost, OK, let's go have a drink.'

"It start differ once they start introducing the guns, about 1973. Then '76 election becomes a violent one, then '79–'80 was the most violent of all. I was shot in that lane in 1977, took seven shots through politics – it was the budding stage of the political violence, so people start segregating, branding and labelling each other. But music was Jamaica's antidote from poverty and hunger. All you need is a little plate of food, some music, and you all right, and the dances were places where respect was shown."

Between the elections of 1976 and 1980, Josey grappled with the allure of 'gangsterism', a way of life for many disenfranchised youth with no other viable means of employment, but his microphone prowess eventually pointed him elsewhere, due partly to U Roy's influence. Yet the deejay insists his path to music was unplanned: had the public not supported him, he might have remained ensconced in gang warfare.

"Most times a Jamaican artist will tell you: 'My mum used to say I could sing from I was six.' But that maybe only happened to three artists out of 500. The other 497 didn't have a clue that they were going to be who they are today. It was something that comes on spontaneous, because music was the only alternative to take us away from poverty. I used to admire U Roy on King Tubby's sound; King Tubby's was the rub-a-dub sound and U Roy's style was more like a sing-jay within that time, the melody and the flow was like riding like a wave. In those days you have one turntable and U Roy used to select and deejay; he had a general selector, but certain dub plates, he'd have them under his arm and then he'd introduce the song – not like today where you hear curse words. It was like: 'The musical disc I'm about to flick is from the man called Mr Alton Ellis, so don't be no rum chemist, this is from the musical specialist.' U Roy is the daddy of all deejays from that time, so I used to want to be like him. Then Claudie Massop was a guy like me, and when I grow a likkle beard, I start to look like him, but people start liking me in the music, and although I have been through a lot of things that could make me look the other way, I chose not to. You used to have a little sound around the corner named Roots Unlimited, people who have their little Friday night discos, but because I am a neighbourhood youth, I always go there and try to be a U Roy.

"I was about 17, because I was mature to the level of being involved in little gang differences, but I was always a respectable gangster with mannerisms and principles. We used to have little confrontations in those days – ratchet knife was the order of the day, and lot of little things transpired which I don't wish to talk about, because those are bad and ugly days. But as the music start to take a hold of me, the badness kind of differ, and the love start pouring out more. This sound was a little disco and King Sturgav was a major disco, so I was in Tower Hill playing one night and U Roy says he like the vibe and that's when we make the collaboration, about 1980–81. When I went to Sturgav, Inspector Willie was my selector, and we didn't have to tell him what to play cause he was a dance man himself. He was a little bit older, but we were all big men. Charlie Chaplin was there as U Roy's apprentice, but I was freelance, just a wild cowboy. Wherever I lay my head, that's my home, and wherever my nose lead me, I just follow."

Josey emphasises the spontaneity and longevity that were key to a deejay's success. "We used to not write songs, like pen them, but up here, you would get 20 songs," he says, tapping his head. "I come to the dance from ten o'clock, and I don't leave the mic until five o'clock the next morning. That's the general way of deejaying, not what you see today, when a guy gets £10–15,000 when he run on stage for 15 minutes and run back to him limo. From ten o'clock until five a.m. was the norm, and you wouldn't be repeating yourself, so you have to be a lyrical individual who can toast the dance for so much hours. My style was different because I was a rough-cut diamond and I was real with the lyrics, like most songs that I have made in those times was about confrontation with me and police: things that are reality, that happened. So I follow that line until this time."

After ruling Sturgav for several years with his chanting style and outlaw persona, Josey Wales finally made his way to the studio in 1982 at the request of Junjo Lawes, then based at McKoy Lane, the skinny road that parallels Payne Avenue, deep inside PNP territory. During this divisive era, differences in political allegiance were not regarded lightly, but Wales knew a good offer when he encountered it, and a string of significant hits followed. 'Leggo Mi Hand' recounted a confrontation with a disrespectful gateman that took liberties with a girlfriend at the entrance to a sound system dance. It was followed by the quasi-religious 'Baby Came To Joseph', the herb smoker's anthem 'Chalice Haffi Burn', and the subdued 'Bobo Dread,' which noted the growing presence of the Rastafari sub-group, whose members sold handmade brooms on the street. Such material made Josey Wales one of Jamaica's most popular deejays during 1982–83, leading to his first overseas appearances, all of which attested to the strong artistic bond fostered between Wales and Junjo, regardless of political differences.

"Junjo was PNP and I was Labourite, so it was a difference of opinion politically, but Junjo wasn't a scaredy-cat, so he approached me and say: 'You are the baddest deejay now, we want you 'pon our thing,' and me say: 'Count out the dollars and we could get it together.' Because I was a brave kid, I started going to McKoy Lane, so we have a musical confrontation where it was just love, drink up we liquor, and the chalice burning all through the night. We went to the studio and I did what he asked me to do."

At the time, Junjo's Volcano sound system had the hardest, freshest deejays. Little John (John McMorris) was a precocious talent that began his recording career at the age of nine; Ranking Toyan (Byron Letts) had stylistic flair reminiscent of Trinity but more geared toward dancehall; Burro Banton (Donovan Spalding) was a gruff-voiced groaner who prefaced a popular style later perfected by namesake Buju Banton; Lui Lepke was a dreadlocked chanter of 'reality' and romance who took his stage name from an American mobster; the young Billy Boyo (Billy Theophilus Rowe) was a slowly drawling toaster who often worked wry humour into his raps; Peter Metro (Peter Clarke), star deejay of the neighbouring Metromedia sound, was a part-time Volcano toaster who often worked bits of Spanish into his lyrics; Lee Van Cleef (Devon Perkins) was another 'outlaw' rated for reliable rhyming skills; Welton Irie (Welton Dobson) cut one of the first full-length 'slack' LPs (*It Feels So Good*), but also voiced plenty of 'reality' tunes; the albino Yellowman, equally fond of the 'rude' and the 'cultural', was one of the first to make an international breakthrough, matching the rudeness of General Echo (Earl Robinson) to the stylistic flair of Lone Ranger. Junjo also had the most dancehall-oriented singers in his camp, including Tony Tuff, the gritty 'reality' singer who got his start in The African Brothers; Frankie Paul, the partially sighted West Kingston singer hailed as Jamaica's Stevie Wonder; and Cocoa Tea, a youth from a small town in Clarendon who was discovered by the Volcano posse at a sound system dance in the countryside – all of which went some way to filling the gap left by Barrington Levy's exit to Britain.

Levy says he moved to the UK in 1982 seeking to broaden his knowledge base. He first travelled to London in 1979 to perform at the Reggae Awards held by noted music newspaper *Black Echoes*, and although his work for Junjo was followed by other chart-toppers for Joe Gibbs, Linval Thompson, Jah Thomas, and others, he decided to emigrate after becoming disappointed by a lack of proper recompense. "When I was down here, all I could see was producers trying to rip you off. They sell your stuff to a record company and you don't know nothing about it. I went to England to learn about the music business, learn about publishing. England teach me a lot about the business aspect."

Meanwhile, Junjo's associate Linval Thompson was creating an impressive series of hits with veteran vocalists. Johnny Osbourne rocked the dancehall with 'Kiss Somebody' in 1981; Freddy McGregor topped the charts with the harmonious 'Big Ship' in 1982, the year The Viceroys made an impact with 'We Must Unite'; and The Meditations conquered America with 'No More Friend' in 1983. "I never feel no way," Thompson says, when asked if it felt strange to be producing such legendary elders. "It's just like a power and everything hit. Greensleeves send for me; everything was cool: they treat me good. When the Father give you a gift, nothing can stop you."

Thompson was also voicing albums as a singer and continuing to record younger talent. "Everybody coming to me: Barry Brown, Wayne Wade, Rod Taylor, Sammy Dread. That time, nobody's talking about those artists." He also produced an intriguing album with Mystic I, a roots trio featuring Anthony Johnson, who later cut popular solo material. "It's some guy in the ghetto who come from the same area, Kingston 13. I hear the sound and I like the sound, so we record them."

Despite his obvious talent for facilitating hits, circumstances forced a long production hiatus. "The business kind of change. It start from a Freddy McGregor album ... a likkle problem moneywise. I also have a Tristan Palmer album, a Cornell Campbell album and an Al Campbell album from that time. Everything get shaky, because I have so much album and no business, through money get tie-up, so we went to America. I had a couple good breaks: that time I get a family and still collecting royalties from Greensleeves, but nothing strong wasn't going on."

In the early 80s, changes in the social fabric of Jamaican society saw several leading performers and producers drop out of action at their peak. On November 22 1980, police killed General Echo after discovering an unlicensed firearm in a car he was travelling in; I Roy described the incident as "coldblooded murder".[1] Robbie Shakespeare faced unlicensed gun

331

charges the same year, while Gregory Isaacs served time in 1982, just as *Night Nurse* was poised to make him the most popular reggae singer in the world. "They transfer me from Harbour Street to Gun Count to General Penitentiary, when they charge I for two unlicensed guns," Isaacs wearily explained. "How the time did really a run, you had to protect yourself. That's the only reason I had them, not to do nothing." This was by no means Isaacs's only conflict with the law: in 1982, he admitted he had already been arrested 27 times.

The clampdown on unlicensed weapons partly resulted from dwindling political patronage: Kingston's endemic violence was now more connected to thievery and drug dealing than political alignment. As the perceived need for 'tribalist' warfare decreased, politicians faced new challenges when their heavily armed 'enforcers' became involved in the cocaine trade. In the late 70s, cocaine appeared in the social circles of the uptown elite and at hedonistic beach parties thrown by tourists in Negril; in the early 80s Jamaica became a way station for Colombian and Peruvian coke destined for North America. In 1984 alone, Jamaican police seized 130 pounds of cocaine, while the Coast Guard intercepted a $45,000,000 shipment. Within a few years the insidious presence of cocaine had drastic consequences on Jamaican society, with the music scene being particularly affected.

Politically and economically, the country was still highly unstable. In 1983 Seaga called a snap election, which was boycotted by rival Michael Manley as Seaga refused to update the archaic electoral register. His policy of Seaganomics, modelled on Reagan's 'trickledown' strategy, was a failure; his removal of price controls but refusal to raise the minimum wage put many basic goods out of the reach of ordinary citizens, and another 20,000 people joined the ranks of the unemployed. Huge IMF loans, which the government had difficulty repaying, resulted in the Jamaican dollar's devaluation in 1984.

Such changes in the social landscape encouraged leading producers to leave the country. The killing of Prince Fari on September 15 1983 was the final element that convinced Roy Cousins to move to Liverpool. "I went blind with cataracts, and I divorce and remarried; me work with Fari and them kill him, and me just decide fi call it a day. Them kill him over a dance: they wanted to keep a dance and him give [a promoter] half of the money and owe him half, but [the promoter's] woman mash up the dance the night, she have a fight, so Fari say him nah pay his other half of the money. Prince is one of the man who come through the system the hard way. Is a man who go to prison in Jamaica, and Jamaica is about survival.

332

Edgewater him live, and him go home to water him garden, and the gunmen watch him, and as soon as him roll up the hose to go in, they go in with him. Them say everybody fi lay down on the floor, and I hear him lay down neatly, him don't put up any resistance, but him wife know the boy them, and she put up resistance. They shoot she first, but she never dead, and they shoot him, kill him like an animal. In the living room, you see the blood with his finger-mark all over the wall, when a person in agony."

As an increasing number of artists and producers joined the exodus, expatriates in New York clamoured for a piece of the evolving dancehall action. The most consistent was Donovan Germain, who cut arresting material with Sly & The Revolutionaries for his Revolutionary Sounds label as the 70s gave way to the 80s. Germain made a strong impact in the USA and UK with a series of notable discs by Cultural Roots. The act was one of the last great harmony groups, showing that a roots sensibility need not be out of place with hard rhythms incorporating Syndrums.[2] Germain's productions were usually marked by a firm drum sound, with bright horn melodies, often arranged by Clive Hunt and Dean Fraser, an equally important component. Both can be heard on The Tamlins' 1982 hit 'Baby Love', a hard reworking of The Sensations' rock-steady classic. Germain would later become one of the island's leading producers after shifting his base of operations back to Kingston.

The Tanka label, also based in New York, made a greater impact initially in the early 80s through a series of hits with singer Roland Burrell, but the label's glory was shortlived. Burrell was another who eased the shift away from harmony groups, raising the primacy of solo vocalists during the early dancehall period. "I used to live down by Trench Town from when I was 14, but I born in Clarendon," Burrell explains, leaning against the ital food counter that is part of Junior Reid's studio complex. Burrell says that during his early days in Kingston he sang informally with members of The Linkers. His professional debut came on Hugh Griffiths's 'Step It In Ballet', a minor hit produced by fellow singer Prince Huntley.[3] "The first show we get, we mash it up, and people start want we; Hugh Griffiths say him want to sing alone, so me just start out 'pon me own and do a tune for Ansel Collins named 'Working Man'. Afterward, a brother from New York come down by Channel One. Ansel Collins bring me to Tanka, and the first tune I sing for him was 'Johnny Dollar'."

The song was based on soul crooner Garnett Mimms's 'A Quiet Place', which had been adapted by The Paragons, Horace Andy, and others during the early 70s. Tanka's bass-heavy re-cut, delivered with clarity by Burrell in a manner more akin to Mimms's original phrasing, simply captivated the Jamaican dancehall audience. "It took off about two years in the dancehall before it came 'pon 45; a dancehall soundman buy it 'pon dub plate and give it to Sly, and Sly put it out, and it took off. That tune really make my name. Afterward, Channel One say they want to do a tune with me, so Tanka give them 'Stormy Night' and it gwan good – in England, it number one. A next brother in New York named Sir Tommy, [fellow singer] Admiral Tibet do an All-Star album for him and we start to do some more 45s. After we make three number-one tunes with Tanka and the *Johnny Dollar* album, then he drop out – some misfortune thing go on."

While the musical entrepreneurs resident in the USA began to exert some influence on sounds being made in Jamaica, a select few Jamaicans were using their time abroad just as constructively. Sugar Minott helped usher in the UK lover's rock craze in the early 80s by cutting soul-oriented material with Jackie Mittoo; he also cut noteworthy discs in New York in 1983–84 at the Bronx studio run by Lloyd 'Bullwackie' Barnes. "I was in Jamaica, struggling," said Minott, "and Roy Allen from Hawkeye records came to Jamaica. We make 'Good Thing Going', an old American song that was a hit for Michael Jackson. The song start to sell in England big and I hit *Top Of The Pops*. Me figure me would catch a different vibes, so me just went to the studio, Easy Street. It was some guy playing rock – he never hear reggae before. The first session at Easy Street, I did four hits."

Jackie Mittoo was instrumental in shaping his work in this era. "Jackie Mittoo was in Canada, playing in some hotel in a tux. When we had 'Good Thing Going', I needed somebody who could just put everything together, so me say: 'Jackie Mittoo is the teacher, that's the man.' The album *Roots Lovers*, some of it was done in New York, like 'Penny For My Song', and even the horns overdub there. 'My Love Is True' – Jackie Mittoo gave me that rhythm from Studio One. Coxsone gave him the rhythm and he gave it to me and was helping me right there, but Coxsone got jealous – he didn't like the alliance."

Minott's most consistent New York connection turned out to be Bullwackies. "My brother-in-law take me down to 'Wackies the first time I went to New York. Me see it was some poor people with some old raggedy stuff, so I figure: what bad can I do if I help these people? I start making songs like 'Herbman Hustling'. [Assistant engineer] Douglas Levy produced that rhythm."

Like 'Oh Mr D.C.', 'Herbman Hustling' was a depiction of those who deal ganja to survive. The original New York version is slow and languorous, but the fast-paced version that Minott subsequently voiced for Sly Dunbar in late 1984 helped steer Jamaican music into another direction, as the rhythm of the Jamaican version (based on Vin Gordon's Studio One instrumental 'Heavenless') was created with a keyboard bass and Oberheim DMX drum machine, and no guitar or other live instrument in sight.

"That's the first computerised rhythm in Jamaica," Minott claimed. "Sly was the first man who had those machines. Sly was ahead of his town: even the bass, it's not bass playing. You put the bass inna the keyboard, that's what he played – him alone play that rhythm. Nobody else could sing on it that day. When Sly start to play that, every singer buck, because it's one chord, too straight, go nowhere. You don't hear no other singing on that rhythm, only Yellowman and Lui Lepke."

Sly used a Roland 808 drum machine on record as early as 1983, initially to supplement his organic drumbeats; in 1984, he used various drum machines in conjunction with an electronic Simmons drum kit. "I bought a 808 first, had it for a while," Sly explains. "I use the clap from the 808 to play on 'Trouble You A Trouble Me' by Ini Kamoze. The same clap was on Dennis Brown's 'Revolution'. The 808 I only use [fully] on one song, Black Uhuru's 'Somebody's Watching You'. I start playing around, but on the same album [*Anthem*] I use the Simmons: I had just bought it, came down to Nassau, took all night to get the sound. The drum machines I started using, I bought the DMX, then the [Synare] SP3. The DMX, I use it to play only a couple songs, because they didn't want me to use it as a drummer because they couldn't play my style, but I used it on 'Herbsman Hustling' for Sugar Minott. Then I use it on 'Taxi Connection'. The action of the DMX was so true, like my action, that's why I loved it so much; a lot of people think I'm playing real drums. I didn't buy the Linn Drum; I liked it, but I preferred the DMX because of the sound, and the Linn Drum action was a bit stiff."

With its synthesizer bass line and purely electronic rhythm, 'Herbman Hustling' was a startling predictor of what would soon be the common form of Jamaican dancehall. However, it is worth remembering that drum machines had long been part of Jamaican music, even if only used intermittently at first. For instance, in 1974–75 both Bob Marley and Lee Perry used a primitive electric rhythm unit on songs like 'So Jah Say', 'Rainbow Country', and 'Dub Revolution', but such equipment was used solely as a percussive element buried beneath live instruments. Augustus Pablo also used drum machines in the 70s, typically during rehearsals, as did Family Man Barrett on some of his productions.

Despite Minott's comments above, the first instance of a totally preprogrammed reggae rhythm created solely by synthesizers and drum machines dates at least to late 1982, when Bunny Wailer collaborated with Marcia Griffiths on the dance number 'Electric Boogie'. Although the song was a major hit in Jamaica, their efforts took time to find favour abroad. "A gig that I-Threes went to do in Toronto didn't turn out too wonderful," Griffiths explains. "I got maybe about $700, and I invested in a keyboard in Canada, and it was the greatest buy I've ever made, because it had every single sound on it. I took it in the studio with brother Bunny, and Bunny was fascinated with the same sound that I loved, which was the piano playing the repeater sound, 'nenga-nenga-nenga-nenga', so that was what we put down first on tape, and then the rhythm, 'boom, baff, boom, baff'. Bunny is a talented songwriter, and one of the greatest producers I know. He took that home in the country, and the following morning he came back with the song 'Electric Boogie'. The song was released coming up to Christmas in 1982 and it went straight to the number-one spot, and ever since there was never a dead period of it not selling anywhere."[4]

As new electronic products sparked further rhythmic experimentation, other notable developments took place in both the ground-level dancehall arena and the international marketplace. As noted by Sly Dunbar, Ini Kamoze was one of the biggest artists to break internationally, thanks partly to the Rhythm Twins' longstanding relationship with Island. Kamoze's distinctively rich tenor, unusual vocal delivery, and general charisma had some hailing him the 'new Bob Marley' after the release of his debut EP and its outstanding single, 'World A Music', in 1984.

On a long-distance telephone call from his current base in Los Angeles, Kamoze, who was born Cecil Campbell, explains that he endured many false starts in the decade before he finally linked with Sly & Robbie. "My father was a policeman and my mother a factory worker, and I grew up between Saint Elizabeth and Spanish Town, where we had aunts and cousins and grandparents. Going through a whole lot of struggles, it was really a period of searching, part of the journey into Rastafari and the cultural aspect of natural living. I wanted to take a new identity, something that I could connect with historically or ancestrally, so I took the name Ini Kamoze, part Amharic and part Swahili, which really means 'At Once' and 'Mountain Of The True God'.

"From 1975 I was working for JAMAL [Jamaica Movement for the Advancement of Literacy], helping to teach adults to read, and I would journey to the recording studios, and I remember Duke Reid pulling his gun and chasing me out of his studio. Then Joe Gibbs was one of the major producers, so in about '79, we found him and played some songs, and we recorded those things, but I can't say what the reason was for them not putting the stuff out. I think we had some encounter with Niney The Observer at the time too, and Bunny Wailer was trying to get me to run through some songs to see what he could do, but me never manifested anything with that either."

After staging an original play called *Runnings* in Spanish Town and cultivating farmland in Saint James, Kamoze joined forces with Jimmy Cliff's nephew, Newton 'Sipho' Merritt, to produce music for their Mogho Naga label.[5] The result was the single 'Trainer's Choice' b/w 'Murteller' (slang for 'murder') and a later effort called 'World Affairs', which proclaimed that reggae's immortality would not be affected by Bob Marley's passing. Both efforts sold poorly, prompting Kamoze to consider abandoning music altogether.

"Even though we got some airplay, you still walk off your shoes heel, and you can only eat a banana for lunch," he recalls. "So I was at the point of just giving up music, but Jimmy Cliff was explaining that he went through the same thing, so just due to the encouragement from Jimmy Cliff, I did six songs on a demo tape, playing a box guitar, and he gave Sly the tape, and that was how that whole thing started." Kamoze's self-titled mini LP and follow-up album, *Statement*, were hugely successful, both on the island and overseas, but he would later break with Sly & Robbie to found his own Selekta label following the poor response to his sophomore album, *Pirate*.

For local audiences, alongside the dramatic success of Frankie Paul, perhaps the biggest dancehall artist to break in 1984 was Cocoa Tea, a tall singer with a distinct and slightly nasal voice who brings a country intonation to his delivery. "The difference between Cocoa Tea and most of the youth whe come from the town, is because I am a country man, I bring this same country folk melody to town and sing," he explains. "Me no change nothing, which is most unusual, so it always capture the people."

Tea is in an unfinished building next door to Roaring Lion, the studio he established during the late 90s near his home in a country town in Clarendon. He says he grew up in the same region. "I was born and raised in Rocky Point, about six miles from here. Born 1959, raised by my mother, because my father migrated to America. I used to sing in choir from a tender age. Them time I couldn't really write a song, but I could sing like a songbird. It steps to a next level when I was about 14: my brethren used to rehearse together and them have a likkle group. As The Clarendonians was from this area, they couldn't say Clarendonians again, so them call themselves The Rockydonians – they were fishermen. Sang Hugh [aka Keith Morgan], he used to rehearse with us too. He's from Westmoreland, but his father, Bongo Son, was living in Rocky Point, so he came here as a young youth. After, he became famous with 'Rasta No Born Yah'."[6]

In his teens, when he was still known by his given name, Calvin Scott, he got his first taste of studio recording after hooking up with popular singer Willie Francis. "Willie Francis sang a song by the name of 'Oh What A Mini' – he became famous and make a transition from singing to producing. He used to come to the country a lot to eat roast fish at Rocky Point, so I became acquainted with him. We went into town and the group did one song, and I did one song, which was 'Searching In The Hills' – Sang Hugh wrote that. We record it at Channel One, about 1974. Style Scott and Flabba Holt was a part of it."

Unfortunately the song sank without trace, despite being licensed to the independent Magnet label in England, and it was "about eternity after that" when Tea next found himself in the studio. "I run around for a while, trying to do other things: went to Caymanas Park, trying to be a jockey, but it was not really my job, so I came back to the country. Growing up, the responsibility thing start to dawn on me: it's getting a little late, so you have to get yourself together, and I started to try my best to write a song – that was my main objective. About 1980, I went back in the studio and did a song by the name of 'Summer Time' for myself, but through lack of promotion, it never did anything, so I came back with another song by the name of 'Big Iron', a cover version of Marty Robbins. There was a record jury that time on the radio in Jamaica, and a man on the radio say: 'Cocoa Tea? This one sound bitter like cerasee tea!'[7] They throw it away and say it was no good."

His command of the mic at sound system events brought Cocoa Tea into the limelight a few years later, catapulting him to fame as the new star in Junjo Lawes's camp. "All sound systems that come to Rocky Point – Metromedia, Killimanjaro, Socialist Roots, Sturgav, Black Harmony – I sing on all of them, so that's where I first link with Junjo. In those days you can't go in a dancehall and sing back a man's song like these youngsters do, you have to come original. I write lyrics and I am equipped with the ability to change my key, which is the most important thing in any music, so any rhythm you put on, me sing 'pon it, so I mash up the dancehall all over the place: Peter Metro, Josey Wales and Charlie Chaplin come, and when them come in, they're hot, but me mash up the dance so they can't hold no mic.

I had a friend who had a girlfriend from Old Harbour by the name of Sonia, and him and Sonia got a big war, so that's why I went about writing a song named 'Lost My Sonia' and every dance I draw that song, it mash up the place.

"Then, when Volcano came to Rocky Point in December 1983, Lui Lepke, Lee Van Cleef, Toyan, Little John and all of them man say: 'Cocoa Tea, you have to come to town and check Junjo.' I went to Junjo in February on Myrie Avenue, start to sing *a capella*. Josey Wales say: 'Any man who sing and make me dance without rhythm must haffe bust in the business.' The first studio Junjo took me to is Harry J. That's when I record the first song, 'Who Are The Champion', then 'Rocking Dolly'. After that came the big hit, 'Lost My Sonia'."[8]

This material finally put Cocoa Tea in the same league as the other quintessential dancehall singers, namely Barrington Levy, Sugar Minott, and contemporaries like Frankie Paul and Half Pint. Although he became one of Junjo's top artists, however, Junjo himself had little involvement with Tea's material. "He just put the money up," Tea says. "First time I was going to the studio he was there, but after that it was people like Steve and Bellow, Junjo's two right-hand man."

Unfortunately, Junjo's efforts would be seriously curtailed after he shifted his base of operations to New York in 1985. "He went to prison for a while," Tea explains. "That's why I say it's hard for people to really trouble hard drugs. Any time you trouble certain things, it mess you up. In Junjo's case, him getting in by distributing it, that's how he wind up in America. I don't know why – he never need it."

"There's an expression: you don't appreciate what you've got till you've lost it," Chris Cracknell suggests, searching for an explanation. "Maybe Junjo felt there was bigger money to be made in other areas, and people get hooked into things, don't they? Maybe he saw that dream, or saw other people around that were making vast sums of money and felt that he could achieve the same. Junjo was also very stylish, very fashionable; he liked to keep up with everything, wanted to drive the nicest cars, dress in the nicest clothes, and he had to maintain that lifestyle.

"For Junjo it was important to show people on the island that he was making it, because he certainly never forgot the people or the places where he grew up, and he supported a lot of people there. When he came to London he would always buy 30 or 40 pairs of Clarks booties to carry back down for everybody, so he never left his people behind. When I went to Jamaica we stayed at his lovely house in the hills, but every morning we went down to the ghetto and there was his BMW parked on the street with no other cars apart from derelict cars with no wheels, but that was where he really loved to be, so he never ever left that ... I suppose in the tradition of Jamaica, very few producers go on forever. Who knows why?"

"The man had the world at his fingertips and just gave it away like that," says Cocoa Tea, "so I move over to Corner Stone, down Greenwich Farm. Michael Chin, that man teach me about money management – he was like a father to me. I did two albums for him: *Mr Cocoa Tea* and *Settle Down*. From there I went to Jammy's."[9]

Once the bulk of Soul Syndicate emigrated to California, Chinna Smith formed The High Times Players with bassist Chris Meredith and drummer Benbow Creary. They became the favourite backing band of the Greenwich Farm producers, while Junjo and Jammy also made use of their talents. "The whole shooting and the violence, some of the man decide them go ah foreign go live," Chinna explains. "Then everybody start branch off. Sly & Robbie start do them own thing and the industry start get selfish. Radics say them nah play with certain man. I realise the music kind of get a way, because no man want to work together again and everybody want to be them own producer, so me go downtown, have me record shop, and put together a little band called High Times Players. Junjo Lawes start come in, do some tunes for Yellowman like 'Mr Chin'. Jammy come back from Canada, me do some bad Dennis Brown for him too. We start do a series of shows downtown, start get into our own production. Mutabaruka come in, do a wicked album, *Check It*."

The High Times sound was marked by Chinna's tastefully melodic arrangements, which naturally made space for his expressive lead guitar, often incorporating jazz elements. Scientist specifically singled out the group for praise: "The musicians that I love working with the most was High Times Players – I could just do what I want. As a result, they got the best sound." This adaptability provided the perfect platform for the recorded work of Mutabaruka, who began setting his poems to music under Chinna's direction at Tuff Gong studio in 1981. "Me know Chinna from just being around music," Muta explains. "I did a show with Jimmy Cliff and he was the guitarist in Jimmy Cliff's band. He produced the first 45, then he produced the album. There is more people that is listening than reading, in Jamaica especially, so in recording the poems, we get a wider audience and get to express ourselves more."

Mutabaruka's vinyl debut was 'Every Time A Ear De Soun', depicting the alienation that Rastas experience in a chaotic society that perpetually rejects its African heritage, prefers the trappings of colonial culture, and gives greater status to foreign disco music than Niyabinghi drumming. "The inspiration comes from different sounds that you hear in your community: the gunshots, woman screaming, the news on the radio about the Russians and the Americans, things people say to Rasta. All of these is expressed very shortly in one poem, to try to make the people get a picture. Them say: 'Comb your head, nasty dread,' them say: 'Drum and bass have no taste.' All of these things is different sounds that you hear."

The acclaimed *Check It*, issued in Jamaica in 1982, established Mutabaruka's name outside Jamaica through its release the following year on the independent Alligator label in the USA. The album contained forceful material that examined issues of identity and spoke out against racial inequality and imperialism. One of the disc's hardest-hitting numbers is 'Whiteman Country', a depiction of immigrant life in Britain. "There was a lot of Jamaicans coming to England in the early 60s on the banana boat, because they were taught that England was a better place to live. There was a time when England was colonising Jamaica and most of the colonial people used to run to the colonial master country. When they come here, they realise that things was not really better than where they were coming from, so that poem was just reiterating that it's not good to stay in a white man's country, knowing that no matter what you do in Britain, you will always be from the Caribbean. That poem was telling black people in England: 'Remember where you're coming from.'"

Delivered without musical backing, 'Sit Dung Pon De Wall' spoke of the peculiar relationship between the wealthy and the destitute, with a rich man's fears noted by the eyes of a benign sufferer. "There's a paranoia between the rich and the poor: poor people always want to be rich and rich people always feel that poor people will soon rise up against them. The rich man is watching the poor with his guns, having all these guards around his house, and the poor man is watching the rich, so it's a vice-versa thing: 'I sit dung 'pon de wall, ah watch him ah watch me.' In feeling that the poor is going to rise up against him, the rich man opens himself up to a whole lot of things that is not really there ... and there is a thing about mad people in Jamaica walking the streets, where people is always feeling that a person who is mad don't understand what is going on, but really the world don't show me that. The 'sane' people is the ones who make the guns, make the nuclear weapons, and they are paranoid that one day these things are going to explode."

The High Times Players were also the first to back Frankie Paul on

341

record. "The first person to bring me into the studio is Earl Chinna Smith, in 1980," the singer reveals during a late-night break from a London recording session. He is a pleasant man to interview, because he constantly bursts into song and often does dramatic impersonations of the characters that have helped him along the way. "I used to live near Tivoli Gardens and I went down there trying to find my school friend. This guy named Stucco heard me singing Larry Graham's 'One In A Million' and he said: 'Youth, you ah waste your talent. Tomorrow morning, come check me.' We went down to High Times, went on the beach, and I started singing the Larry Graham song again, and from that day a whole lot of things start happening. We went to Bob Marley's studio and I recorded one song, 'The Rich And The Poor', an original."

Frankie, born Paul Blake, says Chinna was also responsible for his stage name. "They used to call me Singer Paul back in the days. When I went to High Times I was talking about Frankie Beverley and Frank Sinatra, so Chinna say: 'Why we no call you Frankie Paul?'"

After Chinna's initial promotion, the singer's profile continued to rise. "I perform on stage shows and sing in the streets while coming from school and big crowd draw – everybody know this goddam kid here. People say: 'Me have some brethren at Maxfield Avenue. You ever hear about Channel One?' [Singer] Junior Tucker used to record at Channel One, and Dennis Brown, so it just click to me." Brown was one of Paul's biggest influences, but meeting Stevie Wonder in his formative years had the most direct impact.

"I was born in Kingston, but my parents originally came from Hanover. I used to live between Oxford Street and Oakland Park Road, downtown, Two Miles area. My mom used to keep dances and she used to do higglering, kept it going like a mother and father. From five years of age I went to the Salvation Army School for the Blind, in which I learned how to act and make my music skills better. 1978, Stevie Wonder brought a Braille copier for the school and it was a tremendous evening for all of us. I sang [Johnny Nash's] 'I Can See Clearly Now', both of us together. Then, when I was 14, I went into a band called The Mighty Tides: all policemen, home guards, security, and me the only school kid in that band. I used to sing Tom Jones, [Fats Domino's] 'Blueberry Hill', and [Judy Garland's] 'Somewhere Over The Rainbow'. It was in the Christmas era and I was in a play called *Tamberlaine The Mad Fowl*, choreographed by Hortensia Lindsay from the School of Drama. I was a dog that got up and sang [The Spinners'] 'Working My Way Back To You Babe'."

After cutting early singles for various producers, Frankie recorded his first album, *Strange Feeling*, in 1983. "Winston Riley's niece Sandra was my girlfriend at the time. She brought me down to the shop and he wanted me to do an album." Subsequent albums of equally high standard followed for Joe Gibbs, Channel One, Junjo Lawes, and George Phang, the latter a young man of high social standing in the Concrete Jungle ghetto who wanted to try his hand at record production. Although the Channel One set, shared with Sugar Minott, was the first to bring Frankie Paul to the attention of overseas audiences, the singer says it was Junjo's *Pass The Tu-Sheng Peng*, cut with The Roots Radics, that really boosted him. "When I did that Junjo album, it put me right where I wanted to be: number one, two, three, four in America, number one, two, three in Jamaica, number one, two, three in England."

Of these top-four hits, 'Worries In The Dance' and 'Dem A Talk Bout' reflected Paul's entrenchment in dancehall culture, while 'The Prophet' was a spiritual number that drew from Dennis Brown. The biggest and best of the bunch was the weed-smoker's anthem 'Pass The Tu-Sheng Peng'.[10] But even though Junjo brought Paul to the top of the charts, the singer felt an initial wariness when approached by the producer. "I was very scared working with Junjo at the time, because people that used to hang around Volcano sound was some dangerous coots, and then I didn't know who is who."

While Frankie Paul was working with the Radics for Junjo, The High Times Players were providing the tight and exciting backing for Prince Jammy's emerging stable of stars. Jammy had spent the early part of the decade gradually becoming more self-sufficient. In the front room of his home at 38 Saint Lucia Road, Waterhouse, Jammy installed a two-track machine for basic editing; around 1982, he acquired a four-track and was then able to voice and mix on site. This greater independence reaped fruitful rewards in 1983–84 through lasting hits by aspiring Waterhouse singers Half Pint (Lyndon Roberts) and Junior Reid (Delroy Reid Junior).

Half Pint, a short teenager with a powerful voice, came to Jammy's's attention when he was asked to mix the singer's debut single 'Sally' by John Marshall, an associate of Yabby You who had funded the recording with his partner, Errol Myrie. Recognising the singer's potential, Jammy scored instantly with Pint's 'Money Man Skank', followed by 'Mr Landlord', 'Pouchie Lou', and 'One In A Million'. In 1985 Pint left Jammy's stable for further hits with Sly & Robbie, including 'Hold On', which described the uncomfortable nature of a love triangle; his biggest hit to date came with 'Greetings', one of the proto-digital beats that Sly & Robbie built for George Phang.

Junior Reid made his recording debut at the age of 13 in 1979 for Hugh Mundell, who was then working with Augustus Pablo. Reid's One Blood studio, off a heavily congested Kingston thoroughfare that bisects ghetto neighbourhoods and industrial districts, is one of the spots on the island associated with the promotion of young talent, although plenty of veterans record there too and the central focus is Reid's own creations. As Reid became a follower of Prince Emmanuel Edwards some years ago, many of those hanging out near the food counter wear the distinctive turbans that identify them as 'Bobo Dreads'. It is a lively spot at evenings, with much protracted reasoning and general comradeship.

Inside the small studio, Reid is voicing 'Propaganda', in reference to the 'official' burial given to the supposed remains of Haile Selassie in the year 2000; the rhythm, already over ten years old, was originally Reid's version of Michael Jackson's 'Dirty Diana'. The young Bobo taping the session looks no older than 15; as the mixing board has a chronic fault, he has to keep tapping it to make it work. Despite the large quantities of master tapes, piled high like columns, that are wedged between the oversize mixing board and the room's constrictive walls, an assortment of dreads have crammed themselves into whatever space is left to observe the proceedings. The tensely charged Reid is like a man possessed, arms flailing around his thin, muscular frame as he bounces to the rhythm and pours out his mistrust of the Babylonian media. He is uncertain about some spontaneous lines, and keeps dashing back into the mixing area to demand the opinion of the assembled onlookers. Big Youth, a close associate, is given pride of place.

Eventually, when Reid is satisfied enough to take a short break, he speaks of early group work cut in 1982 for a London-based roots label. "Robert and Michael Palmer, they was Negus Roots. They used to live in Waterhouse, but they went to England, and when they come back down in Jamaica they want to work with me. They put out two singles: 'If I' and 'Sister Dawn'. They want to do an album, and I was moving around with my friends [Sammy Tracy and Terry McDermott]. They like singing, so we just say: 'Why not name ourselves as a band, Voice Of Progress?' We did the album *Minibus Driver*. Then, when we were supposed to do the follow-up album, they was taking up a lot of studio time, screwing up things, so I just went back solo."

Jammy then cut dancehall hits with the singer, notably 'Boom Shack A Lack' and 'Higgler Move'. In Britain, the strongest impact was made with the moving 'Jailhouse', released through North London sound-system operator Ken 'Fatman' Gordon's KG Imperial label. This hit material, plus the album Reid cut for Jammy with The High Times Players, showed the singer establishing his particular interpretation of the Waterhouse vocal style. Reid went on to record for Junjo, but it was after hooking up with Sugar Minott in 1984 that Reid cut his biggest hit: 'Original Foreign Mind', a perceptive take on the lure of emigration, rose high in the Jamaican charts and also impacted the growing American reggae scene. Reid was then drafted into Black Uhuru, following Michael Rose's surprise departure just after the group won a Grammy for *Anthem* – the first such award for a reggae album. ("People start tell me you can fire or hire, so I just say forget this," explains Michael Rose. "From when it start reach them extremes there, I'm turned off.")

"I was asked to join Black Uhuru," Junior Reid states with pride. "It was a great time. I link up with Black Uhuru with a hit song, 'Fit You Haffe Fit'." Reid injected fresh energy into the group, particularly on live performances, but returned to his solo career in the late 80s. He says he left the group "due to music politics"; his ominous description of events is a reminder that, in their heyday, Black Uhuru got more international attention than any contemporary. "After them kill Bob Marley, they never want nothing more so powerful, and Black Uhuru was the next group to get big promotion behind, so they just try to mash up the whole reggae and keep it 'pon a level like how you see them have it now. So me just go forward solo."

Some of the hit material that Half Pint and Junior Reid recorded for Jammy benefited from the hands of Scientist, who became so disgruntled with the state of affairs at Channel One that he left for the 24-track Tuff Gong shortly afterward, opting for the more peaceful environment of the complex at 56 Hope Road. "Nobody really wanted to give me credit, and I'm the only one down there with an electronic background, so if anything get damaged or not working properly I could get it to work some. Everybody getting jealous, because everybody older than me, but I am bringing stuff to the studio that they never did before. I went to Tuff Gong and the sound changed. Before, only uptown bands like Third World going to Tuff Gong, the hardcore dancehall thing was not being done at Tuff Gong. One of my strongest supporters there was Tristan Palmer, and then Early B. All of those dancehall people started going to Tuff Gong; Tuff Gong took away all the customers from Channel One. After that, they closed down, because they lost all their clientele."

Joseph Hoo-Kim says Channel One's demise stemmed partly from his brother Ernest's departure from the music business. "Ernest didn't like the confinement – he couldn't take being in the studio too much, so he began to operate gambling machines again. I bring Kenneth in the business, the same time with Frankie Paul, but it begin to get down when I and Kenneth didn't get along."

Scientist says the atmosphere at Tuff Gong was initially more appealing. "Tuff Gong had Chiao [Ng], a very good maintenance engineer, so the studio was kept very good. Matter of fact, it was the most comfortable place I worked. 'Round at Tubby's and Channel One, you have to deal with all the bad ghetto elements. When I went to Tuff Gong, I could finally breathe and just be an engineer." Unfortunately, such tranquillity was not to last. "I was at Tuff Gong about a year-and-a-half, didn't have to worry about too much of the gangster runnings, but some of the same elements started to come there, because I carry that sound wherever I go. It was becoming too much of a rat race, so I come to America in 1985. My sisters, my mother, everybody was living here." Thus, the last of the classical dub masters made his exit from Jamaica, and a notable decline in dub albums followed.

Meanwhile, other artists were taking reggae's liberating message even further afield. "I'm the first artist to go to Japan, bringing sound system, and Sister Carol go over there and Frankie Paul," said Sugar Minott, ever in touch with the dancehall experience. "They didn't know that there was a thing called sound system – the first time we play, they put this little diagram in the magazine to show you how to hook it up. I have to be the selector at the same time, trying to teach some Japanese youth."

The impact of reggae on the Japanese consciousness was such that acts like the abstract instrumental group Mute Beat would eventually collaborate with the Jamaican artists who inspired them – a strong testimony to the transcendent qualities of a music that has crossed seemingly impenetrable social and linguistic barriers. "Reggae music is the only music in the world that every nation relate to," says Cocoa Tea. "If them don't understand the lyrics, at least the rhythm gets to their mind, their heart – it penetrates."

Ironically, it was a Japanese creation that brought indelible changes to Jamaican popular music at the start of 1985. The Casio company produced a number of inexpensive keyboard instruments, including easily portable models with preset rhythms and built-in melodies. One such preset provided the blueprint for Wayne Smith's 'Under Mi Sleng Teng', a paean to the wonders of marijuana that would change the face of the Jamaican recording scene, causing shock waves all over Jamaica – and, shortly afterward, all over the world.

346

As with much of significance in Jamaican music, the story of 'Sleng Teng' is complex, with contradictory elements provided by different sources. Wayne Smith first worked with Jammy at King Tubby's studio at the dawning of the 80s, recording an early dancehall love song, 'Ain't No Me Without You', when the singer was just 15. Smith learnt to sing in his local Pentecostal church, but was soon hanging around Jammy's sound system, trying to be recognised as a dancehall vocalist. Although the punchy debut single and subsequent album, *Youthman Skanking*, were not particularly strong sellers, the material evidenced the chemistry between singer and producer that would shortly bare noteworthy fruit.

When his early work for Jammy failed to hit, Smith cut a few tunes for Channel One, but these made even less impact, so in 1984 he returned to Jammy to voice 'Come Along', 'Change Your Style', and 'Ain't No Meaning'. Somewhere along the way, Smith bucked up on Noel Davey, another neighbourhood youth trying to make it as a singer. Davey had a Casiotone MT40, and the pair used its 'rock'n'roll' preset to build a basic rhythm for 'Under Mi Sleng Teng'. The lyrics and melody may have been remarkably similar to Barrington Levy's 'Under Mi Sensi', but the song made use of a whole new format that was terribly exciting.

"In the music business, I always like creativeness, so I was wondering what next we were going to do, because everybody was making the same instrumentation, same rhythms, same sound," says Jammy. "Then I was approached by Wayne Smith and Noel Davey, who said: 'King, we have reformed a new sound.' They brought a small Casio keyboard to me and started to play around. They said: 'Here is the sound,' but it sounded crazy to me: it was too fast, no rhythm section, just drum and bass going at 100 miles per hour. So I said: 'I like the sound, but it's not the right tempo for reggae music.' I slowed it down to dancing mode, then we overdubbed some piano, some percussion, and that was the beginning of 'Sleng Teng': we just went inside the studio, recorded the rhythm straight away. I knew it was going to be successful because of the sound of the rhythm, but I didn't know that it would be so much of a big hit."

A few days later, Jammy unveiled the song as his secret weapon at a sound clash against Black Scorpio, a set based on the other side of Sandy Gully in a crowded micro-neighbourhood called Drewsland. This powerful sound, run by a former newspaper seller and racehorse owner known as Jack Scorpio (aka Maurice Johnson), had become the area's most respected set after Jammy's technically outmoded sound system dropped out of circulation in 1980. Now Jammy's Super Power was back in action, bolstered

347

by new equipment brought in from England, and 'Sleng Teng' was the surprise track that flattened the competition.

"We couldn't stop playing it for the night," laughs Jammy. "People were loving it more and more, so I say: 'We've got to get some more artists on this rhythm,' and then we started recording Johnny Osbourne and the rest of the artists, and that changed the whole music scene in the 80s. That was the rhythm that computerised the reggae business, and up until today, people are using computers to build reggae music."

Back in 1985, the effect of 'Sleng Teng' was instantaneous. It unleashed a revolution in reggae by permanently changing the way music was recorded in Jamaica. Every producer went digital, and several dozen versions of 'Sleng Teng' rapidly found their way onto vinyl. "My first number-one Jamaican hit was 'Water Pumpee' by Johnny Osbourne, but 'Sleng Teng' was the biggest hit in Jamaica for me," Jammy emphasises. "I can't tell you the actual number of versions cut by other producers, but I know it was a lot and I think the reason for that is because people were hearing a new sound; everybody else capitalise on it, go on the rhythm and try to do something fi themselves."

The repercussions of the spectacular success of 'Sleng Teng' were many and varied. The song immediately spawned countless re-cuts by raw hopefuls and seasoned talent alike; among the most noteworthy are 'Pumpkin Belly' by rising dancehall singer Tenor Saw, plus Culture's delirious 'Catch A Rasta'. The success of 'Sleng Teng' made Jammy's tiny studio a completely self-sufficient reality; with keyboards, sequencer, and drum machine, he had enough to construct hit rhythms, voicing and overdubbing as necessary. He no longer had to rely on the more established and better-equipped facilities like Harry J. and Channel One: everything could be done right at home, in his converted bedroom.

In time, this approach would revolutionise the way recordings were made in Jamaica, as others began to convert similar spaces. The concept of the bedroom studio was also taken up in places like Chicago and London, where aspiring producers and club deejays used similar set-ups to turn tape loops and sampled sequences into dance music. "The times change," says Jammy of the shift to digital recordings. "You have to go with the time if you want to eat food. If you want to earn a living from the music, you have to do whatever is going on today. In the early 70s, when I used to record at Channel One or Harry J., we used to do live music. Then we just want to experiment, so we did something with 'Sleng Teng' and it changed the whole scene, and that was great for me – even today, everybody is using electronics, computerised drums, drum machine. I really revolutionised that part of the music with 'Sleng Teng'. It was being done a little before 'Sleng Teng', but 'Sleng Teng' was the big hit that made everybody switch over."

In the history of Jamaican popular music, 'Sleng Teng' is a true milestone. Its release marked a turning point in which a new genre was anointed, distinct from any other that preceded it, and although the first noticeable difference was its computerised form, other distinct shifts in content and style resulted from its immediate popularity. 'Sleng Teng' changed Jamaican music overnight, acting as a catalyst more volatile that any other record issued before or since, and it was not only Jamaica that was shaken by this mighty rhythm. By drawing Jamaican music closer to the production values of American hip-hop, a greater exchange of ideas between the two musical cultures resulted, and popular artists in many other lands would eventually draw on its inspiration, not only for salutary tributes cut in a various styles, but also through unauthorised emulation: everyone from 50 Cent and DJ Muggs of Cypress Hill to Parisian house DJ St Germain and Japanese post-punk dub group Little Tempo have worked elements of 'Sleng Teng' into their oeuvres. It is thus no exaggeration to state that 'Sleng Teng' changed the shape of popular music forever.

13

WEAR YU SIZE

Storytelling, slackness, gun talk, and ragga spirituality

"You have different people inna the dance, so you have to please everybody: some man want to hear about gun, some want to hear about punany, then a next man want to hear about Selassie or God. The whole aspect of it is catering to the people that is listening to you." – ADMIRAL BAILEY

"Sometimes I end up doing the same rhythm track for three different producers on the same day ... you wish people would come with ideas of their own, instead of doing the same thing that someone else just did ten minutes ago." – ROBBIE LYN

The success of 'Sleng Teng' had dramatic and far-reaching effects. Previously, singers initiated most reggae songs by bringing lyrics and a melody to a producer, whose session players would construct a musical arrangement. After 'Sleng Teng', most music was constructed by technically proficient keyboard players, or non-musical technicians clever enough to build a basic computer rhythm, to which lyrics were subsequently added. This material was often created without the input of actual musicians, resulting in a rugged form geared toward sound-system devotees. Although the new sound may have baffled overseas listeners, particularly those enamoured with roots reggae, in Jamaica 'Sleng Teng' and its successors made perfect sense. The brash sound of computer drums reflected the harsh reality of modern urban life, providing exciting fuel for the dancehall audience, and the predominant sound had long been heading in this direction through increased use of synthesizers and electronic drumbeats.

In conjunction with the rise of computer rhythms came a shift in form, as the new style was perfectly suited to deejays. Thus, by the end of the decade, traditional singers were on the wane and the new Jamaican superstars were rapping champions of the microphone. Ironically, many of the singers who maintained popularity did so by adapting old American

350

ballads to the new digital beats. Rastafari imagery was also on the wane, as many rising stars were Christian.

Some producers simply could not get their heads around digital music. "What really bother me is: I didn't like computer," says Joseph Hoo-Kim, noting that 'Sleng Teng' signalled the end of Channel One. "When the computer sound come in, I run one session with Sugar Minott and one with Diamonds, and after that I say no. I didn't like the sound and I didn't like one man playing a rhythm, so I didn't run no more session."

Similarly, Sonia Pottinger exited the record business in 1985 to work in ceramics, but other producers had already been making use of technological innovations, so were not displaced by digitisation.[1] For instance, Winston Riley cut an impressive series of hits with upcoming talent in the 'Sleng Teng' aftermath by blending live instruments with partly-computerised rhythms, including 'Boops', Super Cat's hugely popular tale of romantic greed; 'Hold A Fresh', Red Dragon's advice for daily bathing; and smooth crooner Sanchez's forlorn take of Jermaine Jackson's 'Lonely Won't Leave Me Alone' (as 'Loneliness Leave Me Alone'). "Every tune was a hit," Riley explained, "but those wasn't fully computers, because I mostly use live instruments too."

Although the whole of Jamaica was rapidly turning digital, Jammy kept the upper hand by working keenly with Steelie & Clevie, who soon emerged as Jamaica's premier digital rhythm builders. A Trench Town native, Steelie discovered his talent after his mother introduced him to Pablove Black, who taught him the rudiments of the keyboard. He first met Cleveland Browne, a younger brother to Dalton, during the mid 70s, through sound-system events their brother Glen held at the Penthouse club on Red Hills Road. Upon the formation of the family group The Browne Bunch, Steelie became a regular fixture at the Brownes' uptown home, where he and Clevie received more tutelage from Clevie's older siblings, the pair bonding further through a shared love of Studio One. After early session work for Lee Perry, Augustus Pablo, and Sugar Minott, Steelie joined The Roots Radics, with whom he displayed an understated style. Then, following the computerisation that revolutionised Jamaican music overnight, Steelie and Clevie joined forces at King Jammy's studio – Clevie handling drum machines and Steelie on synthesizers – to fashion countless hit rhythms for the rising stars of the dancehall movement. They became an unbeatable team used by every leading dancehall producer, and are estimated to have been responsible for 75 per cent of the Jamaican top 100 during the late 80s.

Jammy remained the undisputed king of the music to the end of the decade, partly because he harnessed Steelie & Clevie early, and also because he used the astute engineer Bobby Dixon, a neighbourhood sound-system operator and electronics technician known as Bobby Digital due to his proficiency with the form. "Growing up, I was a repair technician who fix radios and TVs," says Digital, at his perpetually busy home studio. "I learned by an overseas correspondence course, and my brother has a shop at home, so I get involved. Then we were doing our own little sound system, Heatwave, and I used to follow my friend Michael Jemison to Channel One studio to do some pre-production, trying to do something for Black Crucial and Half Pint, and I was fascinated by how it was done. Michael introduced me to Jammy when I was 19; Jammy was always going abroad, so I just started doing the work, and eventually he said: 'You're going to be in charge.' That was really encouraging. I worked on most of the hits at King Jammy's from the 'Sleng Teng' era, with Wayne Smith, Half Pint, Frankie Paul, Nitty Gritty – you name them."

Although the deejays would soon emerge as predominant, a trio of influential 'bad card' sing-jays made a huge impact with a powerful singing style that came from deep in the gut, using vocal diaphragms for abstract exclamations and dramatic slurring as a new mutation of the Waterhouse style. The first to hit with the method was a West Kingston roughneck called Tenor Saw (aka Clive Bright). Saw made his recording debut, 'Roll Call', for George Phang on a modernised cut of the 'Queen Majesty' rhythm, and recorded impressive tracks for Sugar Minott during 1984–85, finally hitting big the following year with 'Ring The Alarm' on a re-vamped 'Stalag' for Winston Riley, and then voicing the proverb-laden 'Pumpkin Belly' for Jammy – one of the most popular cuts of 'Sleng Teng' ever released.

Saw's unusual delivery and captivating lyrics, which often drew on folk wisdom, was paralleled by the work of his friend, Nitty Gritty (Glen Holness), and eventually adapted by another West Kingston street tough, King Kong (Dennis Anthony Thomas), a rival with a complicated history of musical association. "Tenor Saw was the man who establish the style, and that style is a deep thing," Kong explains at home in Portmore, noting that the two eventually became friends despite initial animosity. "Nitty Gritty adapt the sound and used to say that him originate it, but Tenor Saw was really the youth with that flavour."

Kong is an intense character with plenty of amazing memories. He spices up his tales by frequently breaking into song, and somewhat disconcertingly often refers to himself as "the Gorilla". He explains that his terribly unsettled childhood led him into the wrong crowd, the music happening almost through circumstance. "I was born in Rose Lane, downtown, in the early 60s, where my mother was a higgler. My father and mother have them differences, so the old man take me permanently; him used to cut land, trap bush, and sell bottles, and we move all 'bout. From about nine years old, me live off Lady Musgrave Road, so me used to go to Tuff Gong; Bob Marley was an icon who every youth would want stop at the gate to see. We move to Waterhouse, but inna '73, when the violence start, my father decide it better to go inna the hills to Cavaliers, Saint Andrew, where he's originally from, and where Culture also come from. Them have a youth club up there, so I start to get into acting, and form a group with two other youth, The Black Invaders. Eric Donaldson used to do auditions in him yard, and when we go, him say me should lead. Then we go to Joe Gibbs, the same time when Culture really get them thing together, and Enos McLeod say him love how we sound. After a time, the group mash up, and me did get caught up inna some badness along the way; my father was a man whe beat me for everything, and when you grow without proper guidance, you lick head with the wrong company."

Kong says his casual involvement in the ganja trade led him back to Tuff Gong. "Me start sell weed and link with a brethren named Juicy who say come check him at Tuff Gong. When I go down there with two shopping bags full of weed, I pass the Gong [Marley] and didn't even realise it; the man send fi two boxing gloves fi me and the Gong to fight, but it never worked out, because a youth named Rats & Bats steal somebody's camera, so the whole vibes change. But it was my first little break, since me start to work with Family Man's rehearsals."

Becoming part of the Tuff Gong entourage led to a debut single, 'Pink Eye & Malaria', voiced in the deejay style and credited to Papa King Kong. "Me was a youth whe wash all the cars inna the place, and me voice some tunes for Fams, including 'Pink Eye'. At the time, me was a singer and a deejay, and me used to be 'pon 'nuff little sound, like you have one inna the hills named Ishan, and you have Stereo Pride, and Aires. The first big sound whe me sing 'pon was Stereophonic, with General Echo & Madoo, and after them hear me 'pon that sound there, everybody say: 'You a big singer. You fi sing!'"

Keeping the wrong company landed Kong in General Penitentiary, facing charges for crimes he did not commit, yet even this proved a blessing in disguise. "It all starts inna GP, really, because when me in there, me start bust 'nuff music, and me meet a youth named Barley, who was a bad man in Tower Hill, but him affiliate with music, so him say: 'When you come ah road, come check me, and me carry you round ah Tubby's.' So when me come ah road in '84 and go back up in the hills, me start spar with a youth who have family in Tower Hill, and one day, Barley me see, and him carry me round ah Tubby's and introduce me to the engineer, Professor. So me drop inna that crew there, sleep in an old van in Tower Hill, and start voice some tune like [The Drifters'] 'This Magic Moment'. Me love the vibes and keep inna the trend with the music, until the Tenor Saw sound become familiar in my hearing, and then me bust a tune, 'Sensimania Is Walking', for a brethren from England [a certain T Reuben, who ran the shortlived REM label], and when Tubby hear it, him say: 'When Tenor Saw come round here?' Then me start bust the place with 'Step Pon Mi Corn', which was like the rival of Tenor Saw."

The song, riding a lingering re-cut of 'Stalag' with added synthesizer horn riffs, channelled Tenor Saw's general idiom, but shows Kong's own style in transition. It was not as tight or confident as subsequent material, such as the follow-up hit 'AIDS', a fearsome warning of the terrible disease voiced on a tough cut of Anthony Red Rose's 'Tempo', one of King Tubby's most noteworthy digital hits.[2]

Although Tubby had expanded his Dromilly Avenue studio and installed new equipment just before the digital onslaught, he somehow struggled to keep up with former protégé Jammy in the digital phase. Immediately following the 'Sleng Teng' explosion, Tubby cut Red Rose's 'Under Mi Fat Thing' in an attempt to steal Jammy's thunder, but Jammy got his own back by voicing Nitty Gritty's highly popular 'Hog Ina Me Minty' on a 'Tempo' re-cut. Despite releasing other popular efforts, Tubby largely remained in Jammy's shadow during the following years.

King Kong says financial pressure forced him to moonlight for Bunny Lee during his tenure at Tubby's, yielding impressive tunes released overseas, such as the anti-Apartheid 'Moving On The African Border' and the evocative 'Must Work On Sunday'.[3] But he ultimately drifted out of Tubby's camp, he says, after a domestic debacle. "Me there with a girl at Tower Hill and me and her break up. She move out everything and me there 'pon the floor, so me go check Tubby as the Godfather and say: 'Father Tubbs, me need a bed.' But him say: 'Boy, just gwan and lick it.' That time 'AIDS' bubble 'pon the charts, so me go check Jammy's; him give me a cheque fi three grand, and right away we do 'Legal We Legal' and 'Trouble Again'."

As both were spectacular hits, the move to Saint Lucia Road was obviously the right one. Like many of his peers, Kong really found his feet at Jammy's, voicing the excellent album *Trouble Again* and several other impressive singles in a short space of time. From Jammy's point of view, having all three 'bad card' sing-jays in his camp naturally strengthened things, although each was also voicing elsewhere.

With live musicians falling by the wayside as an army of new computer producers instantaneously emerged, Jammy's digital stable became the focal point for a new set of stars, including baritone toaster Little Twitch (aka Richard Wright), the uniquely talented deejay Tiger (aka Norman Jackson), whose expressive, somewhat exaggerated delivery seemed perfectly suited to digital music, plus singers Colin Roach and Anthony Malvo, rubbing shoulders with better established folk like Cocoa Tea and Frankie Paul. A pivotal moment came when one of Jammy's leading deejays, a tall youth known as Tonto Irie, got so big on the dancehall circuit that he began spending more time abroad, so Bobby Digital coaxed the pot-bellied toaster Admiral Bailey away from the rival King Sturgav sound to join in combination with Chaka Demus (aka John Taylor), a bull-necked toaster whose gruff but well-timed delivery made him one of Jammy's finest deejays. The combination formula worked well on both sound system and record, although Bailey's subsequent solo material was even more popular, keeping him a constant feature of the Jamaican charts during the late 80s.

At King Jammy's studio, a thoroughly relaxed Glendon Bailey says he is currently more active as a football coach, although he still sporadically records. He begins his tale by emphasising that Ranking Joe and Josey Wales were chief role models. "I grow in Olympic Gardens, best recognised as Tower Hill, where it rough on everybody, living with just your mother, who never there for a child. My two big brothers were known as 'shottas' – a badness thing them ah deal with – so me alone just take that other path. I sing as a youth inna the church choir, and then Ranking Joe was my deejay from Sturgav days. Listening to Ranking Joe change me from singing to deejay, because of the uniqueness of how him deliver the message, and from the sound ah string up, that man deejay till the dance done.

"The next deejay whe really make me decide what me want to do was Josey Wales, long before him even start record; before him there 'pon Sturgav, Josey used to deejay 'pon a sound named Roots Unlimited, down ah Mall Road in Olympic Gardens, and from them days we ah listen to Josey till him start deejay 'pon General Graph, a sound whe name themselves similar off of Stereograph. Josey used to deejay slackness and politics – 'nuff man no know that Josey was a slackness deejay, and he used to make it fun, so me and a next youth in school used to compete, who can deejay the best Ranking Joe or Josey Wales lyrics."

As the Admiral was blessed with the ability to readily adapt to any kind of rhythm, he soon began making a name for himself chatting hard-hitting, humorous rhymes on a local sound called Twilight, which led to further appearances on Torpedo, based in rural Saint Mary. "I was doing my original style, the same style me use today, and I think that is one of the things that keep me going. Style ah no something you develop. To me, style ah just something you born with."

The catalyst to bring him to another level was a spontaneous friendship with Josey Wales, which led to greater exposure – and ultimately a shift to Jammy's. "One night Volcano play at Olympic Way and the crowd start bawling for me, so Josey Wales said: 'Them want to hear Admiral, so come in Admiral!' and bring me in 'pon the big sound, and ah pure murder, 'cos the place just mash up. So me no bust yet, but me a slow-leak, 'cos word start to go out. Then U Roy say him want me to deejay 'pon him sound, so me was the warm-up man for Josey Wales and Charlie Chaplin, and me get $300 a night – the biggest money me get out of the business – but me and U Roy couldn't get along. Bobby Digital start to hear of me, and Tonto Irie used to go ah foreign regular, so Jammy did want a next artist fi combine with Chaka Demus. Jammy said: 'Me can give you $100 to play ah town and $150 when we go ah country.' Now, that is cutting my pay in half, but it's like the Father talk to me: 'U Roy have a sound that is now on top, but this man have a sound that is going someplace, plus him have a studio, and the main objective is to start becoming a recording artist.' So it end up to be a good move.

"When I get that job, Chaka Demus and Tullo T. was the big man with Jammy's, so the first night pon Red Hills Road, me no get no mic; them wait till a slow Studio One rhythm start play before them bring me in, because them figure me would drop off, but pity them no know me coming from U Roy, so me tear down the place. Jammy's brother Trevor, Uncle T, bring the report to Jammy, so the second night the sound play ah Harbour View, and Jammy come to the dance because him want to hear me for himself, and me just burn down the place. We had a dance at Portland the following night, with only me and Pompidoo – 'the deejay with the rockstone voice' – and it was a blessing in disguise, because me just burn the place, pure shot a fire, and I bust now inna the sound business. Then me and Chaka Demus become the big man that everybody talk bout."

Bailey's subsequent recording debut, the boastful 'Top Celebrity Man', made no impact in Jamaica, but proved popular with dancehall fans in Britain. The song to elevate him with his home audience was a dancehall update of Amos Milburn's blues standard 'One Scotch', cut in collaboration with Chaka Demus, which topped the Jamaican charts in 1986. "That idea developed by Chaka Demus," Bailey explains, "but every lyrical content that both of us deejay was our own. And it's not like we sit down and write, cause them time there, it's just out of the head."

The following year, Bailey scored a series of even bigger solo hits. The strangely celebratory 'Big Belly Man' was a veritable anthem, saluting the many figures in the music business with a girth as wide as his own. "We there ah Fort Clarence at the Champions in Action concert, with Little Twitch, Josey Wales, and The Sagittarius Band," says Bailey of the tune's debut. "Me's a man who kill you with drama – a man have to know this is entertainment – so it is fun. Inna them days, most of the big man whe people know have big belly – the man who have money, or man whe famous – you ah talk 'bout Jammy, you ah talk 'bout Steelie, you ah talk 'bout me, so me just say me ah go build something where that is concerned, and it hit. I love to build tunes based 'pon what you see around you. That's why those tunes last until today."

Bigger still was the controversial 'Punany', a rude record that points to the rise of sexually explicit 'slackness'. "'Punany' mean the young girl's vagina, no secret there about that, so we no have to go round no corner where that is concerned," laughs Bailey. "We express weself, so I say: 'Give me punany, me want punany,' because me love punany. The tunes that hit and last is tune whe you feel, and it no matter whether the punany good, bad, or whether it ah go kill me, me just want the punany – it's as simple as that."

Although rude records were nothing new in Jamaican music, songs were far more explicit in the early dancehall age. Before he was shot dead by police in 1980, General Echo led the way with singles such as 'Bathroom Sex' and albums such as *Slackest LP In The World*, produced by Winston Riley and issued under the moniker Ranking Slackness. Following close behind was the internationally renowned Yellowman, with songs like 'Cocky Did A Hurt Me' and 'Bedroom Mazuka' for Junjo Lawes. Other early dancehall slackers include Welton Irie, who cut an early X-rated LP for Joe Gibbs, *It Feels So Good*, and Johnny Ringo with tunes like the extremely surreal 'Two Lesbians Hitch' for Tommy Cowan. Then came a flood of cruder efforts stimulated by the 'Punany' craze, with Grindsman offering 'Benz Punany' for L.A. May's Dragon Records in 1989 and Little Lenny warning of 'Punany Tegereg' for Patrick Roberts' Shocking Vibes label the following year.[4] Meanwhile, concurrent with Admiral's groundbreaking hit, Lovindeer's self-produced 'The Oil' and 'Panty Size' both used suggestive humour to make their effect rather than being outright lewd. (His biggest hit of all, 'Wild Gilbert', was a non-slack tune describing the hurricane that caused widespread destruction upon reaching Jamaica in September 1988 – the most powerful storm to hit the island since 1951's Hurricane Charlie.)

The excessive use of foul language was also becoming a problem at stage shows: at the 1988 edition of the annual Sting concert, held at the National Stadium, the microphone was switched off at key intervals, particularly when artists were cursing each other too vigorously. Later, artists like Mad Cobra and Ninjaman would voice discs venerating firearms (the former with 'Shoot To Kill' for Captain Sinbad, the latter with 'Murda Dem' for Steelie & Clevie, plus 'My Weapon' for Cargill Lawrence's Mr Doo label), 'gun talk' rising in tandem with slackness. However, it would be wrong to think of such artists as exclusively gun-oriented, since Cobra cut the occasional 'conscious' tune, too, while much of Ninja's early work for Junior Reid dealt with more constructive topics, such as the biased nature of Jamaican politics and the need for a decent education. The curious 'Bob Marley Way' even looked at the contradictions inherent in Marley's lyrics, as well as in verses of the Bible.

In any case, Admiral Bailey does not see his rude records as being on par with the extremely explicit styles that would emerge in the following years, when the hardcore dancehall or 'ragga' style became cinematically hyper-real. "When a man deejay slackness nowadays, him no keep it discreet or make the mind wonder what him ah talk 'bout – him just say it raw, dry. We used to do it so nice that even the elderly laugh, because them read between the lines. But now man just push it inna your face."

Other chart-toppers from Bailey's peak include 'Two Year Old', a bizarre, semi-slack paean to youth recorded for New York-based producer, Hyman 'Jah Life' Wright, and a series of further anthems for Jammy, including the patriotic 1987 landmark, 'No Way No Better Than Yard', plus a new song on the 'Punany' rhythm called 'Healthy Body' – revived three years later for a return collaboration with Chaka Demus called 'This Is We' – as well as the infectious 'Winey Winey' (1989) and the rude 'Bumper Bottom' (1992).

Bailey ultimately feels his longstanding success is down to versatility, as well as his ability to keep it real. "You have different people inna the dance, so you have to please everybody: some man want to hear gun, some want to hear about punany, then a next man want to hear about Selassie or God, so you have to deejay for everybody. The whole aspect of it is catering to the people that is listening to you."

○

CLOCKWISE FROM TOP LEFT: mellow canary Barrington Levy; Cocoa Tea; Prince Jammy at the controls.

THIS PAGE: Sing-jay gorilla, King Kong; untold stories: Buju Banton.
OPPOSITE: General Trees.

CLOCKWISE FROM TOP RIGHT: Real revolutionary Anthony B.; Mr Vegas; the Messenger, Luciano.

Although every deejay is required to be versatile to succeed, not everyone felt comfortable venturing into risqué territory. "I never used to sing slack songs, 'cos I don't believe in lewdness," says Lieutenant Stitchie, one of the most popular and influential deejays of the period. "You have different markets and people have different tastes, but I believe in subtlety and suggestiveness, not lewndess and slackness. The easiest way out is to speak something derogatory, so most deejays start going that way, but in my book, it wasn't the order of the day, because it is my responsibility as an entertainer to ensure that I impart something positive to the audience at all times."

When I spoke to Stitchie, aka Cleveland Laing, he was holding court at his close friend Bobby Digital's studio, located on an anonymous residential street in Maverley. As well as being readily approachable, he is an obviously intelligent man and, unusually for Jamaica, is very punctual. Like Admiral Bailey, he names Ranking Joe as a key role model, along with the Rasta deejay Brigadier Jerry.

"I was born in Kingston but grew up in Spanish Town, and my father died when I was four, so it was very challenging in a lot of different areas," he says. "I've always done very well in school, but I never had any textbooks, because my mother couldn't afford them. She was very active in the church, so I used to be on the church choir and the school choir, performing in different competitions, like the Jamaica Cultural Development Commission [JCDC] have an annual competition in primary and high schools, and I competed at both levels. But then there was a dance in the area with Sturgav, and the deejay was Ranking Joe; outside the dance, when I first heard him deejaying, I was so impressed, I thought he was reading from a book, but when I got in the dance I realised that he was speaking spontaneously! Then I heard Brigadier Jerry on Jah Love sound system, and I was so impressed by both of them that I started writing my own lyrics."

During the early 80s, while he was working as a biology teacher, Stitchie began performing on a local sound system called Django under the name Ranking Noseworthy. Due to an enduring love of citrus fruits, he was known to friends as Citrus or Citchie, so his debut recording – 'If I Don't Care', recorded for a neighbour called Willie – is said to have credited Ranking Citrus. A later single allegedly credited Stitchie due to a label misprint, the material issued as the deejay made inroads on the highly competitive sound-system circuit.

"I went to another sound system called City Lights," he recalls, "then another called Lightning Super Mix, with Papa San, Major Worries, Anthony Red Rose, and Thriller U. But when everybody went their separate ways, I went to Stereo One, the number-one sound system in Jamaica from 1986–89. It was based in Kingston on Morgan Lane in Grant's Pen, and that's where Stitchie made his name."

Even in these early days, Stitchie's obvious intelligence, poetic phrasing, and knack for storytelling helped set his material apart. For instance, on the 1985 single 'Two Is Better Than Too Many', Stitchie dealt with family planning issues, rather than the wanton topics of other deejays, while 'Story Time' described various neighbourhood characters with cinematic precision. His subsequent recordings may not have achieved much in the way of sales, but they ultimately led him to Jammy's, where his popularity surged.

"I recorded songs with Stereo One like 'Laba Laba' and 'Story Time', and I recorded with Steelie, 'Lover Boy Sess', and I was also on his sound system, Silver Hawk, based in August Town," he says. "It was Steelie that introduced me to Jammy's as an upcoming talent, and I appeared on the Clash Of The Century with Black Scorpio, Metromedia, and Arrows International, where Jammy was crowned the king sound. Then I did my first hit record with Jammy, 'Wear Yu Size'."

The allegorical 'Wear Yu Size' warned of a girlfriend who tried to squeeze into the wrong pair of shoes, its popularity bolstered by a hilarious music video. "That is a humorous song, telling you how modest ladies sometimes want to be, and also us generally getting into a position that we're not really fitting into, so you're biting off more than you can chew," Stitchie explains. "It was totally different from what was happening at the time, because this was in a story format that you could follow, and that wasn't present in deejay music at all." The popularity of the song led to further hits for Stereo One, such as 'Nice Girl', a tale of attempted seduction, and the excellent 'Natty Dread', which describes the discrimination and police brutality faced by Rastas, and was again supplanted by a fine music video (this time with leading Jamaican actor Carl Bradshaw in the title role).

Soon Stitchie bagged a major-label contract, leading to international renown. "I did my first album with Jammy, *Wear Yu Size*, which was a massive success, and then I did a dub plate for Stone Love, 'Old Time Teaching', and an executive from Atlantic Records was at one of the dances and was fascinated by it, because even after the rhythm ended, I was still deejaying, and that was a new style again. I got signed to Atlantic in March 1988 – the first reggae artist signed – and that was the first single released."

Stitchie's five-year tenure with Atlantic produced several hit albums and brought him into new territories through collaborations with rap artists such as LL Cool J, The Youngsters, and Big Daddy Kane, as well as female R&B trio En Vogue and veteran soul singer Teddy Pendergrass. He also opened for Freddy Jackson, Stevie Wonder, and Johnny Gill, and even played with Luther Vandross at Madison Square Gardens. His major-label signing also pointed to dancehall's international potential, leading labels such as Elektra and Sony to sign Jamaican performers, particularly after Maxine Stowe, niece of Clement Dodd and wife of Sugar Minott, joined Sony's A&R team. However, as deejays such as Dillinger and Yellowman had already discovered through previous shortlived deals with A&M and CBS, being signed to a major was inevitably a mixed blessing.

"I did three albums for Atlantic – *The Governor*, *Wild Jamaican Romances*, and *Rude Boy* – but I was basically a guinea pig, because they never knew how to market me," Stitchie laments. "They take me into crevices and corners outside of Jamaica that I would never normally have been in, and I got a lot of exposure from it, but I left Atlantic because you had to be doing a different sort of song to break into a certain market, and that was cutting down on your style – watering down. They treated me extremely well, but there were still limitations, so at some point, I had to break loose."

Back in the late 80s, the storytelling style influenced hits such as Echo Minott's semi-deejayed tale of domestic violence, 'What The Hell', and its deejay answer tune, Major Worries' 'Babylon Boops' – both massive hits for Jammy in 1986. The style also underlines General Trees' 'Gone A Negril', a number-two chart placing the same year that recounted a gold-digging female's fruitless entreaty for Trees to supply her with a foreign visa, despite possessing no passport. At his home in Drewsland, the genial Trees (aka Amos Edwards) emphasises that his songs have always been concerned with reality, and like Stitchie, he refuses to be sidelined by frivolous or negative subject matter.

"I prefer social commentary," he explains in a deep baritone. "That's my thinking with music: see what's going on, put it together, and relate it to people. What you really have in your heart, that's what you push out. Trees nah go talk slackness, and me's a man whe can't really portray gun culture. I move more as a culture person, love to spread a clean message to one and all, no matter what race you might be. At all times, me have something good fi tell them."

After an unsettled youth, Trees found work as a shoemaker but was constantly putting lyrics together. In 1985, a chance meeting with leading local deejay Lord Sassafras brought him onto Black Scorpio sound system, kick-starting his professional career. The stage-name Trees – actually a

365

corruption of Threes – was bestowed on him by radio disc jockey Barry G., who felt he had a trio of voices at his command.

"I born in Kingston but grow partly in Saint Thomas with my aunt, 'cos my mother die from I was about three years old, and my father's a man who run off and left we, so me ah grow wild," Trees recalls. "Then I'm an original shoemaker, and one day Sassafras come for his shoes to fix, and I was running some lyrics, so he said: 'You sound good. I have a sound I'm working on, I could take you there and see what you could do.' The first couple times I go on Scorpio, I just have the crowd jumping and railing, so it's like I was a professional. A few months later, we done the first song, 'Ghost Rider', about a guy who ride at night without lights. Then we come with 'Heart Mind & Soul', another hit, and later 'Gone A Negril', so we have a good relationship with Black Scorpio from those times."

'Ghost Rider' was one of the biggest hits of 1985. Its chorus held slight echoes of the phrasing of both Admiral Bailey's 'Two Year Old' and Josey Wales's massive 'Undercover Lover', but the overall style was all Trees' own. 'Heart Mind & Soul', which became the title track of a 'showcase' album, was a prime example of Trees' fluid, confident toasting style, his lyrics sitting perfectly atop the record's spongy rhythm, the words distinguished by their general constructiveness. 'Mini Bus', another early hit, decried the demise of Jamaica's public bus system, adapting the chorus of Pete Seeger's folk classic, 'Where Have All The Flowers Gone', for his own purposes on a modulated re-cut of 'Freedom Blues'.

Trees' hit material helped Black Scorpio make a dent in Jammy's dominance, as would bigger hits from other artists released by Donovan Germain, but from 1987, the rival to really pose a serious challenge to Jammy's crown was Gussie Clarke, who crafted a very distinctive sound at his newly opened Music Works studio at 56 Slipe Road. "We felt that we were deprived going into other studios," Gussie explains. 'We felt that we needed more time to develop ideas on our own."

During the mid 80s, Gussie typically worked at Channel One with engineer Soljie Hamilton. He cut several albums with The Mighty Diamonds (following the success of 'Pass The Dutchie' on a 'Full Up' re-cut), plus an album of soul covers with Delroy Wilson, *Worth Your Weight In Gold*; a Tetrack album called *Trouble*; and, best of all, Gregory Isaacs's album *Private Beach Party*, recorded at Dynamics and Music Mountain with engineer Noel Hearne.

Never one to rush releases, nor follow dominant trends, Gussie equipped his own studio with unusual components to distinguish it from rival concerns. "I think going against the grain gives one the advantage. Dynamics had the dealership for MCI consoles, so everybody had an MCI, but we went to England and realised that Amek have good consoles. Everybody had a Sony or an MCI tape machine, so we bought Atari, 'cos we just wanted to be different."

Despite its minimal dimensions, Music Works conjured a magical sound whose futurism placed it at the forefront of Jamaican music at the end of the 80s. "We had nothing more than one room, which was an office that we distributed from, so we converted the toilet into a vocal booth, and converted the main room into a control room, so you transact business out on the step."

The hits came thick and fast at Music Works thanks to a devoted team of creative individuals, including Clevie and younger brother Danny on the rhythm-building side (occasionally aided by Steelie); Robbie Lyn on keyboards and Dalton Browne on guitar; the wildcard mixing wizard Steven Stanley in the engineer's chair; and Carlton Hines of Tetrack, fellow singer Hopeton Lindo, and Mikey Bennett from vocal group Home T4 as songwriters and arrangers. This fertile combination generated instantaneous energy, yielding immediate and lasting results from the issue of Gregory Isaacs's 'Rumours' in 1988.

"'Rumours' was the first rhythm track laid," says Gussie proudly. "We were doing a Mighty Diamonds project, and we thought that the song would be perfect for them, but when the song done, we just didn't like it. So we were thinking about who to use for it, and one day, I say: 'Gregory Isaacs,' and Gregory just walk through the door!"

'Rumours' cast Gregory in the role of a suspected drugs 'Don', playing on the outlaw reputation that stemmed from repeated arrests, imprisonment on gun charges, and recent dependence on crack cocaine; the rugged rhythm, punctuated by disjointed synthesizer chords, gave the record an irresistible quality that saw it fill dance floors on both sides of the Atlantic. Further hits rapidly followed based on the same rhythm, including J.C. Lodge's sex-talk exposé, 'Telephone Love', female toaster Lady G.'s 'Nuff Respect', and the group ode cut in celebration of Britain's black community radio stations, 'Pirate's Anthem', featuring Cocoa Tea, Home T, and dancehall toaster Shabba Ranks, one of the most impressive talents to rise in this period. "We created a whole album with the rhythm, *Showcase '88*, and nobody even tried to touch it," Gussie explains. "Our technology and our sound was entirely different from what was happening, so it was difficult to duplicate."

Duplication was a particularly problematic feature of dancehall's digital form. Not only were producers constantly falling back on old Studio One and Treasure Isle rhythms, which were given cursory computerised adaptations, but any producer with a hit found dozens of carbon copies surfacing immediately. "You had producers who kept doing the same thing over and over," Robbie Lyn explains. "If someone come with a hit song, sometimes I end up doing the same rhythm track for three different producers the same day. It was easy money, but looking back on it now, it's not something you're proud of, because you wish people would come with ideas of their own, instead of doing the same thing that someone just did ten minutes ago."

Thankfully, Gussie's team made sure their rhythms were consistently original, keeping Music Works at the top of the heap for a couple of years, until Carlton Hines emigrated to New York and Mikey Bennett joined forces with Patrick Lindsey for a dynamic new production outfit, Two Friends (who soon yielded their own hits). Gussie's broad scope is partly what made his output so appealing. While most producers were concentrating on toasters, Gussie cut noteworthy work with UK-based lover's rock singers Deborahe Glasgow and Peter Hunningale, never neglecting talented vocalists. He also scored a coup by producing Shabba Ranks's first hit album, *Rappin' With The Ladies*, which contained a number of outstanding tracks, including the signature 'Mr Loverman', voiced on a Deborahe Glasgow number.

Shabba (aka Rexton Gordon) was easily the most versatile and charismatic deejay of his generation. The way his smooth rapping flow contrasted with the hardcore focus of his lyrics gave him an outstanding edge, and his popular work for various producers showed that he could captivate an audience with any topic, be it the folk wisdom of 'Peanie Peanie', the macho posturing of 'Wicked In Bed' and 'Trailorload Of Girls', the slackness of 'Caan Done' and 'Love Punany Bad', or the salutation of his iconic predecessors on 'Respect'. He was also adept at the 'combination' style, as evidenced by the huge success of 'Who She Love', which he voiced for Gussie in collaboration with Home T and Cocoa Tea.

"His style's unique," says Bobby Digital, who scored a series of hits with Shabba in the late 80s during the unsettled phase when he broke away from Jammy to become an independent production force. "The way he put his lyrics together and his deliverance was different from the other guys, and he's a commanding fellow, so this is obviously someone who's going to get respect from the public." Hits like 'Peanie Peanie' and 'Trailorload Of Girls' helped Bobby to establish the Digital B label, while Shabba's perpetual rise, aided by a management contract with Clifton 'Specialist' Dillon, soon brought a contract with Sony's Epic subsidiary, leading to collaborative work with hip-hop stars such as KRS-One, Queen Latifah, and Chubb Rock, plus rock'n'roll veteran Chuck Berry and soul crooner Johnny Gill. As the 80s gave way to the 90s, Shabba's resounding success ultimately signalled that dancehall had become a genre of international significance.

It is worth remembering that, despite the overarching popularity of the deejay during this period, a number of veteran singers scored impressive digital hits in the late 80s, including Sugar Minott, Freddy McGregor, Dennis Brown, Leroy Smart, Barrington Levy, Half Pint, and Johnny Osbourne. "You born in the dancehall because there was no TV around," Osbourne says, "and I love anything that's creative. It was a new trend, so I just take the old school with the new school, put them together and make one big school."

Perhaps the most popular singer to successfully survive the digital shift was Beres Hammond, who achieved an incredible string of hits from the mid 80s, following a problematic transition period. "When I left Zap Pow, I went to Joe Gibbs by the advice of Willie Lindo," he explains. "We did an album, *Just A Man*, that had two number-one songs on it, 'I'm Gonna Burn In The Morning Sun' and 'I'm In Love With You', and that's when A&M made an approach, but there was problems with Joe Gibbs, because what he was offering me was pretty disrespectful. Willie Lindo and myself decided to go to Dynamic Sounds to do an album called *Coming At You* – it did well also, but the financial side was still a mystery: how come I'm doing all the right things, but the right thing's not happening to me? The name was growing, but the pocket was slowing, so I decided to do something for myself: I did some harmonies with Pam Hall, saved up to pay musicians, got some time from Aquarius, and started my album, *Let's Make A Song*. I figured that I knew about the music but I didn't know anything about the business, so I brought in a friend to take care of that part, but that never worked out either."

After so many frustrations, the big breakthrough finally came in 1985 with the infectious ballad 'Groovy Little Thing', issued on Beres's own Harmony House label, which sold by the bucket-load, particularly after shop owner, label boss and sound-system veteran Count Shelley picked up the record for overseas distribution. "I was still doing little tracks for myself," Beres explains, "and at this point I decided to put out a reggae single, 'cos all along I was concentrating more on R&B ballads, so I mixed down 'Groovy Little Thing' and it shaped up nicely. Count Shelley was in New York, bought some of the records and said: 'You play this music? You want me to do something with it fi you? We can go to England, me can make 'nuff

369

things happen! All you have to do is give me a stamper and some labels.' So I gave him 3,000 labels, and about a week later he called me and said: 'Record finished.' He send about $4,000 – first time me a get a clump! And I can't tell you how good that felt, so I sent out 5,000 more labels to him, next time him send about, $6,000 for me, and when the song entered the British charts, it must have been about $70,000 – pow!"

Further giant hits followed in quick succession, including 'She Loves Me Now', another self-produced reggae ballad, and the phenomenal 'What One Dance Can Do', produced by Willie Lindo on a minimal re-cut of 'Pressure & Slide'. "Sly Dunbar and Big Youth always said to me: 'Anytime you start sing reggae, you go mash up the place,'" Beres explains, "and 'What One Dance Can Do' went number one everywhere. Then [Donovan] Germain did an answer with Audrey Hall, which went number two in the British charts, which turn the tables for me, as that was when I start seeing some financial compensation."

Unfortunately, just as Beres was finally earning proper remuneration, disaster struck through a near-death experience, symptomatic of Jamaica's escalating crime wave. "Some crazy shit happened to me in the late 80s," he says with a visible shudder. "I was living off Molynes Road and some guys came into the house, tied me up, and robbed me. My woman had some kids, and they just tied up everybody and rolled us in sheets. They wanted to kill me, put a pillow over my head, and I had to find something quick to distract them, so I tell them that police was living next door, and they were trigger happy, so if they hear any noise in the night, they would come and kill everybody. It was horrible, man, and that took a toll on me for about three years. Most of that time I was in New York, afraid to do anything. We later found out who did it, and the guys died: police kill some, bad man kill some, and bad mind kill some."

Beres was certainly not the only artist to face extreme forms of violence in this era. On April 17 1987, drummer Carlton Barrett was murdered outside his home by a lone gunman, apparently dispatched by Barrett's wife and her lover. Less than five months later, on September 11, Peter Tosh was brutally murdered by an associate, Dennis 'Leppo' Lobban, during a robbery at the singer's home in which radio disc jockey Jeff 'Free-I' Dixon was also killed, and drummer Santa Davis and Tosh's wife Marlene seriously injured. Then, on February 6 1989, King Tubby's senseless murder robbed Jamaican music of another of its most creative figures. He was killed outside his home by a group of unknown assailants, apparently during an attempted robbery, and no one has ever been charged for the murder.

Jamaican artists venturing overseas were also troubled by violence, with Tenor Saw reportedly killed by a speeding car in Texas in August 1988. "Tenor Saw was a blessed youth whe come fi do some serious work, but along the wayside get captured by things," says King Kong, who released the self-produced tribute 'He Was A Friend' shortly thereafter. "We become friends ah New York and maybe it's because, at the time, me did touch the coke, and him did touch it too – I think most entertainers all dabble somewhere, and some man just get caught, and the wrong thing happens." Worse still was the death of Nitty Gritty, killed in a shootout with Super Cat that erupted at Count Shelley's Superpower record store in Brooklyn in June 1991 in an incident that allegedly stemmed from a dispute about proceeds from a sound-system event, with Cat apparently firing in self-defence (he signed with Sony shortly after the incident).

It was against a backdrop of out-of-control violence that Jamaica's 1989 general elections were played out, a cowed Michael Manley winning his re-election three days after King Tubby's murder. During Edward Seaga's nine-year reign, a series of restrictive IMF loans had seriously worsened the already faltering economy. With crack cocaine increasingly embedded in the society, many youth became addicts, while the turf wars related to control of its distribution wreaked havoc on the general population, particularly as the former 'enforcers' of party loyalty were now connected to international crime syndicates. Seaga's free-market agenda pleased Washington, but his closeness to the Reagan administration failed to better the lives of ordinary citizens. With high levels of unemployment, rampant inflation, and little scope for betterment, it is no wonder that violent crime escalated, especially as weaponry was readily available.

Following the collapse of the Soviet Union, and with it the broader utopian ideals of socialism, the re-elected Manley brought a far more moderate agenda, especially in terms of private enterprise. He would remain in office for the next three years, during which he was plagued by health problems, as he attempted to reverse the most punitive aspects of Seaga's tenure.

Although most reggae now celebrated romance, sex, or firearms, certain artists remained committed to tackling serious subjects. In the aftermath of the general election, one of the biggest tunes was Junior Reid's 'One Blood', a vibrant, self-produced digital anthem that was a rallying cry for unity.[5] It begins by reminding listeners that they are all part of one human family, regardless of which side of Kingston's political divide they come from. Reid then broadens the scope to apply the same thinking to different nations and ethnicities around the world.

"You could come from Rema, Jungle, Firehouse, or Tower Hill – it's still one blood," Reid says. "Then I unite the world: East, West, North, and South Africa, Europe and all over, link up the Irishman and the Englishman, link the Mexican and Pakistan, and them no like that, because Babylon making so much money to divide the world and cause war. Who is likkle me to come and tell the world that we is one? But because the word is so powerful, I say the word and the word manifest: a lot of people didn't war, and Babylon don't like that."

Reid further explains that the opening line, "Modern vampires of the city sucking blood", symbolised the oppressive forces operating in contemporary societies. "The system that Babylon set up is a vampire, just suck your blood by trying to suffer you, lock you from what you're supposed to live a comfortable life. So when me say 'Modern vampires of the city', it lick a lot of people, because there's a lot of vampires around." The song struck a chord with reggae fans overseas, leading to foreign remixes (and its eventual sampling by Wu-Tang Clan), plus a hit collaboration with Scottish rock act The Soup Dragons for an augmented cover version of The Rolling Stones' 'I'm Free'. Such activity would allow Reid to establish the One Blood studio as a vehicle for rising talent as well as his own material.

The hopeful climate that brought forth 'One Blood' also provided a belated breakthrough for Admiral Tibet, one of the few performers to consistently go against the digital grain by producing solely conscious material. "People been asking me: 'How did you manage in the 80s, when it was just you, Edi Fitzroy, and Cocoa Tea doing conscious music?' It was just a little minority, to the majority with the slackness and the gun lyrics, but me believe in what me doing. I never get tricked. Some artists, if they see that by doing some gun tune they can make some money, they going to do gun tune. So money is one of the main distractions for 'nuff of them."

Holding court on Orange Street, Tibet is obviously a man of great conviction. Born Kenneth Allen in 1960, he reveals that his stage name came from an incident at school, when he and his cousin discovered Tibet in the atlas, and explains that he was compelled to head to Kingston at the end of his teens to pursue music. "I was born in Free Hill, Saint Mary, and I grew up in the adjoining district of Oxford. My father was a postman, my mother was a housewife, and there were five of us kids, so it was a bit rough for my parents. When I leave school at 17 I have to plant cane, carry coconuts, carry bananas, but I just find myself singing, make up my own songs. The first song I write goes: 'I saw a light in me all day and it is before me every night', but I couldn't tell you the meaning of the lyrics. I was singing in the district, and my friends give me compliments; then elderly people hear me and say: 'You have a wonderful voice, the Lord need you with a voice like this! Come to church and sing!' So that give me confidence. I came to Kingston in '81 because I was hearing about Henry 'Junjo' Lawes, and I wanted to make this man produce a song with me. I was staying for three months with a friend at McKoy Lane, near Junjo's corner; Junjo asked me to sing a song, but I couldn't sing, because of nervousness."

After spending the rest of the year back in the countryside, Tibet returned to Kingston in 1982 to work in an electrical-goods factory; although he was more determined than ever to pursue a musical career, he did not reach the recording studio until 1985, after a friend introduced him to upcoming producer Sherman Clatcher, whose Arabic label was attached to a record shop in Cross Roads. The resultant single, 'Babylon War', was funded by Sherman and arranged at Aquarius by co-producer Leon Synmoie. The singer's smooth delivery showed great promise, his potent lyrics delivered in a distinctive tenor.

"That song break me out to the public, so Winston Riley sent for me, and the first song I do for him is 'Woman Is A Trouble' on the 'Stalag' rhythm, and then 'Leave People Business Alone', one of my biggest sellers. People have a habit of spreading rumours, and sometimes it even cause fights, so I just say: 'Leave people business alone and mind your own'. Then I get in touch with Jammy and did 'Serious Time': listening to the news and seeing with my own eyes so many serious things going on, like mother against their own daughter, father against son, brother ah fight against brother, and war down in the Middle East … you have to make the world know what ah gwan."

'Serious Time' is an unusual record in that it hit twice in Jamaica in different formats, with only a short gap between the two. The King Jammy original helped solidify Tibet's reputation in 1987, before the re-vamped 'combination' version, issued by Bobby Digital, became one of the biggest Jamaican chart successes of 1991. "It was remixed with me, Shabba, and Ninjaman for Bobby Digital, a great producer who loves quality," Tibet says. "Me and Bobby did really have an understanding, because he was the engineer at Jammy's on the album I did there, and it get a lot of compliments. Bobby is not like some engineers who just stay frozen – we communicate, so me comfortable working with Bobby. I've voiced for different producers, but Bobby is one of the main."

By the time the reworked 'Serious Time' hit the charts, Beres Hammond had confronted his demons, returned to Jamaica, and begun voicing instant hits for various producers, the biggest coming via Donovan Germain, who had established the popular Penthouse recording studio across the road from Music Works. "I came back in 1990 and I was looking some time around Germain," he recalls. "He says he's all booked up, but he could work out a deal with me: he had a rhythm, and if I could produce something on that rhythm for him, then he would give me studio time. Some girl passed by, I think it was [future vocalist] Patra, before she broke out, and an idea struck me: 'Hey little girl, each time you pass my way I'm tempted to touch.' And three weeks later, that song was mashing up New York. Everything started looking up again, so I did 'Putting Up Resistance' for Tappa Zukie and started doing some things for Fatis Burrell."

'Putting Up Resistance' proved that Beres Hammond was still yielding strong songs of political relevance, in addition to his more common ballads, but even his romantic material could be unusual. The minimal chart-topper 'Emptiness Inside', recorded for upcoming producer and former political 'enforcer' Philip 'Fatis' Burrell, had the spine-tingling, eerie quality of a man trapped in desperation. But the biggest hit was easily the irresistible 'Tempted To Touch', voiced on a rollicking re-cut of 'A Love I Can Feel', which had been crafted for Germain by UK-based rhythm duo Mafia & Fluxy (aka Leroy and David Heywood). The rhythm's infectious quality led to another outstanding hit, Tony Rebel's endearing 'Fresh Vegetable', a sing-jay love song from an ital point of view. "I was telling a lady 'I love you like fresh vegetable', because the men used to call women 'beef' or 'porkie'," Rebel explains, "but as a Rastaman, we wanted to change that."

The radiant sing-jay, born Patrick Barrett, is holding court at Flames Productions, his headquarters in uptown Pembroke Hall. Like Admiral Tibet and many other contemporaries, he migrated to Kingston in pursuit of music. "I was born in Manchester in 1962 and raised mostly by my grandparents, because my mother died in a bus accident when I was four years old. In school, I used to sit at the desk and deejay, and I won the JCDC deejay contest in Manchester in 1983 and 1984. One time I was on a sound called Destiny Outernational in Manchester, run by some people who came from England, and we had a competition with Youth Promotion, and Colourman was saying that I should come to Kingston to join Youth Promotion. Then, when I was 12, I came to Kingston to stay with my uncle in Whitfield Avenue for a short period, and I met Sugar Minott and got a lot of experience around Youth Promotion, but I was in and out, from town to country, where I do farming – plant everything, legal and illegal – until I returned to Kingston in March 1988, to live in this very house, which my aunt owned. I was a big man in my twenties then, with two kids."

Rebel's debut single, 'Casino', pondered the government's reluctance to relax gambling restrictions. It was released on Michael Gentles's Mandeville-based MGB label in 1985; despite making little impact, it is noteworthy because it was already cut in the versatile sing-jay style that would later make him famous. "I always listen to U Roy, U Brown, Trinity, Lone Ranger, but a lot of other deejays used to sound monotonous," he explains. "They did not use melodies, they used to just talk, but I was from that school where I heard U Roy chanting, so I decided that I would get that style in. Brigadier Jerry and Charlie Chaplin sing-jay, but I seem to heighten it a little bit, bring a little more *oomph* to it; I stuck to sing-jay, because people remember a melody more."

Rebel's friend and fellow Destiny Outernational deejay, Garnett Smith, had followed him to Kingston from Manchester hoping to also establish himself in music. In fact, they were working on Youth Promotion together, and Garnett later wound up living with Rebel in Pembroke Hall. Then known as Little Bimbo, he would later achieve greater fame under the name Garnett Silk, once he switched to singing, stimulating great changes in the dominant dancehall style in the process. But Rebel made the initial break upon joining the Penthouse stable, after returning to Kingston full-time, arriving shortly before the label took dancehall to another level during the early 90s.

"I was introduced to Donovan Germain in 1988 by a brethren called Ray Rochester," he recalls. "I went for an audition and Germain was impressed, but more impressed was the engineer, Dave Kelly, who helped me to arrange some of my songs. Germain was a fearless explorer of the music, so he evolutionised the nowadays dancehall with hard, rootsy bass lines and Studio One [re-cuts], doing over those rhythms with Sly & Robbie and Steelie & Clevie, bringing a more modern-day sound to it; those rhythms would hit again, introduced to a next generation. So we were just blessed to connect at the same time, and he was blessed to have some very talented artists in his stable, like Cutty Ranks, Wayne Wonder, Garnett Silk, Beres Hammond, Buju Banton, Marcia Griffiths, and a lot of that success can be attributed to Dave Kelly. We were the Penthouse stable and everybody was just clicking, 'cos it was teamwork."

Of all the artists in the growing Penthouse stable, Buju Banton was the deejay to make the most lasting impact. His peculiar evolution and dramatic transformation probably made him the most controversial as well. At the time of writing, Buju is serving time in an Oklahoma prison, having been convicted of conspiring to set up a cocaine deal, but during an interview conducted before his incarceration, he explained that Germain's dedication is partly what helped dancehall to achieve greater glory. "I linked with Germain through an introduction to Dave Kelly, Wayne Wonder, and the whole Penthouse crew. Working at Penthouse in those era was nice, because we had the studio at our disposal, and everyone would play their part. Nothing comes out of the studio unless Donovan Germain passes it, and he stick with it, 'cos he believe in it."

Although he began recording at a tender age during the mid 80s, Buju Banton's true breakthrough came at Penthouse with 'Love Mi Browning', one of the biggest hits of 1992. As the song was cut in praise of light-skinned women, it caused considerable controversy in Jamaica, prompting Buju to cut 'Love Black Woman' in case listeners thought him anti-black. "People just take the song a wrong way, 'cos some people thought I was talking about a revolver, or about complexion, but it wasn't just a complex. That's why I had to sing 'Love Black Woman', and those songs become hits, so that was my first major step."

When Buju first arrived on the scene, he was a skinny kid with close-cropped hair in a white stringed vest – a very different image to the dreadlocked Rasta figurehead he would become. At his recording studio in Whitehall, a gritty uptown neighbourhood blighted by gang violence, Banton showed initial reticence to the interview process, no doubt because of the many media furores he has faced in relation to 'Boom Bye Bye', his notoriously homophobic record, reportedly penned by Wayne Wonder, and issued on Clifton 'Specialist' Dillon's Shang label not long after 'Love Mi Browning'. Nevertheless, the man born Mark Myrie in 1973 slowly opens up to recount the long process that led to the 'Browning' breakthrough.

"I did have a brother, but him pass off, and I used to live with 13 sisters, but I was raised all 'bout, 'cos my mother is a higgler who had a stall in Barbican Square, where the affluent people from uptown stop, and she wanted to do some farming in the countryside, so I left town about age nine. Then she sent I back to Kingston at age 11 to live with my father – I settle at Whitehall Avenue, right up the road. My father was a tile-maker and singer; him never pursue him musical career, because other responsibilities crept in the way, but I always admire the art of singing.

"I used to attend school in Barbican, and one early morning at the Plaza, joining onto the school, I encountered a champion deejay named Burro Banton. He was exercising on the Plaza, say 'Ribbity-bong' and flash two lyrics, and I stand up amazed. So I call myself Buju Banton, 'cos the name Buju was given to me by my mum: it is a Maroon word for breadfruit, and my mother's mother is a direct descendant of the Maroons from Portland. In that era, I start writing my lyrics, and going down to Chancery Lane and West Street to check Winston Riley, Randy's, and African Museum; in those days, a man could linger and burn a spliff, even as a youth.

"I was on a sound, Rambo International, based on Whitehall Avenue, but play all over the island, with Flourgon, Red Dragon, Daddy Lizard, Sanchez, Clement Irie, Early Black, and Johnny P. Beenie Man used to come through, Shabba pass when him ready, Admiral Bailey and Ninjaman sometimes. There was also a sound me did chat 'pon named Culture Love and another named Seize Love, which become Flourgon's sound; we used to run it with Red Dragon. Clement Irie was the man who bring I into the studio first for a song released 'pon Robert Ffrench's France label ['The Ruler'] – a boom tune in those days."

Another step in the right direction came through material voiced for Techniques (some of which was produced by Winston Riley's sons Kurt and Donahue), including a cut of 'Stalag' called 'Quick' that highlighted the expressiveness of Banton's 'rock-stone' voice as well as his growing lyrical abilities. "In those days it was [future broadcaster/commentator] Sherman Escoffery, Kurt Riley, Donahue Riley, and Ainsworth Williams – all five of us 'pon Chancery Lane, so the musical vibe build from them days, because my brethren control a record shop, and I had the privilege of hearing every song when it first come out, so I think that help me a lot. We used to go to the studio with Father Riley, but me used to work mostly with Kurt, 'cos I a minor in those days, so me used to sit down and watch. 'Stamina Daddy' was with Riley Junior, and 'Quick' was with Riley Senior; I love Winston Riley, because he's the first producer to carry me into the studio as a youth in my khaki, and him never shun I. Everywhere else I go, they lock the gate."

Looking back on his initial recordings, Buju notes that dancehall was largely a "here today, gone tomorrow" scene, with lasting artists something of a rarity. "In those days, most entertainers don't last for two years, or even six months – especially a deejay. In those days I was a youth, so I think like a youth: I never have no children, and I never aspire to own a studio and become a strength to others in the industry." However, he was able to make an impact because of his distinguishing features, namely the appealing gruffness of his voice, and his ability to construct lyrics that made a lasting impression. "My policy from I a youth is that everything I chat is a reality," he emphasises. "Don't care how it may come across, it's reality."

377

Following the formative work for the Techniques family, Buju tried his luck with various producers, until the link with Penthouse brought him into a different league. The Dave Kelly-produced 'Bogle', which celebrated a dance named in honour of the Jamaican national hero, was another early local chart smash; so too was the gal-praising 'The Grudge', cut for Bobby Digital, and the thematically similar 'Gold Spoon', cut earlier at Techniques on a minimalist rhythm.

With the release of his debut album, *Mr Mention*, in 1992, Buju Banton was suddenly the hottest act going, his dynamic performance at the annual Sting festival resulting in a deal with Mercury, then a subsidiary of PolyGram. But just as an international breakthrough seemed imminent, the belated popularity of 'Boom Bye Bye' brought outraged anger from overseas listeners, who objected to the song's enthusiastic call for acts of violence against gays, leading Britain's WOMAD festival to drop Buju from their roster.

Attitudes toward homosexuality in Jamaica are highly complex, and debates about the expression of social mores in dancehall culture have been highly charged. As the situation involves penal codes drafted by colonial authorities, entrenched attitudes stemming from strict – albeit sometimes selective – interpretations of Biblical doctrine, plus other often unspoken issues relating to class and the expression of non-conformity in Jamaica, as well as the anger evoked by what is seen as the dictatorial manner of foreign pressure groups, the matter has sometimes been oversimplified and misrepresented in the media, with spurious allegations raised by either side. It is beyond the scope of this book to adequately address the issues raised by dancehall's anti-gay content, but although Jamaican artists took the region's lead in this expression on CDs and records, the airing of such extreme views should be seen as part of a broader move toward less tolerant forms of religious fundamentalism that have become increasingly common since the early 90s, perhaps most evident in the on-going battles that presently threaten to split the Anglican Church. Furthermore, some cultural commentators have linked the broader backlash to the rise of AIDS, initially painted as a 'gay disease' in the region. "I'm reluctant to do generalisations, but I think it is a fair to say that Jamaica is a homophobic place," says academic/poet Kwame Dawes, who was raised in Jamaica and who has been involved in AIDS awareness projects on the island. "There's a great stigma attached to homosexuality, and also to HIV/AIDS."

In any case, once the growing furore over 'Boom Bye Bye' put Buju on the defensive, Shabba Ranks inadvertently got caught in the controversy during a December 1992 appearance on the British television programme *The Word*. His own strongly worded, anti-gay sentiment would also negatively affect his career, despite a subsequent retraction. Buju Banton is also said to have issued an apology for 'Boom Bye Bye', although he would continue performing portions of the song to sympathetic audiences in years to come, and the controversy initiated by the song has never really died down. Nevertheless, in 1993, the arrival of the more versatile album *Voice Of Jamaica* significantly widened his overseas audience, with songs like the topical 'Deportee', which noted the downgraded status of those forcibly returned to Jamaica, and the safe-sex anthem 'Willy', linked to a local AIDS prevention campaign, both reigning supreme on the Jamaican charts. On songs like 'No Respect', Buju tried out his singing voice, offering further evidence of a growing artistic maturity.

By the time he shifted to Island for the breakthrough set *Til Shiloh* (which included previously released singles, such as the emotive 'Murderer', cut in response to the killing of fellow deejay Panhead, along with new semi-acoustic anthems like 'Til I'm Laid To Rest' and 'Untold Stories'), Buju had begun growing dreadlocks, shifted subject matter to spiritual spheres, and largely recast himself as a singer – all of which stemmed from his surprise adoption of the Rastafari faith. "That part is like a different calling from higher realms that me could never forbid," he explains, "because how be it that this humble man, from a house with such a humble beginning, would be the voice that all the world was listening to, and whatever him utter make sense? This man must have a greater purpose to serve, because they use a great voice and a great sound to sing folly, and keep the nation into a state of degradation, so there is no hope for us, and there is going to be no help for them and those on judgement morning ... it's a rough road, but when you go out into the world, you start to learn that dancehall is a music that is nice, but there's a lot of damage in it, 'cos most of the brethren, they're just singing to earn money. I love my dancehall to the brim, but I nah sing no derogatory song, I nah sing no song that can't play 'pon the radio – let me enjoy myself same way. I would put it as evolution, and evolution is great."

Capleton, otherwise known as Clifton Bailey, was another to undergo a process of transformation. Early on in his career, he was one of the slackest deejays going (as evidenced by 'Good Hole', a collaborative work with Buju), and he also cut a few gun-praising tunes (including 'Gun Talk'), but later shifted focus to matters of spiritual relevance, following his induction to Rastafari. From the latter half of the 90s, he was one of dancehall's most internationally popular deejays, although not without controversy, due to

379

his expression of extreme views in certain lyrics, particularly where same-sex relationships are concerned.

Raised in rural Saint Mary, he became known as Capleton because his ability to argue convincingly reminded of the skills of a prominent local lawyer. Upon moving to Kingston during the mid 80s, heavily influenced by the style of Papa San (and to a lesser degree, Early B. and Ninjaman), he began honing his skills on the African Star sound system, a set formed in Toronto by Stewart Brown, which was based in Jamaica from the mid 80s onward. In 1989, the African Star link brought Capleton to Toronto for a massive live event, and although heavyweight artists such as Ninjaman, Flourgon, Anthony Malvo, and Colin Roach were the main attractions, Capleton stole the show. Back in Jamaica with increased status, he hooked up with Fatis Burrell for the sensational 'Bumbo Red', a song that referenced the enflamed genitalia of sexually active females, and which, like 'Boom Bye Bye', was brutally homophobic. It was followed by 'Number One On The Look Good Chart' for the New York-based Jah Life label, as well as another anti-gay number, 'Lotion Man', for producer Alphonso 'Bravo' Peterkin, who issued an album of the same name in 1991.

The following year, Capleton entered a different league with 'Almshouse', a call for unity on the dancehall circuit (and the standout title track of an album cut for Fatis). The song benefited from a complex tabla-infused rhythm built by Sly Dunbar, inspired by the Bhangra craze in the UK (and also used for dramatic effect on Chaka Demus & Pliers's 'Murder She Wrote', one of the biggest hits of 1992). With its conscious lyrics, 'Almshouse' showed Capleton's growing maturity, as he began aiming toward a more distinctive 'singjay' style.

By the time he cut the chart-topping 'Tour' (1994), which spoke of the senseless killing of fellow deejays Panhead and Dirtsman, Capleton was set for a major transformation. A hip-hop remix of the song reached the *Billboard* charts, bringing him a new set of fans and a contract with Def Jam Records, who teamed him with US rappers such as Method Man and Q-Tip (around the same time that Ini Kamoze scored a stupendous smash with 'Here Comes The Hot Stepper', which permeated world markets via a remix from talented hip-hop engineer Salaam Remi).

The real transformation for Capleton was a personal and spiritual one. By the time Def Jam began issuing his material, he had grown dreadlocks and a beard, substituting his old string-vests and gold jewellery for African robes following his embracement of the radical 'Bobo Dread' branch of Rastafari. He began issuing songs of spiritual fervour, such as 'Don't Dis The

Trinity', and became known as 'The Prophet' for his songs of spiritual focus (as well as 'The Fireman' for lyrics that 'burned' aspects of society he feels to be corruptive).

It is interesting to note that Capleton was among the first Bobo Dreads to rise to prominence on record, for the group's leader, Prince Emmanuel Edwards, generally shunned the reggae and dancehall scenes as 'worldly' pursuits that adherents were not supposed to be part of. Following Emmanuel's death in 1994, however, Bobo Dreads increasingly became part of the dancehall movement, often projecting a similar image to their peers and tackling comparable themes in their recorded works.

In any case, the new Rastafari personae of hardcore artists like Buju Banton and Capleton evidenced a gradual shift taking place in Jamaican music during the mid 90s, as conscious themes came to fore once more. At the same time, more complex rhythms that made use of a mixture of live and computerised instruments began to filter through. Garnett Silk's popularity was a crucial catalyst, his mournful voice retaining the rougher edges of the dancehall style, yet also the smoothness of a great soul man, particularly when singing songs of love or religious devotion. Silk made a massive impact from the stunning debut album, *Its Growing*, cut for Bobby Digital in 1992, and subsequently through hits such as 'Hello Mama Africa' for Richard Bell's Star Trail label, the devotional 'Fill Us Up With Your Mercy' and 'Lord Watch Over Our Shoulders' for King Jammy, and 'Love Is The Answer' for Steelie & Clevie. In 1994, Silk lined up an overseas distribution deal with Atlantic, and was working on an album for the company when both he and his mother tragically died in a fire which is said to have been started when an accidentally discharged bullet struck a propane canister. Nevertheless, he had an indelible impact, and one that shifted Jamaican music toward a different phase.

"Most artists lost their flavour completely," notes Tony Rebel of the period that proceeded dancehall's Rasta renaissance. "They were not singing original songs, just singing over what America did. When Garnett came, we were showing them that all these songs are original, so people went back to basics, starting hitting live instruments again. It was a time when people wanted a change, because they were tired of the gun talk, tired of the slackness, and they wanted the traditional reggae to be there again."

14
LIFT UP YOUR HEAD

Rasta resurgence and hardcore heroes into the new millennium

"At the revolution of the computer, many people got so excited that they lost the favour for the authentic sounds ... our creativity should never be destroyed by the computer, but we can use the computer with our creativity and come up with a sound." – LUCIANO

"Bob Marley do a lot of great reality songs that please everybody, but he still come and say: 'I shot the deputy, but I didn't shoot the sheriff.' So you've got to have a tune that you're sending out to the thugs." – ELEPHANT MAN

Following Garnett Silk's lead, a vibrant Rasta resurgence came into play during the late 90s, and in tandem with the spiritual vibe came an increasingly complex musical backing, as producers began to meld live instruments more frequently onto the predominant foundation of digital beats. Yet as the new millennium approached, the hardcore contingent was far from silent, the content of their lyrics becoming ever more graphic, usually over the barest of minimalist computer rhythms. In the past, one style or the other reigned supreme, yet the two forms now continued in tandem, each with rampantly loyal followings, despite seemingly irreconcilable differences of content and form.

Of the Rastafari faithful to rise to prominence, Luciano was one of the most impressive figureheads to emerge. He was another artist whose embracement of Rasta brought a significant transformation, although as he came from a Seventh Day Adventist background, the shift was from ballads to odes of spirituality, rather than the explicit lyrics of hardcore dancehall.

At his former headquarters, on the western outskirts of Kingston, the man born Jepther McClymont in 1964 explained that his musical evolution was gradual, the transition from the countryside to the capital and the shift from church choir to reggae being part of the early phase. "I started out

382

from a humble family in Davyton, Manchester: my father was a carpenter and my mother do washing, sewing, and was a good midwife, but when I was 11, my father got some sickness and had to move on. I graduated from Manchester High School in 1980 and I came to Kingston when I was 21; I stayed with my brother Mack at Central Village, looking for a job, but I wasn't successful, so I went back to the countryside. My father left a guitar, which he'd built with his own hands, and I used to take the guitar with me to the marketplace, because I see my father play gospel songs on the guitar and always wanted to master it. I was listening to Bob Marley and Dennis Brown, because Bob Marley would say, 'No Woman, No Cry', and many times my momma would break down in tears, and when my momma hear a song like that, it gave her strength, so I grew to appreciate reggae music as roots music. According to my brother, I was playing roots songs, like [Junior Byles's] 'Beat Down Babylon', and Bob Marley songs like 'Work'."

Like so many others, Luciano returned to Kingston in search of work, but with music as an underlying motivation. "Playing my songs, people gave positive criticisms, saying I could go to Kingston and further myself, so I packed my things around '88, '89, and start working at Campbell's Upholstering in the heart of south-central Kingston – a real gun-slinging area – but I knew I had something to do with my life, so in the evenings, if I heard about any band, I would go and try to make an audition, like there was one called the Old Boys downtown, and in Central Village, there was a sound system called Earth Ruler that I would jam with, so this kept the musical vibration moving in me. Normally, as a young artist, you have to pay your dues, because when you go into the dancehall, if you're not a popular deejay, they wouldn't give you a chance, but Shadowman was willing to give me a chance, while the others were saying: 'How this church man want to come to a dance, come sing?'

"After a while, I started realising that I could make a recognition through dub plates, and when I was introduced to Ricky Trooper from Kilamanjaro, I did some dub plates for him; he carried me to Mr Earl Hayles from Aquarius, and things started happening.[1] I started hanging out with [fellow aspiring singer] Presley, and Buju Banton would come through now and again, but he was a little ahead of me; I didn't have any tune on the road, until I did [a cover of Paul McCartney & Stevie Wonder's] 'Ebony & Ivory', which I did for Earl Hayles in the latter part of '92. Then I met Sky High from Mau Mau Productions, so I started doing one and two tracks for Sky High."

These early singles (which credited Luciana) bore the influence of Frankie Paul and Stevie Wonder, but made precious little impact (nor did the Sky High-produced album with Presley, *Stuck On U*). The next stepping stone to success was provided by Dennis Brown's old South London associate, Castro Brown, who had recently returned to Jamaica to establish the New Name label and recording studio. "In '93 at New Name Records, I was rubbing shoulders with musicians like Mikey Spice, Louie Culture, General Degree, and Lady Saw. Castro Brown put some tracks out, like 'Slice Of The Cake' and 'Give Love A Try', which started giving me some recognition in Jamaica, but things didn't work out the way I planned."

More concrete fame resulted from a link with Freddy McGregor, whose Big Ship stable was issuing inspired dancehall material; the outstanding resultant single, 'Shake It Up Tonight', reached the top of the UK reggae charts, and the album of the same name was also well received, despite the problematic circumstances of its creation. "Freddy McGregor invited me to Gussie Clarke's newly built studio [Anchor]," Luciano recalls. "There was a nice sound there, so *Shake It Up Tonight* was a very good album that get me a good recognition, but I realised that when an artist tries to work with another artist, it's kind of hard, because sometimes I would be waiting on Mr Freddy McGregor, who was on tour, so it create frustration."

The answer came through a shift to Fatis Burrell's Exterminator label (later re-named Xterminator), which resulted in a dramatic increase in popularity. Throughout 1994, a series of exceptional singles such as 'Back To Africa', 'Black Survivors', and especially 'One Way Ticket' – one of the year's biggest hits in Jamaica – made Luciano one of the hottest reggae vocalists of the day. By the time he signed to Island for the 1995 album *Where There Is Life*, with its outstanding single, 'It's Me Again Jah', he had swapped string vests for African garb and had dreadlocks sprouting from his head, eventually re-emerging in the new persona of 'The Messenger'.

On the road with Dean Fraser and The Firehouse Crew, Luciano was a veritable powerhouse. His extended live sets, which often saw the singer performing barefoot, turning cartwheels and even climbing the light rig, helped cement his reputation overseas as a leading light of new roots reggae. "I needed a stable, some infrastructure that I knew could really work," he says, "and I think it's one of my bigger moves that I have made. The first song I did for Fatis was 'Chant Out', and he decided to work with me on an exclusive level. Certain songs require a certain kind of harmony, and Fatis had the know-how to pick the right people – like Dean Fraser's the minister for harmony, balance, and overdubbing – so I really have to give the credit to Fatis for that. When I came to town to work in the music fraternity, I didn't see much harmony with the singers, and even the band thing had broken down, but Fatis instilled in us that we needed to have our own band, we have to have our own back-up singers."

In addition to helping Luciano and his peers to strengthen their sounds and internationalise their outlooks, Fatis, who died of a stroke at the age of 57 in 2011, was instrumental in drawing out Luciano's full potential, partly by placing his striking voice over rough and rugged dancehall rhythms, the contrast heightening the dramatic effect of his unusual baritone. "My voice is leant to hardcore roots because the baritone is a more beckoning voice to gather the people, rather than giving a little romance – it has a more commanding vibration to call the people, so I could colour any rhythm and give a different vibes to it. And then I had realised my purpose, because I realised that my singing is not just putting words to the rhythm – I realised that I had to have a meaning."

Ultimately, Luciano feels that the Xterminator phase was crucial to his artistic development, and points out that reggae music generally advanced as the camp evolved. "With *Moving Up*, the first album I built by Fatis, you could not hear much of a concentrated production, as opposed to *Where There Is Life*, so you realise that Fatis had grown, and I had grown with Fatis. And I see that music is like a spirit, 'cos music is still an expression of the inner part of our being, and it seems to me that the very spirit of man moves in cycles: this minute you feel very cheerful, the next minute you might feel sorrowful. People always ask for new ideas and new creations, but at the revolution of the computer, many people got so excited that they lost the favour for the authentic sounds. We have to be knowledgeable to work with technology, but don't let it overthrow our mentality. Our creativity should never be distracted or destroyed by the computer, but we can use the computer with our creativity and come up with a sound."

Although Luciano's contract with Island was not renewed following the release of the excellent 1996 set *Messenger*, he continued cutting fine work for Xterminator to the end of the decade, when friction emerged between Luciano and the radical sing-jay, Sizzla. Following his surprise departure from Xterminator, Luciano established a fledgling operation with fellow singer Mikey General, but was unable to properly sustain it, and has since become somewhat over-recorded, putting forth albums that are perfectly decent but lack the outstanding quality of his peak-period works.

Sizzla Kolanji, aka Miguel Collins, is certainly one of the most controversial of all Jamaican performers. Born in August Town in 1976 to a family of devout Bobo Dreads, he got his start on Caveman sound system, where his unusual vocal style – gentle soprano one moment, barking tenor

385

the next – drew attention. Luciano says he first met Sizzla through Caveman's associate Homer Harris, whose headquarters on Grove Road in Half Way Tree was a meeting point for aspiring artists. Once he had been introduced to Xterminator, a series of singles – including 'True God', with its controversial lyrics about the Almighty's complexion – led to a debut album, *Burning Up* (1995).

The sing-jay's true potential became clear on *Praise Ye Jah*, his sophomore set for Xterminator, and *Black Woman And Child*, an exceptional album of 'reality' tunes produced by Bobby Digital in 1997. Dozens of albums of varying quality have surfaced since, including *The Overstanding*, issued in 2006 by noted hip-hop entrepreneur Damon Dash, but Sizzla has also been the subject of numerous controversies involving unlicensed firearms, clashes with gay rights groups, and, most recently, the granting of land in Zimbabwe, following his performance at Robert Mugabe's 86th birthday celebration. However, there is no doubting Sizzla's widespread popularity, and his Judgement Yard facility in August Town remains a focal point for local ghetto youth, even after his temporary exclusion from the area following the discovery of a cache of automatic weapons during a 2005 police raid.

For every conscious artist to emerge during this period, a hardcore dancehall counterpart became equally popular. In 1994, as Luciano began achieving greater prominence, and shortly before Buju Banton and Capleton made their unexpected conversions, the Jamaican charts were shaken by the presence of Beenie Man, one of dancehall's most dynamic and exuberant performers, as well as by his future rival, Bounty Killer, one of the genre's more dextrous lyricists.

Of all the Jamaican performers to achieve lasting fame, Beenie Man, born Moses Davis in 1973, seems to have started at the youngest age, although the road to greater glory was particularly rocky. As revealed in Milton Wray's detailed biography, *Who Am I? The Untold Story Of Beenie Man*, Beenie's unsettled early years were incredibly harsh. He became semi-wild and lived with open sores on his legs due to malnourishment, before music became his ultimate salvation. In fact, in the rough confines of Waterhouse, entirely saturated with sound systems, the young Davis was already taking the mic at kindergarten age – hence the nickname Beenie Man, a reference to the short trousers he wore.

"I was born and raised in Waterhouse, start in music officially at age five," he explains, while recovering from a typically energetic performance. "I used to be on my uncle's sound, Master Blaster – that's the original sound that I'm from, as an infant." Master Blaster was run by Sidney Wolfe, a percussionist with The Sons Of Negus and Jimmy Cliff's backing band, but despite the family connection, Beenie's mother was not pleased that her son was part of this environment at such a tender age. Nevertheless, she was unable to stop his addiction to sound systems – his main preoccupation ever since.

His debut recording, produced by Junjo Lawes, came about after he won a talent contest sponsored by Tastee Patties. "You used to actually get a recording contract when you win," he laughs, "so I did my first recording when I was about seven or eight." The song was called 'Too Fancy' and it rode the 'Diseases' rhythm, made popular by deejay duo Michigan & Smiley.

By the time Beenie Man began recording a debut album for Bunny Lee, released in 1983 as *The Invincible Beenie Man: The Incredible Ten Year Old DJ Wonder*, he was already a steady fixture on Lee's Unlimited, later switching to Gemini, and eventually Arrows International. The Niney-produced single 'Over The Sea' surfaced the following year; his early work with Barrington Levy was not issued until over a decade later.

Beenie Man's most important link came with Patrick Roberts, whose Shocking Vibes organisation, based in Craig Town (a volatile section of the broader Jones Town area), began issuing singles in the late 80s. In addition to managing his career, Roberts at one point considered becoming Beenie Man's legal guardian. "I've known Shocking Vibes all my life," Beenie says. "We started recording in 1986–87. Shocking Vibes has me concrete, focussed in one way, so I can really get my head on one level."

Beenie's early singles for Shocking Vibes did not make much of an impact, however, and in 1991 he considered retiring from music altogether after a guest spot at the National Arena went awry. During a gala celebration to honour South African icon Nelson Mandela, Beenie was brought on stage by US rapper Doug E. Fresh, only to be booed off for performing a mistimed song about body odour (in which he changed Pinchers' hit 'Bandolero' into the less savoury 'Greendolero'). Coaxed back into the studio by Anthony Malvo, Beenie began to spark interest on the sound-system circuit with songs such as the hyper-violent 'Bad Man Wicked Man', but says such material was cut merely "to get the ears of people, a listening audience, 'cos that's what they was listening to in those times".

Once his name began to garner interest on vinyl, he swiftly stepped up another gear with more versatile material that addressed different topics in a multitude of styles. The ascent proved particularly swift. In 1993, he reached the top of the Jamaican charts with 'Matie', the first of a very long string of hits.[2] He was also crowned Deejay of the Year.

Thereafter, Beenie was seldom out of the charts: 'World Dance', which celebrated the popular dance step of the same name, was one of the biggest tunes of 1994; that same year, the 'combination' album *Guns Out* (aka *Face To Face*) highlighted his feud with Bounty Killer, which reportedly began when Bounty adopted the catchphrase 'People Dead' (which Beenie claims to have originated). He had half a dozen tunes at the top of the charts in 1995, including the suggestive 'Slam', a song so popular that it even spawned a brand of condoms (with Beenie's one-time main squeeze, Carlene The Dancehall Queen, as its chief advertiser), and the braggadocio of 'Tear Off Me Garment'.

The following year yielded 'Nuff Gal', the equally suggestive 'Blackboard', and the defiant 'Ban Mi Fi The Truth', which complained that the authorities were censoring his output. The boastful 'Maestro' was another chart-topper, and the title track to the Greensleeves-issued album that broke him in the UK, leading to a contract with Island for *Blessed*, which reached the *Billboard* top 20. In 1997, 'Who Am I' was another massive hit that boosted his profile overseas, but not without controversy. Despite the boastful nature of a song in which the singer proclaimed himself "the gal them sugar", the peculiar phrasing of the line "How can I make love to a fella?" caused some to speculate about his sexuality – a highly ironic suggestion, since Beenie would later become embroiled in controversy following the 2001 release of his despicably homophonic 'Hand Up Deh'. Nevertheless, he has remained a constant figure in the charts, and has collaborated with numerous overseas stars, including Mya, Wyclef Jean, and Janet Jackson. "I usually do a little bit of everything," he explains. "Music is originality, so you have to come versatile at all times."

It is perhaps fitting that Bounty Killer's career has formed a parallel to Beenie's, since, more often than not, the two have been bitter rivals. Initially known as Bounty Hunter, the adroit wordsmith, born Rodney Price in 1972, took the name Bounty Killer to avoid confusion with a more established rival. Conducting an interview with Bounty in public can be a trying experience, as young females constantly swoon whenever he is spotted, but in person he has a similar directness to Beenie.

"Trench Town was where my parents reside when I was born, but that same year, we moved to Riverton City, and it was really struggling," he explains. "I come from a family of eight kids; my father used to keep dances, have a little gambling house and a shop, and he used to do watchman work on the side, but with so many kids, it was really hard, as we're all in one room. I stop going to school at ninth grade because of financial difficulties and political differences, 'cos the school that I was going to was in some politically motivated community, and the community that I'm from is [aligned to] the rival of that party, so you could get killed just going to school."

As with Beenie Man, Bounty Killer started flexing his musical muscles on sound systems at an early age, thanks in part to family connections. "My father owned a sound system in Riverton City, so that's where my musical influence started. First time I hold a mic, it was my father playing his sound and smoking his chalwa, and when the record finished, I would go and say: 'Ah me name Rodney,' and feel so excited to hear my voice coming through the loudspeakers at seven or eight years old. Then I started to hear deejays like Burro Banton, John Wayne, Super Cat, Admiral Bailey, Shabba Ranks, so I started to get that deejay influence, but in the ghetto, sounds string up on the street, so you don't really have to go to the session to be influenced by music – you can just live down the road, hear the music and be captivated."

Soon, the young Bounty's talents were noticed on a more prominent neighbourhood set. "The first time I hold a mic in public was 1980, on this sound called King Joe. I sing some Junior Reid song, 'Woman Make Your Waistline Roll', and the place tore up. I start to work on styles and lyrics from there, so I start to get my community ratings."

Although Bounty put music on the back burner for a number of years, things reached another level after he moved to nearby Seaview Gardens, another notoriously rough patch of West Kingston, where the presence of Shabba Ranks was a great inspiration. "That's where we start to sight the real international level of it, 'cos Shabba got singed to CBS, and we're living in the same community. Shabba won a Grammy, and dancehall seems like it's gonna take off – the whole country was into dancehall, so everybody who have a little skill of deejaying try to sharpen up, and that's when we started to build back up our little community vibes. Some of my friends was on a little sound system, and one day I go and hold the mic; there was a man that molested his daughter, and it was a big thing in the community, so I make up a song about that and the whole place tore up again. So I start to go on that corner regular, until Shabba was passing one night and decided to deejay, and when Shabba make the place full up, we would get the chance to express our talent, and my song become a favourite in the community. From there, we start to do dub plates for sounds like Black Ark, King Arab, Likkle Gemini, so we start to be known all around the Kingston 11 area, and when we start to go to studios to do dub plates, we get to learn the skills of the professional artists."

The breakthrough came at King Jammy's studio, but the process was far from immediate. "I was doing dub plates in King Jammy's from 1990, but Jammy can't take talk from small people. Someone said: 'Jammy's have this brother who does voicing on Saturdays, maybe you could try to get on one of those rhythms.' So I went and talked to Uncle T., and he said to come the next Saturday, but some bigger acts come, so my thing postpone; I went back the next week and a similar thing happens. But I keep going back until one Saturday, I went and it was empty, so I guess that was my lucky day – February 22 1992."

Bounty says the lyrics he came with went against the grain of the predominant style at Jammy's, but he used his skills of adaptation to swiftly turn things to his favour. "I was voicing some gangster tunes, and the engineer was a Christian; he don't want those type of lyrics, but I'm versatile, so I just come up with an anti-gun song: 'You see the gun, time for it fi done, and if you love live, then you will put down the gun.' Then Uncle T. said: 'What you ah talk 'bout? Him a rude boy, and me want them rude boy song.' So I voiced 'Dip Him', about some deportee, and I become known as Uncle T.'s artist, until Jammy started to hear about this new guy his brother is voicing."

Although Bounty soon began recording for the King, the song that truly broke him almost remained permanently unreleased. 'I start to voice for Jammy, but he is not intrigued to release the songs, until one day, one of the engineers was recording on the 'General' rhythm, and that's when I voice 'Coppershot', but Jammy hear that song and say the gun thing ain't working, so Jammy never released that song. Then Colin Roach voiced another track on the rhythm with Galaxy P., 'Miss Goody Goody', and they find my song on the tape, and Colin Roach liked it, so he mixed off the song, not knowing that Jammy don't want to. VP released it on the flipside of 'Miss Goody Goody' and Jammy heard about 'Coppershot' running away – that's the song that burst, and then Jammy *had* to release it. From there, they never tell me what type of songs to voice – I just voice whatever I decide."

It made sense for Bounty to break through with a song that spoke of gangster living, since it was the life he knew before becoming a professional performer. "I got shot in Seaview Gardens, and I make my songs off of situations, so 'Coppershot' is a situation of my life: a guy get a gun and me and my friends felt like we are untouchable, but it never went that way. I couldn't say I was singing gangster songs first, as there's a few guys before me who sing gangster anthems, like Ninjaman, Cutty Ranks, Mad Cobra, but I guess the way I compose mine was unique, so it stands out. And if you check it now, I've got the most gangster anthems."

With catchphrases such as "Lord a mercy", "OK", and "That's right" peppering most of his output, Bounty Killer remained at King Jammy's to 1995, working solidly with musician Paul 'Jazzwad' Yebuah, yielding the gun-talk album *Roots Reality & Culture* (aka *Jamaica's Most Wanted*), as well as *Down In The Ghetto*, which included the X-rated chart-topper 'Cellular Phone', delivered in a style somewhat influenced by Shabba. A different side of The Killer emerged on the single 'Book Book Book', another chart topper from 1995, which pointed out the need for a good education. This dichotomy grew more pronounced when 'The Warlord', as he became known, started cutting 'reality' tunes as 'The Poor People's Governor'. It was a seemingly schizoid dichotomy, but Bounty says that all of what he records is simply based around "reality".

"People used to have dancehall limited," he explains, "like you only sing about wine-up, shooting people, or smoke some weed, so we start to bring different issues to dancehall, where some of the time, you're going to discuss how our life is. Everybody criticise, saying I'm singing about guns, but I was saying: 'This is reality. It might be dirty, but if someone does something bad, then you must address a bad action.' So if I'm going to sing about something that I've been through, and it's a bad situation, it's not gonna sound good, but I've been through it. If you check *Roots Reality & Culture*, it's all reality, and it's my roots; poverty's a part of my heritage, I know it from I was born, and they have to know that sufferation is a part of Jamaican culture, and now they're making violence become a part of it. But after touring the world, I get to understand that people suffer all over."

Although Bounty Killer had felt comfortable at Jammy's, leaving the stable proved a positive move, in that it allowed for collaboration with key dancehall creators, such as Sly & Robbie and producer/engineer Colin 'Bulby' York. The 1997 album *My Xperience*, his most versatile set to date, became a launching pad to greater international success. "I create my Priceless label, start to record myself, and work with a couple of other producers on the side; then I make the *My Xperience* album and go overseas and link up with The Fugees." Further notable collaborations followed with rap acts such as Busta Rhymes, Mobb Deep, Wu-Tang Clan, Capone-N-Noreaga, and eventually the American ska-rock band No Doubt.

As with many of hardcore dancehall's leading lights, Bounty Killer's career has also been controversial. In the new millennium, he has faced public obscenity charges at performances, been arrested for erratic driving and refusing to be breathalysed, as well as for domestic violence, and had overseas concerts cancelled due to homophobic lyrics. His feud with Beenie Man reached epic proportions when Bounty's main squeeze, the model D'Angel, left him for – and then married – Beenie.

Nevertheless, Bounty Killer remains highly popular, and has also elevated upcoming talent, most recently with a younger set of artists dubbed The Alliance, but first with Scare Dem Crew, a group of aspiring singers and deejays from Seaview Gardens who emerged in the mid 90s. "Me, Harry Toddler, and Boom Dandimite were the three deejays, and Nitty Kutchie was the singer," says Elephant Man, one of dancehall's most flamboyant figures. "We all lived in Seaview Gardens, so we hooked up at Jammy's studio and started rolling with Bounty. Then Bounty formed the Scare Dem Crew, because he wanted to see us eat some food, and all of us wouldn't burst at the same time individually."

Initially known as Dumbo because of his comically oversize ears, Elephant Man was born O'Neil Bryan in Kingston in 1975. Although he came to prominence with Scare Dem, Elephant reminds me that he first scored a minor neighbourhood hit as a solo artist with a song celebrating the Butterfly dance. "I grow up in Seaview Gardens from I was eight or nine, and it was very hard, because my mother hasn't got the money to take care of me and my sisters," he explains, at the Half Way Tree headquarters of the Stone Love sound system. "She used to work at a factory, but stopped because she couldn't afford no bus. When I was about 13, me and my friends Jungle Rat and Peenie Wallie used to love deejaying, and Shabba Ranks lived next door to me, so Shabba and Ninjaman was a big influence. I had a friend named Crack Skull who had a tape recorder, so we start to build up Stereo Two, until we have a studio that he built in his house; then we get 45s and a record changer, so he build up a sound.

"One day my friend Gold Dust said: 'A friend of mine want a Butterfly tune.' They wanted a dancing song, and he had just recorded the tune 'Bun Fi Bun' with Captain Barkey, so they bring me to Mixing Lab and I voiced the first recording I ever did, 'Butterfly', for the Shalom label. Every day that tune played on the radio, and a sound named Black Hawk was stringing up on the corner every Thursday, playing that tune, so everybody said: 'Go to the studio, go to Jammy's!' First I was working with Uncle T., and then I started to record for Jammy."

After Bounty drew Scare Dem together, the Crew's 'Many Many' and 'Bare Gal' were hits on release in 1997, as was Harry Toddler's 'Bad Man

Nuh Dress Like Girl' the following year. Their general popularity spawned rival crews such as the hip-hop influenced Monster Shack trio, as well as the Innocent Kru quartet. Further recognition came via Scare Dem's appearance in the film *Third World Cop* (said to have been loosely based on the exploits of controversial Jamaican 'super-cop' Reneto Adams), although the film surfaced just as Elephant Man opted for a solo career. "I was in Port Morant, performing, and a beef came up with me, Nitty Kutchie, and Boom Dandimite," he recalls. "They went on stage and tried to disrespect me, so I just said: 'I'm gonna move on.'"

Elephant's debut album, *Coming 4 You* (2000), showcased his ability to tackle any subject. "I'm a all-around deejay," he says. "I don't stick to one topic, so I'm talking about girls, but I'm talking about the Lord; I'm talking about rude boys and guns, but I'm talking about the kids, too. I'm just giving everybody a sense of my talent, that I can say anything for anybody." His songs thus recounted super-hardcore tales of thug life, with guns, girls, and religion, while on some of his most popular material, he re-works foreign pop songs in a dancehall milieu. Even in his Scare Dem days, some of Elephant's hardcore lyrics could sound terribly negative – and potentially self-destructive – but as he notes, reggae has always catered to a hardcore element. "Bob Marley do a lot of great reality songs that please everybody, but he still come and say: 'I shot the deputy, but I didn't shoot the sheriff.' So you've got to have a tune that you're sending out to the thugs."

Elephant Man's fast and often shrill raps were further delineated by a lisp and the adopting of catchphrases such as the Disney-style "capiche?" and later "shizzle my nizzle", which he borrowed from gangsta rapper Snoop Dogg. His outrageous stage antics saw him crowned 'The Energy God', with bizarre outfits often incorporating wild fright-wigs or multi-coloured Afros, and simulated sex sometimes part of the onstage equation. "My live performance is off the hook," he boasts. "I start climb places and jump, and I got that in me from birth. The ladies want to touch you – they want to feel the 'anaconda' – so you got to get them involved in what's going on, to let them enjoy their money's worth."

By the time of his sophomore album, *Log On*, Elephant Man was one of the hottest properties in dancehall – and one of the more controversial. The title track was one of several songs to face censure abroad for homophobic content, although Elephant was nonplussed about such unwarranted attention. "I hear that it was a big argument in England, but the tune is about a dance."

In November 2001, Elephant Man faced more serious problems while touring the UK when a violent robbery resulted in the death of his friend, broadcaster Deejay Village, of BBC Radio One. "That's the worst time in my life," he says with a shudder, "but God will take care of everything." He has avoided the UK since, but has gone on to issue a series of even more popular discs and collaborate with a range of rap artists, including Ludacris, Wyclef Jean, and Fat Joe, as well as R&B stars such as Usher, R. Kelly, and Janet Jackson. In 2007, he signed to Bad Boy, Universal's rap subsidiary, for the album *Let's Get Physical*.

○

Some artists are clearly in the 'conscious' camp, some in the 'hardcore' arena, while others seem the embodiment of both, such as the upfront Bobo Dread sing-jay Anthony B, whose work is mostly conscious, yet with an extra bite that lends a hardcore sensibility. "Peter Tosh is who I admire for lyrics, but Ninjaman is one of the great performers, one of those persons who brings life to the music," he says. "Watching a movie and listening to the words, that's like looking at Ninjaman."

Following a blazing live performance, the man born Keith Anthony Blair in 1976 says that music was his dream from an early age. "My parents wanted me to become an accountant, but I want to do music," he laughs, before explaining the circumstances of his upbringing. "I was born in a village called Clark's Town, a little farming community in the Cockpit Country. My grandparents really parent me – they were farming people – and my grandma was a Maroon. When I was about 14, they moved me to Kingston to further my education, so I lived with my uncle, an electrician, and his wife, a teacher, in a district called Cumberland in Portmore. In those days, it was more like the mosquito community, and you wouldn't have to lock your door, but now everybody's living under bars and grills, so it's totally different."

Anthony B. began making live appearances on sound systems from 1988, when he was involved in a regular music session established in the wake of Hurricane Gilbert. "After Gilbert blow, we got to rejuvenate Portmore, so I start a show called The Greatest Show On Earth, every Wednesday night at a place called Newlands, and we start creating a name from there. Shabba Ranking would come through, and Super Cat – people who are already famous." He also began making the journey to Bobo Hill, the spiritual community presided over by Prince Emmanuel Edwards, but was unable to publicly identify himself as a follower. "I couldn't wear a turban," he explains. "Even when I bust, I couldn't just put on a turban, because Emmanuel don't see reggae music as Rasta spiritual music. He see Niyabinghi is the spiritual music and say reggae music is like a business place."

With encouragement from his peers, Anthony B.'s stature dramatically increased. "In the early 1990s, Buju Banton, Bounty Killer, and Beenie Man was my good friend, and then Buju become a superstar, so this convince me that I can do it too. We used to ride bicycle and play ball every evening with Terry Fabulous, and then Terry Fabulous broke out. All of my friends that were at The Greatest Show On Earth start becoming superstars, like Baby Wayne, Josie Stepper, and Reggie Stepper, so the people start to encourage me more. I enter a Reggae Sunsplash competition in 1993, and I win the competition and get to perform on a big show for the first time. Then I did a song called 'Brazil Dance' when Brazil won the World Cup in 1994, and in December of that year, I get the chance to [appear at] Sting, and that's where the break really come – at the time, Bounty Killer and Beenie Man was at war, so I did a song called 'Repentance Time' to baptise Bounty Killer and Beenie Man, so people started calling me the John The Baptist of the music."

Anthony B.'s subsequent recording career was aided by Richard Bell, whose Star Trail label was one of the more impressive imprints during the mid 90s. "I go to Black Scorpio studio with Little Devon, a singer who's a good coach and a strong motivator," he recalls. "He brought me in and I met Richard Bell, who was already recording Beres Hammond and Garnett Silk, but he didn't really have an artist at that moment, so Everton Blender and Anthony B. were really the first two artists signed to the label."

Everton 'Blender' Williams, an expressive baritone singer from Clarendon, released sporadic singles during the early 80s but did not make an impact until the 90s, when his appearance on a Manchester sound system brought familiarity with Garnett Silk, who introduced him to Star Trail in Kingston. 'Lift Up Your Head' was one of the biggest tunes of 1996, and 'Piece Of The Blender' was another popular song to result from the partnership, but Anthony B.'s work made more lasting impact – especially critical efforts such as 'Fire Pon Rome', which received radio bans in Jamaica for directly naming Prime Minister P.J. Patterson and opposition leader Edward Seaga as wrongdoers, censuring as well the Issa and Matalon families, icons of Jamaican business, symbolically linked by B. to the injustices of the Roman Empire.

"We see Rome as a system," he explains, "not literally the Rome now in Italy, but the system that was set up to manipulate the minds of people, and spread injustice and inequality across the world ... and the shotta who grow in the ghetto, he don't even have a birth certificate, but he have a gun that value $500,000 – he never leave his community, but he got a Russian-made gun. How does this get into the country? That's how I see 'Fire Pon Rome': as awareness. It was banned from the radio stations in Jamaica, in fear of what could happen to whoever played the song, because these are powerful people that can order your assassination. In Jamaica, it is known that if you say something against a politician, and they don't like it, you are a dead man. But after 'Fire Pon Rome', the politics frontier change. A politician wouldn't just come and say 'I'm going to give you some light and water'; the promises days are over. Now they have to come with something of substance."

Anthony B.'s strong debut album, *Real Revolutionary*, included further scorchers like 'Raid The Barn', while the 1997 follow-up, *Universal Struggle*, yielded hits like 'Waan Back', which called for a return to dancehall's old-school vibes. "There is too much violence surrounding reggae music," he laments. "I think it's a lot of damaged minds, because a lot of youths come straight into the music out of the ghetto; they don't really go to school and open their minds to read and realise that there's a wide world out there, so it's changing the music from where Bob Marley leave it. I think the dancehall artists need to read a little more, spend a little more time thinking of what they are saying."

With Star Trail largely quiet from the end of the 90s, Anthony B. concentrated on self-produced work, cutting a few discs for producers like Black Scorpio; he also collaborated with rappers such as Snoop Dog, Wyclef Jean, and Bone Crusher, with largely unimpressive results, although his energetic live performances are always greatly anticipated.

Rising up in tandem with Anthony B., albeit by his own circuitous route, the singer Dwight 'Bushman' Duncan was one of the most impressive talents to come to the fore in the mid 90s. His mellow baritone was somewhat reminiscent of Luciano, although both lyrics and delivery set him apart. At the ital 'Rastarant' he runs in Saint Thomas, Bushman explains that music was part of his life for as long as he can remember. "I was born in 1973 in Stanton Housing Scheme, Spring Gardens, grew up in Licence, about three miles from here. My stepfather was a Rastaman who used to go to dances from ancient times, so we used to have Sturgav and Stereo Mars, with Big Youth, Poppa Briggy [aka Brigadier Jerry], John Wayne, and Barry Brown. I hear Little John and Tristan Palmer on dancehall cassettes, and I was introduced to Bob Marley, Dennis Brown, Gregory Isaacs, Sanchez, Thriller U, Al Campbell, Stonewall Jackson, Frankie Paul, Leroy Gibbons, Conrad Crystal, Chuck Turner, Wayne Palmer, so reggae music was all about from I was young. Beres Hammond had a song called 'One Step Ahead' and we used to watch him 'pon *Where It's At*, and I would vision of being in Beres Hammond's shoes; even when I was watching *Miss Lou Ring Ding* on TV, I knew that one day I would go on that TV and perform for the people in Jamaica. And all them vision come true."

Like many of his contemporaries, Bushman says he began to be associated with community sound systems after the destruction caused by Hurricane Gilbert. "I was singing in church choirs in Spring Gardens and Yallahs, from 12 to 14, and when I went back to Licence, that's when Gilbert blew and sound system take over, like Mellow Construction, King Majesty, and Black Starliner. Saint Thomas was like a dancehall plantation then, so we have Black Scorpio, King Jammy's, Chin's International, Point Five Disco, and Metromedia. Then you have contests, so with the ego that you have to hold a microphone and sing, you enter the contest to get the people to recognise you. I would mostly do cover versions, like Tracy Chapman's 'Fast Car' and Sanchez's 'Lonely Won't Leave Me Alone', but I always love to write my own original sounds too."

As was typical of the era, voicing dub plates was a key means for the young vocalist to get heard. "I move to Yallahs when I was 19 and I used to select on Black Starliner, and the dub plate was the strategy to make people know you. Them time I was going by the name of Junior Melody, and we used to go to Arrows dub plate studio on Windward Road to hang for the day; soundman come, and we beg them to let me sing a song, just to make them hear what ah gwan. I even know artists whe *pay* a sound man, just fi do dub plates fi him."

Making the break required considerable determination, however, and football played an unlikely role in the process. "I was between Arrows and Saint Thomas for about five years, and the amount of gates that get closed in our face at different studios, like Black Scorpio, and Anchor with Fatis Burrell ... we forward ah King Jammy's and Colin Roach give I an audition and claim that I wasn't ready. Then, about 1995, Steelie was the man who used to hang out by Arrows, looking for new talent; we used to play football, and he thought I wasn't a good player, but I told him: 'I no come ah studio fi play football, I come ah studio fi sing.' I sing 'Call The Hearse' and him say: 'You sound wicked!' So we made an appointment to meet at his studio, Studio 2000, and I went there and did 'Call The Hearse'."

The graphic lyrics, which described the terrible gun crime that blighted many Jamaican communities, are delivered in incongruously dulcet tones over the barest of computer rhythms. The song made an instant, dramatic

397

impact on the dancehall circuit. "I see it all the while," says Bushman. "Sufferation and poverty make you wise."

Although the partnership worked well, yielding a strong debut album, *Niyaman Chant*, Bushman swiftly moved on following conflict with the production team's management, which significantly delayed the album's release. "It was a learning process," he says. "Certain commitments weren't fulfilled, but Steelie & Clevie's contract was still in effect, so I sit around and never recorded for anyone. After six months, I went to Bobby Digital and told him I wanted to do an album, but he was busy working with Sizzla. Then Saki, Black Uhuru's road manager, told I that King Jammy wanted to see I, and when I went to see King Jammy, I told him: 'I no inna no bag of 45s. I start out doing albums, and that's the way I want to keep it.' So we did the album *Total Commitment*, with some smashing tunes 'pon it, like 'Worries And Problems' and 'Fire Bun A Weak Heart'."

Bushman's arrival at Jammy's came at a time when the studio had been revitalised by new blood, notably engineer Andre 'Suku' Gray, a key studio mainstay of the era that who also active in the popular dancehall rap group, Ward 21 (formed with other young neighbourhood faces helping to transform the place). The resultant *Total Commitment* album was a resounding success, and 'Fire Bun A Weak Heart', on which Bushman warns of the unfairness of the music industry over a hard re-cut of the 'Hypocrites' rhythm (previously used for Half Pint's 1983 hit 'Mr Landlord') was one of its most outstanding tracks. The title track, about the Rastaman's vulnerable side, made waves across the eastern Caribbean, while the meditative 'Worries And Problems' was another subtle gem, and songs like 'Mr Gunis' presented a rougher edge.

"As a youth who left the country to go into the city, I see how the city is set," Bushman notes of the latter. "Ah just gunplay and man dead, and when police come fi investigate, them don't see; the politicians deal with blood money and guns inna the community. Someone will go abroad on farm work, sell some drugs, make good money and say them an 'Area Don' – they have links pon the wharf, and carry in guns and coke. So the Dons and the politicians manipulate the youths. It is one of the greatest problems inna Jamaica today."

Bushman's follow-up album for Jammy, *Higher Ground*, brought forth great songs like 'Fire Pon A Deadas', presenting an ital vegetarian worldview, but its thunder was partially eroded by *A Better Place*, which the singer says was hastily voiced in London for the Stingray label on the advice of his then-manager. In any case, since leaving Jammy's, Bushman's output has slowed.

After a 2002 gun charge took him out of action, he cut some self-produced work and a notable album called *Signs* with producer Iley Dread, while his inspirational live performances keep him in demand overseas.

As this chapter has shown, most upcoming dancehall artists found prominence through the sound-system circuit, with dub-plate specials often an important part of the process. In contrast, Morgan Heritage, one of the most non-standard outfits in reggae history, arrived by very different means. A fully self-contained band of siblings, formed in the USA, Morgan Heritage benefited from the guidance of their father, Denroy, a Jamaican immigrant that scored a big hit in the early 80s with the crossover ballad 'I'll Do Anything For You'. Signed to MCA for a debut album, *Miracles* (1994), they created little impact until they moved to Jamaica with their father the following year and found the proper milieu in which to fully express themselves, free from major-label constraints.

"With Morgan Heritage, you hear roots reggae with a rock edge and an R&B sound, 'cos that's who we are," says vocalist and keyboard player Roy 'Gramps' Morgan, during a break from a recording session at Bobby Digital's studio. "I grew up on bands like Duran Duran, Tears For Fears, Asia, Van Halen, and we learned how to sing off of R&B vocalists such as Stevie Wonder, Donny Hathaway, Sam Cooke, Michael Jackson, James Ingram, Guy, New Edition, Witney Houston, and Sade, plus The Wailers and Frankie Paul."

Gramps's hulking figure and Yankee twang make it easy to picture him as a star football player in an American high school, but as the group interacts with Bobby and his team, patois gradually takes over. While the rest of the group concentrates on overdubbing percussion, Gramps recounts the complex tale that finally resulted in their strong impact on the reggae scene during the mid 90s.

"Everyone in Morgan Heritage was born in Brooklyn, New York, and we were raised in Springfield, Massachusetts, but we would go back and forth to our father's studio in Brooklyn," he begins. "My father was born in May Pen, Clarendon, and went to America in the 60s; he was one of the first artists playing original reggae music in New York City in the 70s, with a band called The Black Eagles, and he later got together with Burt Reid and came up with 'I'll Do Anything For You', which sold over a million copies. Our first influence was listening to his band: he would have rehearsals at home, so we used to mess around with the instruments, and we did a lot of foundation work with the Twelve Tribes Of Israel band, backing artists such as Judy Mowatt and Sister Carol when we was 15 years old. Most of us are

399

self-taught musicians, but at some point we had to take it to the next level, so our father brought in teachers like Jackie Mittoo, Thelonius Monk Jr, and Eugene Gray, the musical director in his band."

Gramps says things improved after a successful Jamaican debut. "In 1992, we played at Reggae Bash in Ocho Rios, and Lee Jaffe from MCA saw our performance. He flew some people down on a Learjet the next day to see us perform at Reggae Sunsplash, and they signed us right off the stage."

Morgan Heritage was then an eight-piece family band, but the disappointing performance of their debut album caused three members to quit. "We did *Miracle* and stayed with MCA for two years, and I think that is a beautiful album, 'cos it was a lot more advanced to what was going on in the reggae scene at the time, but they brought in writers that have worked with Ray Charles, and guys that had written commercials for Michael Jordan, so it was really corporate. At the end of the day, they come up with a product that they couldn't market; they couldn't get the record played on radio in corporate America, so we got right back into the studio in Brooklyn and started 71 Records. And the five that were left held on and said: 'This is what we want to do forever.'"

Significantly, it took a trip to Africa to make the family realise that Jamaica was where they really belonged. "We got invited to do a show in the Ivory Coast in 1995, and it was a real cultural experience that invoked the ancestors," Gramps says. "Feeling that energy, my father said he wanted to go back to Jamaica, 'cos he was tired of trying to make it in America – if we stayed there, the family would probably end up working at Burger King, so we decided to move to Saint Thomas, on the eastern part of the island, one of the most radical and undeveloped parishes. Growing up in the United States, we always had the Jamaican culture, so when we came here, it was already like home, other than getting used to mosquito bites, the heat, and everything on a slower pace."

Shortly after arriving, they began working closely with Bobby Digital and King Jammy, concurrently producing the albums *Protect Us Jah* and *One Calling*, each of which helped establish their reputation as roots reggae contenders, despite being voiced on pre-recorded rhythms rather than on songs made with their own live instruments. "For three months, we would work from eight o'clock till two o'clock in the evening here, then we'd go down to King Jammy's and work till about eight," laughs Gramps. "They would give us the rhythm and we would spit out the lyrics, just like that – nothing was pre-written."

Despite the strength of *One Calling* material such as the catchy title track and the unification anthem 'One Bingi Man', Morgan Heritage found their niche with Bobby Digital, and would continued to work closely with him thereafter. The partnership brought forth popular albums such as *Don't Haffi Dread*, which featured the anthem-like title track, as well as 'Reggae Bring Back Love', a spirited re-cut of The Wailers' 'Bend Down Low'. "King Jammy was like a father, but Bobby Digital is more like a brother," says Gramps, "because he's a young guy, a little more hip, so naturally the chemistry's going to be different."

The group has also issued their own impressive productions, cut with likeminded Rasta artists such as Buju Banton, Anthony B., Junior Kelly, and Luciano and collected on the CD series *Morgan Heritage Family & Friends*, highlights of which include Capleton's 'Jah Jah City' and the Morgan's own 'Rastaman Chant'. Although Bobby Digital has been the mainstay, they have also voiced notable work with other producers. 'Down By The River' – a collaboration with Dean Fraser that rode a digital re-cut of The Cables' 'What Kind Of World' – was one of the biggest hits of 1999, while the R&B ballad 'She's Still Loving Me,' produced by Philip Linton of Arrows, was a huge smash in 2002.

Morgan Heritage's blend of reggae, rock, and R&B has proven highly popular in Jamaica and overseas, where tours with West Coast punk acts like Bad Religion and No FX provided the inspiration for the song 'Jump Around', about the antics of a punk audience. Their younger siblings, LMS, have also impacted with a blend of reggae and hip-hop. Raised within a culture of professionalism, their musical proficiency has given the Morgans an edge in the highly competitive reggae arena, even as recent years have seen longstanding group hiatuses.

Commentators have often noted that the Jamaican music scene is largely dominated by men, both in terms of artistry and production. From the mid 90s, however, the rise of controversial performer Lady Saw opened up new spaces for females in the dancehall. Saw, born Marion Hall in Saint Mary in 1968, came to prominence with raunchy material like the 1994 track 'Stab Up De Meat', while her no-holds-barred stage performances left little to the imagination, featuring simulated sex with hapless audience members. Yet, as with many dancehall performers, it would be wrong to tar all Saw's work with the same brush, since songs like the country-influenced 'Give Me A Reason' found her tackling very different material.

"I don't always agree with her lyrical content, but I really do love her style, and I think she's a very strong female," says Tanya Stephens, one of a wave of women empowered by Saw's success. "When you see a Jamaican woman talk publicly like Lady Saw does, you have to applaud her, even if you don't like what she's saying. I think she's really brave, and I love that. We have a really chauvinistic society, so women are the lesser creatures here; our attitude in Jamaica is, if a woman is strong, she's headfast, and if she does things her way, like any man, she's automatically looked upon as a bitch or a dyke. People get insulted, and that's something that we really need to change."

Although their personal tales are unique, Stephens's musical evolution holds slight echoes of Saw's in that she abandoned ballads for suggestive material, seeking to gain popularity, but her career has been far more versatile. At a café near Kingston's Asylum nightclub, the intelligent and thoughtful vocalist, born Vivienne Tanya Stephenson in 1973, takes time to explain her way into the music business. "I come from a really small town in Saint Mary called Ridgemont," she says. "My father died early, so I was raised by my mother with my brothers and sisters. There were seven of us, of varying ages, and she was a health worker for the government. I moved to Kingston when I was about 17, living in Ziadie Gardens with one of my bigger sisters and going to fashion design school, which sounds much nicer than it is."

She had already written songs in the countryside and hoped to make it as a balladeer, so approaching a recording studio seemed like the best option. "I looked in the phone directory under 'Recording', and Penthouse had a big ad, but they said: 'We don't have space for no new artist, maybe you want to try New Name Music.' So I called them and Derrick Barnet and Noel Browne said: 'You sound like you need some work, but you have some potential' – a diamond in the rough. I did a recording, and I hadn't even turned 17 yet, but it never got released. It was a slow, melancholy ballad, and those songs aren't really welcome in Jamaica from Jamaican artists."

Undaunted by this early false start, Tanya's next port of call was Barry O'Hare's Grove Recording studio, up in Ocho Rios, which yielded more tangible results: a debut album, *Big Things A Gwan*, which contained the popular numbers 'Love How Your Body Tan', 'I Bet You Miss Me', and the hit title track. Mostly sung, but toasted to a lesser degree, the album demonstrated a gradually growing confidence as Tanya worked to settle into her stride, her tenure at Grove bringing concerted artistic development.

"Barry O'Hare and Stephen Stewart are more into developing an artist than developing themselves, and making an album is the best way to do that," she continues. "The environment at Grove felt more like home, and we became something of a family: [fellow vocalists] Prezident Brown and Jack Radics were also there, and Mickey Simpson, before he died, and they were like bigger brothers to me."

At the time, countless production outfits were concentrating on 'one rhythm' albums, with over 20 different artists voicing cuts of the same rhythm, often at basic home recording studios, making maximal output out of minimum input. To record an album of original material with an unknown artist, rather than rushing to voice on pre-recorded rhythms, was an unusual approach. However, at a time when CD sales were dwindling in the face of internet downloads, this approach did not really mean that 'less' equalled 'more.'

"It's far more [financially] feasible to make one rhythm and have several artists on it," Tanya suggests, "but the way producers are looking at it now is a very limited view: if they invested more time and money, you would have a much greater possibility of gain. But we're a very short-term set of people that have evolved into something that is almost impossible to understand. Nobody benefits, because we have become so disposable, and the songs don't last."

Despite the positive aspects of her time at Grove, Tanya soon returned to Kingston, to launch headlong into dancehall. "After living in Kingston, the countryside seems slow, and artists who are based in the country never got no respect. In order to be considered one of *them*, I had to be among them in Kingston. I had songs that people actually knew, so I had offers for management, production, bookings. Then I did some work with Shocking Vibes and I really liked hanging with them, because they were more like a clan.

"At Grove, my work never effected anybody else's, but at Shocking Vibes, it's survival of the fittest, and I really love competition, so I think that helped me to grow too, though I got a lot more progress out of my affiliation with [deejay] Spragga Benz and his crew, as he was the one who kept pushing me. It was tough love, and he was more like a father. I went on the road with him, Baby Cham, Tomahawk, and Sugar Slick – there's a few of us he was dragging around, and he had nothing to gain from it. The first time I ever did a show outside of Jamaica was in Toronto, and I wasn't even on the bill, but he just brought me along."

Tanya took a break from the music in 1994, returning late the following year after the birth of her daughter. Upon reaching Dave Kelly's fledgling Madhouse stable, she made a massive impact with 'You Nuh Ready Fi Dis

Yet', a song of female defiance cut on the highly popular 'Joyride' rhythm (named for Wayne Wonder's hit of the same name, the first to impact on the minimalist, electronic rhythm). "Then everybody stop and took notice," she laughs. "That one was really the turning point. When I first heard the rhythm, I was completely uninspired, but it had that strange, driving rhythm, so I couldn't step away from it. We spent a day in his studio, and [Kelly] has a different work format, 'cos when he's working on an artist, he doesn't have a line outside his door, so you can just work at your own pace. When he asked me what I wanted to put on it, he said: 'What are the things that bother you most?' I said I am really bothered by Jamaican men's egos, and if a girl cheats, it's because the man was lacking in some department."

Tanya's growing popularity resulted in the VP compilation album *Too Hype*, and the Madhouse set *Rough Rider*, which featured another smash, the playfully suggestive 'Big Ninja Bike'. But by the time *Rough Rider* surfaced, Tanya was headed north: unusually for a dancehall performer, she had been working as a songwriter for music publishers Warner Chappell, which prompted a three-year move to Sweden in 1998. She released the *Sintoxicated* album there, but was not particularly happy with it. On trips back to Jamaica, she also began producing artists such as Lady Saw, Spragga Benz, Captain Barkey, Ghost, and Harry Toddler, but with limited success. She has since gone on to release the versatile albums *Gangsta Blues* and *Rebelution*, was one of the few dancehall artists to publicly remind her audience that sexual preference is a private matter, and was probably the first to release a free album, *Infallible*, which was available both as a download and as a freebie with a 2010 issue of Germany's *Riddim* magazine.

In addition to helping Tanya reach a broader audience, Madhouse brought several other hopefuls to prominence during the mid 90s, including her one-time sparring partner, Baby Cham, a baritone toaster who addresses a broad range of topics. Born Damian Dean Beckett in 1977 and now know simply as Cham, the toaster says Madhouse was crucial to dancehall's development. "I knew Dave Kelly by going to Penthouse, but he was a musical genius then, so everyone was just trying to get on a Dave Kelly beat."

Like most of his peers, Cham's sound-system apprenticeship started early. "I was born in Hughenden and spend some of my childhood in Waterhouse, where we had a sound called Studio Mix – that's where I started this whole deejay thing," he recalls. "Artists like Super Cat and John Wayne used to deejay on that sound system, so we used to pirate their songs, till you started trying to make your own rhymes. Me and my friends used to attend the studios: Penthouse, Jammy's, Scorpio, Bobby Digital, Junior Reid, trying to demonstrate our skills to the producers.

"I got the name Baby Cham in 1990 at this deejay contest in Duhaney Park. My friends used to just call me Deanie Man, but it sound too close to Beenie Man, and one of my friends' sisters said: 'What about Baby Champagne?' Then I met Dave Kelly in '92; he had the 'Pepperseed' rhythm mashing up the place, and I wanted to do something on 'Pepperseed' but he wouldn't record me, because I was still attending school. I went back in '95, after I finished school, and he had this new rhythm by the name of 'Stink'. Beenie Man had 'Old Dog' on it, and I voiced 'Funny Man' on it, and we made 'Girls Anthem', singing it like a Michael Jackson song."

The songs to bring him greater recognition were 'The Mass', which mixed different themes together, and the infectious 'Many Many', which spoke of females' propensity to burn through cash. "I was trying to bring a different style with a wider range of music, not just do a song that was debating rude-boy stuff, or religious stuff, or girls stuff – it was all in one. 'The Mass' was the song that really brought me to the front, and 'Many Many' sealed it off."

Cham remained solidly with Madhouse, cutting a debut album, *Wow ... The Story* in 2000. His second album, *Ghetto Story*, was released by Atlantic in 2006, following their successful promotion of the uptown sing-jay Sean Paul.

Sean Paul's surprising leap to fame entailed one of the most momentous major-label signings in the history of reggae. It was probably the most high-profile deal since The Wailers signed to Island decades earlier. He was born Sean Paul Henriques in 1973 to a pair of notable uptown Kingston residents: his father Garth was a water-polo champion, while his mother Fran was a champion swimmer who became renowned for watercolour paintings. Unlike most of his dancehall peers, Paul is essentially a white Jamaican, although his mixed heritage includes Portuguese Jewish, Chinese, and African elements. There are many unusual aspects to the toaster's tale, as he revealed when I spoke to him at an uptown Kingston rehearsal space.

"I grew up in Norbrook in a real suburban, middle-class lifestyle. My father is a businessman, but he went to prison from I was 13 till I was 19, under unfortunate circumstances. That was just a time where I had to be the man around the house and grow up without a father's guidance. My mother and father used to swim for Jamaica in the 60s, and in the early 90s, I was playing water polo for Jamaica, but I wasn't a great student in school. Later, I was a bank teller and I went to hotel management school for two years, but

I always love music. My mum was always playing music in the house, like The Beatles, and I hear reggae music all over the place, plus dancehall, and the hip-hop style started to get into my soul at about the age of 13. I especially liked Super Cat, because him is a bad man, but him turn him life around and become a deejay, and I love the style that him was portraying. I also looked up to Shabba Ranks before Shabba became big in the United States, and I looked up to people like Major Worries, and when I was 17, I started to really check out Bob Marley. I knew one of his kids from school, because Damian Marley, 'Junior Gong', used to go to school with my brother.

"Around 1994, I started to write songs about social issues, and I did demo tapes with those. My father gave them to Cat Coore from Third World, so Cat Coore took me to Rupert Bent's studio in Stony Hill, a small studio that Third World was working out of, to put some proper demos down. After a while, I went to other studios to try and get voiced on the popular rhythms. My brother formed a sound system, Copper Shot, in 1991, so around '95, I started to do dub plates for him and for Renaissance, who were closely linked to Stone Love. I started to do dubs for Stone Love, too, and that broke my career as an artist in the dub plate style. So by 1996, everybody was trying to get dubs from me."

Sean reached the next level once his sound-system apprenticeship brought him to 2 Hard, the production stable established by Jeremy Harding, another uptown youth whose father, Oswald Harding, was a leading lawyer and high-ranking JLP politician. While studying chemical engineering at McGill University, Harding did a two-year music production course, ran a college radio show, and moonlighted as a nightclub deejay. Returning to Jamaica in 1993 to help his father campaign, he established a small studio at his Jack's Hill apartment, building purely electronic rhythms. He has been Sean Paul's manager for the bulk of his career.

"A friend of mine who knew somebody in advertising said he needed jingles, so I started doing jingle work for radio and television," Harding laughs. "I didn't have any intention of producing dancehall, 'cos I actually produced a lot of hip-hop with rap acts in my bedroom in Montreal, but a younger brother of mine started a sound system called Syndicate Disco; they were good friends with Renaissance, Travellers, and Stone Love, so my studio became a nice little spot to do dubs – it wasn't in downtown Kingston, so it was quiet and private. From doing the dub plate sessions, I started to meet all the artists, so one day my brother said: 'Why don't we try putting out a dancehall rhythm?' That first project had Don Yute, Roundhead, General B., Future Troubles, Elephant Man, Harry Toddler, and Sean Paul; Carrot

Jarrett, the percussionist from Third World, used to run this hang-out spot called Raphael's in Kingston, where they would have a live band, and people would come up on the mic and sing or deejay, and Sean had a long association with them. My brother saw him deejay and gave him my card."

"By the end of '96, Jeremy Harding was ready to put out his first rhythm," Sean continues. "I went on it and did 'Baby Girl No Cry No More' – my first song, saying: 'Girl, don't let the man beat you' – which hit in January the next year. Then I did another song called 'Infiltrate', on the 'Playground' rhythm, and that really blew up: Beenie Man's 'Who Am I' was one of the biggest songs on that rhythm, and 'Infiltrate' took me out into the world."

'Infiltrate', a fast-chatted sing-jay track about proper dating etiquette, went against the grain of the menacing 'Playground' rhythm, showing Sean Paul's propensity to hit with celebrations of carnal pursuits and physical expression. "Buccaneer had an opera style, in which he would sing out songs and then deejay, and Beenie Man started to do that too," Sean explains. "So when I started to do that, I found that it really brought a lot more out of me. Then me and Mr Vegas became known as the new sing-jays, and 'Infiltrate' was one of the first where I was singing."

After cutting impressive work for various producers, a debut album was assembled. "I did 'Nah Get No Bly' and 'Deport Them' for Tony Kelly, and I did 'Hot Gal Today' for Steelie & Clevie with Mr Vegas, and by the year 2000, my first album came out, *Stage One*, which contained all of these hits, plus some exclusive songs done between me and my brother, and me and Jeremy Harding. The album was different in that it was strictly dancehall when a lot of people were trying to do hip-hop. 'Deport Them' and 'Hot Gal Today' were both on the *Billboard* charts, so I had popularity in New York with a Spanish-speaking audience."

Party anthem 'Gimme The Light' was the song to turn everything around. This surprise hit eventually brought the deal with Atlantic, making Sean Paul a household name internationally. "'Gimme The Light' is about weed and drinking, and spending money. It's a party vibe, essentially, something I didn't really expect to get that big."

Sean Paul has since issued many other hits, and collaborated with stars of hip-hop and other genres, keeping his profile exceedingly high. The Atlantic deal also involved broader distribution for other artists signed to VP Records and deemed to have crossover potential, although Wayne Wonder's *No Holding Back* gained a similarly lukewarm reception to Cham's *Ghetto Story*, despite the presence of popular singles on each.

In addition to breaking Sean Paul and Cham, Jeremy Harding helped boost Sean's sparring partner, Mr Vegas, into the major league. "2 Hard was where I got my first real break, when I did 'Nike Air (Hands In The Air)'," he explains, during a break from a voicing session at Mixing Lab. "That's the tune that make people in Jamaica really hear this new sound, to say this new youth has a sound of his own."

Vegas was born Clifford Smith on the outskirts of Kingston in 1974. As his older brother Carlton was a longstanding member of The Tamlins, it makes sense that he first tried to make it as a crooner, but Vegas reveals that his shift to sing-jay resulted from a terrible incident. "I grew up in Upper Saint Andrew with my mom and there wasn't much musical activities, like there was maybe just one sound system. When I was about 11, I started sneaking out of school to go to Music Mountain studio, hooked up with a young producer, Zoo Palmer, and did a song called 'Nah Left Me Country', but it never came out.

"Years after, I met up with [deejay] Don Yute, started going to Big Ship, Stone Love, and 2 Hard, and at first I was singing R&B style, but in 1997, some guy tried to have a feud with me, and as I walk away, he use a piece of iron to break my jawbone. It was wired shut for six weeks, and as soon as the wire was taken out, I went straight to Jeremy Harding's studio, but I could not open my mouth as I used to, so I had to stick to a sing-jay style. That was when I did 'Hands In The Air', and it just sounded different. Everybody else was a hardcore deejay, or doing R&B singing, so that was a breath of fresh air."

The track, which saluted the popularity of Nike's Air sneakers in a high-pitched, nasal tone, was an instantaneous and lasting hit, but Vegas did not linger in the 2 Hard camp. Instead, he switched to Danny Browne's Main Street stable, whose status was rising high, following a string of hits with upcoming artists such as Goofy, whose popular 'Fudgie' featured the bicycle horn employed by ice-cream sellers, along with light-skinned toaster Red Rat, whose gimmick was the repeated exclamation "Oh no!"

"Even though I had 'Hands In The Air' and it was creating a big wave in the dancehall, I still have to be begging Danny Browne to go on his next beat," laughs Vegas. "Everyone was saying that beat is going to be the hottest beat for the summer, so I was just begging Danny's wife to let me go on that beat for weeks, and as soon as I started to do 'Heads High', he was like: 'This is the best song on the beat – this is number one.' And that was *the* song for Jamaica for two years straight, so it let me take care of my mum, while touring all over the world."

Although Vegas would have happily remained at Main Street, Danny Browne's surprise conversion to Christianity forced him to work elsewhere. "Then I sought other producers, like Steelie & Clevie, who I did 'Hot Gal Today' for with Sean Paul: we used to link by 2 Hard studio, when he had 'Infiltrate' and I had 'Hands In The Air'." 'Hot Gal Today' was another sweeping success, while Vegas's 2001 album *Damn Right* paved the way for subsequent releases on the American independent, Delicious Vinyl, as well as Universal Records.

Although Vegas formed his own label, In The Streets, with then manager Byron Murray, frustrations with the industry and reported ill health prompted a temporary retirement in 2008. Part of the initial frustration involved standard detrimental practices, such as too many vocalists being forced onto the same rhythms, so that disc jockeys can 'juggle' different cuts of the same beat seamlessly, which Vegas says stifles creativity. "It's hard to break a song in Jamaica with just one song on the beat – there has to be ten or 15 songs on the one beat," he emphasises. "'Gimme The Light' with Sean Paul maybe wouldn't be a big hit if it was just him alone on that beat – there has to be a juggling on the beat when they're playing it in the dance ... and if they want to try something with a different song, it definitely has to be a big record company behind it, with a video, and radio plugs."

Mr Vegas was not the only artist to significantly benefit from a link with Sean Paul. Feisty female toaster Cecile is another, although her initial break came largely through Tanya Stephens. "For the longest time, I followed her around, catching styles and the vibe," she admits, "because I came from a totally different background."

The vocalist, born Cecile Charlton in the rural town of Porus in 1977, went to school in an area called Mile Gully before moving to Mandeville in her teens to live with her father, a wealthy racehorse owner that became mayor of the city before she was born. Upon moving to Kingston in 1995, she found work as a secretary at Steven Ventura's studio, Celestial Sounds, located at Molynes Road. "My dad sent me to Ibo Cooper before I was living in Kingston, and he released one of my songs called 'Beat Of My Heart' when I was still in high school, but it never went anywhere. Then I met Steven Ventura through his cousin, who was looking for an artist at the time, and he actually wanted to manage me, but when he brought me to the recording studio for a production deal, I said that I wanted to work there instead."

Although Cecile was hoping to make it as an R&B balladeer, having been inspired by romantic soul artists such as Anita Baker, like Tanya Stephens and Lady Saw before her she soon found that dancehall tastes required her to change focus and image. "At Celestial Sounds, I was recording stuff, but nothing ever got released," she says. "Steven wanted to groom artists, so if you're recording something and he doesn't think it's ready, he lets you keep on recording to see how you can improve. So I learned while I was working at Celestial Sounds, and I've learned a lot from Tanya. She's the one who really said: 'Yo, do the dancehall thing,' 'cos initially I didn't want to."

Much of Cecile's early work surfaced on Kings Of Kings, a label formed by the Montreal-based Jamaican singer, Iley Dread, who forged important links at Celestial Sounds in the same era. Her new sassy image was based largely on Tanya's, as heard on songs like 'Murder Tonight' and 'Buss Back Sketel', both cut as duets between the two. Cecile's grand breakthrough finally came in 2000 with the song 'Changez', which poked fun at a number of leading sound-system selectors. A massive hit in the dancehall, it was sparked by popular selector Fire Links, although Cecile wound up producing the record herself, in conjunction with engineer/producer Cordell 'Scatta' Burrell, who would shortly oversee Kings Of Kings' dancehall output. "Fire Links wanted me to record a song for a rhythm that he was gonna be producing," Cecile explains, "so I decided I'm going to write a song troubling the selectors in the business. When I finished writing the song, I never had a chorus, but I was singing Mary J. Blige's 'Changes I've Been Going Through', and I thought: this shit can work! And when I finished doing it, I said: 'I'm not giving Fire Links the song, I'm going to produce it myself.'"

Although Cecile voiced some conscious records in her early days, including 'Respect Yuh Wife', written by Tanya Stephens, she was soon associated with titillating material presenting her as a 'bad gal'. Although comfortable with the image, Cecile says that the pressure dancehall artists face to voice material on every rhythm going, sometimes results in sub-standard work. "A few songs, when I listen back to them, I'm like: 'Fuck, what was I thinking?' But when somebody gives you a rhythm, and you have to record on it, sometimes you write crap."

In any case, greater glory awaited: in 2001, her duet with Sean Paul, 'Can Yuh Do Di Wuk', brought wider recognition. "I wrote that song in a minute," she laughs. "'Gimme The Light' was recorded at Celestial Sounds when I used to work there, and then Jeremy just called me and said Sean Paul would like to do something."

Although Cecile signed to Delicious Vinyl following her appearance on Sean Paul's Grammy-winning *Dutty Rock*, the album she was preparing for the label never surfaced. She also began producing upcoming artists, again with limited success, and sees such elements as part of a process of evolution. "I'm still an artist in progress. I've grown since I started, when my performing wasn't all that good, and there's more rungs to climb up the ladder."

In addition to providing Cecile with a launching pad, Celestial Sounds was also the spot where notable producers Scatta Burrell and Iley Dread first made their mark. "I got involved in music because I didn't see any other way out," Scatta explains, during a brief visit to London. "At one point, I was doing some mechanic work, but dancehall music was just drawing me away."

After a particularly unsettled youth, Scatta turned to music by default. "When I was five, my father took off, so it was just my mother and six of us. She was a nurse, and left Jamaica in order to seek better opportunities for us, so we end up staying with one of her church sisters in Grant's Pen – the gangster side of town – for three years: we attended United Pentecostal Church, and that develop my musical ability. Then my aunt came from America and saw the poor living conditions, so she moved us to Constant Spring Gardens for a while, but then that she got sick with sickle cell, so we started moving again. [Future Innocent Kru member] Benzley Hype used to live close to me; his father is [veteran singer] Ainsley Morris, and he had a small studio at the house, so in the evening, we used to fool around in the studio.

"When I leave school, I was living at my uncle's in Mountain View – another terrible area – and he was a mechanic, so that's how I get the mechanic job. Then Benzley Hype said: 'I hear about a studio named Celestial Sounds' – this was about '95. Steven Ventura's father was an advisor to the Prime Minister on Science, and his mother was from Miami, so he studied music in Miami. He came back to Jamaica and set up a studio, but he was new to the whole dancehall thing, so when Benzley and I went there, we brought a little vibes and added to his talent, because we would say: 'Do it *this* way, don't do it *that* way.' He was a cool guy, and I was deejaying for him, but I realised he wasn't feeling my energy that way, because I didn't really have the voice for it. I was modelling myself after Buju Banton, because we used to go to the same church, and he and my cousin Kirk used to go to the same high school."

Although Ventura did not rate Scatta's deejay ability, he eventually nurtured the youth's intuitive engineering skills. "When me see Steven Ventura nah take to my vibes as a deejay, me say: 'Scatta, you need to try and learn this thing.' So I just go there every day and watch him, and if him do anything good, I bop my head: 'Sounds good.' Benzley used to voice songs

411

fi him, and after a while, him accept that I was working along with him, so him started to let me sit around the board. At the time, I was the only one showing interest in being an engineer, and him know a time was going to come when he would really need somebody. He started to hold engineering classes to deal with the bills, and he allowed me to take the class for free. I didn't do so well with the theory, but the hands-on thing, I had it down."

Through family connections, Scatta began working with conscious sing-jay Norris Man, and shortly thereafter Iley Dread, with whom he forged a strong working partnership. Iley was born Colin Levy in Montego Bay in 1966. He was raised between Molynes Road in Kingston, where his mother sold baked goods and clothing, and the northwest town of Chester Castle, where his father ran a club called the Apple Tree Rest, and its resident sound system, Bowzer. After working as a vegetarian chef, Iley moved to Negril, where he sold his original canvas paintings, and began writing songs for artists such as Dennis Brown, John Holt, Gregory Isaacs, Spanner Banner, and Beenie Man. In 1990, Iley migrated to Montreal to help his brother run a restaurant and nightclub; then, after teaming up with engineer Bevin Jackson, a relative of Byron Lee that had worked at Dynamics, he began concentrating on his professional singing career, but Jackson tragically died in a car crash in 1995, leading Iley back to Jamaica the following year, seeking to voice artists on partially completed rhythms initiated with Jackson in Montreal.

"Buju and Syl Gordon had a studio in Ackee Walk called Cell Block," Scatta explains. "Norris Man was at that studio and my cousin Kirk told him to check me at Celestial Sounds, so him come and voice a couple songs. Then Iley Dread came from Canada with ADATs – he go to Buju's studio and they send him to us as well.[3] Steven Ventura mixed a song for him, and he had another song he was working on that him voice Everton Blender, Anthony B., and Uton Green on, but people were telling him that the rhythm was too soft, so he get [keyboardist] Computer Paul to change the rhythm to the 'Gunman' rhythm, but it didn't fit – the chemistry was changed – so them end up going back to the original thing. Him take it down to Dynamics to press, but them send back criticism, say that it should do 'pon 24 track; he had to be in and out of the country, so the man nearly get fed up. But me say: 'Let me try and make it work for you, just give me a couple months.' Him did have a couple of dancehall rhythms he wanted voiced, so I voiced Frisco Kid, Mad Cobra, Anthony B., Terry Ganzie, and mixed them down; they didn't really hit, but he was pleased, because for once he asked for something and it got done properly."

The breakthrough came with Norris Man's 'Persistence', an uplifting number describing the need for endurance. "Norris Man was going through a lot of stress, because him career wasn't going anywhere, and him did have to start sleep at the studio. He build a rhythm for him and [fellow vocalist] Chrisinti at Celestial Sounds, but Chrisinti didn't voice on it as he had to go to Canada, so the rhythm was there. Norris Man voice it and it do wonders for him, so that was my first motivation that me can achieve something. Then Cecile came up with an idea to do over a Jennifer Lopez song ['If You Had My Love'], voice Capleton and Moses I's 'Crazy Look' on it, and them times we set up the Kings Of Kings distribution company, so things was really running well – those songs really break ground."

The situation soon became problematic at Celestial Sounds, however, forcing Scatta to pursue independent music production. "We really hit a rough spot: Cecile was leaving the studio, Norris Man was doing his own thing, Iley's in Canada, so where do I go from here? I was really at a point where I don't just want to be a recording engineer, and I wasn't really making no money. Then, Don McKinley did have a small studio called Exclaim on Constant Spring Road, but he wasn't really using it, and Cecile wanted to do some demos there, so she asked me to come and record. Don McKinley have some rhythm called 'Chiney Gal', and Cecile voiced a song on it, but I wasn't really feeling it ... then the song 'Changez' come up, and she say: 'We nah give Fire Links this.' So we voice it on our rhythm, then we ask Sizzla to voice something on it too, so he do 'Give It To Them', and then Elephant Man nah get left out of nothing, so he do 'New Application', and Beenie Man come with 'Counteract', but we never really have no money, so we no pay anybody – they just did it because Cecile's song was getting airplay and they wanted to be a part of it. From there, we did 'Double Jeopardy' – built by Leftside, Lloyd Parks's son – and it started to cause a little more controversy, because Beenie Man do the song 'Reasoning' about Sting, and then Hawkeye counteract with 'That's My Style', and Elephant Man come with 'Pure Passa Passa', and Kiprich add to it with 'Mek Sure', so I was getting known as a producer. Then Iley said he wants a dancehall album off Sizzla, and I had the 'Martial Arts' rhythm, so Sizzla did 'Karate' and Elephant Man did 'The Bombing', because the World Trade Centre just got bombed."

It is strange to note that Iley Dread was issuing such hardcore material on Kings Of Kings, since he stuck to soft love ballads and traditional Rastafari values in his own work. "I leave the producing to Scatta," Iley explains. "Even though I am paying the bills, Scatta is the man that really go to the studio

413

with the artists, and him mostly concentrate on dancehall, because we both realised there was a faster turnaround for dancehall, and most of the distribution companies were reluctant to license one-drop music."

Thankfully, the hits kept coming thick and fast for Scatta, who was joined in production by his brother Everton around 2001, following the latter's brief internship at Celestial Sounds. That same year, the pair launched the 'Famine' rhythm away from Kings Of Kings, making their own overseas licensing deal with Greensleeves, but Scatta maintained his link with Iley Dread, who still issues the bulk of his creations. Scatta has since created numerous hit rhythms, such as 'Bad Company', 'Coolie Dance', 'Dancehall Rock', 'Fungus', 'Rave', 'Inevitable', and 'Self Defence'.

As the new millennium swung into view, upcoming producers were jockeying for position, with creative forces like Steven 'Lenky' Marsden soon making a concerted impact (particularly in 2002, with his incredibly popular 'Diwali' rhythm), but the frontrunner was Don Corleone, an uptown youth whose Vendetta studio churned out some of the most popular dancehall. Corleone, who was born Donovan Bennett in 1978, says his middle-class background was no hindrance to his dancehall credentials. "I always cling with ghetto people, as we can relate better," he insists, during a break between recording sessions, "and my parents wasn't supporting me, so I had to look out for myself."

Corleone spent his youth between the southwest coastal towns of Whitehouse, Westmoreland, and Santa Cruz, Saint Elizabeth, where he was the selector of a sound system called Studio Two. "My favourite productions were by Steelie & Clevie, Dave Kelly, Bobby Digital, King Jammy. I started deejaying, but then I went to Miami in 1997, to study electronics for four years."

Returning to Jamaica in 2000, Corleone quickly shifted base to the capital, forming the Vendetta sound system in Papine with his cousin, Protoje, music production was the natural next step.[4] "I start the sound system, start deejaying, until one day I made a remix, using my home computer and Cool Edit [software]. Beenie Man and Capleton had a feud at one time, and I made a remix, put them together and make it sound like a real combination, and it was a big thing. Then I opened a little studio at a friend's place in Havendale, recording dub plates for [selectors] Tony Matterhorn, Stone Love, Deejay Khalid, and Bobby Konders, but I wasn't building rhythms then – we would use old 45s instead. Then I used to be a portable dub studio, because I had a laptop and a hard disc recorder, so I used to go up in the hills and check Sizzla. We moved the studio to Garden

414

Boulevard in Mona in 2001, and I started doing a little rhythm building. King Jammy's son, Baby G., had a rhythm named 'The Mexican', and he always said: 'I want to get Sizzla on it, couldn't you get Sizzla for me?' So Sizzla went on the song named 'Come On' – I produced it, Baby G. released it, and it was a big song in Jamaica."

Corleone quickly reached the major league with a little help from a couple of other uptown youth, namely Daniel 'Blaxxx' Lewis, a talented musician who became paralysed from the waist down following a car crash in his teens, and producer/instrumentalist Shiah Coore, son of Cat Coore from Third World. And although the connection would take time to bear tangible fruit, Sizzla Kalonji was a key part of the process, as was upcoming deejay, Vybz Kartel, who had yet to make a proper breakthrough, but who has since become one of Jamaica's most popular and notorious performers.

"Sizzla just came to me one day and said: 'I'm going to give you an album,' so I started to work on *Rise To The Occasion* with the five rhythms that Shiah Coore gave me, and I picked a rhythm out of it, which was the first rhythm I produced, 'Mad Ants'. Shiah Coore built the rhythm, and Blaxxx was involved too: he is a musician I've known from I was a child, who plays keyboards and live drums, but he was producing rap music and I was the first person to introduce him to dancehall. I had quite a number of hits with 'Mad Ants', but the first one came when I discovered Vybz Kartel. One day he came to give me some dubs for my sound, and his style is just tough and fresh, new and different, but nobody was releasing him, so the first song I recorded on the 'Mad Ants' rhythm was 'New Millennium', Vybz Kartel with Wayne Marshall. For my first hit, I discovered Vybz Kartel, and I discovered that I could produce as well."

"The first big commercial success came with Don Corleone," Vybz Kartel confirmed, during a telephone interview. "What I envision as an artist vocally, that's what he envisions as an artist musically, with his instruments. And I like the uptown influence in the music right now, that too has a part to play in the way you hear music: less gun lyrics and more happy tunes and girl songs, because the people determine what the artists say." Kartel, born Adidja Palmer in 1978, would eventually be one of the most controversial artists in dancehall. His X-rated lyrics – notably on his 2008 duet with Spice, 'Romping Shop' – prompted widespread debate about song lyrics, public decency, and the law, while his feud fellow artist Movado degenerated into the Gully versus Gaza war.[5] Even more troubling is his skin bleaching, which drew considerable censure, and at the time of writing, he is currently facing a murder charge. At the time of 'Mad Ants', however, he was just another artist seeking to get his talent heard, his catchphrases 'Up To The Time' and 'Timeless' being part of what made his delivery distinct.

After Corleone's success with 'Mad Ants', the 'Krazy' rhythm soon followed, with another Kartel/Wayne Marshall hit, 'Why You Doing It' (one of the many anti-oral sex songs of the era), as well as Ward 21's amusing 'Rhyme'. Soon after, the more complex 'Egyptian Dance' rhythm showed Corleone's talent for injecting non-standard elements into his dancehall creations. "Me and Vybz Kartel was in the studio and I found this tabla sound and loop it," he says. "I was searching through the same CD and I heard a girl's voice, saying 'umm hmmm', so I sampled it and put it in the rhythm. Then I linked Blaxxx with it and said: 'I want you to play a phrase on this rhythm, so that Kartel can get it for his album.' He had it for about three weeks, playing with it." The result was a complicated rhythm that became the platform for a string of hits with Sean Paul ('Get With It Girl'), Elephant Man ('Egyptian Dance'), Wayne Marshall ('I Will Love The Girls'), and the biggest of all, Vybz Kartel's highly X-rated 'Sweet To The Belly'.

Other hit rhythms to follow include 'Good To Go'; 'Trifecta', which he constructed with Suku from Ward 21; 'Mad Guitar'; 'Cool Fusion', constructed with Leftside and keyboardist Nigel Staff from the Ruff Kut band; and 'French Vanilla', which he co-produced with Jamaican broadcaster DJ Liquid. Elephant Man rode Corleone's creations to massive effect in 2003, particularly on dance anthems like 'Pon Di River, Pon Di Bank', which entered the *Billboard* charts, and 'Signal Di Plane', another of the year's biggest hits. Then, after scoring countless hits in hardcore dancehall mode, Corleone changed tack in 2005 with 'Drop Leaf', a modern, acoustic-guitar driven take on the one-drop sound that yielded a huge hit, 'What Am I Longing For', by singer Jah Cure, who was incarcerated at the time.[6] The similarly emotive 'Seasons', issued the same year, was further evidence of Corleone's drive to broaden dancehall's audience. "Generally dancehall is heading straight across the world," he explains. "Everybody's listening to dancehall now, and dancehall is like the newest craze in music. Dancehall music has a whole different vibe; it's not tied to any other music, it's just there by itself."

As noted throughout this book, Jamaica's dancehall culture has always reflected the desires and tastes of the island's public. I have also tried to show that reggae music has undergone endless cycles of renewal as its creators experiment with new techniques in their quest for fresh sounds and styles that can be created easily under challenging conditions. In this sense, the many facets that have followed the digital explosion can be viewed as part of the music's overall continuity, albeit ones that often perplex roots enthusiasts. 'Sleng Teng' may have loosened the floodgates and brought Jamaican music headlong into the digital age, but the new music was ultimately a continuation of what preceded it, and a vast number of further shifts in style, form, and content have succeeded it right up to the present.

As the artists in the last two chapters have made clear, despite the dominance for a time of sexually suggestive 'slackness' and violent 'gun talk', reggae music came full circle with the new roots movement that came to the fore in 1993 and saw singers and live instruments returning to prominence, as well as a revival of Rastafari elements. These days, however, Jamaican popular music can take any number of bewildering forms: hardcore dancehall deejays like Bounty Killer and Movado perform the Kingston equivalent of American 'gangsta rap' over an electronic version of the ancient Pukumina beat, while artists like Taurrus Riley and Dwayne Stephenson present an updated classical roots, appealing to an international audience through a spiritual message set to a complex backing of live and electronic instruments. Somewhere in between are the fiery Bobo Dread ranters like Capleton and Sizzla, who preach fundamentalist values over rhythms often more akin to heavy metal or punk than anything once known as reggae; forward-thinking females such as Queen Ifrica and Etana take dancehall into new territories, while veterans such as Dwight Pinkney craft easy-listening instrumental re-cuts of classic hits, and performers like Stitchie, Papa San, and Carlene Davis blend reggae and country with gospel. The changes Jamaican music have undergone during the past few years are so numerous, in fact, that another book is surely needed to place these figures in their proper context.

Changing times naturally bring forth different sounds, and although the liberating message that drew many to reggae went underground for a while, by the time Jamaican music went digital, reggae's solid foundation of inspired creativity and devoted religious faith had built a truly global house with many mansions, inspiring a massive audience far beyond its land of origin. I leave the closing words to Cocoa Tea, one of the artists to have consistently sung conscious material, to emphasise reggae's universality:

"Reggae music is the heartbeat of the people. Reggae music highlight the struggles of the people, no matter what race of life people come from, 'cos reggae music come fi make the people get help. It there to uplift the mind and refresh the soul and to teach us how to live in love and harmony.

417

Reggae music preach equal rights and justice. We have to unite black and white: you have your struggles, me have mine, it's only that I have the medium in which to express your struggles and highlight mine at the same time. One song say: 'Not because you live on the hill and I live down there on the flats, everything that you do indirectly affects me whether you know it or not.' So it no matter where you want to live or who you want to be: the war down in Israel, the shooting and killing in Jamaica, election business in America, the AIDS that kill people in Africa: we're going to highlight all of those struggles, because what? It's all of us problem together, me brethren, so we all must come together and try and tackle it, one by one."

ENDNOTES

1 Boogie Rock

1   Reynolds was previously active in the duo Rum & Butter, mainstays of the Glass Bucket in the 30s.

2   The original material was written by Fly's older brother Gerald, aka Geraldo deLeon, a noted pianist and dancer that reportedly caused a sensation in December 1927 by playing piano for 48 hours straight at Astley Clerk's music store, located at 56a King Street. Gerald wrote 'Whai Whai Whai' for Fly in London in 1947.

3   The South African instrumental 'Skokiaan', originally by penny-whistle player August Musurugwa, has been covered internationally many times; highly popular in Jamaica, it was adapted by several reggae artists in the 60s and 70s.

4   Foreshore Road was later renamed Marcus Garvey Drive.

5   The revue featured various performers. "We had Derrick Harriott & The Jiving Juniors, Count Prince Miller & The Downbeats, [singing duo] Bobby & Faye, Sparky & Pluggy dancing, and The Wisdom Brothers balancing on bicycles; Hyacinth Clover would be singing also, which is Bim's wife."

6   'Lover Boy' thus gained the alternate street title of 'S-Corner Rock.'

7   As heard on Gilles Peterson 'Worldwide,' BBC Radio One broadcast, 26 November 1998.

2 Celebration Time

1   KUSF radio broadcast, 4 April 1992; interview conducted by Andrew Rush and Michael Turner.

2   *Lance Haywood At The Half Moon* was ironically recorded at RJR's studio in Kingston, with Ken Khouri's assistance. The pianist's actual surname was Hayward, but he was known as Haywood during his Jamaican sojourn.

3   The winner was Tony Gregory, who recorded extensively for Studio One in the 60s.

4   Morgan says the group was composed of "Bill, Jill, Ken, and myself, all male".

5   The original Lord Koos of Kingston, still alive, is not to be confused with the late Lord Koos who established a sound system and record label in London; as The Matador notes: "All the sound systems in England clone our name."

6   Interview with Steve Barrow, 1994, for the Reggae Archive project.

3 Take It Easy

1   Although the group name points to Dillon's growing awareness of Rastafari, the original name was The Heartaches. "We were very young at them times, not even knowing what Ethiopians really means. Coxsone as a elder man who understands more, he chose and say: 'Ethiopians sound good—the right one that.'"

2   KUSF radio broadcast, 4 April 1992; interview conducted by Andrew Rush and Michael Turner.

3   As Taitt explains: "Lloyd Knibb went into The Skatalites—the Studio One band. They had Jah Jerry, but when Roland have his solo, he got a little lost, so every Sunday I record for The Skatalites, but Jerry was playing out with them. I didn't deal with Coxsone too much, only when The Skatalites were recording on Brentford Road."

4   The non-musical Smart, a manager for Singer sewing machines, was the band's financial backer.

5   The band was comprised of university students: "Kes shake the maracas and sing, and we had three doctors from Barbados, they were at the university, but they were top class musicians: Dr Adrian Clark plays the piano, Dr Basil Robinson was the bandleader, he plays the bass, and Dr Don Torrington plays the tenor."

6   Jarrett says other acts at the event included Gorgeous George, Patti Labelle, Hortense Ellis, Lascelles Perkins, Jimmy Cliff, and Count Prince Miller.

7   In February 1967, machinist Wayne Smellie was shot in in the leg in Denham Town whilst fly-posting for the PNP. He later named Dapper Dan as his assailant.

8   Ken Boothe, who was also featured on the tour, notes that "the band got scrapped in England because of bad arrangements – people weren't getting enough money".

9   Rowe suggests that both 'Stop That Train' and 'Tonight' were "bigger abroad than in Jamaica", while in 1978 Peter Tosh and Mick Jagger scored a much bigger international hit with a version of 'Don't Look Back'.

10 Grant is better known for the roots material he recorded with Augustus Pablo in the late 70s.

11 The Soul Vendors, led by Roland Alphonso, formed from the ashes of The Soul Brothers. Hux Brown, originally from Port Antonio, first came to Kingston circa 1962 to join The Vikings after bandleaders Victor and Sonny Wong requested his membership.

4 Feel The Rhythm

1   Interview with Steve Barrow, March 1994, for the Reggae Archive project.

2   Lee's link with Morgan involves matrimony. "Bunny Lee have children with my cousin Mackie, that's how I get to know him, and since he took on my cousin, I took on his sister Nellie; we married in 1968."

3   Eccles recalls: "Around '62, I start making shows. In '63, I start with the Clarendonians, '64–'65 it was The Wailers at various country theatres, and in 1967, I put back Wailers in the 'Battle of the Stars' at the Ward Theatre, with a whole set of acts."

4   Crooks admits the shows were not always as advertised. "We used to be unfair to the country people, because one time I went to Port Morant School and I brought Blacka Morwell to sing as Delroy Wilson. He did well, but couldn't remember some of the lines. I did that because the country people used to want the artists like mad, and if you can't get them, then you get somebody else to go. On those shows we had Cables, Heptones, Ken Boothe, Alton Ellis, and a

dancer. Sometimes we go to country with a truck and have to come back by a bus because we didn't make any money."

5 Yvonne was featured on the hits 'Meekly Wait And Murmur Not' with Roy Panton and 'Two Roads Before You' with Derrick Morgan. She also performed on stage shows with Jackie Wilson, Byron Lee, and Kes Chin.

6 The single was released on Ronnie Nasrallah's BMN label.

7 Sibbles's other classic lines include Larry & Alvin's 'Mean Girl,' The Abyssinians' 'Satta Massa Ganna' and 'Declaration Of Rights,' The Mad Lads' 'Ten To One,' the adaptation of Eddie Floyd's 'I've Never Found A Girl' known as 'College Rock,' Roy Richards's adaptation of Little Richard's 'Freedom Blues,' John Holt's 'Fancy Make Up,' The Heptones' 'Sweet Talking', and The Soul Vendors' instrumental 'Full Up'. "The Studio One Alton Ellis is me too," Sibbles adds, "plus Dennis Brown's 'No Man Is An Island' [originally by the Van Dykes] and Horace Andy's 'See A Man's Face' and 'Mr Bassie'."

8 Campbell says musicians on those recordings included Jackie Mittoo on piano and organ, Eric Frater on lead guitar and "a youth named Patrick" on rhythm, Boris Gardiner and Leroy Sibbles on bass, plus saxophonists Lester Sterling, Cannonball Bryan, and Roland Alphonso, and Vin Gordon on trombone.

9 For instance, on 'Judge Dread' and Buster's version of James Carr's 'Dark End Of The Street,' Marshall notes that "the harmony is me and Skully and Sticky, and a brother named Trevor from Spanish Town".

10 'Mr Sweet' was released on a Coxsone 45 in 1969.

11 "The headliner for the band was Ken Boothe, and it was the remnants of the Studio One band," Lyn explains. "Fil was the drummer, Eric Frater was the guitarist, and Leroy Sibbles was the bass player. They wanted to do a promotional item associated with the cigarette, so we did this song called 'Without Love,' which is the first recording I played on. It came on the Embassy label, by Ken Boothe & The Swinging Kings; we added the horn section after, which was 'Deadley' Headley Bennett, and Denzil Laing was the percussionist."

12 Featured duets by the pair include 'Ben Johnson Day' and 'Johnny Pram Pram'.

13 According to Collins, other group members to play on the session include a bassist known as Baba and a guitarist called Scotty.

5 Blood & Fire

1 Other members include bassist Earl 'Bagga' Walker, future Wailers keyboardist Earl 'Wire' Lindo, and future Third World bassist Richard Daley on guitar. "We were green, inspired kids who didn't matter about money or anything," Santa recalls.

2 Of Indian Descent, Croucher, known as 'Coolie Boy', faced numerous charges. The most notorious, defended in court by Norman Manley, stemmed from shots he fired at police officers in June 1951 when the officers disrupted an Obeah session held to protect his brother Joscelyn (aka 'Chu Chi'), a fugitive then facing a murder charge.

3 Pratt says the tune was 'Safe Travel,' a song he re-cut on his own in 1968.

4   The song was originally sung by Ken Boothe at Studio One and Holt also recorded a version at Studio One.

5   Tony Chin recalls: "It was me, Max Romeo, Lloyd Charmers, and Santa sing harmony on it in Randy's, and Augustus Pablo plays keyboards."

6   The Chosen Few were Franklyn Spence, Richard 'Richie Mac' MacDonald, Pat Satchmo, and David Scott, who also gained fame as the deejay Scotty.

7   In Jamaican parlance, buzzards are typically called John Crows.

8   Andy initially came to Studio One as part of a duo. "I came with a good friend, Frank, he's the lead singer with Wadada now; we used to sing together, and we pass the audition, but when we went to record, it never work."

9   'I'm Alright' was harmonised by Chinna Smith under the alias Earl Flute.

10 Other notable backing musicians include Leroy Sibbles on bass, Fil Callender on drums, Richard Ace on keyboards, and Vin Gordon on trombone.

11 Daley recalls the care with which the song was put together: "That was an outstanding rhythm – it took us six hours to make that rhythm with 11 musicians on a 24-four track Neave console at Federal." In 1970, Daley constructed a studio of his own at 43 Waltham Park Road, but was unable to equip it properly. 'Yin Mas Gan' is thus a tantalising example of the kinds of sounds he might have created had the facility been fully realised. "It was designed by some Germans, Graeme Goodall know them. I wasn't going for no mediocre equipment – I wanted a Neave console, 24-track. So I spent three months at Neave in Neasden as an engineer, because I was gonna bring down a partially-assembled console, but because of the non-payment of royalties from my investment of my recordings, I had to withhold furnishing my studio."

12 The bands include The Cavaliers, Bobby Demarcado & The Presidents, The Checkmates, The Jamaica Supremes, Los Cavaleros, The Diamonds, The Comets, and The Jets.

13 In addition to Madden and Brooks, The Mystics featured guitarist Lloyd 'Gitsy' Willis, drummer Danny Mowatt, bassist Joe Rugglus, and a vocalist called 'Chuku'.

14 Madden says hired session players on the track include saxophonist Ossie Scott and trombonist Joe McCormack, plus Peter Ashbourne on piano and Aubrey Adams on organ.

6   Merry Up

1   On Louis Armstrong's 1926 recording 'King Of The Zulus', Armstrong's cornet solo is vocally interrupted by an unidentified Jamaican gate-crashing his barbecue. Although the Jamaican's utterance is not exactly in the deejay form, it sets a fascinating precedent to it and I am grateful to James Dillon for pointing out its significance.

2   The song uses an oblique re-cut of Ernie Freeman's 'Live It Up', previously adapted by The Skatalites for 'Beardman Ska'.

3   As Glen recalls: "Cecil Lloyd was Jamaica's number-one piano player. His wife also plays with him on piano – a white lady, but very good." Other band members include bassist Cluette Johnson, guitarist Ernest Ranglin, and alto saxophonist Karl 'Canonball' Bryan. Although talented singers such as Bob Andy

and Shenley Duffus auditioned with the band, Glen says he got the position "because I was quick and could remember".

7 Deejay's Choice

1 On September 1 1957, hundreds of members of the Holy Name Society of Saint Anne's Catholic Church in Kingston made a seaside excursion by train to Montego Bay. On the return journey, the overcrowded train derailed near Kendal, Manchester, killing over 200 and injuring nearly 700, making it one of the worst railway disasters in history.

2 Brenda & The Tabulations' 'Tip Of My Tongue' reached number five on the US charts in 1971; 'Piece Of My Heart' was a substantial hit for Janis Joplin and Big Brother & The Holding Company. Hortense Ellis, then recording as Mahalia Saunders after her marriage to one Mikey Saunders, voiced the reggae versions Tado toasted on.

3 In 1974, Tado cut 'Return Of Muhammed Ali' for "a brethren called Louie"; the following year, he versioned Joy White's 'Dread Out Deh' for Lloyd 'Spiderman' Campbell. Tado also cut some songs for Studio One in this period, plus a song for Joe Gibbs on "one of those 'Joe Frazier' rhythms that he put Big Youth on later", but the material was not released due to conflicts with both producers.

4 The song's cryptic lyrics referred to an advertisement for supermarket poultry.

8 None Shall Escape The Judgement

1 Other band-members include bassist Tony Ramsey, keyboardist Ansel Collins, drummer Neville Grant, and guitarist Philip Grant.

2 Cridland says that circa 1969, The Linkers began as himself and Oswald Grey, a harmony coach at Delacree Lane he was introduced to by members of The Thrillers. "Our first song was for Lloyd Matador, named 'Say Say'; Little Roy was singing for Matador at the time. Another few months after, we met up with Constantine Brown in Jungle [Tivoli Gardens]. Oswald Grey left the group, he more into the Church, so now is me and Con and another brethren we call Peedo as The Linkers, we do 'Loser' for some JLP man named Vin who want to come in the business. From there, I audition with J.J. and we do 'Niyahman Story'."

3 'You Can Run' was issued in the UK without the group's knowledge, credited to The Hurricanes; Danny notes that the vocalists were "me, a guy from Trench Town called Dennis, and Lloyd Forrest—after we split up, he sing with The Jays, and after he left The Jays he start to sing with The Chantells." Clarke also recorded 'Poison Dagger,' issued on the Sheep label; 'Bertha,' done in "kind of a conscious style for this likkle man who used to come by Federal named Mr Lee"; and a self-produced effort at Dynamics called 'This Time'.

9 Natty Dread Taking Over

1 Clarke says The Buccanneers was "a Jamaican group that played dance music and Top 40 for weddings"; The Bluegrass Experience featured drummer

Sparrow Martin, guitarist Eric Frater, and keyboardist Glen Adams.

2   "When they put him in prison and he was coming out, him say: 'After I enter through this door, no one else shall enter,' and no one has entered back through that door," Big Youth recalls. "He said that place is going to be a car park ... and it have to be, because they were the ones that form the constitution of that place, but through him was the darker spade, them push him out."

3   Dennis Brown and Cynthia Richards were also members.

4   Norman worked with Llans Thelwell & The Celestials; Ralston played in a steel band. "I did two LPs with Llans Thelwell in the 60s," Norman reveals. "We were working at the Colony Hotel in Montego Bay, before it turned into the Half Moon; I worked there for six or seven years. Llans Thelwell was an engineer at the airport; he was the bass player. We were singing songs like [The Fifth Dimension's] 'Up, Up, And Away,' and [Jim Reeves's] 'Green Grass Of Home'; we record those songs at Dynamic, and that's where I learned a bit of drumming, one night when the drummer didn't turn up." Adds Ralston: "I was playing in Irving Ellis & The Northcoasters steel band, that was about '68–'70. Irving is the younger brother of Alton Ellis, he came to Falmouth to coach this youth club and give me leadership of the band. I was playing the bass drum first, five big drums, then I play the one they call the guitar pan, it's close to the bass."

5   Norman also recalls cutting unreleased material with Lee Perry in this period, including 'Reggae For Days'.

6   Norman says other group members featured on the album include "Paul Hurlock, he was in The Cardigans and Llans Thelwell & The Celestials with me, and he have his own one-man band at the time; Glen Stair, he's still in Jamaica, one of the cocktail pianists playing in the hotels; Bongo Asher start play percussion with us, he wrote 'Give Rasta Praise' and 'African Liberation'."

7   Singles recorded include 'Gone Me Gone' by Lanford Gilzene, a singer "from the hills, about ten miles from Falmouth"; 'God Bless The Youth' by The Mystics, "Eric Bernard and two of his brethren"; 'Babylon A Fight Rastaman' by 'Allah,' aka Austin Williams, who "used to play a bit of percussion while we were rehearsing"; and 'Whip Them No Skip Them' by toaster Sir Lee of the Screaming Target sound system "from Deeside, about 12 miles from Falmouth", which was particularly popular when issued in Britain.

8   "Glen Marcinick, the guy that owned Tops, he was involved in the original 'It's Not Who You Know'," Norman explains. "He came to Jamaica to cut dubs at the time for [Brixton sound system owner] Lloyd Coxsone, and he went in the studio and make some music; we thought it was Bunny Lee's session. When I came to England, I get to realise he was the one who did it, and I gave him a couple of tracks to release."

9   The material includes 'I'm Tipping' and 'Sweet Sixteen,' with Third World as session musicians.

10 The correct term is Tetrark, denoting an independent portion of a kingdom ruled by a separate leader.

11 "The drummer was Benbow," Hines recalls, "the bass player was Clayton Downie, and Clayton went back and played rhythm guitar; then Pablo put some haunting overdubs on it."

12 "The rhythm was laid at Joe Gibbs or Harry J," Hines notes. "Jacob Miller was playing the drum originally on that, and it was overdubbed by Horsemouth, and Robbie Shakespeare play the bass."

13 Other members include Calman Scott, the brother of Scotty, and Ferris Walters.

10 Oh Lord

1 Backing vocals were provided by Bim Sherman, Mike Brooks, and Pauline Lindsey; musicians include bassist Flabba Holt, drummer Sly Dunbar, guitarist Bingy Bunny, trumpeter Bobby Ellis, trombonist Vin Gordon, plus Bobby Kalphat on piano and Dennis Ferron on organ.

2 "The original name was Soul Attorney and the original owner was Rupert Brown, but because of political things, the sound have to pack up," Brown notes. "Tony Welch bought the sound and it plays for a couple of years as King Attorney, and then they change it to Socialist Roots."

3 "Jack Ruby's was the largest tube amplifier that was ever built in Jamaica – 40 KT88s" says Lloyd Daley, who built it.

4 The rhythm was a re-cut of the Studio One classic 'Death In The Arena', aka 'Whipping The Prince', loosely based on 'Funky Donkey' by prolific American session drummer, Bernard 'Pretty' Purdie, who recorded in Jamaica with The Wailers for JAD.

5 The song was issued by Coxsone in 1964, and later covered by the Specials; Dennis says Andy was "a brethren we meet in Trench Town, his name is Reuben Anderson".

6 Musicians on 'Folk Song' include drummer Cornel Marshall and bassist Lloyd Brevett, plus Gladdy Anderson on piano and Winston Wright on organ.

7 Dennis says Clive became aware of the group through Waterhouse resident Denver Williams, a relative of his stepmother, Patricia Chin. Session players on the disc include drummer Carlton Barrett, bassist Lloyd Parks, and guitarists Chinna Smith and Alva Lewis.

8 "Me get involved in the whole tourist thing with a band named Happiness Unlimited; Beechwood Avenue, at Hummingbird Restaurant, that's where we used to rehearse," Rose recalls. "You have to sing every type of music: the B.B. King thing, R&B, reggae, calypso, dinner music."

9 Rose says the song was backed by a tailor named Winston Samuels (aka 'Thread') and Danny White, "a guitarist whe come from the roots neighbourhood, but them man go ah high school and university".

10 Brown recorded an earlier version, which was also popular in Jamaica, with Niney at Joe Gibbs's in 1972.

11 Nice Up The Dance

1 Joseph Hoo-Kim offered the following thoughts about the trio: "Maxie was Ernest's personal friend, he only take the voices and mix for other producers.

Crucial Bunny usually fix bikes round the bike shop. I would put Bunny Tom-Tom and Maxie as the same type of engineer, but Bunny Tom-Tom was a little more flexible, not as aggressive a mixer. Barnabas live across the road from the studio, so we gave him a try."

2   "With Now Generation, I produced Delroy Wilson with 'I Wish It Was Me', a Tyrone Taylor original," Williams recalls. "Along with that was The Versatiles' 'Stronger Strong' and 'Give Them Bread'; it was [Dudley] Earl, Spanner, and Robert, three brethren from Rollington Town. We went into the studio with The Wailers' band, at that time it was called Rhythm Force, just after the period of The Hippy Boys; it was Family Man, Carly, Glen Adams, Reggie."

3   The earliest-known cut of this rhythm in Jamaica is Dodd's 'College Rock', a melodica instrumental credited to Big Willie; the melodic structure stems from Eddie Floyd's soul hit 'I've Never Found A Girl'.

4   Other notable members include former In Crowd guitarist Michael Murray and bassist 'Professor' Larry Silvera.

5   Ital is a strictly naturalistic way of life propagated by some followers of Rastafari.

12 Under Mi Sleng Teng

1   Interview with David Rodigan, Capital Radio, London, 1981.

2   Cultural Roots was originally composed of Hubert Brooks, Norman Gallimore and Wade Dyce, with Everton Drummond drafted in later; a further incarnation saw Drummond replaced by Devon Russell, and Brooks subsequently left before the group finally split.

3   'Prince' Huntley Dakin, who sang back-up with Burrell on the tune, is operator of the Modern Printry on Maxfield Avenue and founder of the Greedy Puppy label.

4   In 1989 it became a huge hit in Washington DC due to a dance the public created to go with it; a remix by Miami Sound Machine kept the song in the charts.

5   The label borrowed its name from the official title of the King of the Mossi people of Burkina Faso.

6   A sizeable hit in 1974, it was produced by Lloyd F. Campbell with Niney's assistance.

7   Cocoa tea is a sweet breakfast drink, while cerasee tea is a curative beverage made from an extremely bitter vine.

8   This first session almost didn't happen, Tea notes. "The first day I was going to the studio I was held with a spliff. Police stop the car, and me have a draw of weed in me pocket and me get it off, but Lee Van Cliff tell the police is mine I just gave him a spliff, he said he nah go ah jail for no man's weed. The policeman lock me up and carry me to Half Way Tree, and I was lucky, because I got bail the same day."

9   Corner Stone was one of the labels that spun off from Freedom Sounds in the late 70s/early 80s. Another was Church Of Music, formed by Delroy McKoy around 1981.

10 Paul notes that the song was first cut several years earlier for Monica's Records of Toronto.

13 Wear Yu Size

1   In the decades that followed, Pottinger would endure gruelling court battles over the rights to Duke Reid's back catalogue, and suffer from the degenerative Alzheimer's disease, leading to her death in 2010 at the age of 79, shortly after Jamaica's Supreme Court recognized her definitive ownership of Treasure Isle.

2   The title 'Tempo' seems to be a misprint, since the song describes the 'temper' of King Tubby's sound. Kong notes that Tenor Saw accused Red Rose of patterning the song after 'Fever,' which Saw voiced earlier for Sugar Minott.

3   Kong says the latter angered Tenor Saw for adapting/reversing his earlier hit, 'No Work Pon Sunday,' potentially confusing listeners as to which song was which.

4   Tegereg is Jamaican parlance for a loud, rude, or abusive person.

5   It was also a return to local prominence, following an overseas hit collaboration with the British psychedelic dance duo Coldcut, 'Stop This Crazy Thing'.

14 Lift Up Your Head

1   Earl Hayles ran the Aquarius studio following Herman Chin-Loy's migration to Florida.

2   The title refers to women involved in extramarital relationships, a 'matie' being a man's active romantic interest, maintained separately from his wife or regular partner.

3   ADATs are a form of digital audio, not commonly used for recording in Jamaica during the period in question.

4   Born Oje Ken Ollivierre in 1981, rising vocalist Protoje is the son of reggae singer Lorna Bennett and Michael Ollivierre, a calypsonian from Saint Vincent, known as Lord Have Mercy, who coached the Jamaican Olympic track-and-field team during the 90s.

5   The Kartel-Movado feud unfortunately saw violent clashes between supporters, until a public performance between the pair ended the madness.

6   The controversial singer, born Siccature Alcock, served an eight-year sentence for rape, armed robbery, and gun offences, and was released in July 2007; ironically, his popularity has since waned to a certain degree.

427

SELECT BIBLIOGRAPHY

BOOKS

Alleyne, Mervyn *Roots Of Jamaican Culture* (Pluto 1989)

Barrett, Leonard *The Rastafarians* (Beacon 1988)

Barrow, Steve, and Dalton, Peter *The Rough Guide To Reggae* (Rough Guides 2001)

Bishton, Derek *Black Heart Man* (Chatto & Windus 1986)

Booker, Cedella, and Winkler, Anthony *Bob Marley: An Intimate Portrait By His Mother* (Viking 1996)

Bradley, Lloyd *Bass Culture: When Reggae Was King* (Viking 2000)

C., Gordon *The Reggae Files* (Hansib 1988)

Campbell, Horace *Rasta And Resistance* (Hansib 1985)

Chang, Kevin O'Brien, and Chen, Wayne *Reggae Routes* (Temple University Press 1998)

Chevannes, Barry *Rastafari Roots And Ideology* (Syracuse University Press 1994)

Clarke, Sebastian *Jah Music* (Heinemann 1980)

Clifford, Mike (ed) *The Illustrated Encyclopaedia Of Black Music* (Harmony 1982)

Davis, Stephen, and Simon, Peter *Reggae Bloodlines* (Anchor 1977)

Davis, Stephen, and Simon, Peter (eds) *Reggae International* (R&B 1982)

Davis, Stephen *Bob Marley: Conquering Lion Of Reggae* (Plexus 1983)

DeKoningh, Michael, and Griffiths, Marc *Tighten Up: The History Of Reggae In The UK* (Sanctuary 2003)

Faristzaddi, Millard *Itations Of Jamaica And Rastafari* (Judah Anbesa 1987)

Faristzaddi, Millard *The Second Itation* (Judah Anbesa 1991)

Fernando Jr, S. H. *The New Beats* (Anchor 1994)

Foster, Chuck *Roots Rock Reggae* (Billboard 1999)

Gillett, Charlie *The Sound Of The City* (Souvenir 1983)

Goldman, Vivien, and Boot, Adrian *Bob Marley: Soul Rebel – Natural Mystic* (St Martin's 1982)

Goldman, Vivien, and Corio, David *The Black Chord: Visions Of The Groove* (Universe 1999)

Griffiths, Marc *Boss Sounds – Classic Skinhead Reggae* (ST 1995)

Gunst, Laurie *Born Fi' Dead* (Canongate 1995)

Hebdige, Dick *Cut 'n' Mix* (Comedia 1987)

Henzell, Perry *Power Game* (Ten-A Publications 1982)

Hurford, Ray (ed) *More Axe* (Black Star 1987)

Hurford, Ray *The Small Axe Reggae Album Guide* (Black Star 1996)

Jekyll, Walter (ed) *Jamaican Song & Story* (Dover 1966)

Johnson, Howard, and Pines, Jim *Reggae: Deep Roots Music* (Proteus 1982)

Kaski, Tero, and Vuorinen, Pekka *Reggae Inna Dancehall Style* (Black Star 1984)

Katz, David *People Funny Boy: The Genius Of Lee Scratch Perry* (Omnibus 2006)

Katz, David *Jimmy Cliff: An Unauthorised Biography* (MacMillan/Signal 2012)

Kennaway, Guy *One People* (Canongate 1997)

Larkin, Colin (ed), *The Virgin Encyclopedia Of Reggae* (Virgin 1998)

Manley, Michael *Jamaica: Struggle In The Periphery* (Third World Media 1982)
Marre, Jeremy *Beats Of The Heart* (Pluto 1985)
Murrell, Nathaniel, Spencer, William, and McFarlane, Adrian (eds) *Chanting Down Babylon: The Rastafari Reader* (Ian Randle 1998)
Oliver, Paul (ed) *Black Music In Britain* (Open University Press 1990)
Owens, Joseph *Dread* (Sangster's 1976)
Petrie, Gavin (ed) *Black Music* (Hamlyn 1974)
Pollard, Velma *Dread Talk* (Canoe Press 1994)
Potash, Chris (ed) *Reggae, Rasta, Revolution* (Schirmer 1997)
Reel, Penny *Deep Down With Dennis Brown* (Drake Brothers 2000)
Salewicz, Chris *Rude Boy: Once Upon A Time In Jamaica* (Victor Gollancz 2000)
Salewicz, Chris, and Boot, Adrian *Songs Of Freedom* (Bloomsbury 1995)
Salewicz, Chris, and Boot, Adrian *Reggae Explosion: The Story Of Jamaican Music* (Virgin 2001)
Small, Geoff *Ruthless: The Global Rise Of The Yardies* (Warner 1995)
Stolzoff, Norman *Wake The Town And Tell The People: Dancehall Culture In Jamaica* (Duke University Press 2000)
Taylor, Don and Henry, Mike *Marley & Me* (Barricade 1995)
Thelwell, Michael *The Harder They Come* (Grove Weidenfeld 1980)
Thomas, Michael, and Boot, Adrian *Jah Revenge* (Eel Pie 1982)
Thomas, Polly, and Vaitilingam, Adam *The Rough Guide To Jamaica* (Penguin 2000)
Turner, Michael, and Schoenfeld, Robert *Roots Knotty Roots: The Collector's Guide To Jamaican Music* (Nighthawk 2001)
Wallis, Roger, and Malm, Krister *Big Sounds From Small Peoples* (Constable 1984)
Weber, Tom, and Jahn, Brian *Reggae Island* (Kingston Publishers Ltd 1992)
White, Timothy *Catch A Fire: Definitive Edition* (Henry Holt 1998)
Whitney, Malika Lee, and Hussey, Dermott *Bob Marley: Reggae King Of The World* (Kingston Publishers Ltd 1984)

BOOKLETS AND DISCOGRAPHIES
Hurford, Ray (ed) *More Axe 7* (Black Star 1989)
Hurford, Ray *Rhythm Wise* (Black Star 1989)
Hurford, Ray *The Small Axe Files* (Muzik Tree 1992)
Lesser, Beth *King Jammy's* (Black Star 1989)

NEWSPAPERS AND MAGAZINES
A number of periodicals have been consistently useful, most notably *Reggae Swing*, *Roots News*, *Reggae Times*, the *Daily Gleaner*, and the *Observer* from Jamaica; Canada's *Reggae Quarterly*; the *Beat*, *Full Watts*, *400 Years* and *Reggae Calendar* from the USA; *Jahug*, *Echoes*, *Boom Shacka Lacka* and *Mojo* from the UK; France's *Natty Dread* and *Reggae Vibes*; Germany's *Riddim*, Belgium's *Etna*; and Malta's *Reggae World*.

INDEX

Words in *italics* are album titles unless otherwise stated; words in 'quotes' are song titles. Numbers in **bold** refer to illustrations.

440

ACKNOWLEDGEMENTS

I would like to wholeheartedly thank all who consented to be interviewed; your honest recollections and poetic utterances relate the story of reggae's solid foundation. I would also like to thank the fellow journalists, photographers, friends, family members, and other colleagues who assisted with this book. A select few deserve special mention for helping me track down key individuals: in Jamaica, Max Romeo, Winston Jarrett, Gilmour Grant, and the late Bertram Brown; in New York, Clive Chin, and Ras Kush; in England, Doctor Alimantado, Roy Cousins, Linton Kwesi Johnson, and Neil and Holly Fraser. Lee 'Scratch' Perry also receives my unwavering gratitude for initiating the quest for knowledge by insisting I be his ghostwriter in 1987. For providing me with relevant material, contacts, and feedback, I would like to thank various record industry personnel, most notably Steve Barrow, Chris Wilson, Dana Smart, Ray Hurford, Ossi Sillman, the late Tero Kaski, the late Colin Moore, Bruno Blum, Gaylene Martin, Steve Barker, Roger Steffens, CC Smith, Chuck Foster, Michael Turner, Frank Broughton, and David Hill, as well as anyone else not mentioned here that contributed – you know who you are, and your input is greatly appreciated. Furthermore, Tenzing Sonam and Ritu Sarin assisted with Indian surnames, Dave Hallworth helped make an important editorial connection, Chris Menist commented on an early draft of Chapter One, and Kate Pool of the Society of Authors advised on contractual matters. Paula Johnson, Awards Secretary of the Authors' Foundation at the Society of Authors, assisted with the grant that enabled the completion of this revised edition, for which I am most grateful. I also thank all photographers who contributed. For helping shape the original edition, I thank commissioning editor Mike Jones and designer William Webb; for this revised edition, particular thanks are due to Nigel Osborne and Tom Seabrook of Jawbone for seeing things through to fruition. Finally, I thank my partner, Claudia Bernard, for her love and continual support.

PICTURE CREDITS

For other Jawbone titles visit jawbonepress.com

BOWIE IN BERLIN:
A NEW CAREER IN A
NEW TOWN
by Thomas Jerome
Seabrook

ISBN 978-1-906002-08-4

BILL BRUFORD THE
AUTOBIOGRAPHY:
YES, KING CRIMSON,
EARTHWORKS, AND
MORE
by Bill Bruford

ISBN 978-1-906002-23-7

TO LIVE IS TO DIE:
THE LIFE AND DEATH
OF METALLICA'S CLIFF
BURTON
by Joel McIver

ISBN 978-1-906002-24-4

JACK BRUCE:
COMPOSING
HIMSELF: THE
AUTHORISED
BIOGRAPHY
by Harry Shapiro

ISBN 978-1-906002-26-8

RETURN OF THE
KING: ELVIS PRESLEY'S
GREAT COMEBACK
by Gillian G. Gaar

ISBN 978-1-906002-28-2

A WIZARD, A TRUE
STAR: TODD
RUNDGREN IN THE
STUDIO
by Paul Myers

ISBN 978-1-906002-33-6

SEASONS THEY
CHANGE: THE STORY
OF ACID AND
PSYCHEDELIC FOLK
by Jeanette Leech

ISBN 978-1-906002-32-9

WON'T GET FOOLED
AGAIN: THE WHO
FROM LIFEHOUSE TO
QUADROPHENIA
by Richie Unterberger

ISBN 978-1-906002-35-0

THE
RESURRECTION OF
JOHNNY CASH:
HURT, REDEMPTION,
AND AMERICAN
RECORDINGS
by Graeme Thomson

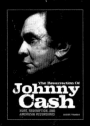

ISBN 978-1-906002-36-7

CRAZY TRAIN: THE
HIGH LIFE AND
TRAGIC DEATH OF
RANDY RHOADS
by Joel McIver

ISBN 978-1-906002-37-4

THE 10 RULES OF
ROCK AND ROLL:
COLLECTED MUSIC
WRITINGS 2005-11
by Robert Forster

ISBN 978-1-906002-91-6

JUST CAN'T GET
ENOUGH: THE
MAKING OF DEPECHE
MODE
by Simon Spence

ISBN 978-1-906002-56-5

GLENN HUGHES
THE
AUTOBIOGRAPHY:
FROM DEEP PURPLE
TO BLACK COUNTRY
COMMUNION
by Glenn Hughes

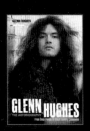

ISBN 978-1-906002-92-3

ENTERTAIN US:
THE RISE OF NIRVANA
by Gillian G. Gaar

ISBN 978-1-906002-89-3

MIKE SCOTT:
ADVENTURES OF A
WATERBOY
by Mike Scott

ISBN 978-1-908279-24-8

SHE BOP: THE
DEFINITIVE HISTORY OF
WOMEN IN POPULAR
MUSIC
by Lucy O'Brien
Revised Third Edition

ISBN 978-1-908279-27-9